FINITE ELEMENT METHOD - SIMULATION, NUMERICAL ANALYSIS AND SOLUTION TECHNIQUES

Edited by **Răzvan Păcurar**

Finite Element Method - Simulation, Numerical Analysis and Solution Techniques
http://dx.doi.org/10.5772/intechopen.69137
Edited by Răzvan Păcurar

Contributors

Horacio Florez, Marcel Janda, Kristyna Jandova, Cristinel Mares, Mutinda Musuva, Toshio Tagawa, Stanford Shateyi, Denson Muzadziwa, Stephen T Sikwila, Viktor Rukavishnikov, Elena Rukavishnikov, Faham Tahmasebinia, Chengguo Zhang, Ismet Canbulat, Onur Vardar, Serkan Saydam, Dario Pitassi, Matteo Benedetti, Enrico Savoia, Vigilio Fontanari, Alberto Molinari, Valerio Luchin, Gianluca Zappini, Zhengyi Jiang, Haibo Xie, Lei-Ming Ma, Xu-Wei Bao, Grzegorz Zboinski, Michal Petrů, Ondřej Novák, Finian McCann, Lechun Xie, Zhou Wang, Chengxi Wang, Liqiang Wang, Chuanhai Jiang, Weijie Lu, Lin Hua, Yan Wen, Lai-Chang Zhang

Published by InTech
Janeza Trdine 9, 51000 Rijeka, Croatia

Publishing Process Manager Teo Kos
Technical Editor SPi Global
Cover InTech Design team

First published February, 2018
Printed in Croatia
Legal deposit, Croatia: National and University Library in Zagreb

Additional hard copies can be obtained from orders@intechopen.com

Finite Element Method - Simulation, Numerical Analysis and Solution Techniques, Edited by Răzvan Păcurar
p. cm.
Print ISBN 978-953-51-3849-5
Online ISBN 978-953-51-3850-1

For EU product safety concerns:
IN TECH d.o.o., Prolaz Marije Krucifikse Kozulić 3, 51000 Rijeka, Croatia,
info@intechopen.com or visit our website at intechopen.com.

Meet the editor

Răzvan Păcurar is a leading researcher within the National Centre of Innovative Manufacturing from the Technical University of Cluj-Napoca, Romania. He holds a PhD title in the Industrial Engineering field and is a specialist in the additive manufacturing domain, with more than 60 articles presented at different international scientific conferences or published within different prestigious journals all over the world (indexed in significant international databases or ISI). He is involved also as a member or director within several national research projects or international grants (FP 7, HORIZON 2020, etc.) in the field of additive manufacturing. He holds the associate professor position at the Department of Manufacturing Engineering from the Faculty of Machine Building at the Technical University of Cluj-Napoca, providing lectures related to computer-aided design, additive manufacturing, nonconventional technologies, and CNC manufacturing domains.

Contents

Preface

During the last decades, the finite element method (FEM) has become a numerical computation tool used more and more extensively by engineers. FEM is based on the principle of building complex objects from simple elements or dividing complex objects into smaller parts that can be easily manipulated.

Applications of this simple concept can be easily found in real life and especially in the engineering domain. Various physical phenomena currently encountered in scientific and engineering domains can be mathematically described using partial derivative equations. In general, finding the exact solutions of such equations by means of analytical methods is impossible for domains with arbitrary geometry. FEM can be used to obtain approximate solutions of partial derivative equations. FEM is based on the selection of approximate functions for solving such equations and can be successfully applied in various engineering fields: static or dynamic analyses of solids, fluids, electromagnetic fields, biomechanics, etc.

This book aims to present results of the applicative research performed using FEM in various engineering fields by researchers affiliated to well-known universities. The book has a profound interdisciplinary character and is mainly addressed to researchers, PhD students, graduate and undergraduate students, teachers, engineers, as well as all other readers interested in the engineering applications of FEM. I am confident that the readers will find information and challenging topics of high academic and scientific level, which will encourage them to enhance their knowledge in this engineering domain having a continuous expansion. The applications presented in this book cover a broad spectrum of finite element applications starting from mechanical, electrical, or energy production and finishing with the successful simulation of severe meteorological phenomena.

Dr. Eng. Răzvan Păcurar
Associate Professor
Technical University of Cluj-Napoca
Cluj-Napoca, Romania

Chapter 1

FEM Analysis of Mechanical and Structural Properties of Long Fiber-Reinforced Composites

Michal Petrů and Ondřej Novák

Additional information is available at the end of the chapter

http://dx.doi.org/10.5772/intechopen.71881

Abstract

This chapter deals with studies of the mechanical properties of samples from long fiber-reinforced composite structures that would contribute to the optimization of the developed constructions made of them. First, the basic issues of composite structures reinforced with long fibers (carbon or glass) and generally of composites with the specification of parameters that would lead to the optimization of mechanical properties with respect to the theoretical strength arc presented. Further, the possibilities and methods of measurements of composite reinforced with carbon and glass fibers are described. This is followed by the introduction of analytical models for the description of the transversal isotropic composite, where these mathematical relations allow the determination of unknown elastic constants and they are also important for the verification of numerical models. Finally, it is comprehensively outlined the problems of creating a numerical model of advanced composite fibrous structure for determining the mechanical properties, both through the description of the continuum, and complex numerical model with a structural configuration enabling approach to allow closer interaction among fibers and matrix. Compared to the averaged values obtained from experimental samples, numerical simulations show a similar trend of stress on strain, with results obtained from simulations.

Keywords: FEM, composite structures, testing, mechanical properties, nonlinear properties

1. Introduction

Studies and analyses of mechanical properties of long fiber-reinforced composites provide important information for future lightweight constructions. First of all, it is important to approach the issues and specifics of long fiber-reinforced composite structures to increase the strength and toughness of the resulting structure. The long fiber-reinforced composite structure is typically formed from two dominant components: carrier fiber reinforcement and a matrix. Ideal arrangement of the final composite (fiber-matrix connection), due to synergy, the high specific properties (high strength, stiffness, and toughness) can be achieved, where none of input components reached. It is that the optimal synergistic effect is characterized by a known "illogical" rule 2 + 3 = 7, which characterizes the sum of the properties of the individual input components (fibers + matrix) achieves a higher value of the specific properties of the newly created structure. In general, the highest specific properties can be achieved if the fibers are stressed up to the strength limit $\sigma_M^f\big|_{F^f \to \max}$ with stress transferred with matrix. The matrix transforms the stress into the fibers, and it also has a significant effect on the bonding with the fibers. Thus, the matrix is the binder component of the composite, creating the final geometry of the composite and at the same time protecting the fibers from wear and damage, which would lead to loss of stability and strength of the resulting composite. The description of the properties of composite structures reinforced with long fibers due to their potential and specific characteristics was given by the authors namely Agarwal et al. [1], Guedes [2], Gay and Gambelin [3], Reifsnider [4], Teply and Reddy [5], Berthelot [6], Gibson [7], or Soden et al. [8]. The authors agree that long fiber-reinforced composite structures are unique materials whose mechanical properties cannot be generally described in an analytical or experimental manner. Theories also differ in mathematical relationships derived for unidirectional composite structures, let alone complete synthesis of mechanical properties for geometrically complex structures of frames with multidirectional fibrous arrangement. This is due to the fact that their properties vary significantly with the type of fibers and a matrix (e.g., physical and mechanical properties, surface treatment, chemical compositions, binding agents, density, thermal expansion, etc.) because only a slight change forms various combinations with significantly different properties in mechanical behavior.[1] Generally, long fiber-reinforced composite structures can be considered as inhomogeneous and heterogeneous structures with anisotropic properties in terms of physical and mechanical behavior. Their heterogeneity is manifested by a large number of combinations of different variants of the resulting structural materials suitable or unsuitable for the specific design requirements and load.[2] If the strength of the composite has to be maximized, the specific surface of the fiber-matrix interface must be high and free of defects. The selection of fiber reinforcement is possible to use a wide range of fibers, whereas their offer is developed and expanded. For structural applications such as frames for machine parts and equipment may be used virtually any organic natural fibers (e.g., coconut, cotton, cellulose fibers, etc.) from a variety of polycrystalline ceramic materials, polymeric fibers, glass, or carbon fibers. The production technology of these fibers is well described by Bareš [9]. Carbon fibers are industrially manufactured with a diameter of 5–12 μm by various methods such as carbonization of organic fibers or pyrolysis. It is generally known that carbon can exist in nature in three forms: diamond, graphite, and glassy (amorphous). Carbon fibers can be

---

[1]This can be mentioned in the example given by Bareš [9]. A simple combination of three homogeneous isotropic light metals to form ternary cast iron is obtained 82,160 possible variants of alloys, if more six metals are combined, more than 300 million different alloy variants could be obtained. (The composite structure reinforced with long fibers has a similar behavior, where the change of the matrix, directional arrangement, and type of fiber significantly affect resulting mechanical properties because it leads to qualitatively different structure [10]).

[2]Transmission of static stress applied to the composite and transferred with fibers is required excellent consistency of fibers and matrix; on the contrary, a dynamic impact requires energy absorption by the crack propagation along fibers.

considered as fibers produced at 800–1600°C, and graphite fibers are produced at >2200°C. However, only fibers obtained from the crystalline form of carbon arranged in a certain direction (production under tension) have a high elastic modulus and other specific design parameters such as a lower density, higher surface area, lower thermal conductivity, higher electrical resistance, and so forth compared to graphite fibers. Glass fibers with diameter of 3.5–20 μm are produced by fast drawing from the melts (the speed reaches up to 400 m min^{-1}). The spinning speed is also influenced by the viscosity (50–100 Pa s), the melting temperature,

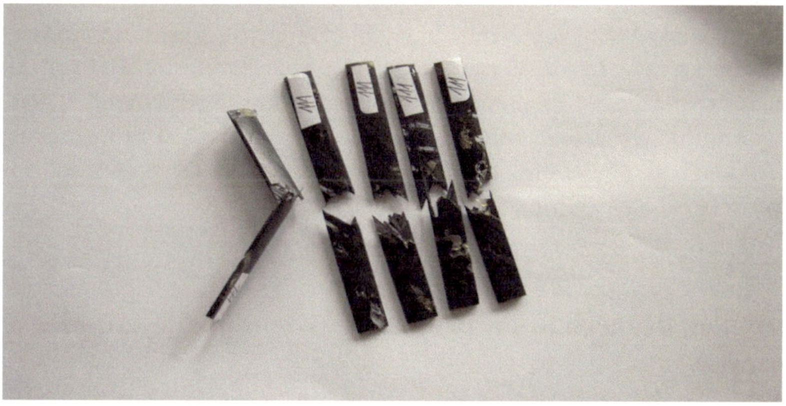

Figure 1. Example: Low strength of the fiber composite structure due to the poor joint of the fiber with matrix.

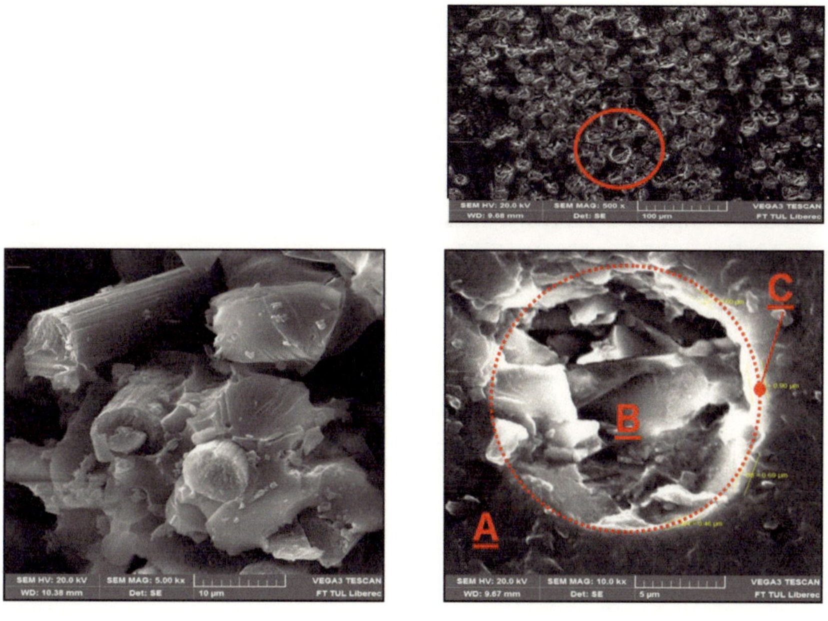

Figure 2. Cross section of composite sample with long fibers (upper), detail: fiber-matrix (bottom left), detail: phase interface (bottom right).

and, of course, the chemical composition of the glass. The matrix, which affects the properties and usability of the resulting composite, has been epoxy used for both the testing sample and design of the developed composite construction. The composite production may result in imperfect bonding of the matrix fibers (e.g., low wettability of the fiber reinforcement in the matrix, bubble formation, etc.), which leads in mechanical defects in the composite structure, which often over grow into critical defects with a significant reduction in strength (**Figure 1**). The resulting strength of the composite structure affects mechanical properties of the selected fiber reinforcement and matrix, which are characterized by mechanical parameters, for example, the elastic modulus, Poisson number, or other parameters such as the creep and fracture properties of the individual components. In terms of strength, a significant role (if not most) plays the interfaces among the fibers and the matrix, which is shown in **Figure 2**. This is due to the fact that the characteristic properties of the interface create a mechanism that apparently causes the synergistic effect that provides their unique mechanical properties to composite structures. Although a number of theories have been compiled, the synergistic mechanism of the phase interface is not yet clear.

2. Measurement of mechanical properties of composite samples with long fiber reinforcing

The determination of unknown parameters of composite materials has to be performed by experimental measurements. These parameters represent input data for numerical simulations. For a complete description of the properties, it is important to make measurements on both the fiber reinforcement (tow) and the matrix as well as on the resulting long fiber-reinforced composite structures (matrix-bonded fibers). Measurement of the mechanical properties of the samples is carried out according to standard laboratory tests, which are divided according to the time course of the applied load. Tests can be divided into static and dynamic. It can thus perform the tensile test at a constant or cyclic loading of the sample, three-point bending strength, and Charpy impact test, as shown in **Figure 3**. The samples may be formed in the "dog bone" shape or, optionally, in the form of a rectangle of defined length L, width b, and thickness h,[3] whereas they can be used for short- or long-term test.

The characteristic physical properties of samples of long fiber-reinforced composites are influenced by weight and volume ratios of individual input components (fiber reinforcement and matrices) that ultimately affect design parameters (mechanical properties and weight of the structure). The mass and volume amounts of the fibers and the matrix in the composite structure sample can be defined according to the following relationships (1–5).

$$m^c = m^f + m^m \tag{1}$$

$$M^f = \frac{m^f}{m^c}, \quad M^m = \frac{m^m}{m^c} \tag{2}$$

[3]Note: geometrical dimensions h, b, L can be also smaller, but it can lead to a problem with clamping of the sample to the jaws of dynamometer.

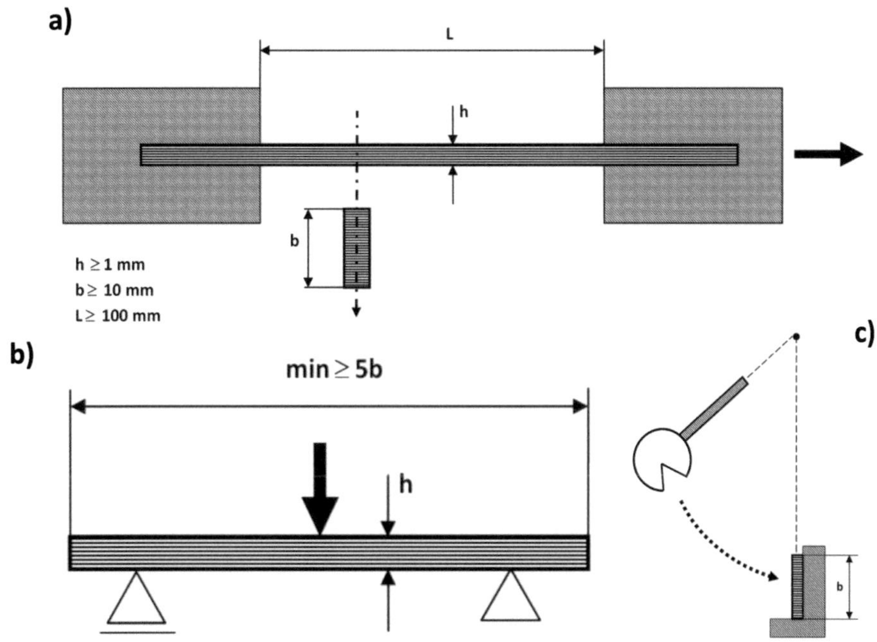

Figure 3. Determination of mechanical properties of composite samples: (a) tensile test, (b) three-point bending test, and (c) Charpy impact test.

$$M^f = 1 - M^m \tag{3}$$

$$V^f = \frac{\mathrm{v}^f}{\mathrm{v}^c}, \quad V^m = \frac{\mathrm{v}^m}{\mathrm{v}^c} \tag{4}$$

$$V^f = 1 - V^m \tag{5}$$

where m^c is the total weight of composite, m^f, m^m is the weight of fibers and matrix, M^f, M^m is the weight amount of fibers and matrix, V^f, V^m is the volume amount of fibers and matrix, v^c is the total volume of composite, and $\mathrm{v}^f, \mathrm{v}^m$ is the volume of fibers and matrix. Volume amount of fibers V^f and matrix V^m can be also expressed with the help of the fiber density ρ^f and matrix density ρ^m, which is applied in Eq. (6). The total density $\rho^c = m^c/\mathrm{v}^c$ can then be expressed as the sum of components, that is, the reinforcement and matrix (7). The characteristic thickness of the composite structure can be expressed according to the relationship (8).

$$V^f = \frac{M^f/\rho^f}{M^f/\rho^f + M^m/\rho^m}, \quad M^f = \frac{V^f\rho^f}{V^f\rho^f + V^m\rho^m} \tag{6}$$

$$\rho^c = \rho^f V^f + \rho^m V^m \tag{7}$$

$$h = m^f \left[\frac{1}{\rho^f} + \frac{1}{\rho^m} \cdot \left(\frac{1 - M^f}{M^f}\right)\right] \tag{8}$$

Gay and Hoa [10] reported that winding of the fibers onto-shaped geometry may achieve the

Name of fibers	m^{f*} [g m^{-2}]	m^{m*} [g m^{-2}]	M^f [%]	M^V [%]	V^f [%]	V^m [%]	ρ^f [g cm^{-3}]	ρ^m [g cm^{-3}]	h [mm]
GF 1600 tex/PUR Huntsman	560	600	48	52	30	70	2.45	1.1	1.2
CF prepreg HEXPLY-M10R	150	91.96	62	38	52	48	1.8	1.2	0.22
CF 24K/PUR Huntsman	213	747	22	78	15	85	1.8	1.1	1.2

Note: m^{f*}, m^{m*} represent area weight, m^{c*} is the total weight of composite.

Table 1. Examples of physical and geometrical parameters of the selected samples of composite structures reinforced with long fibers.

volume fraction of fibers in the composite maximally 55–80% of the total volume of the composite structure. Ideally, these values can be increased by precisely placing fiber tows side by side. A limit state of volume fiber fraction, that is, 100%, cannot be achieved due to the necessity of the presence of the matrix. Also by perfectly precise laying of fiber strands, the strands will always have a certain fill value that will never be equal to 1 in the geometric configuration. Perfectly precise laying of fiber tows does not provide 100% of volume filling due to fiber cross section. However, it should be noted that the optimum ratio of fiber reinforcement is in the range of the synergistic effect, that is, $V^f \approx 0.4 \div 0.65$.

The influence of selected physical parameters on the geometric parameter h of some tested samples from long fiber-reinforced composite structures is shown in **Table 1**. These parameters can then be used to establish numerical models. Other input parameters that are required for the numerical model have to be obtained by measuring the test samples. Other input parameters that are necessary for the numerical model are obtained by testing composite samples.

3. Analytical models for the study of mechanical properties of long fiber-reinforced composites

Numerical modeling of the mechanical properties of the composite is a very difficult problem because there are many unknown parameters that come into model simulations, which are discussed in this chapter. Therefore, some parameters need to be properly verified with analytical models. It is assumed that though mechanical properties of the sample are formed from uniformly spaced transversely isotropic structure, its theoretical description is difficult, as shown in **Figure 4**.

The model of the transverse isotropic fiber composite structure can be defined by six independent elastic constants through the constitutive Eq. (9). The mechanical properties, such as composite structures, are also affected by the volume of fibers V^f and matrix V^m.

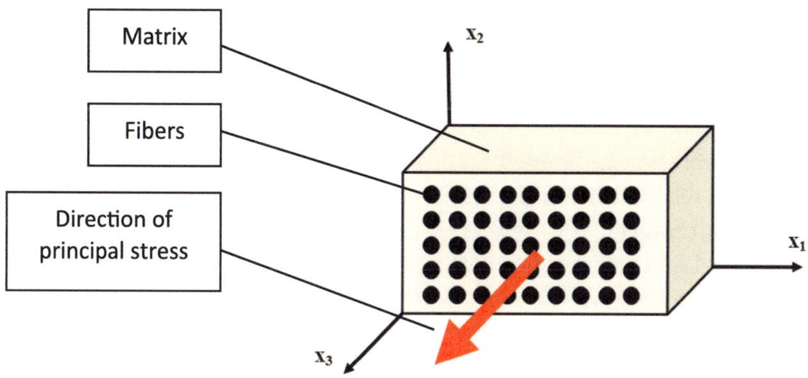

Figure 4. Model of idealized transverse isotropic fiber composite structure.

$$\begin{Bmatrix} \varepsilon_{11} \\ \varepsilon_{22} \\ \varepsilon_{33} \\ \gamma_{12} \\ \gamma_{23} \\ \gamma_{13} \end{Bmatrix} = \begin{bmatrix} 1/E_{11} & -\nu_{12}/E_{11} & -\nu_{12}/E_{11} & 0 & 0 & 0 \\ -\nu_{12}/E_{11} & 1/E_{22} & -\nu_{23}/E_{22} & 0 & 0 & 0 \\ -\nu_{12}/E_{11} & -\nu_{23}/E_{22} & 1/E_{22} & 0 & 0 & 0 \\ 0 & 0 & 0 & 1/G_{23} & 0 & 0 \\ 0 & 0 & 0 & 0 & 1/G_{12} & 0 \\ 0 & 0 & 0 & 0 & 0 & 1/G_{12} \end{bmatrix} \cdot \begin{Bmatrix} \sigma_{11} \\ \sigma_{22} \\ \sigma_{33} \\ \tau_{12} \\ \tau_{23} \\ \tau_{13} \end{Bmatrix} \tag{9}$$

where σ_{ii}, ε_{ii} are the principal stresses and strains in the transversal isotropic composite in individual directions of the coordinate system x_1, x_2, x_3, whereas $\sigma_{11} > \sigma_{22} = \sigma_{33}$, $\varepsilon_{11} \neq \varepsilon_{22} = \varepsilon_{33}$, and $\tau_{12}, \tau_{23} = \tau_{13}$ are the shear stresses in the given planes, $\gamma_{12}, \gamma_{23} = \gamma_{13}$ expresses the shear to individual planes, $E_{11}, E_{22} = E_{33}$ expresses the longitudinal and transverse modulus of elasticity, G_{12}, G_{23} is the shear modulus in the plane of the principal load direction and in a plane perpendicular to the principal load direction, ν_{12} is the Poisson ratio in the principal direction of the load, and ν_{23} is the Poisson ratio in a plane perpendicular to the principal load direction.

For the corresponding model, the interconnection of individual components A, B, C must be included (see **Figure 2**) to create a multiphase system approaching the behavior of composite structures. Therefore, the problem of modeling a composite can be treated as a continuum (a solid model without a geometric arrangement of individual components) or by creating a completely new model with structural parameters, that is, the individual components will be included in the structured unit. The problem of analytical modeling of mechanical properties of general fiber structures through a structural unit is described, among others, by Wyk for the study of interfiber contacts [11] and by Neckář [12]. However, the description of the mechanical properties of the fibrous composite structure is more difficult and has not yet been properly described. This is probably due to the fact that knowledge of the deformation mechanism and damage process is more important for understanding the mechanical properties than the knowledge of the absolute strength that cannot be determined with sufficient precision. This is due to the fact that it is not possible to comprehensively construct a general energy theory (to derive empirical relationships for deformation work) based on statistical characteristics, as can be done with very good accuracy for other anisotropic structures (Petrů et al. [13, 14]). The problem is that the individual components composing the composite structure cannot be reliably quantified even with homogeneous isotropic materials (matrices, glass fibers), let alone anisotropic structures such as carbon fibers (the theoretical value presented in the data sheet is different than value determined experimentally). Therefore, the main problems are related to the complexity of the description and modeling of deformation and the consequent character of the stress (stress concentration under loading). This is mainly due to technological influences in composite production (influence of temperature, humidity, and initial microporosity) that cannot be predicted for model simulations, and it is also relatively difficult to experimentally identify these parameters.[4]

Over time, there have been widespread analytical relationships to form the approach to obtain all elastic constants that can be used by these models, which are given as follows:

- phenomenological models.
- semiempirical models.
- homogenized models.

3.1. Phenomenological models

In the past, phenomenological models have been created as the primary mathematical derivation of the mechanical properties of transversally isotropic fibrous composite structures but can be used well today. Such models include the Voigt and Reuss models. These are models using the mixing rule (mixing of the individual input components, i.e., fibers and matrices), while the Voigt model is very well usable for determining the elastic constants E_{11}, ν_{12} defined by relationships (10 and 11) and is characterized by isotropic strain. The Reuss model is usable for determination E_{22}, G_{12} defined by relationships (12 and 13) and unlike the Voigt model is characterized by isotropic stress.

$$\frac{d\sigma_{11}}{d\varepsilon_{11}} = V^f \frac{d\sigma^f}{d\varepsilon^f} + V^m \frac{d\sigma^m}{d\varepsilon^m} \Rightarrow E_{11} = V^f E^f_{11} + V^m E^m \tag{10}$$

$$\nu_{12} = V^f \nu^f_{12} + V^m \nu^m \tag{11}$$

$$E_{22} = \frac{E^f_{22} E^m}{E^m V^f + E^f_{22} E^m} \tag{12}$$

$$G_{12} = \frac{G^f_{12} G^m}{G^m V^f + G^f_{12} E^m} \tag{13}$$

[4]In the advanced model, simulations can be assembled material models with any parameters, including the statistical parameters, which describe technological production factors, for example, through the theory of random fields as defined by Bittnar and Šejnoha [15]. The problem lies in the identification of the effects and the subsequent statistical evaluation.

where E_{11}^f, E_{22}^f are the longitudinal and transverse modulus of the fiber elasticity, G_{12}^f is a fiber shear module, and ν_{12f} is the Poisson ratio in the plane of the principal direction of the load of the fiber.

3.2. Semiempirical models

Semiempirical models were created later than phenomenological models, and based on the new information and knowledge, they are still being updated. Their development led in particular to the further expansion of the Voigt and Reuss models because these models have been modified by correction factors to specify the resulting elastic constants for the given types of input components. This category includes models that are implemented in certain modifications in finite element softwares such as the Halpin-Tsai model or the Chamis model.

- **Modified model according to the mixing rule**

Modified model according to the mixing rule is derived from Voigt [16] and Reuss [17], and for elastic constants, E_{11}, ν_{12} is defined according to Eqs. (10 and 11). Modification occurs with constants E_{22}, G_{12}, because the resulting difference between the results obtained by the measurements and the relationships (12–13) is usually noticeable. Therefore, it was necessary to make a correction for E_{22}, G_{12} according to Eqs. (14 and 15).

$$\frac{1}{E_{22}} = \frac{\zeta^f V^f}{E_{22}^f} + \frac{\zeta^m V^m}{E^m} \tag{14}$$

$$\frac{1}{G_{12}} = \frac{\frac{V^f}{G_{12}^f} + \frac{\zeta' V^m}{G^m}}{V^f + \zeta' V^m} \tag{15}$$

where ζ^f, ζ^m are correction factors,[5] according to Younes et al. [18].

- Halpin-Tsai model

This is a model that is implemented in a number of numerical programs by using finite element method (FEM). This model is developed as a semiempirical model [19] with correction of E_{22}, G_{12}. Its semiempirical derivation (16–17) using correction factors ζ, ξ has a very good agreement with experiments.

$$E_{22} = E^m \left(\frac{1 + \xi \zeta V^f}{1 - \zeta V^f} \right) \tag{16}$$

$$G_{12} = G^m \left(\frac{1 + \xi \zeta V^f}{1 - \zeta V^f} \right) \tag{17}$$

[5] Correction factors ζ^f, ζ^m can be express as $\zeta^f = \frac{E_{11}^f V^f + \left[\left(1 - \nu_{12}^f \nu_{21}^f\right) E^m + \nu^m \nu_{21}^f E_{11}^f \right] V^m}{E_{11}^f V^f + E^m V^m}$, $\zeta^m = \frac{E^m V^m + \left[(1 - \nu^m \nu^m) E_{11}^f - \left(1 - \nu^m \nu_{12}^f\right) E^m \right] V^f}{E_{11}^f V^f + E^m V^m}$, ζ' is a variable function $0 < \zeta' < 1$, whereas preferred is $\zeta' \approx 0.5 - 0.6$.

where ζ correction factor, for which it is valid $\zeta = \frac{M^f/M^m - 1}{M^f/M^m + \xi}$, ξ is constant, which is for E_{22} equal to 1, and for G_{12} is equal to 2, $M = E$ or G in the case of an expression E_{22} and G_{12} according to Eqs. (12–13).

- Chamis model

This is another semiempirical model [20], which was unlike previous models developed not only for independent elastic constants $E_{11}, E_{22}, G_{12}, \nu_{12}$ but also for G_{23}. The determination of E_{11}, ν_{12} is again based on Voigt and Reusse according to Eqs. (10–11). The Chamis model for calculating other elastic constants introduces a square root of the volume of fiber $\sqrt{V^f}$, which has in Eqs. (18–20), the meaning of fiber incompressibility, which is in line with principle of mass conservation.

$$E_{22} = \frac{E^m}{1 - \sqrt{V^f}\left(1 - E^m/E^f_{22}\right)} \tag{18}$$

$$G_{12} = \frac{G^m}{1 - \sqrt{V^f}\left(1 - G^m/G^f_{12}\right)} \tag{19}$$

$$G_{23} = \frac{G^m}{1 - \sqrt{V^f}\left(1 - G^m/G^f_{23}\right)} \tag{20}$$

where G^f_{23} is the shear modulus of the fiber elasticity in a plane perpendicular to the principle direction of loading.

3.3. Homogenized models

Homogenized models are generalized models that can be used to determine very accurate values of elastic constants for developed composite structures reinforced by longitudinally laid fibers. Such models include, for example, the Mori-Tanaka model [21], a consistent model created by Hill [22] or the Bridging model. Their applicability compared to phenomenological or semiempirical models largely limits the more difficult determination of all constants entering to homogenized models. An example is the Eshelby toughness tensor that can be used for inclusion, which is introduced in both the Mori-Tanaka model and the consistent model. In view of this, from homogenized models, the Brindling model can be used to determine the elastic constants.

- Bridging model

This is a model that is developed to predict the stiffness and strength of transverse isotropic fiber composites. The elastic properties are for the elastic modulus E_{11}, ν_{12} the same as for Voigt and Reusse models (10–11). Elastic constants E_{22}, G_{12}, G_{23} can be expressed using the Bridging model (21–23).

http://dx.doi.org/10.5772/intechopen.71881

$$E_{22} = \frac{\left(V^f + V^m a_{11}\right) \cdot \left(V^f + V^m a_{22}\right)}{\left(V^f + V^m a_{11}\right)\left(V^f S^f_{11} + V^m a_{22} S^m_{22}\right) + V^f V^m \left(S^m_{21} - S^f_{21}\right) a_{12}} \tag{21}$$

$$G_{12} = \frac{\left(V^f + V^m a_{66}\right) \cdot G^f_{12} G^m}{V^f G^m + V^m a_{66} G^f_{12}} \tag{22}$$

$$G_{23} = \frac{1/2\left(V^f + V^m a_{44}\right)}{V^f \left(S^f_{22} - S^f_{23}\right) + V^m a_{44}\left(S^m_{22} - S^m_{23}\right)} \tag{23}$$

where a_{ii}, $S^{f,m}_{ii}$ are the matrix components, which relate to fiber and matrix ratios in the composite structure as reported by Huang [23, 24], where $a_{11} = E^m/E^f_{22}$, $a_{22} = a_{44} = 0,35+ \ (1- \ 0,35)$ E^m/E^f_{22}, $a_{66} = 0,3 + (1 - 0,3)\left[0,5E^m/(1 + v^m)\right]/G^f_{12}$, $a_{12} = \left(S^f_{12} - S^m_{12}\right)(a_{11} - a_{22})/\left(S^f_{11} - S^m_{11}\right)$, $S^{f,m}_{11} = 1/E^{f,m}_{11}, S^{f,m}_{22} = 1/E^{f,m}_{22} S^{f,m}_{12} = S^{f,m}_{21} = -v^{f,m}_{12}/E^{f,m}_{11}, S^{f,m}_{23} = S^{f,m}_{32} = -\, v^{f,m}_{23}/E^{f,m}_{22}$.

4. Numerical models for the study of mechanical properties of long fiber-reinforced composites

Measurement and analytical models of long fiber-reinforced composite structures designed to study mechanical properties are generally able to provide only limited information. This is due to the fact that the measurements are limited by the possibilities of positioning of the sensors and also by the fact that some properties cannot be measured well (e.g., the distribution of the main stress and deformation in the composite structure). The knowledge of the distribution of the main stresses and deformations in the structure is important for assessing how the structure is changed and under which stress. In this case, the corresponding model simulation using numeric methods represents a significant support for the development. Very suitable is to build model simulation in finite element method (FEM), but other numerical methods, such as discrete element (DEM), boundary element (BEM) or finite volume method (FVM) method, are also available. The mechanical loading of composite causes many different processes in the inner structure that varies with the actual deformation. Therefore, it is necessary to simplify or neglect some characteristic features in modeling of such structures. A major problem of mechanical properties modeling of composite structures is in particular the description of the principal stresses in short time $\Delta t = t_{i+1} - t_i$. The solution of problem of composite with boundary conditions under tensile loading lies not only in the specification of the correct boundary conditions and material properties but also in the design of the proposed finite element mesh. The FEM programs are currently very sophisticated and allow the solution of a continuous problem transform into a final solution where the corresponding geometric simple subareas (finite elements) can be designed in the preprocessor. Let $\Omega \subset \mathfrak{R}^3$ is the continuous area of the three-dimensional space in which the problem is solved. Its borders will be denoted Γ, where Γis Lipschitz border and let the approximation of the selected base functions is derived above each finite element of length $l_{element}$, because any continuous function can be represented by a linear combination of algebraic polynomials converging to a continuous solution, that is, $\lim_{l_{element}\to 0} \to 1$. Thus, the FEM method can be understood as a special type of variation method by using the mathematical description of the problem solution. The current commercial software and FEM programs (e.g., Ansys, Abaqus, Permas, LS-Dyna, Marc, PAM CRASH) allow to assemble and subsequently solve a series of problems with nonlinear materials not only with elastic but also plastic behavior corresponding to the properties of the long fiber-reinforced composite.

4.1. FEM simulation of mechanical properties of long fiber-reinforced composite

Model simulations in FEM were performed for different combinations of reinforcement arrangements of long fiber-reinforced composites, which are important for comparison with experiments and analytical relationships. This gives the material properties for numerical simulation of the strength characteristics of whole frames.

This chapter describes the creation of two numerical models and their comparison:

(I) continuum model

(II) extended continuous model with structural unit

The simulations were performed for a complete assessment of the mechanical properties $\sigma_{11}, \sigma_{22}, \varepsilon_{11}, \varepsilon_{22}, \gamma_{12}, \gamma_{23}$ and elastic constants $E_{11}, E_{22}, G_{12}, G_{23}, \nu_{12}, \nu_{23}$, whereas also information explaining the shape changes of the samples observed especially during tensile stress. Model simulations were performed in the following steps:

- creating two model simulations of the long fiber-reinforced composite,
- creating the corresponding mesh of finite elements of the computational model in the preprocessor,
- defining the corresponding initial and boundary conditions,
- assembling a material model of the long fiber-reinforced composite,
- the evaluation and comparison of model simulation results in postprocessor.

4.1.1. Assembling of continuum of the long fiber-reinforced composite model

The FEM model was created in the concept of coherent continuum consisting of a surface geometry corresponding to the test sample with length L = 100 mm, width b = 20 mm, and thickness h = 1.7 mm. The finite element mesh of the numerical model was created from SHELL elements (2D elements) with a constant element size of 2 mm. The boundary conditions affecting the magnitude of the displacements and stress can be defined in two ways, that is, the boundary conditions of the first and second types. The first way is to determine the displacement and stress distributions if force conditions are known, that is, volume forces, surface forces, and nodal loads. The other way is to determine the displacement and tension distribution if the geometric conditions are known, that is, the size of node displacement, the deformations, and so on. Both ways can be also combined. It is mixed boundary conditions, as shown by Li [25]. Boundary and initial conditions for the model were made by the boundary conditions of the second type. One side of the sample was fixed against the displacement and rotation of nodes $U_i = R_i = 0$ in all directions (layout), and the opposite side of the edge of the sample was fixed identically; only in X direction, the movement was allowed, whereas $U_x = 1$ mm that corresponds to the deformation $\varepsilon_x = 1$ %. The strain rate was 2 mm.min^{-1}. The boundary conditions are shown in **Figure 5**.

4.1.2. Assembling of extended continuous composite model of long fiber-reinforced composite

The second numerical FEM model, which was created in the concept of structure unit, is formed from three components: fiber matrix—the interfacial interface, where the microscopic dimensions of such a model are closer to the more real composite. Such a model can be created from a structural unit with the $1, 2, \ldots, n$ fibers, wherein the volume geometric configuration (e.g., structural unit is a cube, cuboid, sphere) can affect the volumetric quantity of fibers and a matrix V^f, V^m, as shown by Neckář [12]. The change in volume ratio V^f can be given on the example of the structural unit of the cuboid, which is shown in the section in **Figure 6**. The structural unit consists of six fibers represented by circles with the same spacing m_i, which are

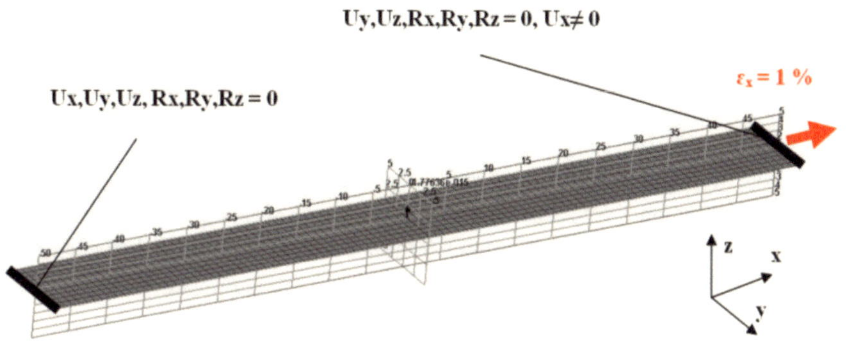

Figure 5. Continuum FEM model of the composite reinforced with long fibers with defined boundary and initial conditions.

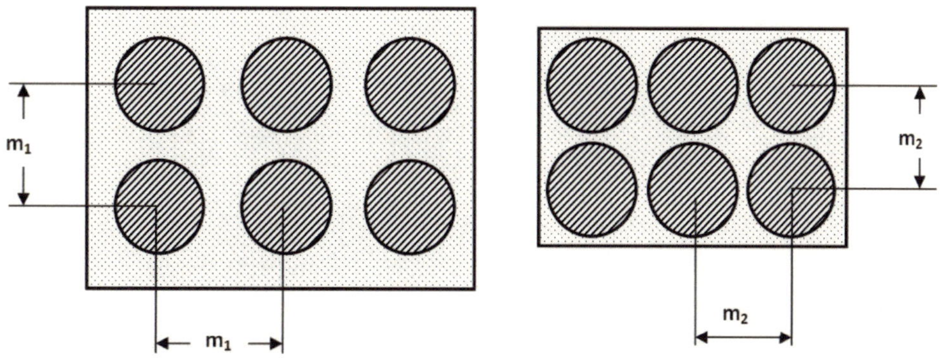

Figure 6. The influence of fiber spacing in the structural unit on V^f fiber volume ratio.

bounded by a matrix (rectangle). By changing of the spacing can then be increased or decreased volume ratio of fibers V^f. The finite element mesh of the numerical model was created from a combination of following elements: BRICK elements (3D elements) with a designed element size of 0.0002 mm defined for fibers and matrix (**Figure 7**).

It will be assumed that $E_{11} = \frac{\sigma_{11}}{\varepsilon_{11}}$, $E_{22} = \frac{\sigma_{22}}{\varepsilon_{22}}$, $G_{12} = \frac{\tau_{12}}{\gamma_{12}}$, $G_{23} = \frac{\tau_{23}}{\gamma_{23}}$.

The problem lies in joining of fibers with the matrix because the interconnections form an interphase. The structural FEM model assembling presents a problem of the determination of appropriate boundary conditions, which is important in terms of accuracy and model verification. Incorrect design may result in concentrators and singularities of stress. The boundary conditions are created by the second type (geometric boundary conditions) as follows: the perimeter surfaces of the model perpendicular to the plane of the stretching direction have defined symmetry conditions on one side (symmetry in axis y and z) and on the opposite side, the boundary conditions are not prescribed. On surfaces in the plane of the stretch direction, that is, in the direction of the X axis, the displacements and rotations were not allowed $U_i = R_i = 0$ in all directions. On the opposite surface of the specimen, the condition was the same, only displacement in the stretching direction was allowed. The displacement was defined constantly to the maximum strain 1%, that is, $U_x = k.|_{\varepsilon_x = 1\%}$, $k. = \text{const.}$, with strain rate 2 mm min^{-1}. Boundary conditions are shown in **Figure 8** and **Table 2**. The material properties applied in both FEM models (I. Continuum Model and the II. Continuum Model with the Structure Unit) are based on the generally known values reported by fiber and matrix manufacturers. The fiber and epoxy matrix parameters are listed in **Table 3**. The results of both numerical simulations have exhibited approximately the same stress at the defined strain $\varepsilon_i = 1\%$ under tensile load in applied direction for a given fiber reinforcement (carbon or glass). The resulting dependence of force on the displacement of the samples obtained from the models showed an approximately linear course, both for carbon and glass fiber-reinforced composite. **Figure 9** shows the tensile test for volume ratio $V^f = 0.3$, where carbon fiber-reinforced composite with the epoxy matrix

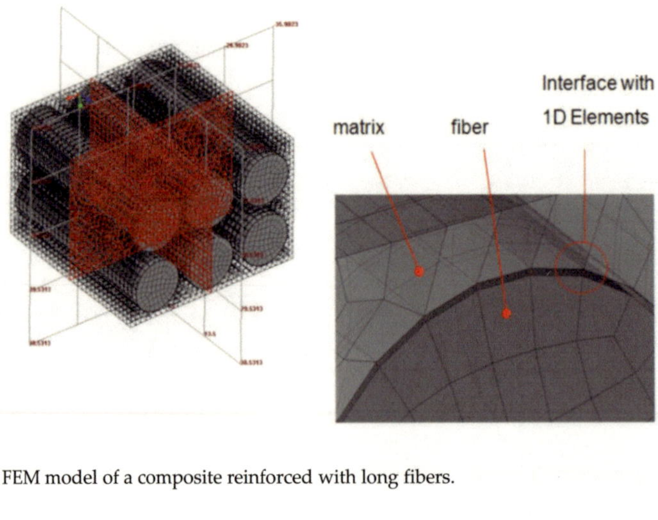

Figure 7. Structural FEM model of a composite reinforced with long fibers.

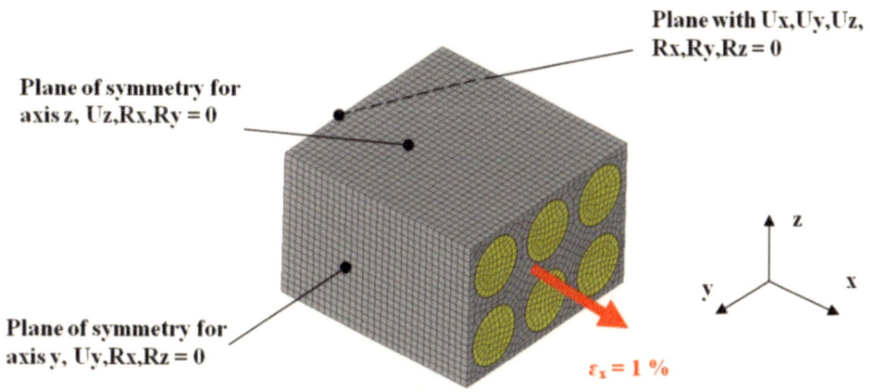

Figure 8. The boundary conditions of the structural FE model of the composite structure reinforced with long fibers.

	Planes in axis x		Planes in axis y		Planes in axis z	
	$+x$	$-x$	$+y$	$-y$	$+z$	$-z$
E_{11}, μ_{12}	$U_x = k.\|_{\varepsilon_x=1\%}$	$U_i, R_i = 0$	$U_y, R_z, R_x = 0$	—	$U_z, R_x, R_y = 0$	—
E_{22}, μ_{23}	$U_x, R_y, R_z = 0$	—	$U_y = k.\|_{\varepsilon_y=1\%}$	$U_i, R_i = 0$	$U_z, R_x, R_y = 0$	—
G_{12}	$U_y = k.\|_{\varepsilon_y=1\%}$ $U_z = 0$	$U_y = 0$ $U_z = 0$	$U_x = 0$ $U_z = 0$	$U_x = 0$ $U_z = 0$	$U_z = 0$	$U_z = 0$
G_{23}	$U_x = 0$	$U_x = 0$	$U_x = 0$ $U_z = 0$	$U_x = 0$ $U_z = 0$	$U_y = k.\|_{\varepsilon_y=1\%}$ $U_x = 0$	$U_x = 0$ $U_y = 0$

Table 2. FEM model boundary conditions for obtaining elastic constants.

Material	Density [kg m^{-3}]	Modulus of elasticity [GPa]		Shear module [GPa]		Poisson's ratio [–]		Tensile strength [GPa]	Elongation [%]
		$E_{11}^{f,m}$	$E_{22}^{f,m}$	$G_{12}^{f,m}$	$G_{23}^{f,m}$	$v_{12}^{f,m}$	$v_{23}^{f,m}$		
Carbon fibers	1750 ± 150	230	15	24	5.4	0.279	0.49	2.3 ± 1.2	1.9 ± 0.6
Glass fibers	2370 ± 230	72.4	72.4	28.7	28.7	0.22	0.22	1.06 ± 0.65	4.8 ± 0.7
Epoxy matrix	1150 ± 370	3.573	3.573	1.31	1.31	0.345	0.345	0.067 ± 0.033	3.6

Table 3. Material and mechanical properties of individual constituent of composite.

exhibits approximately 2.2 times higher force response than the glass fiber-reinforced composite with epoxy matrix.

The obtained results shown in **Figures 10** and **11** can be stated that the continuous model (FE model I) has an approximately steady monotonic course manifested not only in continuous

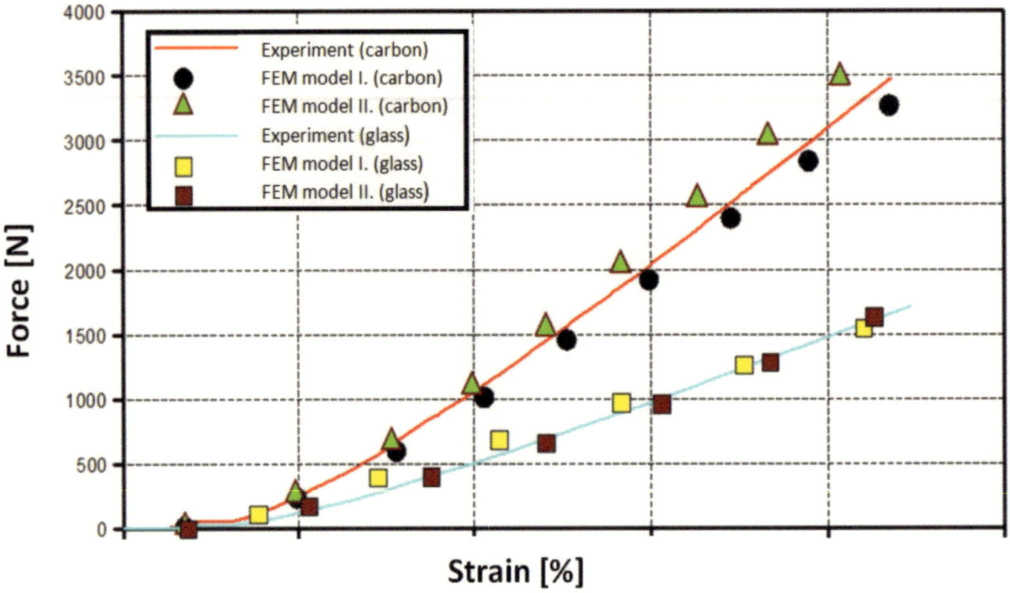

Figure 9. Comparison of experiments and FEM models: Dependence of applied force on sample strain.

distribution of deformation (**Figure 12** above) but also in uniform distribution of the principal stress $\sigma^I = \sigma_{11}$ acting in the load direction (**Figure 12** center).

Due to the simplicity of the FEM model I, it appears to be very suitable for determining the mechanical properties of composite structures and their optimization. However, such a model does not provide information about strain and stress between the fibers and the matrix, let alone the interphase. The continuous model with the structural unit (FEM model II) is significantly more complex, and for some elastic constants, its resultant course is not monotone (G_{23}, ν_{23}); in other words, the resulting dependency is not stable and may not be accurate enough but more complex in terms of results. FEM model II allows to approximate the layout distribution of the structure unit in the loading direction (Z axis) as shown in **Figure 12** (left) and also the principal stress distribution. The principal stress can be determined in isosurfaces or in sequential sections (**Figure 12** right), which allow to analyze the stress distribution between the fibers and the matrix including the interphase. By comparing the maximum values of the stress of 189.1 and 190.9 MPa at same strain $\varepsilon_{11} = 1\%$ and with the volume ratio $V^f = 0.5$ can be stated that the models have significant agreement. This is affected not only by the same material parameters and boundary conditions but also appropriately selected types of elements of the finite element mesh as discussed earlier. FEM model II of the composite structure reinforced with longitudinal fibers with the epoxy matrix is more complex, and the time of the calculation is larger than the FEM model I.

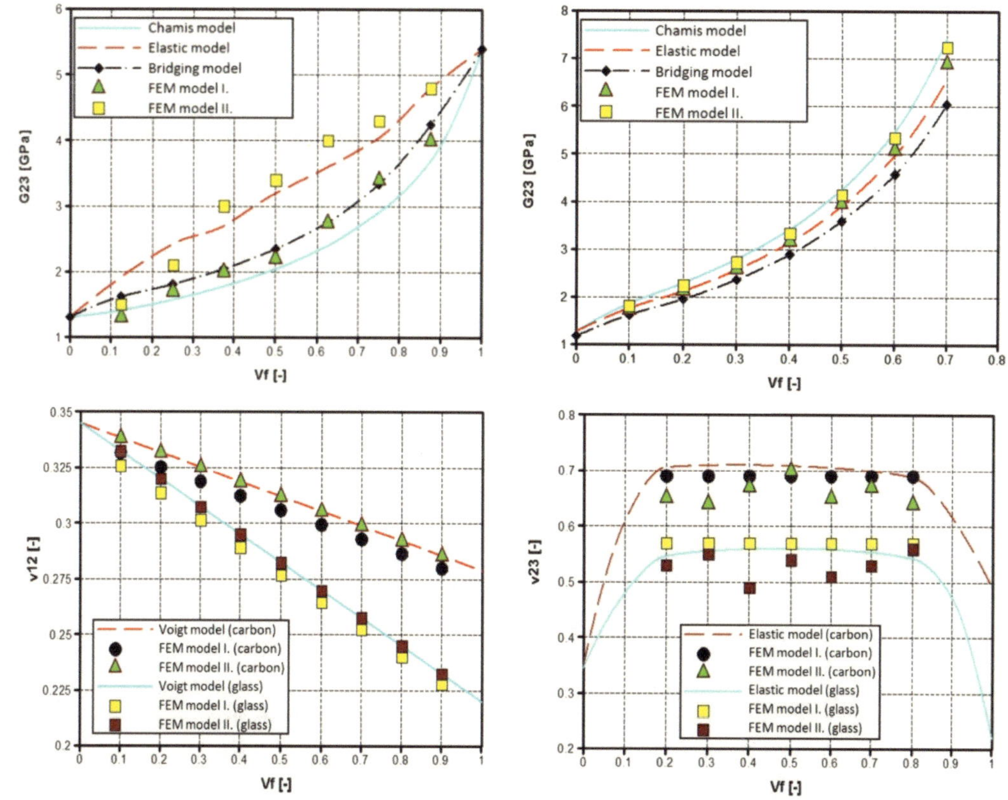

Figure 10. Dependence of modulus G23 (left above), ν_{12} (left below), ν_{23}(right) on V^f of transversally isotropic composites with epoxy matrix and carbon fibers and glass fibers.

However, it must be added that the FEM model II shows valuable scientific knowledge of the approximate distribution of the maximum stress between the fibers and the matrix, which is the largest in the interphase (**Figure 13** left). This confirms the theoretical assumption of the system mechanism (fiber-matrix interphase), where the highest stress transmits newly created component, that is, the interphase, which causes the synergic effect of the resultant construction of the composite structure. **Figure 13** also shows the information that FEM model II shows a nonuniform maximum stress in the composite structure (unlike the FEM model I) and also shows that maximum stress is concentrated only on two fibers (instead of six in the structural unit) of the structural unit. It will reduce the maximum synergic effect that theoretically in the composite structure can occur. The distribution of the interphase in the numerical model and in the real measurement is shown in **Figure 13**. It is necessary to add that from the analyses carried out by measurements on real samples was in all cases evident that the identification of the interphase is very complicated. Due to the

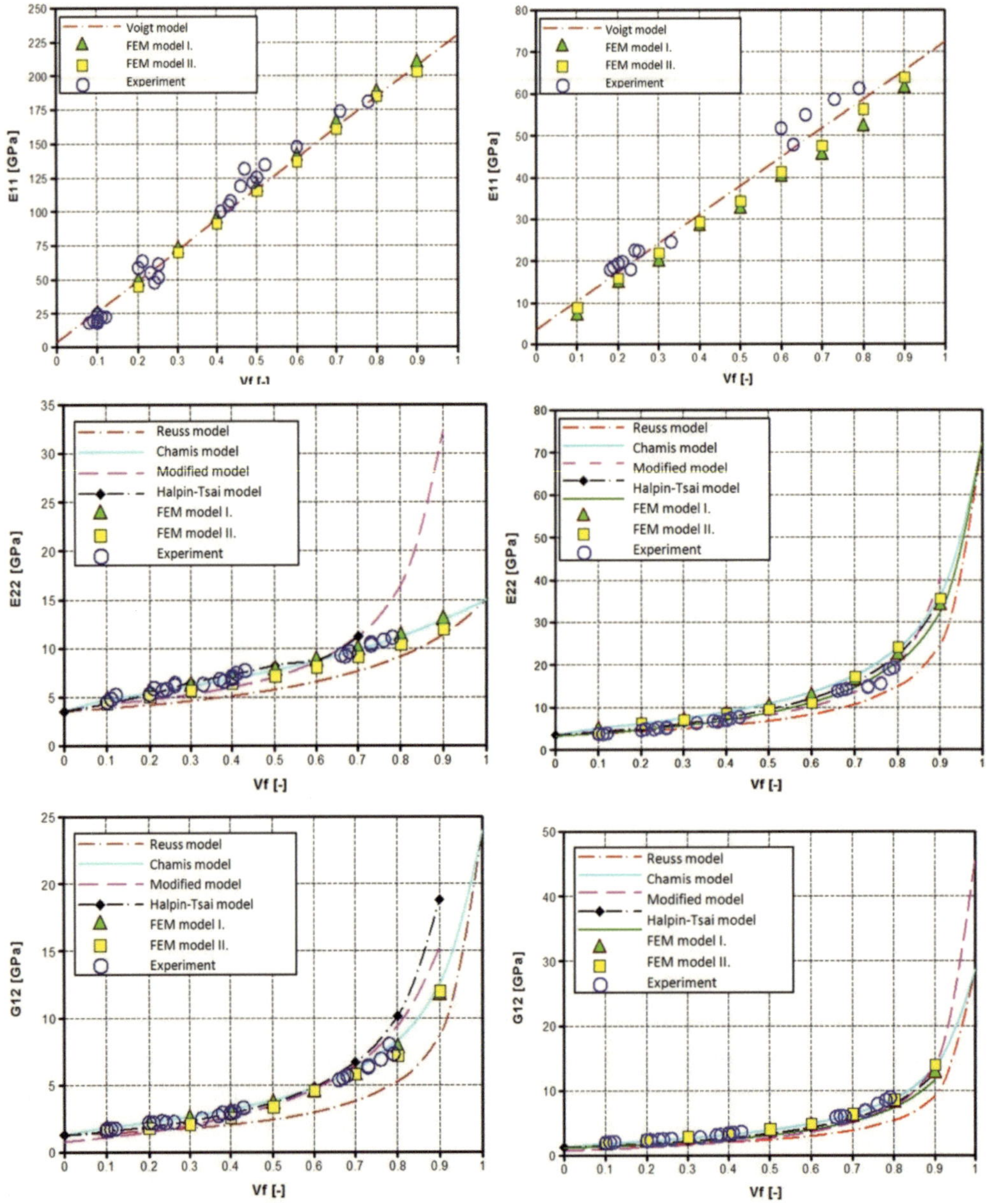

Figure 11. Dependence of modulus *E11, E22, G12* on V^f of transversally isotropic composites with epoxy matrix and carbon fibers (left) and glass fibers (right).

unidentifiable technological process, interphase (third component) could not be created. Also, it is problem to identify and measure the interphase that is important both for verifying of numerical models and for a statistical evaluation how many fibers are involved in synergistic effect.

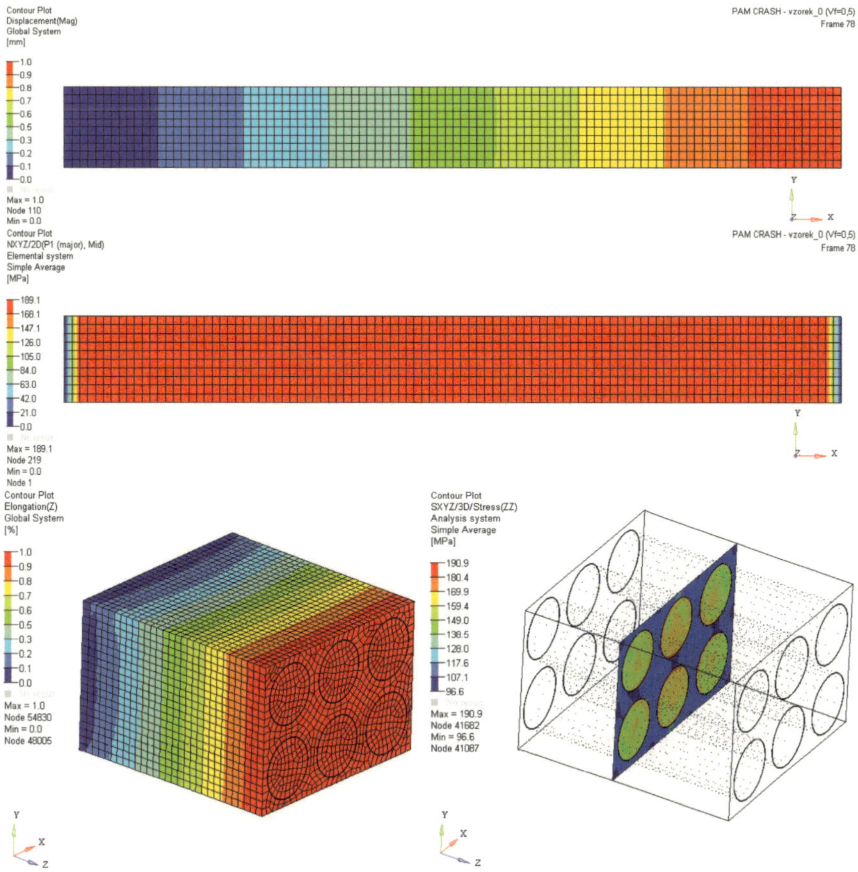

Figure 12. Distribution of deformation (above) and principal stress in the loading direction (center) of the FEM model I of long fiber-reinforced composite with epoxy matrix. The resulting distribution of axial strain (below left) and the principal stress acting in the loading direction (below right) and the FEM model II of composite reinforced with long carbon fiber with epoxy matrix.

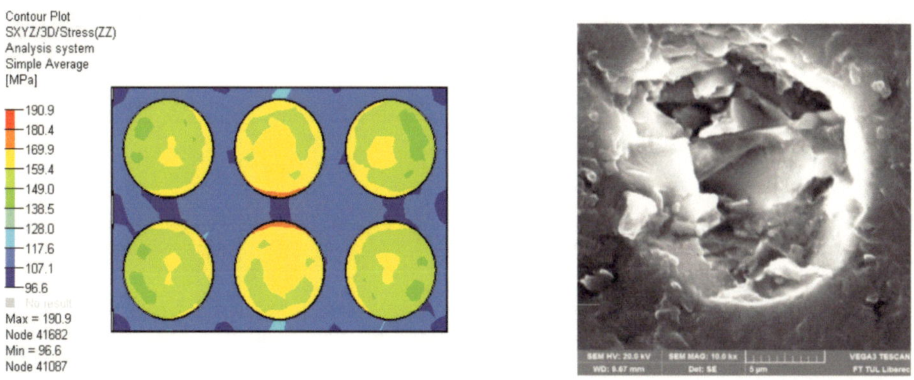

Figure 13. Distribution of principal stress in direction of loading with maximal stress in interphase (left), real sample with visible interphase (right).

5. Conclusion

In this chapter, analyses and numerical simulations of mechanical properties of samples from composite structures were presented. Several studies and experiments have been carried out on samples reinforced with carbon and glass fibers, and mechanical properties allow them to form structural reinforcements of composite materials. Further, analytical models with mathematical relationships (e.g., Voigt, Reuss or Chamis model) allow to determine the unknown elastic constants E_{11}, E_{22}, G_{12}, G_{23}, ν_{12}, ν_{23} of the resulting composite structure. This is followed by a more extensive description of the creation of a numerical model of a composite fiber structure pattern for determining mechanical properties, both through the description of a general continuum and a more complex numerical model with a structural arrangement to allow closer interaction of the fiber and the matrix. From the numerical models, the stress and strain distribution can be determined over a given time interval under chosen packing density V^f as well as the elastic constants. The course of elastic constants has to be compared in some cases only with analytical models because unknown constants cannot be appropriately measured. In summary, the I. continuous model is more user-friendly for numerical simulation and that is suitable for describing the principal stresses, but it does not allow to analyze and study the composite on microlevel. Thus, it does not allow the distribution of the stress between the fiber and the matrix (interphase). This can be done with more complex II. extended continuous model with a structural unit. The results of numerical models establish valuable knowledge and information, including the determination of elastic constants for a particular specific composite design. These results can be used for modeling of large samples and complicated geometries to optimize the design solution.

Author details

Michal Petrů[1]* and Ondřej Novák[2]

*Address all correspondence to: michal.petru@tul.cz

1 Institute for Nanomaterials, Advanced Technology and Innovation, Technical University of Liberec, Liberec, Czech Republic

2 Textile Faculty, Dpt. of Nonwovens and Nanofibrous Material, Technical University of Liberec, Liberec, Czech Republic

References

[1] Agarwal BD, Broutman LJ, Chandrashekhara K. Analysis and Performance of Fiber Composites. 3rd ed. John Wiley & Sons; 2006. p. 576. ISBN: 978-0-471-26891-8

[2] Guedes RM. Creep and Fatigue in Polymer Matrix Composites. Woodhead Publishing; 2011. ISBN: 978-1-84569-656-6

[3] Gay D, Gambelin J. Dimensionnement des Structures, une Introduction. London: Hermes Science Publishing Ltd.; 1999. p. 680. EAN13 : 9782746200494

[4] Reifsnider KL. Fatigue of Composite Materials. Elsevier; 1991. ISBN: 978-0-444-70507-5

[5] Teply JL, Reddy JN. Unified formulation of micromechanics models of fiber-reinforced composites. In: Dvorak GJ, editor. Inelastic Deformation of Composite Materials. New York: Springer; 1990. pp. 341-370

[6] Berthelot JM. Composite Materials: Mechanical Behavior and Structural Analysis. New York: Springer; 1999. pp. 158-181

[7] Gibson RF. Principles of Composite Material Mechanics. New York: Springer: McGraw-Hill, Inc.; 1994. p. 425. ISBN: O-07-023451-5

[8] Soden PD, Hinton MJ, Kaddour AS. Lamina properties, lay-up configurations and loading conditions for a range of fiber-reinforced composite laminates. Composites Science and Technology. 1998;**58**(7):1011-1022. DOI: 10.1016/S0266-3538(98)00078-5

[9] Bareš A. Kompozitní materiály. Praha: SNTL; 1988. p. 356

[10] Gay D, Hoa, SV. Composite Materials – Design and Applications, CRC press, Taylor & Francis Group London, p. 550. ISBN: 978-1-4200-4519-2

[11] Wyk CM. Note on the compressibility of wool. Journal of the Textile Institute. 1946;**37**(12): 285-292

[12] Neckář B, Das D. Modelling of fibre orientation in fibrous materials. Journal of the Textile Institute. 2012;**103**(3):330-340

[13] Petrů M, Novák O, Herák D, Mašín I, Lepšík P, Hrabě P. Finite element method model of the mechanical behaviour of Jatropha Curcas L. bulk seeds under compression loading: Study and 2D modelling of the damage to seeds. Biosystems Engineering. 2014;**127**:50-66. DOI: 10.1016/j.biosystemseng.2014.08.011

[14] Petrů M, Novák O, Herák D, Simanjuntak S. Finite element method model of the mechanical behaviour of Jatropha Curcas L. seed under compression loading. Biosystems Engineering. 2012;**111**:412-421. DOI: 10.1016/j.biosystemseng.2012.01.008

[15] Bittnar Z, Sejnoha J. Numerical Methods in Structural Mechanics, Pitman Monographs and Surveys in Pure and Applied Mathematics. London: Thomas Telford Publications; 1996. p. 442. ISBN: 0-7844-0170-5

[16] Voigt W. Uber die Beziehung zwischen den beiden Elastizitatskonstanten Isotroper Korper. Wiedemanns Annalen der Physik und Chemie (Lepzig). 1889;**38**:573-587

[17] Reuss A. Berechnung der Fliessrense von Mischkristallen auf Grund der Plastizitatsbedingung fur Einkristalle. Zeitschrift Angewandte Mathematik und Mechanik. 1929;**9**:49-58

[18] Younes R, Hallal A, Fardoun F, Chehade FH. Comparative review study on elastic properties modeling for unidirectional composite materials, p. 391-408. Composites and their Properties, INTECH. 2012. DOI: 10.5772/2816

[19] Halpin JC, Kardos JL. The Halpin-Tsai equations: A review. Polymer Engineering and Science. 1976;**16**(5)

[20] Chamis CC. Mechanics of composite materials: Past, present, and future. Journal of Composites, Technology and Research. 1989;**11**(1):3-14. DOI: 10.1520/CTR10143J

[21] Mori T, Tanaka K. Average stress in matrix and average elastic energy of materials with misfitting inclusions. Acta Mettallurgica. 1973;**21**(5):571-574. DOI: 10.1016/0001-6160(73)90064-3

[22] Hill R. Theory of mechanical properties of fibre-strengthen materials – III, self consistent model. Journal of Mechanics and Physics of Solids. 1965;**3**:189-198

[23] Huang ZM. Simulation of the mechanical properties of fibrous composites by the bridging micromechanics model. Composites: Part A. 2001;**32**(3):143-172

[24] Huang ZM, Zhou YX. Strength of unidirectional composites. Advanced Topics in Science and Technology in China. 2012:99-143. DOI: 10.1007/978-3-642-22958-9_4

[25] Li S. Boundary condtions for unit cells from periodic microstructures and their implications. Composites Science and Technology. 2008;**68**(9):1962-1974. DOI: 10.1016/j.compscitech.2007.03.035

Finite Element Dynamic Analysis on Residual Stress Distribution of Titanium Alloy and Titanium Matrix Composite after Shot Peening Treatment

Lechun Xie, Zhou Wang, Chengxi Wang, Yan Wen,
Liqiang Wang, Chuanhai Jiang, Weijie Lu,
Lai-Chang Zhang and Lin Hua

Additional information is available at the end of the chapter

http://dx.doi.org/10.5772/intechopen.73120

Abstract

The residual stress distribution introduced by shot peening (SP) in the deformed surface layer of Ti-6Al-4V and (TiB+TiC)/Ti-6Al-4V were simulated and studied via the three-dimensional (3D) finite element dynamic analysis and the experimental validation. The program of ANSYS/LS-DYNA was utilized, and the 3D homogeneous and inhomogeneous models were set up. The homogeneous model was established for simulating SP process on Ti-6Al-4V. The influence of three important parameters, the shot balls' size, shot velocity and coverage rate on residual stress distribution were investigated. Numerical simulation results showed that these parameters contributed different effects on SP treatment. Using a simplified method, an inhomogeneous model for simulating SP process on (TiB+TiC)/Ti-6Al-4V was set up. The max tensile and compressive residual stress (CRS) was +1155 and −1511 MPa, respectively. Based on this stress distribution, the beneficial effect of reinforcements was indicated during deformation, retarding the damage to the matrix and keeping the adverse tensile stresses in the reinforcements. In order to verify the results of simulation, the residual stress distribution along depth was measured by X-ray diffraction (XRD) method. The residual stress distribution by experiments was agreed with the simulated results, which verified the availability of 3D finite element dynamic analysis.

Keywords: finite element dynamic analysis, residual stress, shot peening, titanium matrix composite, reinforcement, X-ray diffraction

1. Introduction

Shot peening (SP) is an effective surface strengthening method and widely used in industry, which can effectively improve the surface performance of material. The effect of SP depends on the material and parameters during SP process. The small SP intensity will lead to the strengthening effect unobvious, but the excessive SP intensity may result in the formation of micro-cracks and reduce the strength. So, a proper SP intensity should be conducted. Additionally, the improper shot balls will increase the surface roughness of material, which is not benefit to the surface properties. During SP, the shot balls impact the surface of material at a high speed, which transforms the kinetic energy of shot balls into the elastic energy of internal stress. So after SP, the internal energy of material is increased, and it is in the metastable state. While the external environment changes, the material with high energy may be transferred to the low energy state spontaneously, leading to the stress relaxation. For instance, in the high temperature environment, the residual stress will promote the local creep of the material, resulting in reducing the residual stress, which will weaken the effect of SP and be not conducive to the improvement of fatigue properties [1].

Usually, the fatigue strength and fatigue life of cyclically loaded metallic components can be considerably improved due to the compressive residual stress (CRS) and work hardening induced on the surface layer after SP [2]. The distribution of CRS is mainly affected by the parameters of SP and the materials' condition. A significant number of parameters are needed to be regulated and controlled in order to obtain a more beneficial CRS distribution. Therefore, in practical application of SP, the empirical knowledge should be accumulated for getting the appropriate processing parameters, which usually requires time and money consuming. For obtaining the suitable SP parameters and minimizing these trails, the numerical simulation of SP is conducted, building a better understanding of SP process with the aim of study, analyzing and predicting the relationship between the influencing factors and simulation results.

SP simulation has been developed since more than four decades. Some references have indicated that finite element method is a suitable and useful method to predict residual stress distribution after SP [3–7]. The finite element models for SP include 2D and 3D models. Usually, 2D models are adopted to simulate a single impact on a semi-infinite target body, and the simulated accuracy is verified by comparing the simulated stress distribution with the results measured by neutron diffraction and X-ray diffraction (XRD) methods. [8–12]. However, based on the direct comparison of residual stress distribution along the symmetry axis of a 2D model with the experimental results, it is questionable because the measurement area by experiment is different from the impact area of 2D simulation. Generally, the measurement area by some techniques, like XRD, neutron diffraction, and hole drilling, is larger than the diameter of dimple utilized in 2D models, and these techniques just provide macroscopic stress values. Moreover, a very important parameter, the coverage rate, cannot be considered in 2D simulation during the multiple SP process. The shortcomings of 2D models mentioned above lead to the introduction and popular application of 3D models. Because the 3D SP models can show the effect of SP coverage rate on residual stress distribution, they are approaching to the practical work more and become the main choice in recent years, especially 3D models with dynamic analysis. In the overview of SP simulation, some 3D models are adopted with different model descriptions, kinds of material models, kinds of analysis, number of shot balls, and so on [8, 13–20]. On these 3D models, most studies focus on homogeneous material and few work involves 3D inhomogeneous inclusions while establishing models. Even though some researchers have established 3D inhomogeneous models for metal matrix composites using other methods [21–25], few investigation focused on SP.

Composite material is composed of two or more kinds of materials with different chemical and physical properties, and also with different size such as micro or macro. In metal matrix composites, the difference in the properties of metal matrix and reinforcement makes the presence of interface. Due to the mismatch between matrix and reinforcement, the material properties in the vicinity of the interface are not continuous, so that the material properties and microstructure in the vicinity of the interface will vary obviously. The variation of properties has a serious effect on the macroscopic properties of the composites [26]. The size of reinforcement in the composite is typically between several μm and several tens of μm, but the irradiation area of X-ray analysis is about 1 mm^2, therefore, it is difficult to determine the stress distribution around reinforcement in the composite by experimental method. It is a feasible method to carry out numerical simulation using finite element analysis to solve this problem.

As one kind of important metal matrix composites, titanium matrix composites have wide application prospects in the field of aerospace, automobile, and other industries because of their good properties such as high specific strength, good ductility, and excellent fatigue properties, etc. [27–29]. About the residual stress distribution of titanium matrix composites after SP, the experimental investigation has been carried out in our previous work by XRD method [30–33]. However, the measured residual stress by experiments only reveals the average stress of matrix and reinforcements, because the beam size of X-ray is much bigger than the dimension of reinforcement. So, it is hard to directly test the residual stress distribution in and around the reinforcements by experiments, which depends on the method of simulation. In our current work, 3D finite element dynamic analysis of multiple shot impacting is performed on Ti-6Al-4V alloy and titanium matrix composite (TiB+TiC)/Ti-6Al-4V (TiB:TiC = 1:1 (vol%)). The program of ANSYS/LS-DYNA [34] is utilized in the 3D finite element dynamic analysis, and the 3D homogeneous and inhomogeneous models are set up. The systematic study is conducted using this 3D dynamic model to investigate the effect of coverage rate, shot balls' radius, and shot velocity on the residual stress distribution after SP. Moreover, TiC and TiB reinforcements in the composite are constructed in a composite method by the simplified inhomogeneous model. The influence of reinforcements on the stress distribution is analyzed, and the residual stresses in and around reinforcements are obtained and discussed in detail. Moreover, the experimental results by XRD method are compared with the simulation results finally.

2. Finite element simulation on homogeneous SP model

2.1. Homogeneous SP model

2.1.1. Introduction of SOLID164 element

The explicit dynamic analysis of ANSYS/LS-DYNA program provides a rich element library, including 3D bar element (LINK160), 3D beam element (BEAM161), thin shell element (SHELL163), solid element (SOLID164), spring damping element (COMBI165), mass element (MASS166), cable element (Link167), and ten-node tetrahedral element (Tet-Solid168). Each explicit dynamic element has a corresponded linear displacement function, and the default is set to a single point of integration (one of the reduced integrals). It has been proved that the explicit dynamic element with linear displacement function and the element integration can be used for solving the nonlinear problems effectively, such as the cases of large deformation and material's failure [34]. The element utilized in simulation of SP is the SOLID164 element, which is a 3D explicit solid element consisting of eight nodes. Each node in SOLID164 has the degrees of freedom in x, y, z direction of translation, velocity, and acceleration. The geometry, node locations, and the coordinate system for SOLID164 element are shown in **Figure 1** [35]. This element is only used in the dynamic explicit analysis, which supports all licensed nonlinear characteristics. By default, SOLID164 is the single point integral with the viscous hourglass control to speed up the calculation.

In the process of explicit dynamic analysis, the processing of element integral is the most time-consumption, and the processing time by CPU is proportional to the number of integral

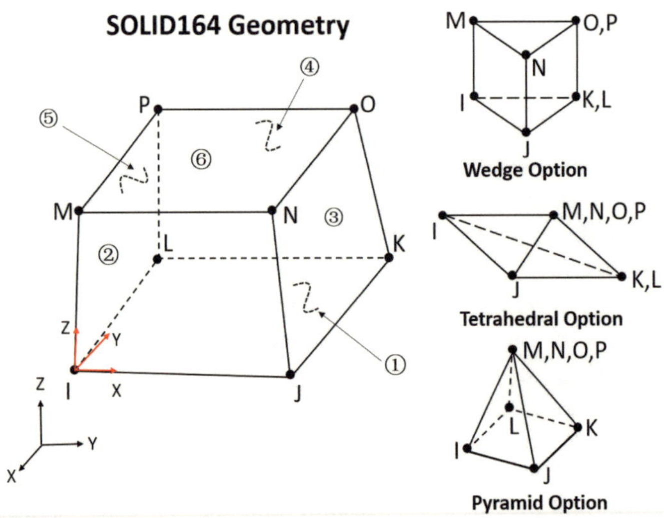

Figure 1. Geometry properties of SOLID164 [35].

points. So, using the simplified integration of elements can save the data storage capacity and reduce the number of calculations greatly, for instance, the single point integral in SOLID164 element, that is, an element has only one integration point, which is in the center of element. The utilization of single points can save a lot of calculation time, but may lead to the hourglass phenomenon. Mesh deformation with an hourglass effect is called the hourglass phenomenon, and in this situation, the typical feature is that the nonrigid element grid is distorted irregularly, resulting in a mathematically stable state but a physically impossible state. The presence of hourglass phenomenon will distort the results of the solution and even the solution cannot be carried out. Therefore, when using the simplified integration of elements, the hourglass phenomenon should be controlled. In ANSYS/LS-DYNA finite element analysis process, if the result of hourglass energy calculated by the model is less than 10% of the total energy, this simulation result and the model can be identified as credible.

2.1.2. *Piecewise linear plasticity model*

The choice of material model is not only related to the success of simulation, but also directly related to the rationality and reliability of calculated results. The process of SP causes a high plastic deformation in the surface layer, so Cowper-Symbols in ANSYS is adopted to achieve 3D finite element dynamic analysis [34]. Cowper-Symbols model is a piecewise linear plasticity model, and the yield stress can be obtained via the strain rate, which is shown in Eq. (1).

$$\sigma_y\left(\varepsilon^p_{eff}, \dot{\varepsilon}^p_{eff}\right) = \sigma_y\left(\varepsilon^p_{eff}\right)\left[1 + \left(\frac{\dot{\varepsilon}^p_{eff}}{C}\right)^{\frac{1}{P}}\right] \tag{1}$$

$\dot{\varepsilon}$ represents the effective strain rate, P and C are the parameters for strain rate, and $\sigma_y(\varepsilon^p_{eff})$ is the original yield stress while the strain rate has not been considered. In this model during simulation, the input data include totally: the density of material ρ, the elastic modulus of material E, Poisson's ratio v, the yield stress, the tangent modulus, the strain rate parameters P and C, and the true stress–strain curve. If the load curve is used, the yield stress and tangent modulus are ignored. If P and C are set to 0, the strain rate effect is omitted.

2.1.3. *Establishment of homogeneous SP model*

Before establishing SP model for (TiB+TiC)/Ti-6Al-4V, the 3D model for homogeneous matrix Ti-6Al-4V should be established firstly. For reducing the number of elements and the calculation time, the symmetry of SP sample and shot balls should be considered, and a 1/2 model can be set up. The 3D homogeneous model established in this work is shown in **Figure 2** [36], including the top four-layer of shot balls, and the bottom of peened target. The dimension of peened target is $12R \times 6R \times 2.1$ mm^3, in which R is the average radius of shot balls. Because of the intensive impacting in the near surface layer, a mesh refinement is adopted and each mesh depth is 0.02 mm. SOLID164 dynamic analysis element is chosen for meshing element, and total mesh number is 120,000.

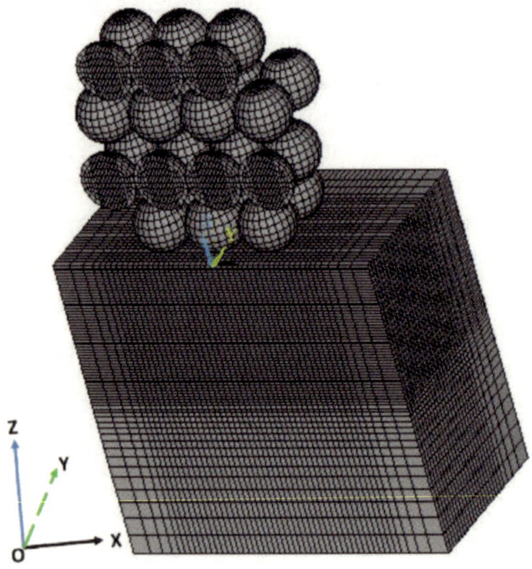

Figure 2. 3D SP model for homogeneous materials [36].

For improving the computational efficiency, the mesh size gradually increases at the model boundary and the lower half. In order to avoid the influence of reflected stress wave within the target on the distribution of residual stress during the process of impacting, nonreflective boundary conditions are implemented on the bottom and flank of the target. Because the XOZ plane is symmetrical, the symmetrical boundary conditions are applied. Because a small size model ($12R \times 6R \times 2.1\ mm^3$) may lead to the nonreal oscillation while simulating the process of impacting, in order to eliminate the effect of nonreal oscillation, the alpha damping constraint is applied to the model in the dynamic analysis. The alpha damping is a damping coefficient proportional to the mass and is very effective for the low frequency oscillations.

In 3D SP model, the top four-layers are shot balls made by case steel, and the hardness and strength of matrix is smaller than that of the case steel balls. The deformability of shot balls is very weak, which hardly affects the results of residual stress distribution. Therefore, the shot balls are defined as rigid bodies. During the explicit dynamics analysis, the degrees of freedom of all nodes in the rigid body are coupled to the mass center of rigid body, thus greatly reducing the computational time of the explicit analysis. Moreover, the corresponding mechanical parameters are given to the rigid body center to describe the dynamic characteristics. In addition, the coverage rate is very important to the distribution of residual stresses after SP. In order to keep the simulation accuracy, the coverage rate is defined and the schematic is shown in **Figure 3** [36]. Four impacts with shot balls are performed in current 3D model. On a single impact, the coverage rate is about 25%, and after four impacts, it approaches 100%. If coverage rate increases to 200%, eight impacts should be carried out in turn.

Because the piecewise linear model is adopted during simulation, the true stress–strain curve is needed. Usually, the stress–strain curve obtained by experiment is the engineering stress–strain curve, which is needed to be transformed into the true stress–strain curve, and the formula of transformation is shown in Eqs. (2) and (3).

$$\sigma_t = \sigma_\varepsilon(1 + \varepsilon_\varepsilon) \tag{2}$$

$$\varepsilon_t = \ln(1 + \varepsilon_\varepsilon) \tag{3}$$

σ_t is the true stress, σ_ε is the engineering stress, ε_t is the true strain, and ε_ε is the engineering strain [37]. The true stress–strain curve is used to provide the corresponding deformation parameters for the shot peened material in the finite element model. Because of the existence of reinforcements in composite and the influences of which on the matrix's residual stress distribution, the strain–stress curves with a single strain rate (10^{-3} s^{-1}) are utilized during simulation. The dynamic stress–strain curves become flatter with increasing strain rate, which reduces the material strain hardening [38]. Thus, considering the variation of strain rates, based on the references [39, 40] and Eq. (1), the parameters C and P are set as $C = 1300$ and $P = 5$.

The true stress–strain curves of Ti-6Al-4V and (TiB+TiC)/Ti-6Al-4V can be obtained from the tensile tests. The dimension of tensile specimens with a gauge section of 4 × 1.8 × 18 mm is shown in **Figure 4(a)**, and the axes direction is parallel to the hot-forging direction. The tensile tests are performed using a Zwick T1-FR020TN test machine in air, and the initial strain rates is 10^{-3} s^{-1}. The true stress–strain curves are shown in **Figure 4(b)**, which are implemented in the simulation process as the elastic–plastic deformation curves. In addition, the typical mechanical parameters of shot balls, target, and reinforcements are shown in **Table 1**.

2.2. Simulated results and discussion

2.2.1. Residual stress distribution on surface

In order to show the deformation of material obviously after SP, the coverage rate of 300% is chosen and the shot velocity is 100 m/s. The simulation results of x-direction principal stress (σ_{xx}) are shown in **Figure 5**. From the **Figure 5(a)**, it can be found that after SP, there is a compressive stress field with a certain depth in the plastic deformation area below the shot balls, and the

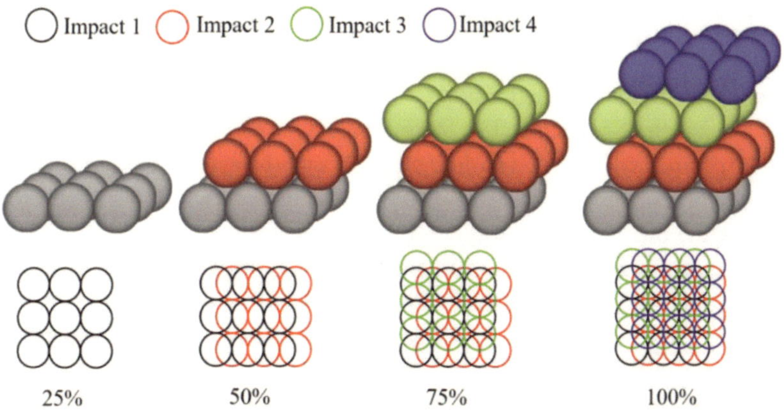

Figure 3. Coverage rate of SP with different impacts [36].

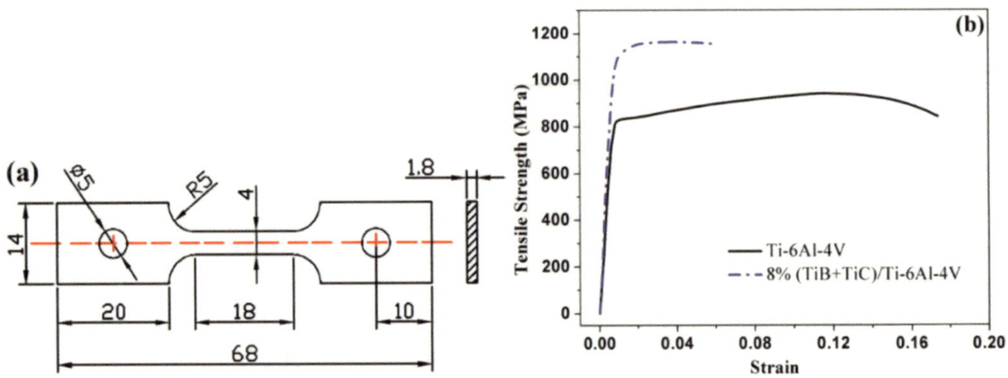

Figure 4. (a) Specimen size for room temperature tests (unit: mm); (b) stress-strain curves of the matrix and composite (strain rate: 10^{-3} s^{-1}).

	Shot balls	Ti-6Al-4V	TiB	TiC
Density ρ (Kg·m^{-3})	7800	4500	4520	4930
Poisson's ratio ν	0.30	0.34	0.14–0.15	0.18–0.2
Young's modulus *E* (GPa)	210	112	371–485	400–460
Constraint of the part	Rigid	Elastic–plastic	Elastic–plastic	Elastic–plastic

Table 1. Typical mechanical parameters of shot balls and target.

distribution of CRS in the plastic deformation zone is uniform, which is about −900 to −1000 MPa. However, in the 2D result of surface in **Figure 5(b)**, the distribution of residual stress is not uniform, and the max CRS is about −1453 MPa, which results from the stress concentration on the impact point of shot ball. In addition, there is tensile residual stress in some area between two craters. As the impacting time of shot ball on material's surface is different, the size of crater on the surface is not consistent, and the area of craters formed firstly is significantly reduced by the extrusion of follow-up craters. In these extruded area, the tensile residual stress is formed, but after repeated SP, the distribution of residual stress is gradually tended to uniform.

Due to the repeated impact and extrusion of shot balls, the plastic deformation appears and many craters are formed on surface. The formation of craters results in the increase of surface area and the appearance of tensile residual stress, which is also the reason that the max CRS does not appear on surface. On surface, the residual stress includes both the compressive stress formed by the plastic deformation and the tensile stress formed by the increase of surface area. With the increase of depth, the tensile residual stress decreases gradually but the CRS is gradually increased, then the max CRS is reached at a certain depth. At last, due to the reduction of plastic deformation, the CRS is gradually reduced to the level of stress before SP. In **Figure 5(b)**, it can be found that there is tensile stress on the surface boundary. The formation of such tensile stress field is mainly due to the limitation of finite element model size (only $12R \times 6R$), and the SP area only $8R \times 4R$ in order to avoid the effect of model boundary

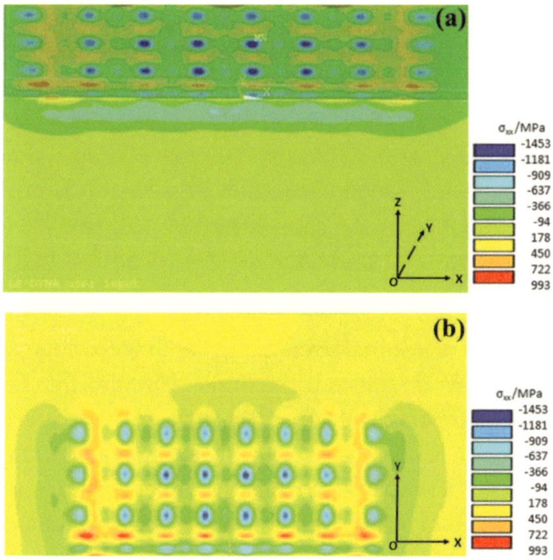

Figure 5. Simulation results of residual stress field of SP (σ_{xx}), (a) 3D result; (b) 2D result of surface.

on the simulation results. So, the tensile stress field of surface boundary has no effect on the residual stress distribution in the plastic deformation zone. Moreover, in the actual SP experiment, the whole surface of material is subjected to SP process, and the uniform CRS can be obtained. The surface tensile stress on the boundary disappears at the same time.

The effect of SP on the residual stress distribution is mainly described by the residual stress variation with the increase of depth and the four characteristic parameters (the surface residual stress, the max residual stress, the depth of residual stress layer, and the depth of max residual stress). Usually, in experiment, after SP, the surface layer of samples are subjected to electrochemical etching and removed layer by layer (each layer is about 15–20 μm), and then the stress value of each layer can be measured by XRD method, and the curves of residual stress variation along the depth are obtained. In order to avoid measurement error, the irradiation area of X-ray on the surface is generally about 1 mm^2, so actually, the measured stress by experiment is the average stress under the statistical of surface area in 1 mm^2. In this numerical simulation, for obtaining the distribution of residual stress along the depth, the stress value of all nodes at a certain depth along Z direction are selected and averaged, which can represent the average stress in a certain depth. Using this method to average the stress values of all nodes, the curve of residual stress distribution with the increase of depth can be obtained.

2.2.2. Influence of coverage rate on residual stress distribution

After SP, the surface coverage rate refers to the ratio of the area occupied by the shot craters to the area of surface required for SP. During the process of SP, the coverage rate is usually required for reaching or exceeding 100%. Moreover, in the experiment, the coverage rate more than 100% can be expressed as a multiple of the time required for a full coverage rate of 100%, for example, the coverage rate of 200% means that the SP time is two times of full coverage.

In order to simplify the model, the collision between two shot balls are not considered, and SP position of each ball can be precisely controlled. Therefore, the different coverage rate can be simulated by the multi-layer shot balls and the coverage increases linearity with the number of layers. In this work, the characteristics of 100% coverage rate (4-layer shot balls), 200% coverage rate (8-layer shot balls), and 300% coverage rate (12-layer shot balls) are simulated. The shot velocity are set as 50 and 100 m/s based on experiment (mentioned in Section 2.2.4), and the average radius of shot balls are chosen as 0.15, 0.3, and 0.6 mm. The influence of coverage rate, radius of shot balls (r), and shot velocity (v) on residual stress distribution are investigated and discussed.

Figure 6 shows the distribution of residual stress along depth with different coverage rates. While the radius and speed of shot balls are constant, the similar variation trend of residual stress can be obtained. With the increase of coverage rate, the CRS and the depth of stress layer are improved. In addition, the depth of max CRS decreases with the increase of coverage rate, which is more obvious in **Figure 6(e)** and **(f)**. Comparing the results under coverage rate of 200 and 300%, it can be found that the increment of surface residual stresses are not obvious with increasing the coverage rate, since the surface of almost all area is covered by craters and the stress field reaches saturation. Though there is a little bit increment of the max CRS while coverage rate increases from 200 to 300%, there is not obvious comparing the coverage variation from 100 to 200%.

The simulated pictures about residual stress distribution under different coverage rates are shown in **Figure 7**, while $r = 0.3$ mm and $v = 100$ m/s. With increasing coverage, the number of craters on surface increases, and the surface residual stresses becomes more uniform. As well, the uniformity of residual stress distribution on subsurface is also improved while viewed from the cross section, and slight tensile stresses in the deep surface decrease gradually and disappear with the increase of coverage rate.

2.2.3. *Influence of shot balls' radius on residual stress distribution*

According to the formula of $m = \frac{4}{3}\pi\rho R^3$, the mass of shot ball is not only linearly related to the density, but also is proportional to R^3. In most of the industrial production, the criterion for choosing the size of shot ball is based on the surface roughness after SP. If it requires high quality of surface (small roughness), the small radius of shot ball is chosen. If there is no high quality requirement of surface, the big radius of shot ball is determined, because the cost of shot balls with small radius are much higher than that of big shot balls. Besides the influence of shot ball's radius on surface roughness, the shot ball also influences the residual stress distribution. So the influence of three kinds of different radius ($r = 0.15$, 0.3, and 0.6 mm) on the residual stress distribution of Ti-6Al-4V is simulated by the model, while the shot velocity is 100 m/s. The results of the residual stress versus depth are shown in **Figure 8**. From the simulation results, it can be found that the surface CRS and max CRS are higher while using small shot balls, but the layer depth of CRS is smaller and the CRS decreases rapidly with increasing depth. When using the big shot balls, both the surface and max CRS are smaller, however, the layer depth of CRS is deeper and CRS decreases slowly with increasing depth.

Some work have shown that when the coverage rate is 100%, the depth of CRS layer has the following relationship with the crater diameter and the shot ball's diameter.

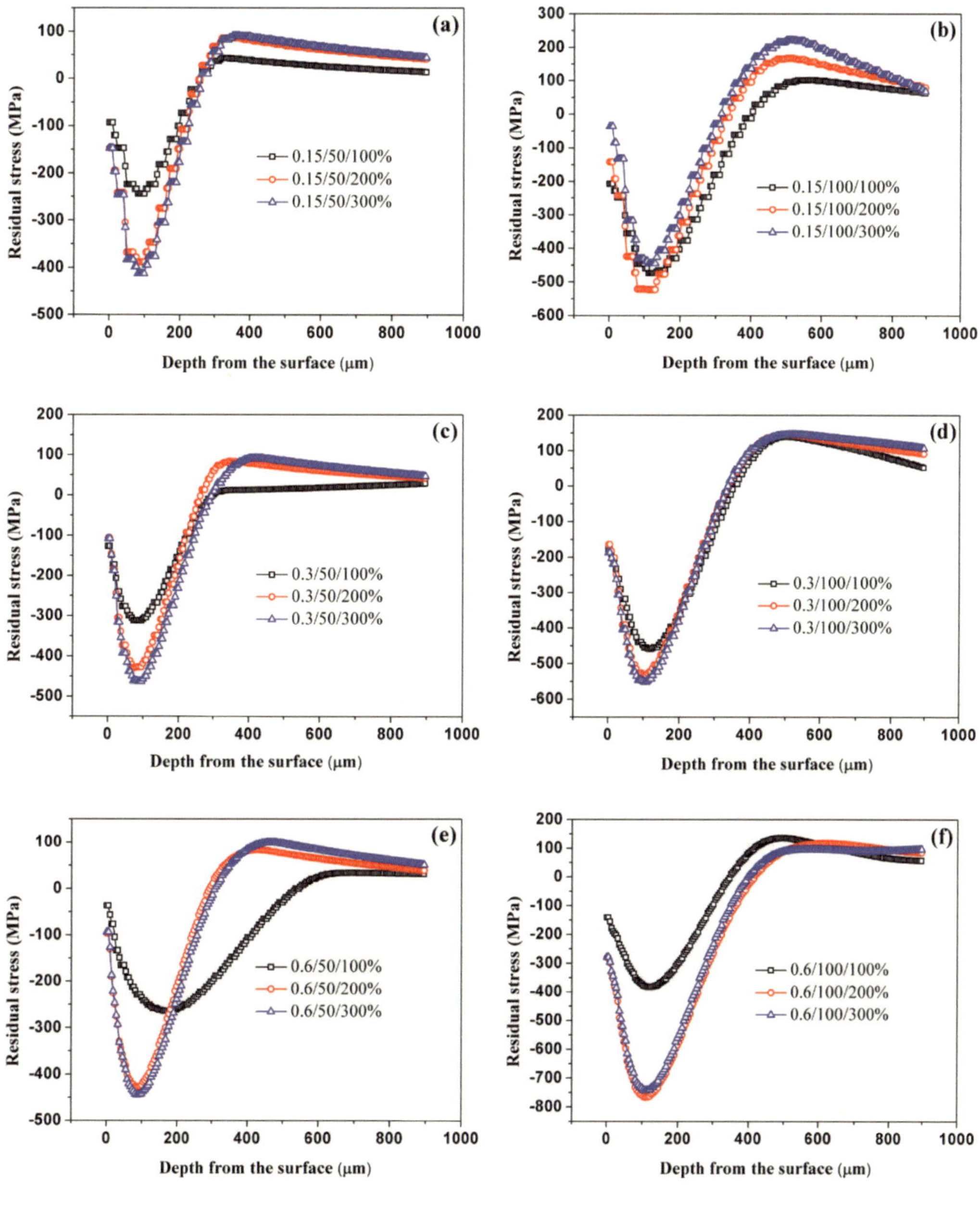

Figure 6. Residual stress distribution in depth with different coverage rates, (a) $r = 0.15$ mm, $v = 50$ m/s; (b) $r = 0.15$ mm, $v = 100$ m/s; (c) $r = 0.3$ mm, $v = 50$ m/s; (d) $r = 0.3$ mm, $v = 100$ m/s; (e) $r = 0.6$ mm, $v = 50$ m/s; (f) $r = 0.6$ mm, $v = 100$ m/s.

$$Z_0 = a \times D - c \times R \tag{4}$$

D is the crater diameter, Z_0 is the depth of CRS layer, R is the shot ball's diameter, and *a*, *c* are constant coefficients. In general, the value of *a* is between 1 and 1.5, and the value of *c* is in

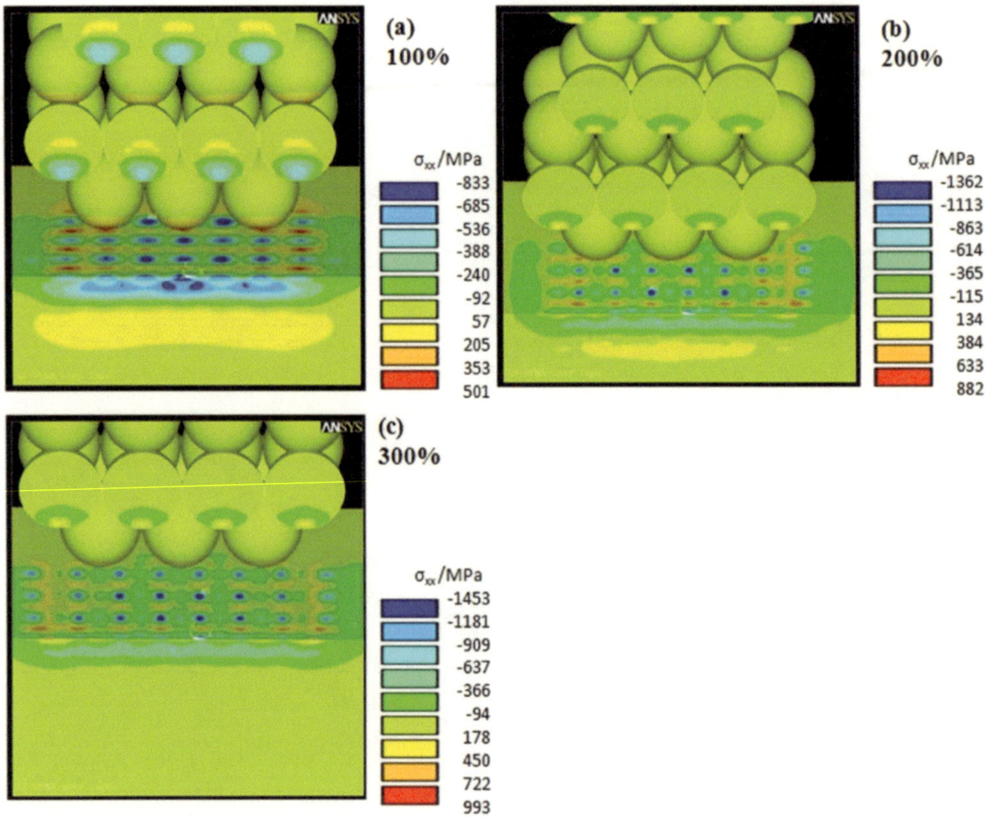

Figure 7. Residual stress distribution after SP with different coverage rates: (a) 100%; (b) 200%; (c) 300%. [36].

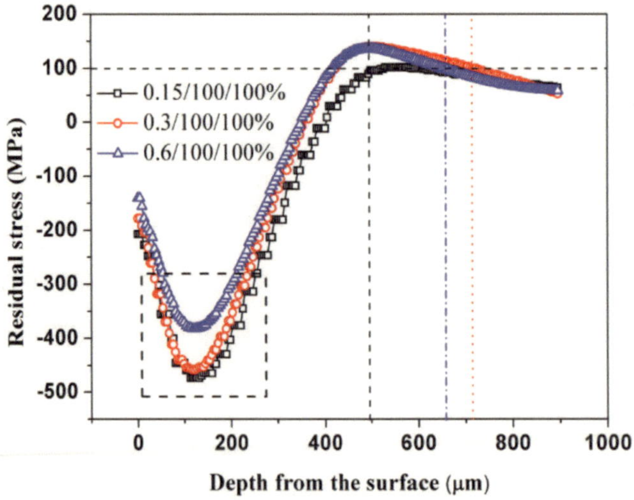

Figure 8. Influence of shot radius on depth distribution of residual stress (v = 100 m/s and coverage = 100%).

the range from 0 to 0.1. In order to obtain the values of a and c, the SP experiment should be carried out. Firstly, the same material as the workpiece is chosen and then the surface of this material is subjected to SP treatment. Secondly, the diameter of crater and the depth of CRS are measured. And at last, the values of a and c are calculated by linear fitting. Based on the values of a and c, the depth of CRS layer can be estimated. At the same shot velocity, the diameter of crater increases with increasing shot diameter, and thus the depth of CRS layer increases.

2.2.4. *Influence of shot velocity on residual stress distribution*

SP is the process of consuming shot balls' kinetic energy and transfer the kinetic energy to the deformation energy of target material. So, after SP, the elastic and plastic deformations are introduced in the surface layer of target material. The shot balls' mass and velocity directly affect the value of kinetic energy. When the material of shot balls is same, the kinetic energy increases with the improvement of shot velocity. In SP experiment by using an air blast machine, the shot velocity can be varied and obtained by adjusting the air pressure. During the flight of shot balls, the velocity will be decreased because of the collision between them and the effect of air resistance, and the attenuation is related to the distance between the nozzle and the material. The smaller diameter of shot ball, the velocity attenuation is more obvious. The attenuation rates of cast shot balls ($\rho = 7.8$ g/cm^3) with different diameters at different shot distances are shown in **Figure 9** [41]. From this figure, it can be found that when the shot distance is less than 2 m, the attenuation rates are proportional to the distance increment.

The shot velocity is also affected by the shot angle in addition to the attenuation with the distance. When the shot balls impact on the surface of workpiece at a certain angle, the velocity can be decomposed into two directions. One is perpendicular to the surface (normal velocity) and the other is parallel to the surface (tangential velocity). The former velocity contributes to the plastic deformation of the surface layer, but the latter only promotes the friction effect. Based on the above analysis, in the experiment of this work, the distance between nozzle and samples is 100 mm (0.1 m),

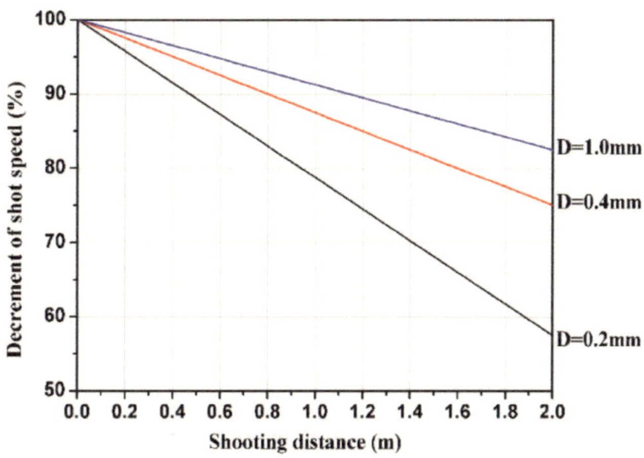

Figure 9. Relationship between decrement of shot velocity and shooting distance [41].

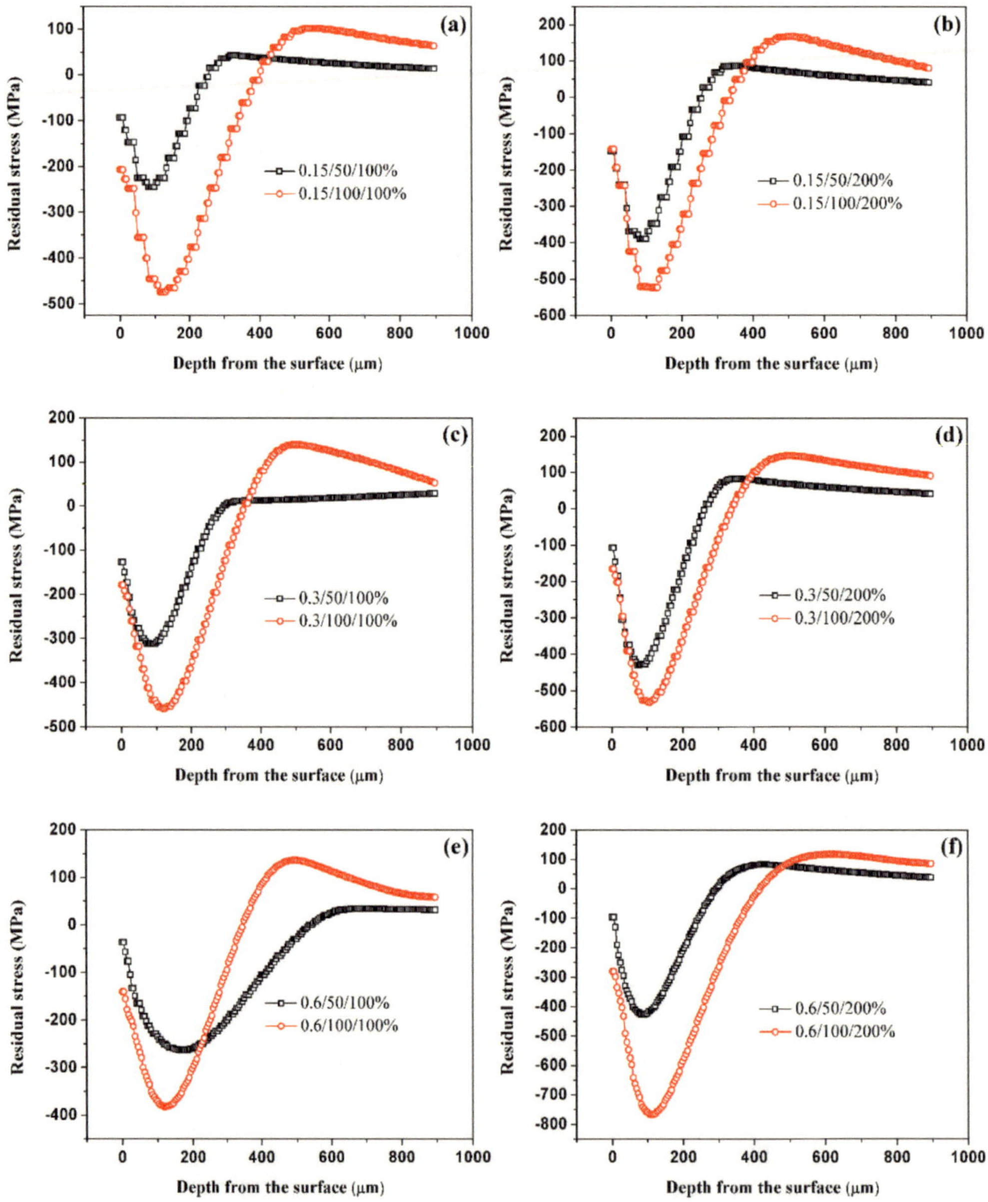

Figure 10. Residual stress distribution in depth with different shot velocities, (a) r = 0.15 mm, coverage = 100%; (b) r = 0.15 mm, coverage = 200%; (c) r = 0.3 mm, coverage = 100%; (d) r = 0.3 mm, coverage = 200%; (e) r = 0.6 mm, coverage = 100%; (f) r = 0.6 mm, coverage = 200%.

in which, the shot velocity on surface is almost the same as initial velocity. Moreover, the direction of peening nozzle is perpendicular to the surface, which can keep the shot velocity perpendicular to the surface and transfer most of kinetic energy to the deformation energy.

In order to simulate the practical process of SP better, the actual shot velocity is estimated by the semi-experiential formula introduced by Dr. Klemenz [42], which is shown in Eq. (5).

$$v = \frac{16.35 \times p}{1.53 \times m + p} + \frac{29.50 \times p}{0.598 \times d + p} + 4.83 \times p \quad (5)$$

m, *p*, and *d* represent the flux of shot balls (kg/min), the jet pressure (bar), and the diameter of shot balls (mm), respectively. In current experiment, the value of *m* is 0.5 kg/min. The different SP parameters are shown: (1) 0.15 mmA (SP intensity), 4 bar (air pressure), 0.5 min (SP time); (2) 0.3 mmA, 10 bar, 0.5 min. The average radius of shot balls $r = 0.3$ mm. Based on above parameters, the approximate shot velocities are estimated as 57 and 92 m/s, corresponding to SP intensities of 0.15 and 0.3 mmA respectively. Thus, the shot velocities of 50 and 100 m/s are considered in this work.

During simulation, the initial shot velocity represents SP intensity. The larger velocity means the higher SP intensity. **Figure 10** indicates the residual stress distribution in depth with different initial velocities. In these figures, the variation trends are similar. While increasing velocity, both the surface and max CRS significantly increase and the depth of deformation layer is also improved. At $v = 100$ m/s, the max depth of CRS in the material reaches 600 μm with $r = 0.6$ mm and coverage = 200% (in **Figure 10(f)**). The surface residual stress is less affected by the shot velocity while $r = 0.3$ and the surface residual stress is around −100 to −200 MPa (in **Figure 10(c)** and **(d)**). Because one part of the kinetic energy is transferred to the deformation energy during SP, while increasing shot velocity, much more kinetic energy can be transferred to the deformation energy, which can result in the surface deformation more severely and the deeper deformation layer can be obtained.

3. Finite element simulation on inhomogeneous SP model

3.1. Establishment of inhomogeneous SP model

In order to set up 3D SP model for inhomogeneous materials, the morphology of reinforcements were observed by scanning electron microscope (SEM, Hitachi S-3400 N, Japan) under 15 kV, 70 μA. Before SEM observation, the samples were ground by abrasive papers, and then by the diamond papers and the aluminum oxide suspensions in order. For acquiring clear morphology of reinforcements, the sample was etched using Kroll's solution (HF: HNO_3: H_2O = 3:5:100 (vol)) for 2–6 s after polishing. All experiments were performed at room temperature. The SEM images of reinforcements in (TiB+TiC)/Ti-Al-4V after etching on surface with different percentage have been shown in **Figure 11** [36, 43]. It is indicated that the reinforcements are distributed uniformly in the composite. The reinforcements like short sticks are TiB, while the equiaxed or near equiaxed particles are TiC. In the following work, the 3D SP model for inhomogeneous materials is based on the microstructure of reinforcements in 8% (TiB+TiC)/Ti-6Al-4V. Based on the simulated results from homogeneous model, the inhomogeneous SP model containing the reinforcements is built in this part and the residual stress distribution in and around the reinforcements are obtained and analyzed. In this model, the parameters of $v = 100$ m/s, $r = 0.3$ mm and coverage = 200% are chosen as the initial parameters.

The 3D SP model for inhomogeneous materials is shown in **Figure 12** [36] based on the microstructure observation of reinforcements. In the figure, the green part represents the matrix, the

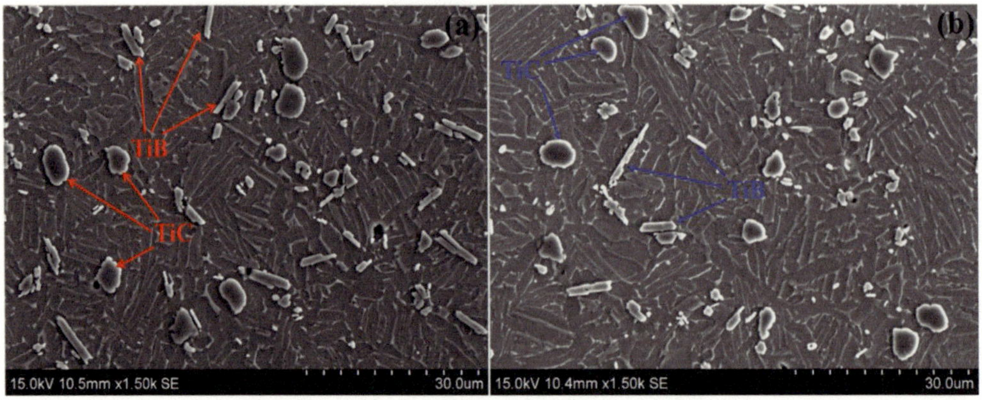

Figure 11. SEM images of reinforcements in (TiB+TiC)/Ti-Al-4V after etching on surface with different percentage; (a) 8% (TiB+TiC) [36]; (b) 5% (TiB+TiC) [43].

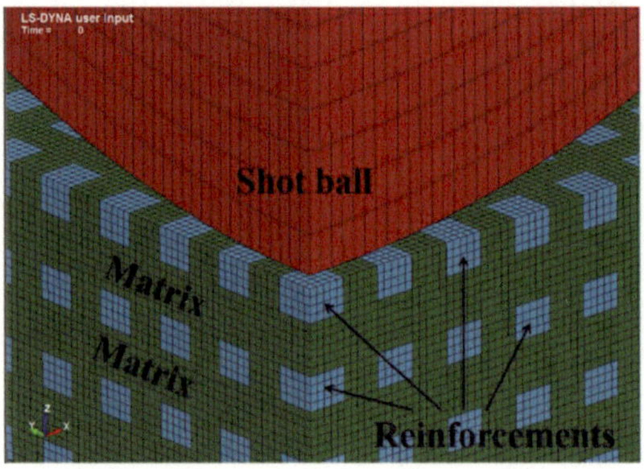

Figure 12. 3D SP model for inhomogeneous materials [36].

blue parts with disjunction distribution represent the reinforcements TiB and TiC, and the red and 1/4 spherical object is the shot ball. Because the mechanic parameters of these two reinforcements are similar, one kind of mesh is used in this model to simplify the calculation. Moreover, the whole mesh number reaches 320,000. In addition, a combination of two kinds of materials is built, one is the matrix Ti-6Al-4V, and the other is the average parameters of TiB and TiC. Wherein the relatively large area of plastic deformation, actually the directly impact area, the quite fine mesh is introduced. In this inhomogeneous model, the volume percentage of reinforcement is set as 8% based on the microstructure of material. The 1/4 symmetry model is set up and the nonreflecting boundary conditions on flank of model are applied. The symmetric boundary conditions are also applied on the symmetry plane in order to avoid the effect of stress wave.

3.2. Residual stress distribution

The residual stress distribution (σ_{xx}) of plastic deformation area is shown in **Figure 13** after SP. In the plastic deformation zone, there are both CRS and tensile stresses, the max CRS is

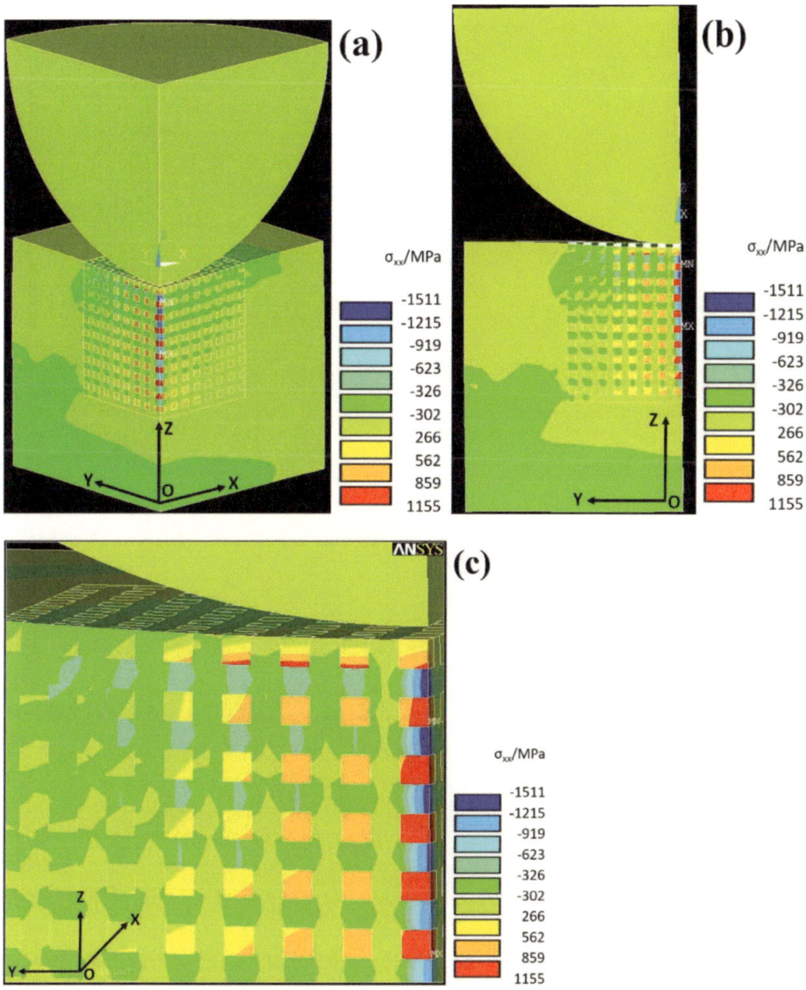

Figure 13. Residual stress distribution in depth simulated from inhomogeneous SP model (σ_{xx} direction); (a) 3D result; (b) 2D result; (c) magnification of 2D result.

−1511 MPa and the max tensile residual stress is +1155 MPa. Moreover, the CRS exist in the matrix, but there are tensile residual stresses in the reinforcements, which reveal that the reinforcements withstand the tensile stresses, and this stress distribution indicates the higher yield strength of reinforcements. The stress distribution indicates the effect of reinforcements, keeping the adverse tensile stresses in reinforcements and retarding the damage to matrix. The different residual stress distributions between the matrix and reinforcements are resulted from the different mechanical properties, consisting with the desired results after SP treatments.

The simulation results of residual stress field of SP (σ_{xx}) on the whole surface are shown in **Figure 14**. The similar stress distribution as **Figure 13** has been shown, in and around the reinforcement. Tensile residual stress appears and the stress concentration exists, but between the reinforcements, there are CRS and the distribution of CRS is uniform below the subsurface (in

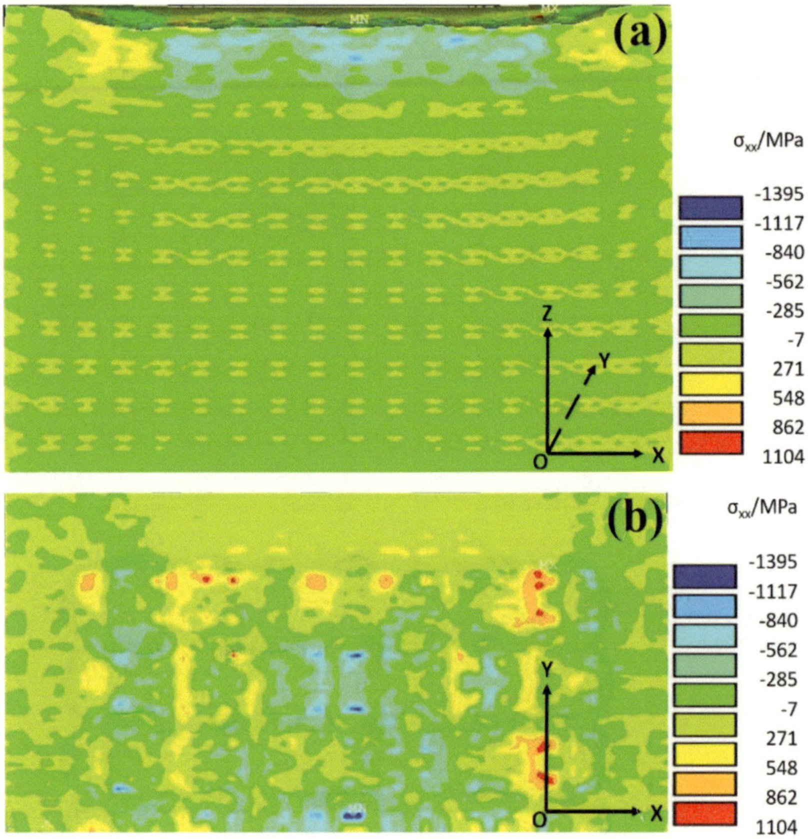

Figure 14. Simulation results of residual stress field of SP (σ_{xx}) on the whole surface; (a) 3D result; (b) 2D result of surface.

Figure 14(a)). In addition, it is obvious that the max CRS appears in the subsurface, and after SP treatment of 200% coverage rate, the deformation of surface layer can be observed from the cross section (in **Figure 14(a)**) and the surface (in **Figure 14(b)**). Comparing with the residual stress distribution on the surface of homogeneous material in **Figure 5**, the stress distribution on surface of composite in **Figure 14(b)** is not uniform because the influence of reinforcements. The value of max CRS and tensile residual stress in **Figure 14(b)** are increased a little comparing the results in **Figure 5(b)**. The detailed discussion will be carried out in the following section.

3.3. Influence of reinforcements on residual stress distribution

The stress difference between the reinforcement and matrix is mainly due to the large mechanical differences between them. During the SP process, the matrix material and the reinforcement are deformed by the pressure caused by the impact of shot balls. The matrix material is deformed easily due to the small Young's modulus and yield strength. But the Young's modulus of the reinforcement is very large. The reinforcement in the surface undergoes bending under the vertical impact of shot balls, the reinforcement in the deeper area of plastic deformation zone is mainly deformed elastically. Some of the surface reinforcements are deformed in the plastic and result in high tensile residual stress (in **Figure 14(a)**). After SP, there is still high compressive stress in the plastic deformation zone even though the elastic recovery occurs. Meanwhile, the elastic recovery of matrix is limited by the reinforcement, which also makes the CRS in matrix further improved.

During SP process, the matrix material in the composite undergoes the severe plastic deformation and the compressive stress is introduced. The tensile stress in whisker reinforcements is produced with a symmetrical distribution due to the bending deformation. In the top region where the whisker is strengthened, also the compressive stress is produced, but it is significantly less than the stress between the whisker reinforcements. After SP, the material will spontaneously show the elastic recovery and both the compressive and tensile stress are reduced. While the elastic recovery is completed, the compressive stress region is obtained in the matrix between the whisker reinforcements and the tensile stress is retained in the reinforcements (in **Figure 14**). Since the tensile stresses in reinforcement are much lower than the strength of reinforcement, it is reasonable to believe that these tensile stresses have no detrimental influences on the fatigue properties of shot peened composites. In order to verify the simulated results obtained by 3D finite element dynamic analysis, the experimental investigation on residual stress distribution of Ti-6Al-4V and 8% (TiB+TiC)/Ti-6Al-4V after SP are carried out via XRD method.

4. Experimental validation on residual stress distribution

4.1. Experimental process

SP treatment was performed using an air blast machine (Carthing Machinery Company, Shanghai, China). The SP intensities were: 0.15, 0.30, and 0.45 mmA. The distance between nozzle and samples was 100 mm and the diameter of peening nozzle was 15 mm. The shot media was cast steel ball with hardness of 610 HV and average radius of 0.3 mm. In order to obtain the uniform stress field on surface, the coverage rate of SP process was 200%. Residual stresses were measured by X-ray stress analyzer (LXRD, Proto, Canada) with Cu-*Ka* radiation under 30 kV/25 mA and Ni filter. The diffraction peak of Ti (213) was detected in the measurements and then the residual stresses were determined according to the $\sin^2\psi$ method [44] and the range of tilting angles was 0–45°. The schematic figure of residual stress measurement coordinate was shown in **Figure 15(a)** and the photo of residual stress measurement using X-ray stress analyzer was presented in **Figure 15(b)**. For obtaining the stress distribution along the depth, the thin top surface layer was removed one by one via chemical etch method with a solution of distilled water, nitric acid, and hydrofluoric acid in proportion of 31:12:7.

4.2. Residual stress distribution of Ti-6Al-4V

The CRS distribution of Ti-6Al-4V under three different SP intensities is shown in **Figure 16(a)**. The residual stresses are compressive stresses and the values increase to max and then decrease, close to the simulated results by the homogeneous SP model. When the SP intensity increases from 0.15 to 0.45 mmA, the depths of max CRS are located at 50, 50, and 75 μm, corresponding to the intensity of 0.15, 0.30, and 0.45 mmA, respectively. The surface deformation layers are 275, 325, and 400 μm depth, which show that the deformation layer depth increases gradually with increasing SP intensity. In addition, with the increase of SP intensity, the CRS of surface is enhanced from

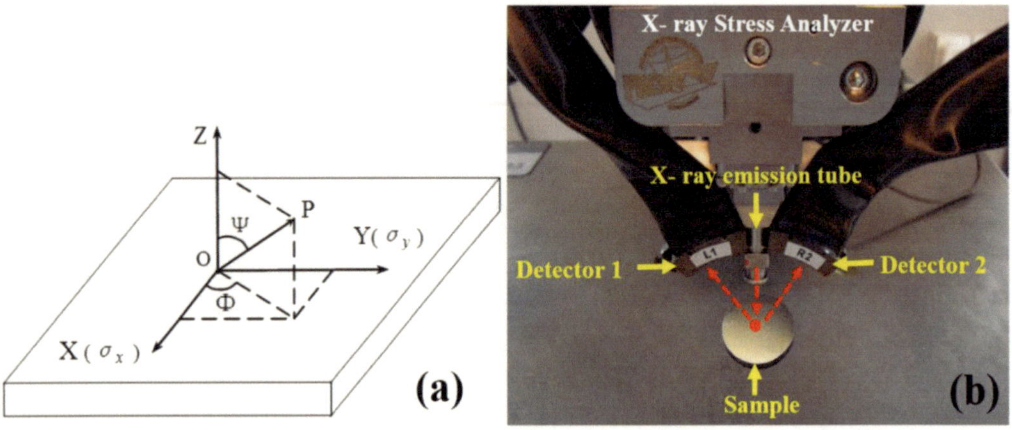

Figure 15. (a) Schematic figure of residual stress measurement coordinate; (b) photo of the residual stress measurement using X-ray stress analyzer.

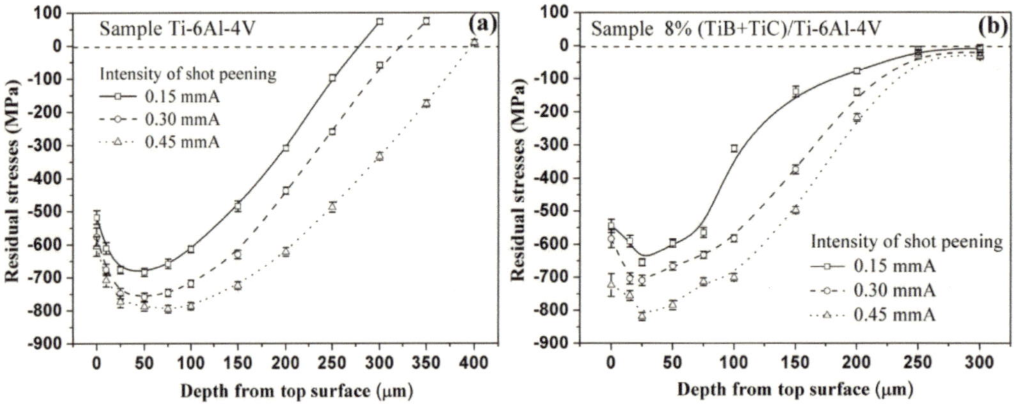

Figure 16. Depth distribution of CRS on the matrix and composite under three different SP intensities [36], (a) Ti-6Al-4V; (b) 8% (TiB+TiC)/Ti-6Al-4V.

−517 to −605 MPa, which is improved by 17%. The max CRS varies from −684 to −794 MPa and the increase rate is about 16%. It is mainly due to the improved shot velocity after increasing SP intensity, which can cause more severe plastic deformation on surface, the deeper surface deformation layer and the larger CRS. Comparing the results by simulation and experiment, it reveals that the variation trends of residual stress by simulation are similar with the results from experiment.

4.3. Residual stress distribution of 8% (TiB+TiC)/Ti-6Al-4V

Figure 16(b) shows the experimental results of residual stress distribution on the composite 8% (TiB+TiC)/Ti-6Al-4V. From the figure, the depths of surface deformation layer are 200, 250, and 300 μm corresponding to 0.15, 0.30, and 0.45 mmA, which are shallower than the matrix's. The difference is resulted from the existence of reinforcements' resistance to the deformation of surface. Moreover, SP intensity has direct relation to the shot velocity. The larger impact velocity, the higher impact kinetic energy, and the depths of surface deformation layer are deeper.

At the same depth, the higher of SP intensity, the values of CRS are bigger. These variation trends of residual stresses are similar to **Figure 16(a)**, and the depths of max CRS are located at 25 μm, which are shallower than the matrix's under the same SP intensity. The CRS of surface is enhanced from −545 to −724 MPa and the max CRS varies from −655 to −819 MPa. Contrasting the results from experiment and simulation, the ranges of residual stress measured via experiments are good agreement with the simulated results by 3D finite element dynamic analysis shown in **Figure 13**. The difference between simulation and experiment are inevitable, because the irradiation area of X-ray is larger than the dimension of reinforcement, and the tested residual stresses show the average values of the matrix and reinforcements. Based on all results, analysis and discussion, 3D finite element dynamic analysis is an effective method to simulate the residual stress distribution of metal matrix composite after SP treatment, especially to obtain the residual stress distribution in and around the reinforcements in the composite.

5. Conclusions

In order to study the effect of various parameters on the residual stress distribution after SP, LS/DYNA analysis module in ANSYS is utilized to establish the finite element model for Ti-6Al-4V and (TiB+TiC)/Ti-6Al-4V, and both 3D homogeneous and inhomogeneous models are set up. The influence of coverage rate, shot radius, and shot velocity on residual stress distribution is studied using the multi-layer shot balls to simulate the actual SP process. The main results are concluded as the following:

1. The influence of different coverage rates on residual stress distribution is investigated. With increasing coverage rate, the number of craters on the surface is increased obviously, and the uniformity of surface residual stresses is improved a lot. Comparing the results under coverage rate of 200 and 300%, the increment of surface residual stresses are not obvious, since the surface of almost all covered by craters and the stress field reaches saturation.

2. The influence of cast steel shot balls with different radius on the residual stress distribution is simulated when the shot velocity is 100 m/s. The CRS induced by smaller shot balls is higher, but the depth of residual stress layer is smaller and decreases rapidly. While increasing radius, the surface and max CRS are smaller, while the depth of residual stress layer decreases slowly.

3. The simulation results of different shot velocities show that the higher CRS and the deeper residual stress layer can be obtained under higher velocity. At 100 m/s, the max depth of CRS reaches 600 μm with r = 0.6 mm and coverage = 200%. The surface residual stress is less affected by shot velocity, while the radius of shot balls is 0.3 mm and the surface residual stress under two kinds of velocities is around −100 to −200 MPa.

4. The residual stress distribution in the plastic deformation zone, and in and around the reinforcements are obtained. Due to the different mechanic properties between the reinforcement and matrix, the elastic deformation of the reinforcement is mainly caused by SP, and a large tensile residual stress is formed in the body of reinforcement. Meanwhile, the plastic deformation of the matrix occurs and CRS are formed. After the elastic recovery, there is still high CRS remained in the matrix.

5. The results obtained from the inhomogeneous SP model reveal that the compressive and tensile residual stresses are introduced in (TiB+TiC)/Ti-6Al-4V. The max CRS and tensile residual stress are −1511 and +1155 MPa, respectively. CRS appear in matrix, but the tensile residual stresses gets generated in the reinforcements, which reveals the higher yield strength of reinforcements. This stress distribution indicates the effect of reinforcements, keeping the adverse tensile stresses in reinforcements and retarding the damage to matrix.

6. The experimental results from XRD method are shown that the surface CRS increased from −545 to −724 MPa and the max CRS varies from −655 to −819 MPa. The ranges of residual stress distribution in experiments are in good agreement with the simulated results by 3D finite element dynamic analysis.

From all results and discussion, using 3D finite element dynamic analysis to simulate the residual stress distribution of titanium matrix composite is reasonable, especially for the stress distribution in and around the reinforcements.

Acknowledgements

This work is supported by the projects of "Chu Tian Scholar" of Hubei Province in China (CTXZ2017-05), The 111 Project (B17034), National Natural Science Foundation of China (No. 51302168, No. 51405356 and No. 51502142), 973 Program (No. 2014CB046701) and Shanghai Pujiang Program (No. 15PJD017). The financial support of the Jiangsu Higher Education Institutions of China (No. 15KJB430021) and the Startup Foundation for Introducing Talent of NUIST (No. 2014r036) are gratefully appreciated. The financial support of Research Fund for the Doctoral Program of Higher Education of China (No. 20130143120015), Medical Engineering Cross Research Foundation of Shanghai Jiao Tong University (No. YG2014MS02), Shanghai Jiao Tong University Chenxing Program (No. 15X100080069) are appreciated.

Author details

Lechun Xie[1,2]*, Zhou Wang[1], Chengxi Wang[3], Yan Wen[1], Liqiang Wang[3]*, Chuanhai Jiang[3], Weijie Lu[3], Lai-Chang Zhang[4] and Lin Hua[1]

*Address all correspondence to: lechunxie@yahoo.com and wang_liqiang@sjtu.edu.cn

1 Hubei Key Laboratory of Advanced Technology for Automotive Components, School of Automotive Engineering, Wuhan University of Technology, Wuhan, Hubei Province, P.R. China

2 Institute for Frontier Materials, Deakin University, Geelong, VIC, Australia

3 State Key Laboratory of Metal Matrix Composites, School of Materials Science and Engineering, Shanghai Jiao Tong University, Shanghai, P.R. China

4 School of Engineering, Edith Cowan University, Perth, WA, Australia

References

[1] Bruno G, Fernández R, Gonzalez-Doncel G. Relaxation of the residual stress in 6061Al-15 vol.% SiC w composites by isothermal annealing. Materials Science and Engineering A. 2004;**382**:188-197

[2] Schulze V. Characteristics of surface layers produced by shot peening. In: Proceeding of the Eighth International Conference on Shot Peening ICSP-8 in Garmisch-Partenkirchen DGM, Citeseer. 2002. pp. 145-160

[3] Kim K-H, Kim Y-C, Jeon E-C, Kwon D. Evaluation of indentation tensile properties of Ti alloys by considering plastic constraint effect. Materials Science and Engineering A. 2011;**528**:5259-5263

[4] Benedetti M, Fontanari V, Monelli B. Numerical simulation of residual stress relaxation in shot peened high-strength aluminum alloys under reverse bending fatigue. Journal of Engineering Materials and Technology. 2010;**132**:011012

[5] Kim T, Lee JH, Lee H, Cheong S-k. An area-average approach to peening residual stress under multi-impacts using a three-dimensional symmetry-cell finite element model with plastic shots. Materials & Design. 2010;**31**:50-59

[6] Prasannavenkatesan R, Zhang J, McDowell DL, Olson GB, Jou H-J. 3D modeling of subsurface fatigue crack nucleation potency of primary inclusions in heat treated and shot peened martensitic gear steels. International Journal of Fatigue. 2009;**31**:1176-1189

[7] Guagliano M. Relating Almen intensity to residual stresses induced by shot peening: A numerical approach. Journal of Materials Processing Technology. 2001;**110**:277-286

[8] Rouhaud E, Ouakka A, Ould C, Chaboche J, Francois M. Finite elements model of shot peening, effects of constitutive laws of the material, Proceedings ICSP-9, Paris, France. 2005

[9] Ould C, Rouhaud E, François M, Chaboche JL. A kinematic hardening finite elements model to evaluate residual stresses in shot-peened parts, local measurements by X-ray diffraction. In: Mater. Sci. Forum Trans Tech Publ. 2006. pp. 161-166

[10] Baragetti S, Guagliano M, Vergani L. A numerical procedure for shot peening optimisation by means of non-dimensional factors. International Journal of Materials and Product Technology. 2000;**15**:91-103

[11] Boyce B, Chen X, Hutchinson J, Ritchie R. The residual stress state due to a spherical hard-body impact. Mechanics of Materials. 2001;**33**:441-454

[12] Evans R. Shot peening process: Modelling, verification, and optimisation. Materials Science and Technology. 2002;**18**:831-839

[13] Levers A. A. Prior, finite element analysis of shot peening. Journal of Materials Processing Technology. 1998;**80**:304-308

[14] Meguid S, Shagal G, Stranart J, Daly J. Three-dimensional dynamic finite element analysis of shot-peening induced residual stresses. Finite Elements in Analysis and Design. 1999;**31**:179-191

[15] Majzoobi G, Azizi R, Nia AA. A three-dimensional simulation of shot peening process using multiple shot impacts. Journal of Materials Processing Technology. 2005; **164**:1226-1234

[16] Frija M, Hassine T, Fathallah R, Bouraoui C, Dogui A, de Génie Mécanique L. Finite element modelling of shot peening process: Prediction of the compressive residual stresses, the plastic deformations and the surface integrity. Materials Science and Engineering A. 2006;**426**:173-180

[17] Wang T, Platts M, Wu J. The optimisation of shot peen forming processes. Journal of Materials Processing Technology. 2008;**206**:78-82

[18] Hong T, Ooi J, Shaw B. A numerical simulation to relate the shot peening parameters to the induced residual stresses. Engineering Failure Analysis. 2008;**15**:1097-1110

[19] Kim T, Lee H, Jung S, Lee JH. A 3D FE model with plastic shot for evaluation of equibiaxial peening residual stress due to multi-impacts. Surface and Coating Technology. 2012;**206**:3125-3136

[20] Meo M, Vignjevic R. Finite element analysis of residual stress induced by shot peening process. Advances in Engineering Software. 2003;**34**:569-575

[21] Böhm HJ, Han W. Comparisons between three-dimensional and two-dimensional multiparticle unit cell models for particle reinforced metal matrix composites. Modelling and Simulation in Materials Science and Engineering. 2001;**9**:47

[22] Böhm HJ, Eckschlager A, Han W. Multi-inclusion unit cell models for metal matrix composites with randomly oriented discontinuous reinforcements. Computational Materials Science. 2002;**25**:42-53

[23] Han W, Eckschlager A, Böhm HJ. The effects of three-dimensional multi-particle arrangements on the mechanical behavior and damage initiation of particle-reinforced MMCs. Composites Science and Technology. 2001;**61**:1581-1590

[24] Duschlbauer D, BÖhm HJ, Pettermann HE. Computational simulation of composites reinforced by planar random fibers: Homogenization and localization by unit cell and mean field approaches. Journal of Composite Materials. 2006;**40**:2217-2234

[25] Borbely A, Biermann H, Hartmann O. FE investigation of the effect of particle distribution on the uniaxial stress–strain behaviour of particulate reinforced metal-matrix composites. Materials Science and Engineering A. 2001;**313**:34-45

[26] Su X-fC, Hao-ran, Wang, Li-min, Relations of the mesoscopic damage mechanisms with the macroscopic properties of metal matrix composites. Acta Metallurgica Sinica(English letters). 1999;**16**:88-93

[27] Kuruvilla A, Prasad K, Bhanuprasad V, Mahajan Y. Microstructure-property correlation in AlTiB2 (XD) composites. ScMM. 1990;**24**:873-878

[28] Ranganath S. A review on particulate-reinforced titanium matrix composites. Journal of Materials Science. 1997;**32**:1-16

[29] Zhang L-C, Attar H. Selective laser melting of titanium alloys and titanium matrix composites for biomedical applications: A review. Advanced Engineering Materials. 2016; **18**:463-475

[30] Xie L, Jiang C, Lu W, Chen Y, Huang J. Effect of stress peening on surface layer characteristics of (TiB + TiC)/Ti–6Al–4V composite. Materials & Design. 2012;**33**:64-68

[31] Xie L, Jiang C, Lu W, Zhan K, Chen Y. Investigation on the residual stress and microstructure of (TiB + TiC)/Ti–6Al–4V composite after shot peening. Materials Science and Engineering A. 2011;**528**:3423-3427

[32] Xie L, Jiang C, Lu W. The influence of shot peening on the surface properties of (TiB+ TiC)/Ti–6Al–4V. Applied Surface Science. 2013;**280**:981-988

[33] Xie L, Jiang C, Lu W, Feng Q, Wu X. Investigation on the surface layer characteristics of shot peened titanium matrix composite utilizing X-ray diffraction. Surface and Coating Technology. 2011;**206**:511-516

[34] ANSYS. Ansys Ls-Dyna User's Guide. ANSYS, Inc: Canonsburg; 2008

[35] ANSYS, Release 11.0: Element Reference., in, ANSYS Inc, 2007

[36] Xie L, Wang C, Wang L, Wang Z, Jiang C, Lu W, Ji V. Numerical analysis and experimental validation on residual stress distribution of titanium matrix composite after shot peening treatment. Mechanics of Materials. 2016;**99**:2-8

[37] Dowling NE. Mechanical Behavior of Materials: Engineering Methods for Deformation, Fracture, and Fatigue. Pearson; 2012

[38] Symonds PS. Viscoplastic behavior in response of structures to dynamic loading. In: Huffington NJ, editor. Behavior of Materials under Dynamic Loading. New York: American Society of Mechanical Engineers; 1965. pp. 106-124

[39] Jones N. Structural aspects of ship collisions. In: Wierzbicki NJ, editor. Structural Crashworthiness. Butterworth; 1983. pp. 308-337

[40] Aljawi A. Plastic deformation of thin plates subjected to quasi-static and dynamic loadings. The Journal of Engineering Research [TJER]. 2004;**1**:59-74

[41] Fang B. Controlled Shot Peening and Residual Stress Theory (in Chinese). Shandong Science and Technology Press; 1991

[42] Klemenz M. Anwendung der Simulation der Randschichtausbildung beim Kugelstrahlen auf die Abschätzung der Schwingfestigkeit gekerbter Bauteile, in. Shaker, Aachen: Universität Karlsruhe; 2009

[43] Xie L, Feng Q, Wen Y, Wang L, Jiang C, Lu W. Surface microstructure characterization on shot peened (TiB+ TiC)/Ti–6Al–4V by Rietveld whole pattern fitting method. Journal of Materials Research. 2016;**31**:2291-2301

[44] Withers P, Bhadeshia H. Residual stress. Part 1–measurement techniques. Materials Science and Technology. 2001;**17**:355-365

Chapter 3

Multiscale Wavelet Finite Element Analysis in Structural Dynamics

Mutinda Musuva and Cristinel Mares

Additional information is available at the end of the chapter

http://dx.doi.org/10.5772/intechopen.71882

Abstract

Over the recent past, various numerical analysis techniques have been formulated and used to obtain approximate solutions for numerous engineering problems to aid predict the behaviour of systems accurately and efficiently. One such approach is the Wavelet Finite Element Method (WFEM) which involves combining the classical Finite Element Method (FEM) with wavelet analysis. The key desirable properties exhibited by some wavelet families, such as compact support, multiresolution analysis (MRA), smoothness, vanishing moments and the 'two-scale' relations, make the use of wavelets in WFEM advantageous, particularly in the analysis of problems with strong nonlinearities, singularities and material property variations present. The wavelet based finite elements (WFEs) of a rod and beam are formulated using the Daubechies and B-spline wavelet on the interval (BSWI) wavelet scaling functions as interpolating functions due to their desirable properties, thus making it possible to alter the local scale of the WFE without changing the initial model mesh. Specific benchmark cases are presented to exhibit and compare the performance of the WFEM with FEM in static, dynamic, eigenvalue and moving load transient response analysis for homogenous systems and functionally graded materials, where the material properties continuously vary spatially with respect to the constituent materials.

Keywords: multiresolution, wavelets, wavelet finite element (WFE), eigenvalue analysis, moving load problem, functionally graded material (FGM)

1. Introduction

In the analysis of complex structural problems, it is often challenging to formulate and apply exact closed-form solutions, as the realistic nature of such engineering systems exhibits varying complexities, high gradients and strong irregularities, e.g., suddenly varying loading conditions, contrasting material composition or geometric variations. Based on the existing mathematical tools available, such systems may require certain assumptions and generalisations to be implemented in order to simplify the model, which may lead to inability to correctly describe the properties and behaviour of the system under described conditions. However, the preferred approach is to find an approximate numerical solution, whilst retaining these complexities as accurately as possible, to better describe and predict the behaviour of such systems. This has given rise to numerical methods such as the classical Finite Element Method which employs polynomial interpolating functions to obtain approximate solutions for various engineering problems. Although this numerical analysis technique has grown in popularity, its use to tackle problems with regions of the solution domain where the gradient of the field variables are expected to vary suddenly or fast, bring on difficulties in the analysis of a complex system [1]. In order to improve on the accuracy and better represent the system's behaviour, higher order polynomial interpolating functions or finer meshes may be employed and this in turn significantly increases the computational costs; which is undesirable. Moreover, the resolution of the elements can only be analysed to a specific scale once the orders of the governing polynomial functions have been selected. Subsequently, overcoming these challenges has been the driving force in the formulation of other numerical approximation techniques such as the Wavelet Finite Element Method [1–6].

The initial development of wavelet analysis came from separate efforts that led to the foundation of modern wavelet theory. Grossman and Morlet [7] used wavelet analysis as a tool for signal analysis of seismic data and are credited with the introduction of the term and methodology of wavelets as it is known today. Ingrid Daubechies is recognised for her major breakthrough and contribution by constructing a family of orthonormal wavelet with compact support known as the Daubechies wavelets [8]. Wavelet analysis was used mainly by mathematicians as a decomposition tool for data functions and operators and its application has vastly grown in various disciplines at an exponential rate e.g., medicine [9], finance [10] and astronomy [11]. Likewise, the range of wavelet families and bases available for selection has also increased and this is credited to the properties of wavelets that allow it to be tailored to suite numerous avenues for design manipulation to meet the necessary and specific requirements for its application. The properties of different wavelet families vary, and therefore the decision on which family is the 'most adequate', is paramount to its application. Nevertheless, the more general aspects of wavelets formulations make it an important and convenient tool for mathematical manipulation allowing for the decomposition of a function into a set of coefficients that are dependent on scale and location. The 'two-scale' relation gives rise to one of the most key features of wavelet theory, multiresolution analysis (MRA), which allows for the convenient transformation of wavelet basis functions between different resolution scales [8]. Furthermore, the compact support property of wavelets ensures that the wavelet basis functions are finitely bound (non-zero over a finite range). The vanishing moments of wavelets allow the basic functions of wavelets to represent polynomials and other complex functions.

These desirable properties of wavelets have led to the use of wavelet basis functions as interpolating functions, in contrast to conventional polynomial functions as used in classical FEM, in the formulation of the wavelet based finite element method. For example, MRA permits for specific WFEs to be selected and analysed locally at finer scales without altering the initial system model, thus improving the accuracy of the solution, particularly in areas with high gradients or singularities present. Furthermore, rapid convergence of the method and compact support lead to a reduction in computational costs since fewer elements are required to achieve acceptable levels of accuracy [4, 5]. Due to the adaptability of wavelets, different wavelet families are being developed and customised for specific problems. However, it must be noted that when selecting a particular wavelet basis function for WFEM, key requirements, such as compatibility, completeness and convergence, must be satisfied and should allow for the easy implementation and treatment of boundary conditions.

The Daubechies wavelet based finite element was first introduced to solve a 1D and 2D second order Neumann problem via the formulation of a tensor product finite element [2]. The Daubechies wavelet Galerkin finite element was then used to analyse the bending of plates and beams [12] giving rise to the formulation of a wavelet based beam finite element [6] and two dimensional Daubechies wavelet plate finite element [13] for static analysis. The Daubechies wavelet base finite element stiffness matrices and load vectors were presented by Chen et al. at multiresolution scale $j = 0$ [14] and different multiresolution scales [4]. The Daubechies plate finite element was developed by Diaz et al. for the static analysis of plates based on Mindlin-Reissner plate theory [15], where shear deformation is taken into consideration through the thickness of the plate, and compared it with Kirchhoff plate theory formulations [16]. This wavelet family has also been used in the analysis of many other structural problems, including formulation of the Rayleigh-Euler and Rayleigh-Timoshenko beam elements [17], the wavelet based spectral finite element to study elastic wave propagation in 1-D connected waveguides [18] and also to investigate the thermal stress distribution along the vertical direction of the tank wall [19]. Overall, the wavelet family performed decently in providing accurate solutions for the various structural analysis problems tackled. However, the Daubechies wavelet lacks an explicit expression for the wavelet and scaling functions and possesses unusual smoothness characteristics, particularly for lower orders, making it challenging to evaluate the numerical integrals necessary for the formulation of the element matrices and load vectors. The evaluation of the connection coefficients is therefore necessary for the formulation of these element matrices and vectors.

In a bid to overcome the limitations presented by the Daubechies wavelet, further research has been carried out to identify other potential wavelet families that can be implemented in WFEM. Basic spline functions were initially used as interpolating functions for the free vibration analysis of frame structures [3]. Chui and Quak [20] constructed the semi-orthogonal B-spline Wavelet on the Interval, which has the desirable properties of multiresolution, compact support, explicit expressions, smoothness and symmetry. The BSWI was employed to construct the wavelet based C^0 type plane elastomechanics element and Mindlin plate element [21] as well as truncated conical shell wavelet finite elements [22]. Xiang et al. [5] significantly contributed to the use of BSWI in WFEM by constructing the axial rod, beam (Timoshenko and Euler Bernoulli) and spatial bar WFEs with a multiresolution lifting scheme. Furthermore, this research was extended to the static and dynamic analysis of plates based on Kirchhoff plate theory using BSWI based wavelet finite elements [23, 24]. Xiang et al. [25] were able to illustrate that the shear-locking phenomenon of a rotating Rayleigh-Timoshenko shaft was significantly eliminated when the BSWI based WFEs were employed. Majority of the problems examined by this point were of static analysis and this led Musuva and Mares [26] to develop and implement the Daubechies and BSWI homogenous beam WFEs for the analysis of dynamic response and moving load problems. The vibration and dynamic response analysis was carried out for frame structures using the two wavelet families [27] and the WFEM was compared with an analytical wavelet approach using coiflets for the analysis of vehicle-bridge interaction for fast moving loads [28]. Furthermore, the Daubechies and BSWI wavelets were used to construct a functionally graded beam wavelet finite element under various moving load conditions [29, 30].

Other different wavelet families have been selected and employed in the formulation of the WFEM to solve a wide variety of structural analysis problems and research in this field is still ongoing. The trigonometric Hermite wavelet, which can be explicitly expressed, was used to construct beam [31] and thin plate WFEs [32] for static and free vibration analysis. The Hermite Cubic Spline Wavelet on the Interval (HCSWI), polynomial wavelets [33] and the second generation wavelets [34] are other wavelet based approaches that have been introduced and researched on. A more comprehensive synthesis and summary of wavelet based numerical methods for various engineering problems is presented in [35].

A generalised Wavelet based Finite Element Method framework is presented based on the BSWI and Daubechies wavelet families to derive rod and beam WFEs for homogenous and functionally graded materials for static and dynamic structural problems. A brief introduction of wavelet analysis is described in Section 2, with emphasis given to the Daubechies wavelets, BSWI, multiresolution and connection coefficients formulations. In Section 3, the wavelet based finite elements for a rod, Euler Bernoulli homogeneous beam and transversely varying functionally graded beam are presented. The evaluation of the element matrices and various load vectors, including the WFEM moving load formulation, are presented. A comparison on the performance of the Daubechies and BSWI WFEMs are highlighted via numerical examples for a variety of static and dynamic structural problems in Section 4 followed by conclusions.

2. Wavelet and multiresolution analysis

Wavelets are a class of basic functions that represent functions locally, both in space and time, and allow for the analysis of functions to be carried out at different resolutions (scales) [36]. The wavelet basis emanates from a set of wavelet coefficients associated with a particular location in time and different multiresolution scales. The scaling and wavelet functions stem from multiresolution analysis (MRA), which is a key and desirable property of wavelets, and refers to the simultaneous appearance of multiple scales in function decompositions in the Hilbert space $L^2(\mathbb{R})$ using a sequence of closed subspaces V_j, which is represented mathematically as [36]:

$$\cdots V_{-2} \subset V_{-1} \subset V_0 \subset V_1 \subset V_2 \subset \ldots \tag{1}$$

Therefore in principle, in order for multiresolution to occur, the closed subspaces V_j satisfy the following properties:

$$\overline{\bigcup_{j\in\mathbb{Z}} V_j} = L^2(\mathbb{R}) \tag{2}$$

$$\bigcap_{j\in\mathbb{Z}} V_j = \{0\} \tag{3}$$

http://dx.doi.org/10.5772/intechopen.71882

$$\begin{aligned} &f_2(x) = f(2x)\forall x \\ &f \in V_j \Leftrightarrow f_2 \in V_{j+1} \qquad j \in \mathbb{Z} \end{aligned} \tag{4}$$

$$\begin{aligned} &f_n(x) = f(x-n) \\ &f \in V_0 \Leftrightarrow f_n \in V_0 \qquad n \in \mathbb{Z} \end{aligned} \tag{5}$$

The orthogonal complement subspace W_j of V_j contains the additional 'detail' for subspace V_{j+1} i.e., $V_{j+1} = V_0 \oplus W_0 \oplus W_1 \oplus W_2 \cdots \oplus W_j$. The union of the subspaces V_j leads to the space $L^2(\mathbb{R})$ from the condition in Eq. (2) [36]. The scaling $\phi(x) \in L^2(\mathbb{R})$ and wavelet $\psi(x) \in L^2(\mathbb{R})$ functions correspond to the subspaces V_j and W_j respectively. The difference between current subspace V_j and subsequent subspace V_{j+1} is represented by the wavelet space W_j which becomes automatically orthogonal to all other W_j for $k < j$ due to the inclusion in and orthogonality to V_j. For the fundamental space V_0, the scaling function $\phi(x)$ and its translates $\phi(x-k)$ produce an orthonormal basis for V_0. The orthonormal basis for the next space V_1 is the rescaled function $\sqrt{2}\phi(2x-k)$. Thus, the orthonormal basis of V_j is defined as:

$$\phi_k^j(x) = 2^{\frac{j}{2}}\phi\left(2^j x - k\right) \qquad k \in \mathbb{Z} \tag{6}$$

Provided Eq. (6) and the above mentioned properties are satisfied, the wavelet orthonormal basis for subspace W_j at scale j is

$$\psi_k^j(x) = 2^{\frac{j}{2}}\psi\left(2^j x - k\right) \qquad k \in \mathbb{Z} \tag{7}$$

The orthogonal subspaces W_j result from the decomposition of $L^2(\mathbb{R})$ and subsequently the functions within these subspaces inherit the scale and shift invariance properties from the scaling function subspaces V_j and are orthonormal [8]. The projections of a function $f \in L^2(\mathbb{R})$ at scale j in the subspaces V_j and W_j, defined as $P_j f$ and $Q_j f$ respectively, are expressed as:

$$\begin{aligned} P_j f &= \sum_k a_k^j \phi_k^j(x) \\ Q_j f &= \sum_k b_k^j \psi_k^j(x) \end{aligned} \tag{8}$$

where a_k^j and b_k^j are coefficients in the subspaces V_j and W_j respectively. Thus, if all the conditions described above are met, then the scaling and wavelet functions satisfy [8]

$$\begin{aligned} &\int_{-\infty}^{\infty} \phi(x)dx \neq 0 \\ &\int_{-\infty}^{\infty} \psi(x)dx = 0 \end{aligned} \tag{9}$$

2.1. Daubechies wavelet

Daubechies wavelets are compact supported orthonormal wavelets developed by Ingrid Daubechies and for order L, the scaling and wavelet functions are described by the 'two-scale' relation [8]:

$$\phi_L(x) = \sum_{k=0}^{L-1} p_L(k)\phi_L(2x-k) \tag{10}$$

$$\psi_L(x) = \sum_{k=0}^{L-1} q_L(k)\phi_L(2x-k) \tag{11}$$

The scaling and wavelet functions have the supports $[0, L-1]$ and $\left[1-\frac{L}{2}, \frac{L}{2}\right]$ respectively. The normalised wavelet function filter coefficients $q_L(k)$ and scaling function filter coefficients $p_L(k)$ have the relation $q_L(k) = (-1)^k p_L(1-k)$. The multiresolution scaling and wavelet basis functions corresponding to the subspaces V_j and W_j are defined as:

$$\phi^j_{L,k}(x) = 2^{\frac{j}{2}}\phi_L\left(2^j x - k\right) \tag{12}$$

$$\psi^j_{L,k}(x) = 2^{\frac{j}{2}}\psi_L\left(2^j x - k\right) \tag{13}$$

The scaling and wavelet functions defined in Eqs. (10)–(13) satisfy the following properties [8]:

$$\int_{-\infty}^{\infty} \phi_L(x)dx = 1 \tag{14}$$

$$\int_{-\infty}^{\infty} \phi^j_{L,k}(x)\phi^j_{L,l}(x)dx = \delta_{k,l} \tag{15}$$

$$\int_{-\infty}^{\infty} \psi^j_{L,k}(x)\psi^j_{L,k}(x)dx = \delta_{k,l} \tag{16}$$

$$\int_{-\infty}^{\infty} \phi^j_{L,k}(x)\psi^j_{L,l}(x)dx = 0 \tag{17}$$

$$\int_{-\infty}^{\infty} x^m\psi_L(x)dx = 0 \qquad m = 0, 1, \ldots, \frac{L}{2} - 1 \tag{18}$$

Certain wavelet families have no explicit formulation, as is the case with the Daubechies wavelets. Therefore, Eq. (10) gives rise to a system of equations that require a normalising equation obtained from Eq. (14) to evaluate the scaling functions. The Daubechies wavelet of order L has $\frac{L}{2} - 1$ vanishing moments from property (18) and consequently the scaling functions at scale j can represent a polynomial of order x^m where $0 \le m \le \frac{L}{2} - 1$, i.e., [37]

$$x^m = \sum_k M_k^{j,m}\phi^j_{L,k}(x) \tag{19}$$

The coefficients $M_k^{j,m}$ denote the moments of the scaling function and it translates at V_j. The derivatives of the Daubechies wavelet scaling functions are evaluated by differentiating the refinement Eq. (10) m times, and are obtained as [12]:

$$\phi_L^{(m)}(x) = 2^m \sum_{k=0}^{L-1} p(k)\phi_L^{(m)}(2x-k) \tag{20}$$

A normalising condition is required to evaluate Eq. (20) which is obtained from the moments of the scaling functions.

$$\sum_{k=-\infty}^{k=\infty} k^m \phi^{(m)}(x-k) = m! \tag{21}$$

2.2. Daubechies connection coefficients

As earlier mentioned, the Daubechies functions cannot be computed analytically and their derivatives are highly oscillatory, particularly at low wavelet orders and/or high order derivatives. Therefore, the integral of the products of the scaling functions and/or derivatives are computed as what is commonly known as connection coefficients [37]. There are two forms of connection coefficients that are of relevance to this study; the multiscale two-term connection coefficient ${}_{a,b}\Gamma_{k,l}^{j,d_1,d_2}$ and multiscale connection coefficient $\Upsilon_k^{j,m}$. We define the two-term connection coefficient [30]

$${}_{a,b}\Gamma_{k,l}^{j,d_1,d_2} = 2^j \int_{-\infty}^{\infty} \mathcal{X}_{[0,1]}(\xi)\phi_a^{(d_1)}(2^j\xi-k)\phi_b^{(d_2)}(2^j\xi-l)d\xi \tag{22}$$

where a and b are the orders of the scaling function at multiresolution j, while the values d_1 and d_2 denote the order of the derivative of the scaling functions. $\mathcal{X}_{[0,1]}(x) = \begin{cases} 1 & 0 \le x \le 1 \\ 0 & otherwise \end{cases}$ is the characteristic function. The formulation presented is a modified algorithm of that described in [4] and allows for the evaluation of the connection coefficients for different values of a and b at different multiresolution scales j. From the 'two-scale' relation presented in Eq. (10),

$$\phi_L(2^j\xi-k) = \sum_r p(r)\phi_L(2^{j+1}\xi-2k-r) \tag{23}$$

Differentiating Eq. (23) m times

$$2^{jm}\phi_L^{(m)}(2^j\xi-k) = 2^{(j+1)m}\sum_r p(r)\phi_L^{(m)}(2^{j+1}\xi-2k-r) \tag{24}$$

Substituting Eq. (24) into Eq. (22) and applying the 'two-scale' relation of the characteristic function, the two-term connection coefficient can be expressed as:

$${}_{a,b}\Gamma_{k,l}^{j,d_1,d_2} = 2^{d_1+d_2-1}\sum_{r,s}\left[p_a(r-2k)p_b(s-2l) + p_a(r-2k+2^j)p_b(s-2l+2^j)\right]\Gamma_{r,s}^{j,d_1,d_2} \tag{25}$$

where $2-a \le k, r \le 2^j - 1$ and $2-b \le l, s \le 2^j - 1$. Eq. (25) can be expressed in matrix form as:

$$
\begin{aligned}
&_{((a+2^j-2)(b+2^j-2)\times 1)}\left\{{}_{a,b}\boldsymbol{\Gamma}^j\right\}= \\
&\qquad 2^{d_1+d_2-1}{}_{((a+2^j-2)(b+2^j-2)\times(a+2^j-2)(b+2^j-2))}\left[{}_{\mathrm{a,b}}\boldsymbol{P}\right]_{((a+2^j-2)(b+2^j-2)\times 1)}\left\{{}_{a,b}\boldsymbol{\Gamma}^j\right\}
\end{aligned}
\tag{26}
$$

where the square matrix $\left[{}_{a,b}\boldsymbol{P}\right]$ contains the filter coefficients as expressed in Eq. (25) and $\left\{{}_{a,b}\Gamma^j\right\}$ contains the connection coefficients. To uniquely determine the connection coefficients, normalising conditions are required to generate a sufficient number of inhomogeneous equations via the multiscale moment condition from Eq. (19)

$$
\xi^m = 2^{\frac{j}{2}}\sum_k {}_L M_k^{j,m}\phi_L\left(2^j\xi - k\right) \tag{27}
$$

Defining the second form of the connection coefficient

$$
\Upsilon_k^{j,m} = 2^{\frac{j}{2}}\int_0^1 x^m\phi_L\left(2^j\xi - k\right)d\xi = 2^{\frac{j}{2}}\int_{-\infty}^{\infty}\mathcal{X}_{[0,1]}(\xi)\xi^m\phi_L\left(2^j\xi - k\right)d\xi \tag{28}
$$

Substituting Eq. (27) into (28)

$$
\Upsilon_k^{j,m} = 2^j\sum_l M_l^{j,m}\int_{-\infty}^{\infty}\mathcal{X}_{[0,1]}(x)\phi_L\left(2^jx - l\right)\phi_L\left(2^jx - k\right)dx \tag{29}
$$

However,

$$
{}_{L,L}\Gamma_{k,l}^{j,0,0} = 2^j\int_{-\infty}^{\infty}\mathcal{X}_{[0,1]}(x)\phi_L\left(2^jx - l\right)\phi_L\left(2^jx - k\right)dx \tag{30}
$$

Thus

$$
\Upsilon_k^{j,m} = \sum_l M_l^{j,m}{}_{L,L}\Gamma_{k,l}^{j,0,0} \tag{31}
$$

where ${}_{L,L}\Gamma_{k,l}^{j,0,0}$ are the two-term connection coefficients with $a = b = L$ and $d_1 = d_1 = 0$ and $M_l^{j,m}$ are the moments earlier described.

2.3. B-spline wavelets on the interval [0,1] (BSWI)

The BSWI are a family of wavelets that emanate from Basis splines functions (B-Splines) and the basic functions in subspace V_j of order m and scale $j > 0$ are expressed as [20]

$$
B_{m,k}^j(x) = \left(t_{k+m}^j - t_k^j\right)\left[t_k^j, \ldots, t_{k+m}^j\right]_f (t - x)_+^{m-1} \tag{32}
$$

with the knot sequence

$$
\begin{gathered}
\left\{t_k^j\right\}_{k=-m+1}^{2^j+m-1} \\
t_k^j \le t_{k+1}^j
\end{gathered}
\tag{33}
$$

$\left[t^j_k, t^j_{k+1}, \dots, t^j_{k+m}\right]_t$, is the mth divided difference of the truncated power function $(t-x)^{m-1}_+$ with respect to variable t. The general B-splines take the form

$$B^j_{m,k}(x) = \frac{x - t^j_k}{t^j_{k+m-1} - t^j_k} B^j_{m-1,k}(x) + \frac{t^j_{k+m} - x}{t^j_{k+m} - t^j_{k+1}} B^j_{m-1,k+1}(x)$$
$$B^j_{1,k}(x) = \begin{cases} 1 & k \le x \le k+1 \\ 0 & otherwise \end{cases} \tag{34}$$

and have support $_{supp}B^j_{m,k}(x) = \left[t^j_k, t^j_{k+m}\right]$. The B-spline basis function has simple knots inside the unit interval and m-tuple knots at 0 and 1, as expressed in Eq. (33). The knots at 0 ad 1 coalesce and form multiple knots for BSWI while the internal knots are simple hence smoothness is unaffected. For the knot sequence on [0,1], t^j_k is given as [38]:

$$t^j_k = \begin{cases} 0 & -m+1 \le k < 1 \\ 2^{-j}k & 1 \le k < 2^j \\ 1 & 2^j \le k \le 2^j + m - 1 \end{cases} \tag{35}$$

The number of inner scaling functions present in the formulation of BSWI is determined by the scale j. There must be at least one inner scaling function on the interval [0,1] and this gives rise to the minimum value of j necessary to ensure this condition is met and is defined as j_0:

$$2^{j_0} \ge 2m - 1 \tag{36}$$

The basis $B^j_{m,k}(x)$ from the inner knots corresponds to the mth cardinal B-splines, $N_m(x)$, at multiresolution j [38]:

$$N_m(x) = m[0, 1, \dots, m](t-x)^{m-1}_+ \tag{37}$$

$$\phi^j_{m,k}(x) = B^j_{m,k}(x) = N_m\left(2^j x - k\right) 0 \le k < 2^j - m + 1 \tag{38}$$

where $\phi^j_{m,k}(x)$ is the BSWI scaling function which can be differentiated m times. The corresponding B-wavelet with support $_{supp}\psi^j_{m,k}(x) = \left[\frac{k}{2^j}, \frac{k+2m-1}{2^j}\right]$ is expressed as:

$$\psi^j_{m,k}(x) = \frac{1}{2^{m-1}} \sum_{l=0}^{2m-2} (-1)^l N_{2m}(l+1) B^{j+1,(m)}_{2m,2i+l}(x) \tag{39}$$

$B^{j+1,(m)}_{2m,k}(x)$ is the mth derivative for the B-spline of order $2m$ and scale $j+1$ and can be evaluated explicitly from Eq. (34). Given that the requirement $j > j_0$ ensures at least one inner B-wavelet is present, the scaling and wavelet function of the BSWI are obtained as [39]:

$$\phi_{m,k}^{j}(x) = \begin{cases} B_{m,k}^{j_0}\left(2^{j-j_0}x\right) & -m+1 \le k \le -1 \\ B_{m,0}^{j_0}\left(2^{j-j_0}x - 2^{-j_0}k\right) & 0 \le i \le 2^j - m \\ B_{m,2^j-k-m}^{j_0}\left(1 - 2^{j-j_0}x\right) & 2^j \le i \le 2^j + m - 1 \end{cases} \tag{40}$$

$$\psi_{m,k}^{j}(x) = \begin{cases} \psi_{m,k}^{j_0}\left(2^{j-j_0}x\right) & -m+1 \le k \le -1 \\ \psi_{m,0}^{j_0}\left(2^{j-j_0}x - 2^{-j_0}k\right) & 0 \le i \le 2^j - m \\ \psi_{m,2^j-k-2m+1}^{j_0}\left(1 - 2^{j-j_0}x\right) & 2^j \le i \le 2^j + m - 1 \end{cases} \tag{41}$$

and the scaling function derivatives can be evaluated directly by differentiating Eq. (40).

3. The wavelet finite element method

3.1. Axial rod wavelet finite element

Assume each WFE is divided into equal segments, n_s, connected by $r = n_s + 1$ elemental nodes, as shown in **Figure 1**, with axial deformation u_i. The total number of degrees of freedom (DOFs) within each WFE is denoted by $n = r$ for $n, r \in \mathbb{N}$. Vector $\{\boldsymbol{u_e}\} = \{u_1 u_2 \cdots u_{r-1} u_r\}^T$ contains all the axial DOFs in physical space, as illustrated in **Figure 2(a)**, where $u_i = u(x_i)$ represents the elemental node axial deformation DOF at node i corresponding to coordinate position x_i. The nodal natural coordinates is $\xi_i = \frac{x_i - x_1}{L_e}$ $(0 \le \xi_i \le 1,\ 1 \le i \le r)$. The Daubechies and BSWI scaling functions $\phi_{z,k}^{j}(x)$ are used as the interpolating functions and for a family of order z at multiresolution scale j, the axial deformation

$$u(\xi) = \sum_{k=h}^{2^j-1} a_{z,k}^{j} \phi_{z,k}^{j}(\xi) \tag{42}$$

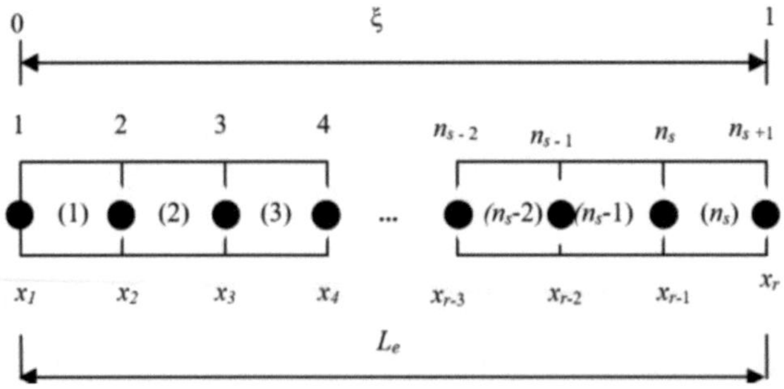

Figure 1. Wavelet finite element layout.

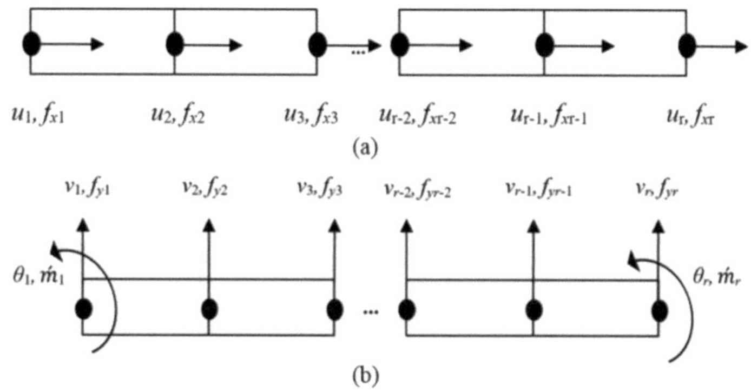

Figure 2. (a) Axial rod and (b) Euler Bernoulli beam wavelet finite element layout.

contains the unknown wavelet coefficients $a^j_{z,k}$. This gives rise to the vector $\{u_e\}$ containing the axial deformations at all elemental nodes in physical space.

$$_{(n\times1)}\{u_e\} = {}_{(n\times n)}\left[R^w_r\right]_{(n\times1)}\{a_e\} \tag{43}$$

The matrix $\left[R^w_r\right] = \left[\{\Phi^j_z(\xi_1)\} \quad \{\Phi^j_z(\xi_2)\} \quad \cdots \quad \{\Phi^j_z(\xi_{r-1})\} \quad \{\Phi^j_z(\xi_r)\}\right]^{\mathrm{T}}$ contains the scaling function vectors $\{\Phi^j_z(\xi_i)\}$ approximating the axial deformation at the corresponding elemental nodes and $\{a_e\} = \left[a^j_{z,h} \quad a^j_{z,h+1} \quad \cdots \quad a^j_{z,2^j-2} \quad a^j_{z,2^j-1}\right]^{\mathrm{T}}$. The axial deformation at any point along the rod element can be generalised as:

$$u(\xi) = {}_{(1\times n)}\left\{\Phi^j_z(\xi)\right\}_{(n\times n)}\left[T^w_r\right]_{(n\times1)}\{u_e\} \tag{44}$$

The matrix $\left[T^w_r\right] = \left[R^w_r\right]^{-1}$ is the axial rod wavelet transformation matrix with the scripts r and w denoting rod and wavelet respectively. The wavelet based axial rod shape functions can be evaluated as $\{N_{r,e}(\xi)\} = \left\{\Phi^j_z(\xi)\right\}\left[T^w_r\right]$ within each element.

Suppose the axial rod is subjected to nodal point loads f_{xi} and distributed loading $f_d(x)$, then the potential energy within the axial rod Π^a can be generally expressed as [40]:

$$\Pi^a = \int_0^l \frac{EA}{2}\left(\frac{du(x)}{dx}\right)^2 dx - \sum_i u(x_i)f_{xi} - \int_0^l f_d(x)u(x)\,dx \tag{45}$$

where E is the Young's modulus, A is the cross-sectional area and l is the length of the rod. Therefore, given the relation highlighted in Eq. (44), the axial stain energy U^a_e within each WFE of length L_e is expressed in natural coordinates as:

$$U^a_e = \frac{1}{2}\frac{EA}{L_e}\{u_e\}^T\int_0^1\left[T^w_r\right]^T\left\{\frac{d\Phi^j_z(\xi)}{d\xi}\right\}^T\left\{\frac{d\Phi^j_z(\xi)}{d\xi}\right\}\left[T^w_r\right]d\xi\{u_e\} \tag{46}$$

The stiffness matrix of the rod element in wavelet space, $\left[k^w_{r,e}\right]$ is computed using the first derivative of the scaling functions and is symmetric.

$$_{(n\times n)}\left[k^{w}_{r,e}\right]=\int_{0}^{1}\{\Phi'^{j}_{z}(\xi)\}^{T}\{\Phi'^{j}_{z}(\xi)\}d\xi \tag{47}$$

In order for one to obtain the stiffness matrix in physical space, the element properties and transformation matrix $[T^{w}_{r}]$ are applied to the wavelet space stiffness matrix in Eq. (47).

$$_{(n\times n)}\left[k^{p}_{r,e}\right]=\frac{EA}{L_e}\,_{(n\times n)}\left[T^{w}_{r}\right]^{T}\,_{(n\times n)}\left[k^{w}_{r,e}\right]_{(n\times n)}\left[T^{w}_{r}\right] \tag{48}$$

The load vector containing the axial point loads of the WFE in physical space is obtained as:

$$_{(n\times 1)}\left\{f^{n,p}_{r,e}\right\}=\sum_{i}\left[T^{w}_{r}\right]^{T}\{\Phi^{j}_{z}(\xi_i)\}^{T}f_{xi} \tag{49}$$

and the equivalent nodal load vector for the distributed load $f_d(x)$ in physical space is

$$_{(n\times 1)}\left\{f^{d,p}_{r,e}\right\}=L_e\int_{0}^{1}f_d(\xi)\left[T^{w}_{r}\right]^{T}\{\Phi^{j}_{z}(\xi)\}^{T}d\xi \tag{50}$$

When applying the Daubechies wavelet family, the WFE has a total of $n=2^j+L-2$ DOFs. The wavelet space stiffness matrix is evaluated from the multiscale two-term connection coefficients $_{a,b}\Gamma^{j,d_1,d_2}_{k,l}$ $a=b=L$ and $d_1=d_1=1$ and is given as:

$$_{((2^j+L-2)x(2^j+L-2))}^{D}\left[k^{w}_{r,e}\right]=2^{2j}\left[\Gamma^{j,1,1}\right] \tag{51}$$

where (2^{2j}) is the normalising factor and the matrix $[\Gamma^{j,1,1}]$ has the entries $_{L,L}\Gamma^{j,1,1}_{k,l}$ for the limits $2-L\le k,l\le 2^j-1$. Similarly, the distributed forces acting on the element require the form $\Upsilon^{j,m}_{k}$ for limits $2-L\le k,l\le 2^j-1$ of connection coefficients and the value of m depends on the order of the function $f_d(x)$ of the forces. In the case of the BSWI formulations, the total DOFs is $n=2^j+m-1$ and the condition $j\ge j_0$ must be satisfied. Therefore, the wavelet space stiffness matrices of the BSWI axial rod are computed as:

$$_{((2^j+m-1)\times(2^j+m-1))}^{BS}\left[k^{w}_{r,e}\right]=\int_{0}^{1}\{\Phi'^{j}_{m}(\xi)\}^{T}\{\Phi'^{j}_{m}(\xi)\}d\xi \tag{52}$$

3.2. Euler Bernoulli beam wavelet finite element

According to Euler Bernoulli beam theory, it is assumed that the shear deformation effects are neglected because before and after bending occurs, the plane cross-sections remain plane and perpendicular to the axial centroidal axis of the beam. The beam WFE of length L_e, is divided into n_s equally spaced elemental segments connected by r elemental nodes at coordinate values $x_i\in[x_1,x_r]$ and $i\in\mathbb{N}$ as illustrated in **Figure 1**. The WFE has the transverse displacement v and rotation θ taken into account, with corresponding transverse forces f_y and moments $\acute{m}$ respectively. The transverse displacement and rotation DOFs must be present at each elemental end node to ensure inter-element compatibility [4–6]. However, the DOFs at the internal elemental nodes can be tailored according to the desired requirements and this in turn will affect the total number of elemental segments and nodes present in each element. In this case the internal WFE nodes only have the transverse displacement present and the total number of DOFs within each beam element is n as illustrated in **Figure 2(b)**. Therefore, there are $n-2$ displacement DOFs and 2 rotation DOFs in total for each WFE and consequently $r=n-2$ elemental nodes and $n_s=n-3$ elemental segments. Let the vector $\{v_e\}=\{v_1 \quad \theta_1 \quad v_2 \quad v_3 \quad \cdots \quad v_{r-2}\, v_{r-1}\, v_r\theta_r\}^T$ denote all the physical DOFs within the beam element. The displacement and rotation DOFs corresponding to coordinate position $x_i \in [x_1, x_r]$ $i \in \mathbb{N}$ and $(1 \le i \le r)$ in local coordinates are denoted as $v_i = v(x_i)$ and $\theta_i = \theta(x_i)$. The nodal natural coordinate $\xi_i = \frac{x_i - x_1}{L_e}$ $(0 \le \xi_i \le 1,\ 1 \le i \le r)$. The deflection and rotation at any point of the wavelet based beam finite element can be approximated by applying the wavelet scaling functions $\phi^j_{z,k}(x)$ of order z at multiresolution scale j as interpolating functions.

$$
\begin{aligned}
v(\xi) &= \sum_{k=h}^{2^j-1} b^j_{z,k} \phi^j_{z,k}(\xi) \\
\theta(\xi) &= \frac{\partial v(\xi)}{\partial x} = \frac{1}{L_e} \sum_{k=h}^{2^j-1} b^j_{z,k} \frac{\partial \phi^j_{z,k}(\xi)}{\partial \xi}
\end{aligned}
\tag{53}
$$

Therefore, the DOFs present within the entire beam element can be represented as

$$
{}_{(n\times 1)}\{\boldsymbol{v}_e\} = {}_{(n\times n)}\left[\boldsymbol{R}^w_b\right]_{(n\times 1)}\{\boldsymbol{b}_e\} \tag{54}
$$

$\left[\boldsymbol{R}^w_b\right] = \left[\{\boldsymbol{\Phi}^j_z(\xi_1)\} \quad \frac{1}{L_e}\{\boldsymbol{\Phi}'^j_z(\xi_1)\} \quad \{\boldsymbol{\Phi}^j_z(\xi_2)\} \quad \cdots \quad \{\boldsymbol{\Phi}^j_z(\xi_{r-1})\} \quad \{\boldsymbol{\Phi}^j_z(\xi_r)\} \quad \frac{1}{L_e}\{\boldsymbol{\Phi}'^j_z(\xi_r)\} \right]^{\mathrm{T}}$ and vector $\{\boldsymbol{b}_e\}$ contains the unknown wavelet coefficients $b^j_{z,k}$ representing the beam wavelet space DOFs.

From Eq. (54), the transverse displacement and rotation at any point of the beam element can be expressed as:

$$
\begin{aligned}
v(\xi) &= {}_{(1\times n)}\left\{\boldsymbol{\Phi}^j_z(\xi)\right\}_{(n\times n)}\left[\boldsymbol{T}^w_b\right]_{(n\times 1)}\{\boldsymbol{v}_e\} \\
\theta(\xi) &= \frac{1}{L_e}{}_{(1\times n)}\left\{\boldsymbol{\Phi}'^j_z(\xi)\right\}_{(n\times n)}\left[\boldsymbol{T}^w_b\right]_{(n\times 1)}\{\boldsymbol{v}_e\}
\end{aligned}
\tag{55}
$$

where $\left[\boldsymbol{T}^w_b\right] = \left[\boldsymbol{R}^w_b\right]^{-1}$ is the beam wavelet transformation matrix which is used to obtain the wavelet based shape functions for the beam $\{\boldsymbol{N}_{b,e}(\xi)\} = \{\boldsymbol{\Phi}^j_z(\xi)\}\left[\boldsymbol{T}^w_b\right]$. The potential energy Π^b within a Euler Bernoulli beam subjected to concentrated forces f_{yi}, distributed force $f_d(x)$ and bending moments $\acute{m}_i$ can be generally expressed as [40]:

$$
\Pi^b = \int_0^l \frac{EI}{2}\left(\frac{d^2v}{dx^2}\right)^2 dx - \sum_i f_{yi} v(x_i) - \int_0^l f_d(x) v dx - \sum_k \acute{m}_k \frac{dv(x_k)}{dx} \tag{56}
$$

where E is the Young's modulus, I is the moment of inertia and l is the length of the beam. The strain energy U^b_e within each beam element of length L_e can expressed in terms of the approximation of the transverse displacement via scaling functions as highlighted in Eq. (55).

$$U_e^b = \frac{1}{2}\frac{EI}{L_e^3}\{v_e\}^T \int_0^1 [T_b^w]^T \left\{\frac{d^2\Phi_z^j(\xi)}{d\xi^2}\right\}^T \left\{\frac{d^2\Phi_z^j(\xi)}{d\xi^2}\right\} [T_b^w] d\xi \{v_e\} \tag{57}$$

This gives rise to the beam WFE stiffness matrix in wavelet space

$$_{(n\times n)}\left[k_{b,e}^w\right] = \int_0^1 \{\Phi_z''^j(\xi)\}^T \{\Phi_z''^j(\xi)\} d\xi \tag{58}$$

The vector $\left\{\Phi''^j_z(\xi)\right\} = \left\{ \phi''^j_{z,h}(\xi) \quad \phi''^j_{z,h+1}(\xi) \quad \cdots \quad \phi''^j_{z,2^j-2}(\xi) \quad \phi''^j_{z,2^j-1}(\xi) \right\}$ contains the second derivative of the scaling functions. Taking into account the material properties of the beam, the wavelet space stiffness matrix is transformed into physical space via the transformation matrix $[T_b^w]$.

$$_{(n\times n)}\left[k_{b,e}^p\right] = \frac{EI}{L_e^3} {}_{(n\times n)}[T_b^w]^T {}_{(n\times n)}\left[k_{b,e}^w\right] {}_{(n\times n)}[T_b^w] \tag{59}$$

The transverse kinetic energy of the beam element is expressed as

$$\Lambda_e^b = \frac{1}{2}\rho A L_e \int_0^1 \dot{v}(\xi)^T \dot{v}(\xi) d\xi \tag{60}$$

where $\dot{v}(\xi) = \frac{\partial v(\xi)}{\partial t}$, ρ is the density and A is the cross-sectional area of the beam. Applying the scaling functions to approximate the displacements within the beam, the kinetic energy becomes

$$\Lambda_e^b = \{\dot{v}_e\}^T \frac{1}{2}\rho A L_e \int_0^1 [T_b^w]^T \{\Phi_z^j(\xi)\}^T \{\Phi_z^j(\xi)\} [T_b^w] d\xi \; \{\dot{v}_e\} \tag{61}$$

The mass matrix in physical space of the Euler Bernoulli beam element, $\left[m_{b,e}^p\right]$, can be evaluated as:

$$\left[m_{b,e}^p\right] = \rho A L_e [T_b^w]^T \int_0^1 \{\Phi_z^j(\xi)\}^T \{\Phi_z^j(\xi)\} d\xi [T_b^w] \tag{62}$$

The vectors containing the element concentrated point loads, bending moments and equivalent distributed loads in physical space respectively are subsequently evaluated as:

$$\begin{aligned}
_{(n\times 1)}\left\{f_{b,e}^{n,p}\right\} &= \sum_{i=1}^{r} {}_{(n\times n)}[T_b^w]^T {}_{(n\times 1)}\{\Phi_z^j(\xi_i)\}^T f_{yi} \\
_{(n\times 1)}\left\{f_{b,e}^{m,p}\right\} &= \sum_{k} {}_{(n\times n)}[T_b^w]^T {}_{(n\times 1)}\{\Phi_z'^j(\xi_k)\}^T \acute{m}_k \\
_{(n\times 1)}\left\{f_{b,e}^{d,p}\right\} &= L_e \int_0^1 f_d(\xi) {}_{(n\times n)}[T_b^w]^T \{\Phi_z^j(\xi)\}^T d\xi
\end{aligned} \tag{63}$$

In various engineering problems, the loading conditions analysed vary in location and/or magnitude with respect to time, e.g., a train travelling over a track, and this is generally referred to as moving load problems. Assume a moving load of magnitude P travels across a beam element, as illustrated in **Figure 3**, from the left at a constant speed of c m·s^{-1} and is represented by the function $(x, t) = P\delta(x - x_0)$ [41]. $\delta(x)$ is the Dirac Delta function and x_0 is the distance travelled by the moving load at time t. The potential work of the load at this instant at position $\xi_0 = \frac{x_0}{L_e}$ in natural coordinates is [1, 30]:

$$\Omega_e^b(\xi_0) = \int_0^1 P\delta(\xi - \xi_0)v(\xi)d\xi = P\{\boldsymbol{v}_e\}^T\left[\boldsymbol{T}_b^w\right]^T\{\boldsymbol{\Phi}_z^j(\xi_0)\}^T \tag{64}$$

Therefore, the element load vector in physical space is evaluated as

$$\left\{\boldsymbol{f}_{b,e}^{p,p}(t)\right\} = P\left[\boldsymbol{T}_b^w\right]^{T\ t}\{\boldsymbol{\Phi}_z^j(\xi_0)\}^T \tag{65}$$

Assuming the moving load transverses to a new position ξ_0 within the same WFE, the numerical values of the shape functions, and consequently load vector, will change accordingly. All other WFEs representing the system with no loading present have zero entries within the load vectors at that particular time t. When the moving load is acting on a new WFE, the scaling functions corresponding to the WFE subjected to the moving load are used to obtain the load vector for that particular element.

When applying the Daubechies wavelet family of order L at multiresolution j, the total DOFs within a single element is $n = 2^j + L - 2$ and for this specific layout, the total number of elemental nodes is $r = 2^j + L - 4$ and corresponding elemental segments $n_s = 2^j + L - 5$. The Daubechies wavelet space stiffness and mass matrices of the Euler Bernoulli beam WFE are obtained from the connection coefficients and are expressed as:

$$_{((2^j+L-2)\times(2^j+L-2))}^{D}\left[\boldsymbol{k}_{b,e}^w\right] = 2^{4j}\left[\boldsymbol{\Gamma}^{j,2,2}\right] \tag{66}$$

$$_{((2^j+L-2)\times(2^j+L-2))}^{D}\left[\boldsymbol{m}_{b,e}^w\right] = \left[\boldsymbol{\Gamma}^{j,0,0}\right] \tag{67}$$

Correspondingly, the connection coefficients of the form $\Upsilon_k^{j,m}$ for $2 - L \le k \le 2^j - 1$ are used to evaluated the distributed loads and the value of m is based on the load function $f_d(x)$. For the

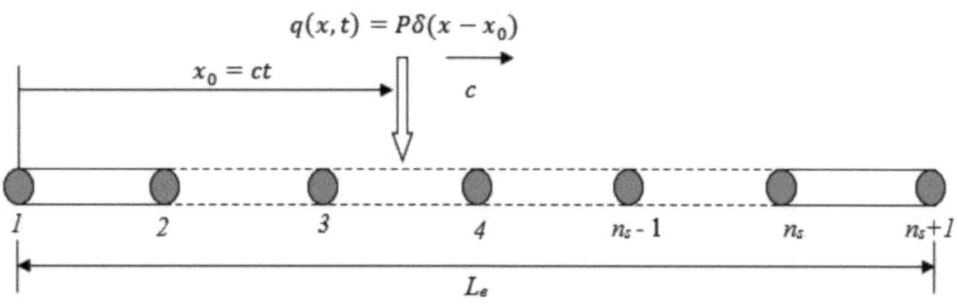

Figure 3. Layout of a beam WFE subjected to a moving point load.

BSWI family of order m and at scale j, there are $n = 2^j + m - 1$ total DOFs, $r = 2^j + m - 3$ elemental nodes and $n_s = 2^j + m - 4$ elemental segments within the each WFE for this layout. The stiffness and mass matrices in wavelet space can be evaluated directly and are obtained as:

$$ {}^{BS}_{((2^j+m-1)\times(2^j+m-1))}\left[k^{w}_{b,e}\right] = \int_0^1 \{\Phi''^{j}_{m}(\xi)\}^T\{\Phi''^{j}_{m}(\xi)\}d\xi \tag{68} $$

$$ {}^{BS}_{((2^j+m-1)\times(2^j+m-1))}\left[m^{w}_{b,e}\right] = \int_0^1 \{\Phi^{j}_{m}(\xi)\}^T\{\Phi^{j}_{m}(\xi)\}d\xi \tag{69} $$

3.3. Transversely varying functionally graded Euler Bernoulli beam wavelet finite element

Functionally graded materials are a recent evolution of composite materials where the material constituents, hence properties, vary continuously in the desired spatial directions. The need for such revolutionary materials arose to overcome limitations of conventional composite materials, for instance, desirable properties would diminished when applied to highly intense thermal environments or material debonding due to increased stress concentration at material interfaces [42]. In the formulation of the wavelet based functionally grade beam as presented in **Figure 4(a)**, of height h, length l and width b, the material distribution is modelled based on the power law of transverse gradation [43]

$$ P(y) = P_{lo}\left(\left[P_{ratio} - 1\right]\left(\frac{y}{h} + \frac{1}{2}\right)^n + 1\right) \tag{70} $$

As illustrated in **Figure 4(b)**, the transverse variation of the effective material properties $P(y)$ (Young's modulus) can be infinitely altered via the non-negative volume fraction power law

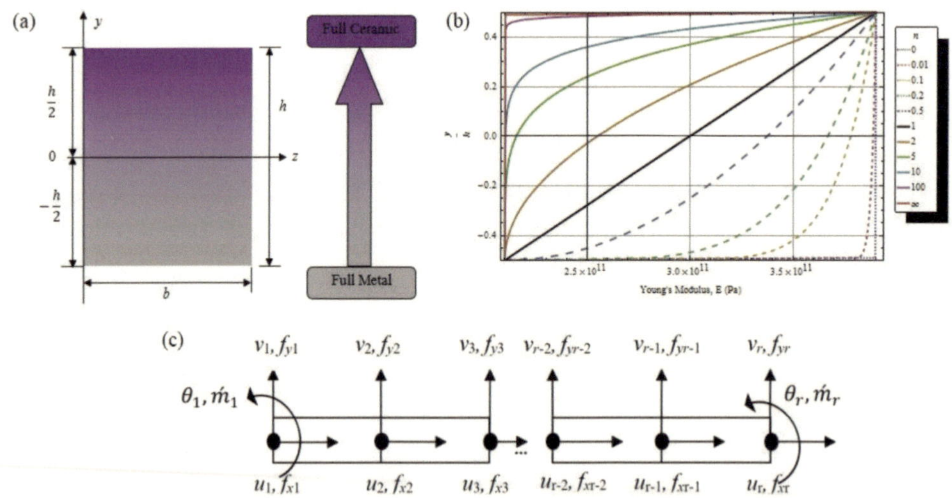

Figure 4. (a) Cross-section of transversely varying functionally graded beam. (b) Effective Young's modulus variation of steel-alumina functionally graded beam for different n. (c) Functionally graded beam layout.

exponent, n. P_{ratio} is the ratio of the upper and lower surface material properties P_u and P_{lo} respectively.

The beam WFE has axial deformation u_i and transverse deflection v_i DOFs at all elemental nodes and rotation θ_i DOFs only present at elemental end nodes with corresponding axial forces f_{xi}, transverse forces f_{yi} and bending moments θ_i as illustrated in **Figure 4(c)**. The wavelet scaling functions are implemented as interpolating functions and the axial deformation, deflection and rotation at any point of the beam element are described by Eqs. (42) and (53) respectively. However, in order to ensure that the defined DOFs are positioned correctly, the layout of the element determines the order of scaling functions selected. In this case, the order of the scaling functions selected to approximate the axial displacement is $z-2$ if the scaling function order approximating the bending DOFs is z. The vector containing the total number of DOFs, s, present in the functionally graded beam element is $\{\boldsymbol{h}_e\} = \{u_1 \quad v_1 \quad \theta_1 \quad u_2 \quad v_2 \quad u_3 \quad v_3 \quad \cdots \quad u_{r-1} \quad v_{r-1} \quad u_r \quad v_r \quad \theta_r\}^T$ and subsequently

$$u(\xi) = {}^{a}_{(1\times s)}\left\{\boldsymbol{\Phi}^{j}_{z-2}(\xi)\right\}_{(s\times1)}\{\mathbf{c}_e\}$$

$$v(\xi) = {}^{t}_{(1\times s)}\left\{\boldsymbol{\Phi}^{j}_{z}(\xi)\right\}_{(s\times1)}\{\mathbf{c}_e\}$$

$$\theta(\xi) = \frac{\partial v(\xi)}{\partial x} = \frac{1}{L_e}\frac{\partial v(\xi)}{\partial \xi} = \frac{1}{L_e}{}^{t}_{(1\times s)}\left\{\boldsymbol{\Phi}'^{j}_{z}(\xi)\right\}_{(s\times1)}\{\mathbf{c}_e\} \tag{71}$$

where the vector $\{c^e\}$ contains the unknown wavelet space element DOFs and

$${}^{a}_{1\times s}\left\{\boldsymbol{\Phi}^{j}_{z-2}(\xi)\right\} = \left\{\phi^{j}_{z-2,h}(\xi) \quad 0 \quad 0 \quad \phi^{j}_{z-2,h+1}(\xi) \quad 0 \quad \cdots \quad 0 \quad \phi^{j}_{z-2,2^j-1}(\xi) \quad 0 \quad 0\right\}$$

$${}^{t}_{1\times s}\left\{\boldsymbol{\Phi}^{j}_{z}(\xi)\right\} = \left\{0 \quad \phi^{j}_{z,i}(\xi) \quad \phi^{j}_{z,i+1}(\xi) \quad 0 \quad \cdots \quad 0 \quad \phi^{j}_{z,2^j-2}(\xi) \quad \phi^{j}_{z,2^j-1}(\xi)\right\} \tag{72}$$

$${}^{t}_{1\times s}\left\{\boldsymbol{\Phi}'^{j}_{z}(\xi)\right\} = \left\{0 \quad \phi'^{j}_{z,i}(\xi) \quad \phi'^{j}_{z,i+1}(\xi) \quad 0 \quad \cdots \quad 0 \quad \phi'^{j}_{z,2^j-2}(\xi) \quad \phi'^{j}_{z,2^j-1}(\xi)\right\}$$

Therefore, the DOFs present within the entire beam element can be represented as

$${}_{s\times1}\{\boldsymbol{h}_e\} = {}_{s\times s}\left[\boldsymbol{R}^{w}_{p}\right]_{s\times1}\{\boldsymbol{c}_e\} \tag{73}$$

and consequently

$$u(\xi) = {}^{a}_{(1\times s)}\left\{\boldsymbol{\Phi}^{j}_{z}(\xi)\right\}_{(s\times s)}\left[\boldsymbol{T}^{w}_{p}\right]_{(s\times1)}\{\boldsymbol{h}_e\}$$

$$v(\xi) = {}^{t}_{(1\times s)}\left\{\boldsymbol{\Phi}^{j}_{z}(\xi)\right\}_{(s\times s)}\left[\boldsymbol{T}^{w}_{p}\right]_{(s\times1)}\{\boldsymbol{h}_e\}$$

$$\theta(\xi) = \frac{1}{L_e}{}^{t}_{(1\times s)}\left\{\boldsymbol{\Phi}'^{j}_{z}(\xi)\right\}_{(s\times s)}\left[\boldsymbol{T}^{w}_{p}\right]_{(s\times1)}\{\boldsymbol{h}_e\} \tag{74}$$

The wavelet transformation matrix $\left[\boldsymbol{T}^{w}_{p}\right] = \left[\boldsymbol{R}^{w}_{p}\right]^{-1}$. The strain energy of the functionally graded beam element, U_e, is defined as

$$U_e = \frac{b}{2}\int_{-\frac{h}{2}}^{\frac{h}{2}}\int_0^1 E(y)\left[\frac{1}{L_e}\left(\frac{\partial u(\xi)}{\partial \xi}\right)^T\left(\frac{\partial u(\xi)}{\partial \xi}\right) - \frac{y}{L_e^2}\left(\frac{\partial^2 v(\xi)}{\partial \xi^2}\right)^T\left(\frac{\partial u(\xi)}{\partial \xi}\right)\right.$$
$$\left. - \frac{y}{L_e^2}\left(\frac{\partial u(\xi)}{\partial \xi}\right)^T\left(\frac{\partial^2 v(\xi)}{\partial \xi^2}\right) + \frac{y^2}{L_e^3}\left(\frac{\partial^2 v(\xi)}{\partial \xi^2}\right)^T\left(\frac{\partial^2 v(\xi)}{\partial \xi^2}\right)\right] d\xi\, dy \tag{75}$$

where L_e is the length of the element and $E(y)$ the effective Young's modulus obtained from Eq. (70). Let

$$^{A}E_e = \int_{-\frac{h}{2}}^{\frac{h}{2}} E(y)dy = \int_{-\frac{h}{2}}^{\frac{h}{2}} [E_u - E_l]\left(\frac{y}{h}+\frac{1}{2}\right)^n + E_l dy$$
$$^{B}E_e = \int_{-\frac{h}{2}}^{\frac{h}{2}} y\, E(y)dy = \int_{-\frac{h}{2}}^{\frac{h}{2}} y\left([E_u - E_l]\left(\frac{y}{h}+\frac{1}{2}\right)^n + E_l\right)dy \tag{76}$$
$$^{C}E_e = \int_{-\frac{h}{2}}^{\frac{h}{2}} y^2 E(y)dy = \int_{-\frac{h}{2}}^{\frac{h}{2}} \left(y^2[E_u - E_l]\left(\frac{y}{h}+\frac{1}{2}\right)^n + E_l\right)dy$$

$^{A}E_e$, $^{B}E_e$ and $^{C}E_e$ denote axial, axial-bending coupling and bending stiffness of the WFE respectively. The wavelet based physical space elemental stiffness matrix of the beam, $\left[k_e^w\right]$, is

$$\underset{(s\times s)}{^{A}}\left[k_e^w\right] = \int_0^1 \frac{b\,^{A}E_e}{L_e}\left[T_p^w\right]^T {}^{a}\left\{\frac{\partial \Phi^j_{z-2}(\xi)}{\partial \xi}\right\}^T {}^{a}\left\{\frac{\partial \Phi^j_{z-2}(\xi)}{\partial \xi}\right\}\left[T_p^w\right] d\xi$$
$$\underset{(s\times s)}{^{B}}\left[k_e^w\right] = \int_0^1 \frac{b\,^{B}E_e}{L_e^2}\left[T_p^w\right]^T {}^{t}\left\{\frac{\partial^2 \Phi^j_{z}(\xi)}{\partial \xi^2}\right\}^T {}^{a}\left\{\frac{\partial \Phi^j_{z-2}(\xi)}{\partial \xi}\right\}\left[T_p^w\right] d\xi$$
$$\underset{(s\times s)}{^{C}}\left[k_e^w\right] = \int_0^1 \frac{b\,^{B}E_e}{L_e^2}\left[T_p^w\right]^T {}^{a}\left\{\frac{\partial \Phi^j_{z-2}(\xi)}{\partial \xi}\right\}^T {}^{t}\left\{\frac{\partial^2 \Phi^j_{z}(\xi)}{\partial \xi^2}\right\}\left[T_p^w\right] d\xi$$
$$\underset{(s\times s)}{^{D}}\left[k_e^w\right] = \int_0^1 \frac{b\,^{C}E_e}{L_e^3}\left[T_p^w\right]^T {}^{t}\left\{\frac{\partial^2 \Phi^j_{z}(\xi)}{\partial \xi^2}\right\}^T {}^{t}\left\{\frac{\partial^2 \Phi^j_{z}(\xi)}{\partial \xi^2}\right\}\left[T_p^w\right] d\xi$$
$$\underset{(s\times s)}{}\left[k_e^p\right] = {}^{A}\left[k_e^p\right] - {}^{B}\left[k_e^p\right] - {}^{C}\left[k_e^p\right] + {}^{D}\left[k_e^p\right] \tag{77}$$

The kinetic energy of the functionally graded beam element, Λ_e, is defined as

$$\Lambda_e = \frac{1}{2}\int_0^b dz\int_{-\frac{h}{2}}^{\frac{h}{2}}\int_0^1 \rho(y)\left(L_e(\dot{u}(\xi,t)\dot{u}(\xi,t)) - y\left(\dot{u}(\xi,t)\frac{\partial \dot{v}(\xi,t)}{\partial x}\right) - y\left(\frac{\partial \dot{v}(\xi,t)}{\partial \xi}\dot{u}(\xi,t)\right)\right.$$
$$\left. + \frac{y^2}{L_e}\left(\frac{\partial \dot{v}(\xi,t)}{\partial x}\frac{\partial \dot{v}(\xi,t)}{\partial x}\right) + L_e(\dot{v}(\xi,t)\dot{v}(\xi,t))\right) d\xi\, dy \tag{78}$$

$\rho(y)$ is the effective density also obtained from Eq. (70). Let the inertial coefficients be denoted as:

$$
\begin{aligned}
{}^{A}\rho_e &= \int_{-\frac{h}{2}}^{\frac{h}{2}} \rho(y)dy = \int_{-\frac{h}{2}}^{\frac{h}{2}} [\rho_u - \rho_l]\left(\frac{y}{h}+\frac{1}{2}\right)^n + \rho_l dy \\
{}^{B}\rho_e &= \int_{-\frac{h}{2}}^{\frac{h}{2}} y\rho(y)dy = \int_{-\frac{h}{2}}^{\frac{h}{2}} y\left([\rho_u - \rho_l]\left(\frac{y}{h}+\frac{1}{2}\right)^n + \rho_l\right) dy \\
{}^{C}\rho_e &= \int_{-\frac{h}{2}}^{\frac{h}{2}} y^2\rho(y)dy = \int_{-\frac{h}{2}}^{\frac{h}{2}} \left(y^2[\rho_u - \rho_l]\left(\frac{y}{h}+\frac{1}{2}\right)^n + \rho_l\right) dy
\end{aligned}
\tag{79}
$$

The wavelet based physical space elemental mass matrix of the beam, $[m_e^p]$, is

$$
\begin{aligned}
{}^{A}_{(s\times s)}[m_e^w] &= \int_0^1 b^A\rho_e L_e \left[T_p^w\right]^T {}^a\left\{\Phi_{z-2}^j(\xi)\right\}^T {}^a\left\{\Phi_{z-2}^j(\xi)\right\}\left[T_p^w\right]^T d\xi \\
{}^{B}_{(s\times s)}[m_e^w] &= \int_0^1 b^B\rho_e \left[T_p^w\right]^T {}^a\left\{\Phi_{z-2}^j(\xi)\right\}^T {}^t\left\{\frac{\partial\Phi_z^j(\xi)}{\partial\xi}\right\}\left[T_p^w\right]^T d\xi \\
{}^{C}_{(s\times s)}[m_e^w] &= \int_0^1 b^B\rho_e \left[T_p^w\right]^T {}^t\left\{\frac{\partial\Phi_z^j(\xi)}{\partial\xi}\right\}^T {}^a\left\{\Phi_{z-2}^j(\xi)\right\}\left[T_p^w\right]^T d\xi \\
{}^{D}_{(s\times s)}[m_e^w] &= \int_0^1 b^C\rho_e \left[T_p^w\right]^T {}^t\left\{\frac{\partial\Phi_z^j(\xi)}{\partial\xi}\right\}^T {}^t\left\{\frac{\partial\Phi_z^j(\xi)}{\partial\xi}\right\}\left[T_p^w\right]^T d\xi \\
{}^{E}_{(s\times s)}[m_e^w] &= \int_0^1 b^A\rho_e L_e \left[T_p^w\right]^T {}^t\left\{\overline{\Phi}_z^j(\xi)\right\}^T {}^t\left\{\overline{\Phi}_z^j(\xi)\right\}\left[T_p^w\right]^T d\xi \\
{}_{(s\times s)}[m_e^p] &= {}^{A}[m_e^p] - {}^{B}[m_e^p] - {}^{C}[m_e^p] + {}^{D}[m_e^p] + {}^{E}[m_e^p]
\end{aligned}
\tag{80}
$$

4. Numerical examples

Example 1: A uniform axial cantilever rod (free-fixed) subjected to linear varying load $q(x) = -q_0\, x$ has a uniform cross sectional area, $A = A_0$, Young's Modulus, $E = E_0$ and length l. The exact solution for displacement at a particular point x can be obtained by solving $u(x) = \frac{1}{EA}\int_0^x P(x)dx = \frac{1}{E_0A_0}\int q_0 \frac{x^2}{2}\, dx$ [40]. One WFE is used to represent the rod using Daubechies and BSWI WFEM approaches and the results are compared with the exact, h-FEM and p-FEM formulations. The governing equation of the system for FEM and WFEM is

$$[K_r]\{U_r\} = \{F_r\} \tag{81}$$

where $[K_r]$ is the system stiffness matrix, $\{U_r\}$ is the system vector containing the DOFs and $\{F_r\}$ is the loading vector of the system. The axial deformation of the rod is analysed at the arbitrary point $0.1l$ and the rate of convergence of the different approaches is compared in **Figure 5**. The plot shows the absolute relative error of the axial deformation and corresponding number of DOFs. The FEM (h-FEM) solution involves increasing the number of elements, p-FEM involves increasing the order of the polynomials (one element only) and

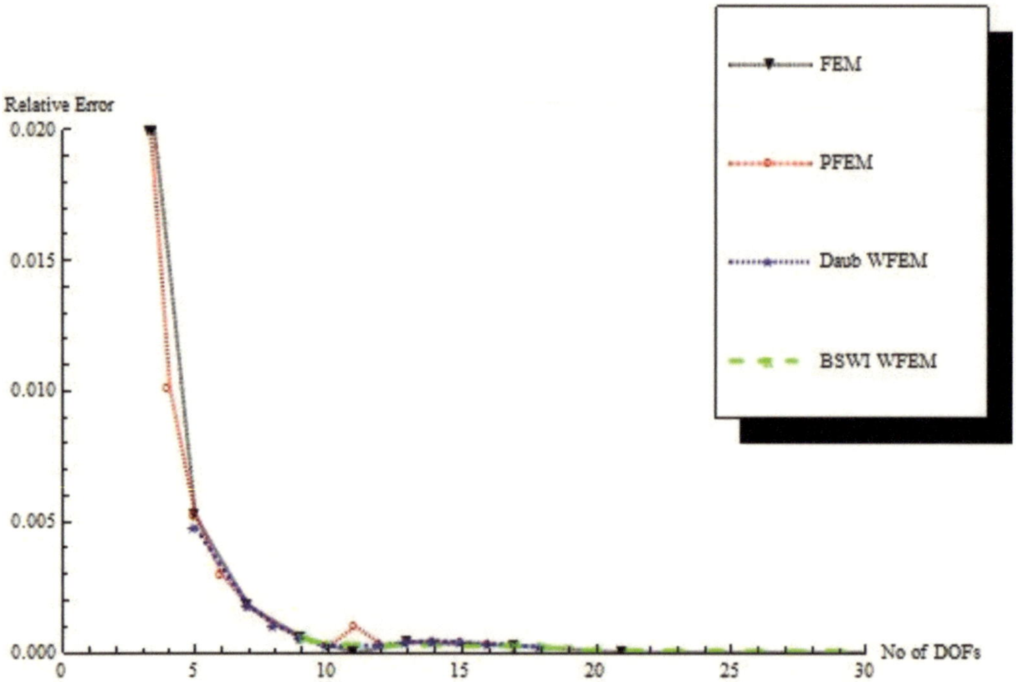

Figure 5. Comparison of the convergence of the axial deformation at point $x = 0.1l$.

both Daubechies and BSWI WFEMs have the order and/or multiresolution scale j increased. The results show that although the rates of convergence of all the methods are similar, the WFEM approaches have a slightly improved rate with only one element employed.

Example 2: A simply supported two-stepped beam of length $2l$ has non-uniform flexural stiffness represented by the unequal cross sections; the bending stiffness of the right and left half is given as $E_1 I_1 = E_0 I_0$ and $E_2 I_2 = 4\,E_0 I_0$ respectively. The entire beam is subjected to a uniformly distributed load $q(x) = 1$. The flexural stiffness function is expressed as [44]:

$$E(x)I(x) = E_0 I_0 \left[1 - \gamma\,\widehat{H}(x - x_0)\right] \tag{82}$$

where $\gamma = 0.75$ is defined as the decrement of discontinuity intensity and satisfies the condition $0 \le \gamma \le 1$ to ensure positivity of the flexural stiffness. $\widehat{H}(x - x_0)$ is the Heaviside function for $0 \le x_0 \le 2l$. The general analytical governing equation is

$$\left\{E_0 I_0 \left[1 - \gamma\,\widehat{H}(x - x_0)\right] v''(x)\right\}'' = q(x) \tag{83}$$

The FEM and WFEM governing equation is summarised as:

$$[\boldsymbol{K_b}]\{\boldsymbol{V_b}\} = \{\boldsymbol{F_b}\} \tag{84}$$

The vector $\{\boldsymbol{V_b}\}$ contains the system DOFs within the entire beam, $[\boldsymbol{K_b}]$ is the beam stiffness matrix and $\{\boldsymbol{F_b}\}$ is the equivalent system load vector. The h-FEM (FEM-8; 8 elements), p-FEM of order 9 (p-FEM-9; 2 elements), Daubechies WFEM of order $L = 10$ and scale $j = 1$ ($D10_1$; 2 elements) and the BSWI WFEM of order $m = 3$ and scale $j = 3$ ($BSWI3_3$; 2 elements) are selected for comparison with the exact solution governed by Eq. (83). Each approach has a total of 18 DOFs within the beam. The deflection and rotation across the beam is presented in **Figure 6(a)** and **(b)** respectively. The percentage errors of the deflections are compared for the different approaches and presented in **Figure 6(c)**. All numerical approaches describe the deflection and rotation across the beams very accurately. However, given that both the Daubechies and BSWI WFEM deflection solutions have a maximum error of 1.28% in comparison to 3.82% from the h-FEM and p-FEM approaches, the WFEMs exhibit better convergence to the exact solution. Furthermore, improved accuracy is attained with fewer elements implemented than the h-FEM and p-FEM and this results in reduced computational time.

Example 3: A steel-alumina functionally graded beam of length l and uniform cross-sectional area $A = 0.36$ m^2 (height $h = 0.9$ m and width $b = 0.4$ m) is fully alumina at the upper surface and fully steel at the lower surface with material properties; $E_u = 3.9 \times 10^{11}$ Pa, $\rho_u = 3.96 \times 10^3$ kg·m^{-3} and $E_l = 2.1 \times 10^{11}$ Pa, $\rho_l = 7.8 \times 10^3$ kg·m^{-3} respectively ($E_{\text{ratio}} = \frac{E_u}{E_l}$; $\rho_{\text{ratio}} = \frac{\rho_u}{\rho_l}$). E and ρ denote the Young's modulus and density respectively. The slenderness ratio for the beam is $l/h = 100$. The free vibration of the steel-alumina beam is analysed for the boundary conditions pinned-pinned (PP), pinned-clamped (PC), clamped-clamped (CC) and clamped-free (CF), for

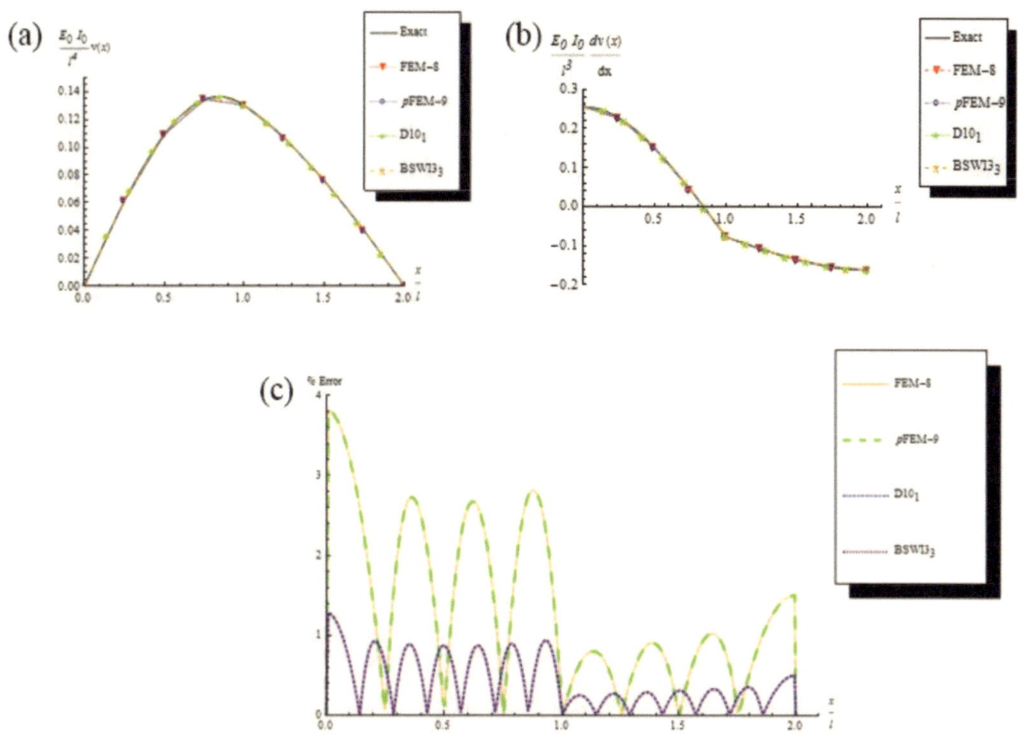

Figure 6. (a) Deflection and (b) rotation (c) comparison of the deflection percentage error across a simply supported stepped beam subjected to a uniformly distributed load $q(x) = 1$.

different values of n in Eq. (70). The free vibration of the functionally graded beam is governed by [45]

$$[[\boldsymbol{K}] - \omega^2[\boldsymbol{M}]]\left\{\acute{\boldsymbol{U}}\right\} = 0 \tag{85}$$

The matrices $[\boldsymbol{K}]$ and $[\boldsymbol{M}]$ are the stiffness and mass matrices for the functionally graded beam, ω is the natural frequency and $\left\{\acute{\boldsymbol{U}}\right\}$ is the vector containing the DOFs within the entire beam. The ith non-dimensional frequency λ_i of the FGM beam is evaluated from the relation $\lambda_i^2 = \omega_i l^2 \left(\frac{12\,\rho_l}{E_l h^2}\right)^{\frac{1}{2}}$. The functionally graded beam is modelled for the different approaches using 2 Daubechies WFEs ($L = 12$; $j = 0$; 37 DOFs); one BSWI ($m = 5$; $j = 4$; 38 DOFs) WFE and 12 h-FEM elements (39 DOFs). The results of the first 3 non-dimensional natural frequencies of the beam are presented in **Table 1** for different boundary conditions and material distributions. It is

			$n = 0$	$n = 0.1$	$n = 0.5$	$n = 1$	$n = 5$	$n = 10$	$n = 10^4$
λ_1	PP	BSWI5_5	4.34462	4.1943	3.84903	3.65795	3.37139	3.29504	3.33251
		FEM	4.34463	4.19431	3.84912	3.65811	3.3715	3.2951	3.33258
		D12_0	4.34462	4.1943	3.84903	3.65795	3.37139	3.29504	3.33251
		BSWI5_4	4.34462	4.1943	3.84903	3.65795	3.37139	3.29504	3.33251
	PC	BSWI5_5	5.43022	5.24233	4.81079	4.57197	4.21381	4.11838	3.92681
		FEM	5.43024	5.24238	4.81112	4.57253	4.21419	4.11856	3.92682
		D12_0	5.43023	5.24234	4.8108	4.57197	4.21382	4.11839	3.92681
		BSWI5_4	5.43022	5.24233	4.81079	4.57197	4.21381	4.11839	3.92681
	CC	BSWI5_5	6.54131	6.31498	5.79514	5.50745	5.07601	4.96105	4.73028
		FEM	6.54137	6.31509	5.79585	5.50867	5.07685	4.96145	4.73028
		D12_0	6.54132	6.31498	5.79514	5.50745	5.07601	4.96106	4.73028
		BSWI5_4	6.54131	6.31498	5.79514	5.50745	5.07601	4.96105	4.73028
	CF	BSWI5_5	2.59318	2.50345	2.29737	2.18333	2.01229	1.96671	1.87523
		FEM	2.59318	2.50346	2.2974	2.18337	2.01232	1.96673	1.87523
		D12_0	2.59318	2.50345	2.29737	2.18333	2.01229	1.96671	1.87523
		BSWI5_4	2.59318	2.50345	2.29737	2.18333	2.01229	1.96671	1.87523
λ_2	PP	BSWI5_5	8.68871	8.38806	7.69754	7.31541	6.74237	6.58969	6.66461
		FEM	8.68894	8.38834	7.69844	7.31684	6.74338	6.59024	6.66537
		D12_0	8.68968	8.389	7.6984	7.31623	6.74313	6.59043	6.66535
		BSWI5_4	8.68871	8.38806	7.69754	7.31541	6.74238	6.58969	6.66461
	PC	BSWI5_5	9.77473	9.4365	8.65966	8.22977	7.58512	7.41335	7.06849
		FEM	9.77513	9.43702	8.66145	8.23263	7.58713	7.41442	7.06879
		D12_0	9.7765	9.43821	8.66124	8.23127	7.5865	7.4147	7.06977

			$n = 0$	$n = 0.1$	$n = 0.5$	$n = 1$	$n = 5$	$n = 10$	$n = 10^4$
		$BSWI5_4$	9.77473	9.4365	8.65967	8.22977	7.58512	7.41335	7.06849
	CC	$BSWI5_5$	10.8597	10.4839	9.62083	9.14322	8.42702	8.23619	7.85305
		FEM	10.8604	10.4848	9.62387	9.14808	8.43044	8.238	7.85355
		$D12_0$	10.8636	10.4877	9.62433	9.14655	8.43009	8.23918	7.8559
		$BSWI5_4$	10.8597	10.4839	9.62083	9.14322	8.42702	8.23619	7.85305
	CF	$BSWI5_5$	6.49133	6.26671	5.75083	5.46534	5.03722	4.92315	4.69413
		FEM	6.49138	6.2668	5.75131	5.46615	5.03778	4.92342	4.69417
		$D12_0$	6.49134	6.26673	5.75084	5.46535	5.03723	4.92316	4.69415
		$BSWI5_4$	6.49133	6.26671	5.75083	5.46534	5.03722	4.92315	4.69413
λ_3	**PP**	$BSWI5_5$	13.0317	12.5808	11.545	10.9719	10.1125	3.29504	3.33251
		FEM	13.0334	12.5826	11.5489	10.9774	10.1166	3.2951	3.33258
		$D12_0$	13.0461	13.5947	11.5578	10.984	10.1237	3.29504	3.33251
		$BSWI5_4$	13.0317	12.5808	11.545	10.9719	10.1125	3.29504	3.33251
	PC	$BSWI5_5$	14.1176	13.629	12.507	11.8861	10.9551	10.7071	10.209
		FEM	14.1201	13.6318	12.5131	11.895	10.9617	10.711	10.2108
		$D12_0$	14.1444	13.655	12.5308	11.9088	10.9761	10.7275	10.2284
		$BSWI5_4$	14.1176	13.629	12.507	11.8861	10.9551	10.7071	10.209
	CC	$BSWI5_5$	15.2034	14.6773	13.4689	12.8003	11.7977	11.5306	10.9942
		FEM	15.2071	14.6813	13.4779	12.8135	11.8074	11.5364	10.9968
		$D12_0$	15.2662	14.7379	13.5247	12.8533	11.8466	11.5783	11.0396
		$BSWI5_4$	15.2034	14.6773	13.469	12.8003	11.7978	11.5306	10.9942
	PC	$BSWI5_5$	10.8611	10.4853	9.62205	9.14437	8.42814	8.2373	7.85409
		FEM	10.8618	10.4861	9.62437	9.14797	8.4307	8.23872	7.85458
		$D12_0$	10.8667	10.4907	9.62702	9.1491	8.43249	8.24155	7.85814
		$BSWI5_4$	10.8611	10.4853	9.62206	9.14438	8.42815	8.2373	7.8541

Table 1. The non-dimensional frequencies of a steel-alumina FG beam for different transverse varying distributions and boundary conditions.

observed that all approaches give highly accurate results with respect to the reference ($BSWI5_5$), particularly for the fundamental frequencies. Furthermore, the BSWI WFEM solution exhibits better levels of accuracy than the Daubechies WFEM and *h*-FEM solutions for the higher frequencies. Both WFEM solutions achieve high levels of accuracy with the described layout of having the rotation DOFs present at elemental and nodes and using fewer elements that the *h*-FEM approach.

Assume the same beam, with simply supported boundary conditions and length $l = 20$ m, is subjected to a moving load of magnitude $P = 1 \times 10^5$ N travelling across at c m·s^{-1}. The behaviour of the beam is described using Euler Bernoulli beam theory and is assumed to be undamped. The governing equation describing the dynamic behaviour of the system is given by [45]:

$$[\mathbf{M}]\left\{\ddot{\mathbf{U}}(t)\right\} + [\mathbf{K}]\{\mathbf{U}(t)\} = \{\mathbf{F}(t)\} \tag{86}$$

where $\left\{\ddot{\mathbf{U}}(t)\right\}$ and $\{\mathbf{U}(t)\}$ represent the system acceleration and displacement vectors at time t. $\{\mathbf{F}(t)\}$ is the moving load vector. The deflection of the beam $v(x,t)$, as the moving load travels across, is normalised as a non-dimensional parameter $v(x,t)/v_0$ where $v_0 = \frac{Pl^3}{48E_lI}$ is the deflection at the centre of the simply supported functionally graded beam when subjected to a static load of magnitude P at the centre. The maximum normalised deflection mid-span of the beam is analysed over a moving load velocity range $0 < c \leq 300$ m·s^{-1} at increments of 1 m·s^{-1} to identify the critical velocity for the different variations of the constituent materials as illustrated in **Figure 7**. The results present are obtained from the BSWI (2 element; $m = 4$; $j = 3$; 37 DOFs) WFEM solution. The h-FEM (12 elements; 39 DOFs) and Daubechies (2 elements; $L = 12$; $j = 0$; 37 DOFs) WFEM solution gives similar results. The values of the critical moving load velocity and corresponding maximum non-dimensional displacement are presented in **Table 2** for the different values of n for all approaches. The results are compared with those presented in [46]. Both the Daubechies and BSWI WFE M solutions very accurately yield the correct values.

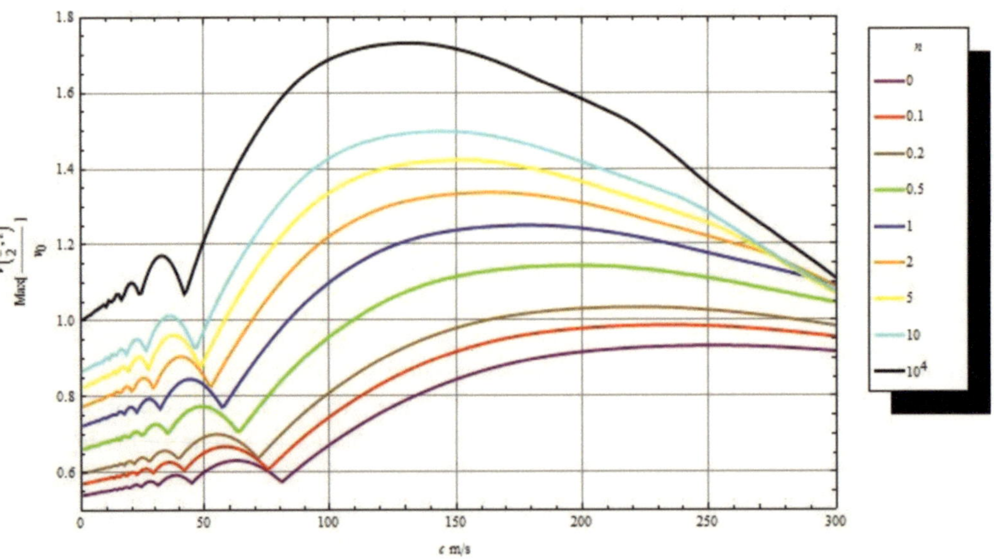

Figure 7. Variation of the maximum non-dimensional vertical displacement at the centre of a simply supported steel-alumina beam with respect to moving load velocities, for different n.

n	Critical velocity c m·s^{-1}				Max $\left[\frac{v(\frac{l}{2},t)}{v_0}\right]$			
	Ref. [46]	FEM	$D12_0$	$BSWI4_3$	Ref. [46]	FEM	$D12_0$	$BSWI4_3$
0	252	252	252	252	0.9328	0.9322	0.9323	0.9322
0.1	–	235	235	235	–	0.9863	0.9864	0.9863
0.2	222	222	222	222	1.0344	1.0340	1.0340	1.0340
0.5	198	198	198	198	1.1444	1.1435	1.1437	1.1436
1	179	178	178	178	1.2503	1.2491	1.2495	1.2493
2	164	164	164	164	1.3376	1.3363	1.3368	1.3365
3	–	157	158	158	–	1.3747	1.3751	1.3748
5	–	151	151	152	–	1.4217	1.422	1.4218
7	–	148	148	148	–	1.4567	1.4570	1.4568
10	–	145	145	145	–	1.4974	1.4976	1.4974
10^4	132	132	132	132	–	1.7308	1.7309	1.7308

Table 2. The non-dimensional frequencies of a steel-alumina FG beam for different transverse varying distributions and boundary conditions.

5. Conclusions

A generalised formulation framework for the construction of an axial rod, Euler Bernoulli beam and functionally graded two-dimensional wavelet based finite elements is presented. The Daubechies and BSWI families are selected due to their desirable properties, particularly compact support, 'two-scale' relation and multiresolution. It is illustrated via a set of numerical examples that the WFEMs perform exceptionally well when compared to conventional h-FEM and p-FEM where high levels of accuracy are achieved with fewer elements required and the approaches converge more rapidly to the exact solution. Furthermore, the methods are able to accurately describe the behaviour of static and dynamic systems with singularities, variation in material properties and loading conditions present. This exhibits the vast potential of the method in the analysis of more complicated systems and the ability to alter the multiresolution scales without affecting the original mesh allows effective and efficient avenues solution accuracy improvement.

Author details

Mutinda Musuva and Cristinel Mares*

*Address all correspondence to: cristinel.mares@brunel.ac.uk

Department of Mechanical, Aerospace and Civil Engineering, College of Engineering, Design and Physical Sciences, Brunel University, London, England, UK

References

[1] Musuva M. The multiscale wavelet finite element method for structural dynamics [thesis]. London: Brunel University; 2015

[2] Ko J, Kurdila AJ, Pilant M. A class of wavelet-based finite element methods for computational mechanics. In: Proceedings of the 35th Structures, Structural Dynamics and Materials Conference, South Carolina; 1994

[3] Chen W-H, Wu C-W. A splines wavelets element method for frame structures vibration. Computational Mechanics. 1995;**16**(1):11-21

[4] Chen X, He Z, Xiang J, Li B. A dynamic multiscale lifting computation method using Daubechies wavelet. Journal of Computational and Applied Mathematics. 2006;**188**(2): 228-245

[5] Xiang JW, Chen XF, He ZJ, Dong HB. The construction of 1D wavelet finite elements for structural analysis. Computational Mechanics. 2007;**40**(2):325-338

[6] Ma J, Xue J, Yang S, He Z. A study of the construction and application of Daubechies wavelet-based beam element. Finite Elements in Analysis and Design. 2003;**39**(10):965-975

[7] Grossmann A, Morlet J. Decomposition of Hardy functions into square integrable wavelets of constant shape. SIAM Journal of Mathematical Analysis. 1984;**15**(4):723-736

[8] Daubechies I. Orthonormal bases of compactly supported wavelets. Communications on Pure and Applied Mathematics. 1988;**41**(7):909-996

[9] Rabbani H, Nezafat R, Gazor S. Wavelet-domain medical image denoising using bivariate Laplacian mixture model. IEEE Transactions on Biomedical Engineering. 2009;**56**(12):2826-2837

[10] Ramsey JB. The contribution of wavelets to the analysis of economics and financial data. Philosophical Transactions of the Royal Society. 1999;**357**(1760):2593-2606

[11] Starck J-L, Bobin J. Astronomical data analysis and sparity: From wavelets to compressed sensing. Proceedings of the IEEE. 2010;**98**(6):1021-1030

[12] Zhou Y, Wang J, Zheng X. Applications of wavelet Galerkin FEM to bending of beams and plate structures. Applied Mathematics and Mechanics. 1998;**19**(8):745-755

[13] Chen X, Yang S, Ma J, He Z. The construction of wavelet finite element and its applications. Finite Elements in Analysis and Design. 2004;**40**(5–6):541-554

[14] Chen M-Q, Hwang C, Shih Y-P. The computation of wavelet-Galerkin approximation on a bounded interval. Journal for Numerical Methods in Engineering. 1996;**39**(17):2921-2944

[15] Diaz LA, Martin MT, Vampa V. Daubechies wavelet beam and plate finite elements. Finite Elements in Analysis and Design. 2009;**45**(3):200-209

[16] Diaz LA, Vampa V, Martin MT. The construction of plate finite elements using wavelet basis functions. Revista Investigacion Operacional. 2009;**30**(3):193-204

[17] Wang YM, Chen XF, He ZJ. Daubechies wavelet finite element method and genetic algorithm for detection of pipe crack. Nondestructive Testing and Evaluation. 2011;**26**(1):87-99

[18] Mitra M, Gopalakrishnan S. Spectral formulated wavelet finite element for wave propagation and impact force identification in connected 1D waveguides. International Journal of Solids and Structures. 2005;**42**(16–17):4695-4721

[19] Zhao B, Wang K. The application of the wavelet finite element method on the temperature field and thermal stress analysis of the petroleum tank. Journal of Information and Computational Science. 2011;**8**(7):1103-1111

[20] Chui CK, Quak E. Wavelets on a bound interval. Numerical Methods of Approximation Theory. 1992;**9**:53-57

[21] Xiang J, Chen X, He Y, He Z. The construction of plane elastomechanics and Mindlin plate elements of B-spline wavelet on the interval. Finite Elements in Analysis and Design. 2006;**42**(14–15):1269-1280

[22] Xiang J, He Z, Chen X. The construction of wavelet-based truncated conical shell element using B-spline wavelet on the interval. Acta Mechanica Solida Sinica. 2006;**19**(4):316-326

[23] Xiang J, Chen X, He Y, He Z. Static and vibration analysis of thin plates by using finite element method of B-spline wavelet on the interval. Structural Engineering and Mechanics. 2007;**25**(5):613-629

[24] Xiang J, Chen X, He Z, Zhang Y. A new wavelet-based thin plate element using B-spline wavelet on the interval. Computational Mechanics. 2008;**41**(2):243-255

[25] Xiang J, Chen D, Chen X, He Z. A novel wavelet-based finite element method for the analysis of rotor-bearing systems. Finite Element in Analysis and Design. 2009;**45**(12):908-916

[26] Musuva M, Mares C. The wavelet finite element analysis of a beam subject to a moving load. In: Proceedings of the First International Conference on Railway Technology: Research, Development and Maintainance, Stirlingshire, UK; 2012

[27] Musuva M, Mares C. Vibration analysis of frame structures using wavelet finite elements. In: Journal of Physics: Conference Series 382, Bristol; 2012

[28] Musuva M, Koziol P, Mares C, Neves M. The analysis of beams subject to moving loads using: Coiflets, the wavelet finite element method and the finite element method. In: Proceedings of the Second International Conference on Railway Technology: Research, Development and Maintenance, Stirlingshire, UK; 2014

[29] Musuva M, Mares C. The dynamic analysis of functionally graded materials (FGM) using the wavelet finite element method (WFEM). In: Proceedings of the 26th International Conference on Noise and Vibration Engineering, Leuven, Belgium; 2014

[30] Musuva M, Mares C. The wavelet finite element method in the dynamic analysis of a functionally graded beam resting on a viscoelastic foundation subjected to a moving load. European Journal of Computational Mechanics. 2015;**24**(5):171-209

[31] He W-Y, Ren W-X. Finite element analysis of beam structures based on trigonometric wavelet. Finite Elements in Analysis and Design. 2012;**51**:59-66

[32] He W-Y, Ren W-X. Trigonometric wavelet-based method for elastic thin plate analysis. Applied Mathematical Modelling. 2013;**37**(4):1607-1617

[33] Castro LMS. Polynomial wavelets in hybrid-mixed stress finite element models. International Journal for Numerical Methods in Biomedical Engineering. 2010;**26**(10):1293-1312

[34] Wang YM, Chen XF, He ZJ. An adaptive inverse iteration algorithm using interpolating multiwavelets for structural eigenvalue problems. Mechanical Systems and Signal Processing. 2011;**25**(2):591-600

[35] Li B, Chen X. Wavelet-based numerical analysis: A review and classification. Finite Elements in Analysis and Design. 2014;**81**:14-31

[36] Chui CK. An Introduction to Wavelets. 1st ed. London: Academic Press Limited; 1992

[37] Latto A, Resnikoff HL, Tenenbaum E. The evaluation of connection coefficients of compactly supported wavelets. In: Proceedings of the French-USA Workshop on Wavelets and Turbulence, New York; 1991

[38] Quak E, Weyrich N. Decomposition and reconstruction algorithms for spline wavelets on a bounded interval. Applied and Computational Harmonic Analysis. 1994;**1**(3):217-231

[39] Goswami JC, Chan AK, Chui CK. On solving first-kind integral equations using wavelets on a bounded interval. IEEE Transactions on Antennas and Propagation. 1995;**43**(6):614-622

[40] Logan DL. In: James H, editor. A First Course in the Finite Element Method. 4th ed. Toronto: Nelson; 2006

[41] Fryba L. In: Stott E, editor. Vibration of Solids and Structures under Moving Loads. 3rd ed. London: Thomas Telford Ltd.; 1999

[42] Carrera E, Giunta G, Petrolo M. Beam Structures: Classical and Advanced Theories. Wiley; 2011

[43] Wakashima K, Hirano T, Niino M. Space applications of advanced structural materials. In: European Space Agency: Proceedings of an International Symposium, Paris, France; 1990

[44] Bondi B, Caddemi S. Closed form solutions of Euler-Bernoulli beams with singularities. International Journal of Solids and Structures. 2005;**42**(9–10):3027-3044

[45] Bathe KJ. Finite Element Procedures. 1st ed. New Jersey: Prentice Hall; 1996

[46] Simsek M, Kocaturk T. Free and forced vibration of a functionally graded beam subjected to a concentrated moving harmonic load. Composite Structures. 2009;**90**(4):465-473

Chapter 4

Numerical Analysis of Hot Polymer-Coated Steel Pipeline Joints in Bending

Finian McCann, Guido Ridolfi, Erwan Karjadi,
Harm Demmink and Helen Boyd

Additional information is available at the end of the chapter

http://dx.doi.org/10.5772/intechopen.72262

Abstract

A numerical method to analyse the effect of the application of polymer coatings on the bending resistance of steel pipeline joints is presented. Experiments were conducted by Heerema Marine Contractors at Heriot Watt University to investigate the influence of the thickness of polymer field joint coatings and the cooldown time provided after applying the coating on the behaviour of pipeline joints when being bent during reeling operations. Temperature readings were obtained from thermocouples inside the polymer field joint coating during the application process, and pipeline ovality measurements were taken during mechanical testing. Thermal modelling of the coating application procedure was developed using COMSOL Multiphysics; this model was validated against the thermocouple readings, while a mechanical model simulating the pipe being bent to a reel was developed in Abaqus finite element modelling software. The temperature outputs, areas of stress concentration and pipe ovalities obtained from the experiments are shown to be predicted accurately by the numerical models. Upon successful validation of the numerical models, a parametric study was conducted assessing the influence of field joint coating thickness and cooldown times, in order to find an optimal design solution to reduce the cooldown time required prior to bending the pipe without buckling.

Keywords: nonlinear mechanics, polymers, reel-lay method, steel pipelines, subsea engineering, thermo-mechanical modelling

1. Introduction

In the field of subsea engineering, the reel-lay method offers logistical and technical advantages over alternative pipe laying methods such as J-lay as S-lay [1]. A considerable length of pipeline is fabricated and coated onshore from pipe segments, which are welded together to form individual stalks, as shown in **Figure 1a**. The stalks are spooled continuously onto a reel situated on a barge (see **Figure 1b** and **c**) docked at an onshore production facility, with tie-in welds performed to join consecutive stalks together to form a contiguous pipeline typically numerous kilometres in length. The barge then transports the loaded reel out to a construction vessel offshore, such as Heerema Marine Contractors' deepwater construction vessel DCV *Aegir* (see **Figure 2a**), where it is installed onto the vessel. The pipe is fed over the aligner wheel on the lay tower, through a straightener and through the moonpool in the deck of the vessel, then subsequently unspooled and laid on the seabed (see **Figure 2b**). In the case of the *Aegir*, logistical advantages are offered by three reels being available. While a reel is being unspooled onboard the vessel and pipe being laid offshore, another reel can be loaded with another pipeline back onshore, with yet another reel in transit either to or from the vessel. Compared to the J-lay method where the pipeline is fabricated onboard the vessel by welding successive 50 to 75 m-long segments together, the onshore fabrication process is far less susceptible to the suspension of operations due to adverse weather conditions, and the overall process of unspooling and laying the pipe is considerably quicker and thus also less likely to be affected by scheduling or weather delays [2].

In order to provide mechanical protection, corrosion protection and thermal insulation for the product conveyed within, the steel pipes are coated with a polymer linepipe coating. In order to maintain the temperature of production fluids during operation and shutdown conditions, thicker coatings have had to be employed to enhance the thermal performance of the pipeline solution [3]. There are considerable challenges inherent to installing pipes with such thick coatings; it has been found previously [4] that combinations of coating thickness, pipe wall thickness and mismatch in material properties across a field joint can result in buckling. These challenges are especially present when employing the reel-lay method where the pipeline, welds and coatings typically undergo a number of bending events during fabrication, spooling, unspooling and eventual touchdown on the seabed. Previous projects have seen Heerema successfully reel and lay pipelines with a 53 mm-thick multiple layer polypropylene (MLPP) coating; the

a) b) c)

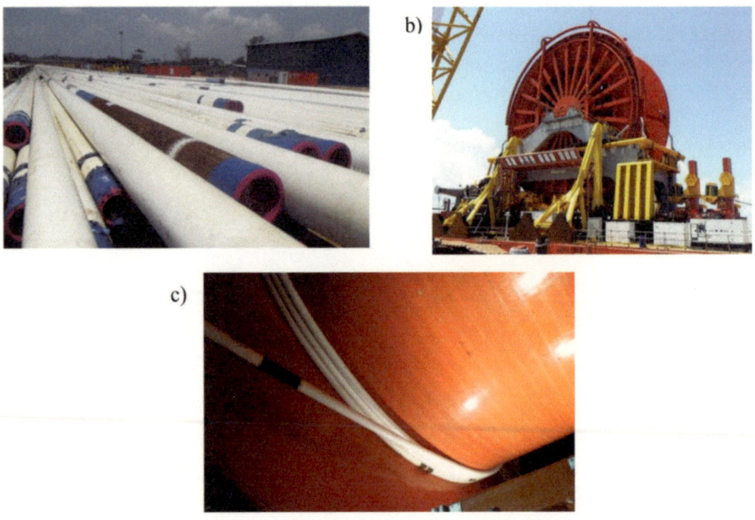

Figure 1. (a) Stalks prepared onsite; (b) empty reel drum onboard a barge; (c) reeling of pipeline stalks.

http://dx.doi.org/10.5772/intechopen.72262

Figure 2. (a) DCV *Aegir*, owned and operated by Heerema Marine Contractors, capable of reel-lay and J-lay; (b) schematic of reel-lay system onboard the *Aegir*.

impetus for the investigation described in the current chapter was to ascertain whether this capacity could be extended to considerably thicker coating systems. Extending the envelope to encompass these coating solutions would allow Heerema to employ the reel-lay method to lay pipeline in ever more challenging environments and greater water depths. The current chapter focuses on pipelines with a 9LPP coating with an overall thickness of 100 mm.

In order not to damage the polymer coating when welding pipe segments together, it is necessary to cut back the coating approximately 300 mm either side of the weld, typically with a 30° chamfer to provide a smooth transition between the linepipe coating and the field joint coating and avoid stress raisers due to geometric and material discontinuities. After the weld has been performed and passed inspection, an injection-moulded polypropylene (IMPP) field joint coating (FJC) is applied around the weld in order to replace the coating material that had been cut back prior to welding. The IMPP application process (described in more detail in Section 2.2) involves heating the steel to above 200°C. Since steel loses strength and stiffness with increasing temperature, the field joint is left to cool down so that the steel pipe can regain its strength and be bent to the reel without buckling or deforming excessively.

It is thus necessary to determine how long is required for the field joint to cool down sufficiently before reeling can take place safely. For field joints within a single stalk this is not an issue since the stalks are fabricated well in advance of reeling and so the field joints will have cooled down and regained full strength. However, during continuous reeling the stalks are joined together while the pipeline is being spooled with reeling paused while the weld is performed.

The pipeline is thus subject to barge motions and the associated fatigue effects which can further weaken the welds. It is advantageous that reeling is paused for a short time as possible so that allowances made for fatigue effects need not be too onerous; current best practice is to pause reeling at least overnight.

One of the primary factors dictating the cooldown time is the thickness of the insulating IMPP field joint coating, which can be controlled by using a specially-shaped mould for the IMPP, creating either hourglass or full FJCs (see **Figure 3**). A thinner coating allows for a quicker cooldown time and hence the strength of the steel is regained sooner. However, thicker FJCs contribute noticeably to the overall resistance of the field joint, even though the elastic stiffness and the strength of steel are orders of magnitude greater than those of the polymer coatings; although the steel yields at a strain of around 0.2% and loses much of its stiffness thereafter, the polymers

a) b)

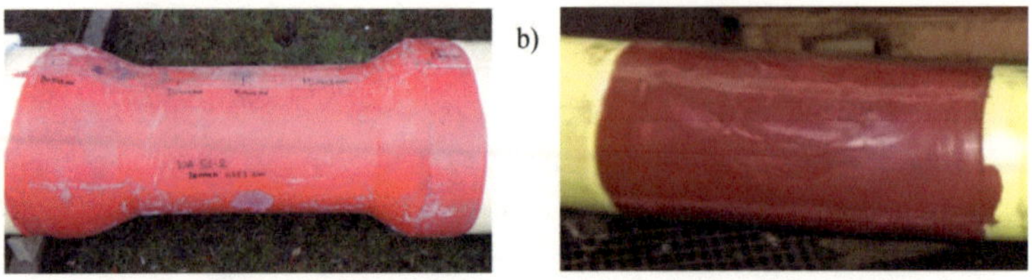

Figure 3. (a) Hourglass field joint coating; (b) full field joint coating.

maintain their elastic stiffness up to strains of approximately 2%, and thus contribute to the stability of the steel pipe when it is deforming plastically and help to prevent buckling. Thus, an optimal field joint coating thickness can be found where a balance is struck between steel strength being regained sooner and the contribution of the polymer material to the resistance of the joint.

In the current chapter, the experimental campaign is described and results presented, followed by a description of the thermal and mechanical numerical models developed to simulate the behaviour of the hot tie-in field joints. After successful validation of the models against the experimental results, a parametric study was conducted varying the thickness of the FJC and the cooldown time prior to bending, providing a matrix of viable coating and cooldown combinations upon which an appropriate operational envelope could be defined for the pipeline system.

2. Experimental investigation

Following successful qualification and commissioning of 12.75″ pipelines with 53 mm-thick five-layer polypropylene (5LPP) coating for a previous project, it was initially decided to investigate the behaviour of a pipeline with 100 mm-thick nine-layer polypropylene (9LPP) coating in order to expand the reel-lay capacity envelope for the *Aegir*. Given that the inner radius of the reel is 8 m, the outer diameter of bare or thinly-coated reel-laid pipes is typically limited to 16″ so that strains in the innermost layer of pipe around the reel are limited to 2.5% in accordance with DNV guidelines [5]. For thicker coatings, the strains in the outer surface of the coating increase accordingly, with a greater risk of damage to the pipe walls and coating. Thus, the primary aim of the experimental investigation was to assess whether these higher levels of strain could be withstood satisfactorily by the steel pipe and coating materials.

2.1. Specimens

Factory-coated test specimens were prepared comprising three pipe segments of grade X65 steel (yield strength f_y = 450 N/mm²), with 20 mm girth-welded field joints. The field joints were 3.45 m apart in order to test two FJCs at the same time on the rig. The outer diameter of the pipes was nominally 327 mm, while the wall thickness was 15.7 mm, giving a diameter-to-thickness ratio of 20.8; the pipes were intentionally chosen to be this slender in order to provide a more onerous combination of pipe wall thickness and coating thickness [3]. The composition of the 9LPP coating is shown in **Figure 4**; after a thin three-layer polypropylene (3LPP) base layer is applied, alternating layers of foam and solid polypropylene are provided in order to combine the enhanced thermal insulating performance of the foam with the

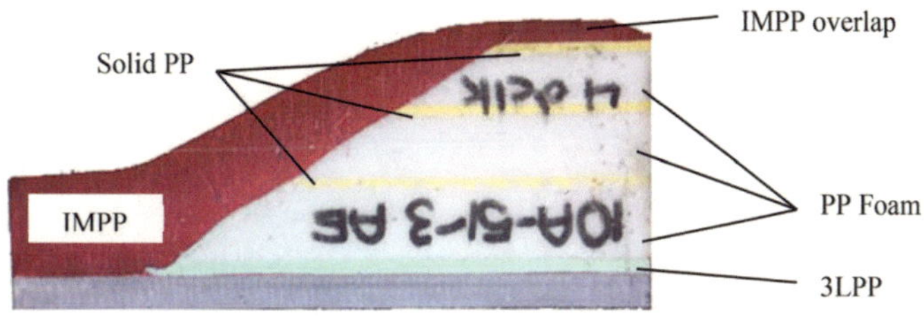

Figure 4. Chamfer section of 9LPP linepipe coating and IMPP field joint coating.

relative stiffness and strength of the solid polypropylene layers. Material fingerprinting was undertaken in parallel to the experimental investigation in order to characterise the thermal and mechanical properties of the various materials used in the pipeline system.

While the majority of specimens prepared were intended for full mechanical bend testing, a number of specimens were reserved in order to measure the heat evolution occurring within the liquid IMPP after injection. The temperatures were recorded using thermocouples, which were arranged as shown in **Figure 5**, in order to calibrate and validate thermal numerical models.

Three different FJC geometries were investigated: full, with a nominal thickness of 108 mm to include a 50 mm long, 8 mm thick overlap at the top of the chamfer, a thick hourglass with a nominal thickness of 50 mm, and a thin hourglass with a nominal thickness of 40 mm. A bare pipe with no FJCs was also tested in the bend rig as a control specimen. Temperature readings recorded by the thermocouples are presented and discussed in Section 3.2.3.

2.2. Setup and procedure

The tests were conducted at Heriot Watt University, Edinburgh, from November 2014 to January 2015. A coating station was installed onsite; for the specimens being used solely for temperature development measurement, the thermocouples were installed in the coating station also. The ambient temperature was recorded during each test.

The IMPP application process involves heating the bare steel substrate to temperatures around 240°C with an induction heater, then applying a thin layer of fusion bonded epoxy (FBE) followed by thin layers of chemically-modified polypropylene (CMPP) to encourage bonding between the steel substrate and the IMPP. The chamfers of the linepipe coating are reheated to encourage bonding with the IMPP, and a mould is then fitted around the field joint. The liquid polypropylene is then injected at 200°C into the mould, which is removed after some solidification of the polypropylene.

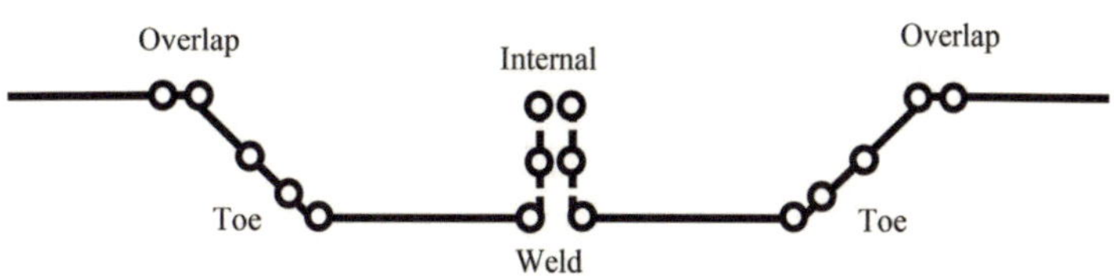

Figure 5. Schematic of thermocouple locations within the FJC.

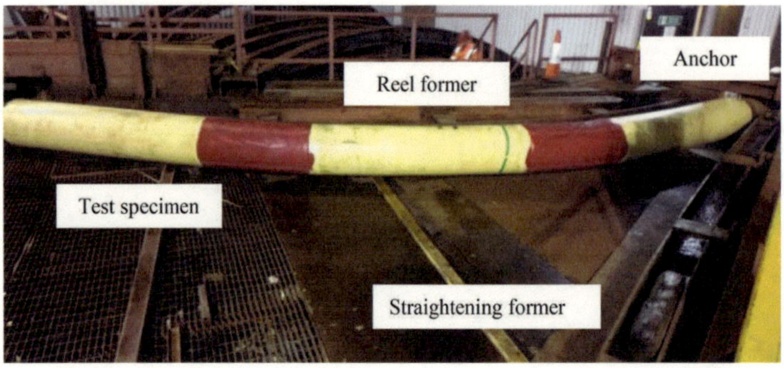

Figure 6. Bend test rig at Heriot Watt University, with a test specimen bent to the reel former.

The bending rig consisted of a reel former with a radius of curvature equal to 8 m, and a straightening former with a radius of curvature equal to 55.84 m (see **Figure 6**); these radii are representative of those of the reel drum and straightener employed onboard DCV *Aegir*. After coating of the field joints was completed in the coating station, the pipe specimen was installed into the bending rig. One end of the pipe was anchored with a pin, while the other end of the pipe was attached to a pull head, which was translated between the two formers by means of a cable attached to a crane.

After a pre-defined cooldown period, the test procedure was initiated, whereby the specimen underwent five full bending cycles, with each cycle consisting of a number of steps: (i) the pipe is bent to the reel former and held; (ii) the pipe is released, (iii) the pipe is bent to the straightening former and (iv) the pipe is finally released again. The pipe was held to the reel former overnight in order to simulate the effect of the IMPP cooling down on the reel prior to resumption of reeling operations. The pipe is subjected to five full cycles during qualification testing in order to ensure that pipe integrity is maintained during initial spooling, straightening, bending over the aligner wheel and pipelay, along with contingencies for weather delays or the possibility of requiring to recover the pipe back onto the reel and then to unspool again. Ovality measurements were taken at salient locations after each cycle step, where the ovality is defined according to DNV design guidance [5] as:

$$\text{ovality} = (D_{max} - D_{min})/(D_{nom}) \tag{1}$$

where D_{max} is the maximum diameter of the deformed pipe, D_{min} is the minimum diameter of the deformed pipe and D_{nom} is the original nominal diameter of the pipe. The ovality measurements were taken using optical metrology equipment inserted inside the pipe; thus, the values used in Eq. (1) relate to the inner diameter of the steel pipes with D_{nom} = 295.7 mm.

3. Numerical modelling

Finite element modelling was used during the planning phase of the campaign in order to select suitable specimens, coating thicknesses and cooldown times for the tests; these models were refined further and validated against the experimental results. In the current section, the modelling techniques employed are described.

3.1. Modelling approach

In order to model the behaviour of the hot tie-in field joints, a thermo-mechanical model was required. Although coupled thermo-mechanical modelling is available in commercially-available finite element modelling software such as Abaqus [6], it is computationally expensive. An alternative approach employed in the current work is to separate the analysis into a thermal model to simulate the process of applying the IMPP, followed by a mechanical model simulating the process of bending the pipe that incorporates the temperature field predicted by the thermal model along with temperature-dependent material models.

Thermal modelling was performed using COMSOL Multiphysics [7], with the temperature fields around the field joint exported at a number of defined intervals of cooldown. These fields were then mapped onto an Abaqus mechanical model that simulated bend testing of the pipe. Given that the cooldown times are in the order of hours and that the bending events were performed in a number of minutes, there is a difference in orders of magnitude between the cooldown rates and the strain rate during the bend tests. Thus, it is reasonable to assume that heat flow within the field joints during bending was negligible and so can be accurately modelled by assuming a static temperature field in the mechanical models, thus achieving a considerable degree of efficiency over a fully-coupled thermo-mechanical model.

3.2. Thermal modelling

A time-dependent thermal model was developed in COMSOL Multiphysics, which was chosen due to its relative computational efficiency and modelling flexibility when compared to thermal modelling in comparable finite element modelling software. A section of the pipe around a particular field joint was represented by two-dimensional models assuming axisymmetric conditions about the longitudinal axis, with symmetry also assumed at the weld plane. The models relating to the three different FJC geometries are shown in **Figure 7**. It was found from sensitivity analysis that the change in temperature was negligible at a distance of 2 m from the weld, and thus the extent of the models reflects this. Triangular elements were used

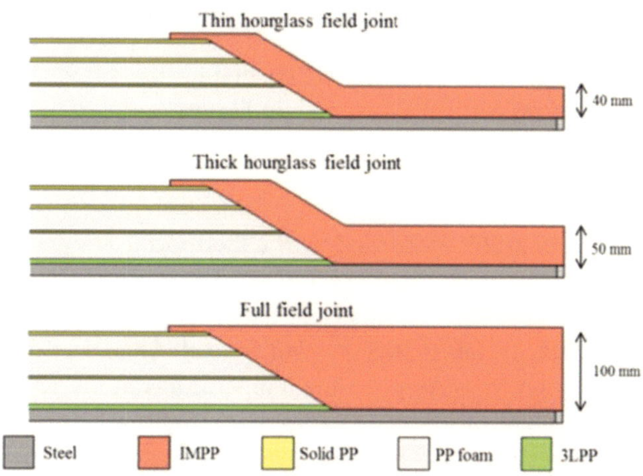

Figure 7. Modelling of field joints in COMSOL.

to mesh the model. Temperature-dependent thermal conductivities and heat capacities from an extensive campaign of material fingerprinting of coating materials and steel pipe materials conducted by Heerema Innovation were applied in the numerical models.

3.2.1. *Boundary conditions*

An air cooling boundary heat flux was imposed on external surfaces, with the convection transfer coefficient set equal to 10 W/m^2/K. When validating the numerical model against the experimental data, the ambient temperature was set equal to that recorded onsite on the day of testing; for the subsequent parametric study, the ambient temperature was set equal to 20°C.

Initially, it was assumed that internal airflow was negligible and so no boundary heat flux was defined along internal surfaces; this assumption is accurate for considerably long lengths of pipe where air flow is practically non-existent. However, for the shorter test specimens, the effects of internal air cooling on the temperature within the field joint coating are significant since heat is drawn from the polymer coating by the relatively highly-conductive steel pipe, which is being continually cooled by the air. It was found from sensitivity analysis that applying a temperature of 18°C and a heat transfer coefficient of 3 W/m^2/K along the internal surfaces of the models provided appropriate cooldown rates.

3.2.2. *Analysis steps*

The analysis was divided into a number of steps representing the IMPP application procedure as conducted onsite. Firstly, induction heating of the steel was modelled using a body heat flux defined appropriately to raise the temperature of the steel pipe to 240°C within the recorded operating time. Next, domains representing the layers of FBE and CMPP were added to the model and the analysis was resumed in order to simulate cooling of the steel substrate to 190°C. Reheating of the chamfers was simulated by applying a surface heat flux to the relevant surfaces in the model, defined appropriately so as to replicate reheating to between 140 and 150°C during the time recorded onsite.

In the final step of the thermal analysis, the IMPP was included at an initial temperature of 200°C. The model was run to simulate 16 h of cooldown to provide comparison with the thermocouple data. Three separate models were created for the full, thick hourglass and thin hourglass FJC geometries, respectively, as shown in **Figure 7**.

3.2.3. *Validation of thermal model*

The temperature evolution profiles recorded by the thermocouples (located at the positions indicated in **Figure 5**) for the thick hourglass FJC specimen are shown in **Figure 8** as solid lines. It can be seen that, as would be expected, temperatures recorded closer to the outer surface of the FJCs at the overlap reduce quicker than those located internally. Owing to thermal conduction through the steel pipe, the temperatures at the weld and toe locations reduce quicker than at the internal thermocouples where the insulating polymer slows down heat flow considerably. This effect was noticeably more pronounced in the full FJC than in the hourglass FJCs, with the temperature reducing quickest in the thin hourglass FJC.

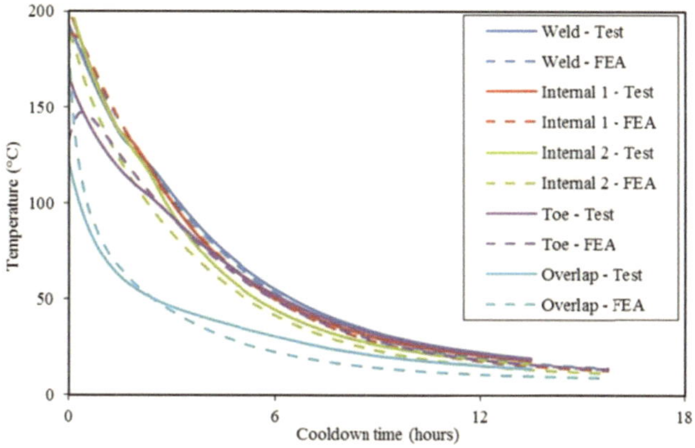

Figure 8. Experimental and numerical temperature evolutions for the thick hourglass FJC specimen.

The predictions of the numerical models are shown as dashed lines in **Figure 8**. Good agreement is observed between the experimental observations and the numerical predictions, particularly at the weld and toe locations and also at the internal thermocouples, while some discrepancy is observed to develop at the external overlap locations; this behaviour was also observed in the full FJC and thin hourglass FJC models. This can most likely be attributed to the overestimation of the convection transfer coefficient for the external boundary cooling coefficients. It is noticeable that since this discrepancy is more prevalent on the external boundaries rather than in the rest of the model, the majority of temperature loss in the IMPP is due to conduction through the steel, rather than from air convection. Overall, the accuracy of the numerical predictions is confirmation of the suitability of the modelling techniques and the material models used, and allows for the temperature fields to be applied to the mechanical models in the next stage of the analysis.

3.3. Mechanical modelling

Modelling of the bend test procedure was performed using Abaqus 6.12 [6]. For validation of the model, the measured geometry of the test specimens was used, while for the parametric study, nominal dimensions were used. Temperature-dependent material models were used in the simulations as outlined in Section 3.3.2, with the temperature fields predicted by the thermal modelling mapped to the Abaqus models using the procedure outlined in Section 3.3.4. The model was validated successfully against the experimental results for ovality and stress distributions, which then allowed a parametric study to be conducted to identify combinations of FJC thickness and cooldown time where buckling is avoided.

3.3.1. Model geometry and boundary conditions

The model of the bend test rig is shown in **Figure 9**, with a combination of shell and solid instances used to model the pipe and coating materials, with two FJCs centred at 20 mm girth welds. A pipe with no FJCs was also modelled in order to provide validation against the bare pipe tested onsite.

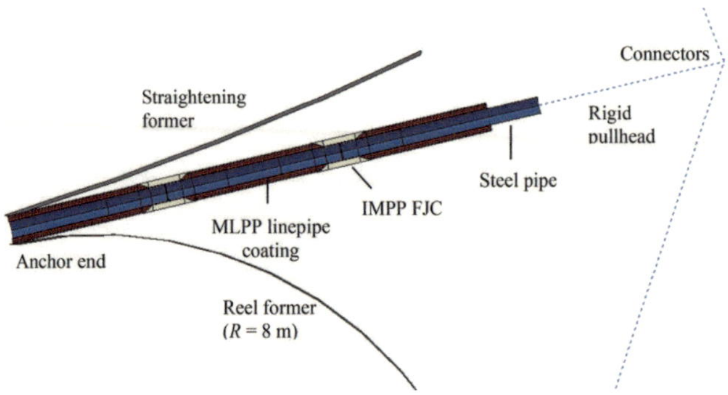

Figure 9. Model of the bend test rig and pipe specimen in Abaqus.

Analytical rigid instances were used to model the reel former and straightening former, each with a radius of curvature equivalent to those used onsite, respectively. Pin-ended conditions were defined at the anchor end, permitting only rotation in the plane of the rig. Connector elements were used to model the cables from the pullhead to the crane with appropriate displacements imposed on them in order to simulate the pipe being bent to the formers across the various analysis steps.

Contact interactions were defined between the outer surface of the coating and the former surfaces, with a coefficient of friction of 0.3 to define the tangential behaviour and a pressure overclosure to define the normal behaviour.

3.3.2. Material modelling

As part of a campaign of material fingerprinting conducted by Heerema Marine Contractors, moduli of elasticity and full stress-strain curves for the various polymer and steel materials used in the pipes were obtained at a number of ambient temperatures and strain rates. A typical set of stress-strain curves is shown in **Figure 10** for the IMPP material, with testing performed at 5 mm/min; these curves were converted to true stress and true strain prior to their use in the numerical models. For temperatures outside the tested range, the material curves were based on extrapolation. For the polypropylene materials, an elastic-plastic material model with isotropic hardening was assumed, in keeping with previous studies [8]. Although polypropylene exhibits viscoelastic behaviour in practice, given the strain rates and hold times being modelled in the current study, it was not necessary to model changes in stress owing to viscous flow of the material.

The moduli of elasticity of the various coating materials were modelled as temperature-dependent, while the Poisson's ratio was set at 0.45. The coefficient of thermal expansion for the three polypropylene materials was temperature-dependent and based on manufacturers' recommendations.

The X65 material was also modelled using an elastic-plastic material model albeit with non-linear kinematic hardening, and based on test data obtained across a range of temperatures. For temperatures outside the tested range, material curves were extrapolated based on derating the material in accordance with DNV guidelines [5]. The resulting true stress-true strain curves are shown in **Figure 11**. The stress-strain relationship for the welds was assumed to be similar to that of the parent steel, albeit with isotropic hardening and a strength overmatch of

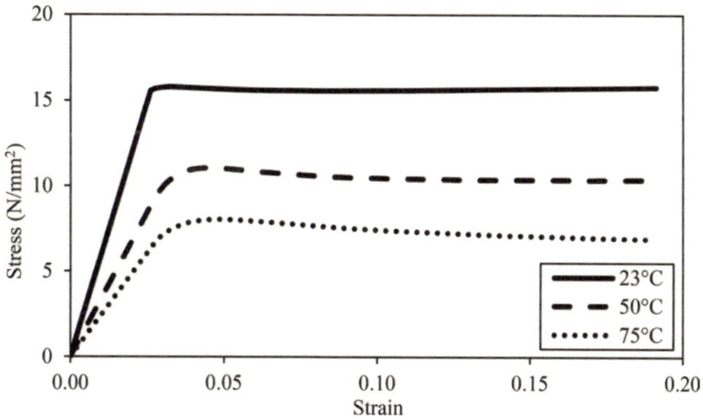

Figure 10. Stress-strain curves for the IMPP material obtained from tensile testing.

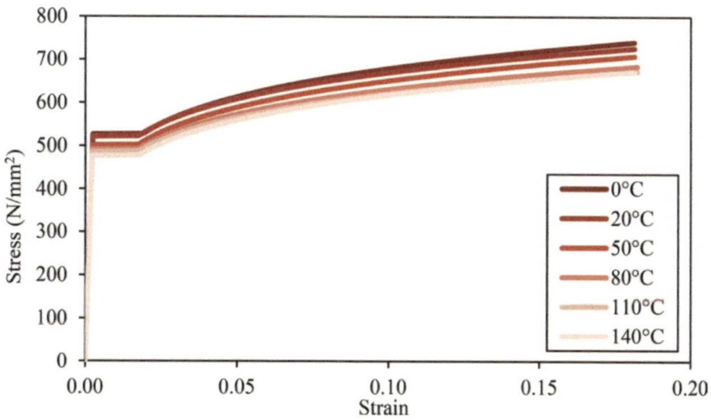

Figure 11. Stress-strain curves for X65 steel at a range of temperatures.

80 N/mm^2 based on previous project experience. The modulus of elasticity of the steel materials was assumed to be 210,000 N/mm^2 with a Poisson's ratio equal to 0.3. The coefficient of linear expansion was set equal to 13×10^{-6}.

3.3.3. *Elements and meshing*

In the interests of computational efficiency, the mechanical model employed a combination of quadrilateral shell S4R elements for the steel pipe, and solid C3D8R elements for the thicker coating materials. The steel pipe elements were in fact composite layups in order to include the thin layers of FBE and CMPP. A nominal element size of 15 mm was used, with the mesh density increased in the area of interest around the weld.

3.3.4. *Mapping of temperature fields*

The thermal analysis was performed using two-dimensional axisymmetric models with triangular meshes, while the mechanical analysis used three-dimensional solid brick and quadrilateral shell elements. In order to map the temperature field correctly, an algorithm was developed whereby the COMSOL temperature field was centred on a weld plane and then

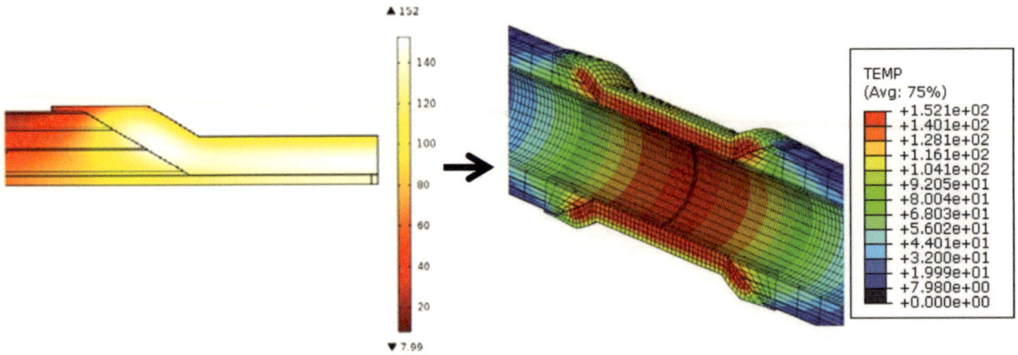

Figure 12. Example of transferral of COMSOL temperature output to a discrete field in Abaqus.

translated and rotated to cylindrical coordinates. A least-squares node-matching routine then identified the nodes in the COMSOL mesh closest to each node in the Abaqus mesh within longitudinal neighbourhoods of 100 mm. The resulting field was then inputted as a discrete field into the Abaqus model. An example of the result of running the algorithm is shown in **Figure 12**, with the COMSOL temperature output on the left hand side and the resulting temperature field in Abaqus shown on the right. For the validation of the numerical models against the experiments, temperature fields were outputted at the appropriate cooldown times related to the time after IMPP application recorded during the bend tests. Since there was a half hour to an hour difference in application time between the two FJCs for a particular test pipe, and thus a noticeable difference in temperature, separate temperature fields were mapped around the two joints.

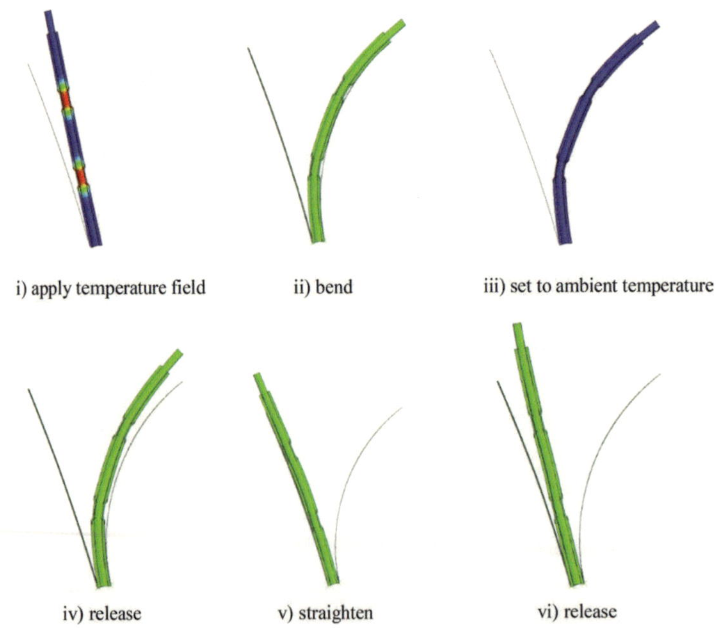

Figure 13. Bend cycle steps modelled in Abaqus.

3.3.5. Analysis procedure

A geometrically-nonlinear static analysis was employed, divided into a number of steps, as shown in **Figure 13**: (i) firstly, the temperature field was applied to the model; (ii) next the pipe was bent to the reel former and held; (iii) the temperature field was then set equal to the appropriate ambient temperature (either that recorded onsite for the validation study, or 20°C for the parametric study) in order to simulate the pipe and FJCs cooling down; (iv) next, the pipe was released, then (v) bent to the straightening former, and finally (vi) released again, thus completing the first bend cycle. The model simulated five full bending cycles in total (the latter four all with the temperature field set equal to the appropriate ambient temperature). As can be seen in **Figure 13**, after a full bend cycle there is a noticeable amount of plastic deformation present in the pipe after straightening; limiting this plastic deformation and avoiding buckling of the pipe and tearing of the coating are two of the main challenges posed by the reel-lay procedure.

4. Results and comparisons

In this section, the results of the bend tests are discussed, and comparison is made with the predictions of the numerical model.

4.1. Pipe deformation, buckling and ovality

A bare pipe with no FJCs was tested first in the bend rig as a control specimen, whereupon it buckled at the first bend to the reel former, as shown in **Figure 14a**; this early onset buckle can be attributed to the stiffness mismatch between the full linepipe coating and the bare steel pipe causing strains to concentrate within the bare steel. It can also be seen that the point of initiation of the buckle is located to the left of the weld. The strain field predicted by the numerical model is shown in **Figure 14b**, where the strain concentration can indeed be observed in the uncoated region of the pipe. It can be seen that the pipe was also predicted to buckle after the first bend to the reel, albeit with the point of initiation of the buckle located closer to the weld. Given the high imperfection sensitivity of cylindrical shells in compression, this discrepancy in buckle location is likely down to a localised thinning of the pipe wall in the area around the buckle due to corrosion. It can be seen that, in areas in the steel pipe away from the buckle, the tensile strain is approximately 2.5%, in keeping with analytical predictions.

Despite the presence of the polymer coating, one of the field joints on the pipe with the thin hourglass FJC also buckled on the first bend to the reel. During initial simulations prior to the test campaign, ovalities in excess of 10% were expected; based on previous experience [9] this level of ovality is a strong predictor of the occurrence of buckling. The buckled field joint is shown in **Figure 15a**; as can be seen, there is noticeable lift-off from the reel former. In **Figure 15b**, the equivalent numerical prediction of the stress field is shown, with rippling observable in the compression zone.

The pipes with the thick hourglass and full FJCs did not buckle throughout the five bending cycles; the numerical models also predicted that no buckling would occur. In **Figure 16**, the ovalities recorded along the length of the pipe with the thick hourglass FJC after the first bend

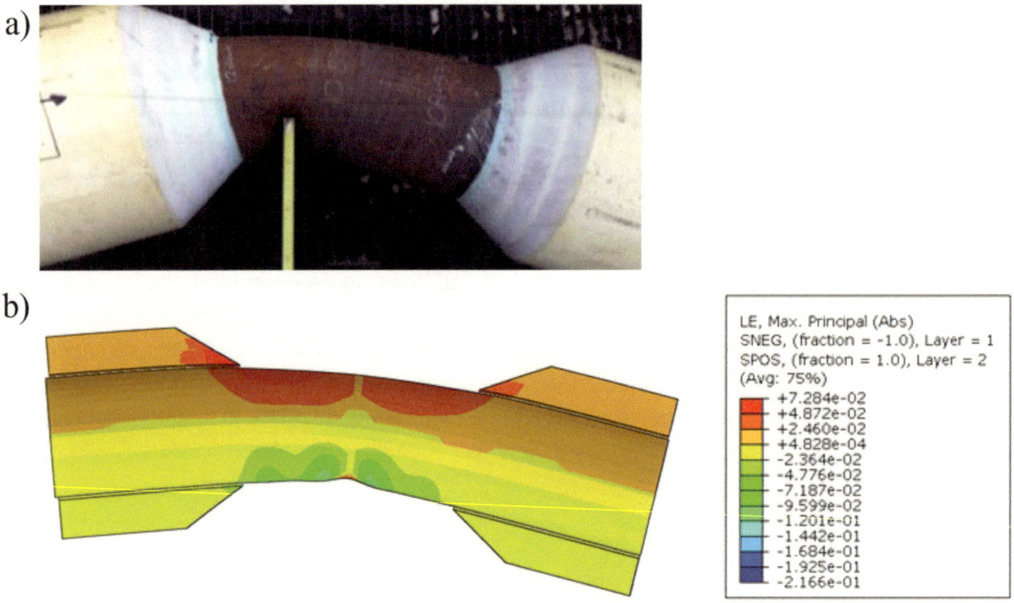

Figure 14. Bending of field joint with no coating; (a) experimental observation and (b) numerical prediction of strain field.

to the reel are compared with numerical predictions, with the ovalities calculated using Eq.(1). The two peaks in the ovality distributions coincide with the location of the field joints. As can be seen, there is particularly good agreement in the region around the field joint furthest from the anchor end, while the predictions of ovality are underestimated at the field joint closest to the anchor end. This can be attributed to some relaxation of contact stress towards the anchor end during the simulation as the point of contact progresses along the pipe. Similar accuracy was obtained across all the tested pipes, thus increasing confidence in the ability of the numerical model to predict pipe deformations and ovalities but most importantly whether the field joints can withstand five full bending cycles without buckling. The results of the experimental investigations and the numerical analysis showed that, provided the correct FJC thickness is applied, reeling of pipelines with 100 mm-thick MLPP coatings is indeed achievable.

4.2. Stress whitening

During testing of the specimens with FJCs applied, a phenomenon known as stress whitening was observed. Stress whitening occurs when the molecule chains within a polymer become damaged due to excessive tensile stresses causing plastic deformation, with holes and tears forming as the molecular structures are altered [10]. Light incident upon the affected zones is then diffused and scattered more readily, appearing as white discolorations on the surface of the polypropylene. In the following discussion, comparisons are made after the first bend to the reel former and holding in position overnight, i.e., after the field joint has cooled down fully.

Owing to the inherent difficulty of installing stress measuring instrumentation into the coating and retrieving it afterwards, visual identification of stress whitening was used as an indicator of tensile stress concentrations within the IMPP material. In **Figure 17**, the appearance

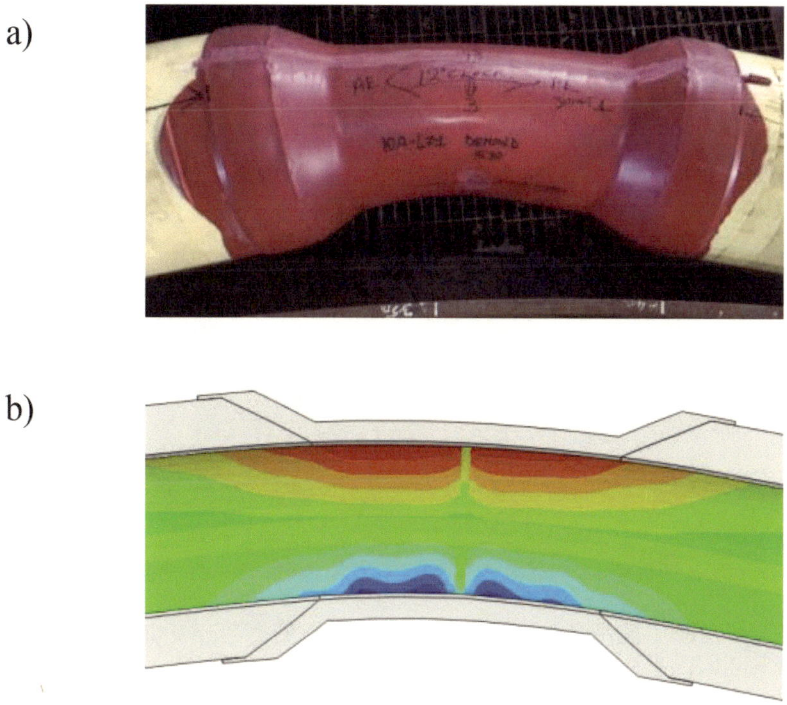

Figure 15. Pipe with thin hourglass FJC; (a) experimental observation, (b) simulated stress field with rippling observable.

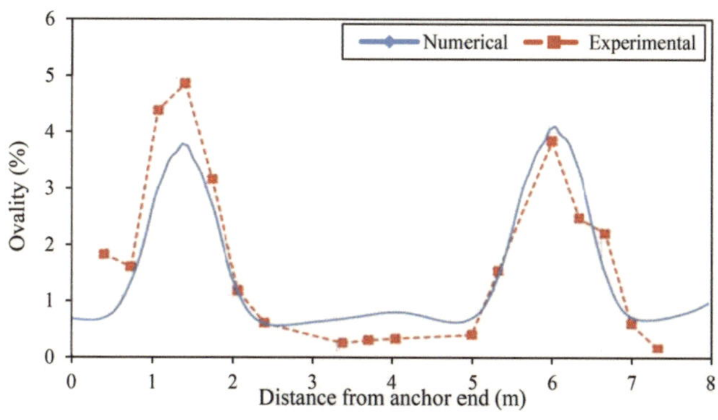

Figure 16. Comparison of measured and predicted ovality distributions in the pipe with the thick hourglass FJCs after the first bend to the reel.

of stress whitening in the thick hourglass FJC is compared to the numerical prediction of the principal stress field. Given that the yield stress is approximately 16 N/mm^2 it can be seen that the location of areas where plastic deformation has occurred agree very well with the location of stress whitening above the chamfer toes observed onsite.

In the case of the thin hourglass FJC, as can be seen in **Figure 18a**, the level of stress whitening was not as prevalent or as noticeable, indicating that much less plastic deformation has occurred than in the thick hourglass FJC. This corroborates with the predicted stress field

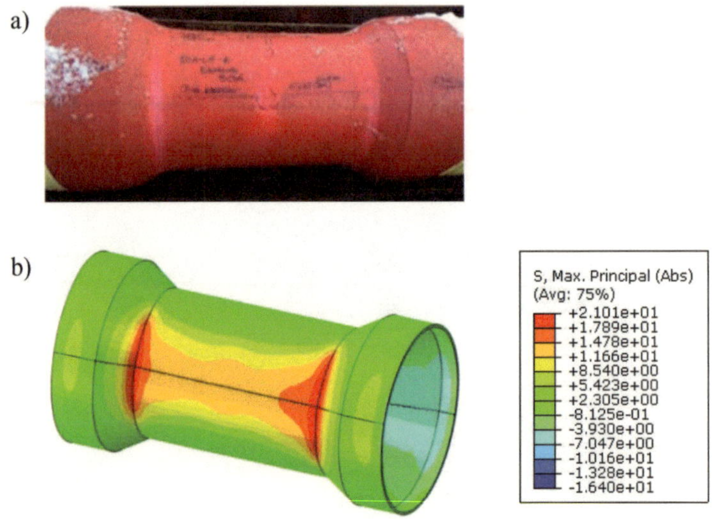

Figure 17. Thick hourglass FJC; comparison of (a) stress whitening observed during test with (b) numerical prediction of stress.

shown in **Figure 18b** where the maximum stress is 13.85 N/mm^2, suggesting that the material has not yielded yet (although in practice some polymer chains may have been damaged already when the material was hotter and therefore less strong, as evidenced by the material curves shown in **Figure 10**). While it may be counter-intuitive that less stress whitening has occurred in the thin hourglass FJC rather than in the thick hourglass FJC, this can be explained by considering the reduction in longitudinal strain on the outer surface of the thin hourglass FJC since it is closer to the neutral axis of the section than the outer surface of the thick hourglass FJC. It can be seen that the areas of peak stress above the chamfer toe coincide with the lightest areas on the external surface of the tested pipe.

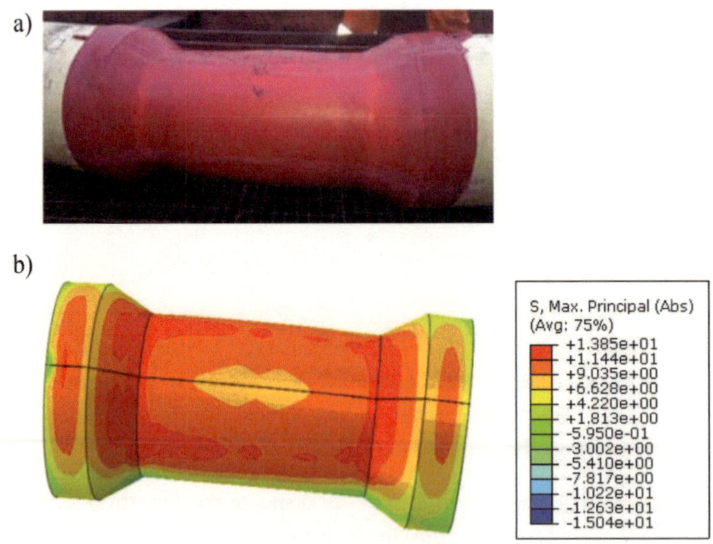

Figure 18. Thin hourglass FJC; comparison of (a) stress whitening observed during test with (b) numerical prediction of stress.

In the full FJC, stress whitening was observed after testing as shown in **Figure 19a**; stress concentrations were also predicted in the numerical model above the chamfers, as shown in **Figure 19b**. Although the agreement is not as clearly observable as in the hourglass FJCs, the level of stress predicted in the areas of stress whitening is commensurate with the yield stress of the material.

Finally, in addition to the three pipes with hot tie-in field joints, another pipe with full FJCs was tested after it had fully cooled down to the ambient temperature. As can be seen in **Figure 20a**, there was no evidence of stress whitening visible in this specimen, and as shown in **Figure 20b**, the numerical model also predicted a uniform stress field with no concentrations, with maximum stresses of approximately 15 N/mm^2 in the IMPP.

Bending of the steel when it is still hot and weakened leads to higher strains and deformations around the field joint as a whole. The thin hourglass field joint would have cooled quicker than the thick hourglass field joint, allowing the steel to regain relatively more strength and thus limiting the amount of strain. The increased deformation in the thick field joint has led to higher stresses in the pipe as well as the field joint coating, which can be observed upon comparison of **Figures 17b** and **18b**.

In the each of the three hot tie-in field joints, it can be seen that stress concentrations and areas of stress whitening occur above the chamfers, particularly above the chamfer toe. One explanation is that there is a stiffness mismatch either side of the chamfer that causes stress to accumulate at this point; however, the transition between the IMPP field joint coating and the MLPP linepipe coating occurs quite gradually over the length of the chamfer (approximately 175 mm), and so sudden peaks in stress would not be expected. Upon inspection of the evolution of the distribution of ovality along the length of the pipe specimens during the bend test, a correlation between the ovality gradient and the peaks in stress was apparent. In **Figure 21**, the distribution of ovality gradient along the length of the thick hourglass FJC specimen, as predicted by the numerical model, is shown. The locations of the chamfers and field joints are also overlaid on the graph. It can be seen that areas of peak ovality gradient coincide with the toes of the chamfer, where

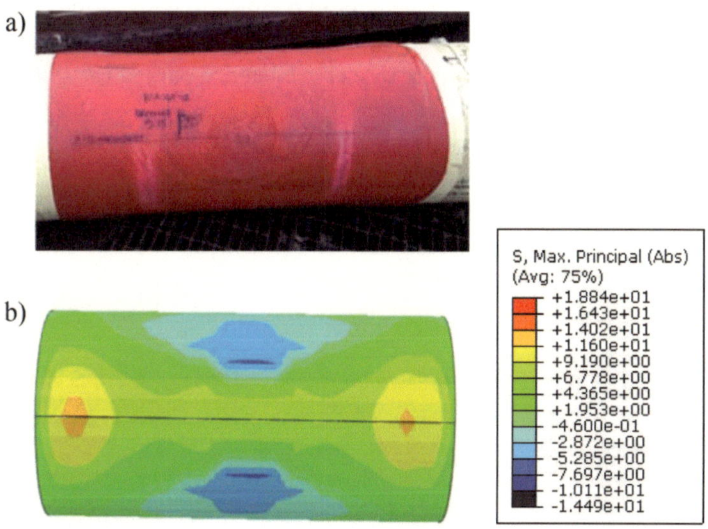

Figure 19. Full hourglass FJC; comparison of (a) stress whitening observed during test with (b) numerical prediction of stress.

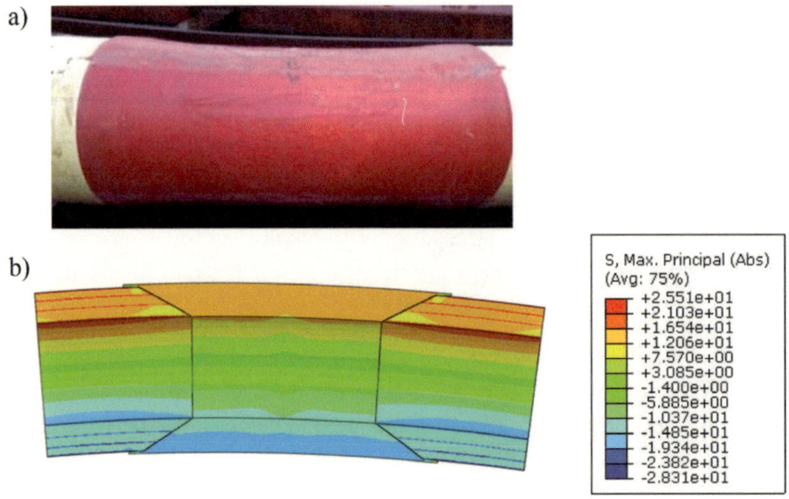

Figure 20. Full hourglass FJC bent after being fully cooled down; comparison of (a) stress whitening observed during test with (b) numerical prediction of stress.

stress whitening was also observed very clearly in the test pipe, as shown in **Figure 17a**. In addition, although stresses close to yield were predicted by the numerical model in the full FJCs of the pipe that was bent after fully cooling down, since the stress distribution and also ovality distribution were quite uniform, i.e., with a small gradient, there was no stress whitening visible. This agreement between peak ovality gradient and areas of stress whitening can be attributed to the higher levels of strain associated with sudden large deformations in the steel pipe, which would cause associated large strains, and hence stresses, in the coating materials.

4.3. Parametric study

As demonstrated by the comparisons between the experimental observations and the numerical results, the thermal and mechanicals models are capable of accurately predicting the behaviour of hot tie-in field joints in bending. With the model validated, a parametric study was conducted

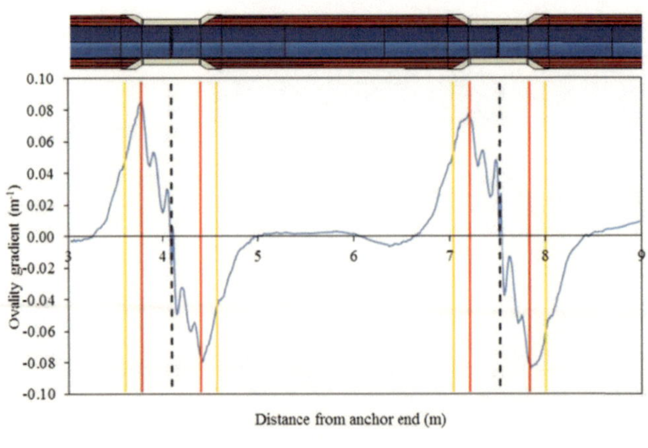

Figure 21. Ovality gradient along the length of the pipe with the thick hourglass FJC with chamfer locations overlain.

varying the thickness of the FJCs and the amount of cooldown time. Bend tests on pipes with FJC thicknesses from 20 mm up to a full FJC and cooldown times from 1 hour up to 24 hours were simulated and assessed to ascertain whether five full bend cycles could be completed without the pipe buckling. The results of the parametric study showed that an optimal thickness and cooldown time existed that represented significant material and time savings compared to current practice.

5. Conclusions

Finite element models simulating the thermal and mechanical behaviour of hot tie-in field joints during coating application and bending have been developed. Experimental investigations recording the temperature evolution profiles within the field joint coatings after pouring and the mechanical behaviour of the field joints during bend testing were used as a basis for calibration and validation of the numerical models. Three separate field joint coating geometries were tested in order to examine the influence of coating thickness on the overall behaviour of the field joint.

Thermal modelling in COMSOL Multiphysics employed temperature-dependent thermal properties obtained from material fingerprinting. It was found that it was necessary to model internal air cooling in the test specimens, which would not normally be required when modelling longer pipeline sections. Close agreement was observed upon comparison of temperature evolutions recorded onsite with those predicted by the numerical models, allowing for the predicted temperature fields to be subsequently applied to mechanical models.

Numerical models were developed in Abaqus to simulate bend testing of the various pipe specimens, employing temperature-dependent material models obtained from material fingerprinting. Temperature fields obtained from the thermal numerical models were mapped onto the mechanical models and the process of bend testing over five full bend cycles simulated. The numerical predictions for pipe ovality and coating stress distributions were compared with the experimental results, with close agreement observed. It was also found that ovality gradient can be used as a predictor of the occurrence of stress whitening in the coating materials. The numerical analysis, coupled with the results of the experimental investigation, showed that reeling of pipes with 100 mm-thick coating is possible.

The successful validation of the numerical models allowed for an extensive parametric study to be conducted, varying the field joint coating thickness and the cooldown times provided after application of the IMPP. It was found that an optimal FJC thickness existed that balanced the quicker cooldown times associated with thinner FJCs with the material strength benefits of thicker FJCs. The results of the study showed that use of this optimal FJC thickness can result in significant time savings when conducting reeling operations in practice.

Acknowledgements

The authors wish to thank the team at the Innovation Department of Heerema Marine Contractors for their assistance during the planning and execution of the experimental campaign, and also to David Haldane and the technical staff at Heriot Watt University for their support throughout testing.

Author details

Finian McCann[1]*, Guido Ridolfi[2], Erwan Karjadi[2], Harm Demmink[2] and Helen Boyd[2]

*Address all correspondence to: mccannf@lsbu.ac.uk

1 School of the Built Environment and Architecture, London South Bank University, UK

2 Heerema Marine Contractors, Netherlands

References

[1] Smith SN, Clough T. Deepwater pipeline installation by reel-lay method. In: Proceedings of the Offshore Technology Conference 2010, 3-6 May 2010, Houston, TX; 2010

[2] Karjadi E, Boyd H, van Rooijen R, Demmink H, Balder T. Development of Aegir reeling pipeline analyses by test validation. In: Proceedings of the 32nd International Conference on Ocean, Offshore and Arctic Engineering, 9-14 June 2013, Nantes, France; 2013

[3] Ridolfi G, Boyd H, Karjadi E, Demmink H, McCann F, de Bode A. Extension of the reel-ability envelope of the Aegir: synergy between analysis and full-scale testing. In: Proceedings of the 25th International Ocean and Polar Engineering Conference, 21-26 June 2015, Hawaii, USA; 2015

[4] Crome T. Reeling of pipelines with thick insulation coating: finite-element analysis of local buckling. In: Proceedings of the Offshore Technology Conference 1999, 3-6 May 1999, Houston, TX; 1999

[5] Det Norske Veritas. DNV-OS-F101: Submarine Pipeline Systems. DNV. 2013. Vol. 2013

[6] Abaqus. 2012. ABAQUS analysis user's manual, v6.12.3. USA: Dassault Systems Simulia Corp., Providence; 2012

[7] COMSOL, Inc. COMSOL Multiphysics 4.2a. COMSOL, Inc. 2011; 2011

[8] Karjadi E, Boyd H, Demmink H, Thibaux P. Reeling pipeline material characterization – testing, material modeling and offshore measurement validation. In: Proceedings of the 34th International Conference on Ocean, Offshore and Arctic Engineering, 31 May–5 June 2015, St. Johns, Canada; 2015

[9] Karjadi E, Boyd H, van Rooijen R, Demmink H, Balder T. Development on Aegir reeling pipeline analyses by test validation. In: Proceedings of the 32nd International Conference on Ocean, Offshore and Arctic Engineering, 9-14 June 2013, Nantes, France; 2013

[10] Pae KD, Chu H-C, Lee JK, Kim J-H. Healing of stress-whitening in polyethylene and polypropylene at or below room temperature. Polymer Engineering & Science. 2000;**40**(8): 1783-1795

Chapter 5

Application of Finite Element Analysis in Multiscale Metal Forming Process

Zhengyi Jiang and Haibo Xie

Additional information is available at the end of the chapter

http://dx.doi.org/10.5772/intechopen.71880

Abstract

The application of finite element analysis has been presented in multiscale metal forming process. A 3D finite element method (FEM) has first been proposed to analyze the deformation mechanism of thin strip cold rolling with the consideration of friction variation in deformation zone. The crystal plasticity finite element method (CPFEM) is applied on the simulation of surface asperity flattening in the uniaxial planar compressing process. 3D Voronoi tessellation and frictional modeling have been applied in microforming processes. All simulation results from the proposed modeling have been validated by the related experimental results.

Keywords: multiscale, metal forming, FEM, friction variation, Voronoi tessellation, size effect

1. Introduction

Process modeling for the investigation and understanding of deformation mechanics has become a major concern in research, and the application of the finite element method (FEM) has been tremendously increased, particularly in the modeling of forming processes. There are many research studies on the principles and fundamentals of the simulation of metal forming, but only a few studies describe the application of FEM to the analysis and simulation of multiscale forming processes. The main objective of this chapter is to present the applications of FEM in metal forming analysis from macroscale to microscale.

Friction at the strip-roll interface is an important consideration in the metal-forming process. Traditionally, the frictional force is assumed to be proportional to the normal force, and the friction coefficient keeps the same in the roll bite. This assumption conflicts with the research results where the friction is changeable in the roll bite [1], and the rolling pressure and model control accuracy will be influenced significantly. The deformation mechanics of thin foil [2] and the foil rolling with constant friction during cold rolling [3] have been investigated. The finite element method has been proposed in special-shaped strip rolling [4–6], particularly with variable friction models [5, 6]. Considering modeling accuracy, a friction variation model should be introduced in the cold rolling simulation of thin strip.

The application of crystal plasticity finite element method (CPFEM) has been introduced in the simulation of surface asperity flattening in cold quasistatic uniaxial planar compression process. Rate-dependent crystal plasticity constitutive models have been established on the basis of experimental conditions [7], and the influences of the reduction and strain rate on the surface roughness are investigated using the 3D crystal plasticity finite element method [8]. The experimental results are also employed in the 3D CPFEM model and compared with the simulation results.

Microforming differs from the conventional forming technology in terms of materials, processes, tools, and machines and equipment due to the miniaturization nature of the whole microforming system [9]. It is impossible to scale down all parameters in the microforming process according to the theory of similarity due to the existence of size effects in microforming processes. A number of unexpected problems in key aspects of mechanical behavior, tribology, and scatter of material behavior are encountered [10, 11]. Challenges remain in the high efficiency manufacturing of high-quality microproducts due to the common problem of microscale size effects [9, 11], complexity of processes for making microproducts, and the ever increasing requirement to improve product quality and performance.

In Section 4, novel material model with grained heterogeneity in 3D Voronoi tessellation has been developed in the simulation of micro cross wedge rolling, springback analysis in micro flexible rolling and the micro V-bending processes considering grain boundary and generation process of grains in the workpiece [12–16]. The modified FE model in microforming has been applied with the consideration of size effects including material characterization, friction/contact characterization, and other size-related factors presented in Section 5. Open and closed lubricate pocket (OCLP) theory and size-dependent friction coefficient are proposed in micro deep drawing (MDD) and micro hydromechanical deep drawing (MHDD) [17–19]. Real microstructures and Voronoi structures are applied in microstructural models through the image-based modeling method [20, 21].

2. FEM analysis applied to thin strip rolling

The three-dimensional (3D) finite element method (FEM) has been used in the analysis of strip rolling, shape rolling, and slab rolling, and Jiang et al. [4–6, 22] used this finite element method to solve special-shaped strip rolling. This is a major drawback to producing accurate and reliable models for the cold rolling of thin strip due to the lack of well-defined friction boundary conditions. The 3D rigid plastic FEM has been proposed to solve the thin strip rolling considering friction variation in the deformation zone, and the comparison between the computed results and measured values has also been made.

In the friction variation model, the friction varies along the contact length of the deformation zone. The frictional shear stress model is modified as [5]:

$$\tau_f = K_i \frac{m_1 \sigma_s}{\sqrt{3}} \left(\frac{2}{\pi} tan^{-1} \left\{ \frac{V_g}{k_i} \right\} \right) \tag{1}$$

where m_1 is the friction factor; σ_s yields stress; K_i is a coefficient of the friction shear stress changes with K_1 and K_2 for forward slip zone and backward slip zone, respectively; k_i is a positive constant with k_1 and k_2 for forward slip zone and backward slip zone, respectively; V_g is relative slip velocity between the strip and the roll and can be obtained by:

$$V_g = \sqrt{(v_x sec\beta - V_R)^2 + v_y^{\,2}} \tag{2}$$

where v_x and v_y are the velocity components in the x and y directions, respectively, β is the angular position of the node, V_R is the tangential velocity of the roll, and the distribution of these frictional shear stress models is shown in **Figure 1**.

As shown in **Figure 2**, a quarter of the strip was studied. Isoparametric hexahedral elements were applied with eight Gauss points throughout the deformed workpiece. The element number in x, y, and z directions are 10, 8, and 5, respectively, and totally there are 594 nodes and 400 elements.

From the simulation with low carbon steel, **Figures 3** and **4** show the effect of reduction on rolling pressure and spread of strip for different k_2 and constant k_1 = 0.1. k_2 influences the simulation results significantly where the rolling pressure increases with decreased k_2. When k_2 value is below 0.1, the rolling pressure calculation value is in agreement with the measured one. The spread calculation value for k_2 = 0.1 is also close to the measured one when the reduction is less than 43%. For k_2 = 0.1, the change of k_1 also has an effect on the simulation results, as shown in **Figures 5** and **6**. It can be seen that the calculated results are in good agreement with the measured values for k_1= 0.1. Therefore, the simulation results are close to measured values when k_1 and k_2 are less than 0.1.

The rolling of copper strip is simulated with work roll diameter 158.76 mm, width of strip 76.2 mm, rolling speed 0.16 m/s, and friction factor m_1 = 0.4. For case 1, $K_1 = K_2$ = 1.0 and $k_1 = k_2$ = 0.1

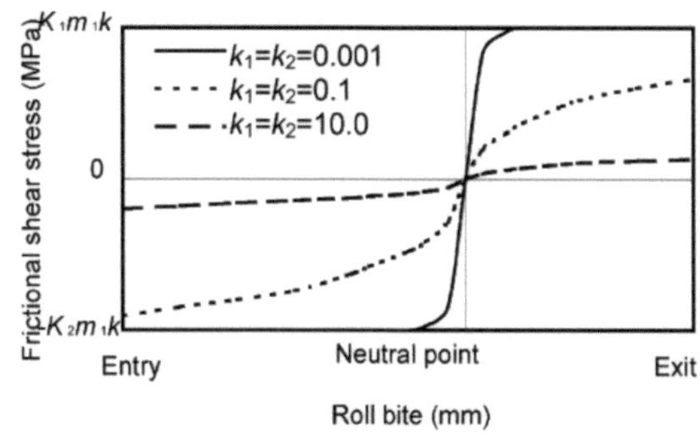

Figure 1. Frictional shear stress models.

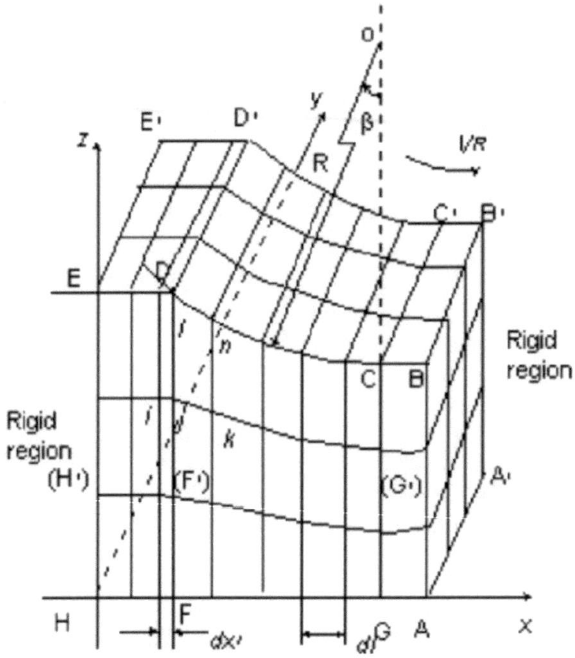

Figure 2. One-quarter of the deforming workpiece.

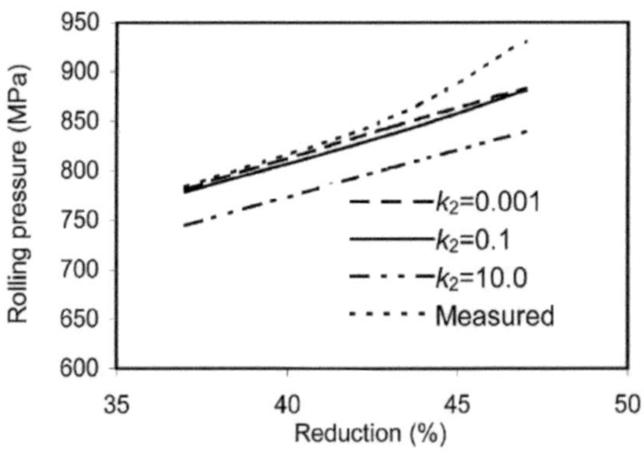

Figure 3. Effect of K_2 on rolling pressure.

and case 2, K_1= 0.7, K_2 = 1.4, and $k_1 = k_2 = 0.1$. The friction variation in the roll bite has a significant effect on the spread as shown in **Figure 7**, where the spread calculated through the constant friction model is greater than the result obtained from the friction variation one, and the spread increases with an increase of reduction. The spread decreases when K_1 increases and K_2 decreases (in case 2) due to the increased forward slip as shown in **Figure 8**, more metal flows along the rolling direction, resulting in a decrease of the transverse flow of metal. It is found in **Figure 7** that the effect of friction variation on spread is not significant for reduction < 25%.

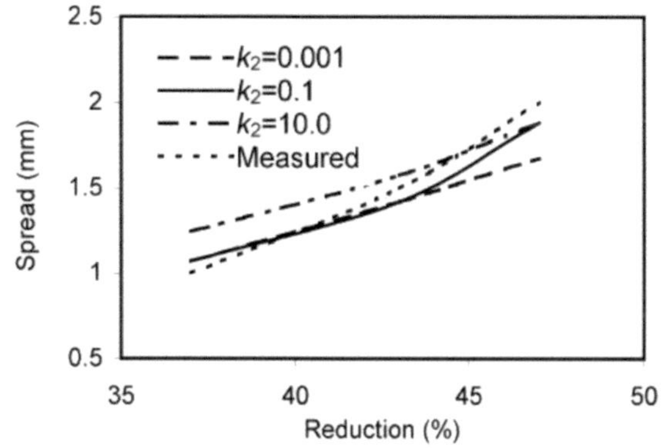

Figure 4. Effect of K_2 on spread.

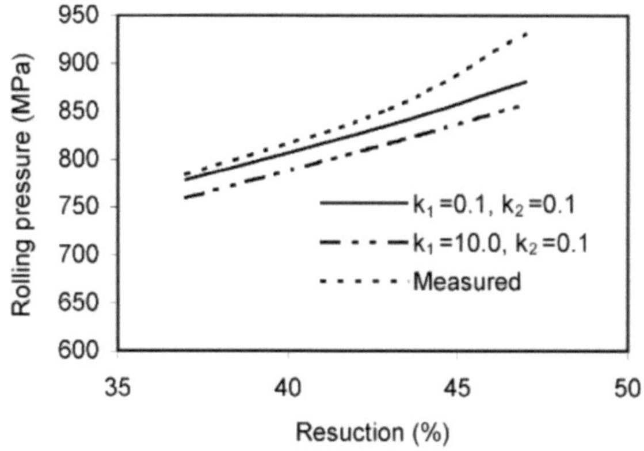

Figure 5. Effect of K_1 on rolling pressure.

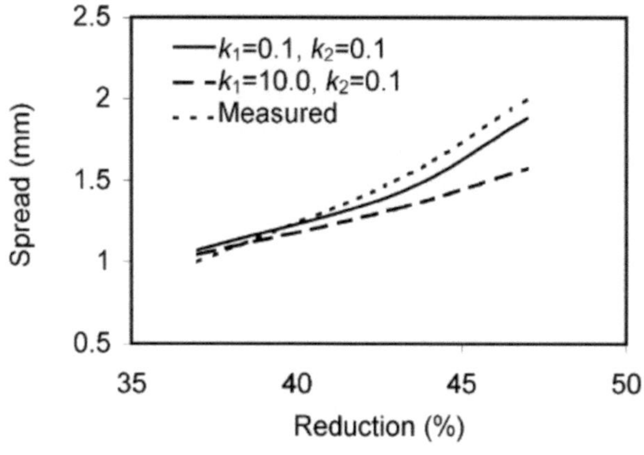

Figure 6. Effect of K_1 on spread.

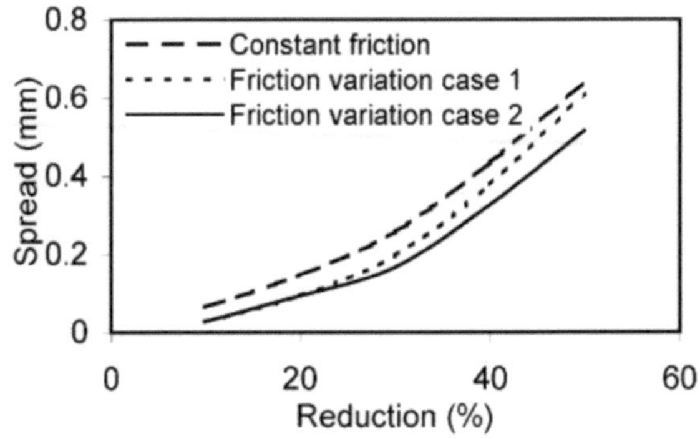

Figure 7. Effect of reduction on spread.

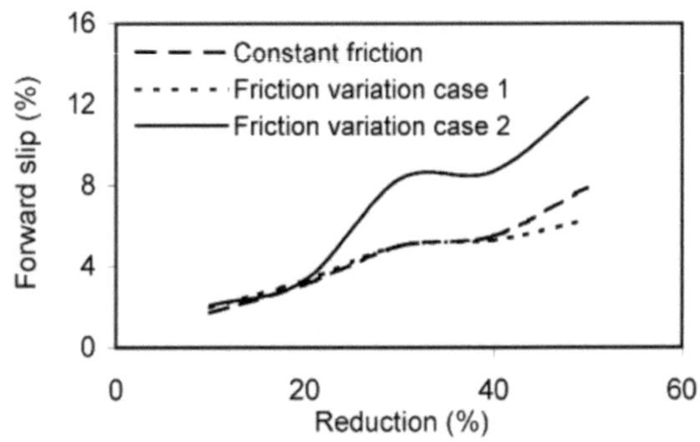

Figure 8. Effect of reduction on forward slip.

3. Application of crystal plasticity finite element method (CPFEM)

Little research has been done on the surface development of constraint surface (surface asperity flattening process) with CPFEM. Most current CPFEM research focus on the development of free surface (surface roughening) by uniaxial and biaxial tensile deformation. In particular, there are almost no reports that mention the relationship between the orientation of surface grains and surface roughness. The texture development of the constraint surface is also a very interesting topic. In metal forming, the strain rate contributes significantly to the workpiece work hardening, but there is little research on how the strain influences the surface roughness. A physical simulation has been conducted on an INSTRON servo-hydraulic testing machine by using a channel die. The relationship between the surface roughness and related parameters such as gauged reduction, friction, texture (grain orientation), and grain size and strain rate has been identified.

The methodology of crystal plasticity finite element modeling (**Figure 9**) follows the rules as: rate-dependent crystal plasticity constitutive models will be written into the UMAT and then used in the ABAQUS main program (geometric model). The geometric model is established based on experimental conditions (reduction, strain rate, friction, original surface roughness, and original texture information). The modeling results will be compared with the

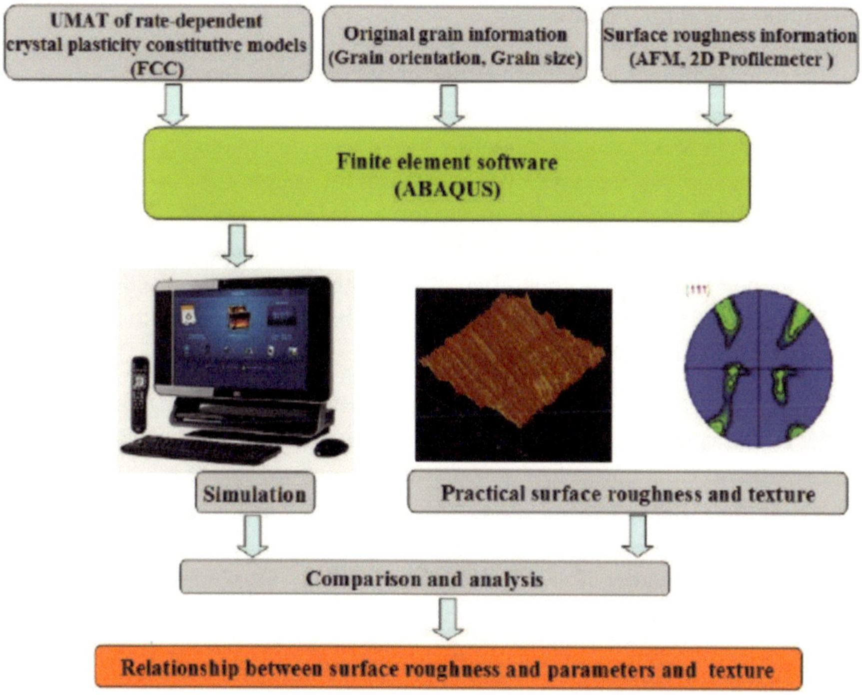

Figure 9. Methodology of crystal plasticity finite element modeling.

experimental results. Furthermore, the relationship between the surface asperity flattening process (surface roughness) and the above-mentioned parameters will be investigated. The mechanism of surface asperity flattening will be analyzed.

Flow rule of plastic deformation gradient F^p can be expressed [7]:

$$\dot{F}^p F^{p^{-1}} = \sum_{\alpha=1}^{n} \dot{\gamma}_{(\alpha)} S_{(\alpha)} \otimes m_\alpha \quad (3)$$

where $\dot{\gamma}_{(\alpha)}$ is the plastic shear rate of the αth slip system.

The relationship between the shear rate $\dot{\gamma}_{(\alpha)}$ and the resolving shear stress $\tau_{(\alpha)}$ is formulated below [7]:

$$\dot{\gamma}_{(\alpha)} = \dot{\gamma}_0 \, sgn\,(\tau_{(\alpha)}) \left| \frac{\tau_{(\alpha)}}{S_{(\alpha)}} \right|^{1/m} \quad (4)$$

For cubic metal, the hardening equation of the slip system can be simplified as [7]:

$$\dot{S}_{(\alpha)} = \sum_{\beta=1}^{n} h_{\alpha\beta} \left| \dot{\gamma}_{(\beta)} \right| \quad (5)$$

where $h_{\alpha\beta}$ is the hardening matric of the slip system α led by the slip system β.

3.1. Three-dimensional (3D) model

A three-dimensional model based on crystal plasticity finite element (CPFE) is proposed according to the atomic force microscopy (AFM) experimental values where the results are sorted and applied in MATLAB for modeling the surface morphology. Every four neighboring elements at the top surface have one orientation for keeping the weight function of orientation in the model. Some elements on the top surface are refined. There are 840 C3D8R integration elements; among them 280 elements are with 70 Euler angle triplets and the others are featured by one element with one orientation. Both the tool and mold have 460 discrete rigid elements. A spatial orientation distribution has been assigned for the workpiece based on the electron backscatter diffraction (EBSD) experimental results.

The relationship between the AFM measured results, the MATLAB calculated results, and 3D CPFE model is shown in **Figure 10**. Direction 1 corresponds to the rolling direction, direction 2 to the normal, and direction 3 to the transverse direction. The three-dimensional model is 100 μm × 100 μm × 100 μm in size. Due to the small size of the sample, only a quarter of practical samples were chosen for simulation. It is considered that during the modeling, the combined slip system includes 12 {110} <111> slip systems (slip planes and slip directions). A total of 630 Euler angle triplets from the experimental results were input into ABAQUS as the initial crystallographic condition of the 3D model [7, 8]. All the parameters of simulation are taken from **Table 1** as a reference.

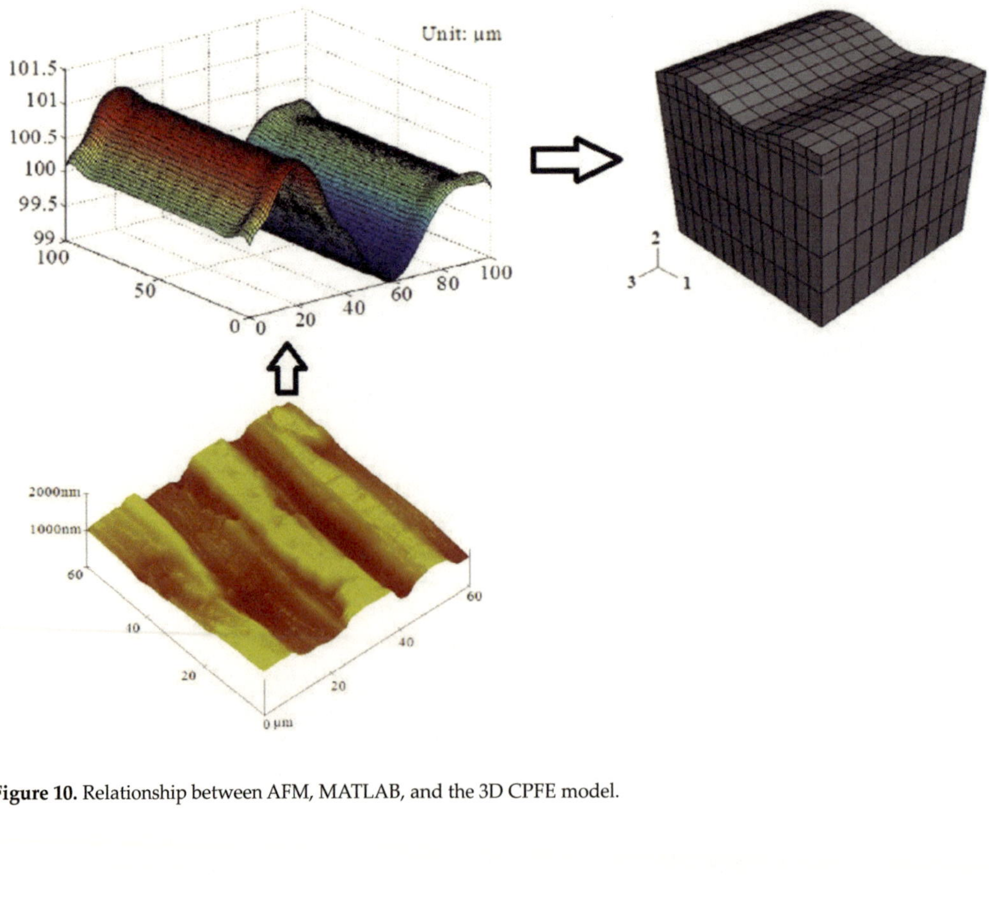

Figure 10. Relationship between AFM, MATLAB, and the 3D CPFE model.

Parameter	Value	Parameter	Value
C_{11}	106,750 MPa	s_0	12.5 MPa
C_{22}	60,410 MPa	h_0	60 MPa
C_{44}	28,340 MPa	s_s	75 MPa
$\dot{\gamma}_0$	0.001	a	2.25
m	0.02	q_1	1.0 (coplanar)
			1.4 (no coplanar)

Table 1. Material parameter of aluminum.

3.2. Results and discussion

3.2.1. Influence on surface roughness

Figure 11 shows that the surface asperity of the samples tends to be flattened with an increase of reduction. With an increase in reduction, the sample with a higher strain rate has a higher flattened rate of surface asperity than the sample with a lower strain rate. Increasing the applied macroscopic strain rate will increase the shear rate of lip systems in the surface area. Then under the same reduction, the sample deformed at a higher strain rate will activate more slip systems in the surface area. When the reduction is 40%, the surface roughness R_a of the sample with a higher strain rate is 0.16 μm, while the sample with a lower strain rate is only 0.09 μm.

3.2.2. Influence of the strain rate on hardness

Figure 12 shows the influence of the strain rate on the hardness of the sample, and the influence is nonlinear. There are different stages in the evolution of hardness because when the

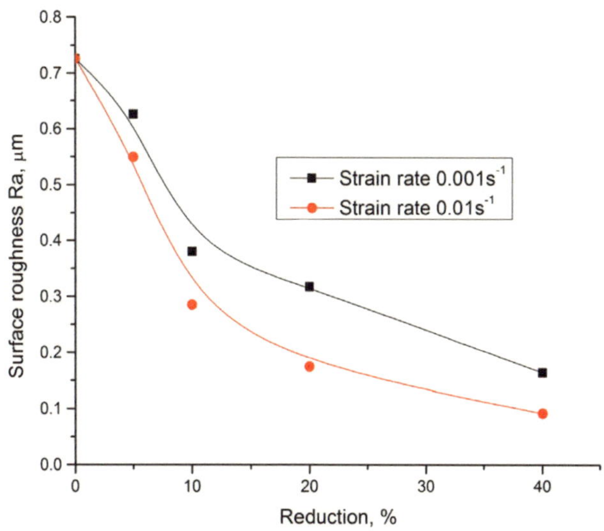

Figure 11. Influence of strain rate on surface roughness.

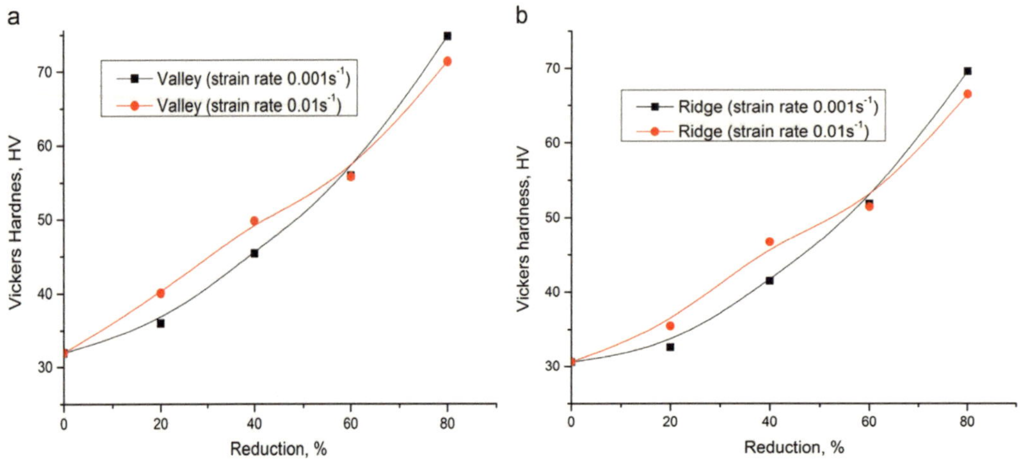

Figure 12. Influence of the strain rate on hardness (a) valley and (b) ridge.

reduction is lower (less than 60%), increasing the strain rate generally increases the hardness. At a larger reduction, increasing the strain rate will decrease the hardness under the same reduction [23]. When the reduction is lower, increasing the strain rate can increase the shearing rate of slip systems and also increase the density of dislocation. However, when reduction exceeds a certain value, the dislocation motion will overcome the barrier of grain boundary. In some areas, the density of dislocation decreases.

3.2.3. *Effect of strain on surface roughness (R_a)*

In **Figure 13**, both the experimental and simulation results show the same tendency that increasing the strain rate can lead to a decrease in surface roughness under the same reduction. When reduction is less than 10%, the effect of the strain rate on surface roughness is insignificant, where mostly elastic deformation influences the flattening behavior of surface asperity. In this case, the increase of strain rate affects insignificantly the elastic deformation surface roughness. Plastic deformation plays an important role on surface area when the reduction exceeds 10%. When slip is the only deformation mode, the increased strain rate can result in more slip through the increased slip shear rate. Therefore, the surface roughness will decrease greatly with an increase in the strain rate.

3.2.4. *Effect of the strain rate on texture*

Figure 14 shows that the influence of strain rate on the pole figures with at strain rate of 0.001 s^{-1} and 0.01 s^{-1} is not significant. In this case, every experiment has been carried out at room temperature, and the two applied strain rates are quite small. Deformation under the two strain rates belongs to the quasistatic deformation, and the difference between the two applied strain rates is small compared to the other dynamic deformation.

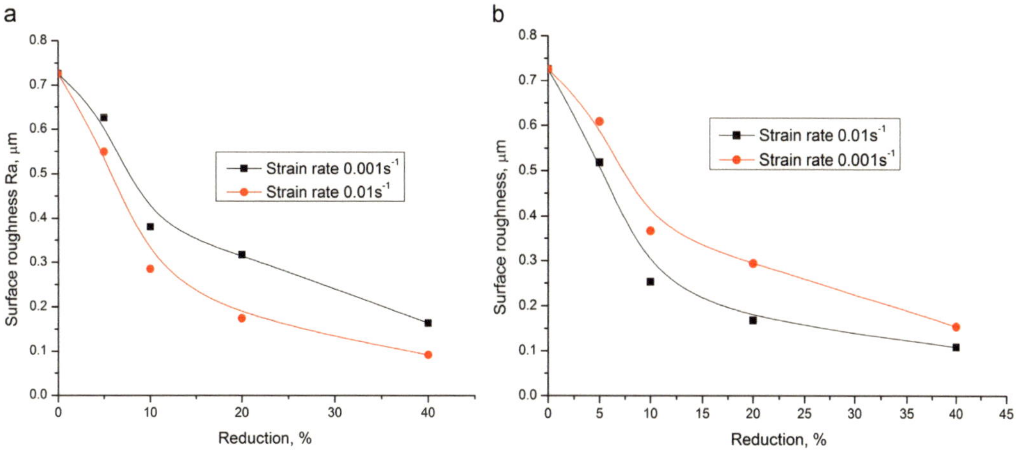

Figure 13. Effect of the strain rate on surface roughness R_a: (a) experimental and (b) simulation.

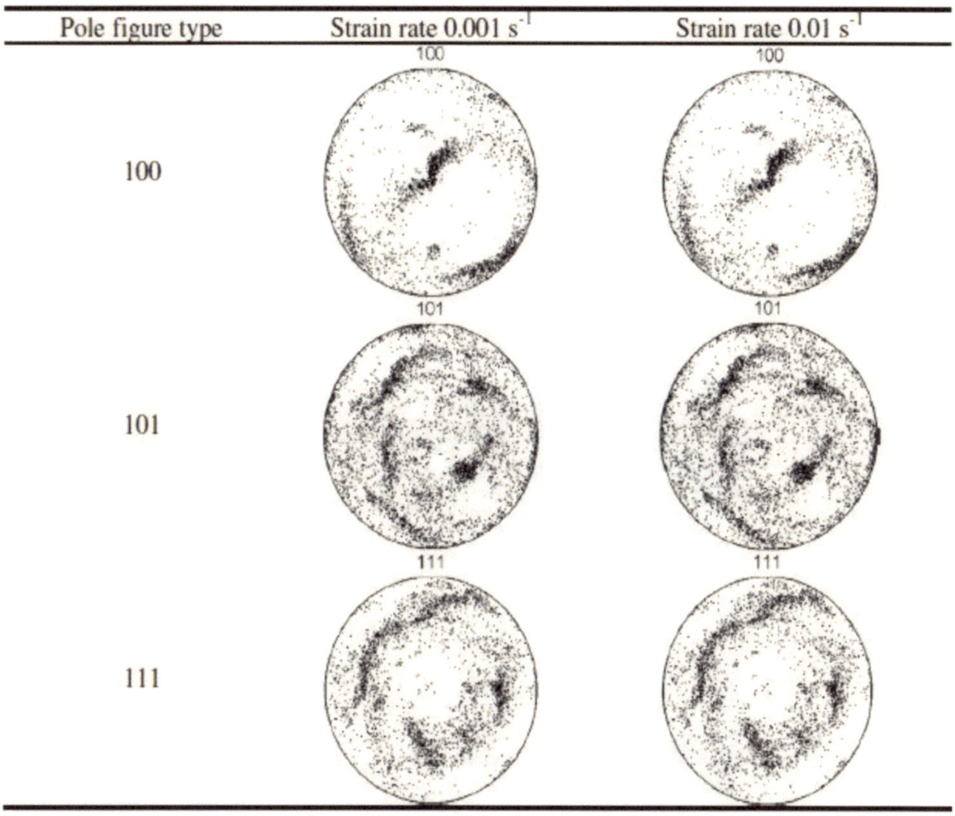

Figure 14. Effect of the strain rate on texture (reduction 60% without lubrication).

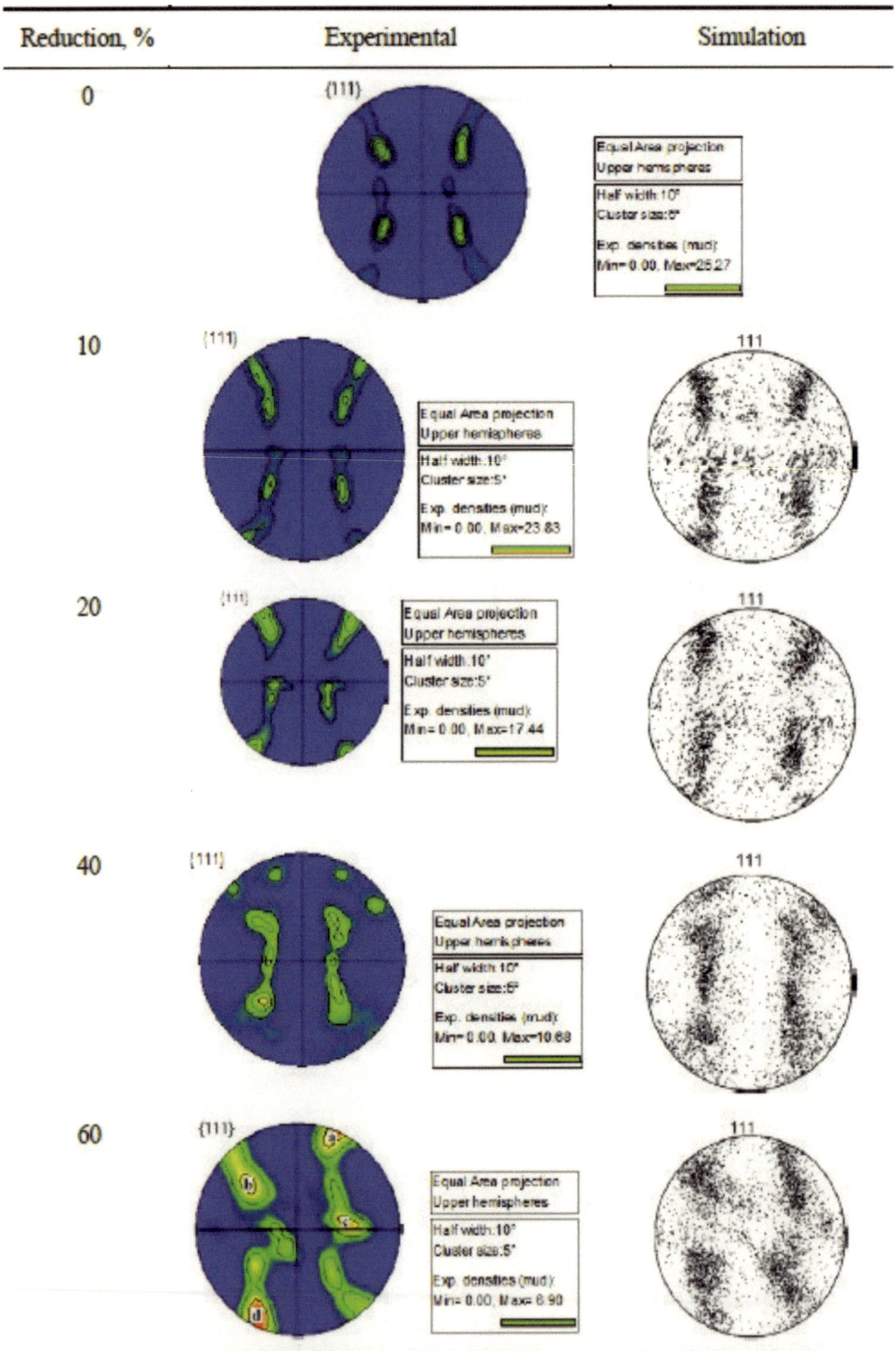

Figure 15. Comparison of the experimental pole figures with the simulation results.

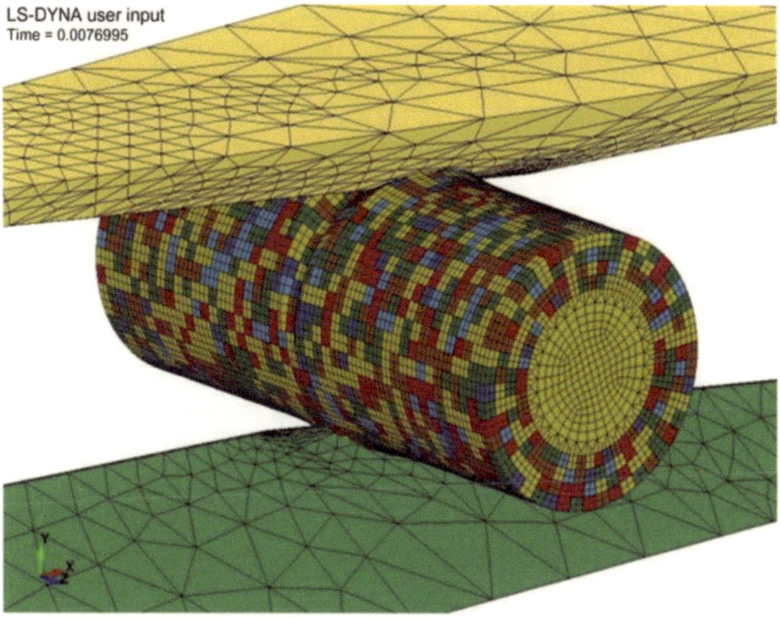

Figure 16. FE model in grained heterogeneities of workpiece in MCWR.

3.2.5. Analysis of pole figure

Normally, the close-packed plane in FCC metal is {111}. In this case, the pole figure {111} is used for the analysis. Before compression, the sample has a cubic texture {111}<001> as shown in **Figure 16**. The predicted result has been compared to the experimental result; both of them show the same texture development. In the pole figure {111}, with an increased reduction, the brass orientation {110}<112> of silk texture becomes obvious while the cubic texture {001}<100> gets weaker. When the reduction reaches 60%, the brass orientation {110}<112> of silk texture shows extreme strong around a and d areas shown in **Figure 15**. Additionally, some S orientations {123}<634> can be seen in b and c areas. These results are basically in the agreement with the Sarma and Dawson's results [7, 8], which show a consistent development in hardness and grain size.

4. Novel material model based on Hall-Petch relationship in microforming

Size effects in microforming cannot be conveyed by the classical theory of continuum plastic mechanics, which is scale-independent. The specimen size effects on the flow stress of polycrystalline Cu-Al alloy have been investigated, and the fact that the flow stress decreases with the dimensional reduction of specimen has been explained by the proposed affect zone model [24]. A flow stress model, a function of the ratio of the sheet thickness to grain size, has been established based on Hall-Petch relationship, dislocation pile-up theory, and affect zone model [25]. A mixed material model based on modified Hall-Petch relationship, surface layer model, and grained heterogeneity is proposed, and the 3D aggregate of polycrystalline is represented by a Voronoi tessellation. The effect of grain size on flow stress is an important aspect of polycrystalline metal plastic deformation. The simulation of microforming processes (micro cross wedge rolling (MCWR), micro flexible rolling and micro V-bending) have been conducted with the consideration of size effects from grain size and feature size. The validation of the proposed material model will be conducted by physical experiments through the comparison between experimental results and simulation ones.

Fundamentals have been developed to build up a FE model considering the occurrence of size effects at microscale by using the ANSYS/LS-DYNA program. The newly developed material model is implemented considering grained heterogeneity. As shown in **Figure 16**, two forming tools and a cylindrical workpiece of 0.831.2 mm^2 are meshed in solid element 164 with an 8-noded structure. In order to reduce computational time and ensure stability in large deformation, viscous hourglass control and one-point integration were applied for all elements. For each grain size, 10 different polycrystalline aggregates of workpiece were generated stochastically by the algorithm of 3D Voronoi tessellation. The simulation was performed by applying equal and opposite velocities to forming tools in the horizontal (x) direction. In whole process, the workpiece is left unconstrained, and the tools are held in the vertical (y) direction and in the out-of-plane (z) direction [12]. **Figure 17** shows the process of forging shape during micro cross wedge rolling.

Laminar cricoid distribution of strain is typical in conventional CWR with homogeneous material properties and also exists in MCWR where billet material is homogeneous (**Figure 18a**). However, the grained heterogeneity effects on the metal deformability and strain distribution should be considered in microscale forming. It is shown in **Figure 18b–d** that the continuous laminar distribution of strain in the workpiece has been disturbed due to the inhomogeneous

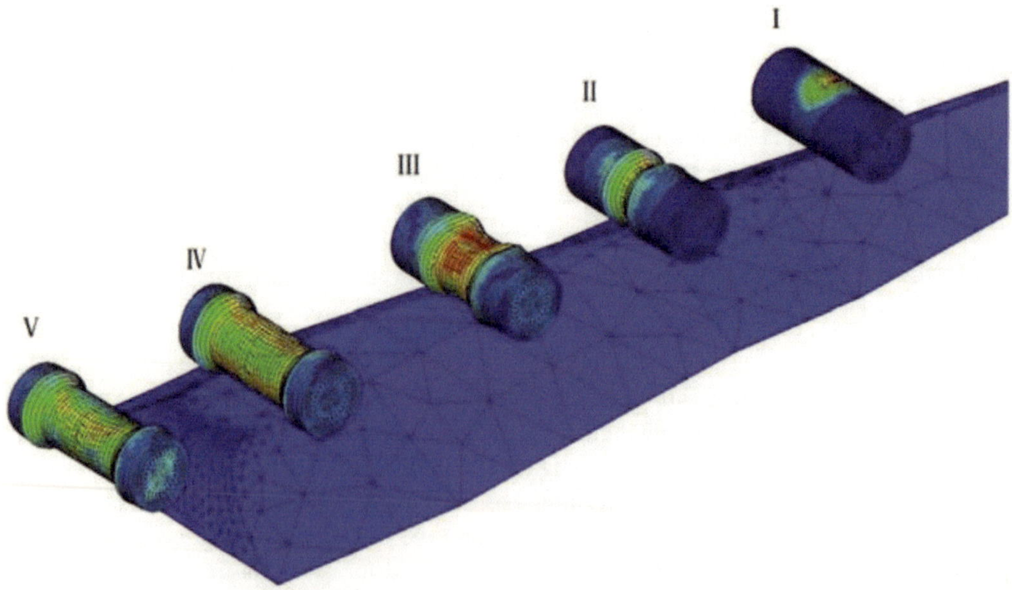

Figure 17. Process of forging shape during MCWR.

http://dx.doi.org/10.5772/intechopen.71880

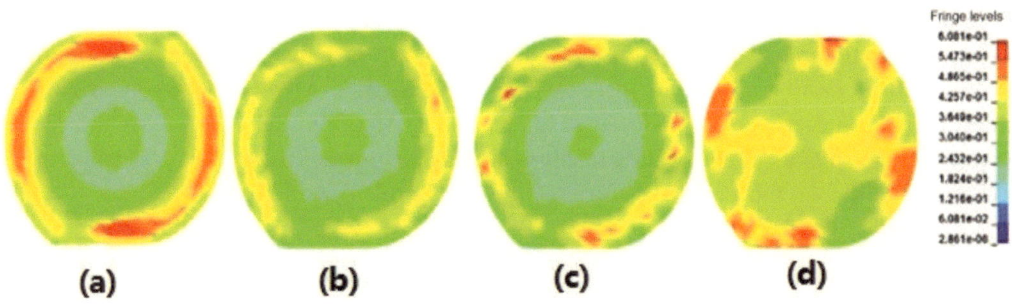

Figure 18. Distribution of effective strain of the medial section in axial direction (a) uniform material properties and (b, c, d) inhomogeneous material properties with grain sizes of 6, 40, and 120 μm, respectively.

mechanical properties [12–14]. The location of the maximum strain and stress cannot be determined easily as that in the conventional CWR process.

The stress and strain distribution on the profile for the halved 250 μm thick workpiece consisting of grains with the average grain size of 250 μm is illustrated in **Figure 19**. The stress-strain distribution is inhomogeneous because only some grains are in plastic regime while others still undergo elastic strain regime during the flexible rolling process [15].

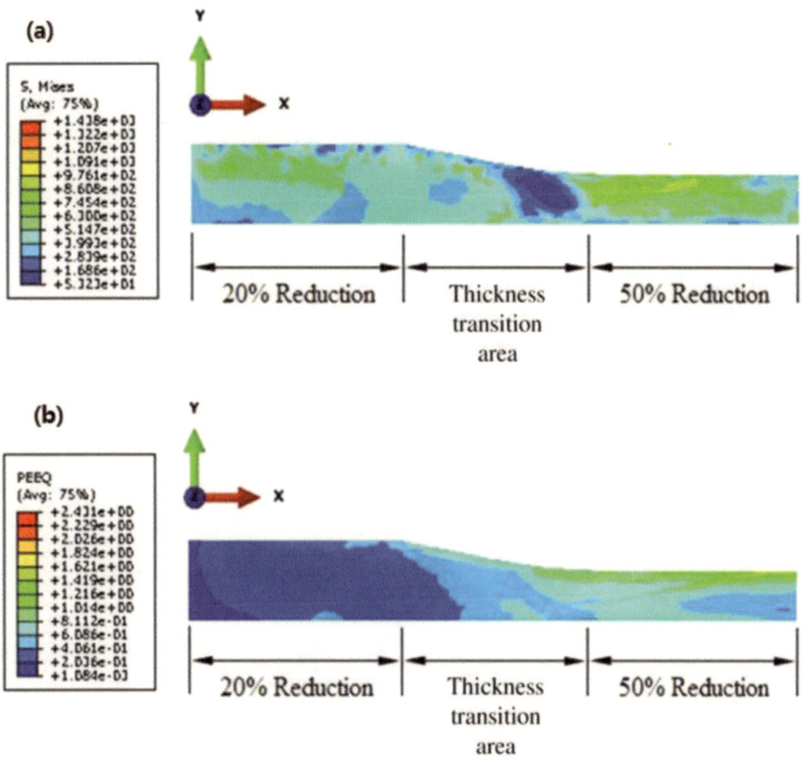

Figure 19. Stress-strain distribution on the profile after springback in micro flexible rolling: (a) von Mises stress distribution and (b) equivalent plastic strain distribution.

Figure 20 shows the tension effect on the average springback from the proposed models. Regardless of the initial thickness and pass reduction, the springback decreases moderately when the front and back tensions increase in increments of 25 MPa from 0 to 100 MPa. For thicker workpiece, front and back tensions have a significant influence on eliminating the springback due to that front and back tensions are able to improve metal flow and relax residual stresses and then increase the thickness precision of rolled workpiece.

In **Figure 21**, it can be seen that the thickness springback increases as the initial workpiece thickness decreases. For a certain grain size, the grain number decreases in thickness direction for less thick workpiece. Therefore, the effect of each single grain plays a very significant role on the springback resulting in larger springback value. For each thickness, the curves are in similar trends under different reductions, and the springback difference is below 10.5% for each grain size, which is close to the simulation result.

Micro V-bending process is simulated with an implicit FEM package: ABAQUS/Standard. The processing parameters in the simulation are the same as those in physical experiments, and the value of coefficient of friction is set to be 0.02. The FE model of micro V-bending with Voronoized specimen is shown in **Figure 22a**. **Figure 22b** illustrates the grain heterogeneity in Voronoized specimen, among which different colors represent different mechanical properties of grains. It is shown in **Figure 23** that the upper bound grain plastic property is illustrated by dark blue (six grains), while light blue (six grains) is for the lower bound grain plastic property [16]. The FE model is close to real physical test condition as the right and the left sides of the sample are not equal in terms of grain size and the scatter of mechanical properties of grains, rather than set up as a traditional asymmetrical one.

Figure 24 shows the simulation result of micro V-bending. The inhomogeneous deformation occurs significantly during bending process. The different colors in middle deformation zone represent that different grains have undergone different deformation because of grain heterogeneity. In the bending process, some grains first reach their yield stress and undergo plastic deformation prior to other grains. Even the workpiece has started the plastic deformation, some grains with higher yield stress may still be under elastic stress condition. This sort of grain heterogeneous deformation could influence the springback significantly and should be taken into account in numerical simulation of microforming [16].

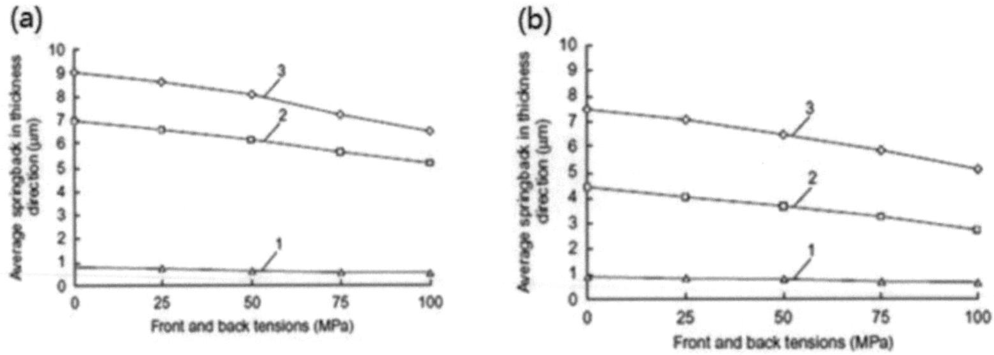

Figure 20. Relationship between average springback in thickness direction and front and back tensions for initial workpiece thickness of 100, 250, and 500 μm: (a) 20% reduction and (b) 50% reduction.

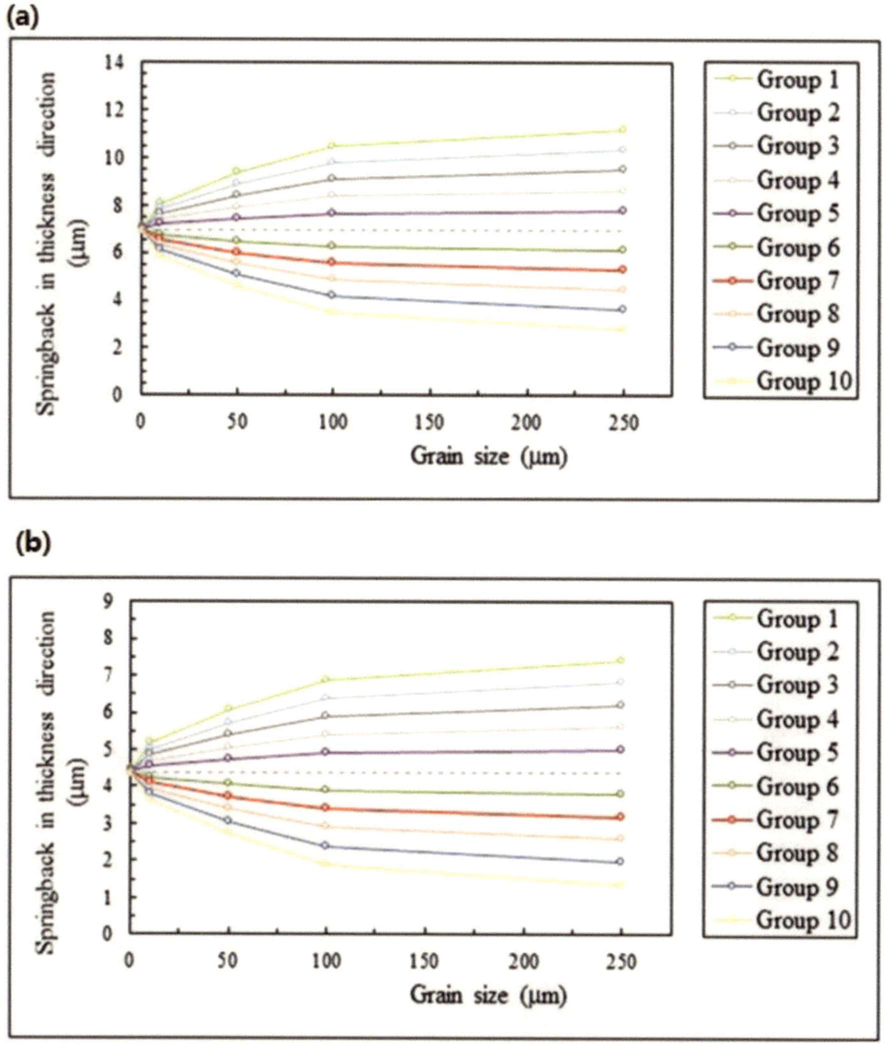

Figure 21. Springback in thickness direction versus gain size for initial workpiece thickness of 100 μm: (a) 20% reduction and (b) 50% reduction.

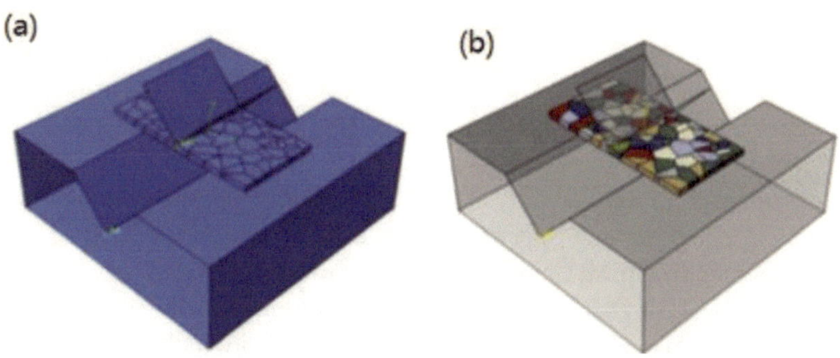

Figure 22. FEM simulation of micro V-bending with (a) Voronoi tessellations and (b) grain heterogeneity.

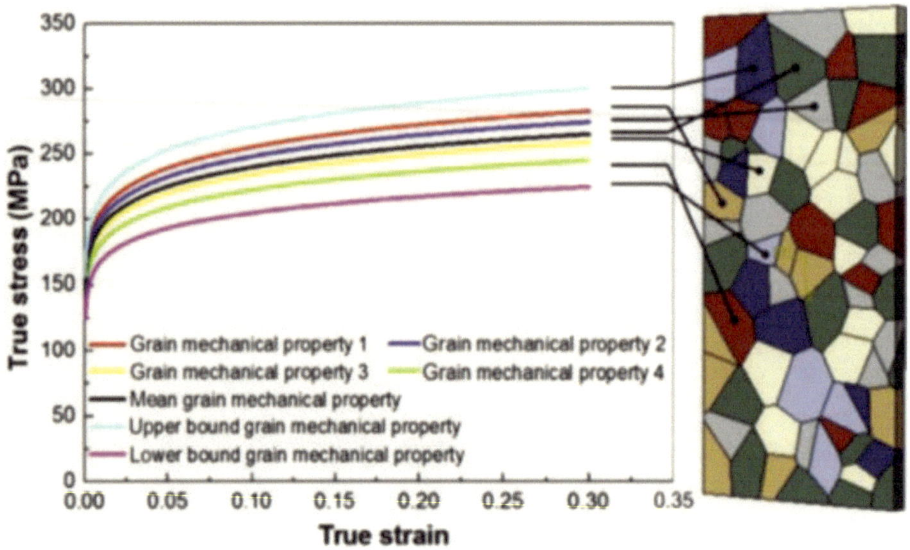

Figure 23. Grain properties randomly assigned on a Voronoized bending sample.

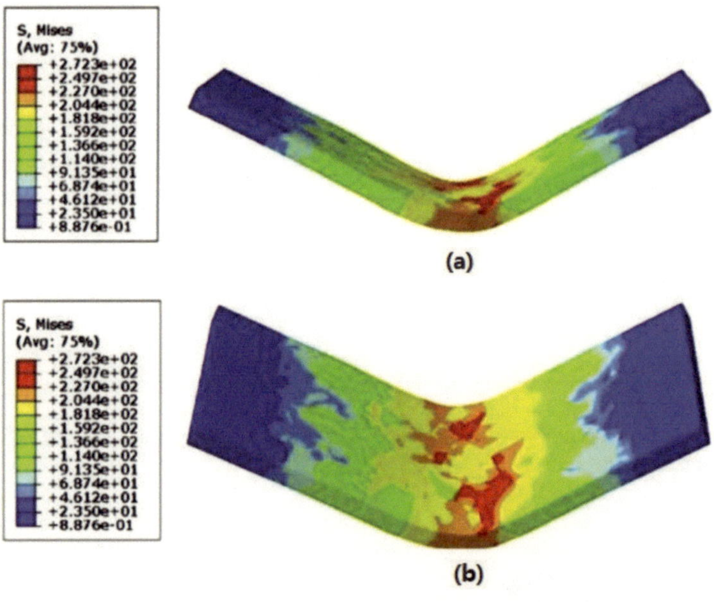

Figure 24. (a) Final angle after springback and (b) von Mises stress distribution.

Seven plastic properties are obtained by experiment and calculation, and they are randomly distributed in bending specimens. Specimens with different random grain heterogeneity distributions are exhibited in **Figure 25**, which are called models "1," "2," "3," "4," "5," "6," and "7," respectively. Seven groups of micro V-bending FE simulations have been conducted with above-mentioned seven specimens individually. Springback angles of seven simulations and an average value are measured and calculated, as shown in **Table 2**.

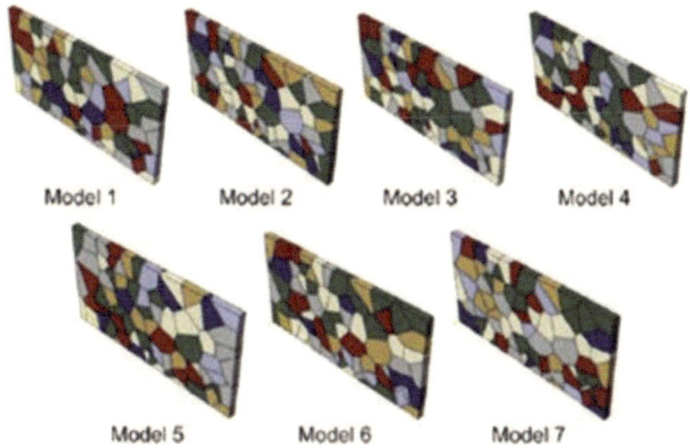

Figure 25. Bending specimens with different gain heterogeneity distributions.

Distribution group	1	2	3	4	5	6	7	Average
Springback angle	30.52	27.37	32.09	31.78	33.44	28.65	34.12	31.14

Table 2. Springback angles from FE simulation (degree).

5. Modified FEM with the consideration of material and lubrication characterization in MDD and MHDD

Figure 26 represents a typical EBSD microstructure. First, the EBSD image was input into the MATLAB software, and the binary image was obtained with black grain boundaries and white grains. Noise and small holes were eliminated in the transformation. Then, the Moore-Neighbor tracing algorithm modified by Jacob's stopping criteria was applied in the binary image treatment. As shown in **Figure 26b**, the information of grains and individual closed subareas, including single grain's area, geometrical center and geometrical orientation, was detected and sorted in MATLAB. The blue ports in **Figure 26b** are the grain's geometrical centers [9, 20, 21].

Figure 27 displays the Voronoi structures and their corresponding FE models with average grain sizes of 10, 20, and 40 μm, respectively.

After annealed at 1100°C, the 50 μm thick blanks, with equiaxed crystals microstructure and average grain size of 40 μm, were drawn into micro cups. The drawn cup mouth is shown in **Figure 28a**, and the maximum thickness distributions of drawn cups are illustrated in **Figure 28b–d**, which represented the new developed model, a Voronoi model without the consideration of grain boundaries and a normal model in homogeneous material properties, respectively. The comparison of the maximum wall thickness between the simulation and the experimental results has been conducted. The localized deformation is ignored, and the maximum thickness was averaged with the lowest peak thickness values for all the simulation cases. It can be seen that the new model and the Voronoi model considered microscopic heterogeneity have higher maximum thickness than that in the normal model [9], where the largest thickness is obtained from the Voronoi model without grain boundaries buffer.

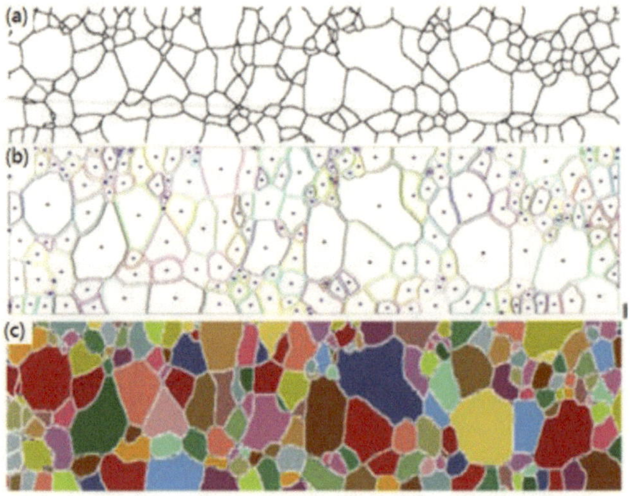

Figure 26. (a) Microstructure of a sample from EBSD, (b) its corresponding geometry detected by MATLAB and (c) corresponding simulation model.

The material surface consists of lots of peaks and valleys called roughness in microforming. The roughness and the extent of the valleys get larger compared to the scaled down workpiece size. As shown in **Figure 29**, the lubricant cannot be retained in the valleys connected to the edge of the blank, and this area is called open lubricant pockets (OLPs) [9, 18, 19]. The fraction of OLPs increases with the decrease in specimen size. The friction force increases because the lubricant cannot be kept during microscale forming process. Therefore, the OLPs must be taken into account when studying the tribological behavior of microforming.

Figure 30 shows schematic of evaluation test for OLPs utilizing liquid where the blank is compressed by the tools under approximately 20 MPa contact pressure. During experiment, the liquid is filled into the tool first, and the liquid intruded area is colored. Then the blank

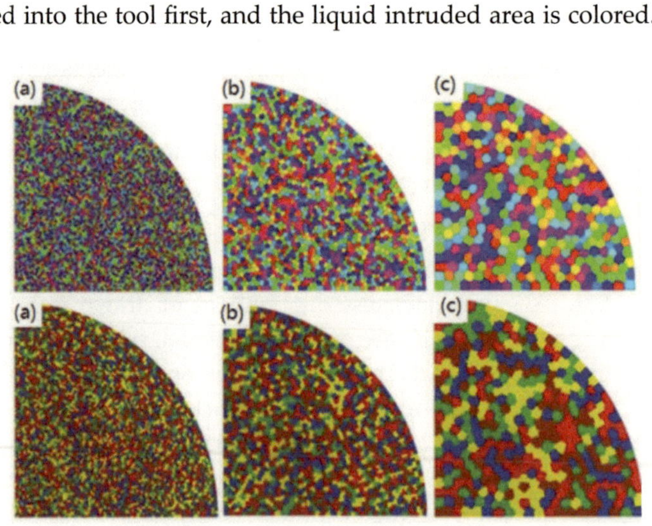

Figure 27. Voronoi structures (in the first line) and their corresponding FE models (in the second line): average grain sizes of (a) 10, (b) 20, and (c) 40 μm.

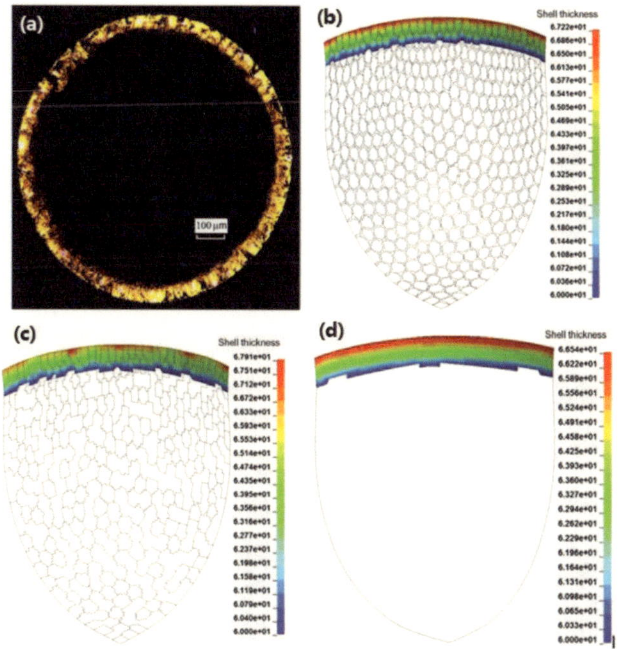

Figure 28. (a) Drawn cup with 1100°C annealed blank and maximum thickness distribution from the simulation with (b) the developed new model, (c) the Voronoi model, and (d) the normal model.

with visualized, and liquid intruded area is taken out when the liquid dries out. After this, the blank surface is observed under a digital microscope, and the pictures are digitized [9, 17].

Figure 31 illustrates the effects of scale factor on the normalized punch force-stroke curves at MDD with lubrication and MHDD with radial pressure. The shape of punch force-stroke curves in $\lambda = 1, 2$ is as similar as that with $\lambda = 50$ at MDD and MHDD. In these conditions, only the inner or outer pockets exist in the flange area. Therefore, the coefficient of friction in the flange area is almost uniform. On the other hand, in $\lambda = 5$, the inner and outer pockets are

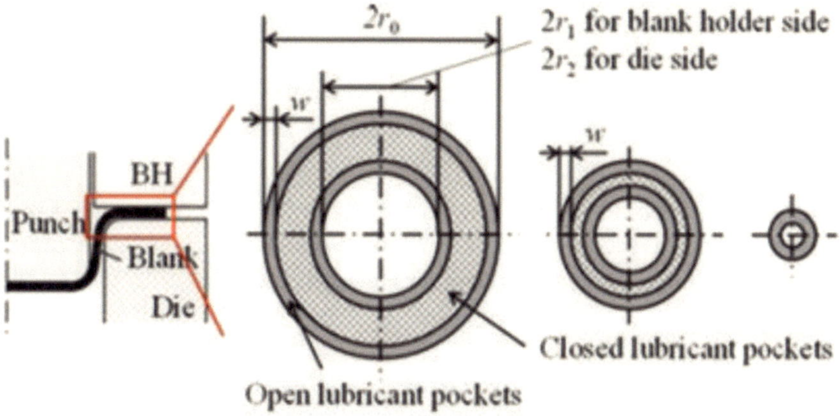

Figure 29. The change of fraction of OLPs in flange area with the decrease of blank size.

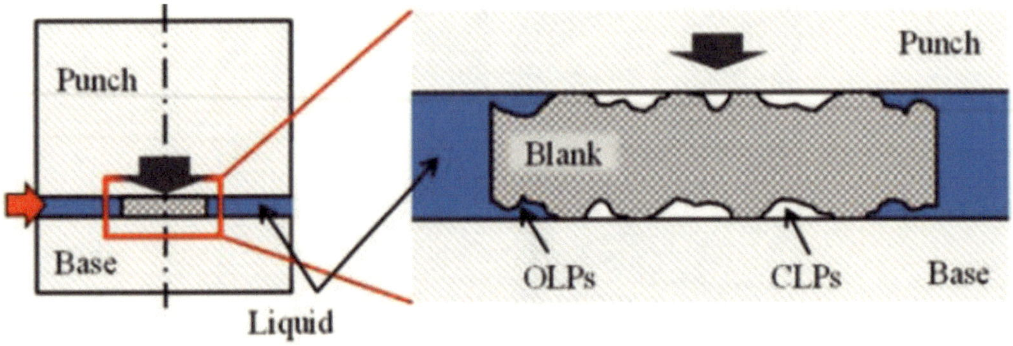

Figure 30. Schematic of evaluation test for OLPs utilizing liquid.

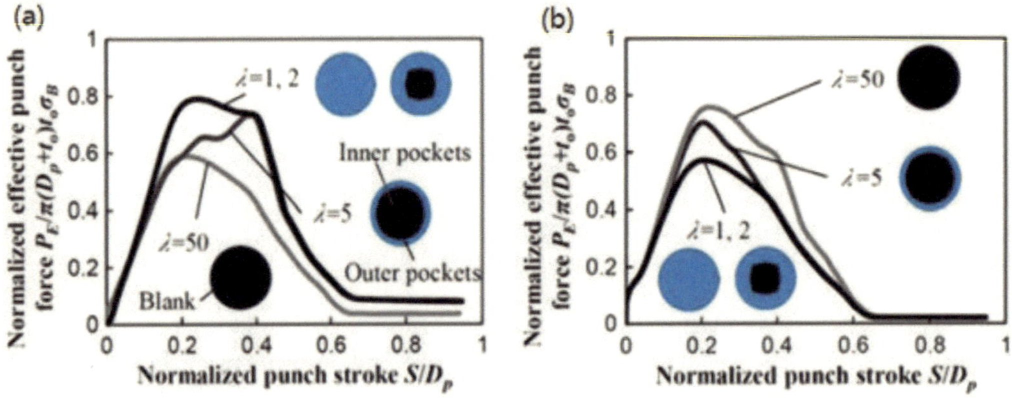

Figure 31. Effects of scale factor λ on normalized punch force-stroke curve at different lubrication conditions (a) MDD with lubrication, and (b) MHDD with radial pressure.

mixed in the flange area. In the initial process, the inner pockets mainly exist at die shoulder and flange area and affect the tribological behavior significantly. Therefore, the punch force-stroke curves are as similar with that in macroscale. However, in the middle process, the ratio of outer pockets increases. As a result, the tribological behavior shifts to that in microscale. This behavior appears at both MDD and MHDD. This causes the maximum punch force shifts as shown in **Figure 31a**. These results indicate the ratio of the outer pockets to the flange area during the forming process influences the tribological behavior of the MHDD as shown in **Figure 31b**.

Figure 32a shows the tribological size effects in MDD and MHDD. With the decrease in the size, the friction force increases in case of MDD with lubrication because the ratio of outer pockets increases. When λ = 1, 2, the maximum effective punch forces in MDD with the dry friction and lubrication become the same because only the outer pockets exist at flange area. On the other hand, with the decrease in the size, the friction force in MHDD decreases. It can be seen the tribological size effects in MHDD have an opposite behavior with MDD. In MHDD, the fluid medium is provided to the outer pockets whose ratio is high in microscale. This

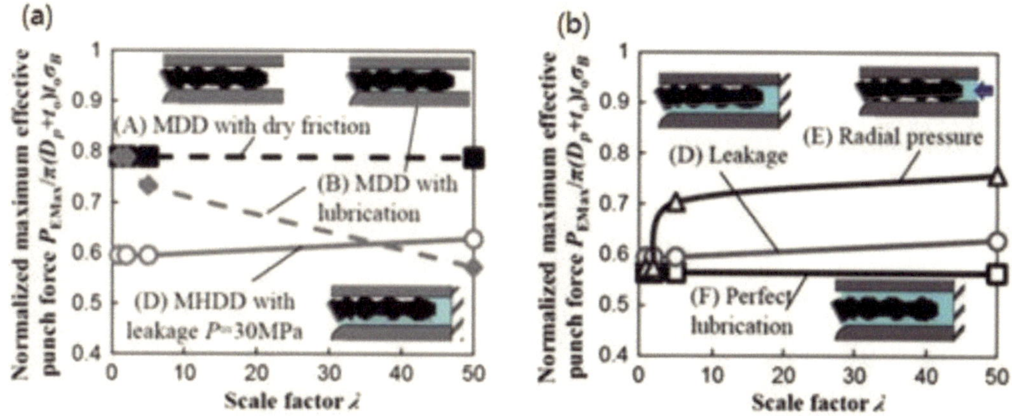

Figure 32. Tribological size effects at different lubrication conditions in MDD and MHDD.

caused the decrease in friction force in MHDD. **Figure 32b** shows the effect of the lubrication type on friction force in MHDD. The decrease of friction force in radial pressure condition is much larger than that in leakage condition. Also in radial pressure condition, the friction force significant decreases from λ = 5–1. It is because the contact pressure between the blank and die at die shoulder is higher than that between the blank and blank holder in the small D_p/t. Therefore, the decrease in coefficient of friction at die shoulder is especially important to decrease the friction force in MHDD. According to the above-mentioned results, the friction force can decrease with the decrease in size in MHDD, while it only increases in MDD. The friction force can be reduced by filling the fluid medium in the outer pockets in MHDD [19].

6. Conclusions

This chapter presents the applications of FEM in metal-forming analysis from macroscale to microscale, including FEA software programs used, simulation approach and results obtained, and their validation for metal-forming processes. A 3D rigid plastic FEM is used with the consideration of friction variation models in the case of work roll kiss occurrence during cold rolling of thin strip. The modeling of the friction variation can produce a more accurate model that can improve the accuracy of simulation results. In the CPFEM, the simulation results show that with an increase in reduction, the cubic texture {001}<100> is weak, while the brass orientation {110}<112> becomes strong. The simulation result agrees with the experimental one. When reduction exceeds 60%, most grains have plastic slips. With an increase in reduction, both the grain size and surface roughness decrease while the flow stress increases. Novel material model with grained heterogeneity in 3D Voronoi tessellation has been developed in the simulation of micro cross wedge rolling, springback analysis in thickness direction during micro flexible rolling process and the micro V-bending process considering grain boundary and generation process of grains in the workpiece. Real microstructures and Voronoi structures are applied in microstructural models through image-based modeling method and modified FE with the consideration of size effects including material characterization, friction/contact characterization, and other size-related factors. Open and closed lubricate pocket theory and size-dependent coefficient of friction are also proposed in micro deep drawing and micro hydromechanical deep drawing.

Author details

Zhengyi Jiang* and Haibo Xie

*Address all correspondence to: jiang@uow.edu.au

School of Mechanical, Materials, Mechatronic and Biomedical Engineering, University of Wollongong, Wollongong, NSW, Australia

References

[1] Liu Y, Tieu A, Wang D, Yuen W. Friction measurement in cold rolling. Journal of Materials Processing Technology. 2001;**111**:142-145. DOI: 10.1016/S0924-0136(01)00541-6

[2] Zhang L. On the mechanics of cold rolling thin foil. International Journal of Machine Tools and Manufacture. 1995;**35**:363-372. DOI: 10.1016/0890-6955(94)E0028-H

[3] Fleck N, Johnson K, Mear M, Zhang L. Cold rolling of foil. Proceedings of the Institution of Mechanical Engineers, Part B: Journal of Engineering Manufacture. 1992;**206**:119

[4] Jiang Z, Tieu A. Modelling of rolling of strips with longitudinal ribs by 3-D rigid visco-plastic finite element method. ISIJ International. 2000;**40**:373-379. DOI: 10.2355/isijinternational.40.373

[5] Jiang Z, Tieu A. A 3-D finite element method analysis of cold rolling of thin strip with friction variation. Tribology International. 2004;**37**:185-191. DOI: 10.1016/S0301-679X(03)00049-5

[6] Jiang Z, Tieu A. A method to analyse the rolling of strip with ribs by 3-D rigid visco-plastic finite element method. Journal of Materials Processing Technology. 2001;**117**:146-152. DOI: 10.1016/S0924-0136(01)01087-1

[7] Li H. A Study of Surface Roughness in the Metal Forming Process [Thesis]. Australia: University of Wollongong; 2012

[8] Li H, Öchsner A, Wei D, Ni G, Jiang Z. Crystal plasticity finite element modelling of the effect of friction on surface asperity flattening in cold uniaxial planar compression. Applied Surface Science. 2015;**359**:236-244. DOI: 10.1016/j.apsusc.2015.10.043

[9] Jiang Z, Zhao J, Xie H. Microforming Technology: Theory, Simulation and Practice. Elsevier; 2017. 452 p. ISBN: 9780128112120

[10] Vollertsen F, Hu Z. Tribological size effects in sheet metal forming measured by a strip drawing test. CIRP Annals. 2006;**55**:291-294. DOI: 10.1016/S0007-8506(07)60419-3

[11] Chan W, Fu M, Lu J, Liu J. Modelling of grain size effect on micro deformation behavior in micro-forming of pure copper. Materials Science and Engineering A. 2010;**527**:6638-6648. DOI: /10.1016/j.msea.2010.07.009

[12] Lu H. A Study on the Micro Cross Wedge Rolling of Metals [Thesis]. Australia: University of Wollongong; 2013

[13] Jiang Z, Lu H, Wei D, Linghu K, Zhao X, Zhang X. Finite element method analysis of micro cross wedge rolling of metals. Procedia Engineering. 2014;**81**:2463-2468. DOI: 10.1016/j.proeng.2014.10.351

[14] Lu H, Wei D, Jiang Z, Wu D, Zhao X. Study on the influence of temperature on the surface asperity in micro cross wedge rolling. AIP Publishing. 2013:1032-1037

[15] Qu F, Jiang Z, Lu H. Analysis of micro flexible rolling with consideration of material heterogeneity. International Journal of Mechanical Sciences. 2016;**105**:182-190. DOI: 10.1016/j.ijmecsci.2015.11.004

[16] Fang Z, Jiang Z, Wei D, Liu X. Study on springback in micro V-bending with consideration of grain heterogeneity. International Journal of Advanced Manufacturing Technology. 2015;**78**:1075-1085. DOI: 10.1007/s00170-014-6697-3

[17] Sato H, Manabe K, Wei D, Jiang Z. Numerical modeling of size effect in micro hydromechanical deep drawing. AIP Conference Proceedings. 2013;**1567**:926 http://dx.doi.org/10.1063/1.4850121

[18] Sato H, Manabe K, Ito K, Wei DB, Jiang ZY. Development of servo-type micro-hydromechanical deep-drawing apparatus and micro deep-drawing experiments of circular cups. Journal of Materials Processing Technology. 2015;**224**:233-239. DOI: 10.1016/j.jmatprotec.2015.05.014

[19] Sato H, Manabe K, Wei D, Jiang Z, Alexandrov S. Tribological behaviour in micro-sheet hydroforming. Tribology International. 2016;**97**:302-312. DOI: 10.1016/j.triboint.2016.01.041

[20] Luo L, Jiang Z, Wei D, Manabe K, He X, Li P. An experimental and numerical study of micro deep drawing of SUS304 circular cups. Manufacturing Review. 2015;**2**:27. DOI: 10.1051/mfreview/2015029

[21] Luo L, Jiang Z, Wei D, Manabe K, Zhao X, Wu D. Effects of surface roughness on micro deep drawing of circular cups with consideration of size effects. Finite Elements in Analysis and Design. 2016;**111**:46-55. DOI: 10.1016/j.finel.2015.11.005

[22] Jiang Z, Tieu A. Modelling of thin strip cold rolling with friction variation by a 3-D finite element method. JSME International Journal, Series A. 2003;**46**(3):218-223

[23] Li H, Jiang Z, Wei D, Zhang X. Microtexture based analysis of surface asperity flattening behavior of annealed aluminum alloy in uniaxial planar compression. Tribology International. 2013;**66**:282-288. DOI: 10.1016/j.triboint.2013.04.011

[24] Miyazaki S, Shibata K, Fujita H. Effect of specimen thickness on mechanical properties of polycrystalline aggregates with various grain sizes. Acta Metallurgica. 1979;**27**:855-862. DOI: 10.1016/0001-6160(79)90120-2

[25] Leu D. Modelling of size effect on tensile flow stress of sheet metal in microforming. ASME Journal of Manufacturing Science and Engineering. 2009;**131**:0110021-0110028. DOI: 10.1115/1.3039520

Finite Element Thermal Analysis of Metal Parts Additively Manufactured via Selective Laser Melting

Dario Pitassi, Enrico Savoia, Vigilio Fontanari,
Alberto Molinari, Valerio Luchin,
Gianluca Zappini and Matteo Benedetti

Additional information is available at the end of the chapter

http://dx.doi.org/10.5772/intechopen.71876

Abstract

In this chapter, a three-dimensional finite element model is developed to simulate the thermal behavior of the molten pool in selective laser melting (SLM) process. Laser-based additive manufacturing (AM) is a near net shape manufacturing process able to produce 3D objects. They are layer-wise built through selective melting of a metal powder bed. The necessary energy is provided by a laser source. The interaction between laser and material occurs within a few microseconds, hence the transient thermal behavior must be taken into account. A calibration procedure is carried out to fit the numerical solution with the experimental data. Once the calibration has corrected the thermal parameters, a dynamic mesh refinement is applied to reduce the computational cost. The scanning strategy adopted by the laser is simulated by a path simulator built using MatLab®, while numerical analysis is carried out using ANSYS®, a commercial finite element software. To improve the performance of the simulation, the two codes interact each other to solve the analysis. Temperature distribution and geometrical feature of the molten pool under different process conditions are investigated. Results from the FE analysis provide guidance for setting up the optimization of process parameters and develop a base for further residual stress analysis.

Keywords: selective laser melting, titanium, CAD geometry, nonlinear transient thermal analysis, dynamic mesh refinement, parameters calibration

1. Introduction

Additive manufacturing is a 3D manufacturing process able to produce prototypes directly from a CAD file. Powder bed fusion (PBF) processes were, among others, the first commercialized AM processes. Nowadays, the most important powder bed fusion process is selective

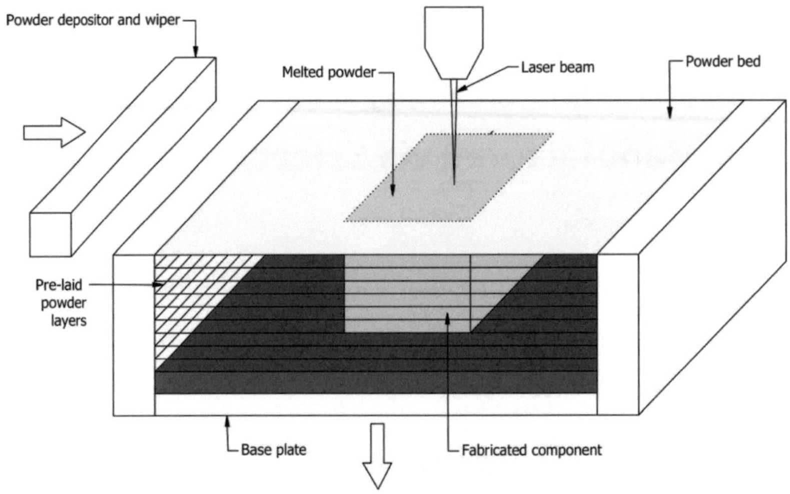

Figure 1. Schematic drawing of SLM process.

laser melting (SLM). Its basic method of operation is schematically shown in **Figure 1** and, generally, all other powder bed fusion processes follow the same basic approach.

The process fuses thin layers (typically 30÷60 μm thick) of metallic powder, which has been spread across the build area using a powder depositor and a leveler (wiper). The building area is enclosed in a chamber filled with inert gas to minimize oxidation and degradation of the powdered material. The base plate is heated in order to maintain the powder and the fabricated component at high temperature. Sometimes, infrared heaters are placed above the build platform to increase the temperature around the part being formed. The temperature within the chamber must be controlled to minimize the laser power requirements of the process (when preheating, less laser energy is required for fusion) and to prevent warping of the part due to non-uniform thermal expansion (curling).

Once the layer has been deposited and adjusted by the wiper, a laser beam is directed onto the powder bed and is moved using galvanometers in such a way that it thermally fuses the material to form the slice cross-section. Surrounding powder remains loose and serves as a support for subsequent layer deposition. After completing a layer, the build platform (base plate) is lowered and a new layer is laid. The beam scans the subsequent slice cross-section and the process repeats until the complete part is built. A cool-down period is typically required to allow the parts to uniformly achieve an adequately low temperature to be handled and exposed to ambient atmosphere. Finally, the parts are removed from the powder bed, loose powder is cleaned off the parts, and further finishing operations, if necessary, are performed.

Since the introduction of PBF, each new technology developer has introduced competing terminology to describe the mechanism by which fusion occurs, with variants of *sintering* and *melting* being the most popular. However, the use of a single word to describe the powder fusion mechanism is problematic as multiple mechanisms are possible. There are four different fusion mechanisms that are present in PBF processes. These include solid-state sintering, chemically-induced binding, liquid-phase sintering, and full melting [1, 2].

Since the attention of this chapter is mainly focused on SLM, the only full melting mechanism will be considered in detail. Full melting is indeed the mechanism most commonly associated with PBF processing of engineering metal alloys. In SLM, the entire region of material subjected to the heat source is melted to a depth exceeding the layer thickness. The thermal energy of subsequent scans of a laser is typically sufficient to remelt a portion of the previously solidified material. As a consequence, this type of melting is very effective at creating well-bonded, high-density structures.

Use of optimum process parameters is extremely important for producing satisfactory parts using PBF processes. Among them, special attention must be paid to the scanning strategy, viz. the movements applied by the laser on the powder surface. The path followed by the laser greatly influences the surface heat distribution, as it is responsible for highly localized temperature peaks. Scanning often occurs in two modes, contour and fill mode, as shown in **Figure 2**.

In contour mode, the outline of the part cross-section is scanned. This is typically done for surface finishing reasons around the perimeter. The rest of the cross-section is then scanned using a raster technique, whereby one axis is incrementally moved across the part being formed and the other axis is continuously swept back and forth. The contour can be scanned

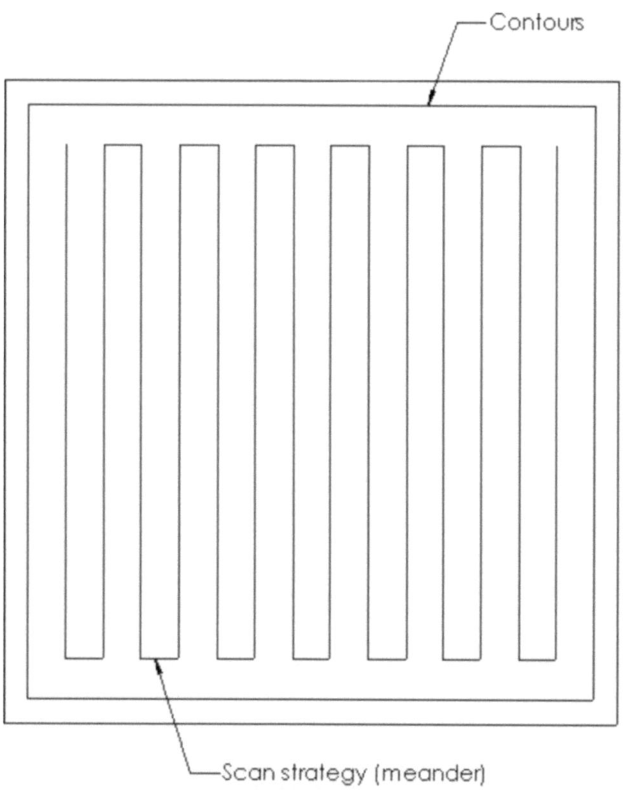

Figure 2. An example of scanning strategy: fill mode and contour mode.

either before or after the cross-section, depending on the surface characteristics of the part being done. Multiple scanning strategies are available for the fill section as shown in **Figure 3**.

Since high thermal gradients result in large residual stresses, a great effort must be made to well define the movement of the heat source on the surface. The choice of the path is not unique and it must be done trying to find the most suitable one depending on the cross-section characteristics. Moreover, the scan strategy rotates at each subsequent layer as it is explained in **Figure 4**.

The rotation helps to balance the temperature of the working area. Despite the rotation, the path increment in horizontal direction remains constant and opposite to the gas flux. Consequently, the working area is kept clean because the melting slags drop far from the loose powder. The user can set the rotation angle. The angle used in this study has been suggested by the machine manufacturer and it is equal to 67°, so the rotation scheme repeats every 180 layers.

Nowadays, SLM specifically permits to manufacture highly customized products that are almost ready to use rather than mere prototypes. An object with very complex shape, which is almost impossible to produce with traditional technologies, can be easily created saving cost and time. Despite the benefit, these manufacturing processes are very problematic to control because of the high number of involved parameters. The numerical simulation helps to reduce the number of experimental trial-and-error tests necessary to optimize the process, minimizing the time and cost of manufacture of the final product while maintaining its quality unmodified. The thermal

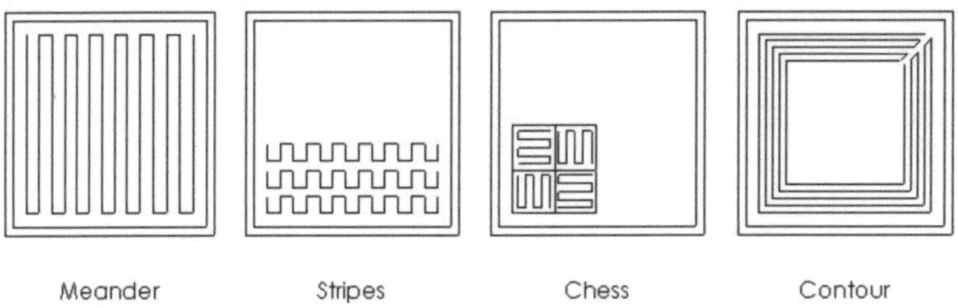

Figure 3. The four different scanning strategies: meander, stripes, chess, and contour.

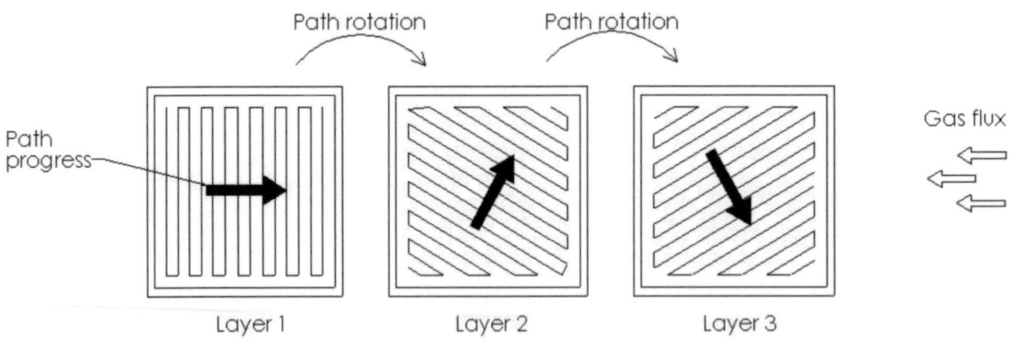

Figure 4. The meander path rotation and the oriented path progress.

behavior of the molten pool is one of the most critical factors influencing the reliability of the part, as it affects geometrical accuracy, material properties, and residual stresses. In addition, the heat exchange between laser and powder is a very complex process that involves a lot of variables. Despite direct measurements of the thermal field are available, this is not enough to fully understand the molten pool behavior. Finite element analysis (FEA) is a powerful tool to gather more information about the process [3].

The first studies about numerical simulation applied to PBF were developed during the 1990s of the last century. In 1998, Williams and Deckard [4] were the first that setup a framework for the numerical analysis applied to PBF. The numerical model was able to study the effects of process parameters on the selective laser sintering (SLS). Afterward, Shiomi and Yoshidome proposed a model where melting and solidifying process could be studied, using FE analysis [5]. In this chapter, the behavior of a molten pool due to a single laser spot is considered. The laser works in pulse mode and the melted part of the powder are assumed to change into a sphere that increases the dimensions after each pulsed irradiation. Fisher and Romano [6] investigated the variation in sintering process using pulse and continuous heat source. They noticed that during continuous wave interaction, the grains are homogeneously heated (the authors use an analogy to distinguish between different heating: they say that with homogeneously heating, the grains are *cooked*), while during pulsed laser interaction, the heating is no longer homogeneous (the grains are *roasted*). As mentioned before, the interaction of laser radiation with powder bed is a very complex mechanism greatly responsible for the mechanical characteristics of the final product. Gusarov et al. made a great effort in developing a numerical model that is able to simulate the heat transfer between laser and powder [7, 8]. It is worth mentioning that all the new models developed for the SLM simulation always refer to the models that have just been developed for the welding process [9] inasmuch SLM can be considered as a series of micro welding processes. Among all the numerical frameworks proposed in the literature, it seems that the most powerful tool for the process simulation is the finite element method. The first example of 3D finite element analysis is the paper of Contuzzi and Campanelli [10]. The aim of this study is to evaluate the temperature evolution in a 3D part being formed with SLM process. The molten liquid phase is considered by introducing the specific latent heat while the thermal properties are kept constant, aiming to reduce the computational cost of the analysis. The model proposed by Kolossov and Boillat [11] instead, allows for the nonlinear behavior of thermal conductivity and specific heat due to the temperature change and phase transformation. Introducing nonlinear behavior for the material increases the reliability of the simulation. However, the measurements of the thermal properties are greatly affected by uncertainty. The thermal properties can be directly measured [12–14] or calculated with thermal models [15]. A more precise thermal conductivity of the powder bed, named effective thermal conductivity, can be calculated using the relation proposed by Dai and Shaw [16]. Their model encompasses the effect of temperature- and porosity-dependent thermal conduction and radiation as well as the temperature-dependent natural convection. Not only material properties but also heat source definitions greatly affect the numerical results. Hashemzadeh and Chen [17] collected a variety of heat distributions that can be used to model the heat exchange. Articles [11] and [18] are an example where the heat source can be easily modeled as a 2D flux applied on the powder surface, neglecting the effect of the laser penetration into the powder. Li and Wang [19] explained how a 3D heat flux can be modeled in order to improve the numerical results related to the molten pool depth. Despite the great accuracy of all the previous models, results coming from the numerical simulations are slightly different from the experimental evidence. This is due to the high complexity of the physics involved in SLM and indeed to a large number of simplifications needed to simulate the process. Hu and Kovacevic [18] tried to reduce the mismatch between numerical and experimental data with a calibration procedure that adjusts the process parameters in order to fit the molten pool dimension retrieved from the simulation with the experimental measurements. It can be noticed from the previous papers that the discretization of the domain is always kept constant so that all the analysis must be applied to microscopic scale in order to keep the computational time low. Patil, Pal et al. [20, 21] explained how the dynamic mesh refinement can be applied to reduce the computational cost needed to solve such problems (like SLM), where different levels of mesh density are required to capture the localized phenomena.

Despite the strong reduction in computational time due to the dynamic mesh refinement, it is not feasible to simulate the thermal field evolution of an entire object, also for very small components. This is due to the extremely large number of spots that are required to melt the cross-section of a single layer. This problem can be partially solved with an analytical solution of the thermal field [22, 23]. Nevertheless, this solution returns the global temperature of a single layer and it is not possible to distinguish between different heat distributions due to the multiple scanning strategies. Therefore, the simulation presented in this chapter is mainly focused on the study of the thermal evolution of a microscale domain. The FEA domain presented here includes only one layer of powder and its dimensions are chosen to reduce as much as possible the number of elements. A model that is able to simulate the thermal evolution of a complete part, taking also into consideration the effect of the scanning strategy, is still an open challenge.

SLM technology is widely used in different domains of the industry, such as aerospace, automotive, and consumer goods. However, the most important industrial application is the medical and surgical field. In this context, SLM is acting a major transformation of the traditional production techniques, more and more surgical implants are fabricated with PBF technologies. Since the industrial applications of SLM are continuously increasing, numerical simulations of the process become fundamental to predict the mechanical properties of the parts starting from the behavior of the thermal field. ANSYS® and ABAQUS® are an example of general purpose software that is widely used for the FE simulation of SLM process. Moreover, the industries are so interested in the new manufacturing possibilities offered by the SLM, so that numerical simulations were no more confined to academic research but became a powerful tool for the companies willing to develop new commercial products. As a result, specific software has launched onto the marketplace, for example, 3DSIM (based on dynamic adaptive mesh refinement [24]), SIMUFACT (based on the inherent strain theory [25, 26]), and NETFABB.

The framework presented in this chapter involves both ANSYS® and MatLab® to perform the FE analysis of a SLM process on a titanium alloy powder. At the beginning, all the process parameters needed for the simulation are collected. Then, the laser path is simulated using MatLab®. This permits the definition of each point of heat application. Their spatial coordinates are imported into ANSYS® to apply the thermal load into the FE model. The performances of the simulation are improved through a tight interaction between MatLab® and ANSYS®. The main analysis environment is ruled by MatLab® and ANSYS®, which is launched in batch mode only when it is needed. Moreover, a dynamic mesh refinement is applied to the model to reduce the computational cost of the simulation. Finally, a calibration procedure is proposed to correct the titanium alloy properties.

2. Process parameters

Thermal residual stresses are greatly affected by the temperature distribution. Moreover, the thermal field is greatly affected by laser characteristics and scanning strategies. Therefore, a proper setup of machines parameters is a key issue in reducing thermal residual stresses. Even if different scanning strategies can be adopted, the meandering path only will be considered in the following as it seems to be the most reliable one, ensuring a uniform thermal field and a low machining time. In this configuration, the laser scans the powder with the trajectory shown in **Figure 2**. The most important process parameters that are related to the different laser scanning strategies are listed below:

- Laser power [150÷500 W]
- Hatch distance [50÷105 μm]
- Point distance [20÷75 μm]
- Path rotation [0÷90°]
- Layer thickness [30÷60 μm]
- Time exposure [30÷70 μs]
- Powder absorbance [0.3÷0.5]

Changing these parameters can lead to different material characteristics, for example, material density, surface roughness, and porosity. All these characteristics are directly responsible for the mechanical properties of the sample. It is important, indeed, to have a powerful tool that is able to predict the thermal field with respect to different laser parameters.

The SLM machine available for this study is a Renishaw® model AM250. The main characteristic of this machine is the pulsed laser technology. The process parameters used in the simulation are collected in **Table 1** and refers to the machine setup.

2.1. Material properties

The most suitable metallic material for surgical implants is Ti-6Al-4 V and the data collected in the subsequent tables always refer to this alloy. Ti-6Al-4 V is a titanium alloy with 6% of

Process parameters	
Laser power (W)	160
Hatch distance (μm)	50
Point distance (μm)	20
Layer thickness (μm)	60
Path rotation (°)	67
Time exposure (μm)	30
Powder absorbance	0.5

Table 1. Process parameters used in the simulation.

aluminum and 4% of Vanadium. It has excellent biocompatibility properties, as well as good mechanical properties [12].

Since the melting and cooling process is governed by nonlinear phenomena, the material properties used in the simulation must be temperature dependent. The parameters needed for the FE thermal analysis are thermal conductivity, density, and specific heat. In addition, for the processes involving phase changes, enthalpy is requested as well to account for the latent heat of the material. Specifically, the enthalpy (H) is related to density (ρ), specific heat (c), and temperature (T) according to Eq. (1):

$$H = \int \rho c(T) dT \tag{1}$$

The thermal properties of Ti-6Al-4 V can be easily found in the technical literature [12, 13]. However, these properties are defined only for the solid bulk state and are not suitable to represent the material behavior in powder form or above the melting point. Regarding the properties of the liquid phase, the following simplifying assumptions are taken:

- The apparent powder density is assumed to be 60% of that of the bulk material [27, 28].
- The powder's thermal conductivity might be calculated from the modified Zehner-Schlunder's equation [15] or from the Dai and Shaw's model [16]. Nevertheless, constants involved in the equation are given in the literature with a high uncertainty; therefore, accurate results are not straightforward. Despite the presence of those analytical models, thermal conductivity is simply supposed to be one order of magnitude less than the corresponding parameter for bulk material. In general, the powder is a worse heat conductor than the solid.
- The numerical model requires the definition of thermal parameters for the whole temperature domain, even though thermal conductivity has no real meaning in liquid and vapor phase. Starting from the consideration that thermal gradients are hindered in the liquid phase (and even more in vapor) since crystal lattices are randomly oriented, a first trial conductivity can be half of the value at the transition point. Moreover, the thermal conductivity is supposed to remain constant through liquid and vapor phase. The lack of reliability caused by these assumptions will be reduced by the calibration procedure.

- A distinction between powder and bulk thermal properties holds only in the solid-phase. Above the melting point, the thermal behavior is the same both for powder and bulk.

As a result, thermal conductivity below melting point is experimentally measured while for high-temperature simplifications apply. Data are shown in **Table 2**.

While the conductivity value is taken from experimental data (or from literature), the enthalpy is calculated from Eq. (1). Variables needed for the equation are collected in **Table 3**.

The integration domain from Eq. (1) is divided into steps, from reference temperature (0°C) to limit temperature (5000°C). Each step corresponds to a different alloy phase: solid, liquid, and vapor. In order to reduce the computational cost, the density is kept constant throughout the temperature domain. The specific heat changes as a function of the temperature, but it is considered constant at each integration step. As a consequence, the enthalpy behavior is linear and can be easily calculated from the equations below.

$$C_{avg} = \frac{C_s + C_L}{2} \quad \text{(average specific heat)} \tag{2}$$

$$C^* = C_{avg} + \left(\frac{L}{T_L - T_S}\right) \quad \text{(specific heat for transition)} \tag{3}$$

$$H_S = \rho C_S (T_S - T_0) \quad \text{(enthalpy at solid temperature)} \tag{4}$$

$$H_L = H_S + \rho C^* (T_L - T_S) \quad \text{(enthalpy at liquid temperature)} \tag{5}$$

$$H_+ = H_L + \rho C_L (T - T_L) \quad \text{(enthalpy above liquid temperature)} \tag{6}$$

Thermal conductivity (W/mK)		
Temperature (°C)	**Solid**	**Powder**
0	6.1874	0.6187
19	6.5660	0.6566
399	12.2620	1.2262
800	18.1490	1.8149
1198	23.4590	2.3459
1499	27.8010	2.7801
1605	29.9134	2.9913
1660	14.9567	14.9567
3265	14.9567	14.9567
3295	7.4784	7.4784
5000	7.4784	7.4784

Table 2. Variation of thermal conductivity with temperature.

Thermal parameters	Solid	Powder
Density (kg/m^3)	4220	2532
Solidus temp (°C)	1605	1605
Liquidus temp (°C)	1660	1660
Vapor temp (°C)	3265	3265
Saturation temp (°C)	3295	3295
Specific heat for solid (J/kgK)	708.8	708.8
Specific heat for liquid (J/kgK)	1000	1000
Specific heat for vapor (J/kgK)	1500	1500
Latent heat of fusion (J/kg)	365,000	365,000
Latent heat of vapor (J/kg)	9,376,200	9,376,200

Table 3. Thermal parameters.

where C_L: specific heat of solid; ρ: density; T_S: solidus temperature; T_L: Liquidus temperature; T_0: reference temperature; T: saturation temperature; and L: latent heat.

Table 4 shows the values of enthalpy calculated with the previous equations. The column named *equation* refers to previously numbered equations used for the calculation.

2.2. Heat source

The heat source can be modeled both as a surface or a volumetric thermal load [17]. In order to keep the computational cost as low as possible, the heat source is considered as a 2D heat flux applied on the surface of the powder bed. The thermal load transferred by the laser is called *laser irradiance* and can be represented as a Gaussian distribution [18]:

$$I = \frac{2AP}{\pi r_{max}^2} \cdot e^{\left(-2\frac{r^2}{r_{max}^2}\right)} \tag{7}$$

Enthalpy (J/m^3)			
Temperature (°C)	**Solid**	**Powder**	**Equation**
0	0	0	
1605	4.8008e + 9	2.8805e + 9	Eq. 3
1660	6.5398e + 9	6.5398e + 9	Eq. 4
3265	1.3312e + 10	1.3312e + 10	Eq. 5
3295	1.4210e + 10	1.4210e + 10	
5000	6.5237e + 10	6.5237e + 10	

Table 4. Variation of enthalpy with temperature.

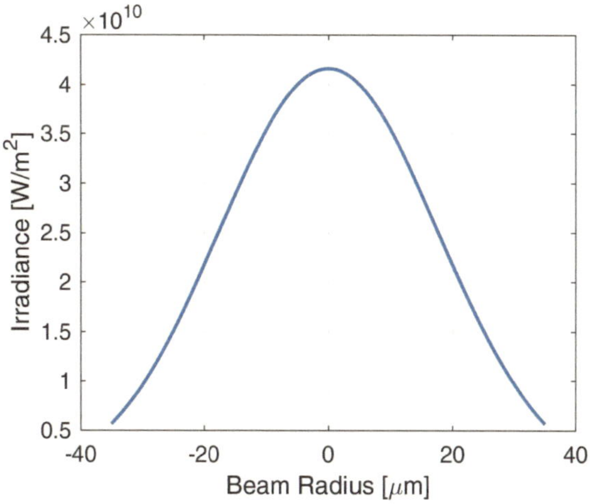

Figure 5. Laser beam irradiance with a Gaussian distribution.

where A: powder absorbance; P: laser powder; and r_{max}: laser beam radius is defined as the radius in which the power density is reduced from the peak value by a factor of e^2 [29].

Figure 5 shows irradiance values of the laser heat source. The laser radius is 35 μm.

3. Path simulation

A good knowledge of the heat source movements is fundamental to develop a reliable simulation that is able to predict the temperature distribution into the working area. The simulation is developed using MatLab® and takes a CAD file storing the geometry of the part in STereo Lithography interface format (STL) as input. This file extension describes volumes through raw unstructured triangulated surfaces (*tessellation*). For each triangle, the unit normal and vertices (ordered by the right-hand rule) are collected using a three-dimensional Cartesian coordinate system. **Figure 6** shows an example of tessellation.

Even if the simulation can analyze any kind of CAD geometry, a simple square block was chosen for the sake of simplicity. Since a non-uniform heat distribution is greatly responsible for thermal residual stresses, different scanning strategies can be used to reduce temperature peaks on the powder bed. Among them, the most suitable paths are: meandering, stripes, chess, and contour (**Figure 3**). The strategy chosen for the simulator is the meandering path, since it is a good trade-off between high deposition rate and low-temperature gradients. Moreover, for further reduction in local temperature peaks, the laser path changes orientation at each layer. Path simulation carried out with MatLab® takes into account all these characteristics. At the beginning, a slicing algorithm is formulated to slice the 3D-geometry into a given number of layers as requested by the real process. Once having the spatial location and orientation of the triangles (from STL files), it is possible to intersect their triangular surfaces with horizontal planes (layers) using geometrical properties. **Figure 7** explains the working principle of the slicing algorithm.

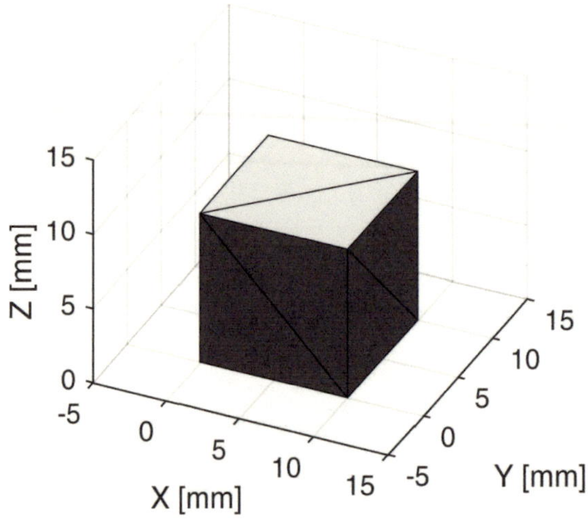

Figure 6. An example of CAD model tessellation.

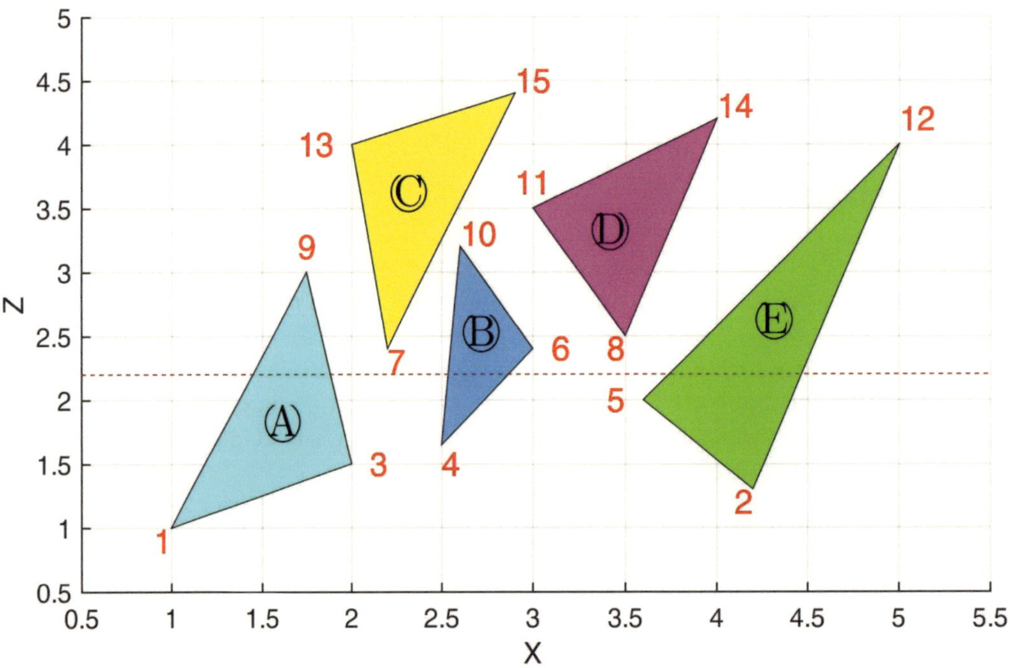

Figure 7. A 2D example of a triangles tessellation.

Instead of a three-dimensional example, the triangles are sketched in 2D-space. The dashed line represents the slicing plane. Vertices are grouped with respect to Z-coordinates as listed in **Table 5**.

The triangles having the Z-coordinate higher than the height of the slicing plane belong to the upper vertices group, while the remaining belongs to the other group. The triangles that share

http://dx.doi.org/10.5772/intechopen.71876

Vertices below the slicing plane	Vertices above the slicing plane
1 → A	9 → A
2 → E	10 → B
4 → B	12 → E
7 → C	14 → D
8 → D	15 → C

Table 5. Vertices are grouped with respect to the slicing plane.

vertices in both groups are those involved in the slicing procedure. Contour related to each cross-section is calculated from the intersection between the plane and the triangle surfaces as it is shown in **Figure 8**. Coordinates of the intersection point are called Z_p and X_p.

As a result, being the contour related to all cross-sections, the meandering path is applied to each layer. Since the path rotates at each layer, meandering slope changes and also the intersection between the path and the contour. Instead of a straightforward rotation of the path, it seems preferable to apply first a geometrical transformation to the contour and then apply the path, keeping its slope horizontal. This indeed allows a simple evaluation of the intersection points. **Figure 9** shows an example that can help to understand the procedure.

Referring to **Figure 9**, a square contour (blue) must be filled with a meandering contour tilted first with a slope of 45° and then 67°. Instead of tilting the path, the contour is rotated (cyan) by an angle corresponding to the desired slope of the path. Then, the contour is stretched so that the meander path is held constant and the hatch distance is kept unitary. Notice that the number of

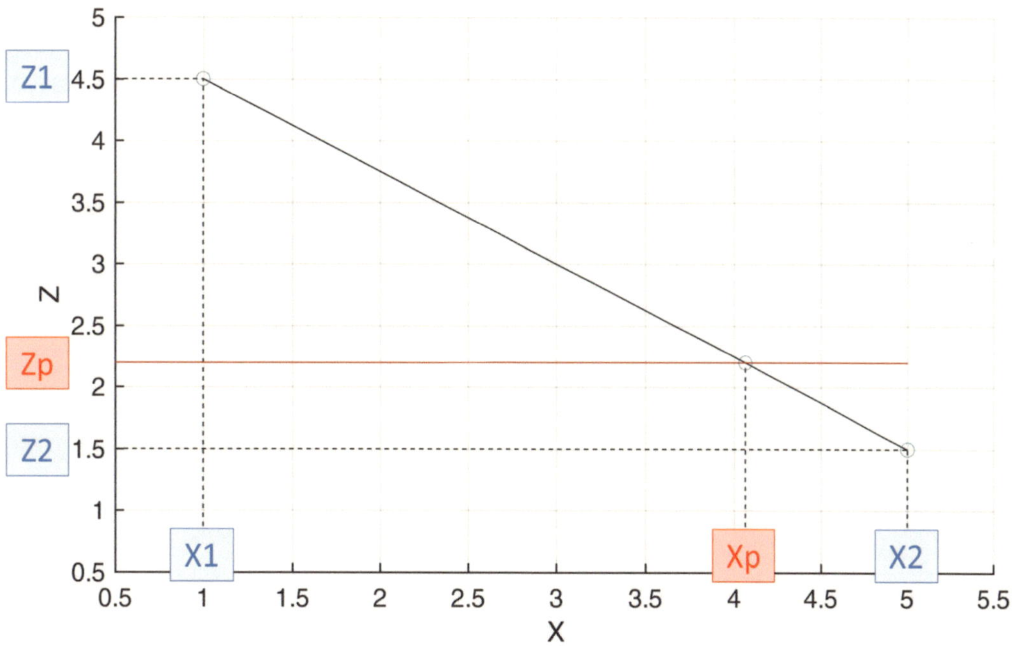

Figure 8. The intersection points are determined through geometrical relations.

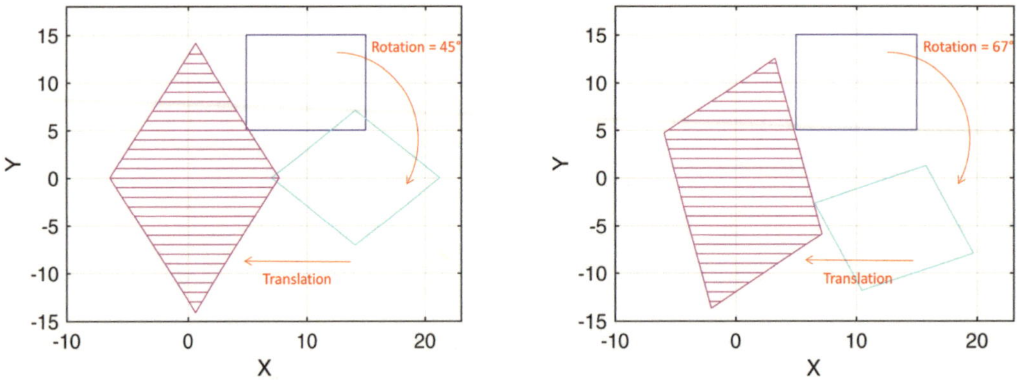

Figure 9. The geometrical transformation applied to cross-section for two different path rotations.

hatch spaces has been previously calculated, and keeping a unitary hatch distance will result in a more reliable intersection procedure.

The result of the slicing procedure is illustrated in **Figure 10**.

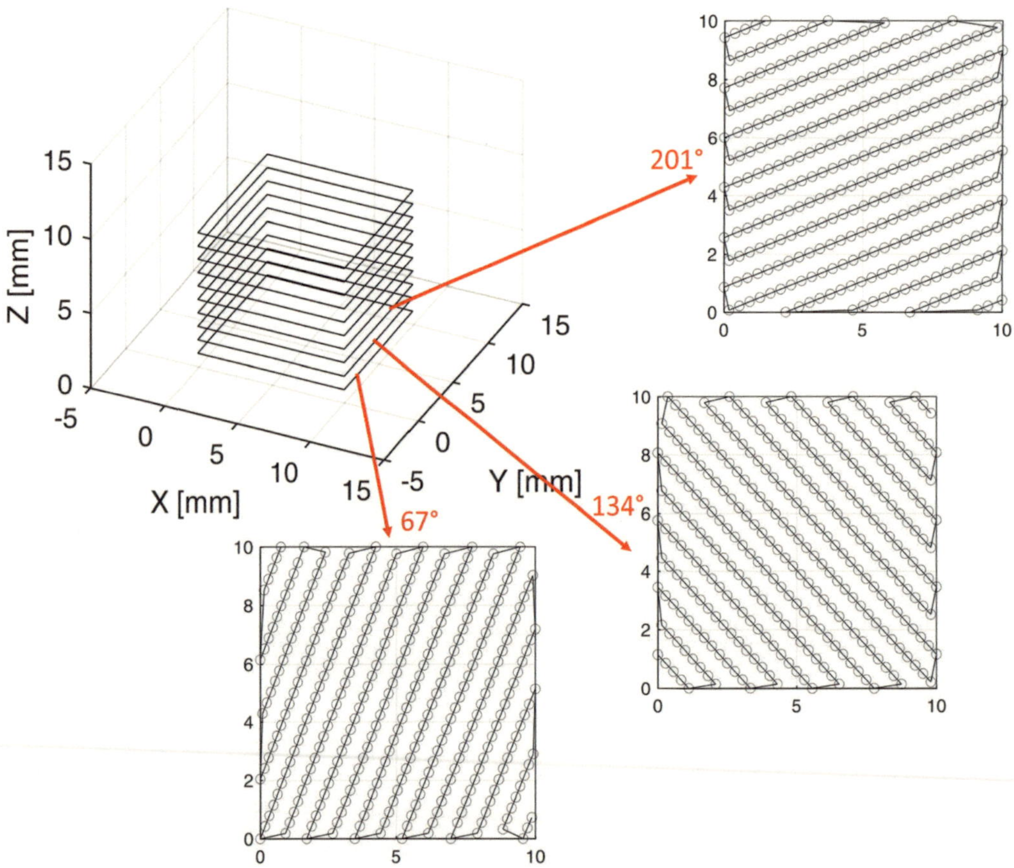

Figure 10. Results from the path simulator.

http://dx.doi.org/10.5772/intechopen.71876

As shown in **Figure 10**, the scanning strategy is defined for each layer with a sequential rotation (multiple of 67°). The dots represent the laser spot locations and the line used to connect them is indicated to emphasize the meandering path. The coordinates of the laser spot are stored into a file and can be used by ANSYS® for the heat source application. Notice that distances between laser spots in **Figure 10** are not in true scale. Meandering paths are shown just for illustrating how the laser moves on the powder surface.

4. Modeling approach

In SLM, the energy needed to melt the powder bed is provided by a laser source. The portion of material under the laser is heated because of the interaction between electromagnetic waves and powder grains. This type of heat transfer occurs in a very short time interval (microseconds) and provokes material modifications due to both phase (liquid and solid) and aggregation (powder and bulk) state changes. When the laser heats the surface, powder grains undergo very rapid heating that melts the material in the localized region surrounding the irradiated spot. After that, the laser is moved forth and the molten pool starts cooling and solidifying. At the end, the material has changed its aggregation state from powder to bulk. Since the path meanders on the surface, the material undergoes multiple reheating processes, sometimes above the melting point.

All previous characteristics would lead to a very complex and cumbersome simulation unless some simplifications are applied to the numerical model. The simulation is formulated taking into consideration all the SLM features, even if they are applied in a simpler way. For example, with the aim of reproducing both phase (solid-liquid-vapor) and aggregation state (bulk-powder) transformations, only material properties are defined, rather than complex thermodynamic models. Applications involving phase change can be approached using ANSYS® through elements with enthalpy property capabilities.

The thermal transient analysis is necessary to take into account the high heating and cooling rate. Moreover, since the laser works in pulsed mode, the analysis is fully solved for each application point. The iterative algorithm forces the analysis to be solved, deleted, and restarted at each step. Consequently, nodal results must be continuously saved and uploaded through a mapping procedure as will be extensively explained later.

4.1. Numerical model

The governing heat transfer equation can be written as:

$$-\left(\frac{\partial q_x}{\partial x}+\frac{\partial q_y}{\partial y}+\frac{\partial q_z}{\partial z}\right)+Q=\rho c\frac{\partial T}{\partial t} \tag{8}$$

where q_x, q_y and q_z are components of heat flow through unit area. According to Fourier's law:

$$q_x=-k_x\frac{\partial T}{\partial x}$$

$$q_y=-k_y\frac{\partial T}{\partial y}$$

$$q_z = -k_z \frac{\partial T}{\partial z}$$

Notice that for isotropic, material thermal conductivity is the same: $k_x = k_y = k_z$.

General formulation of governing differential equation can be obtained substituting Fourier's law component in Eq. (8):

$$\mathrm{div}([k] \cdot \nabla T) + Q = \rho c \frac{\partial T}{\partial t} \tag{9}$$

where $[k] = k[I]$ is the thermal conductivity matrix.

Eq. (9) can be decomposed into a weak formulation [30] as the following system of differential equation of first order in t:

$$[C_{\text{thermal}}]\{\dot{T}(t)\} + [k_{\text{thermal}}]\{T(t)\} = \{F(t)\} \qquad t \in \{0, t'\} \tag{10}$$

A description of the three matrices in Eq. (10) is given below:

i. The thermal stiffness matrix $[k_{\text{thermal}}]$ is expressed as follows:

$$[k_{\text{thermal}}] = \int_V [B_{\text{thermal}}]^T [k][B_{\text{thermal}}] dV + \int_S h[N]^T N ds \tag{11}$$

where $[B_{thermal}]$ is the matrix containing the first derivatives of shape functions. The size of this matrix related to a brick element comprised of eight integration points is 3×8. Once computed, $[k_{thermal}]$ has dimension 8×8. dV denotes the volume of the element. The surface integral is valid when the bulk is exposed to convection boundary conditions (i.e., boundary condition with imposed flux). h is the convective heat transfer coefficient which has been assumed to be 12.5 w/m^2K for Argon [20].

ii. The thermal specific heat matrix $[C_{\text{thermal}}]$ is expressed as follows:

$$[C_{\text{thermal}}] = \int_V [N]^T [N] \, \rho c \, dV \tag{12}$$

where $[N] = [N_1 N_2 N_3 \ldots N_8]$ are the three-dimensional nodal shape functions of size 1×8. Once computed, $[C_{thermal}]$ has dimension 8×8. ρ is the mass density and c is the specific heat.

iii. The thermal flux vector $\{F(t)\}$ is expressed as follow:

$$\{F(t)\} = \int_S (\mathbf{q}(\mathbf{x}, \mathbf{t}) \cdot \widehat{\mathbf{n}}) \cdot [N]^T dS + \int_S h[N]^T T_f \, dS \tag{13}$$

where $\mathbf{q}$ is the input heat flux depending on boundary conditions and $\mathbf{x} = \{x, y, z\}^T$ is the position vector. dS denotes the surface area of the element. The second surface integral in Eq. (13)

is valid only when the convection boundary conditions apply. T_f is the temperature of the environment into the working chamber.

Simulation reliability is subjected to the accuracy of the numerical model. Although geometrical features try to reproduce as much as possible the real SLM environment, simplifications must be taken regarding the boundary and loading conditions in order to reduce the computational cost. The attention is mainly focused on the melting process of one single powder layer, even if the algorithm allows for the simulation of multiple layers. Adding more layers, the number of elements grows as well as the number of spots; hence, the computational cost dramatically increases. As it will be presented in Section 5, dynamic mesh refinement is a powerful way to reduce the number of elements and, therefore, the time needed for the numerical solution, while preserving results accuracy.

The FE model is based on SLM real workspace. The geometry, as it is shown in **Figure 11**, is divided into two regular and constant meshes. The first one is at the surface and it is finer because it simulates the powder bed (1 mm x 0.2 mm x 0.06 mm) where the temperature variations are more important. To reduce the computation time, the base plate

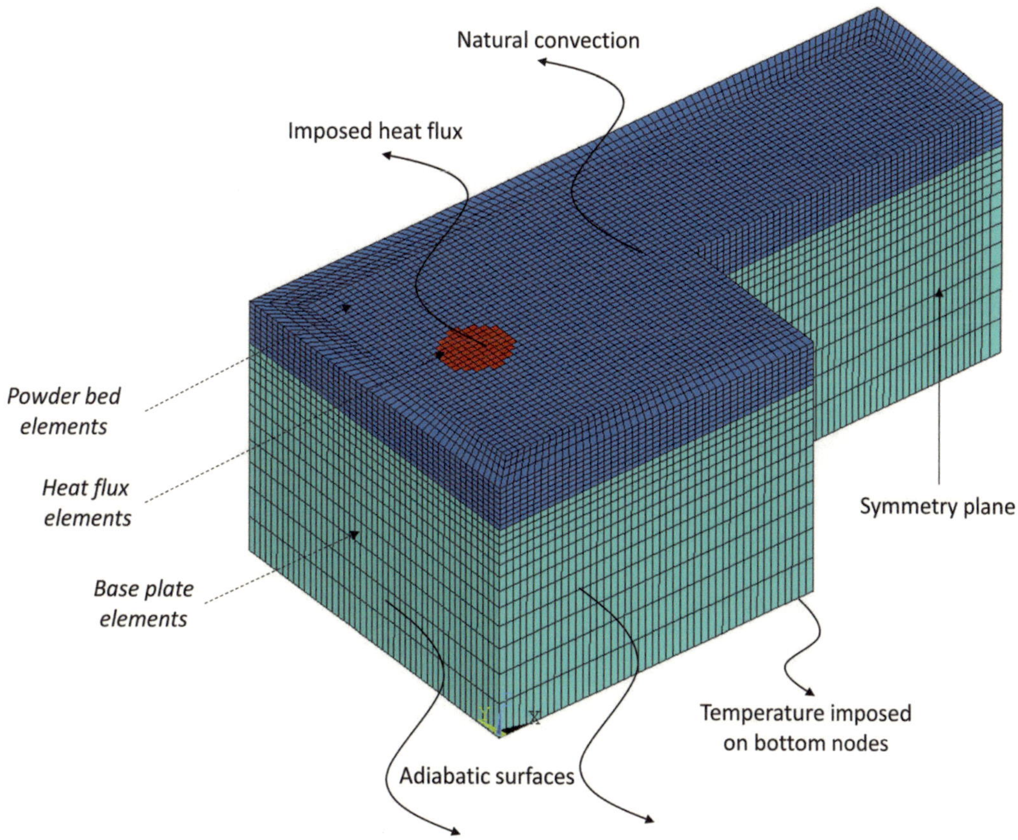

Figure 11. Boundary condition and different material properties: molten pool (red elements circular area on the top), powder bed (blue elements, fine-meshed volume on the top), and base plate (cyan elements, coarse-meshed volume on the bottom).

(1 mm x 0.2 mm x 0.3 mm) is discretized with a coarser mesh. The height must ensure that the bottom border will not interfere with the surface temperature. Mapped mesh guarantees nodal consistency at the interface between powder and base. Convergence analysis has been done to validate the mesh size. Powder elements affected by the heat source, are assigned with different material properties, as it is shown in **Figure 11**.

A mapped mesh employing hexahedral 8-node elements is adopted to reduce the computational cost while maintaining high thermal field resolution. Specifically, thermal brick elements called *SOLID70* with the following characteristics are used:

- Conduction and enthalpy capabilities
- Eight nodes (no mid-edge node capability)
- Applicable to a 3-D transient thermal analysis
- Mapped mesh

Different thermal properties can be associated with the same element type, hence it makes it possible to distinguish the different behavior of powder, base plate, and molten pool. Referring to **Figure 11**, the base plate elements (cyan) are associated with constant thermal properties, as it is supposed that the base plate is not affected by the thermal field. This assumption helps to reduce the non-linearity. Different element properties are also associated with the layer in order to distinguish between the inert powder bed (blue elements) and the grains that undergo the melting process. These elements are depicted in red and represent the dimension of the molten pool. Different thermal properties have just been explained in Section 2.1.

As mentioned before, the algorithm is iterative and the system must be solved at each laser spot application. The diagram in **Figure 12** shows how the solving algorithm is carried out.

4.2. Boundary condition

The system of equations resulting from Eq. (10) can be solved once the prescribed boundary conditions (BCs) have been substituted. In FE thermal analysis, the possible BCs are:

1. Imposed temperature
2. Imposed heat flux
3. Flux due to convection ruled by the temperature difference
4. Flux due to radiation ruled by the fourth power of the absolute temperature

Boundary conditions depend on how the system interacts with the external environment:

i. Top surface:

   The working chamber is filled with Argon to reduce the alloy powder oxidation. Natural convection applies overall on the top surface, apart from the localized area where the

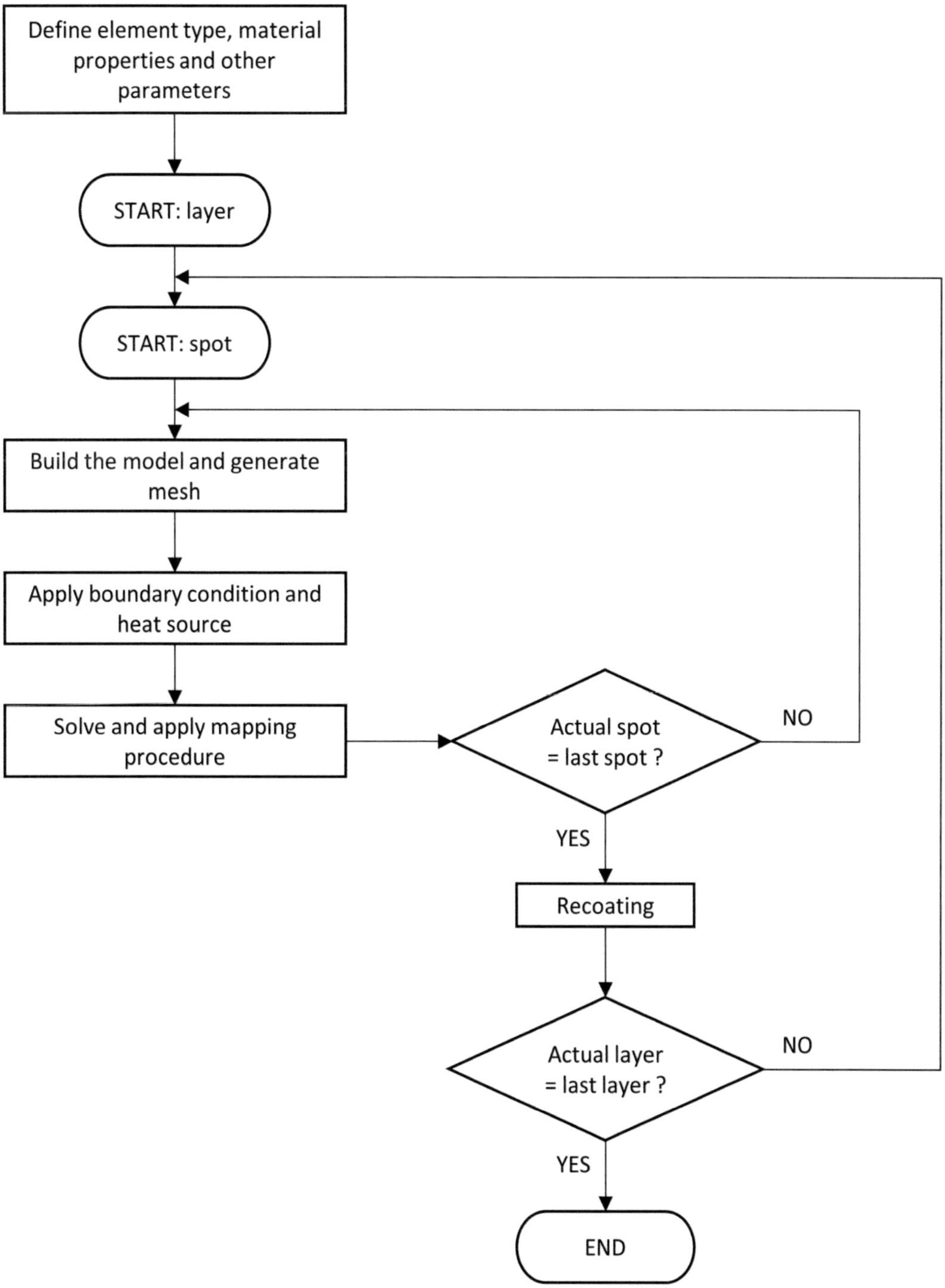

Figure 12. A flow chart representing the main algorithm.

laser heat flux is imposed. Since the emitting radiation flux makes the analysis highly nonlinear, its effect is not considered here. To solve this problem, an empirical relationship has been proposed [9, 18], which combines the effect of radiation and convection into a *lumped* heat transfer coefficient.

ii. Lateral surfaces:

Since the powder conductivity is very low, lateral surfaces can be considered as adiabatic, hence the heat flux imposed is equal to zero ($\mathbf{q}(\mathbf{x}, t) = 0$).

iii. Bottom surface:

In SLM machines, the base plate is heated between 80°C and 130° C, depending on the machine model. Bottom nodes are constrained with imposed temperature or with convection conditions. In this work, the bottom surface is constrained with convection boundary condition. As a consequence, a convection coefficient must be chosen in order to reproduce the convective exchange conditions into the base plate.

BC applied to the numerical model is summarized in **Figure 11**.

Not only boundary conditions, but also initial conditions (ICs) are requested to solve the numerical model. Initial conditions can be imposed setting up a starting temperature for all the nodes. These temperatures are used in transient solutions as the first step temperatures, hence at a time equal to zero:

$$T(\mathbf{x}, t = 0 \ldots t') = T_0(\mathbf{x}) \tag{14}$$

Moreover, since transient solution occurs at each cycle, initial condition must also be set at the beginning of each load step. It follows that initial condition applied to load step *n* are the nodal temperature obtained from the solution at step *n-1*.

4.3. Mapping procedure

Element undergoing phase change must be continuously updated with different material properties to simulate the melting and cooling process. When the average temperature of an element is higher than the melting point, the element is provided with different material properties that allow tracking the molten pool behavior. ANSYS® cannot easily change material properties while the transient solution is running, not even using restart options. Therefore, it is mandatory to solve the analysis before modifying material properties. During post-processing, the temperatures of each element are analyzed and the material properties are changed accordingly.

The iterative algorithm helps to keep the analysis simple, even if it requires the element properties to be deleted at the end of each iteration so that they must be continuously saved and resumed at the beginning of the next iteration. Moreover, the mesh and, hence, the element spatial location are not constant throughout the iteration due to the dynamic mesh refinement (see Section 5). In fact, the FE environment is rebuilt iteratively with different element densities depending on the laser location, as it is shown in **Figure 13**.

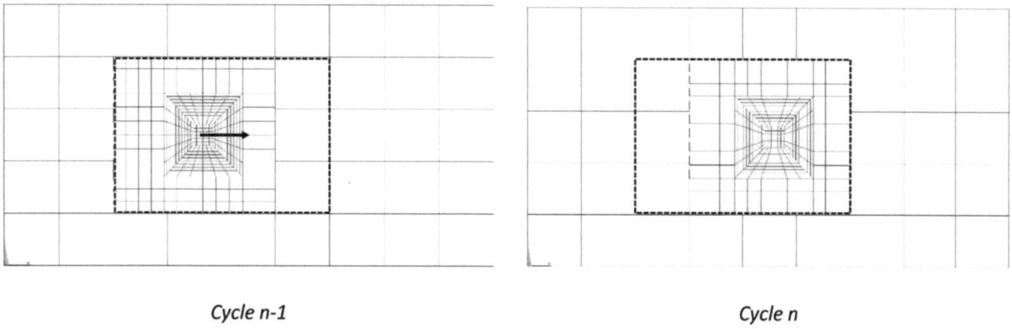

Figure 13. Comparison between OLD_MESH and NEW_MESH.

OLD_MESH and NEW_MESH refer to listed mesh entities. Each row of the list contains elements and nodes tracking number, their spatial coordinates, and the related properties.

The procedure able to assign correctly the temperature and material properties between two different mesh environments is called mapping procedure and is carried out in sequence by MatLab® and ANSYS®. A mapping algorithm is a useful tool that is able to save nodal temperatures from the previous load step, evaluate and assign material type with respect to the element average temperature, and finally, restore the data in the subsequent iteration as initial conditions. To avoid misunderstanding, it is worth noticing the difference between nodal and element properties: temperatures are the values assigned to nodes, while the material number is assigned to the elements. Due to ANSYS® programming language, different thermal behaviors can be assigned to the same element type using material numbers. This is the reason why in this work the expression material properties has been used with the same meaning as thermal properties.

The flowchart presented in **Figure 14** helps to understand the mapping algorithm.

At the beginning, the elements and nodes are listed by ANSYS® in a file with the related material number and temperature. This occurs in the post-procedure step related to the n cycle (NEW_MESH). The file is imported into MatLab® and compared with the previous mesh file, just saved before from the n-1 cycle (OLD_MESH). Referring to **Figure 13**, elements and nodes are compared with respect to their spatial location and divided into two groups: common and uncommon entities. The dashed squares in **Figure 13** highlight the difference between common and uncommon mesh.

Data coming from the previous analysis (step n-1) are assigned to the next one (step n) regardless of the grouped entities. Since the common elements and nodes share the same spatial location, the properties are simply transferred from the OLD_MESH to the NEW_MESH. The mapping algorithm takes the (element and node) spatial coordinates from OLD_MESH and searches the corresponding location in NEW_MESH (notice that the reference point for the element localization is the centroid). The mapping based on spatial coordinates is needed as the common entities share the same location but not the same tracking number because of the different meshes. Consequently, the temperatures and material numbers are transferred to NEW_MESH and can be simply assigned as the initial condition with respect to the entities number.

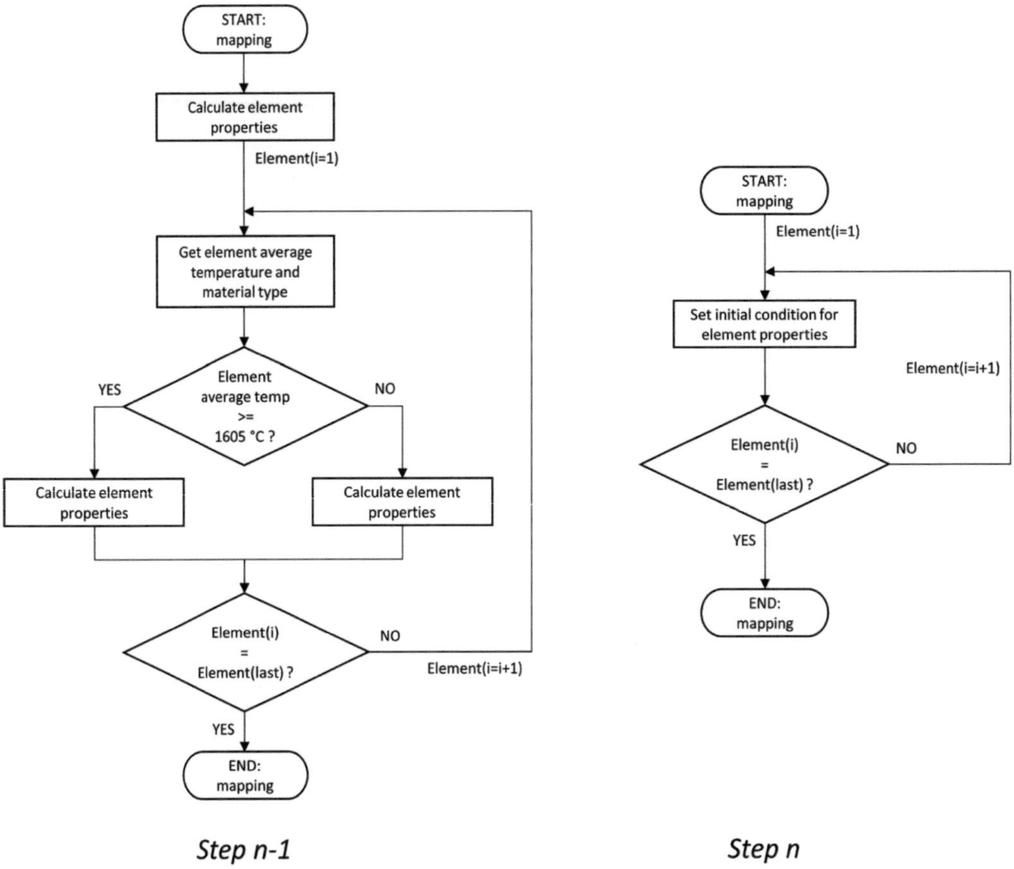

Figure 14. A flowchart illustrating the mapping procedure between two subsequent spots.

Regarding the uncommon entities, their properties cannot be directly transferred to the model because there is a spatial mismatch between the two meshes. The solution is to perform an interpolation. The elements and nodes locations from OLD_MESH are the input values, while the NEW_MESH entities are the target. The interpolation scheme scans all the elements (nodes) in the NEW_MESH, searching for the location that suits better the elements (nodes) belonging to the OLD_MESH. When the best solution is found, the properties can be interpolated between the two meshes. A different interpolation scheme is applied for temperature and material properties. The material number is assigned to the target with respect to the nearest OLD_MESH element and no interpolation is needed. However, the temperatures are assigned to target nodes with a more complicated scheme: not only the nearest node from OLD_MESH is chosen, but also a group of surrounding nodes that properly fit the target. Therefore, the temperature is assigned by means of an interpolation scheme that can be performed on a surface (2D interpolation) or on a volume (3D interpolation) regardless of the precision requested in the analysis. Finally, the interpolated value can be transferred to NEW_MESH and used for the initial condition.

The framework for the mapping procedure requests a lot of time for being set up, because it needs a strong interaction between ANSYS® and MatLab®. MatLab® is used for grouping the entities and for mapping the common entities. ANSYS® is chosen for the uncommon nodes taking advantage of the in-built powerful interpolation algorithm. Despite the complexity, a mapping method based on common and uncommon entities guarantees a strong reduction in the computational cost. The bottleneck of a traditional mapping procedure is the time-consuming interpolation algorithm. With this solution, the interpolation is applied only to a limited number of elements and not to the entire domain.

5. Mesh refinement

FEA is a useful tool to return an approximation of physics variables. Obviously, the computation time is a decisive factor to make numerical simulations competitive with respect to trial-and-error experiments. Traditionally, the bottleneck of a transient FEA is the time requested to compute the temperature field at each laser beam position. This gets even worse considering nonlinear material properties, the high amount of load steps, and elements number. In fact, every load step is divided into sub-steps to satisfy transient time integration rules. Consequently, the factor mainly responsible for the prolonged simulation time is the amount of elements and sub-steps; thus, in order to minimize the computational cost, this must be reduced as much as possible.

Suppose that the model has been built applying a uniform mapped mesh to the entire domain. Moreover, the mesh density has been increased as much as possible since FEM can predict more accurate results when the number of elements is high. Generally, it is often recommended to increase the elements density in the neighborhood of a certain zone where the results are requested to be more accurate. A typical example is when the stress concentration factor of a shouldered shaft subjected to an axial force needs to be determined. In such a case, the elements are concentrated in the vicinity of the fillet in order to obtain more reliable results.

However, the simulation time is proportional to the elements number and expected to increase enormously. One possible solution to overcome this long computing time is to use the dynamic mesh refinement (DMR) approach. It involves an independent mesh refinement of multiple sub-domains. This strategy allows to further refine, independently, the meshes in a hierarchic manner to reach a higher resolution.

It is mainly composed of two parts:

- Mesh refinement: increase element density in a region while having a coarse mesh in the remaining domain.
- Dynamic: the mesh is dynamically adapted according to the problem's nature, e.g., boundary conditions, constitutive laws or geometry.

We will adopt a dynamic mesh refinement so as to adjust the local mesh refinement to the position of the laser spot. This has the great advantage of solving load steps with much fewer elements, hence the simulation time will benefit too. The dynamic part is a priority in this case, since there is a need to iteratively update the mesh at the end of each load step according to the laser spot position. The mesh can be rearranged in many ways; one option is to divide the mesh into different levels of refinement. As shown in **Figure 15**, three levels of increasing refinement degree have been implemented, namely level 1,2, and 3.

There are essentially two methods in order to build the mesh with different refinement levels, viz. *bottom-up* and *top-down* approaches. The former builds the entire domain starting with the coarsest mesh (level 1) and subsequently digs and removes the elements in order to generate a mesh of level 2 and so on for all the refinement levels. The latter method differs inasmuch as the finest mesh is built at the beginning and the remaining meshes are generated accordingly. ANSYS® does not let the user modify the mesh once it is created, thus the second method was preferred over the first one.

5.1. Bonded contact technique

In order to impose discontinuous mesh levels to work properly, there is a need to connect the two parts to restore the continuity of the field variable. As it can be seen from **Figure 15,** mesh level 2 and 3 do not share the same nodes; hence, there is no mesh continuity between the two parts. Mesh compatibility was intentionally lost in order to further reduce the number of elements outside the heat-affected zone (HAZ). As a matter of fact, there are two main techniques to ensure continuity between incompatible meshes: bonded contact and constraint equations. Since the latter introduces additional constraint equations thus increasing the computational cost and the memory request, DMR based on bonded contact is preferred. The state of these contact elements never changes throughout the simulation, whereby not introducing additional sources of nonlinearity.

DMR requires an additional routine that permits data transfer from the previous mesh to the newly created and adapted mesh, as it has been explained in Section 4. **Figure 16** shows the

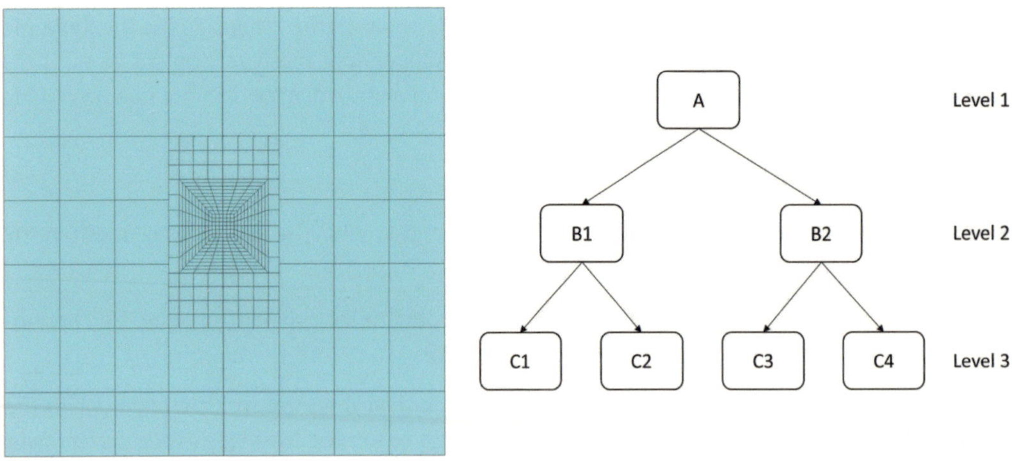

Figure 15. An example of dynamic mesh refinement approach.

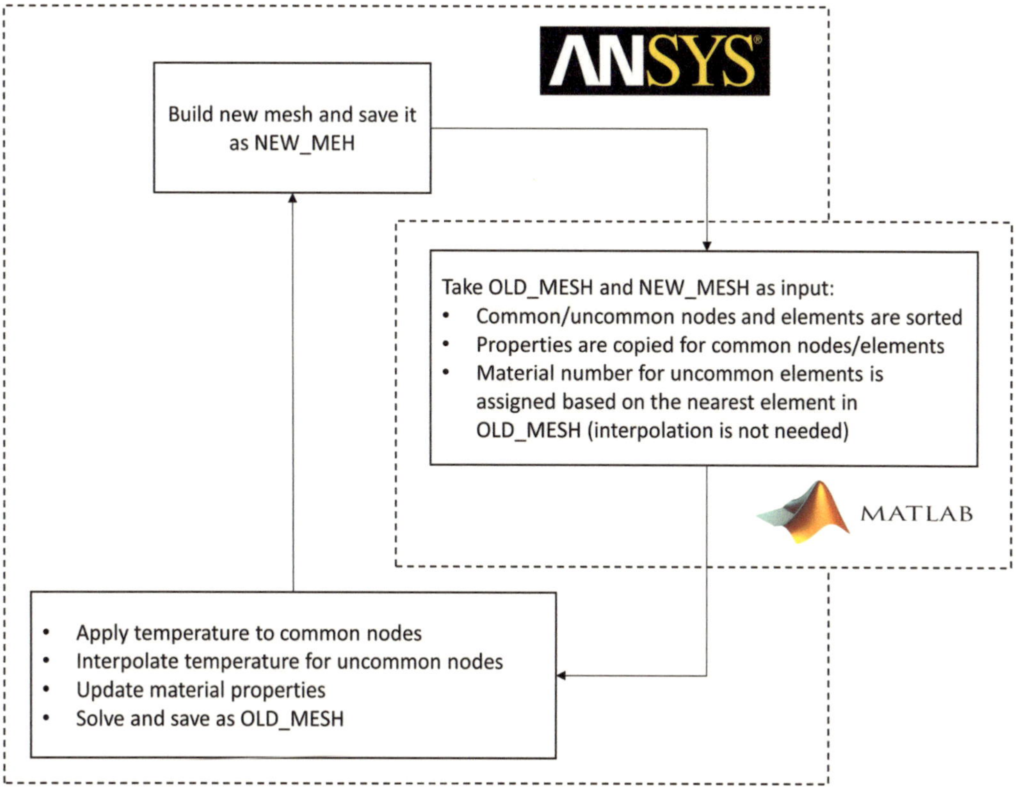

Figure 16. A flow chart for the mesh refinement procedure.

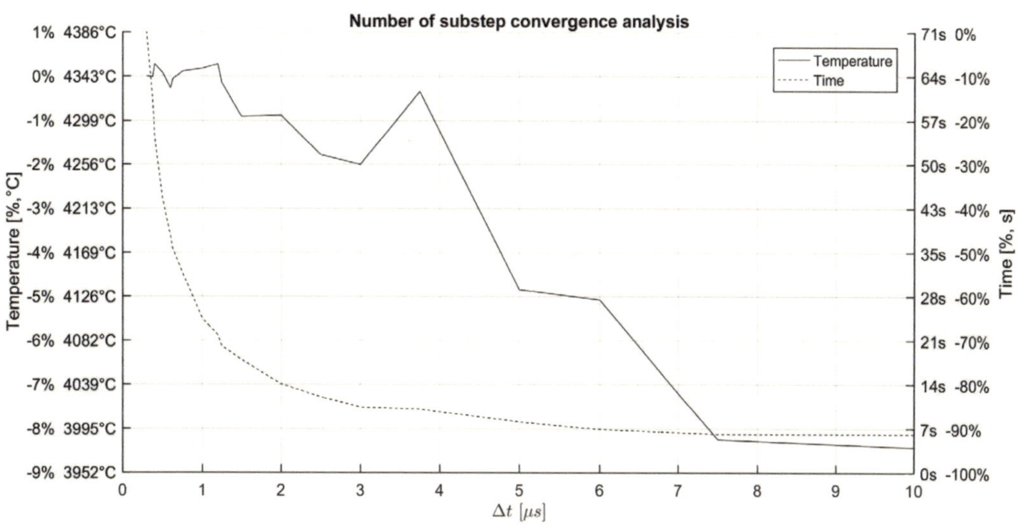

Figure 17. Time consumption and maximum temperature trend.

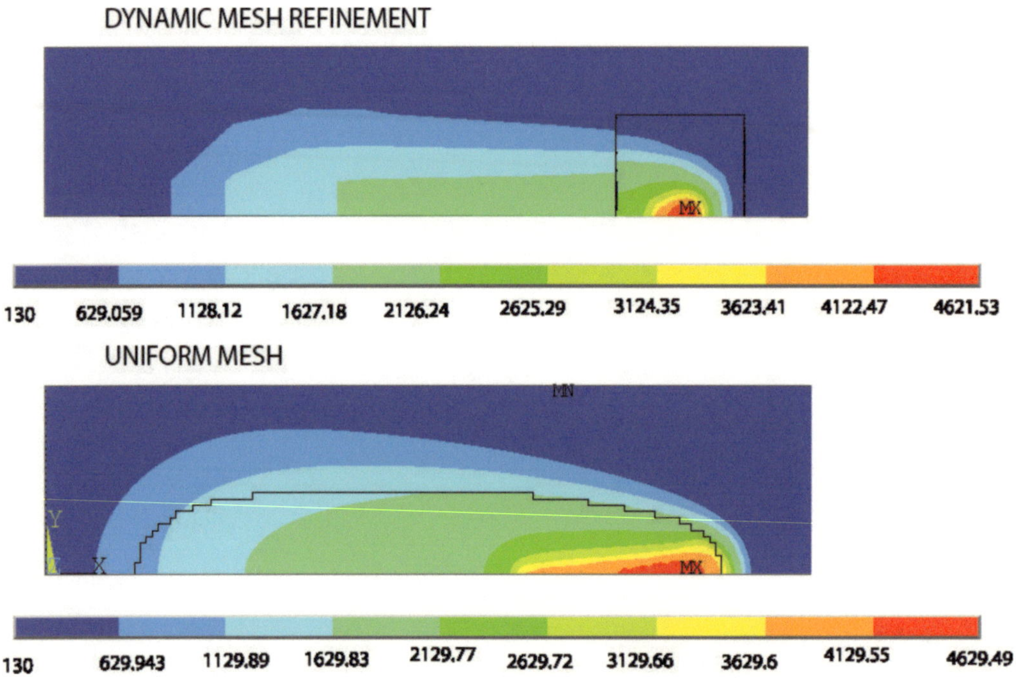

Figure 18. Comparison between the constant mesh and the dynamic mesh refinement.

flowchart related to the DMR procedure. Moreover, it helps to understand how the mapping procedure is matched to well-fit the DMR requirements.

At the beginning, the ANSYS® simulation of the first laser spot is solved and data including mesh and nodal temperature are stored in the external file OLD_MESH. Subsequently, the spot position is moved and the mesh is updated and saved as NEW_MESH. At this point, ANSYS® stops working and MatLab® ad-hoc procedure will take OLD_MESH and NEW_MESH as inputs. The routine will sort nodes as common and uncommon and will return the information

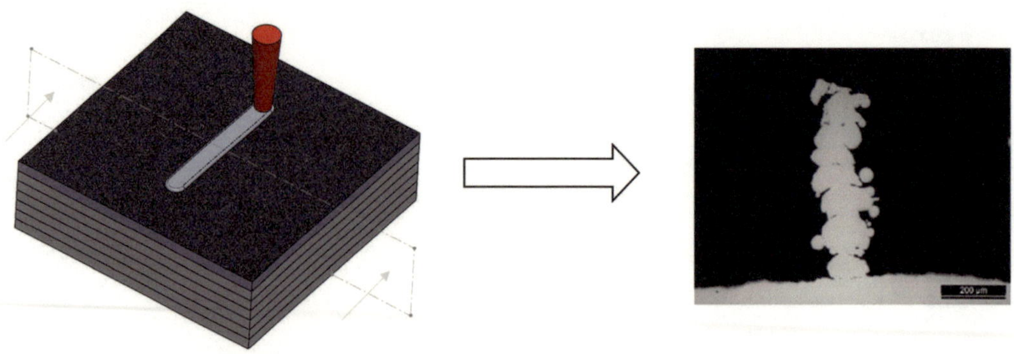

Figure 19. Micrograph of a single molten seam.

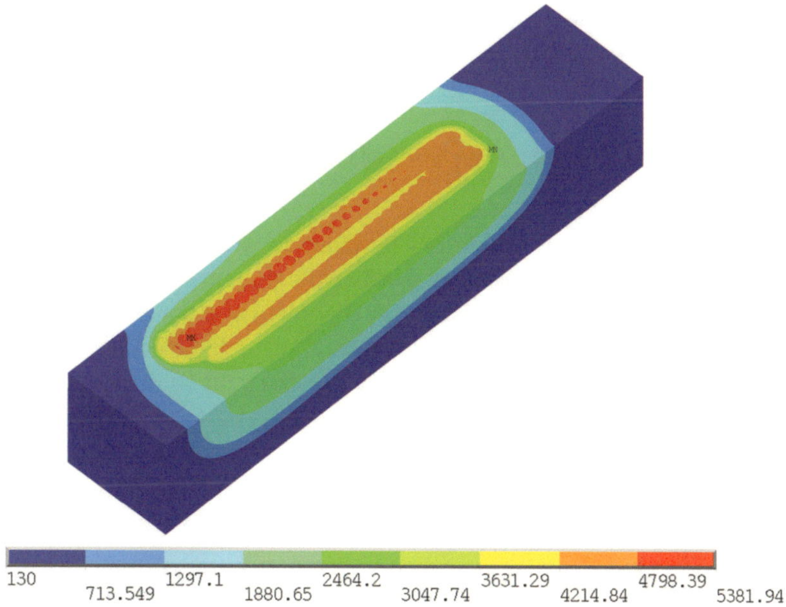

Figure 20. Thermal behavior of the molten pool.

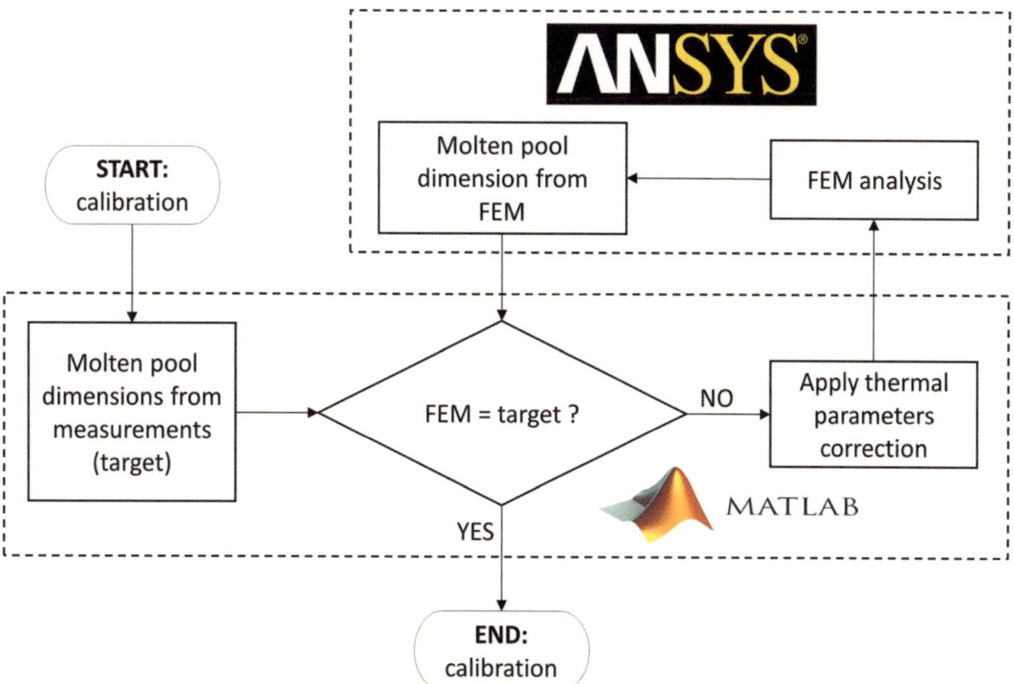

Figure 21. A flow chart for the calibration procedure.

to ANSYS®. At this point, the temperature field of the previous mesh can be applied to the new mesh as an initial condition in the following way:

- Common new nodes will have the same temperature as the old ones
- Uncommon new nodes will have an interpolated temperature from the old ones due to the *MOPER APDL command.

As a result, the simulation time dropped from 15 minutes/spot to 71 seconds/spot reducing the calculation time by 92%. As already mentioned before, the main parameter, which greatly affects the simulation time, is the number of substeps. The optimal value thereof was found through a convergence analysis based on the plot shown in **Figure 17**. It can be noted that an increment in the time step size Δt has a much more pronounced effect on the solution time rather than on maximum nodal temperature (a measure of the solution accuracy). A reasonable trade-off between accuracy and simulation time is a time step size of 3 μs, allowing for 1% error in maximum temperature estimation and a computation time reduction of 80%. It is worth noting that the overall time reduction, due to mesh refinement and time step size reduction, is equal to 98.5%.

The uniform mesh model and the one implementing DMR was tested applying a laser beam on a straight line and the results are shown in **Figure 21**. It can be seen that the temperature scale has only some little negligible variations. The DMR model well represents the physical phenomena and is a trade-off between result accuracy and computation time.

6. Calibration

It has been proven that the computational performances can be strongly enhanced using a simplified numerical model. Nevertheless, results are greatly affected by the lack of accuracy due to several simplifications applied to the model. A calibration procedure is necessary to reduce this issue: the material properties and the boundary conditions can be modified trying to fit numerical results with experimental data. The comparison is based on the molten pool dimension measured from a solidified seam. Moreover, since only a single seam is needed for the calibration, the geometrical domain can be halved along the symmetry plane, saving computational cost. The main reason for the calibration is that ANSYS® does not consider elements which behave as *liquid* elements. The only way to simulate melting and cooling is to change the material properties and in particular thermal conduction and enthalpy, even though conduction does not apply for liquids.

As a consequence, the thermal properties are not well-defined for temperatures above the melting point. In this situation, a convective parameter should be used. This consideration permits the change of the parameters as needed, trying to simulate the convective behavior with a fictitious conduction parameter. The calibration procedure aims to adjust the thermal properties (only above the melting point) whereby fitting the molten pool size to the experimental data. The parameters adjusted by the calibration are enthalpy and thermal conductivity: the enthalpy is modified to control the temperature field while the conductivity is mainly responsible for the size of the molten pool. Specifically, metallographic inspections, as shown in **Figure 19**, are used to estimate width and depth of the molten pool.

Figure 18 shows a single molten seam obtained overlapping multiple layers. The seam was melted using the process parameters listed in **Table 1**. It has been cut and analyzed in order to gather information about the width and depth of the molten pool. Measured values are:

- Width = 183 ± 38 μm
- Depth = 107 ± 38 μm

The deviation related to measurements is mainly related to the narrow geometry and tiny dimensions of the object. Its width is only 4-5 times larger than the dimensions of the metal powder particles; therefore, the profile is not regular. It represents the minimum thickness that can be obtained with a single scan of the laser beam on the powder bed. Notice from **Figure 19** that the molten seam undergoes the re-melting process with the application of successive layers and therefore the depth is not a reliable parameter. Nevertheless, the object is helpful in order to evaluate the real width of the molten pool.

6.1. Calibration results

Due to the uncertainty related to the depth, only the molten pool width is taken into account, while the former issue will be addressed in future work. At the beginning, a trial simulation is carried out to check how the temperature field is sensitive to the parameters change. A directly measured thermal field is not available for this work; hence, the comparison is done with respect to results retrieved from the literature [20]. The enthalpy is indeed modified to keep the thermal field under control. New values for enthalpy are shown in **Table 6**. Only the last enthalpy value is modified increasing the specific heat for vapor by a factor of 10. This helps to decrease the maximum nodal temperature.

The thermal behavior of molten pool is shown in **Figure 20**, which gives an idea about how elevated is the temperature of the zone irradiated by the laser.

This is due to the fact that the molten pool width is narrower than the experimental data and the conductivity needs to be increased. The calibration is, in a nutshell, an iterative algorithm that changes the conductivity with a trial factor as long as the numerical data well reproduce the experimental measurement. The algorithm involves MatLab® and ANSYS® as it is shown in the diagram presented in **Figure 21**.

The correction factor for conductivity is shown in **Table 7**. Notice that the correction is applied only to those values above the melting temperature.

Results coming from calibration are shown in **Figure 22**.

Enthalpy (J/m^3)		
Powder	**Solid**	**Powder**
5000	5.2448e + 11	5.2448e + 11

Table 6. Calibrated value for enthalpy.

Thermal conductivity (W/mK)		
Temperature (°C)	**Solid**	**Powder**
1660	14.9567*5	14.9567*5
3265	14.9567*5	14.9567*5
3295	7.4784*5	7.4784*5
5000	7.4784*5	7.4784*5

Table 7. Calibrated value for thermal conductivity.

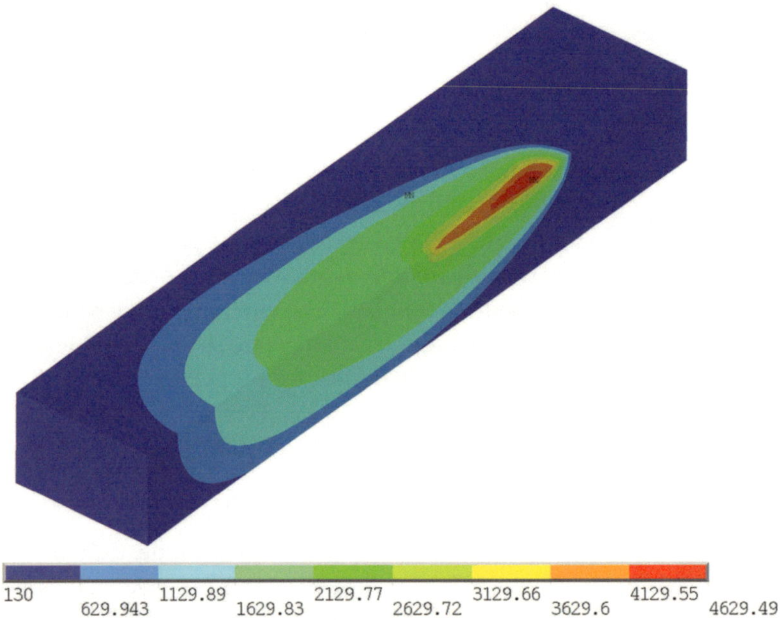

Figure 22. Molten pool behavior with calibrated parameters.

7. Results

After parameters calibration, the simulation of a SLM process can be carried out. Because of the high number of laser spots, the simulation must be applied only to a small portion of the powder bed. Only one layer is considered and the adopted laser scanning strategy is the meander path. In order to gather information about the thermal field evolution into the bed powder, the time evolution of the temperature field is sampled on a spot selected as a temperature probe. The corresponding results are shown in **Figure 23**. The small window shows powder bed and meandering path. The black point along the meandering path represents the probe, which the temperature graph refers to.

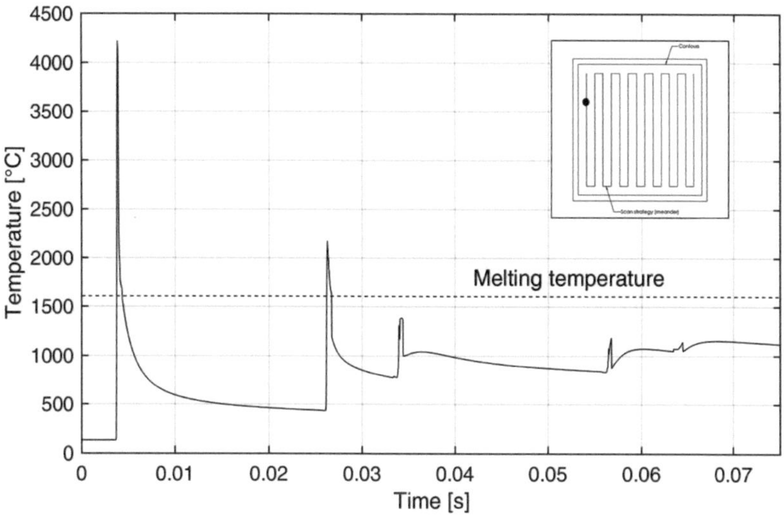

Figure 23. Temperature development of a point at the surface of the powder bed.

A very narrow temperature peak can be noticed in **Figure 23**. The highest peak is due to the heat source applied directly onto the probe. The other peaks are related to the reheating of the solidified area as the heat source is applied on the surrounding areas. In this example, the scan element is subject to remelting only once. The melting and cooling process occurs with very high gradients and this is the main source of the thermal residual stresses affecting the as-built parts.

8. Conclusions

A three-dimensional FE model is developed using ANSYS® to study the thermal behavior of the molten pool in building a single layer via SLM process. At the beginning, the scanning strategy adopted by the laser is simulated by a path simulator built using MatLab. Then, the FE analysis framework is extensively explained with special regard to thermal properties applied to the model. Dynamic mesh refinement is used to reduce the computational cost of the simulation. Special care is taken in devising a mapped mesh discretization scheme, ensuring that the traveling subdomain centered on the laser spot changes as less as possible the mesh of the remaining subdomain. Finally, a calibration procedure is applied to fit the numerical results with the experimental measurements. The simulation results agree reasonably well with experimental and literature results and give some insight into the mutual interaction among the process parameters. Useful indications can be gained to optimize the process parameters, to estimate the adhesion between the layers, and to identify the best building strategy. This model can be further developed by incorporating the nodal temperature field into a structural analysis for predicting the resulting stress and strain field.

Acknowledgements

This work is part of the *FAMAC Research Project*, co-sponsored by *Eurocoating S.p.A.* and *Provincia Autonoma di Trento* (Regional Public Authority).

Author details

Dario Pitassi[1], Enrico Savoia[1], Vigilio Fontanari[1], Alberto Molinari[1], Valerio Luchin[2], Gianluca Zappini[2] and Matteo Benedetti[1]*

*Address all correspondence to: matteo.benedetti@unitn.it

1 University of Trento, Department of Industrial Engineering, Trento, Italy

2 Eurocoating S.p.A., Pergine Valsugana, Trento, Italy

References

[1] Gibson I, Rosen DW, Stucker B. Additive Manufacturing Technologies. Rapid Prototyping to Direct Digital Manufacturing. 1st ed. New York: Springer; 2010. DOI: 10.1007/978-1-4419-1120-9

[2] Kruth J-P, Mercelis P, Van Vaerenbergh J, Froyen L, Rombouts M. Binding mechanism in selective laser sintering and selective laser melting. Rapid Prototyping Journal. 2005;**11**(1): 26-36. DOI: 10.1108/13552540510573365

[3] Zeng K, Pal D, Stucker B. A review of thermal analysis methods in laser sintering and selective laser melting. In: 23rd Annual International Solid Freeform Fabrication Symposium - An Additive Manufacturing Conference, SFF 2012. 2012. pp. 796-814

[4] Williams JD, Deckard CR. Advances in modelling the effects of selected parameters on the SLS process. Rapid Prototyping Journal. 1998;**4**(2):90-100. DOI: 10.1108/13552549810210257

[5] Shiomi M, Yoshidome A, Abe F, Osakada K. Finite element analysis of melting and solidifying processes in laser rapid prototyping of metallic powders. International Journal of Machine Tools and Manufacture. 1999;**39**(2):237-252. DOI: 10.1016/S0890-6955(98) 00036-4

[6] Fischer P, Romano V, Weber HP, Kolossov S. Pulsed laser sintering of metallic powders. Thin Solid Films. 2004;**453**:139-144. DOI: S0040609003016729

[7] Gusarov AV, Yadroitsev I, Bertrand P, Smurov I. Heat transfer modelling and stability analysis of selective laser melting. Applied Surface Science. 2007;**254**(4):975-979. DOI: S0169433207011907

[8] Gusarov AV, Smurov I. Modeling the interaction of laser radiation with powder bed at selective laser melting. Physics Procedia. 2010;**5**:381-394. DOI: S1875389210004918

[9] Vinokurov VA. Welding Stresses and Distortion: Determination and Elimination. 1st ed. London, UK: British Library Lending Division; 1977. 317 p. DOI: 9780853501664

[10] Contuzzi N, Campanelli SL, Ludovico AD. 3D finite element analysis in the selective laser melting process. International Journal of Simulation Modelling. 2011;**10**(3):113-121. DOI: 10.2507/IJSIMM10(3)1.169

[11] Kolossov S, Boillat E, Glardon R, Fischer P, Locher M. 3D FE simulation for temperature evolution in the selective laser sintering process. International Journal of Machine Tools and Manufacture. 2004;**44**(2):117-123. DOI: 10.1016/j.ijmachtools.2003.10.019

[12] Boyer R, Collings EW, Welsch G. Materials Properties Handbook: Titanium Alloys. Novelty, OH, USA: ASM International; 1994. 1169 p

[13] Boivineau M, Cagran C, Doytier D, Eyraud V, Nadal M-H, Whiltan B, Plottlacher G. Thermophysical properties of solid and liquid Ti-6Al-4V (TA6V) alloy. International Journal of Thermophysics. 2006;**27**(2):507-529. DOI: 10.1007/PL00021868

[14] Basak D, Overfelt RA, Wang D. Measurement of specific heat capacity and electrical resistivity of industrial alloys using pulse heating techniques. International Journal of Thermophysics. 2003;**24**(6):1721-1733. DOI: 10.1023/B:IJOT.0000004101.88449.86

[15] Hsu CT, Cheng P, Wong KW. Modified Zehner-Schlunder models for stagnant thermal conductivity of porous media. International Journal of Heat and Mass Transfer. 1994;**37**(17):2751-2759. DOI: 10.1016/0017-9310(94)90392-1

[16] Dai K, Shaw L. Thermal and mechanical finite element modeling of laser forming from metal and ceramic powders. Acta Materialia. 2004;**52**(1):69-80. DOI: 10.1016/j.actamat.2003.08.028

[17] Hashemzadeh M, Chen B-Q, Guedes Soares C. Comparison between different heat sources types in thin-plate welding simulation. In: Guedes Soares C, Lopez Pena F, editors. Developments in Maritime Transportation and Exploitation of Sea Resources. UK: Francis & Taylor Group London; 2013. DOI: 10.13140/2.1.3250.1123

[18] Hu D, Kovacevic R. Modelling and measuring the thermal behaviour of the molten pool in closed-loop controlled laser-based additive manufacturing. In: Proceedings of the Institution of Mechanical Engineers, Part B: Journal of Engineering Manufacture. 2003. pp. 441-452. DOI: 10.1243/095440503321628125

[19] Li C, Wang Y, Zhan H, Han T, Han B, Zhao W. Three-dimensional finite element analysis of temperatures and stresses in wide-band laser surface melting processing. Materials & Design. 2010;**31**(7):3366-3373. DOI: 10.1016/j.matdes.2010.01.054

[20] Patil N, Pal D, Khalid Rafi H, Zeng K, Moreland A, Hicks A, Beeler D, Stucker B. A generalized feed forward dynamic adaptive mesh refinement and derefinement finite element framework for metal laser sintering. Journal of Manufacturing Science and Engineering. 2015;**137**(4):041001-041001-15. DOI: 10.1115/1.4030059

[21] Zeng K, Pal D, Patil N, Stucker B. A new dynamic mesh method applied to the simulation of selective laser melting. In: Solid Freeform Fabrication Proceeding. Austin: University of Texas; 2013. pp. 549-559

[22] de La Batut B, Fergani O, Brotan V, Bambach M, El Mansouri M. Analytical and numerical temperature prediction in direct metal deposition of Ti6Al4V. Journal of Manufacturing and Materials Processing. 2017;**1**(1). Article number 3. DOI: 10.3390/jmmp1010003

[23] Fergani O, Berto F, Welo T, Liang SY. Analytical modelling of residual stress in additive manufacturing. Fatigue and Fracture of Engineering Materials and Structures. 2016;**40**(6): 971-978. DOI: 10.1111/ffe.12560

[24] Zeng K, Pal D, Gong HJ, Patil N, Stucker B. Comparison of 3DSIM thermal modelling of selective laser melting using new dynamic meshing method to ANSYS. Materials Science and Technology. 2015;**31**(8):945-956. DOI: 10.1179/1743284714Y.0000000703

[25] Keller N, Ploshikhin V. New method for fast predictions of residual stress and distortion of AM parts. In: Solid Freeform Fabrication Symposium. Austin, Texas. p. 2014

[26] Song X, Xie M, Hofmann F, Illston T, Connolley T, Reinhard C, Atwood RC, Connor L, Drakopoulos M, Frampton L, Korsunsky AM. Residual stresses and microstructure in powder bed direct laser deposition (PB DLD) samples. International Journal of Material Forming. 2015;**8**(2):245-254. DOI: 10.1007/s12289-014-1163-1

[27] Thijs L, Verhaeghe F, Craeghs T, Van Humbeeck J, Kruth J-P. A study of the microstructural evolution during selective laser melting of Ti–6Al–4V. Acta Materialia. 2010;**58**(9): 3303-3312. DOI: 10.1016/j.actamat.2010.02.004

[28] Abe F, Osakada K, Kitamura Y, Matsumoto M, Shiomi M. Manufacturing of titanium parts for medical purposes by selective laser melting. In: Proc. 8th Int. Conf. Rapid Prototyping. 2000. pp. 288-293

[29] Martin V. Allmen, Blatter A, editors. Laser-Beam Interactions with Materials. 2nd ed. Vol. XII. 196 p. Berlin, Germany: Springer-Verlag Berlin Heidelberg; 1995. DOI: 10.1007/978-3-642-57813-7

[30] Zienkiewicz O, Taylor R, Zhu JZ, editors. The Finite Element Method: Its Basis and Fundamentals. 7th ed. Vol. 2013. Oxford, UK: Butterworth-Heinemann. p. 756

Chapter 7

Adaptive Modeling and Simulation of Elastic, Dielectric and Piezoelectric Problems

Grzegorz Zboiński

Additional information is available at the end of the chapter

http://dx.doi.org/10.5772/intechopen.72265

Abstract

In this chapter, theoretical and implementation details of the algorithms of hierarchical modeling and hierarchical *hp*-approximations, residual error estimation methods and four-step adaptive procedures are considered in the context of their application to modeling and simulation of the problems of elasticity, dielectricity and piezoelectricity. In the hierarchical modeling, 3D-based hierarchical elastic and dielectric models are applied. The adaptive discretization process is based on the hierarchical shape functions and the constrained approximations. In the error estimation, the equilibrated residual method is applied, which serves the total and approximation error assessment. These errors control the model and *hp*-adaptivity. In the case of adaptive algorithms, four-step procedure is utilized. It includes global solutions on the initial mesh, mesh modified in order to remove some undesired numerical phenomena, the intermediate *h*-refined mesh and the final (or target) *p*-enriched mesh. Examples demonstrating the effectivity of the mentioned modeling and approximation, error estimation and adaptivity control parts of the overall simulation algorithm in the three classes of problems are presented.

Keywords: adaptivity, modeling, simulation, finite elements, hierarchical models, hierarchical approximations, error estimation, adaptivity control, algorithms, effectivity, elasticity, dielectricity, piezoelectricity

1. Introduction

This chapter constitutes a continuation and extension of the previous work [1] on theoretical and implementation difficulties in application of the adaptive hierarchical modeling and *hp*-adaptive finite element analysis to elasticity, dielectricity and piezoelectricity. In the cited work, the 3D-based elastic, dielectric and piezoelectric hierarchies of models were elucidated. These models are based on either three-dimensional theories or reduced models polynomially constrained through the thickness. In the mentioned work, also the hierarchical approximations for the three classes of hierarchical models are presented. The rules for ordering the hierarchical models and approximations are described. Then, the a posteriori error estimation, based on the equilibrated residual method (ERM) applied to the three classes of problems, is presented. The similarities and differences between the element (local) problems necessary for the element error estimation for these three cases are addressed. Finally, the three- and four-step error-controlled adaptive procedures for the three classes of problems are proposed. The procedures require the global problem solution on the initial, modified, intermediate (h-refined) and final (p-enriched) meshes.

In this chapter, attention is paid to the effectivity of the algorithms for adaptive modeling and simulation of three considered classes of physical phenomena, that is, elasticity, dielectricity and piezoelectricity. Effectivity of hierarchical approximations within elastic, dielectric and piezoelectric media is compared. For this purpose, convergence curves for the analogous model problems within three mentioned classes of problems are generated and assessed. Also, the exemplary comparative results of the approximations are presented for these three classes of model problems. In the case of the error estimation, the global and local (element) effectivity indices for the total, approximation and modeling errors, where the latter is the difference of the former two, in the exemplary model problems of elasticity, dielectricity and piezoelectricity are calculated and compared. The exemplary distribution of the element error indicators and the global values of the error estimators for the model problems of three classes are presented and compared. In the case of the adaptive procedures, the model- and hpq-adaptive algorithms, where h represents the element size parameter, while p and q stand for the element longitudinal and transverse orders of approximation, are of our interest. These algorithms are controlled with the estimated values of the modeling, approximation and total errors. In order to check the effectivity of these algorithms, results necessary for the obtainment of the hp-adaptive convergence curves for the mentioned three model problems of elasticity, dielectricity and piezoelectricity are produced. The convergence is assessed in the context of obtainment of the target values of the errors in subsequent steps of the adaptive calculations for three classes of problems. Also, the comparative results of the adaptive solutions of the model problems of three classes are presented.

1.1. Research objectives

The main objective of this research is to demonstrate the effectivity of our generalizing algorithms [1] adapted, modified or developed for the problems of elasticity, dielectricity and piezoelectricity. Also, the issue of comparison of the corresponding effectivities for these three classes of problems is of our interest. In relation to these objectives, the presented general approach to adaptive modeling and simulation is numerically tested in the context of the approximation algorithms, error estimation algorithms and adaptivity control algorithms as well.

1.2. State-of-the-art issues

In this brief survey, the issues of hierarchical modeling, hierarchical approximations, error estimation and adaptivity control are addressed. The survey is limited to the numerical techniques used in this chapter and the papers directly utilized for this research—no general overview of the four mentioned issues is presented. The interested readers can find such overviews in some of the publications cited below.

The 3D-based hierarchical shell models utilizing three-dimensional degrees of freedom (dofs) and conforming to higher order shell theories were firstly proposed in [2] and repeated in [3]. The conventional hierarchical shells, employing mid-surface dofs, were proposed in [4]. The 3D-based approach was extended onto the first-order shell and shell-to-shell theories in [3, 5]. The latter works also extend the 3D-based hierarchical modeling onto 3D elasticity and solid-to-shell transition models. The author of this chapter is not aware of any hierarchical models of linear dielectricity. Some hierarchic piezoelectric models were presented in [6] in the context of multilayered plate structures. Suggestions on introduction of the 3D-based hierarchical dielectric and piezoelectric models were formulated in [1, 7].

The hierarchical and constrained approximations necessary for *p*- and *h*-adaptivity, respectively, are adopted in our work and were proposed in [8]. Hierarchical approximations for conventional shells were developed in [4], for 3D-based shells in [2, 9] and for complex structures in [5]. The last paper collects partial results presented in [9–12]. Classical and hierarchical approximations for piezoelectric problems were elaborated in [6, 13]. Hierarchical approximations for the complex 3D or 3D-based hierarchical models of dielectrics and piezoelectrics were proposed in the works [1, 7].

The general considerations on error estimation based on the equilibrated residual method can be found in [14]. Application of this method to 3D elasticity was described in [15]. The method was also applied to the hierarchical shells of conventional character in [16]. The analogous approach for the 3D-based first-order shells was developed in [17, 18]. The method was also utilized to error estimation in the 3D-based complex structures [19]. Application of the method to dielectric and piezoelectric problems was suggested in [1, 20].

Finally, adaptivity control by means of the three-step strategy for simple structures was presented in [21]. Within this strategy, three subsequent meshes are generated—initial, intermediate (or *h*-refined) and target (or *p*-enriched) ones. The method was applied to adaptive analysis of conventional hierarchical models of shell- and plate-like structures in [16]. In that work, the third step is split into two, that is, q and p enrichments are performed in sequence. The original three-step strategy was then extended in [3] by addition of the fourth step in which the mesh is modified to get rid of the numerical consequences of the improper solution limit, numerical locking and edge effect. The model adaptivity is performed along with the *h*-step and p and q enrichments are performed simultaneously. Such a four-step adaptive strategy is applied to modeling and simulation of complex elastic structures in [19]. Adaptive simulation in electric or electromechanical problems is less advanced. Adaptivity for simple piezoelectrics was introduced in [22]. Application of the three- or four-step strategies to the analysis of simple and complex dielectrics and piezoelectrics was suggested in [1].

1.3. Novelty of the research

The main novelty of the presented research consists in application of the chosen techniques of hierarchical modeling and approximation, error estimation and adaptivity control, effective in the adaptive modeling and simulation of the elasticity problems, to the adaptive analysis of dielectric and piezoelectric phenomena.

The novelty of this particular chapter is the direct comparison of the robustness of the modeling and simulation algorithms of the coupled problem of piezoelectricity and the problems of pure elasticity and pure dielectricity.

2. Model problems

The following model problems are considered in this chapter: the linear static problem of elasticity, the linear electrostatic problem and the linear problem of stationary piezoelectricity. For each of the model problems, the appropriate finite element formulation is presented. For this purpose, the standard engineering matrix notation is applied.

2.1. Elastostatics

Here, the problems of a three-dimensional (solid) and 3D-based shell or solid-to-shell bodies are considered. Such problems were presented in [1]. In that work, the local (strong) and variational (weak) formulations of the problems are given. These formulations take advantage of the former considerations from [2, 23, 24] and are repeated in [3]. Using the variational formulation presented therein, one can derive the global finite element equations of the problem under consideration and write them in the following form:

$$\boldsymbol{K}_M \boldsymbol{q}^{q,hp} = \boldsymbol{F}_V + \boldsymbol{F}_S \tag{1}$$

where $\boldsymbol{K}_M$ is the global stiffness matrix, while $\boldsymbol{F}_V$ and $\boldsymbol{F}_S$ represent the global vectors of the volume and surface nodal forces. The vector $\boldsymbol{q}^{q,hp}$ stands for the global displacement degrees of freedom (dof), corresponding to hpq approximation, and is composed of the element (local) displacement dof vectors $\overset{e}{\boldsymbol{q}}$ of the elements $e = 1, 2, \ldots, E$, where E is the total number of elements within an elastic body. These vectors are defined later in this chapter.

The global stiffness matrix is composed (aggregated) of the element stiffness matrices of the form

$$\overset{e}{\boldsymbol{k}} = \int_0^1 \int_0^1 \int_0^{-\xi_2+1} \overset{e}{\boldsymbol{B}}{}^T \boldsymbol{D} \overset{e}{\boldsymbol{B}} \det(\boldsymbol{J}) \, d\xi_1 d\xi_2 d\xi_3 \tag{2}$$

where $\boldsymbol{D}$ denotes the elastic constants matrix, $\overset{e}{\boldsymbol{B}}$ represents the strain-displacement matrix, and $\det(\boldsymbol{J})$ is the Jacobian matrix determinant. The limits and coordinates of the integration correspond to the normalized coordinates ξ_i, $i = 1, 2, 3$ of the prismatic elements applied in [1]. The specific forms of the strain-displacement matrix can be found in the works [9, 10, 12] for the 3D-based versions of the prismatic solid (and hierarchical shell), first-order shell and solid-to-shell (and shell-to-shell) adaptive elements, respectively.

The nodal mass forces vector can be defined in the standard way

$$\overset{e}{\boldsymbol{f}}_M = \int_0^1 \int_0^1 \int_0^{-\xi_2+1} \overset{e}{\boldsymbol{N}}^T \boldsymbol{f} \det(\boldsymbol{J})\, d\xi_1 d\xi_2 d\xi_3, \tag{3}$$

where $\overset{e}{\boldsymbol{N}}$ and $\boldsymbol{f}$ represent the element shape functions matrix and the mass loading vector, respectively.

The element nodal forces vector due to the surface traction $\boldsymbol{p}$ can be defined in the following two forms

$$\begin{aligned} \overset{e}{\boldsymbol{f}}_S &= \int_0^1 \int_0^{-\xi_2+1} \overset{e}{\boldsymbol{N}}^T \boldsymbol{p}\, \mathrm{wsp}(\boldsymbol{J})\, d\xi_2 d\xi_1 \\ \overset{e}{\boldsymbol{f}}_S &= \int_0^1 \int_0^1 \overset{e}{\boldsymbol{N}}^T \boldsymbol{p}\, \mathrm{wsp}(\boldsymbol{J})\, d\xi_3 d\eta_i \end{aligned} \tag{4}$$

corresponding to the bases and sides of the prismatic element. Above the element, bases and sides are defined with the normalized longitudinal coordinates ξ_j, $j = 1, 2$, or the transverse normalized coordinate ξ_3 and the coordinates η_i, $i = 1, 2, 3$ tangential to the sides of the element [3, 9]. The term $\mathrm{wsp}(\boldsymbol{J})$ is the coefficient defined with the components of the Jacobian matrix $\boldsymbol{J}$ (see [3, 9] again).

2.2. Electrostatics

The general formulations of the problems of electrostatics can be found in [25]. Here, classical linear dielectric models are applied to such problems. The local and variational formulations for this case was presented in [1] for any 3D or 3D-based geometry (bulky, symmetric-thickness or transition ones). The corresponding finite element equations read:

$$\boldsymbol{K}_E \boldsymbol{\varphi}^{\rho, h\pi} = \boldsymbol{F}_Q \tag{5}$$

In Eq. (5), $\boldsymbol{K}_E$ represents the global characteristic matrix of dielectricity, while $\boldsymbol{F}_Q$ stands for the global characteristic electric charges nodal vector. The vector $\boldsymbol{\varphi}^{\rho, h\pi}$ is the unknown global nodal vector of electric potentials. This vector definition results from the applied $\rho, h\pi$-approximation, where ρ and π represent the transverse and longitudinal orders of approximation. The global potential vector is composed of the element potential vectors $\overset{e}{\boldsymbol{\varphi}}$, which are described later in this chapter. The global matrix $\boldsymbol{K}_E$ is the result of summation of the element contributions

$$\overset{e}{\boldsymbol{k}}_E = \int_0^1 \int_0^1 \int_0^{-\xi_2+1} \overset{e}{\boldsymbol{b}}^T \gamma \overset{e}{\boldsymbol{b}} \det(\boldsymbol{J})\, d\xi_1 d\xi_2 d\xi_3 \tag{6}$$

with γ and $\overset{e}{\boldsymbol{b}}$ denoting the electric (or permittivity) constants matrix and the matrix of the relation between the electric field components and the nodal electric potentials (or shortly field-potential matrix). The specific form of the latter matrix in the case of the prismatic element can be found in the work [26].

The nodal electric charges vector of the element e has to be defined in a different way on the prismatic element bases and sides, that is,

$$\overset{e}{f}_Q = \int_0^1 \int_0^{-\xi_2+1} \overset{e}{n}^T c \, \mathrm{wsp}(J) \, d\xi_2 d\xi_1 \tag{7}$$

and

$$\overset{e}{f}_Q = \int_0^1 \int_0^1 \overset{e}{n}^T c \, \mathrm{wsp}(J) \, d\xi_3 d\eta_i \tag{8}$$

where $\overset{e}{n}$ and c are the element shape functions vector and the scalar density of the surface electric charges.

2.3. Stationary piezoelectricity

The local and variational formulations of linear piezoelectricity combine our former considerations concerning the linear elasticity and linear dielectricity [13, 27]. This approach was repeated in [1]. The corresponding finite element formulation can be written in the form a coupled system of equations. The coupling is represented by the matrix K_C in the following way

$$\begin{aligned} K_M q^{q,hp} - K_C \varphi^{\rho,h\pi} &= F_V + F_S, \\ K_C^T q^{q,hp} + K_E \varphi^{\rho,h\pi} &= F_Q \end{aligned} \tag{9}$$

The coupling term can be called the global characteristic matrix of piezoelectricity, while the rest terms retain their previous meaning. The additional remark concerns special or simplified versions of the above equation. The inverse or direct piezoelectric problems can be considered here with the right-hand side terms equal to zero in the first and second equation, respectively. It is also worth mentioning that different pq and $\pi\rho$ adaptive approximations of the vectorial displacement and scalar electric fields are proposed in (9), with the common h-approximation.

The global matrix of piezoelectricity introduced above can be obtained through the standard finite element summation procedure, where the following element contributions are employed

$$\overset{e}{k}_C = \int_0^1 \int_0^1 \int_0^{-\xi_2+1} \overset{e}{B}^T C \overset{e}{b} \, \det(J) \, d\xi_1 d\xi_2 d\xi_3 \tag{10}$$

with C representing the piezoelectric (coupling) constants matrix.

The element contributions to the other terms of (9) are defined as before, that is, in accordance with (2)–(4) and (6)–(7). Note that the different shape functions matrices, $\overset{e}{N}$ and $\overset{e}{n}$, for the displacements and potential fields are employed here due to the different orders of approximations, pq and $\pi\rho$, within both fields. Thanks to this, the corresponding adaptation processes within both fields can be performed independently.

3. The applied numerical techniques

3.1. Hierarchies of models

The presented elastic, dielectric and piezoelectric models are all based on the 3D-based approach, which results in the application of the three-dimensional or 3D-based degrees of freedom (dofs) only. The mechanical shell and transition models are also equipped with such dofs. This means that mid-surface degrees of freedom of the conventional shell and transition models are not applied. The so-called through-thickness dofs are employed instead. Also, some constraints are imposed on the three-dimensional displacements field of the shell and transition models so as to obtain the equivalence of the conventional and 3D-based descriptions. The related issues are presented in detail in the works [3, 5]. Analogously, in [7], the 3D-based hierarchy of dielectric models was proposed. It includes the three-dimensional and symmetric-thickness hierarchical models. Three-dimensional and 3D-based through-thickness dofs are employed in these models. In the latter work, also the 3D-based mechanical and dielectric models were combined, so as to obtain the 3D-based hierarchy of the piezoelectric models. This idea was also recalled in [1]. Note that all the presented 3D-based models, either elastic, dielectric or piezoelectric ones, can be treated as the 3D models polynomially constrained through the thickness.

The mechanical hierarchy M of the 3D or 3D-based elastic models M reads:

$$M \in \mathrm{M}, \quad \mathrm{M} = \{3D, MI, RM, 3D/RM, MI/RM\} \tag{11}$$

with $3D$ denoting three-dimensional elasticity, MI representing hierarchical shell models of higher order, RM being the first-order shell model corresponding to Reissner theory of shells and $3D/RM$ and MI/RM standing for the transition models of solid-to-shell or shell-to-shell character. The hierarchical shell and shell-to-shell models constitute two sub-hierarchies:

$$\begin{aligned} MI &= \{M2, M3, M4, \ldots\}, \\ MI/RM &= \{M2/RM, M3/RM, M4/RM, \ldots\} \end{aligned} \tag{12}$$

where I represents the order of the hierarchical model MI. This order is equivalent to the order of polynomial constraints defining the transverse displacement.

Subsequently, the hierarchy E of 3D-based dielectric models E includes:

$$E \in \mathrm{E}, \quad \mathrm{E} = \{3D, EJ\} \tag{13}$$

where $3D$ represents three-dimensional theory of dielectricity, while EJ denotes the 3D-based hierarchical models. The latter models constitute the following subhierarchy:

$$EJ = \{E1, E2, E3, \ldots\} \tag{14}$$

with J standing for the order of the hierarchical dielectric theory (the polynomial order of the through-thickness constraints of electric potential).

The 3D-based hierarchy P of piezoelectric models P consists of the following component models:

$$P \in \mathrm{P}, \quad \mathrm{P} = \{(M, E) : M \in \mathrm{M}, E \in \mathrm{E}\} \tag{15}$$

The hierarchy is composed of all combinations (M, E) of the elastic models M from (11) and (12) and dielectric models E defined in (13) and (14), that is,

$$\begin{aligned} \mathrm{P} = \{&(3D, 3D), (MI, 3D), (RM, 3D), (3D/RM, 3D), (MI/RM, 3D) \\ &(3D, EJ), (MI, EJ), (RM, EJ), (3D/RM, EJ), (MI/RM, EJ)\} \end{aligned} \tag{16}$$

3.2. Hierarchical and constrained approximations

In the proposed approach, each of the 3D or 3D-based elastic, dielectric and piezoelectric models is approximated with the three-dimensional hierarchical shape functions. The functions applied in this work are originated from [8]. Their main feature is that they allow different orders of approximation on each of the element edges and sides. Such different orders are necessary for the local (element) q- and p-adaptivity. These different orders are obtained due to the shape function definition based on tensor products of the directional (longitudinal and transverse) shape functions of different orders. The specific form of the directional and three-dimensional functions for the case of the 3D solid and 3D-based hierarchical shell elements was presented in [3, 9]. The case of the solid-to-shell and shell-to-shell elements is addressed in [3, 12], while the first-order shell element shape functions are shown in [3, 10]. The analogous functions for the three-dimensional and hierarchical symmetric-thickness dielectric elements are given in [26]. In the case of the piezoelectric elements, the idea is to combine the elastic elements of various mechanical models with the dielectric elements. This idea is implemented in [1, 26]. Some details concerning shape functions of the component (elastic and dielectric) and combined (piezoelectric) elements are presented in the following paragraphs.

The displacement field of the elastic and piezoelectric elements is defined through the interpolation function $\boldsymbol{u} = \boldsymbol{u}(\boldsymbol{\xi})$ describing displacements $\boldsymbol{u} = (u_1, u_2, u_3)^T$ of any point $\boldsymbol{\xi}$ of the normalized geometry of the element. This interpolant is a sum of four component functions:

$$\boldsymbol{u}(\boldsymbol{\xi}) = \boldsymbol{u}^1(\boldsymbol{\xi}) + \boldsymbol{u}^2(\boldsymbol{\xi}) + \boldsymbol{u}^3(\boldsymbol{\xi}) + \boldsymbol{u}^4(\boldsymbol{\xi}) \tag{17}$$

The first component function $\boldsymbol{u}^1(\boldsymbol{\xi})$ of the element vertices is defined as a product of the linear vertex node shape function matrix $\mathbf{N}_v$ and the corresponding vector of nodal threesomes of directional dofs, that is,

$$\boldsymbol{u}^1(\boldsymbol{\xi}) = \mathbf{N}_v(\boldsymbol{\xi})\,\boldsymbol{q}_v \tag{18}$$

where the mentioned vector is: $\boldsymbol{q}_v = \left[\ldots, q_{1,i}, q_{2,i}, q_{3,i}, \ldots\right]^T$, and where $i = 1, 2, \ldots, I_v$ with I_v being the number of vertex nodes within the element.

http://dx.doi.org/10.5772/intechopen.72265

The second component interpolant $\boldsymbol{u}^2(\xi)$, corresponding to the element edges, is equal to the product of the higher-order shape function matrices, $\boldsymbol{N}_h$ and $\boldsymbol{N}_u$, of the element horizontal and vertical (upright) mid-edge nodes and the corresponding dof vectors:

$$\boldsymbol{u}^2(\xi) = \boldsymbol{N}_h(\xi)\boldsymbol{q}_h + \boldsymbol{N}_u(\xi)\boldsymbol{q}_u \tag{19}$$

The mentioned vectors of degrees of freedom at the horizontal and vertical nodes are as follows: $\boldsymbol{q}_h = \left[\dots, q_{1,i,k}, q_{2,i,k}, q_{3,i,k}, \dots\right]^T$, $\boldsymbol{q}_u = \left[\dots, q_{1,j,l}, q_{2,j,l}, q_{3,j,l}, \dots\right]^T$, $i = 1, 2, \dots, I_h$, $j = 1, 2, \dots, I_u$, where I_h and I_u are the numbers of the horizontal and upright mid-edge nodes, while k and l represent numbers of dofs at these nodes.

The subsequent interpolant $\boldsymbol{u}^3(\xi)$ corresponds the higher order mid-base and mid-side nodes of the element. The function is obtained through the multiplication of the shape function matrices, $\boldsymbol{N}_b$ and $\boldsymbol{N}_s$, by the corresponding dofs vectors in accordance with

$$\boldsymbol{u}^3(\xi) = \boldsymbol{N}_b(\xi)\boldsymbol{q}_b + \boldsymbol{N}_s(\xi)\boldsymbol{q}_s \tag{20}$$

where the vectors of nodal dofs are equal to: $\boldsymbol{q}_b = \left[\dots, q_{1,i,k}, q_{2,i,k}, q_{3,i,k}, \dots\right]^T$, $\boldsymbol{q}_s = \left[\dots, q_{1,j,l}, q_{2,j,l}, q_{3,i,l}, \dots\right]^T$ with $i = 1, 2, \dots, I_b$ and $j = 1, 2, \dots, I_s$. Here, I_b and I_s denote the numbers of the mid-base and mid-side nodes, while k and l are dof numbers at these nodes.

The last component interpolant $\boldsymbol{u}^4(\xi)$, assigned to the element higher order middle node, is defined as a product of the shape function matrix $\boldsymbol{N}_m$ and the corresponding dof vector:

$$\boldsymbol{u}^4(\xi) = \boldsymbol{N}_m(\xi)\boldsymbol{q}_m \tag{21}$$

where the dof vector is: $\boldsymbol{q}_m = \left[\dots, q_{1,k}, q_{2,k}, q_{3,k}, \dots\right]^T$, with k standing for a dof number at this node.

With $\overset{e}{\boldsymbol{N}} = [\boldsymbol{N}_v(\xi), \boldsymbol{N}_h(\xi), \boldsymbol{N}_u(\xi), \boldsymbol{N}_b(\xi), \boldsymbol{N}_v(\xi), \boldsymbol{N}_m(\xi)]$ and $\overset{e}{\boldsymbol{q}} = \left[\boldsymbol{q}_v, \boldsymbol{q}_h, \boldsymbol{q}_u, \boldsymbol{q}_b, \boldsymbol{q}_s, \boldsymbol{q}_m\right]^T$ Eq. (17) can be written in the alternative standard form

$$\boldsymbol{u}(\xi) = \overset{e}{\boldsymbol{N}}(\xi)\overset{e}{\boldsymbol{q}} \tag{22}$$

The function $\phi = \phi(\xi)$ interpolating electric potential at any point ξ of the normalized dielectric or piezoelectric element is also defined as a sum of four components

$$\phi(\xi) = \phi^1(\xi) + \phi^2(\xi) + \phi^3(\xi) + \phi^4(\xi) \tag{23}$$

The linear interpolant $\phi^1(\xi)$ of the element vertices is equal to the product of the vector $\boldsymbol{n}_v$ of shape functions for the vertices and the corresponding nodal vector of scalar dofs, that is,

$$\phi^1(\xi) = \boldsymbol{n}_v(\xi)\boldsymbol{\varphi}_v \tag{24}$$

where $\boldsymbol{\varphi}_v = [\ldots, \varphi_i, \ldots]^T$ and $i = 1, 2, \ldots, J_v$, with J_v denoting the number of vertices within the element.

The higher order interpolant $\phi^2(\xi)$, corresponding to horizontal and vertical (upright) mid-edge nodes, is equal to a product of the shape function vectors $\boldsymbol{n}_h$ and $\boldsymbol{n}_u$ and the corresponding vectors of nodal dofs:

$$\phi^2(\xi) = \boldsymbol{n}_h(\xi)\boldsymbol{\varphi}_h + \boldsymbol{n}_u(\xi)\boldsymbol{\varphi}_u \tag{25}$$

with $\boldsymbol{\varphi}_h = [\ldots, \varphi_{i,k}, \ldots]^T$, $\boldsymbol{\varphi}_u = [\ldots, \varphi_{i,l}, \ldots]^T$, $i = 1, 2, , \ldots, J_h$, $j = 1, 2, \ldots, J_u$. Above, the numbers of the horizontal and upright mid-edge nodes are equal to J_h and J_u, respectively, while k and l are numbers of the consecutive dofs at these nodes.

The next higher order interpolation function $\phi^3(\xi)$, dealing with the mid-base and mid-side nodes, can be calculated with the multiplication of the shape function vectors $\boldsymbol{n}_b$ and $\boldsymbol{n}_s$ of these nodes and the respective vectors of nodal dofs:

$$\phi^3(\xi) = \boldsymbol{n}_b(\xi)\boldsymbol{\varphi}_b + \boldsymbol{n}_s(\xi)\boldsymbol{\varphi}_s \tag{26}$$

while $\boldsymbol{\varphi}_b = [\ldots, \varphi_{i,k}, \ldots]^T$ and $\boldsymbol{\varphi}_s = [\ldots, \varphi_{i,l}, \ldots]^T$. Additionally, $i = 1, 2, \ldots, J_b$ and $j = 1, 2, \ldots, J_s$ with J_b and J_s standing for the numbers of the mid-base and mid-side nodes, respectively, and k, l being dofs numbers at these nodes.

The last component function $\phi^4(\xi)$, assigned for the middle node, needs multiplication of the shape function vector $\boldsymbol{n}_m$ of the node and the corresponding vector of the nodal dofs

$$\phi^4(\xi) = \boldsymbol{n}_m(\xi)\boldsymbol{\varphi}_m \tag{27}$$

where $\boldsymbol{\varphi}_m = [\ldots, \varphi_k, \ldots]^T$, and k represents the number of a hierarchical dof at the middle node.

Note that when $\overset{e}{\boldsymbol{n}} = [\boldsymbol{n}_v(\xi), \boldsymbol{n}_h(\xi), \boldsymbol{n}_u(\xi), \boldsymbol{n}_b(\xi), \boldsymbol{n}_s(\xi), \boldsymbol{n}_m(\xi)]$ and $\overset{e}{\boldsymbol{\varphi}} = [\boldsymbol{\varphi}_v, \boldsymbol{\varphi}_h, \boldsymbol{\varphi}_u, \boldsymbol{\varphi}_b, \boldsymbol{\varphi}_s, \boldsymbol{\varphi}_m]^T$, Eq. (23) can be written in the well-known general form

$$\phi(\xi) = \overset{e}{\boldsymbol{n}}(\xi)\overset{e}{\boldsymbol{\varphi}} \tag{28}$$

Here, we discuss on the constrained approximation. Such an approximation is necessary for h-adaptivity, which results in neighborhood of the element of different sizes, that is, the undivided elements e of the initial mesh are adjacent to the divided elements f of the h-adapted mesh. A further consequence of the different sizes is the constrained (or hanging) nodes of the smaller elements, which do not possess their counterparts in the neighboring bigger elements. In order to assure continuity of the field of displacements and the electric potential field between such elements, the constraining relations have to be introduced to the contributions of the smaller elements f to Eqs. (1), (5) and (9), before the assemblage of the global matrices and vectors. The constraining relation for the case of displacements reads:

$$\overset{f}{\boldsymbol{q}} = \begin{bmatrix} \overset{f}{\boldsymbol{q}}_s \\ \overset{f}{\boldsymbol{q}}_u \end{bmatrix} = \begin{bmatrix} \boldsymbol{I} & \boldsymbol{0} \\ \boldsymbol{0} & \overset{fe}{\boldsymbol{C}}_q \end{bmatrix} \begin{bmatrix} \overset{f}{\boldsymbol{q}}_s \\ \overset{e}{\boldsymbol{q}}_w \end{bmatrix} \tag{29}$$

where the parts $\overset{f}{\boldsymbol{q}}_s$ and $\overset{f}{\boldsymbol{q}}_u$ of $\overset{f}{\boldsymbol{q}}$ include the unconstrained and constrained dofs of the smaller element f, $\overset{e}{\boldsymbol{q}}_w$ contains displacements of the constraining nodes of the bigger neighbor e, while $\overset{fe}{\boldsymbol{C}}_q$ and $\boldsymbol{I}$ represent the constraint coefficient matrix and the unity matrix. In the case of the electric potential, the analogous relation reads:

$$\overset{f}{\boldsymbol{\varphi}} = \begin{bmatrix} \overset{f}{\boldsymbol{\varphi}}_s \\ \overset{f}{\boldsymbol{\varphi}}_u \end{bmatrix} = \begin{bmatrix} \boldsymbol{I} & \boldsymbol{0} \\ \boldsymbol{0} & \overset{fe}{\boldsymbol{C}}_\varphi \end{bmatrix} \begin{bmatrix} \overset{f}{\boldsymbol{\varphi}}_s \\ \overset{e}{\boldsymbol{\varphi}}_w \end{bmatrix} \tag{30}$$

The general rules for the constrained approximation are presented in [8]. These rules are applied in [3, 14, 26] where the methods of obtainment of the constraint coefficients for the two-dimensional and three-dimensional cases are described.

3.3. Error estimation

The equilibrated residual method of error estimation [14–16, 19] applied to solid mechanics is based on the solution of the approximated local (element) problems of mechanical equilibrium. The corresponding equilibrium condition, written in the language of finite elements, takes the form:

$$\overset{e}{\boldsymbol{k}}_M \overset{e}{\boldsymbol{q}}^{Q,HP} = \overset{e}{\boldsymbol{f}}_V + \overset{e}{\boldsymbol{f}}_S + \overset{e}{\boldsymbol{f}}_R \tag{31}$$

with $\overset{e}{\boldsymbol{k}}_M$ standing for the element stiffness matrix, $\overset{e}{\boldsymbol{f}}_V$ and $\overset{e}{\boldsymbol{f}}_S$ denoting the nodal mass and surface forces vectors, and $\overset{e}{\boldsymbol{f}}_R$ representing the nodal forces vector due to the equilibrated interelement stress loadings. In (31), $\overset{e}{\boldsymbol{q}}^{Q,HP}$ is the solution displacements vector in the approximated local problem. Note that the discretization parameters H, P and Q (the element size, and the longitudinal and transverse approximation orders in the local problems) can be different to their global counterparts h, p and q. The element solutions from the above relation give the global error estimate, which upper-bounds the true error [15, 16, 19]. In the presented approach, the above relation is applied to both the approximation and total errors estimation. However, different values of the discretization parameters are applied in both cases, that is, $H = h$, $P = p + 1$, $Q = q$ and $H = h$, $P = p + 1$, $Q = q + 1$, respectively. The modeling error is calculated as the difference of the previous two errors.

As demonstrated in the work [20], application of the equilibrated residual methods to dielectric problems needs solution of the local (element) electric equilibrium problems. Such equilibrium, expressed in the language of finite elements, can be written in the following way:

$$\overset{e}{\boldsymbol{k}}_E \overset{e}{\boldsymbol{\varphi}}^{\mathrm{P},H\Pi} = \overset{e}{\boldsymbol{f}}_Q + \overset{e}{\boldsymbol{f}}_H \tag{32}$$

In the above-mentioned equation, the term $\overset{e}{\boldsymbol{k}}_E$ stands for the element characteristic matrix of dielectricity, $\overset{e}{\boldsymbol{f}}_Q$ is the element nodal vector due to surface charges, while $\overset{e}{\boldsymbol{f}}_H$ represents nodal forces due to the equilibrated interelement charges. The vector $\overset{e}{\boldsymbol{\varphi}}^{\mathrm{P},H\Pi}$ is the solution vector of electric potential in the local problem. The solution is approximate and the corresponding discretization parameters H, Π, P (the element size and longitudinal and transverse approximation orders) can be different to their global counterparts h, π, ρ. In the cases of the approximation and total errors, the values of $H = h$, $\Pi = \pi + 1$, $\mathrm{P} = \rho$ and $H = h$, $\Pi = \pi + 1$, $\mathrm{P} = \rho + 1$ are applied, respectively. Again, the collection of the local solutions obtained by means of (32) leads to the error estimate, which upper-bounds the true total and true approximation errors, and the modeling error is defined as the difference of these two errors.

Generalization of the equilibrated residual methods onto piezoelectric problems was proposed and developed in [1, 20, 26]. In accordance with this proposition, the above mechanical and electrical local equilibria Eqs. (31) and (32) have to be replaced by the coupled equations describing electromechanical equilibrium. Such equations take the following finite element form:

$$\begin{aligned} \overset{e}{\boldsymbol{k}}_M \overset{e}{\boldsymbol{q}}^{Q,HP} - \overset{e}{\boldsymbol{k}}_C \overset{e}{\boldsymbol{\varphi}}^{\mathrm{P},H\Pi} &= \overset{e}{\boldsymbol{f}}_V + \overset{e}{\boldsymbol{f}}_S + \overset{e}{\boldsymbol{f}}_R \\ \overset{e}{\boldsymbol{k}}{}_C^T \overset{e}{\boldsymbol{q}}^{Q,HP} + \overset{e}{\boldsymbol{k}}_E \overset{e}{\boldsymbol{\varphi}}^{\mathrm{P},H\Pi} &= \overset{e}{\boldsymbol{f}}_Q + \overset{e}{\boldsymbol{f}}_H \end{aligned} \tag{33}$$

The coupled local solutions $\overset{e}{\boldsymbol{q}}^{Q,HP}$ and $\overset{e}{\boldsymbol{\varphi}}^{\mathrm{P},H\Pi}$ of the above set have one disadvantage. It lies in the lack of the upper-bound property of the total, approximation and modeling errors by the residual-based global estimators obtained from the local solutions of (33).

In the works [1, 26], the decoupled version of the above set was also proposed as a simpler alternative:

$$\begin{aligned} \overset{e}{\boldsymbol{k}}_M \overset{e}{\boldsymbol{q}}^{Q,HP} &= \overset{e}{\boldsymbol{k}}_C \overset{e}{\boldsymbol{\varphi}}^{\rho,h\pi} + \overset{e}{\boldsymbol{f}}_V + \overset{e}{\boldsymbol{f}}_S + \overset{e}{\boldsymbol{f}}_R \\ \overset{e}{\boldsymbol{k}}_E \overset{e}{\boldsymbol{\varphi}}^{\mathrm{P},H\Pi} &= -\overset{e}{\boldsymbol{k}}{}_C^T \overset{e}{\boldsymbol{q}}^{q,hp} + \overset{e}{\boldsymbol{f}}_Q + \overset{e}{\boldsymbol{f}}_H \end{aligned} \tag{34}$$

In Eqs. (31) and (32) and in the above two sets of equations, the vectors of the equilibrated nodal forces and charge are defined in accordance with:

$$\overset{e}{\boldsymbol{f}}_R = \int_{S_e \backslash S} \overset{e}{\boldsymbol{N}}{}^{\mathrm{T}} \langle \boldsymbol{r}_e(\boldsymbol{u}^{hpq}) \rangle \, dS_e = \sum_f \int_{S_{ef}} \overset{e}{\boldsymbol{N}}{}^T \langle \boldsymbol{r}_e(\boldsymbol{u}^{hpq}) \rangle \, dS_{ef} \tag{35}$$

and

$$\overset{e}{\boldsymbol{f}}_H = \int_{S_e \backslash S} \overset{e}{\boldsymbol{n}}{}^{\mathrm{T}} \langle h_e(\phi^{h\pi\rho}) \rangle \, dS_e = \sum_f \int_{Sef} \overset{e}{\boldsymbol{n}}{}^{\mathrm{T}} \langle h_e(\phi^{h\pi\rho}) \rangle \, dS_{ef} \tag{36}$$

where S_e and S are the element and body surfaces, while $\langle \boldsymbol{r}_e(\boldsymbol{u}^{hpq}) \rangle$ and $\langle h_e(\phi^{h\pi\rho}) \rangle$ denote the equilibrated interelement (between element e and any of its neighbors f) stress vector and the equilibrated interelement charge density acting on the common sides S_{ef} between the elements. Some more details on how to calculate the equilibrated stresses and charge can be found in [3, 19, 26].

3.4. Adaptive strategy

The adaptive strategy applied in this chapter takes advantage of the Texas three-step strategy [21]. The original strategy is assigned for structures of simple geometry (a single geometrical part of one type) and simple physical description (one model). Such a strategy is designed for *hp*-adaptivity and consists of three steps: initial, intermediate and final ones, where three subsequent global problem solutions are obtained. In this strategy, the solution on the initial mesh is followed by the error estimation and error-controlled *h*-adaptation (element refinement). In this way, the intermediate mesh is formed. The solution on this mesh is then followed by the error estimation and the error-controlled *p*-adaptivity (element approximation order enrichment). The problem solution on this mesh is followed by the error estimation again.

The original strategy was extended in three ways [3, 26]. First, structures of complex geometry and complex physical description can be analyzed in the presented approach. Second, the *h*-step of the adaptation is enriched with the model adaptivity, while the *p*-step of the strategy is completed with *q*-adaptivity (enrichment of the element transverse approximation order) [19] in the way different to the earlier proposition of [4]. Third, the strategy is enhanced through the addition of one more adaptation step called the modification one. In this step, the initial mesh is modified so as to remove the undesired numerical phenomena, such as the improper solution limit, numerical locking or boundary layers [28]. The extended strategy can be applied to elastic [3, 19], dielectric [1] and piezoelectric [1, 26] problems. Some difficulties in the application of the strategy to the cases of piezoelectricity are described in [1]. The analogous comments for the case of elasticity can be found in [29, 30].

Description of the error-controlled adaptivity for elastic, dielectric and piezoelectric structures is started with the *h*-adaptivity within the mechanical field (hence index *M*). In accordance with [19, 21], the new number of elements n_{I_M} in the intermediate mesh (denoted with index *I*), which replace an element of the initial mesh, is equal to:

$$n_{I_M}^{2\mu_{0_M}/d+1} = \frac{\eta_{0_M}^2 E_I}{\gamma_{a,I}^2 \|\boldsymbol{u}_0\|_U^2} \tag{37}$$

where η_{0_M} is the estimated value of the approximation error from the initial mesh, μ_{0_M} represents the known or assumed *h*-convergence rate, *d* denotes dimensionality (equal to 2 or 3) of the adapted geometrical part. Additionally, E_I is the total number of elements in the intermediate mesh, $\|\boldsymbol{u}_0\|_U^2$ is the strain energy norm of the solution from the initial mesh, while the coefficient $\gamma_{a,I}$ determines the expected relative value of the global approximation error within the intermediate mesh.

In the case of the mechanical field, local (element) p-enrichments are controlled with the longitudinal (or overall) element approximation order p_T of the final (or target) mesh (marked with the index T). The longitudinal order corresponds to thin-walled structures, while the overall order to three-dimensional bodies. The following common formula [19, 21] determines this parameter:

$$p_T^{2\nu_{0M}} = \frac{p_0^{2\nu_{0M}} \eta_{I_M}^2 E_I}{\gamma_{a,T}^2 \| \boldsymbol{u}_0 \|_U^2} \tag{38}$$

with η_{I_M} representing the estimated value of the approximation error from the intermediate mesh, ν_{0_M} being the given p-convergence rate, p_0 denoting the longitudinal approximation order from the initial mesh and $\gamma_{a,T}$ standing for the expected relative value of the global approximation error in the target mesh.

In the case of q-adaptivity within the mechanical field of the thin-walled structures, the target values of the element transverse approximation orders q_T can be defined in accordance with [3, 19]:

$$q_T = q_0 - \frac{1}{2} \log_{t/2l} \frac{\theta_{I_M}^2 E_I}{\gamma_{m,T}^2 \| \boldsymbol{u}_0 \|_U^2} \tag{39}$$

Above, q_0 is the element transverse order from the initial mesh, t and $2l$ represent the thickness and length of the thin-walled part of the structure, θ_{I_M} is the estimated value of the modeling error from the intermediate mesh and $\gamma_{m,T}$ denotes the expected relative value of the modeling error in the target mesh.

The h-adaptivity within the electric field needs determination of the new number (denoted with index E) of elements, n_{I_E}, in the intermediate mesh (marked with index I again). Such a number has to be determined for each element of the initial mesh. This number is equal to:

$$n_{I_E}^{2\mu_{0_E}/d+1} = \frac{\eta_{0_E}^2 E_I}{\gamma_{a,I}^2 \| \phi_0 \|_W^2} \tag{40}$$

Above, the quantity η_{0_E} stands for the estimated value of the approximation error in the initial mesh, the exponent μ_{0_E} is the assumed h-convergence rate and the norm $\| \phi_0 \|_W^2$ represents the electrostatic energy corresponding to the initial mesh.

Note that in the case of piezoelectricity, for each element, the final subdivision is determined with

$$n_I = \max\left(n_{I_M}, n_{I_E}\right) \tag{41}$$

as the common mesh division is applied for the mechanical and electric fields (see [1]).

The value of the longitudinal (or overall) approximation order π_T within the electric field of an element of the target (final) mesh can be calculated from [26]:

$$\pi_T^{2\nu_{0M}} = \frac{\pi_{0_E}^{2\nu_{0_E}} \eta_{I_E}^2 E_I}{\gamma_{a,T}^2 \|\phi_0\|_W^2} \tag{42}$$

where η_{I_E} is the estimated approximation error value from the intermediate mesh, ν_{0_E} is the assumed problem-dependant p-convergence rate and π_0 is the longitudinal approximation order within the initial mesh.

Finally, in the case of q-adaptivity of thin dielectric or piezoelectric body, the element transverse order of approximation of the electric potential field in the final mesh has to be determined. The following formula can be proposed for this purpose [26]:

$$\rho_T = \rho_0 - \frac{1}{2} \log_{t/2l} \frac{\theta_{I_E}^2 E_I}{\gamma_{m,t}^2 \|\phi_0\|_W^2} \tag{43}$$

where ρ_0 is the element transverse approximation order applied in the initial mesh, t and $2l$ are the transverse and longitudinal dimensions of a thin member (body or part) and θ_{I_E} is the modeling error estimated value of a finite element of the intermediate mesh.

4. Numerical examples

In this section, some comparative examples for problems of elasticity, dielectricity and piezoelectricity are presented. Attention is focused on the comparison of effectiveness of three main algorithms applied in our generalizing approach to adaptive modeling and analysis of the problems of three mentioned classes. The tested numerical procedures include hierarchical approximations, error estimation and error-controlled adaptivity. In the first case of hierarchical approximations, convergence curves for the three classes of problems are compared. In the second case of error estimation with the equilibrated residual method, effectivities of the global estimators in three problems are presented. In the third case of adaptive procedure, effectivity of the adaptation is checked through the comparison of the adaptive convergence curves. Also, the ability to reach the assumed admissible error in problems of three types is assessed.

4.1. Model structures

Here, the same domain geometry is considered in the problems of elasticity, dielectricity and piezoelectricity. Its square longitudinal dimensions are equal to $2l = 3.1415 \cdot 10^{-2}$ m, while its thickness equals $t = 0.01 \cdot 10^{-2}$ m. The domain thickness may change if necessary. This domain can represent a plate structure in the mechanical case, a thin dielectric in the electric case and a thin piezoelectric structure in the electromechanical case.

So as to be able to compare three different physical problems, physical properties of the materials and the external load and charge are assumed such that the induced mechanical and electric potential energies are of the same order. The isotropic mechanical properties of the plate structure and thin piezoelectric correspond to a typical piezoelectric material and are taken from [27].

Young's modulus is assumed to be equal to $E = 0.5 \cdot 10^{11}$ N/m^2, while the applied Poisson's ratio is $\nu = 0.294$. The isotropic dielectric properties of the dielectric and piezoelectric are characterized with the permittivity equal to $\delta = 0.1593 \cdot 10^{-7}$ F/m. The nonzero anisotropic piezoelectric constants are $d_{13} = d_{23} = -0.15 \cdot 10^{-9}$ C/N, $d_{33} = 0.3 \cdot 10^{-9}$ C/N and $d_{52} = d_{61} = 0.5 \cdot 10^{-9}$ C/N (compare [27] again). The surface load of magnitude $p = 0.4 \cdot 10^6$ N/m^2 is applied to the upper surface of the elastic and piezoelectric structures. Furthermore, the surface electric charge of density $c = 0.2 \cdot 10^{-1}$ C/m^2 is applied to the upper surface of the dielectric and piezoelectric domains.

The kinematic boundary conditions within the mechanical field of displacements of the elastic and piezoelectric structures assume all edges (lateral sides) clamped—no displacements on these edges are present. In the case of the electric field of potential within the dielectric and piezoelectric domains, grounding is assumed around the domain (zero potential on the lateral sides).

In the next sections, only symmetric quarters of the structures are shown due to the symmetry of the applied geometry, load and charge distributions and boundary conditions.

4.2. Convergence of hierarchical approximations

Figures 1 and **2** illustrate distributions of the effective value (*sef*) of a stress tensor (effective stress) and the electric displacement vector magnitude (*dm*) for the purely mechanical and electric problems, while **Figures 3** and **4** present the same quantities corresponding to the electromechanical problem. The displayed values are obtained due to solution of the corresponding global problems, either (1) or (5) or (9). Comparing **Figure 1** with **Figure 3** as well as **Figures 2** and **4**, one can notice that the stresses in the piezoelectric case are changed with

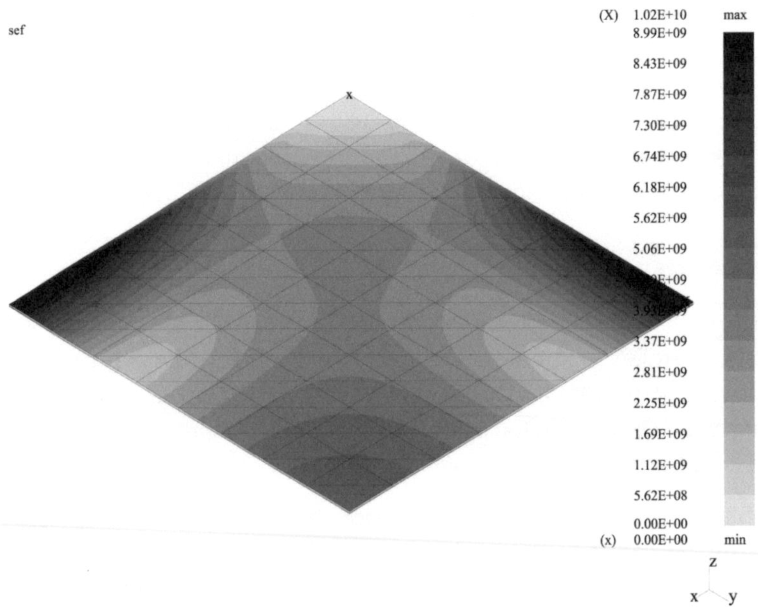

Figure 1. Effective stress in the purely mechanical case.

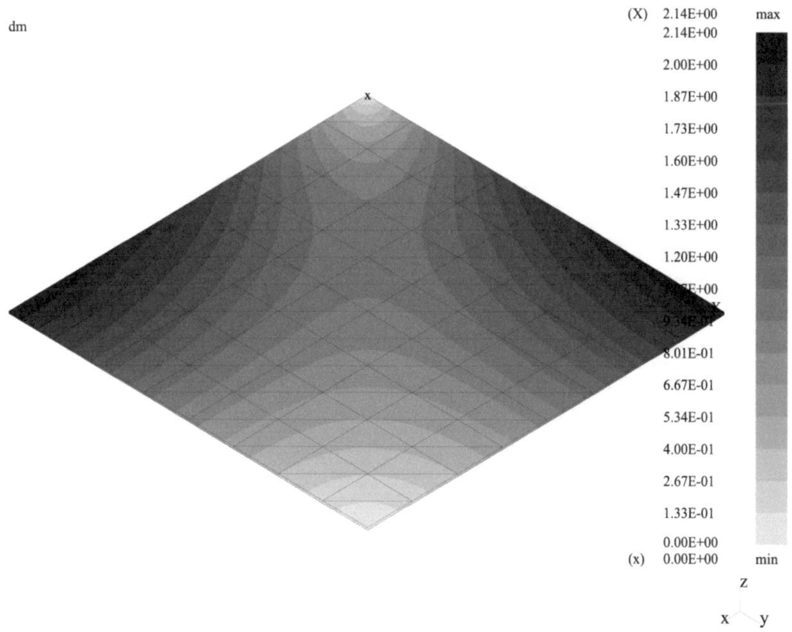

Figure 2. Magnitude of electric displacement in the purely electric case.

respect to the purely elastic case due to the presence of the electromechanical coupling. Similarly, the electric displacements of the piezoelectric case look different to those of the purely dielectric example due to the influence of the coupled mechanical displacements field.

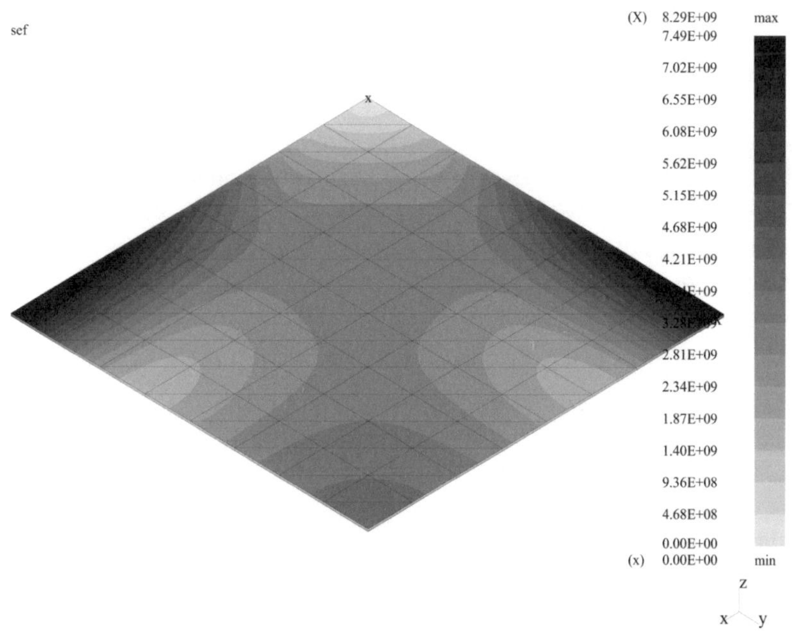

Figure 3. Effective stress in the coupled problem.

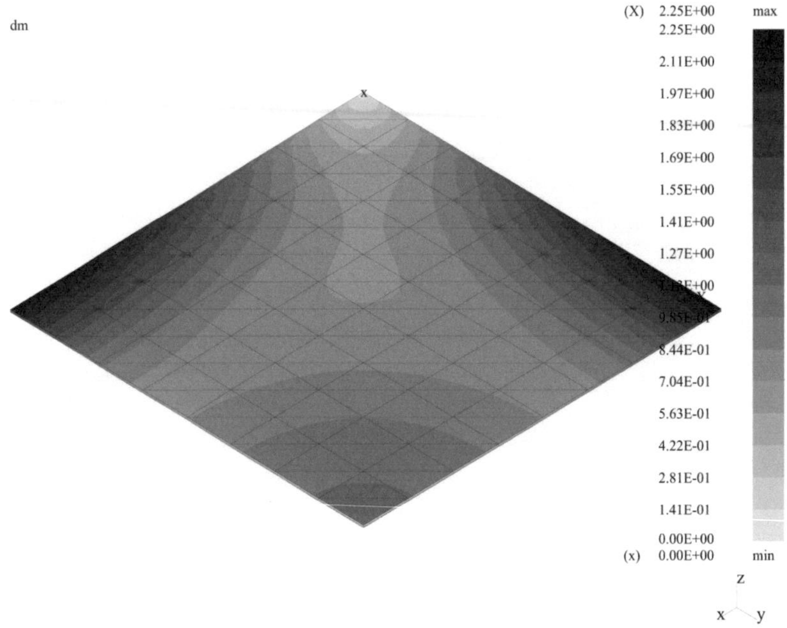

Figure 4. Magnitude of electric displacement in the coupled problem.

The h- and p-convergence curves for the elastostatic case are presented in **Figures 5** and **6**. The electrostatic problem solution h- and π-convergence curves are displayed in **Figures 7** and **8**. The solution convergence curves for the stationary piezoelectricity are shown in **Figures 9** and **10**. In these figures, the absolute values of the approximation errors are plotted versus the number N of the applied degrees of freedom. The number of degrees of freedom changes due to the increase in either the number of subdivisions $m = l/h$ (the case of h-convergence) or the longitudinal approximation order p or π (the case of p-convergence). The applied values of the discretization parameters of the uniform meshes are $m = 1, 2, \ldots, 8$, $p = \pi = 1, 2, \ldots, 6$ while the transverse orders of approximation are kept constant and equal to $q \equiv I = 2$ or/and $\rho \equiv J = 2$, with $\pi \equiv pi$ and $\rho \equiv rho$. The error is calculated as a square root of the difference of the potential energy of the numerical solution and the exact value of this energy in three cases: mechanical, electric or electromechanical. As the exact values of the solutions to three problems are not known, these values are replaced by the best numerical ones obtained from the meshes of $p = \pi = 9$, $h = 9$, $q = \rho = 2$.

The following findings can be formulated based on the analysis and comparison of the drawings. The convergence curves for the purely mechanical problem consist of three parts. The first part, almost horizontal and flat, corresponds to the presence of the numerical locking. The second part of the highest slope corresponds to the so-called asymptotic convergence. The third part of worse convergence is affected by the influence of the boundary layer. Such a picture of convergence is typical for elastic problems and displacement finite element formulation (compare [5]). In the case of the pure dielectricity, the curves consists of two parts only—the second and third ones. No locking is observed for this problem. In the case of the coupled problem of piezoelectricity, three parts of the curves appear again. As far

http://dx.doi.org/10.5772/intechopen.72265

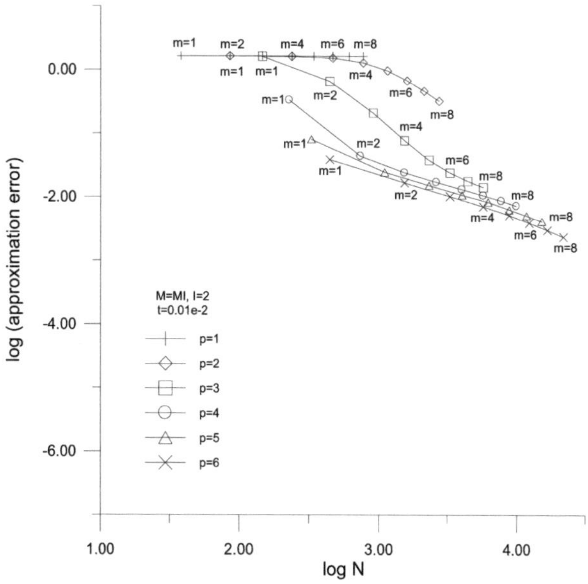

Figure 5. *h*-Convergence in the purely elastic problem.

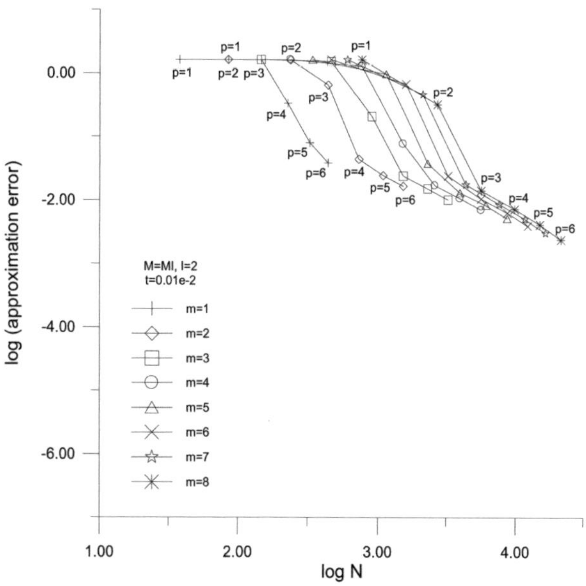

Figure 6. *p*-Convergence in the purely elastic problem.

as the asymptotic convergence range is concerned, it should be noticed that in the purely electric case, the convergence is much higher (slopes are more steep) than in the purely mechanical problem. Additionally, the boundary layer effect in the dielectric problem is less severe than in the mechanical one—the slopes of the third parts of the curves are higher in the former case.

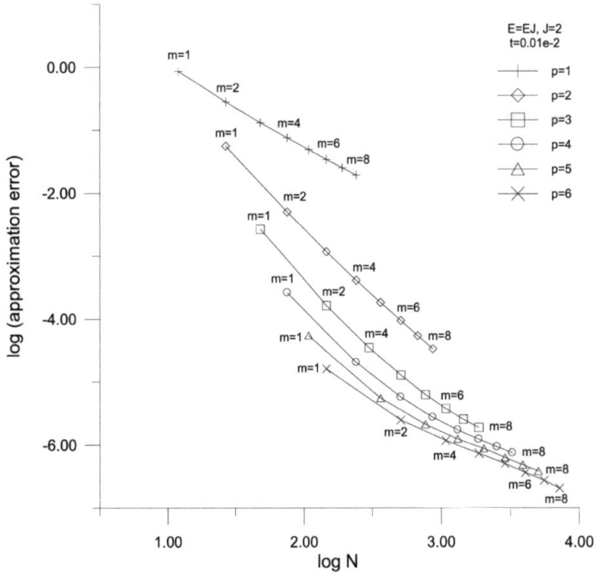

Figure 7. *h*-Convergence in the purely dielectric problem.

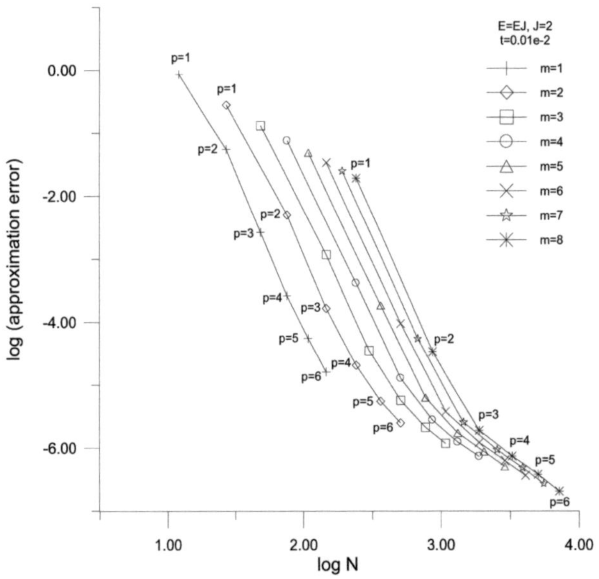

Figure 8. *p*-Convergence in the purely dielectric problem.

As it comes to the piezoelectricity, the following observations can be seen. The first parts of the convergence curves in the case of the coupled problem are not flat but are bent, that is, the monotonic character of these parts is not retained. This observation reflects the fact of change

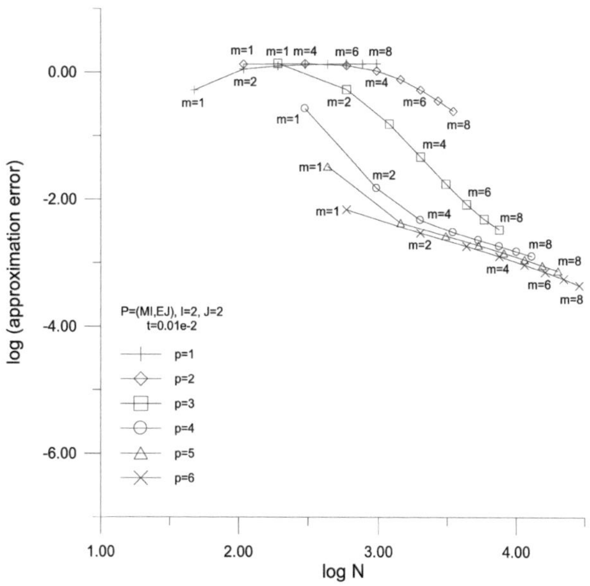

Figure 9. h-Convergence in the coupled piezoelectric problem.

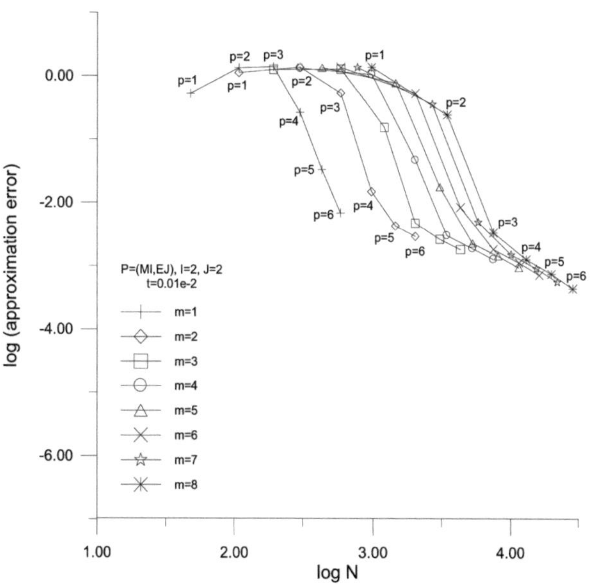

Figure 10. p-Convergence ($\pi = p$) in the coupled problem.

of the sign of the potential energy, which is composed of mechanical, electric and coupling contributions of different signs. The solution convergence curves of the piezoelectric problem, in the asymptotic and boundary-layer ranges, lie just between the corresponding curves of the pure problems, with a tendency to be closer to the purely mechanical case.

4.3. Effectivity of error estimation

In this section, results concerning application of the equilibrated residual method to the analogous model problems of elastostatics, electrostatics and stationary piezoelectricity are presented. The data of the problems are taken from Section 4.1. The thickness of the analyzed domains is now equal to $t = 0.15 \cdot 10^{-2}$ m. The surface traction equals now $p = 4.0 \cdot 10^6$ N/m^2. This value has changed due to the thickness change so as to assure the same order of the electric and mechanical potential energies, as well as the same order of the electric and mechanical parts of this energy, in the tests concerning three mentioned problems of elasticity, dielectricity and piezoelectricity. Presentation of the results starts with the purely elastic case. In **Figure 11**, the chosen example of the estimated total error distribution is presented for the uniform mesh discretization parameters $m = 3$, $p = 4$ and $q = 2$. The level of the relative estimated total errors in elements (denoted as $(M)\,nt$) for the mechanical problem can be seen in the figure, as well as the average global value of the error estimator, marked as *avr*. The estimated local errors represent the square root of the difference between the mechanical potential energies of the numerical global solution under consideration, determined by (1), and the solution obtained from the local problems (31). In the case of a local error indicator, these energies are limited to a single element, while in the case of the global error estimator, the energies of all elements are taken into account. **Figure 12** presents effectivity indices of the global error estimators as a function of the longitudinal approximation order p. The effectivity indices are calculated as ratios of the global estimators by the global values of the true total, approximation and modeling errors. The global values of the errors are equal to the square root of the difference of the appropriate energies. As the exact values of the solutions,

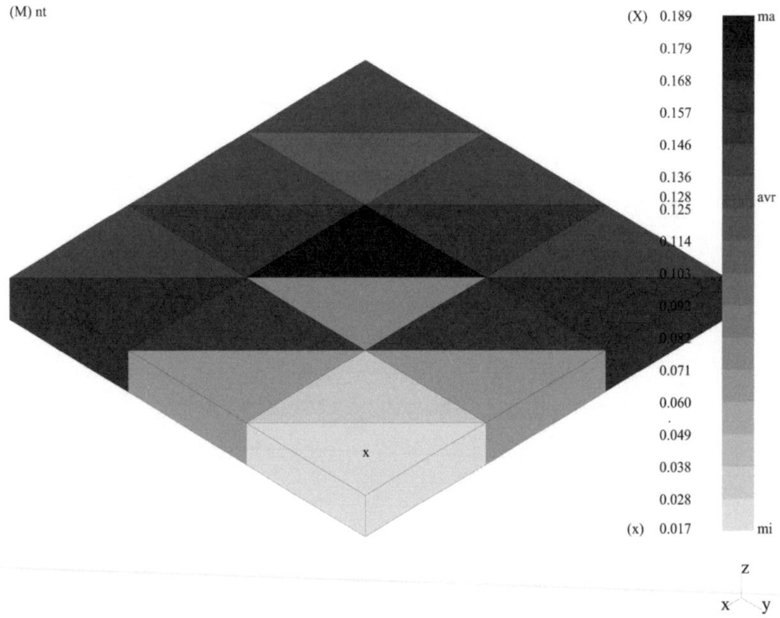

Figure 11. Estimated total errors in the purely mechanical case.

necessary for the exact energy values, are not known, they are replaced with the numerical values obtained by using (1), from the finest and richest meshes possible, that is, with $m = 9$, $p = 9$ and $q = 2$ or $q = 6$ in the cases of the approximation and total errors calculations, respectively.

Figures 13 and **14** display the analogous results for the electrostatic case. The first figure shows the exemplary distribution of the locally estimated relative total errors (denoted as $(E)nt$), and also the average error estimate (marked with *avr*), for $m = 3$, $\pi \equiv pi = 4$, $\rho \equiv rho = 2$. The global solution to the problem (5) and the solutions to the local problems (32) are employed for the determination of two electric potential energies. These energies correspond to the numerical solution and the estimate of the exact solution. As far as the second figure is concerned, it illustrates the change of the effectivity indices of estimation of the total, approximation and modeling errors as a function of the longitudinal order of approximation π. In order to obtain the necessary exact values of the energies, the global problem (5) was applied again, with $m = 9$, $\pi = 9$ and $\rho = 2$ or $\rho = 6$, for the calculation cases of the approximation and total errors, respectively.

The analogous estimated error distributions and the analogous plots of the effectivity indices versus $p = \pi$ for the piezoelectricity case are shown in **Figures 15–18**. Here, the numerical and estimated values of the mechanical and electric parts of potential energies, necessary for the exemplary local and average estimated error values determination, are obtained from (9), with $m = 3$, $p = \pi = 4$, $q = \rho = 2$ and (33), respectively. The exact energy values necessary for effectivity calculations are obtained through the global numerical approximation (9), with $m = 9$, $p = \pi = 9$ and $q = \rho = 2$ or $q = \rho = 6$ and $\pi \equiv pi$, $\rho \equiv rho$.

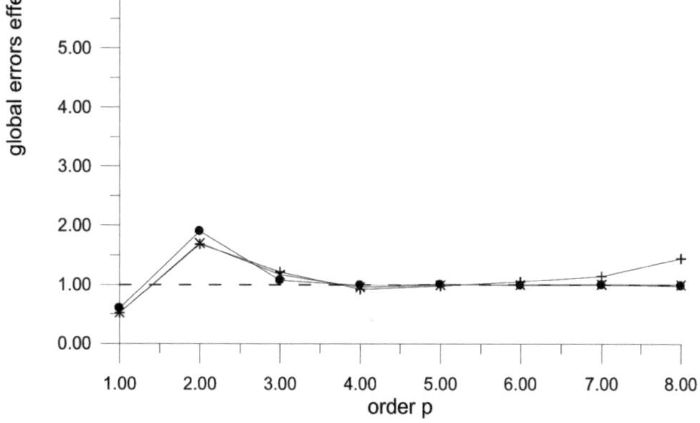

Figure 12. Effectivities of the estimators in the purely mechanical case.

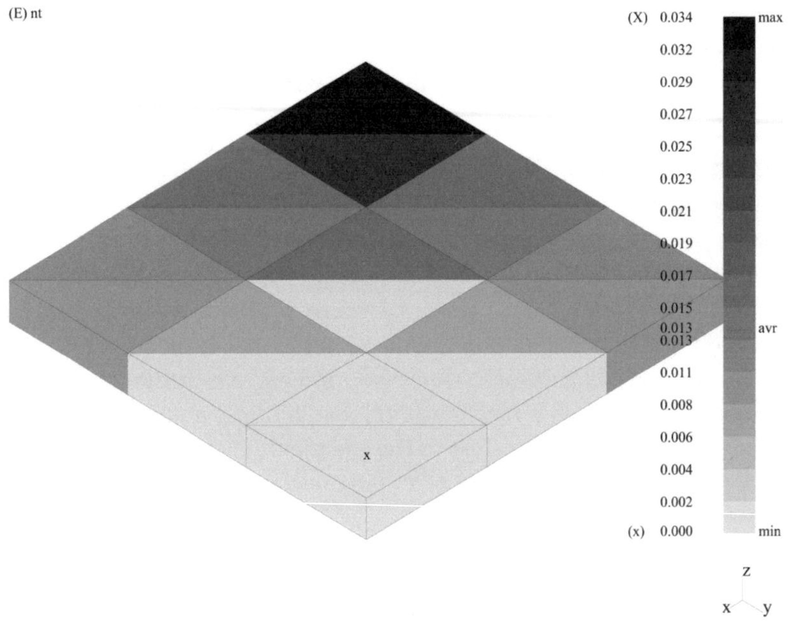

Figure 13. Estimated total errors in the purely electric case.

Comparing **Figures 11, 13, 15** and **17**, one can notice that the estimated total error level for the cases of elasticity and dielectricity are not the same for the corresponding model problems, as the latter problem produces the lower local and global error estimates. The average relative

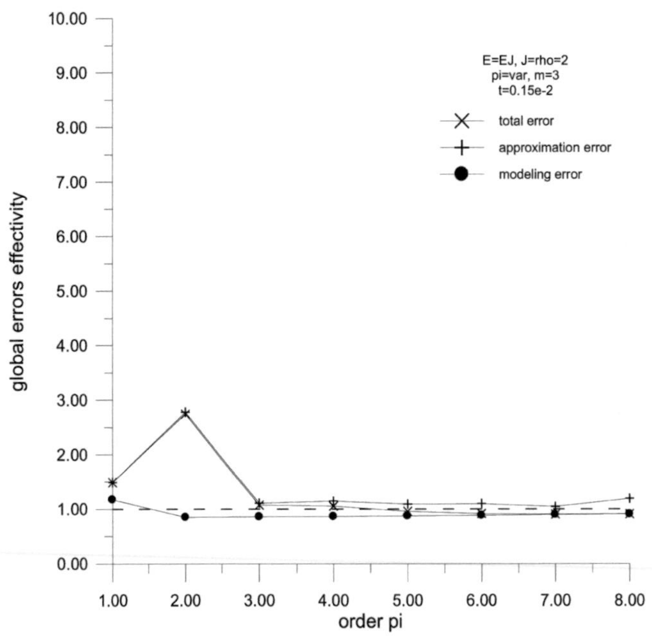

Figure 14. Effectivities of the estimators in the purely electric case.

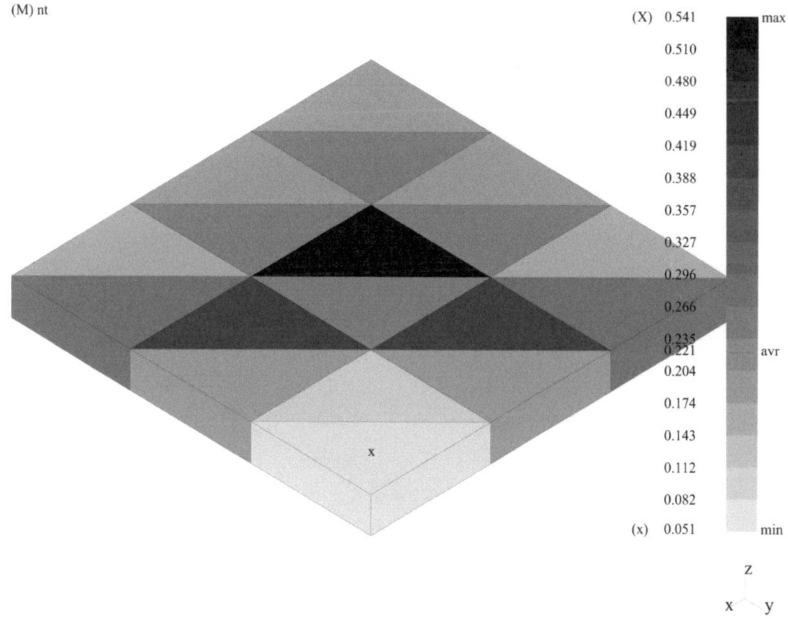

Figure 15. Mechanical parts of the estimated total errors (piezoelectricity).

values of the total error estimates for these two cases are equal to 0.128 and 0.013, respectively. In the case of the piezoelectricity, the estimated local and global error values are higher than in the previous two cases. The mechanical and electric parts of the average total error estimate are

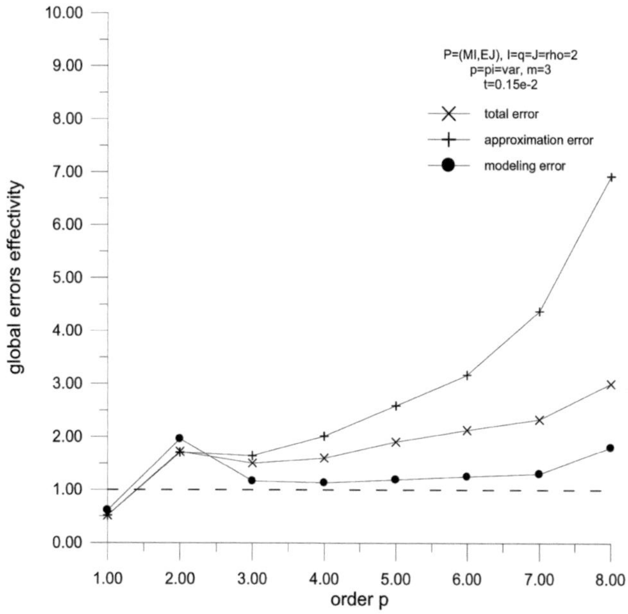

Figure 16. Effectivities of estimators' mechanical parts (piezoelectricity).

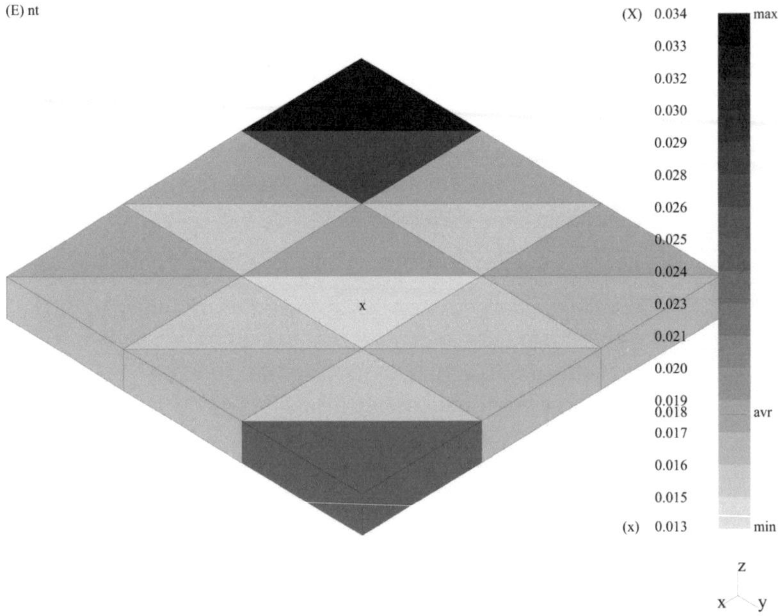

Figure 17. Electrical parts of the estimated total errors (piezoelectricity).

equal to 0.221 and 0.018, respectively. As far as the effectivities for three model problems from **Figures 12, 14, 16, 18** are concerned, one can see that the pure problems deliver very similar effectivities—in both problems close to the desired values of 1. The values are almost everywhere

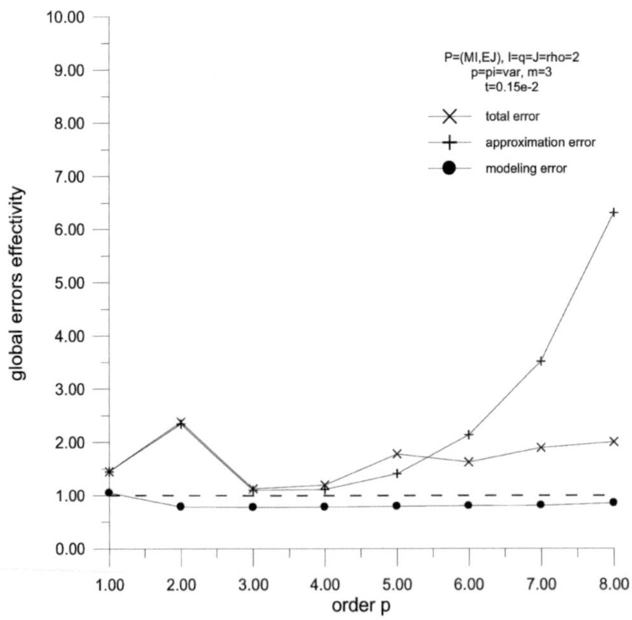

Figure 18. Effectivities of estimators' electrical parts (piezoelectricity).

larger than 1, and this result is consistent with the upper bound property of the estimation present in the pure problems (compare [19]). In the case of the coupled piezoelectric problem, global effectivities are much greater than 1, that is, the estimated global error values are much overestimated. This suggests that some additional techniques should be applied in the error estimation by the equilibrated residual method if one wants the effectivities to become closer to 1. A remedy can be the application of the higher order equilibration [14] in the piezoelectricity problems, instead of the linear equilibration used in this work and usually applied to pure problems.

4.4. Convergence of *hp*-adaptivity

In **Figures 19–24**, the results illustrating both *hp*-adapted meshes and convergence of the corresponding adaptation processes are presented for three model problems of elasticity, dielectricity and piezoelectricity. In these problems, the original data are recalled from Section 4.1. The thickness of the domains is equal to $t = 0.15 \cdot 10^{-2}$ m, as in the previous test. In this way, the influence of the error estimation, performed in the previous subsection, on effectiveness of the mesh adaptation presented here can be assessed. Also, it is worth noticing that for the applied thickness value, the locking and boundary layer phenomena do not influence convergence very much. Note also that the presented adaptation is controlled with the estimated values of the element approximation errors within the displacements and electric potential fields by means of the formulas (37), (38) or/and (40), (42).

In the first two figures, the purely elastic case is presented. **Figure 19** presents the mesh obtained in the three-step adaptive process. Both the changes of the mesh density and the

Figure 19. Final *hp*-adapted mesh in the purely mechanical case.

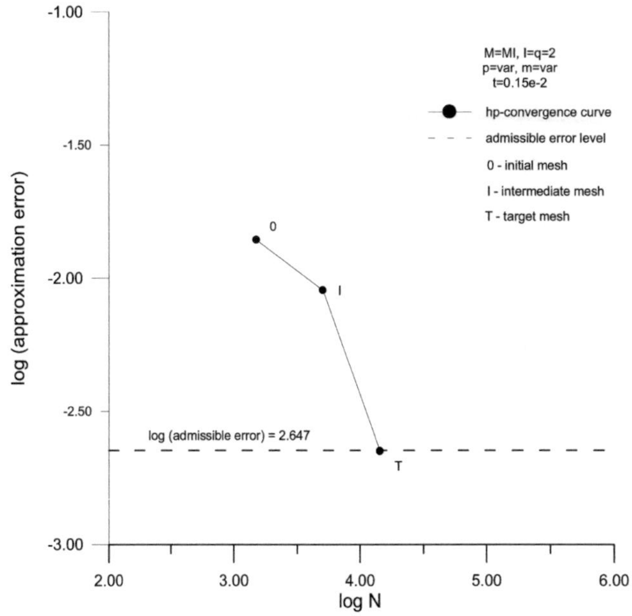

Figure 20. *hp*-Adaptive convergence in the purely mechanical case.

element changes of the longitudinal order of approximation can be seen in **Figure 19**. The initial mesh (not displayed) corresponds to the discretization parameters $m = 3$, $p = 4$ and $q = 2$. In this mesh, the longitudinal approximation order equal to $p = 4$ is applied in order to

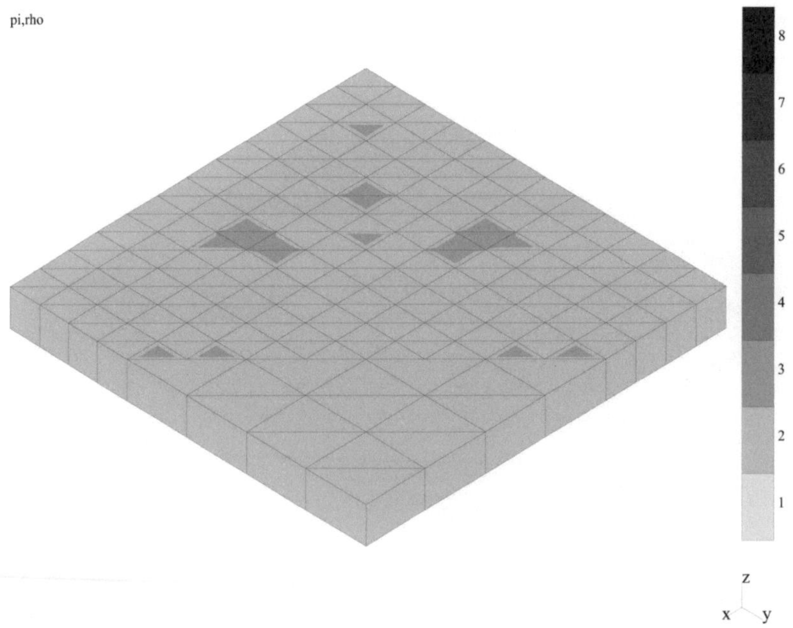

Figure 21. Final $h\pi$-adapted mesh in the purely electric case.

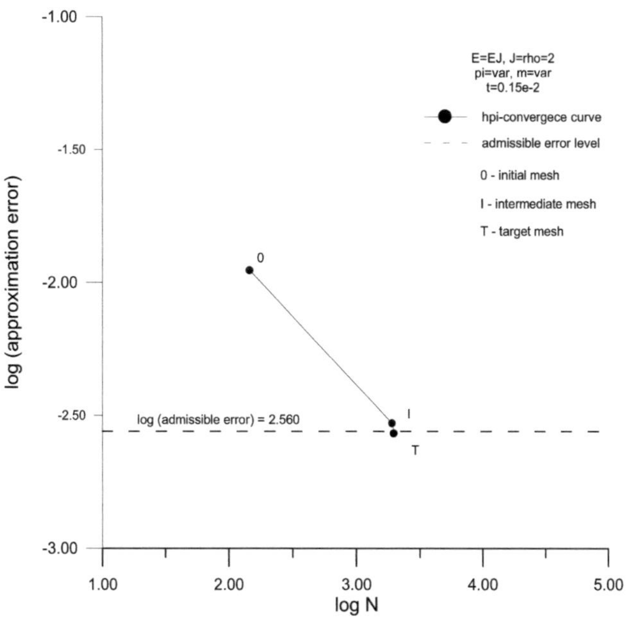

Figure 22. *hπ*-Adaptive convergence in the purely electric case.

remove the influence of the locking phenomenon present in purely mechanical problems. The target approximation error for the final mesh is assumed to be 0.1 with the ratio of the errors from the intermediate and final meshes equal to 2. The next **Figure 20** displays the

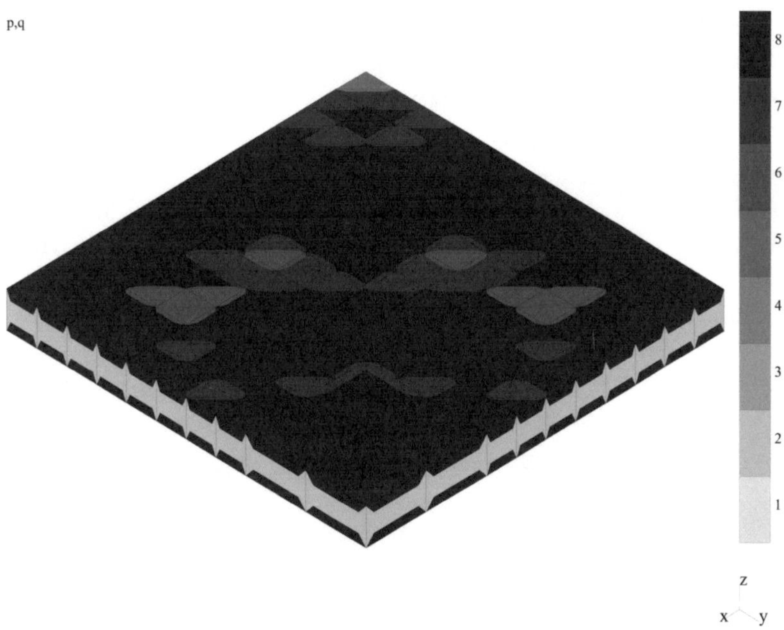

Figure 23. Final *hp*-adapted mesh in the coupled problem.

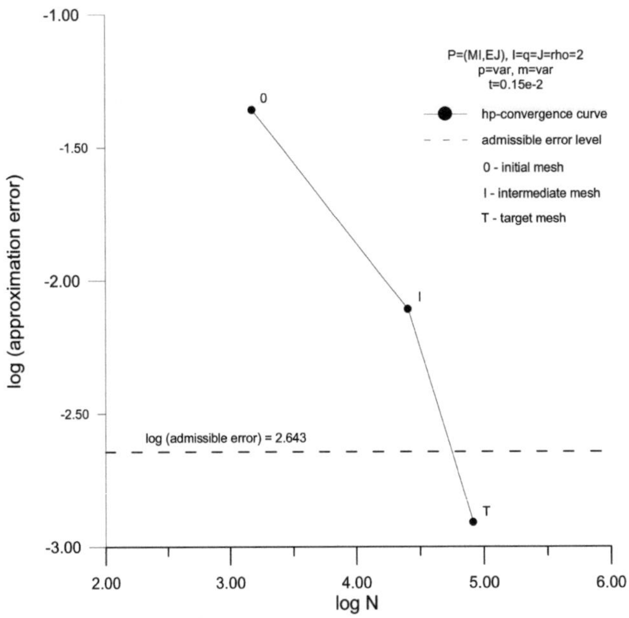

Figure 24. *hp*-Adaptive convergence in the coupled problem.

hp-convergence of the solution during the adaptation process. In the error calculations, the exact value of the energy is replaced with the value obtained for the best numerical discretization of the second-order ($q = 2$) hierarchical shell model, where $m = 9$ and $p = 9$. The final true error value corresponds to the lowest (third) point of the convergence curve. This value can be compared with the horizontal dotted line corresponding to the admissible error level.

Figures 21 and **22** present the similar results for the purely electric case. The first of them displays the final mesh resulting from the three-step adaptation. The only difference within the applied discretization parameters is $\pi = 2$ within the electric potential field of the initial mesh. This value replaces $p = 4$ in the displacements field of the previous example. The assumption of $\pi = 2$ results from lower error level within the former field and the lack of the numerical locking within dielectric problems. Subsequently, the second figure illustrates the $h\pi$-convergence curve of the adapted solution. The curve can be compared with the admissible error level again. The exact solution, necessary for the error calculations, is approximated by the numerical solution corresponding to $m = 9$, $\pi = 9$ and $\rho = 2$.

The next two couples, **Figures 23** and **24**, as well as **Figures 25** and **26**, present exactly the same results, that is, final meshes and adaptive convergence curves for the displacements and electric potential fields, respectively, in the case of the coupled problem of piezoelectricity. For both fields, exactly the same initial mesh and error control parameters are applied as for the pure problems of elasticity and dielectricity. The presence of locking in piezoelectric problems is taken into account, hence $p = 4$ and $\pi = 2$ are set within the initial meshes of the corresponding fields. In the case of the adaptive convergence curves, the admissible error levels are marked with the dotted lines

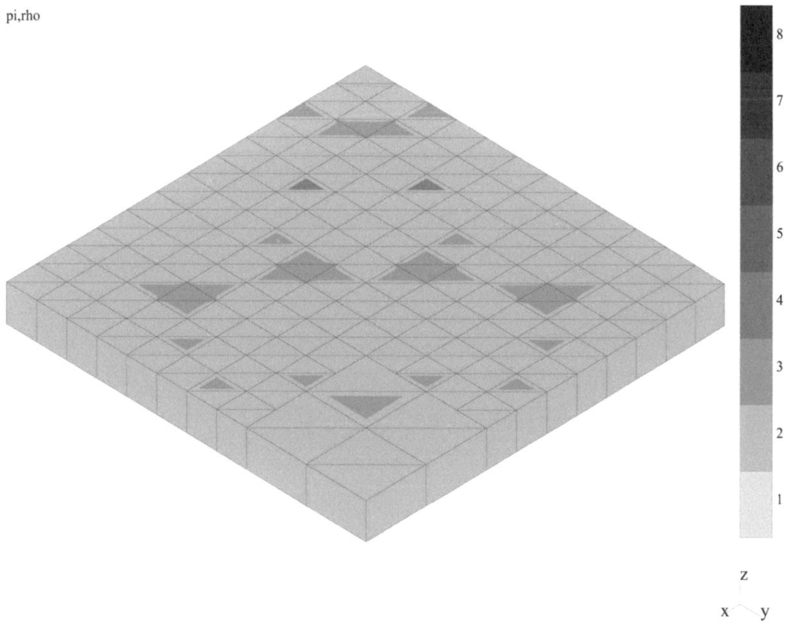

Figure 25. Final $h\pi$-adapted mesh in the coupled problem.

again. The numerical approximation of the exact solution entering the error calculations is obtained from the discretization based on $m = 9, p = \pi = 9, q = \rho = 2$.

Discussion of the obtained numerical results can be concluded in the following way. In the case of the pure elasticity, the admissible error value is reached in three steps. The estimated average approximation error relative value for the initial mesh is 0.084. A relatively rare h-mesh is generated as the error is relatively low in the initial mesh and overestimation for $p = 4$ does not occur (compare **Figure 12**). Then the mesh is well p-enriched.

In the case of the pure dielectricity, the relatively fine h-mesh is produced because of the error overestimation for $\pi = 2$ (see **Figure 14**) present in the initial mesh. The estimated average approximation error relative value for the initial mesh is moderate and equal to 0.124. As a result, the p-enrichment is reduced (barely visible). The admissible error is reached, however.

In the case of the piezoelectricity, the changes in the common h-mesh come from the relatively large errors of the displacements field in the initial mesh. The corresponding average error value for the displacements field is equal to 0.227, while for the electric potential field, it equals 0.127. The displacements field errors in elements are larger than those of the electric potential field. As a result, the common h-mesh is too fine for the electric potential. This effect is enforced by the overestimation for $\pi = 2$ (**Figure 18**). The following π-enrichment is weak. However, the admissible error level is reached for the potential field. This demonstrates that the idea of the common h-mesh for both fields works well also in the case of the field of lower errors. As far as the displacement field is concerned, one can notice that the error overestimation for $p = 4$ (see **Figure 16**) in the common h-mesh produces too rich p-mesh for displacements and thus the

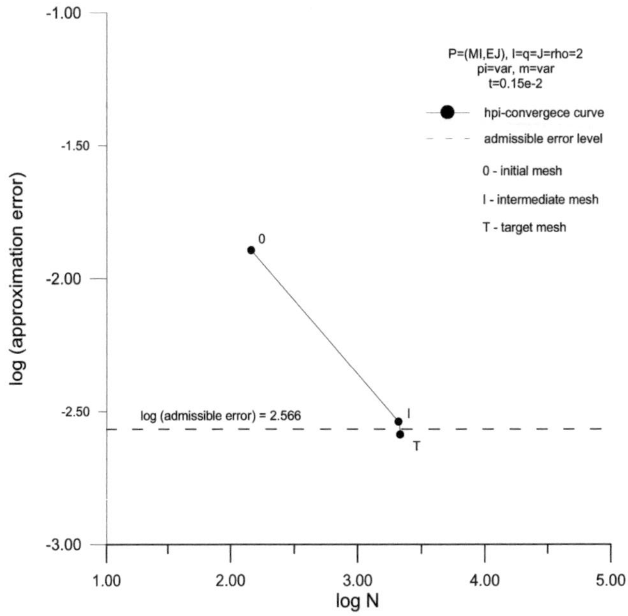

Figure 26. $h\pi$-Adaptive convergence in the coupled problem.

corresponding admissible error value is far exceeded. The obtained solution for displacements is better than expected.

5. Conclusions

In this chapter, the algorithms of hierarchical modeling, hierarchical approximations, error estimation and adaptivity control, so far utilized successfully for elastic problems, are applied to the problems of dielectricity and piezoelectricity. To the best knowledge, no examples of such application had been reported in the existing literature.

This chapter shows how to assess effectivity of the algorithms of hierarchical approximations, equilibrated residual method of error estimation and three-step adaptive procedure, originally applied to elasticity and possible also in dielectricity and the coupled piezoelectric problems.

The observations from the tests concerning hierarchical *hp*-approximations allow for the following generalizations. The applied hierarchical approximations can be effective in modeling and simulation of all three classes of problems. The *h*- and *p*-convergence rate is the highest for the purely dielectric problems and the lowest for the analogous purely elastic ones. The convergence of the piezoelectric problems is located between the convergences of the corresponding pure problems. In the case of the pure problems, the convergence curves are monotonic, while in the case of the coupled problems of piezoelectricity, the loss of monotonicity can happen because of the sign change of the electromechanical potential energy.

The general conclusions concerning the applied error estimation method are as follows. In the pure problem of elasticity, the effectivities of the modeling, approximation and total errors are all close to 1.0, except for the cases of poor discretization ($p = 1, 2$). In the pure dielectric problems, the values of the effectivities are between 0.9 and 1.0. For the cases of poor discretization, these values are close to 2.0. In the case of piezoelectricity, the indices are close to their values from the pure problems for low values of the approximation order, that is, for $p \leq 3$ or/and $\pi \leq 3$. For higher values of the approximation order, the corresponding effectivities are much higher than 1.0 for the approximation error. A bit smaller overestimation can be seen in the case of the total error. It can be concluded that for rich discretizations, some additional techniques are necessary in the case of piezoelectricity, so as to enforce values of the effectivities closer to 1.0.

Generalizations related to the applied adaptivity control algorithms can be formulated in the following way. For the analogous mechanical, electric and electromechanical problems, the three-step adaptive strategy leads to similar convergence results as it comes to the final mesh true error level, even though the *hp*-path in each of three cases can be different. The final error values are usually smaller or close to the admissible error level. In the case of piezoelectricity, too fine or/and too rich meshes may be generated, if overestimation, coming from the error estimation procedure, occurs.

The results concerning the effectivity of the application of the mentioned three algorithms to the dielectric and piezoelectric problems as well as the comparative effectivity analysis of the analogous mechanical, electric and electromechanical problems are unique—no other examples of such results can be found in the related literature.

Acknowledgements

Partial financial support of the Polish Scientific Research Committee (now the National Science Centre) under the research grant no. N N504 5153 040 is thankfully acknowledged.

Author details

Grzegorz Zboiński[1,2]*

*Address all correspondence to: zboi@imp.gda.pl

1 Institute of Fluid Flow Machinery, Polish Academy of Sciences, Gdańsk, Poland

2 Faculty of Technical Sciences, University of Warmia and Mazury, Olsztyn, Poland

References

[1] Zboiński G. Problems of hierarchical modelling and *hp*-adaptive finite element analysis in elasticity, dielectricity and piezoelectricity. In: Petrova R, editor. Perusal of the Finite Element Method. Rijeka: InTech; 2016. Ch. 1. pp. 1-29

[2] Szabó BA, Sahrmann GJ. Hierarchic plate and shell models based on *p*-extension. International Journal for Numerical Methods in Engineering. 1988;**26**:1855-1881

[3] Zboiński G. Hierarchical Modeling and Finite Element Method for Adaptive Analysis of Complex Structures [D.Sc. thesis, in Polish]. 520/1479/2001. Gdańsk, Poland: Institute of Fluid Flow Machinery; 2001. 304 p

[4] Oden JT, Cho JR. Adaptive *hpq* finite element methods of hierarchical models for plate- and shell-like structures. Computer Methods in Applied Mechanics and Engineering. 1996;**136**:317-345

[5] Zboiński G. Adaptive *hpq* finite element methods for the analysis of 3D-based models of complex structures: Part 1. Hierarchical modeling and approximations. Computer Methods in Applied Mechanics and Engineering. 2010;**199**:2913-2940

[6] Carrera E, Boscolo M, Robaldo A. Hierarchic multilayered plate elements for coupled multifield problems of piezoelectric adaptive structures: Formulation and numerical assessment. Archives of Computational Methods in Engineering. 2007;**14**(4):384-430

[7] Zboiński G. Hierarchical models for adaptive modelling and analysis of coupled electro-mechanical systems. In: Łodygowski T, Rakowski J, Litewka P, editors. Recent Advances in Computational Mechanics. London: CRC Press; 2014. pp. 339-334

[8] Demkowicz L, Oden JT, Rachowicz W, Hardy O. Towards a universal *hp* adaptive finite element strategy. Part 1. A constrained approximation and data structure. Computer Methods in Applied Mechanics and Engineering. 1989;**77**:113-180

[9] Zboiński G. Application of the three-dimensional triangular-prism *hpq* adaptive finite element to plate and shell analysis. Computers & Structures. 1997;**65**:497-514

[10] Zboiński G, Jasiński M. 3D-based *hp*-adaptive first order shell finite element for modelling and analysis of complex structures: Part 1. The model and the approximation. International Journal for Numerical Methods in Engineering. 2007;**70**:1513-1545

[11] Zboiński G. 3D-based *hp*-adaptive first order shell finite element for modelling and analysis of complex structures: Part 2. Application to structural analysis. International Journal for Numerical Methods in Engineering. 2007;**70**:1546-1580

[12] Zboiński G, Ostachowicz W. An algorithm of a family of 3D-based solid-to-shell transition, *hpq*/*hp*-adaptive finite elements. J. Theoret. Appl. Mech. 2000;**38**:791-806

[13] Lammering R, Mesecke-Rischmann S. Multi-field variational formulation and related finite elements for piezoelectric shells. Smart Materials and Structures. 2003;**12**:904-913

[14] Ainsworth M, Oden JT. A Posteriori Error Estimation in Finite Element Analysis. New York: Wiley; 2000

[15] Ainsworth M, Oden JT, Wu W. A posteriori error estimation for *hp* approximation in elastostatics. Applied Numerical Mathematics. 1994;**14**:23-55

[16] Cho JR, Oden JT. A priori error estimations of *hp*-finite element approximations for hierarchical models of plate- and shell-like structures. Computer Methods in Applied Mechanics and Engineering. 1996;**132**:135-177

[17] Zboiński G. A posteriori error estimation for *hp*-approximation of the 3D-based first order shell model: Part I. Theoretical aspects. Applied Mathematics, Informatics and Mechanics. 2003;**8**(1):104-125

[18] Zboiński G. A posteriori error estimation for *hp*-approximation of the 3D-based first order shell model: Part II. Implementation aspects. Applied Mathematics, Informatics and Mechanics. 2003;**8**(2):59-83

[19] Zboiński G. Adaptive *hpq* finite element methods for the analysis of 3D-based models of complex structures: Part 2. A posteriori error estimation. Computer Methods in Applied Mechanics and Engineering. 2013;**267**:531-565

[20] Zboiński G. Application of the element residual methods to dielectric and piezoelectric problems. In: Kleiber M et al., editors. Advances in Mechanics: Theoretical, Computational and Interdisciplinary Issues. London: CRC Press; 2016. pp. 605-609

[21] Oden JT. Error estimation and control in computational fluid dynamics: The O. C. Zienkiewicz lecture. In: Proc. Math. of Finite Elements (MAFELAP VIII). Uxbridge: Brunel University; 1993. pp. 1-36

[22] Vokas C, Kasper M. Adaptation in coupled problems. International Journal for Computation and Mathematics in Electrical and Electronic Engineering. 2010;**29**(6):1626-1641

[23] Ciarlet PG. Mathematical Elasticity, Three-Dimensional Elasticity. Vol. 1. Amsterdam: North-Holland; 1988

[24] Ciarlet PG. Plates and Junctions in Elastic Multi-Structures. Berlin, Paris: Springer-Verlag, Masson; 1990

[25] Ramsey AS. Electricity and Magnetism: An Introduction to Mathematical Theory. Cambridge: Cambridge University Press; 2009

[26] Zboiński G. Adaptive Finite Element Method for Analysis of Electro-Mechanical Sensor/Actuator-Structure Systems: Report of the Research Project PB 5153/B/T02/2011/40 [in Polish]. Report no. 282/2015. Gdańsk, Poland: Institute of Fluid Flow Machinery; 2015

[27] Preumont A. Mechatronics: Dynamics of Electromechanical and Piezoelectric Systems. Dordrecht: Springer; 2006

[28] Zboiński G. Numerical tools for a posteriori detection and assessment of the improper solution limit, locking and boundary layers in analysis of thin-walled structures. In: Diez P, Wiberg NE, editors. Adaptive Modeling and Simulation 2005. Barcelona: CIMNE; 2005. pp. 321-330

[29] Zboiński G. Unresolved problems of adaptive hierarchical modelling and *hp*-adaptive analysis within computational solid mechanics. In: Kuczma M, Wilmański K, editors. Advanced Structural Materials, Computer Methods in Mechanics. Vol. 1. Berlin: Springer-Verlag; 2010. Ch. 7. pp. 111-145

[30] Jasiński M, Zboiński G. On some *hp*-adaptive finite element method for natural vibrations. Computers and Mathematics with Applications. 2013;**66**:2376-2399

Chapter 8

Vibration Simulation of Electric Machines

Marcel Janda and Kristyna Jandova

Additional information is available at the end of the chapter

http://dx.doi.org/10.5772/intechopen.72266

Abstract

This chapter deals with the basics of vibration calculations in electrical machines. It includes a brief introduction to the sources of vibration in electrical machines. In addition, the construction of electric machines is briefly summarized. It also describes the influence of individual parts of electric machines on vibration generation. The chapter also deals with the important steps that need to be taken when calculating vibration signal waveform using finite element method (Ansys). The individual sections summarize the most important requirements for setting the vibration calculation and it also deals with minimizing the calculation errors.

Keywords: vibration, finite element method, electric machines, vibration simulation, vibration sources, Ansys, Maxwell

1. Introduction

The vibration of electric machines is one of the causes of the function of electric machines. This is an undesirable phenomenon that cannot be completely separated. The vibrations of electric machines are very depending on the operating state of the electric machine. In the diagnostics of electrical machines, vibrations are used to identify failures of both electrical machines as well as mechanical connections to other machines and power failures. In practice, electrical machines can experience many types of malfunctions that can affect the function of the electrical machine itself or even destroy it. In some cases, vibrations generated by electrical machine failures can also damage other machinery near this machine. For this reason, prevention and early detection of malfunctions is important. In electrical machines, most of the progressive failures begin gradually to appear on the level or frequency spectrum of vibrations. Each failure has other symptoms (other vibration frequencies, direction, size, etc.). This makes it possible to determine the type of failure based on long-term tracking. In order to be able to identify in a timely manner, the type of malfunction that arises, it is necessary to know the manifestations of the individual faults. In earlier times, the only possibility of tracking and measuring the development of malfunctions was done on real machines. On the basis of this experience, the same foreseeability disturbances could be assumed in other machines. This process has been simplified with the onset of computing and finite element utilization. It is now possible to simulate the physical models in electrical machines in full extent. It is possible to interface individual types of models (mechanical, electromagnetic, thermal) and then achieve very accurate results. The Ansys program is a program that allows to solve physical phenomena in electrical machines. Thanks to the individual modules, it is possible to make electromagnetic, thermal and mechanical design of any electrical machine and then simulate its behavior in different operating states. Especially today, when using many types of inverters, it is a great advantage to connect a model to an electrical circuit. It allows to solve the influence of different methods of power supply on electric machine. For example, what effect the vibrations of the electric machine will have on higher harmonic generated inverter.

The problem of calculating vibrations in electrical machines is very complex due to the number of physical phenomena, and it is necessary to handle a large amount of information from many areas (mechanics, magnetism, etc.). For this reason, this chapter focuses on a basic approach to solution issues. In solving a particular problem, it is necessary to take into account the time requirement of individual calculations and to perform a sufficient amount of calculation simplifications which are based on the results requirements analysis. Simplification may involve adjustments to a particular model that is used for the calculations. Another simplification may be the neglect of some of the vibration sources that operate in the electric machine, and so on. The main requirement is that the simplification of the model does not cause the error to be calculated. Therefore, it is necessary to familiarize themselves with the construction of the simulated machine, the sources of vibration, the functions of individual parts and their effect on the propagation of vibrations [1, 2].

2. Vibration fundamentals

Vibrations are a mechanical phenomenon. It can be said that this is the movement of a flexible body or environment whose individual body vibrates around the equilibrium position.

The forces acting on the vibrating body define the motion equation:

$$m.\frac{d^2x}{dt^2} = F(t) - k.x - b.\frac{dx}{dt} \tag{1}$$

where m is body mass, x is deviation from the steady state of the body, $F(t)$ is force dependent on time, k is stiffness of the spring, and b is coefficient of damping.

The forces acting on any system create the oscillation itself. In a simple case, the oscillation has a harmonic character. This occurs when system is exposed to a single source with a constant exciting force. For the description of harmonic oscillation, the relationship is used:

$$x(t) = x_{max}.\sin(2.\pi.f.t) \tag{2}$$

where $x(t)$ is displacement value, x_{max} is maximum displacement value and f is vibration frequency.

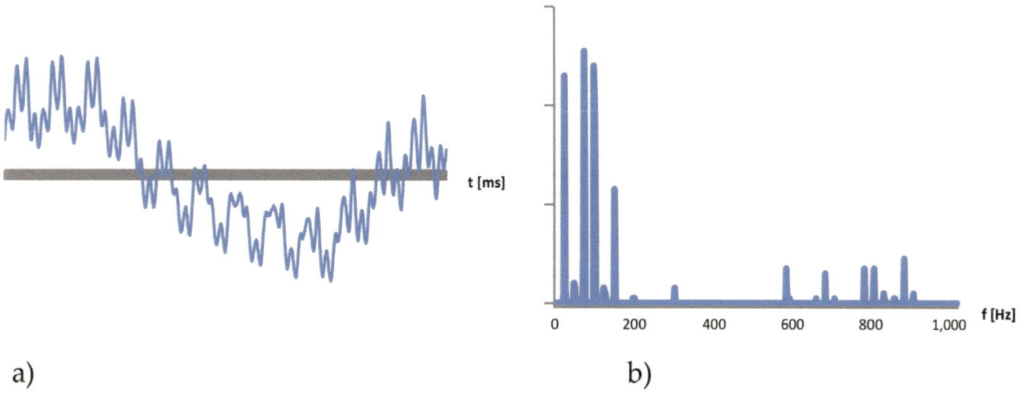

Figure 1. Induction motor vibration - a) Displacement of electric machine. b) FFT of vibration signal

This relationship applies to very simple oscillations. There are a number of sources and influences in electric machines that affect the vibration generation. The actual course of vibration displacement is, therefore, the sum of forces that change over time with different frequencies. The vibration displacement of the electric machine is shown in **Figure 1**. Fast Fourier Transformation is used to convert the signal into the frequency area and the result of this transformation is shown in **Figure 1**. **Figure 1** also shows the proportion of individual harmonics on the vibration signal [2–4].

3. Electric machine construction

For the calculation of vibrations in electrical machines, it is necessary to get basic information about their basic construction. The electric machine consists of a magnetic circuit. The magnetic circuit focuses most of the magnetic field into a defined area. The magnetic circuit itself is made of steel plates connected to the stator, respectively into the rotor. There are grooves cut on the internal circumference of the stator, into which the winding is inserted. The winding itself is one of the most important parts of electric machines. Copper with good electric conductivity and with 99% purity is used as a material of winding. In some applications, aluminum alloy of similar purity is used as a material. All electric motors have many other mechanical parts. These include a shaft on which the rotor plates are mounted. Although the shaft is, in most cases, a simple component that is made of a machined steel rod, it can have a great effect on the vibration of the machine. The main parameter that can affect the vibration is the quality of the processing and the quality of the whole rotor balancing. Due to the possible inhomogeneity of the material, the so-called mass unbalance can occur, causing the unwanted vibrations generated by the machine. The vibration level and frequency depend on the rotation speed of the rotor itself. Rotors are balancing in production to reduce this phenomenon.

Another important part of electrical machines is bearings. Many types of bearings are used in electrical machines. Ball bearing or roller bearings are commonly used. Nowadays, electromagnetic bearings are also used in special applications. From the vibration point of view, two separate phenomena occur in the bearings. The first is generating vibrations. This is in trouble-free condition caused, for example, by skipping the balls. The fault condition is the result of a missing lubricant. Failures can also be caused by poor quality lubricants. The second factor that affects the vibration of the electric machine is transmission between the rotor and the stator. Depending on the design of the bearings, they are partially damped.

The bearings are located in a bearing shield that is attached to the frame of the electric machine. A stator of the electric machine is also placed in the frame. There are several types of frames. The most commonly used are foot frame or flanges frame. Based on the type of frame, the machine is mechanically connected to the device. Again, the method of attachment of the machine affects the propagation or, respectively, vibration damping in the electrical machine. A terminal box is also attached to the frame and it serves to connect the power supply. The power supply method of the electric machine is another important factor. Electric machines are divided according to the following types of power supply:

- Asynchronous: Electric machines powered by AC voltage, either in one or in three phases. These are the most commonly used machines in the industry. They have different rotations of the magnetic field in the stator and the rotor.
- Synchronous: Electrical machine whose rotating speed is proportional to the frequency of the alternating current supply and independent of the load. Synchronous machines are very often used as a generator
- DC machines: Electrical machine powered by direct current. In most cases, it works with a static field in static machine parts. Permanent magnets may appear in their construction.

As can be seen from the brief description of the construction of the electric machine, it is a mechanically and intricately complex device with many variations. Various factors can affect the formation or propagation of vibrations. For this reason, it is always necessary to determine which parameters and structural elements are inserted into the calculation process and which are neglected [5–7, 10, 11].

3.1. Electrical machine failures

The generation of vibrations in an electric machine influences several design parameters. The influence on the generation of vibrations is mainly due to components design, mainly their shape and quality of production. With the time of use of the electrical machine in operation, vibration and wear of individual components increase.

Vibration sources are identified in vibration spectrum. Each vibration source takes effect of specific frequency in the spectrum. The amplitude is proportional to the degree of damage. For each source that causes the peaks at corresponding frequencies with increasing deviation, the value of peaks increases [2, 8].

Examples of electrical machine faults that can be modeled with finite element method are:

- Unbalance of the rotor: The unbalance depends on the distribution of the center of gravity of the rotor relative to its axis of rotation. Because of the uneven distribution of matter, the imbalance causes centrifugal force, noise and rotor vibration. With higher speeds, vibration is increasing.

- Eccentric rotor: Eccentricity occurs especially when the rotary axis is shifted relative to the geometric axis. Because of the eccentric rotor, there is a variable air gap between the stator and the rotor that generates pulsating vibrations. The greatest vibration reaches the first harmonic component. The rotor eccentricity contributes to vibration and noise. It causes an unbalanced pull of magnetic force in the rotor and bending the shaft.

There are two types of eccentricity:

Static eccentricity: Situation, when the rotor is deflected from the center of the engine and still rotates around its own axis of rotation. This is because of the static eccentricity. The size of the air gap is not constant over its entire circumference, resulting in stronger interactions between the stator and rotor magnetic fields in places with a smaller air gap.

Dynamic eccentricity: In the latter case, dynamic eccentricity occurs when the rotor rotates in the geometric center of the engine but does not rotate around its own axis of rotation. The air gap is a function of both position and time. The variable air gap rotates at a frequency equivalent to the rotational speed of the rotor.

- Bent shaft: The cause of the shaft deformation is the difference between the geometric axis and the axis of rotation. The geometric axis of the bent shaft has the shape of a curve. If the axis of rotation is not a straight line, it is a bend shaft. If the center of gravity does not lie on the rotary axis, the rotor is unbalanced [2, 8].

4. Vibration sources

For any calculation of the vibration level, it is necessary to become familiar with the various sources that generate these vibrations in electric machines. According to the physical principle, sources of vibration can be divided into several groups:

- Electromagnetic sources
- Mechanical sources
- Aerodynamic sources

Vibrations of electromagnetic and mechanical origin occur in all rotating electric machines. As a source of aerodynamic origin, it is usually a fan. Fan is often not a part of the construction of electric machines. For this reason, this chapter does not deal with the problem of calculating the vibrations thus generated [1].

4.1. Electromagnetic sources

Part of the vibration of electric machines is of electromagnetic origin. Their cause is the oscillation of the machine frame and its parts caused by electromagnetic forces. These forces are due to higher harmonics of the supply current, magnetic saturation, phase asymmetry, magnetostriction or disturbances in the magnetic circuit or electrical component of the machine.

The frequency spectrum of these vibrations has discrete character. Vibrations caused by the electrical causes occur mainly in the radial direction. Vibrations are occurred in the case of more varied air gap size in the axial direction, for example, due to non-symmetrical rotor mounting [1].

4.2. Mechanical sources

Mechanical vibrations are mainly caused by bearings, rotor balancing, machining of rotating parts and rotor mounting. Mechanical vibrations produced into electrical machines are also caused by connected devices. These external vibration sources include clutch misalignment or gearing, wedge gears or vibrations caused by connected loads [1].

4.3. Aerodynamic sources

The basic aerodynamic source of vibration is the fan in electric machine. Any obstruction that is exposed to air flow can generate vibration. The main cause of fan noise is the formation of turbulent airflow around the fan blades [1, 2, 4].

5. Vibration simulation using finite element method (FEM)

As already indicated in the previous sections of the chapter, the vibration of electric machines is a phenomenon that interferes with several physical areas (mechanics, electromagnetism, etc.) [8–10]. Therefore, the entire calculation process needs to be divided into several parts:

a. Determining Vibration Sources: at first, it is necessary to decide which resources to count. In the case of this chapter, the calculation is simplified only for the occurrence of vibrations by the effect of a time-dependent electromagnetic field. For this reason, it is possible to use Maxwell 2D or Maxwell 3D. This module allows to calculate the time-varying effect of the force in the magnetic circuit depending on the change of the electric current. The use of this program also allows to connect to a simulator of electrical circuits (program Simplorer). After connecting the supply current to the Maxwell model on the simpler electric circuit, it is possible to calculate the changes in the magnetic circuit caused by the control logic, that is, speed control.

b. Model creation: creating a model of an electric machine is one of the most important parts of the calculation itself. The user must choose between 2D and 3D model. The 2D model is much simpler, and therefore, the calculation itself takes a very short time. On the other hand, this is a great simplification of the calculation. The 3D model will allow for a more accurate calculation and consideration of the more influences affecting the calculation. However, the calculation of 3D models is considerably more demanding for computational power, and therefore, the calculation time is considerably longer.

c. Calculation of forces caused by selected sources: the next step is to determine the forces that act on the electrical machine. In this chapter, this is defined as a force of electromagnetic

http://dx.doi.org/10.5772/intechopen.72266

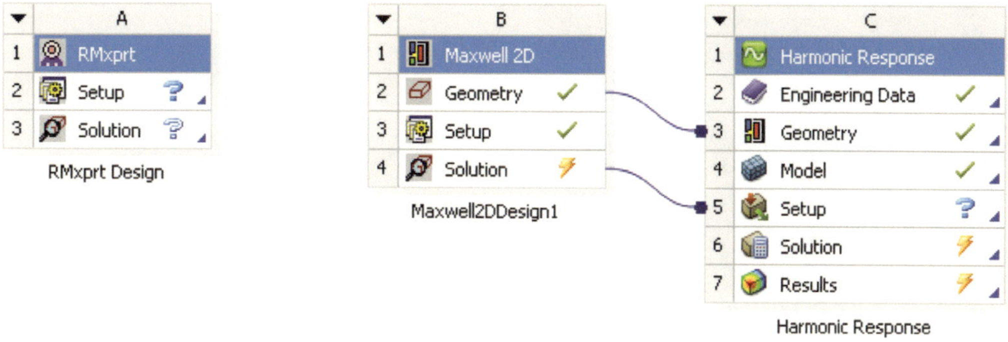

Figure 2. The Ansys workbench modules.

origin. The Maxwell program is used to determine them. These calculations can be supplemented by the calculation of the actual frequencies of the electric machine and also by external influences (such as asymmetry, etc.). An important factor is determining the right time step.

d. Determining vibration on the model: determination of vibration on a particular model is the result of a mechanical analysis [8–10] (**Figure 2**).

6. Model creation

The model of an electric machine can be made in several ways. One of them is the use of modern CAD systems to create geometry and its subsequent import into the computing environment. Another option is to create a model directly in the Ansys (using DesignModeler).

Another choice is to use the RMxprt environment. This module is primarily designed for rapid calculations of electrical machines. It features an environment for fast input of electrical machine dimensions. At the beginning of the job, the user selects a template that matches the specific machine type. The user then enters the main machine dimensions, slot size and slot type, and other parameters using simple tables.

RMxprt contains the following electrical machine templates:

- Synchronous machine
- Permanent magnet DC motor/DC machine
- Claw-pole alternator
- DC machine
- Single-phase/three-phase induction machine
- Universal motor

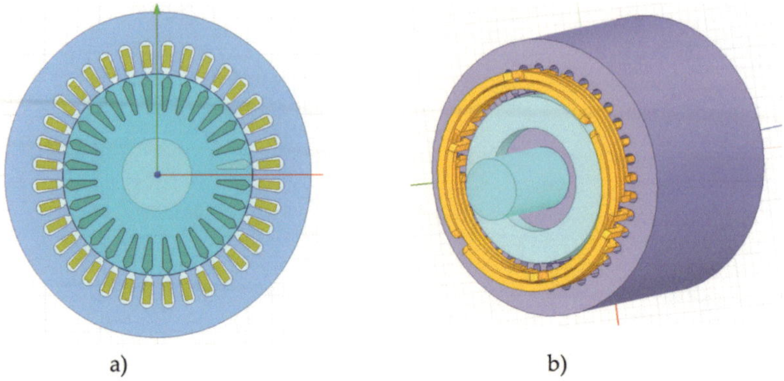

Figure 3. Models of induction machine generated by RMxprt: a) 2D model and b) 3D model.

User needs to know a lot of information to create a model in RMXprt. One of the items to know is the basic design dimensions. Furthermore, it is necessary to know how to place the windings in the grooves and also the dimensions of the individual wires. All of these parameters affect the end result [10] (**Figure 3**).

7. Determining the time step

When calculating the vibration of an electrical machine, it is important to note, as in the case of its measurement, the need to take into account the sampling frequency of the search signal. In the case of finite element calculation, this sampling frequency is represented by the time step of the individual calculations.

Results of transient analysis are linear approximate in the Ansys program. This can cause data loss. Example of choosing a time step or sampling frequency is shown in **Figure 4** on the simple signal. The used signal shows the sinus function with frequency 1 Hz. When selecting a large time step (specifically 3 Hz), this function is approximated by a straight line. There is a complete loss of function. When there is use 5 values on signal sampling and there is use linear interleaving function for his reconstruction, then constructed signal has triangle waveform. The calculated signal is the same as the original function only when using a sampling frequency of 36 Hz (and higher). This example shows how the time step can affect the results of the time waveform

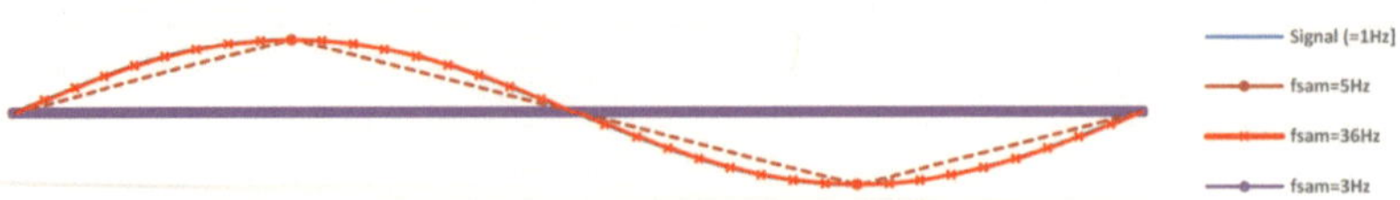

Figure 4. Linear approximation of sin signal.

calculations of primitive function. Even greater influence can be experienced on the course of the calculated waveforms of the vibrational signals, which are much more complicated.

For the sampling of the general signal, the so-called Nyquist condition is mentioned in the literature. This indicates that each frequency-limited time function can be replaced by samples taken with the T_{sam} period, which is equal to half of the overturned value of the $f_{\max}$, the highest frequency contained in the sampling signal. Therefore:

$$f_{sam} = \frac{1}{T_{sam}} \geq 2.f_{\max} \tag{3}$$

where f_{sam} is sampling frequency and $f_{\max}$ is maximal frequency included in the signal.

As shown in **Figure 4**, when this state is used for a complex signal (such as the vibration are complex), there has been a strong deformation of the entire calculated waveform. Determining the time step requires some experience and knowledge that leads to a compromise between the quality of the result and the time consumption of the calculation [4].

8. Electromagnetic simulation

Electromagnetic simulation is a possible solution in the Maxwell program, which is one of the Ansys software package modules. Maxwell module is used to calculate the magnetic field on 2D and 3D models. The calculation itself is based on Maxwell's equations. These equations can be written in a differential form:

$$\nabla x E = -\frac{\partial B}{\partial t} \tag{4}$$

$$\nabla . B = 0 \tag{5}$$

$$\nabla x H = J + \frac{\partial D}{\partial t} \tag{6}$$

$$\nabla . D = \rho \tag{7}$$

where E is electric field intensity, B is magnetic flux density, H is magnetic field intensity, J is current density on surface, D is electric flux density, and ρ is volume charge density.

Some of these parameters depend on the properties of the used material:

$$B = \mu_0 . \mu_r . H \tag{8}$$

where μ_0 is permeability of vacuum and μ_r is relative permeability of material.

$$D = \varepsilon_0 . \varepsilon_r . E \tag{9}$$

where ε_0 is permittivity of vacuum and ε_r is permittivity of magnetic material.

$$J = \sigma.E \tag{10}$$

where σ is electric conductivity.

To determine the vibrations in the electric machine model, the force acting between the rotor and the stator must be determined from the magnetic field in the air gap. For the calculation of these forces, it is possible to use the Maxwell stress tensor. Based on this, it is possible to write for two components electromagnetic forces on a 2D model equation:

- For radial direction

$$F_{rad} = \frac{L_{stk}}{2.\mu_0}.\oint_l (B_n^2 - B_t^2)dl \tag{11}$$

- For tangential direction

$$F_{\tan} = \frac{L_{stk}}{2.\mu_0}.\oint_l B_n.B_t\,dl \tag{12}$$

where B_n is normal component of flux density, B_t is tangential component of flux density, l is length of stator edge, and L_{stk} is stack length of the motor [2, 8, 9].

In the Maxwell environment, the following relationships to determine the individual power components [3] can be used:

$$F_{rad} = F_x.\cos\Theta_{tip} + F_y.\cos\Theta_{tip} \tag{13}$$

$$F_{\tan} = -F_x.\cos\Theta_{tip} + F_y.\cos\Theta_{tip} \tag{14}$$

The radial force component acts perpendicularly to each tip, and the teeth cause radial deformation and vibration. Meanwhile, the tangential force acts on the rotor and produces rotational torque and also causes torsional strains.

When determining the behavior of an electrical machine, the time course of the supply voltage is decisive. This chapter deals with the calculation of vibrations on an asynchronous motor. This type of machine is powered by three-phase alternating voltage. For the simplest case, the time course is harmonious, containing one harmonic. In many real cases, the supply voltage is not smooth. The effect on these waveforms may be the power supply or the function of the inverter connected to the electric machine.

For calculation, the voltage was given in the following phases:

- Phase A: Umax * sin(2*pi*50*time)
- Phase B: Umax * sin(2*pi*50*time-2*pi/3)
- Phase C: Umax * sin(2*pi*50*time-4*pi/3)

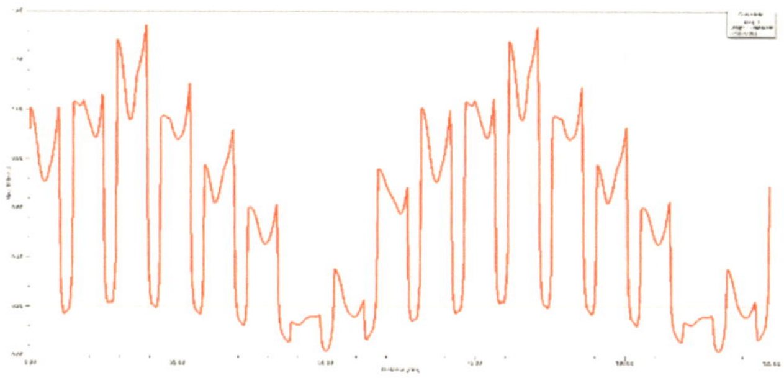

Figure 5. Magnetic field density in the air gap.

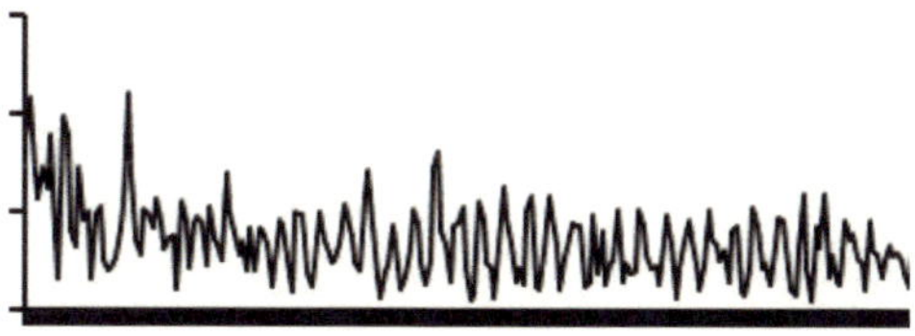

Figure 6. The time course of forces in the electric machine.

From the point of view of the electromagnetic calculation of electrical machines, the magnetic magnet induction is the most important variable in the air gap. This magnitude depends on the design of the particular electric machine (number of slots, etc.). The figure of this magnitude at half the length of the air gap is shown in **Figure 5**. It is seen that magnetic flux density waveform is not as smooth as the supply voltage waveform. This waveform is displayed on a line representing the half of the air gap. It is clear that the quality of this process is very dependent on the quality of the mesh. The number of elements can affect the resulting signal waveform and also its frequency spectrum. Generally, it is recommended to use at least four elements representing the width of the air gap. Since the width of the air gap of the electric machine can range from tens to millimeters, it is a factor that can greatly influence the solving time and calculation difficulty.

The total time course of the absolute value of the forces in the electric machine is shown in **Figure 6**. As shown in **Figure 6**, the influence of linear approximation between the individual time steps is evident [2, 8, 9].

9. Mechanical simulation

The mechanical analysis itself in the Ansys program serves to determine the deformations based on the forces applied to the model. The main variable, which in this case describes the vibration, is the displacement of the individual components of the model. It also serves to determine a deformation and displacement of the body at each point in the mesh when finite element method is used. The calculation is based on the following equation:

$$[M].\{a\} + [C].\{v\} + [K].\{x(t)\} = \{F(t)\} \tag{15}$$

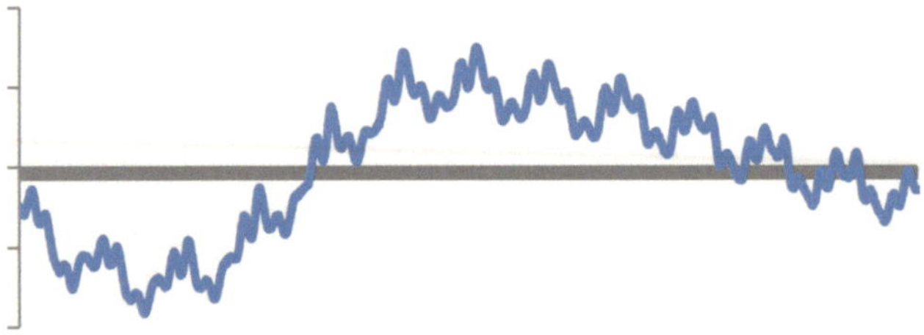

Figure 7. Vibration results from FEM.

where $F(t)$ is load vector, M is mass, C is damping, K is stiffness, x is displacement vector, a is acceleration vector ($a = \ddot{x}(t)$), and v is velocity vector ($v = \dot{x}(t)$).

On the basis of this equation, the individual displacements of the bodies are then determined. Several other parameters have to be taken into account to set the calculation correctly. One of the things that need to be set is the material properties of the individual parts of the simulated machine. The material properties are the material density, the Poisson's ratio and the Young's modulus for mechanical analysis. These material properties can be found on the Internet or requested from the material supplier.

Another parameter that affects the quality of the result is the final set-up of the mesh. There is a need to focus on to focus on where forces work or where there is a small cross-section on model. At these points of the model, it is necessary to manually adjust the strength of the mesh to avoid any unwanted effect on the result.

Another parameter is to determine the properties of the contact surfaces. Particularly, for more complex models, results are poor where there is a poor contact surface setting. The Ansys mechanical analysis module uses five types of contact surfaces such as bounded, without separation, without friction, friction and pulping. Their choice depends on the knowledge of the construction of the electrical machine and on the way of the mechanical connection of its individual parts [4, 8] (**Figure 7**).

10. Conclusions

Since the vibration of electric machines is a carrier of information about its state, the issue of vibration calculation is very topical. When designing any electrical machine, the designer must reach to a certain standard of vibration which is given by the norm. In many cases, when designing a new machine, there were problems with vibration. This problem occurs only after the prototype has been created. By using finite element methods in vibration determination, designer can achieve very interesting results that can help minimize the vibration of electrical machines at the design stage. It can mean considerable savings for the manufacturing company.

The calculation of vibrations using the Ansys program is a very complex issue. The correct setup of electromagnetic computation requires experience not only with calculating electrical machines but also with program Maxwell's control and adjustment. The actual modeling of the machine itself is also quite demanding. Whether the user uses a classical CAD system or RMxprt, it needs a lot of information that can have a detrimental effect on the calculation. One of the most important information is the dimensions of the electric machine. This information can be obtained from the technical documentation. Another factor that can influence the calculation is the knowledge of the materials used and especially their properties. Much information about these materials can be found on the Internet. In many cases, the values of material properties are measured in specific conditions (e.g., at temperature 22°C) and then these values do not have to match the calculation conditions. The ideal source of information on material properties is the supplier of construction materials.

Once a model has been created, it is necessary to set-up individual analyses. It should be noted that, for example, electromagnetic analysis has different mesh quality requirements than mechanical analysis. There are automatic features for mesh creation in Ansys Workbench and Maxwell environment. For vibration calculations, it is necessary to edit the quality mesh on certain parts of the model manually in many cases. However, this requires knowledge not only of the procedures for both types of calculations but also of some experience with different types of analyses. Another non-negligible part of the calculation is the time step selection for transient analysis. If the time step is too long, there is a loss of data that could be critical to the calculation. Conversely, when setting a small time step, an unreasonable load on the computing hardware will occur and an increase in the computational time will be necessary. Given the number of calculations that need to be made to achieve the relevant results, a minor change may mean an extension of day calculations.

It can be said that modern programs using finite element methods allow the calculation of a wide range of physical problems. As far as the calculations of vibrations of electric machines are concerned, it is a very complex issue, which affects many areas (electricity, magnetism, mechanics, thermal). The calculation of the complete vibrational spectrum of the electric machine with all vibration sources is possible, but it is very time consuming. Therefore, it is always necessary to focus on solving a certain part of this issue. Based on the analysis of the results, requirements and the analysis of the input parameters, it is possible to simplify the solution considerably, which allows to achieve reasonable results in a sufficiently short time. An ideal solution to the vibration problem of electric tools using finite element method is to build a team of workers with knowledge and experience from different industries who will cooperate.

Acknowledgements

This research work has been carried out in the Centre for Research and Utilization of Renewable Energy (CVVOZE). Authors gratefully acknowledge the financial support from the Ministry of Education, Youth and Sports of the Czech Republic under NPU I program (project No. LO1210).

Author details

Marcel Janda* and Kristyna Jandova

*Address all correspondence to: janda@feec.vutbr.cz

Faculty of Electrical Engineering and Communication, Brno University of Technology, Brno, Czech Republic

References

[1] Jacek FG, Wang C, Lai JC. Noise of polyphase electric motors. Boca Raton, FL: CRC/ Taylor & Francis; 2006. ISBN 9780824723811

[2] Nemecek P, Elias T. Vibrační diagnostika základních závad strojů [online]. Liberec: Technicka univerzita v Liberci; 2010 Available from: http://www.kvm.tul.cz/getFile/id:1851

[3] XIN GE. Simulation of Vibration in Electric Machines for Hybrid-Electric Vehicles [Thesis]. Goteborg, Sweden: Chalmers University of Technology; 2014. p. 56

[4] Vijayraghavan P, Krishnan R. Noise in electric machines: A review. In: proceedings of the IEEE Industry Applications Conference; 1 Oct 12-15; vol. 1, St. Louis, MO; p. 251-258

[5] Clarence W. de Silva, editor. Vibration and Shock Handbook. [Online-Ausg.]. Hoboken: CRC Press; 2005. ISBN 9781420039894

[6] Michael R, Hatc H. Vibration Simulation Using Matlab And Ansys. London: Chapman & Hall/CRC; 201. 656 p. ISBN: 1-58488-205-0

[7] Chapman S J. Electric Machinery Fundamentals. Fourth ed. Australia: BAE SYSTEMS; 2004. 323 p

[8] Ansoft Maxwell 3D – Electromagnetic and Electromechanical Analysis, User's guide; 2006

[9] Ansys, Inc. Theory Reference. 10th ed. ANSYS Incorporated; 2005

[10] Hughes A, Bill D. Electric Motors and Drives - Fundamentals, Types and Applications. 4th ed. Burlington: Elsevier Science; 2013. ISBN 9780080993683

[11] Boldea I, Nasar S A. The Induction Machine Handbook. Hoboken: CRC Press; 2001. ISBN 9781420042658

Chapter 9

Numerically and Analytically Forecasting the Coal Burst Using Energy Based Approach Methods

Faham Tahmasebinia, Chengguo Zhang,
Ismet Canbulat, Onur Vardar and Serkan Saydam

Additional information is available at the end of the chapter

http://dx.doi.org/10.5772/intechopen.71879

Abstract

Coal burst is referred to as the violent failure of overstressed coal, which has been recognised as one of the most critical dynamic failures in coal mines. This chapter aims to analytically and numerically evaluate the energy transformation between the different strata and coal layers. An accurate closed-form solution is developed. Due to the complexity of the causes and mechanisms contributing to the coal burst occurrence, 3D finite element modelling as well as discrete element models will be developed to validate the suggested analytical assessments of rock/coal burst occurrence. The energy concept is emphasised in order to improve the understanding of the underlying mechanisms of coal burst. Only with enhanced understanding of the driving mechanisms, a reliable coal burst risk assessment can be achieved.

Keywords: analytical modelling, numerical modelling, released energy, coal burst, failure mechanism

1. Introduction

One of the critical engineering problems faced by the coal mining industry is coal burst. It is caused by a dynamic release of energy within the overstressed rock mass/coal during the mining process. It occurs under the effects of complex environments of geology, stress and mining conditions. It has been recognised that the unstable releases of potential energy of the rock around the excavations, mainly in the form of kinetic energy, contributes to the coal burst occurrence. Interactions between the coal and rock interface, as well as the confinement, can completely determine the failure mode and the ultimate bearing capacity of coal pillars, influencing the amount of stored energy within a pillar. Many authors define rock/coal burst as a sudden, rapid rupture of the rock mass with a violent, explosive release of elastic/strain energy from the surface of an excavation, which is generally associated with a seismic event and produces rock particle ejections [1–5]. The coal burst source is the mechanism that triggers or induces the damage mechanism visible on the excavation surface. The coal burst source is generally associated with a seismic event that can be performed at a wide range of local magnitudes, normally ranging from undetectable up to 5 [6]. Indeed, mining-induced seismicity can reach moderate values of ground velocity and acceleration, and in some cases its effects on the surface can be compared with low-intensity earthquakes [7]. The mechanism that produces the seismic event is a sudden release of the strain energy that has been stored above a critical level within the rock/coal mass. Some portion of this energy is demolished by crack development, and the rest of the energy is converted into the kinetic energy [8, 9]. When the energy source is located near the roadway, the released energy may lead to coal fragmentation. At the place of the source of the energy, where it is located in a plane of weakness inside the coal mass, the released energy provokes shear displacement along the plane, which in revolve generate vibrations that persuade coal ejections when they are situated near the excavation boundaries [7]. Tarasov and Randolph [6] have explained a number of special and inconsistent behaviours of hard rock at the significant depth that are directly related to rock failure mechanisms in deep excavations. They determined that the procedures of the shear failure, with respect to the significant low friction, can be classified as the main reason to release energy. Based on the suggested frictionless mechanism, the level of the brittleness of the confined rock/coal masses might be increased under high stress conditions. This may result in reducing the overall ductility which would in line with the abrupt fracture failure. Under an energy-balance approach, the methods to predict coal burst risk are based on energy indexes such as energy release rate (ERR) [8–10], energy storage rate (ESR), strain energy storage index (WET) [11], potential energy of elastic strain (PES) or strain energy density (SED) (i.e., the elastic strain energy in a unit volume of the coal mass, which can be computed by the uni-axial compressive strength of the coal and the relevant unloading tangential modulus), and burst potential index (BPI). A combination of both analytical as well as numerical methods, where they can comprehensively evaluate the structural performance of the mine scale, would be broadly addressed in the current research. Thus, the following aims explicitly will be addressed.

1. Develop a full 2D and 3D finite element as well as discrete element models to compute the inducted energies in a single pillar with different high to width ratios. In this approach, different loading conditions varying from the static, quasi-static as well as dynamic loading will be exclusively examined.

2. Considering the effect of the energy transformations between the rock/coal layers due to the different contact/joint properties.

3. Suggest empirical equations to predict the amount of the released strain energy due to the mining activities.

The main novelty of this research is to simulate the effect of the failure and post-failure of the engaged material as well as joint/contact properties on the energy transformation.

2. Numerical modelling strategy

Numerical simulations can be considered as an individual tool to predict possible failure modes and the actual capacity of the mining setting. It is mostly useful to undertake parametric and sensitivity analyses to gain better understanding the nature and level of indecision, or remaining hazard, associated with design process.

First, a finite element model is developed by taking advantage from the commercial software package ABAQUS/Explicit. All the geotechnical components, including the rock and coal, were modelled by the eight-node linear brick element (C3D8R) available in the ABAQUS library. Element C3D8R relies on reducing integration and hourglass control. The assigned meshes were established by using the structured technique available in ABAQUS. The solution to the nonlinear problem was sought using the explicit dynamic analysis procedure available in ABAQUS. In the current study, **Figure 1** presents a quarter of a single pillar.

Thus, by taking advantage from the symmetrical boundary conditions, a finer mesh was assigned to the model. Finding the right input material properties would be a significant assumption, which has not been appropriately studied in the available literature. Modelling of mechanical behaviour of the coal under both compression and shear stresses would be very complicated, since there are no articulated reports which might be concerned with the uni-axial and tri-axial behaviour of coal under both static and dynamic loading conditions. According to

Figure 1. Illustration of a typical single pillar model using ABAQUS/Explicit.

the elastic analysis, the stress analysis and energy computations were organised in line with the linear relationship between the stress and the strain in coal and overburden properties. The peak and post-peak behaviour of coal and surrounding rock masses will be ignored. Therefore, in the current literature, the computed stress, strain and kinetic energy have been noticeably overestimated. At the second stage, a combination of the 2D and 3D discrete element models using UDEC and 3DEC was developed. **Figure 2** illustrates the pillar model incorporating half of coal, roof and floor along the symmetrical centre-line of the pillar. The height of the roof and floor was 20 m and the mining height was fixed at 3 m, while the pillar widths varied in order to simulate the pillars with width to height (w/h) ratios from 1 to 5.

A Mohr-Coulomb (MC) material that presents a constant strength after failure and a Mohr-Coulomb strain-softening material that can reach the peak strength and then decrease to a residual strength have been considered. A quasi-static loading condition as a velocity was applied on the top and bottom of the model. The applied velocity was started with a very small, constant velocity to represent a relative loading system to promote a model of a coal failure that progresses slowly. Simulating a proper loading/displacement condition is significantly crucial, specifically, gaining a sound understanding of the structural reaction of a single

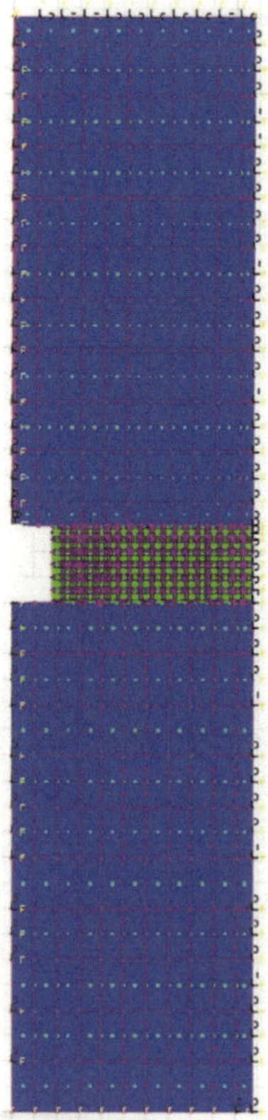

Figure 2. Geometry and zoning of coal pillar model using UDEC.

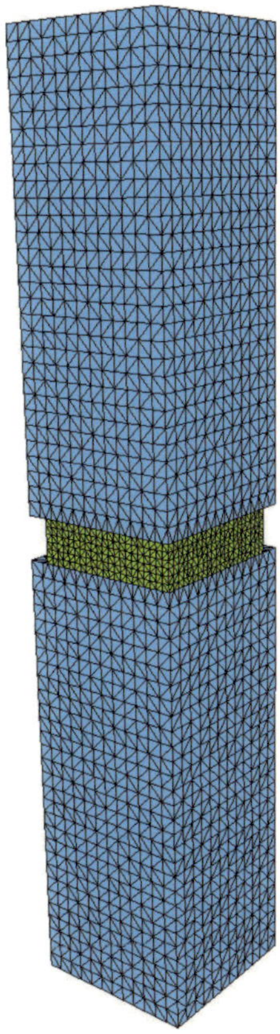

Figure 3. Geometry and zoning of coal pillar model using 3DEC.

coal sample under dynamic or quasi-static loading conditions. Consideration was also given to defining a joint interface. A Coulomb Slip (CS) joint interface property, where it is represented by displacement softening parameters, was taken into account to simulate the interface properties between the different joints.

The uniform zone size of 0.1 m was applied to the coal, and a smooth variation of zoning from the coal to the boundaries was used for roof and floor with appropriate aspect ratios to avoid numerical instability. Roller boundaries were applied along the side of the roof and floor, the bottom of the floor and the vertical line. The same trend was applied to develop the three-dimensional discrete element using 3DEC (see **Figure 3**).

3. Analytical approach

An analytical method is developed to evaluate shear stress and strain distributions between the engaged surfaces throughout different joint layers by considering the beam theory method in different directions with respect to the different planes, where it can independently calculate shear forces between the different layers and shear strain as well as the curvature distribution along the different layers that have been extracted. The main concept to derive the following equations was extracted from [12, 13]. The cross-sectional analysis is based on the assumption of the Euler-Bernoulli beam model. The strain distribution across the section can be calculated by $\varepsilon = \varepsilon_r - y \times \kappa$, where ε_r is the strain at the reference point (which can be determined at any point), y is the distance between the selected point and location of the neutral axis of the cross-section and κ is the curvature across the section in different strata layers. A vector can be introduced by $K(D)$ which will be included in the internal action N (axial forces) and M (internal moment). External loads, which might be due to the effect of the self-weight of the strata layers as well as the possible applied forces due to the vertical or horizontal displacement in the different layers, can induce the external axial force N_e and external moment M_e. The relationship between the internal and external actions can be presented by:

$$\varepsilon = \begin{bmatrix} \varepsilon_r \\ \kappa \end{bmatrix} \tag{1}$$

$$r(\varepsilon) = \begin{bmatrix} N \\ M \end{bmatrix} \tag{2}$$

$$r_e = \begin{bmatrix} N_e \\ M_e \end{bmatrix} \tag{3}$$

$$r(\varepsilon) = r_e \quad \text{(This is the vector for strain)} \tag{4}$$

By considering the nonlinear interactions, the presented equations can be re-written by:

$$r\left(\varepsilon^{(i+1)}\right) = r\left(\varepsilon^{(i)}\right) + r_t\left(\varepsilon^{(i)}\right) \times \Delta\varepsilon^{(i)} = r_e \tag{5}$$

$$r_t\left(\varepsilon^{(i)}\right) \times \Delta\varepsilon^{(i)} = r_R^{(i)} \tag{6}$$

$$r_R^{(i)} = r_e - r\left(\varepsilon^{(i)}\right) \tag{7}$$

$$\frac{\partial N\left(\varepsilon_r^{(i)}, \kappa^{(i)}\right)}{\partial \varepsilon_r} \times \Delta\varepsilon_r^{(i)} + \frac{\partial N\left(\varepsilon_r^{(i)}, \kappa^{(i)}\right)}{\partial \kappa} \times \Delta\kappa = N_R^{(i)} \tag{8}$$

$$N_R^{(i)} = N_e - N\left(\varepsilon_r^{(i)}, \kappa^{(i)}\right) \tag{9}$$

$$M_R^{(i)} = M_e - M\left(\varepsilon_r^{(i)}, \kappa^{(i)}\right) \tag{10}$$

All the equations can be re-presented in matrix format:

$$r_t\left(\varepsilon^{(i)}\right) = \begin{bmatrix} \dfrac{\partial N\left(\varepsilon_r^{(i)}, \kappa^{(i)}\right)}{\partial \varepsilon_r} & \dfrac{\partial N\left(\varepsilon_r^{(i)}, \kappa^{(i)}\right)}{\partial \kappa} \\ \dfrac{\partial M\left(\varepsilon_r^{(i)}, \kappa^{(i)}\right)}{\partial \varepsilon_r} & \dfrac{\partial M\left(\varepsilon_r^{(i)}, \kappa^{(i)}\right)}{\partial \kappa} \end{bmatrix} \tag{11}$$

$$\Delta\varepsilon^{(i)} = \begin{bmatrix} \Delta\varepsilon_r^{(i)} \\ \Delta\kappa^{(i)} \end{bmatrix} \quad \text{(Changing strain and curvature)} \tag{12}$$

$$r_R^{(i)} = \begin{bmatrix} N_R^{(i)} \\ M_R^{(i)} \end{bmatrix} \tag{13}$$

The partial derivatives of N and M with respect to ε_r and κ can be re-arranged in a more practical form, recalling the definitions of internal actions as:

$$\frac{\partial N\left(\varepsilon_r^{(i)}, \kappa^{(i)}\right)}{\partial \varepsilon_r} = \int \frac{\partial \sigma}{\partial \varepsilon_r} dA \tag{14}$$

$$\frac{\partial N\left(\varepsilon_r^{(i)}, \kappa^{(i)}\right)}{\partial \kappa} = \int \frac{\partial \sigma}{\partial \kappa} dA \tag{15}$$

$$\frac{\partial M\left(\varepsilon_r^{(i)}, \kappa^{(i)}\right)}{\partial \varepsilon_r} = -\int y \frac{\partial \sigma}{\partial \varepsilon_r} dA \tag{16}$$

$$\frac{\partial M\left(\varepsilon_r^{(i)}, \kappa^{(i)}\right)}{\partial \kappa} = -\int y \frac{\partial \sigma}{\partial \kappa} dA \tag{17}$$

where the values of the stress depend on the constitutive models adopted for the materials and on the magnitude of the strain

$$\frac{\partial N\left(\varepsilon_r^{(i)}, \kappa^{(i)}\right)}{\partial \varepsilon_r} = \int \frac{\partial \sigma}{\partial \varepsilon_r} dA = \int \frac{\partial \sigma}{\partial \varepsilon} \times \frac{\partial \varepsilon}{\partial \varepsilon_r} dA = \int \frac{\partial \sigma}{\partial \varepsilon} \times \frac{\partial(\varepsilon_r - y \times \kappa)}{\partial \varepsilon_r} dA = \int \frac{\partial \sigma}{\partial \varepsilon} dA \tag{18}$$

$$\frac{\partial N\left(\varepsilon_r^{(i)}, \kappa^{(i)}\right)}{\partial \kappa} = \int \frac{\partial \sigma}{\partial \kappa} dA = \int \frac{\partial \sigma}{\partial \varepsilon} \times \frac{\partial(\varepsilon_r - y \times \kappa)}{\partial \kappa} dA = -\int y \times \frac{\partial \sigma}{\partial \varepsilon} dA \tag{19}$$

$$\frac{\partial M\left(\varepsilon_r^{(i)}, \kappa^{(i)}\right)}{\partial \varepsilon_r} = -\int y \times \frac{\partial \sigma}{\partial \varepsilon_r} dA = -\int y \times \frac{\partial \sigma}{\partial \varepsilon} \times \frac{\partial(\varepsilon_r - y \times \kappa)}{\partial \varepsilon_r} dA = -\int y \times \frac{\partial \sigma}{\partial \varepsilon} dA \tag{20}$$

$$\frac{\partial M\left(\varepsilon_r^{(i)}, \kappa^{(i)}\right)}{\partial \kappa} = -\int y \times \frac{\partial \sigma}{\partial \varepsilon_r} dA = -\int y \times \frac{\partial \sigma}{\partial \varepsilon} \times \frac{\partial(\varepsilon_r - y \times \kappa)}{\partial \kappa} dA = \int y^2 \times \frac{\partial \sigma}{\partial \varepsilon} dA \tag{21}$$

$$\sigma = E \times \varepsilon \quad \text{for} \quad |\varepsilon| \leq \varepsilon_p \ \text{(elastic strain)} \tag{22}$$

$$\sigma = f_p \quad \text{for} \quad |\varepsilon| > \varepsilon_p \ \text{(plastic strain)} \tag{23}$$

$$\frac{\partial \sigma}{\partial \varepsilon} = \frac{\partial (E \times \varepsilon)}{\partial \varepsilon} = E \quad \text{for} \quad |\varepsilon| \leq \varepsilon_p \ \text{(elastic strain)} \tag{24}$$

$$\frac{\partial \sigma}{\partial \varepsilon} = \frac{\partial \left(f_p\right)}{\partial \varepsilon} = 0 \quad \text{for} \quad |\varepsilon| > \varepsilon_p \ \text{(plastic strain)} \tag{25}$$

$$N\left(\varepsilon_r^{(i)}, \kappa^{(i)}\right) = \int \sigma dA = \sum_{j=1}^{n_j} \sigma\left(y_j, \varepsilon_r^{(i)}, \kappa^{(i)}\right) \times A_j \tag{26}$$

$$M\left(\varepsilon_r^{(i)}, \kappa^{(i)}\right) = -\int y \sigma dA = -\sum_{j=1}^{n_j} y_j \times \sigma\left(y_j, \varepsilon_r^{(i)}, \kappa^{(i)}\right) \times A_j \tag{27}$$

$$\frac{\partial N\left(\varepsilon_r^{(i)}, \kappa^{(i)}\right)}{\partial \varepsilon_r} = \int \frac{\partial \sigma}{\partial \varepsilon} dA = \sum_{j=1}^{n_j} \frac{\partial \sigma\left(y_j, \varepsilon_r^{(i)}, \kappa^{(i)}\right)}{\partial \varepsilon} \times A_j \tag{28}$$

$$\frac{\partial N\left(\varepsilon_r^{(i)}, \kappa^{(i)}\right)}{\partial \kappa} = -\int y \times \frac{\partial \sigma}{\partial \varepsilon_r} dA = -\sum_{j=1}^{n_j} y_j \times \frac{\partial \sigma\left(y_j, \varepsilon_r^{(i)}, \kappa^{(i)}\right)}{\partial \varepsilon} \times A_j \tag{29}$$

$$\frac{\partial M\left(\varepsilon_r^{(i)}, \kappa^{(i)}\right)}{\partial \varepsilon_r} = -\int y \times \frac{\partial \sigma}{\partial \varepsilon_r} dA = -\sum_{j=1}^{n_j} y_j \times \frac{\partial \sigma\left(y_j, \varepsilon_r^{(i)}, \kappa^{(i)}\right)}{\partial \varepsilon} \times A_j \tag{30}$$

$$\frac{\partial M\left(\varepsilon_r^{(i)}, \kappa^{(i)}\right)}{\partial \kappa} = \int y^2 \times \frac{\partial \sigma}{\partial \varepsilon} dA = \sum_{j=1}^{n_j} y_j^2 \times \frac{\partial \sigma\left(y_j, \varepsilon_r^{(i)}, \kappa^{(i)}\right)}{\partial \varepsilon} \times A_j \tag{31}$$

$$\mathrm{r}\,(\mathrm{x}, \mathrm{d_e}) = \begin{bmatrix} \mathrm{N}(\mathrm{x}, \mathrm{d_e}) \\ \mathrm{M}(\mathrm{x}, \mathrm{d_e}) \end{bmatrix} = \begin{bmatrix} \int_A \sigma(\mathrm{x}, \mathrm{y}, \mathrm{d_e}) \mathrm{dA} \\ -\int_A \mathrm{y}\sigma(\mathrm{x}, \mathrm{y}, \mathrm{d_e}) \mathrm{dA} \end{bmatrix} = \begin{bmatrix} \sum_{j=1}^{n_j} \sigma(\mathrm{x}, \mathrm{y}, \mathrm{d_e}) \mathrm{A_j} \\ -\sum_{j=1}^{n_j} \mathrm{y_j}\sigma(\mathrm{x}, \mathrm{y}, \mathrm{d_e}) \mathrm{A_j} \end{bmatrix} \tag{32}$$

$$I = \int_a^b f(x) dx = \left(\frac{b-a}{2}\right) \times \int_{-1}^{1} f\left(\frac{a+b}{2} + \frac{b-a}{2} \times \overline{x}\right) = \left(\frac{b-a}{2}\right) \times \sum_{k=1}^{n_G} w_k \times f\left(\frac{a+b}{2} + \frac{b-a}{2} \times \overline{x_k}\right) \tag{33}$$

$$\mathrm{k_e}(x, \mathrm{d_e}) = \int_L \mathrm{B^T}(x) \mathrm{r}(\mathrm{x}, \mathrm{d_e})\, \mathrm{dx} = \frac{\mathrm{L}}{2} \sum_{\mathrm{k}=1}^{n_G} w_k \mathrm{B^T}(x_k) \mathrm{r}(x_k, \mathrm{d_e}) \tag{34}$$

$$\mathrm{q_e} = \int_L \mathrm{N_e^T(x)p(x)dx} = \frac{\mathrm{L}}{2}\sum_{\mathrm{k=1}}^{n_\mathrm{G}} w_k \mathrm{N_e^T}(x_k)p(x_k) \quad x_k = \frac{\mathrm{L}}{2}(\overline{x_k}+1) \tag{35}$$

$$\begin{bmatrix} u(x) \\ v(x) \end{bmatrix} = \begin{bmatrix} N_{u1}(x) & 0 & 0 & N_{u2}(x) & N_{u3}(x) & 0 & 0 \\ 0 & N_{v1}(x) & N_{v2}(x) & 0 & 0 & N_{v3}(x) & N_{v4}(x) \end{bmatrix} \times \begin{bmatrix} u_L \\ v_L \\ \theta_L \\ u_M \\ u_R \\ v_R \\ \theta_R \end{bmatrix} = \mathrm{N_e(x)d_e} \tag{36}$$

$$N_{u1}(x) = 1 - \frac{3x}{L} + \frac{2x^2}{L^2} \tag{37}$$

$$N_{u2}(x) = \frac{4x}{L} + \frac{4x^2}{L^2} \tag{38}$$

$$N_{u3}(x) = -\frac{x}{L} + \frac{2x^2}{L^2} \tag{39}$$

$$N_{v1}(x) = 1 - \frac{3x^2}{L^2} + \frac{2x^2}{L^3} \tag{40}$$

$$N_{v2}(x) = x - \frac{2x^2}{L} + \frac{x^3}{L^2} \tag{41}$$

$$N_{v3}(x) = \frac{3x^2}{L^2} - \frac{2x^3}{L^3} \tag{42}$$

$$N_{v4}(x) = -\frac{x^2}{L} + \frac{x^3}{L^2} \tag{43}$$

$$\begin{aligned} u(x) &= N_{u1}(x)u_L + N_{u2}(x)u_M + N_{u3}(x)u_R \\ v(x) &= N_{v1}(x)v_L + N_{v2}(x)\theta_L + N_{v3}(x)v_R + N_{v4}(x)\theta_R \end{aligned} \tag{44}$$

$$B(x) = \begin{bmatrix} N'_{u1}(x) & 0 & 0 & N'_{u2}(x) & N'_{u3}(x) & 0 & 0 \\ 0 & N''_{v1}(x) & N''_{v2}(x) & 0 & 0 & N''_{v3}(x) & N''_{v4}(x) \end{bmatrix} \tag{45}$$

$$N'_{u1}(x) = -\frac{3}{L} + \frac{4x}{L^2} \tag{46}$$

$$N'_{u2}(x) = \frac{4}{L} - \frac{8x}{L^2} \tag{47}$$

$$N'_{u3}(x) = -\frac{1}{L} + \frac{4x}{L^2} \tag{48}$$

$$N''_{v1}(x) = \frac{12x}{L^3} - \frac{6}{L^2} \tag{49}$$

$$N''_{v2}(x) = \frac{6x}{L^2} - \frac{4}{L} \tag{50}$$

$$N''_{v3}(x) = \frac{6}{L^2} - \frac{12x}{L^3} \tag{51}$$

$$N''_{v4}(x) = \frac{6x}{L^2} - \frac{2}{L} \tag{52}$$

$$\mathrm{k_e}\left(x, \mathrm{d_e^{(i)}}\right) = \frac{\mathrm{L}}{2}\sum_{\mathrm{k}=1}^{n_\mathrm{G}} w_k \mathrm{B}^\mathrm{T}(x_k)\mathrm{r}^{(\mathrm{i})}\left(x_k, \mathrm{d_e^{(i)}}\right) = \frac{\mathrm{L}}{2}\sum_{\mathrm{k}=1}^{n_\mathrm{G}} w_k \times \begin{bmatrix} N'_{u1}(x_k) & 0 \\ 0 & N''_{v1}(x_k) \\ 0 & N''_{v2}(x_k) \\ N'_{u2}(x_k) & 0 \\ N'_{u3}(x_k) & 0 \\ 0 & N''_{v3}(x_k) \\ 0 & N''_{v4}(x_k) \end{bmatrix} \times \begin{bmatrix} \mathrm{N}\left(x_k, \mathrm{d_e^{(i)}}\right) \\ \mathrm{M}\left(x_k, \mathrm{d_e^{(i)}}\right) \end{bmatrix} \tag{53}$$

$$\mathrm{q_e} = \frac{\mathrm{L}}{2}\sum_{\mathrm{k}=1}^{n_\mathrm{G}} w_k \times \begin{bmatrix} N_{u1}(x_k) & 0 \\ 0 & N_{v1}(x_k) \\ 0 & N_{v2}(x_k) \\ N_{u2}(x_k) & 0 \\ N_{u3}(x_k) & 0 \\ 0 & N_{v3}(x_k) \\ 0 & N_{v4}(x_k) \end{bmatrix} \times \begin{bmatrix} n(x_k) \\ w(x_k) \end{bmatrix} \tag{54}$$

$$\mathrm{N}\left(x_k, \mathrm{d_e^{(i)}}\right) = \sum_{j=1}^{n_j} \sigma\left(\mathrm{x_k}, \mathrm{y_i}, \mathrm{d_e^{(i)}}\right)\mathrm{A_j} \tag{55}$$

$$\mathrm{M}\left(x_k, \mathrm{d_e^{(i)}}\right) = -\sum_{j=1}^{n_j} \mathrm{y_j}\sigma\left(\mathrm{x_k}, \mathrm{y_i}, \mathrm{d_e^{(i)}}\right)\mathrm{A_j} \tag{56}$$

Thus, by calculating stress and strain at the different points in the different layers of the overburden, the internal axial forces as well as internal moments can be calculated. It was assumed that the strain energy can be calculated by:

$$A = \frac{1}{2} \times \iiint \left(\sigma_{xx} \times \varepsilon_{xx} + \sigma_{yy} \times \varepsilon_{yy} + \sigma_{zz} \times \varepsilon_{zz} + \sigma_{xy} \times \varepsilon_{xy} + \sigma_{xz} \times \varepsilon_{xz} + \sigma_{yz} \times \varepsilon_{yz} \right) dxdydz \quad (57)$$

where $\sigma_{xx} \times \varepsilon_{xx}, \ldots\ldots, \sigma_{yz} \times \varepsilon_{yz}$ can be calculated, according to the principal of the virtual work and virtual deformation $\delta A = \delta R_1 + \delta R_2$, when the induced stresses and strains cannot be directly extracted from the simulated model.

4. Energy calculation based on the numerical approach

According to Xie et al. [14], the coal burst proneness of a coal can be determined by the coal burst proneness assessments. Special attentions were devoted by the number of researchers to develop coal burst proneness indexes, which are broadly utilised, such as elastic energy, impact energy, dynamic failure time as well as elastic deformation and stiffness ratio indexes. The elastic energy index WET is defined as the ratio of the elastic strain energy and the strain energy dissipation at point E (75–85% of the peak strength). As shown in **Figure 4**, the ratio of the area SEAC (between the unloaded line EA and the strain axis) and the area SEOA (between the load and unload line) is the elastic energy index

$$W_{ET} = \left(\frac{S_{EAC}}{S_{EOA}} \right) \quad (58)$$

The impact energy index KE is defined as the ratio of the pre-peak area and the post-peak area, KE namely, the ratio of energy in the pre-peak stage and the energy released in the post-peak stage.

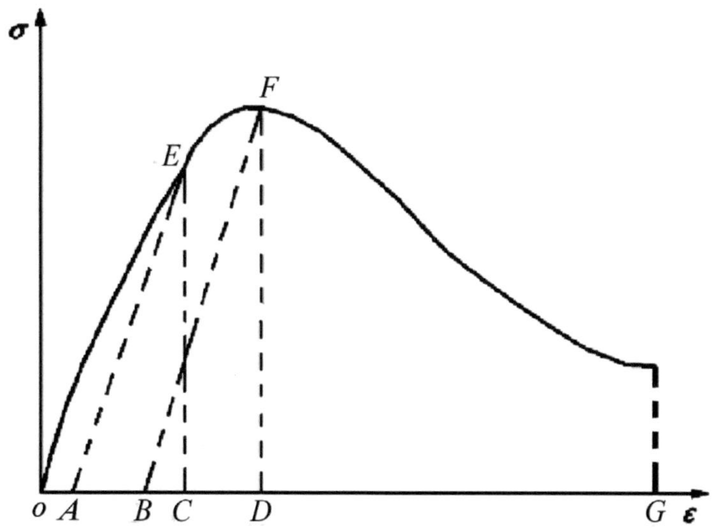

Figure 4. A typical stress-strain curve.

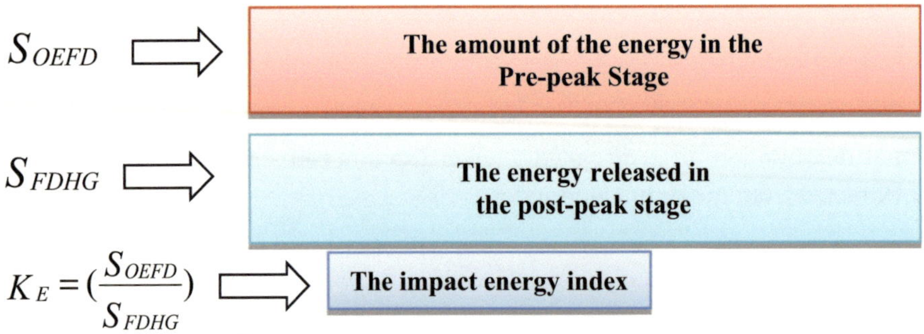

5. Energy calculation based on the analytical approach

According to Xie et al. [14], dissipated and released energy can play a significant role which may result in coal deformation and failure. Based on the failure mechanism, the fracture procedure of a coal mass might be started from a partial fracture which would be followed by local damage. This procedure will be finally resulting in collapsing the mining structures. The failure process is thermodynamically permanent, which includes released and dissipated energy. The dissipated energy can cause damage as well as a permanent deformation of the coal mass, which is followed by weakening of strength. A sudden release of the strain energy may lead to a catastrophic failure, which clearly indicates a certain condition where the coal mass collapses. The released and dissipated energy from the coal mass, individually, plays an essential role in the relevant sudden failure, which would be one of the major requirements to investigate the procedure of the deformation and failure of a coal mass. **Figure 5** is a typical compression curve of coal under a constant displacement.

Figure 5 explicitly demonstrates the calculation of the dissipated, released and residual energies. With respect to the constant development of the inner micro-defects, energy dissipation is an indispensable characteristic of the deformation and failure of the coal mass. The evolution declines the strength of the coal, which may result in total failure. In this content, the dissipated energy is directly concerned with the damage as well as mitigating strength of the coal.

$$u_{d1} = \int_0^{\varepsilon_1} (\sigma_a d\varepsilon) = \sum_0^{\varepsilon_1} \left[\left(\varepsilon_{1(i)} - \varepsilon_{1(i-1)} \right) \times \left(\frac{\sigma_{a(i)} + \sigma_{a(i-1)}}{4} \right) \right] \quad \text{Dissipated energy before peak} \tag{59}$$

$$u_{d2} = \int_{\varepsilon_3}^{\varepsilon_4} (\sigma_c d\varepsilon) = \sum_{\varepsilon_3}^{\varepsilon_4} \left[\left(\varepsilon_{(j)} - \varepsilon_{(j-1)} \right) \times \left(\frac{\sigma_{c(j)} + \sigma_{c(j-1)}}{4} \right) \right] \quad \text{Dissipated energy after peak} \tag{60}$$

$$u_r = \int_{\varepsilon_1}^{\varepsilon_2} (\sigma_m d\varepsilon) = \sum_{\varepsilon_1}^{\varepsilon_2} \left[\left(\varepsilon_{(k)} - \varepsilon_{(k-1)} \right) \times \left(\frac{\sigma_{m(k)} + \sigma_{m(k-1)}}{4} \right) \right] \quad \text{Released elastic energy} \tag{61}$$

http://dx.doi.org/10.5772/intechopen.71879

$$u_{ed} = \int_{\varepsilon_2}^{\varepsilon_3} (\sigma_p d\varepsilon) = \sum_{\varepsilon_2}^{\varepsilon_3} \left[(\varepsilon_{(l)} - \varepsilon_{(l-1)}) \times \left(\frac{\sigma_{p(l)} + \sigma_{p(l-1)}}{4} \right) \right] \quad \text{Residual elastic energy} \tag{62}$$

Tables 1 and **2** presents a comparison between the different elastic and post-failure energy components using UDEC and 3DEC output results as well as semi-close form solutions. As it can be found, there is a good agreement between the suggested semi-analytical methods as well as the calculated key energy components which were extracted from the UDEC and 3DEC output results.

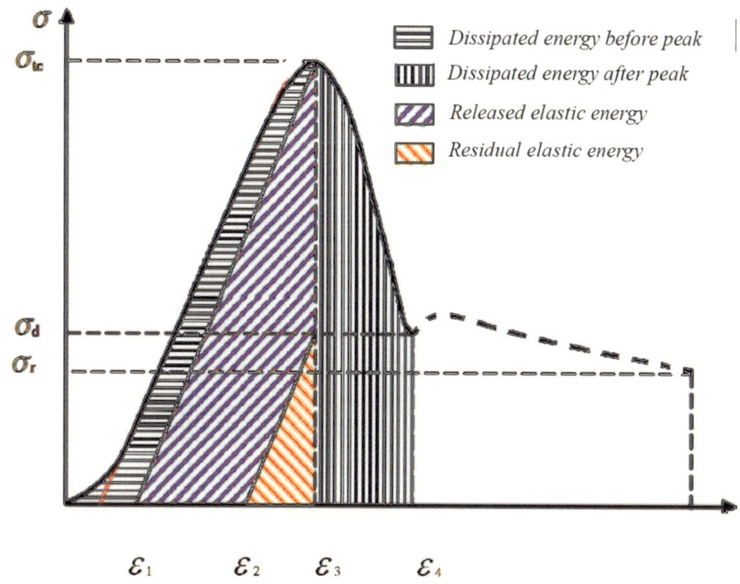

Figure 5. Analytically calculation of dissipated energy and released energy (Xie et al. [14]).

	Elastic strain energy (kJ/m^3)		Dissipated elastic strain energy (kJ/m^3)		The amount of the energy in the pre-peak stage (kJ/m^3)		The energy released in the post-peak stage (kJ/m^3)	
Ratio (w/h)	UDEC	Analytic	UDEC	Analytic	UDEC	Analytic	UDEC	Analytic
1	1.56	1.63	0.78	0.77	3.61	3.73	12.47	10.59
1.5	1.92	1.35	0.8	0.78	7.89	7.44	12.48	11.03
2	2.0621	2.004	0.991	0.92	10.22	9.83	18.31	17.09
2.5	4.70	4.82	1.16	1.11	14.47	13.43	21.17	23.14
3	11.13	10.58	2.51	2.41	35.825	32.87	11.73	10.6
4	14.72	13.27	4.07	4.60	60.26	55.00	56.34	70.02
5	16.63	16.24	5.334	5.37	75.83	73.67	91.19	84.04

Table 1. A comparison between the different energy components (UDEC and the analytical solution).

	Elastic strain energy (kJ/m^3)		Dissipated elastic strain energy (kJ/m^3)		The amount of the energy in the pre-peak stage (kJ/m^3)		The energy released in the post-peak stage (kJ/m^3)	
Ratio (w/h)	**3DEC**	**Analytic**	**3DEC**	**Analytic**	**3DEC**	**Analytic**	**3DEC**	**Analytic**
1	2.58	2.65	1.767	1.55	4.91	4.77	14.87	14.77
1.5	2.94	2.37	1.88	0.78	8.88	8.46	16.56	15.23
2	4.24	4.01	2.891	2.92	12.55	11.98	21.23	20.14
2.5	6.72	6.84	3.18	3.11	15.37	15.41	24.35	23.99
3	13.15	12.62	5.51	5.44	37.15	36.87	28.45	27.68
4	16.76	16.27	7.07	7.20	60.26	62.33	59.11	57.88
5	19.83	19.28	8.334	8.22	76.22	75.12	96.54	92.66

Table 2. A comparison between the different energy components (3DEC and the analytical solution).

6. Progress of the failure in different pillar ratios

Different loading conditions varying from the quasi-static to dynamic loading has been applied to the coal pillar with the different width to height (w/h) ratio to determine the pillar capability as well as the possible observed failure modes. A strain-based criterion, as a major failure criterion, was implemented in the ABAQUS/Explicit to predict of the cracking path due to the different applied loadings as well as different pillar geometrical properties. A quarter

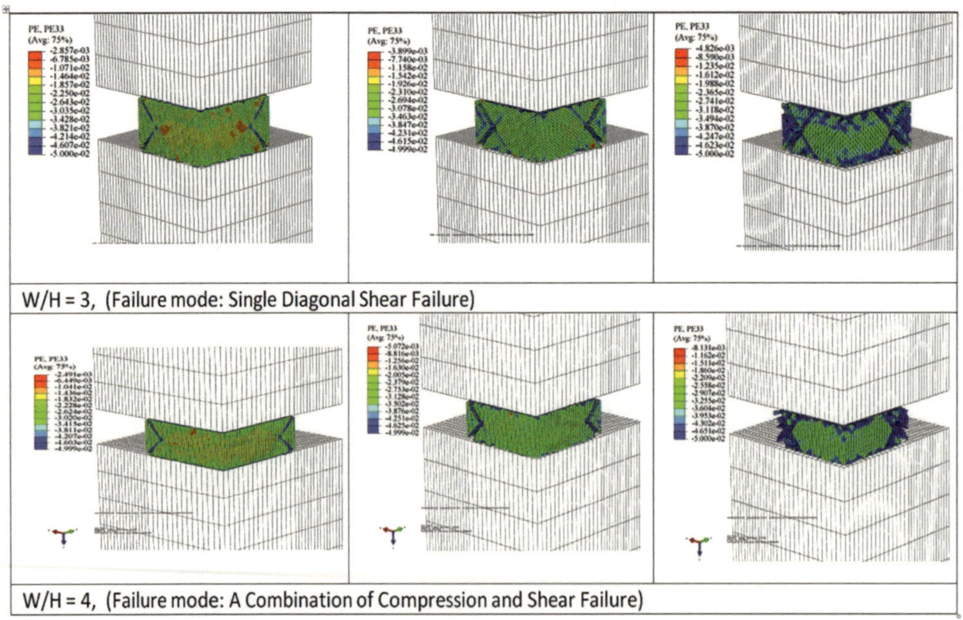

Figure 6. Failure mode of a single pillar with the different w/h ratios.

coal pillar model based on the symmetrical boundary conditions with respect to the different width by height (w/h) ratios of 1–10 were developed. It was observed that when the w/h ratios are less than 4, the failure mode of pillar can be either a double or a single diagonal shear failure in which the trajectory cracking starts from the edges and progresses towards the centre of the pillar. While the w/h ratios are greater than 4, the obtained possible failure mode would be a combination of the shear and compression failure modes. Thus, the trajectory of the cracking due to the pure compression failure would be propagated from the centre to the corners where a pillar gradually starts towards fully squashed (see **Figure 6**).

7. Remarkable conclusions

Analytical method is an important part of coal burst evaluation and forecasting. Analytical forecasting methods, either alone or combined with numerical simulations, can be used to estimate both *in situ* stress and induced stress, which leads to the prediction of failure-prone areas and calculation of critical values of the energies. The behaviour of a single pillar under different applied loads ranging from the quasi-static towards the dynamic loading conditions was simulated using commercial finite element package ABAQUS/Explicit. A strain-based failure condition was evaluated to determine the failure modes in a single pillar by respecting to the different w/h ratios. The observed numerical failure modes can be classified by shear and compression failures as well as a combination of both shear and compression were comprehensively illustrated. The released energy or residual energy is either transferred into kinetic energy or dissipated energy in non-elastic behaviour such as joint shear and fracturing. The unstable release of potential energy of the coal around the excavations, mainly in the form of kinetic energy, causes coal burst.

Author details

Faham Tahmasebinia*, Chengguo Zhang, Ismet Canbulat, Onur Vardar and Serkan Saydam

*Address all correspondence to: faham.tahmasebinia@sydney.edu.au

School of Mining Engineering, University of New South Wales, Sydney, Australia

References

[1] Linkov AM. Rockbursts and the instability of rock masses. International Journal of Rock Mechanics and Mining Sciences & Geomechanics Abstracts. 1996;**33**(7):727-732

[2] Gong QM, Yin LJ, SY W, Zhao J, Ting Y. Rock burst and slabbing failure and its influence on TBM excavation at headrace tunnels in Jinping II hydropower station. Engineering Geology. 2012;**124**(1):98-108

[3] Li S, Feng XT, Li Z, Chen B, Zhang C, Zhou H. *In situ* monitoring of rockburst nucleation and evolution in the deeply buried tunnels of Jinping II hydropower station. Engineering Geology. 2012;**137–138**:85-96

[4] Cai M. Principles of rock support in burst-prone ground. Tunnelling and Underground Space Technology. 2013;**36**:46-56

[5] Ortlepp WD, Stacey TR. Rockburst mechanisms in tunnels and shafts. Tunnelling and Underground Space Technology. 1994;**9**(1):59-65

[6] Tarasov BG, Randolph MF. Frictionless shear at great depth and other paradoxes of hard rocks. International Journal of Rock Mechanics and Mining Sciences. 2008;**45**(3):316-328

[7] Wang JA, Park HD. Comprehensive prediction of rockburst based on analysis of strain energy in rocks. Tunnelling and Underground Space Technology. 2001;**16**(1):49-57

[8] Cook NGW. Origin of rockbursts. In: Richards L, editor. Rockbursts; Prediction and Control. London: Institute of Mining and Metallurgy; 1983. pp. 1-9

[9] Wattimena RK, Sirait B, Widodo NP, Matsui K. Evaluation of rockburst potential in a cut-and-fill mine using energy balance. International Journal of the Japanese Committee for Rock Mechanics. 2012;**8**(1):19-23

[10] Mitri HS, Tang B, Simon R. FE modelling of mining-induced energy release and storage rates. The Journal of the South African Institute of Mining and Metallurgy. 1999;**99**(2):103-110

[11] Novozhilov VV. Foundations of the Nonlinear Theory of Elasticity. Graylock. Mineola, New York; 1999

[12] Ranzi G, Gilbert R. Structural Analysis: Principles, Methods and Modelling. Boca Raton. Florida: CRC Press; 2015

[13] Ranzi G, Dall Asta A, Ragni L, Zona A. A geometric nonlinear model for composite beams with partial interaction. Engineering Structures. 2010;**32**(5):1384-1396

[14] Xie HP, Li L, Peng R, Ju Y. Energy analysis and criteria for structural failure of rocks. Journal of Rock Mechanics and Geotechnical Engineering. 2009;**1**(1):11-12

Chapter 10

Linear Thermo-Poroelasticity and Geomechanics

Horacio Florez

Additional information is available at the end of the chapter

http://dx.doi.org/10.5772/intechopen.71873

Abstract

Most engineering applications estimate the deformation induced by loads by using the linear elasticity theory. The discretization process starts with the equilibrium equation and then develops a displacement formulation that employs the Hooke's law. Problems of practical interest encompass designing of large structures, buildings, subsurface deformation, etc. These applications require determining stresses to compare them with a given failure criteria. One often tackles this way a design or material strength type of problems. For instance, Geomechanics applications in the oil and gas industry assess the induced stresses changes that hydrocarbon production or the injection of fluids, i.e., artificial lift, in a reservoir produce in the surrounding rock mass. These studies often include reservoir compaction and subsidence that pose harmful and costly effects such as in wells casing, cap-rock stability, faults reactivation, and environmental issues as well. Estimating these stress-induced changes and their consequences require accurate elasticity simulations that are usually carried out through finite element (FE) simulations. Geomechanics implies that the flow in porous media simulation must be coupled with mechanics, which causes a substantial increase in CPU time and memory requirements.

Keywords: elasticity, single-phase flow, geomechanics, Dirichlet-Neumann, mortar methods, continuous Galerkin

1. Introduction

This chapter presents a continuous Galerkin FE formulation for linear isotropic elasticity. It covers in detail how to derive such formulation beginning with the equilibrium equation and the virtual work statement. It also discretizes the continuity equation for slightly compressible single-phase flow to show how to couple different physics with elasticity. It discusses several coupling approaches such as the monolithic and iterative ones, i.e., loosely coupled. This chapter also mentions the affinity of the poroelastic case with the thermoelastic one. It thus also includes thermoelasticity in the treatment herein. It shows concrete numerical examples covering two- and three-dimensional problems of practical interest in thermo-poroelasticity. The sample problems employ triangular, quadrilateral, and hexahedral meshes and include comments about implementing boundary conditions (BCS). An introduction to domain decomposition ideas such as iterative coupling by the BCS, i.e., Dirichlet-Neumann domain decomposition and mortar methods for non-matching interfaces is included.

The treatment herein demonstrates that the continuous Galerkin formulation for linear isotropic elasticity is the foundation to develop codes for mechanics. Indeed, after discretizing linear elasticity is straightforward to extend the implementation to nonlinear mechanics such as rate-independent plasticity. It thus provides some comments about such extension. Applications of practical interest show that industrial size problems will require domain decomposition techniques to handle such simulations in a timely fashion. Unquestionably, domain decomposition techniques can exploit current parallel machines architectures which brings high-performance computing into the picture. For instance, recently the author showed that the Dirichlet-Neumann scheme could handle problems at the reservoir field-level as well as the mortar method decoupled by this last one. Its current results are backed up by papers published in peer-reviewed journals and conferences thus this book chapter summarizes that effort.

2. Mathematical model for thermo-poroelasticity

This section discusses the governing equations for linear homogeneous isotropic thermo-poroelasticity and their FE formulation. It skips details for the sake of brevity thus a more detailed treatment can be found in [1–4]. The mathematical formulation considers a bounded domain $\Omega \subset \mathbb{R}^n, n = 2, 3$ and its boundary is $\Gamma = \partial\Omega$, and a time interval of interest $]0, \Im[$. Let $\mathcal{T}_h$ be a non-degenerate, quasi-uniform conforming partition of Ω composed of triangles or quadrilaterals for two-dimensional problems, and hexahedra or tetrahedra for three-dimensional problems. For instance, Gai [5] thesis showed that deformable porous media, i.e., the reservoir matrix, the single-phase flow model equation derives from the continuity equation, i.e., a mass balance statement, for slightly incompressible single-phase flow and Darcy's law which yields:

$$\frac{\partial \phi^*}{\partial t} + \nabla \cdot \left(-\frac{1}{\mu} \underline{\underline{K}} (\nabla p - \rho g \nabla z) \right) = q, \tag{1}$$

where the equation's parameters are ϕ^*, a model specific porosity, $\underline{\underline{K}}$ represents the absolute permeability tensor. The dynamic viscosity is μ, while ρ is the fluid density, as well as g, is the gravity acceleration constant, p is the fluid pressure, and q represents sources and sinks. This latter notation is standard in fluid mechanics and reservoir simulation. Finally, the algorithmic porosity ϕ^* is defined by:

$$\phi^* = \phi^0 + \alpha \cdot \left(\nabla \cdot \underline{u} - \varepsilon_v^0 \right) + \frac{1}{M} \left(p - p^0 \right), \tag{2}$$

where the additional parameters are accordingly α which is the Biot's constant, $\underline{u}$ represents the displacement vector, while ε_v^0 is the initial volumetric strain. Herein M is the Biot's modulus [6], while ϕ^0 and p^0 define for a reference or initial state. The common BCS for the pressure equation imply Neumann or no-flow namely:

$$\nabla p \cdot \widehat{\underline{n}} = 0 \text{ on } \Gamma, \tag{3}$$

one should also consider an initial or reference pressure distribution in the whole domain. Sources and sinks simulate injector and producer wells, respectively. Herein $\widehat{\underline{n}}$ is the outer unitary normal vector as usual. For the mechanics part, one begins from the equilibrium equation for a quasi-steady process, i.e., Newton second law, which means that one discards the acceleration term:

$$\begin{aligned} -\nabla \cdot \underline{\underline{\sigma}} &= \underline{f} \;\text{ in }\; \Omega \;\; ; \;\; \Gamma = \Gamma_D^u \cup \Gamma_N^u \\ \underline{u} &= \underline{0} \;\text{ on }\; \Gamma_D^u \\ \underline{t} &= \underline{\underline{\sigma}} \cdot \widehat{\underline{n}} \;\text{ on }\; \Gamma_N^u \end{aligned} \tag{4}$$

where $\underline{\underline{\sigma}}$ is the stress tensor, $\underline{f}$ corresponds to the vector of body forces, such as gravity and electromagnetic effects, for instance. One can decompose BCS in Dirichlet type, i.e., Γ_D^u, and Neumann type BCS, i.e., Γ_N^u, where the external tractions are known or prescribed. Hooke's law combined with Biot's poroelastic theory defines $\underline{\underline{\sigma}}$ by the following expression:

$$\underline{\underline{\sigma}} = \underline{\underline{C}} : \underline{\underline{\varepsilon}} - \left[\alpha\left(p - p^0\right) + 3K\beta\left(T - T^0\right)\right]\underline{\underline{\delta}} \, ; \; \underline{\underline{C}} = \lambda \underline{\underline{\delta}} \otimes \underline{\underline{\delta}} + 2G\underline{\underline{I}}, \tag{5}$$

where $T = T(x, t)$ is the temperature, $\underline{\underline{C}}$ is the elastic moduli, β corresponds to the coefficient of thermal dilatation while K is the bulk modulus. The Kronecker delta becomes $\underline{\underline{\delta}}$ while λ, and G, are the Lamé constants, and $\underline{\underline{I}}$ represents the fourth-order identity tensor. The strain tensor $\underline{\underline{\varepsilon}}$ is given by:

$$\underline{\underline{\varepsilon}} = \nabla^s \underline{u} = \frac{1}{2}\left[\nabla \underline{u} + (\nabla \underline{u})^T\right]. \tag{6}$$

One can derive a weak form by substituting Eq. (2) into Eq. (1) and then multiplying by a test function $v \in H_0^1(\Omega)$ and integrating over Ω and using the Gauss-divergence theorem, this yields:

$$\begin{aligned} &\int_\Omega \left(\frac{1}{M}\frac{\partial p}{\partial t} v + \alpha v \nabla \cdot \underline{\dot{u}} + \frac{1}{\mu}\underline{\underline{K}} \cdot \nabla p (\nabla v)^T\right) \cdot dx = \int_\Omega q \cdot v dx + \\ &\int_\Omega \left(\frac{\rho g}{\mu}\underline{\underline{K}} \cdot \nabla z (\nabla v)^T\right) dx + \int_{\partial\Omega_N^p} v \frac{1}{\mu}\underline{\underline{K}}(\nabla p - \rho g \nabla z) \cdot \widehat{\underline{n}}^T ds. \end{aligned} \tag{7}$$

A weak form for the equilibrium Eq. (4) can be derived in a similar way, by testing against a given virtual displacement, $\underline{\chi}$. One arrives at:

$$\int_{\Omega} \left(\nabla \underline{\chi}\right)^{T} : \underline{\underline{\sigma}} d\Omega = \int_{\partial\Omega_{N}^{u}} \underline{\chi}^{T} \cdot \underline{t} ds + \int_{\Omega} \underline{\chi}^{T} \cdot \underline{f} d\Omega \tag{8}$$

where $\underline{t} = \underline{\underline{\sigma}} \cdot \underline{\widehat{n}}$ are the tractions applied as Neumann BCS. This is the well-known virtual work statement. The FE space can be taken as a finite-dimensional subspace of the continuous Sobolev spaces [7], thus:

$$\mathcal{C}_{k}(\mathcal{T}_{h}) = \{v \in L^{2}(\Omega) \;\; : \;\; \forall e \in \mathcal{T}_{h}, v|_{e} \in \mathbb{P}_{k}(e)\} \tag{9}$$

where $\mathbb{P}_{k}(e)$ represents the space of polynomials of total degree less than or equal to k, $\mathcal{C}_{k}(\mathcal{T}_{h})$ is called test functions that are continuous along the given element's edges. Let one represents the primary variables in the element e, i.e. displacements and pressure, as nodal values multiplied by shape or interpolation functions [8]:

$$p_{e}^{h}(\underline{x}) = (\underline{\Pi}^{e})^{T} \cdot \underline{p}^{e} \; ; \underline{u}_{e}^{h}(\underline{x}) = \underline{\underline{\Psi}}^{e} \cdot \underline{u}^{e} \tag{10}$$

where $\underline{\Pi}^{e}$ and $\underline{\underline{\Psi}}^{e}$ are matrices of shape functions given by:

$$\begin{aligned} &\Pi_{i}^{e} = \psi_{i}^{e}(\underline{x}) \\ &\Psi_{ij}^{e} = \begin{cases} \psi_{k}^{e}(\underline{x}) & \text{if } j = \underline{\mathrm{j}} \\ 0 & \text{otherwise} \end{cases} \\ &\underline{\mathrm{j}} = \mathrm{nDOF} \cdot (k-1) + i \; ; k = 1 \ldots nn \end{aligned} \tag{11}$$

here nn is the number of nodes in the given element, $i = 1 \ldots nn$ $j = 1 \ldots nn \cdot n$ and nDOF is the number of degrees of freedom which equals the space dimension, n. Now the engineering strain $\widehat{\underline{\varepsilon}}$ is defined by:

$$\widehat{\underline{\varepsilon}} = \underline{\underline{B}} \cdot \underline{u}^{e} \;\; ; \;\; \underline{\underline{B}} = \underline{\underline{D}} \cdot \underline{\underline{\Psi}}^{e} \tag{12}$$

where $\underline{\underline{D}}_{(n)}$, $n = 2, 3$ is defined as:

$$\underline{\underline{D}}_{(2)}^{T} = \begin{bmatrix} \partial_{x} & 0 & \partial_{y} \\ 0 & \partial_{y} & \partial_{x} \end{bmatrix}; \; \underline{\underline{D}}_{(3)}^{T} = \begin{bmatrix} \partial_{x} & 0 & 0 & \partial_{y} & \partial_{z} & 0 \\ 0 & \partial_{y} & 0 & \partial_{x} & 0 & \partial_{z} \\ 0 & 0 & \partial_{z} & 0 & \partial_{x} & \partial_{y} \end{bmatrix}. \tag{13}$$

Finally substituting the generalized Hooke's law Eq. (5) into Eq. (8) and using Eq. (7) leads to the FE model for linear isotropic poroelasticity, thus:

$$\begin{bmatrix} 0 & 0 \\ \underline{\underline{\mathrm{Q}}}^{T} & \underline{\underline{\mathrm{S}}} \end{bmatrix} \frac{d}{dt} \left\{ \begin{array}{c} \underline{u} \\ \underline{p} \end{array} \right\} + \begin{bmatrix} \underline{\underline{\mathrm{K}}} & -\underline{\underline{\mathrm{Q}}} \\ 0 & \underline{\underline{\mathrm{H}}} \end{bmatrix} \left\{ \begin{array}{c} \underline{u} \\ \underline{p} \end{array} \right\} = \left\{ \begin{array}{c} \underline{f}_{u} \\ \underline{f}_{p} \end{array} \right\}. \tag{14}$$

One can obtain the loose coupling approach in different ways. Eq. (15) shows one possible choice, where one solves the displacements first by taking the pressures from the previous time step. Next, one updates the pressures by using the newest displacements:

$$\begin{aligned}
\underline{\underline{K}} \cdot \underline{u}^{k+1} &= f_u + \underline{\underline{Q}}\left(\underline{p}^k - \underline{p}^0\right) \\
\underline{\underline{S'}} \cdot \underline{p}^{k+1} &= \underline{\underline{S''}} \cdot \underline{p}^k + \underline{f_p} \cdot \Delta t - \underline{\underline{Q}}^T\left(\underline{u}^{k+1} - \underline{u}^k\right) \\
\underline{\underline{S'}} &= \underline{\underline{S}} + \theta \cdot \Delta t \cdot \underline{\underline{H}} \\
\underline{\underline{S''}} &= \underline{\underline{S}} - (1-\theta) \cdot \Delta t \cdot \underline{\underline{H}},
\end{aligned} \tag{15}$$

where expressions for the matrices are provided in Eq. (16) and θ is the implicitness factor that lies between 0 and 1, while Δt represents the time-step size. One can define an iterative coupling scheme in different ways, but they all derive from the loose coupling scheme with incorporating an internal iteration to update lagged quantities. For further details please refer to [4]. Also notice that for thermal stresses, one can derive an equivalent pressure drop, after Eq. (5), that renders Eq. (15) unchanged.

$$\begin{aligned}
&\underline{\underline{S}} = \int_\Omega \frac{1}{M} \underline{\Pi} \cdot \underline{\Pi}^T dx \; ; \; \underline{\underline{Q}} = \int_\Omega \underline{\underline{B}}^T \alpha \underline{\omega}_{(n)} \cdot \underline{\Pi} dx \\
&\underline{\underline{K}} = \int_\Omega \underline{\underline{B}}^T \underline{\underline{C}} \; \underline{\underline{B}} dx \; ; \; \underline{f_u} = \int_{\partial\Omega_N^u} \underline{t} \cdot \underline{\underline{\Psi}}^T ds + \int_\Omega \underline{\underline{\Psi}}^T \underline{f} \cdot dx \\
&\underline{\underline{H}} = \int_\Omega \frac{1}{\mu} \underline{\underline{K}} \nabla \underline{\Pi} \cdot (\nabla \underline{\Pi})^T dx \; ; \; \underline{\omega}_{(2)} = (1,1,0)^T \; ; \; \underline{\omega}_{(3)} = (1,1,1,0,0,0)^T \\
&f_p = \int_{\partial\Omega_N^p} \left(\frac{1}{\mu} \underline{\underline{K}} \nabla p \cdot \underline{n}\right) \cdot \underline{\Pi} ds + \int_\Omega \underline{\Pi}^T q \cdot dx + \int_\Omega \left(\frac{\rho g}{\mu} \underline{\underline{K}} \cdot \nabla \underline{\Pi} (\nabla z)^T\right) dx.
\end{aligned} \tag{16}$$

This section completes with a comment about the Continuous Galerkin (CG) formulation for the pressure (1). It is well-known that the formulation that was presented above for flow it is not locally mass conservative, and thus the resulting fluxes are not continuous across the element edges. But it is also true that accurate flow simulations require the latter, especially for multi-phase flow, though. Nevertheless, one can utilize post-processing techniques to recover locally conservative mass fluxes [2]. This chapter, though, for convenience has restricted its focus to CG methods for flow but has realized that the coupled formulation may be modified to consider mixed FE methods and finite volumes for flow as well as changing CG by post-processing. The author already showed for the simple flow cases reported herein that CG yields to physical pressure fields that can be employed for geomechanics purposes. The precise numerical comparison among CG and Discontinuous Galerkin (DG) solutions was performed in [2] to demonstrate that CG can compute pressures accurately.

3. Nonlinear heat transfer equation

The transient nonlinear heat conduction in a given body is as follows [9–11]:

$$\begin{aligned} \rho C_p \frac{\partial T}{\partial t} &= \nabla \cdot (\kappa \nabla T) + Q_T \;\; on \;\; \Omega \times]0, \mathfrak{J}[, \\ T &= g \;\; on \;\; \Gamma_D^T \times]0, \mathfrak{J}[, \\ n \cdot (\kappa \nabla T) &= h \;\; on \;\; \Gamma_N^T \times]0, \mathfrak{J}], \\ T(x, 0) &= T_0(x) \forall x \in \Omega. \end{aligned} \tag{17}$$

In (17), C_p is the heat capacity to constant pressure and $\kappa = \kappa(T)$ is the thermal conductivity. Q_T represents heat sources. Neumann BCS imply heat transfer via Fourier's law: adiabatic or no-flux BCS; $h = 0$ of most domain boundaries.

One can derive a FE formulation for model problem (17) by multiplying by a test function and integrate by parts and applying the Gauss-divergence theorem to arrive at the following bilinear form:

$$m(T, v) + k(T, v) - q(Q_T, v) - f(h, v) = 0, \tag{18}$$

where the functions are:

$$\begin{aligned} m(T, v) &= \int_{\Omega^e} v \rho C_p \partial_t T \cdot dx, \\ k(T, v) &= \int_{\Omega^e} \kappa (\nabla T)^T \cdot \nabla v \cdot dx, \\ q(Q_T, v) &= \int_{\Omega^e} v \cdot Q_T \cdot dx \;\; ; \;\; f(h, v) = \int_{\Gamma_h^e} v \cdot h \cdot ds. \end{aligned} \tag{19}$$

Time discretization renders the local residual for the element e:

$$\begin{aligned} \underline{R} \equiv \underline{\underline{M}} \cdot \left(\underline{T}^{(\ell)} - \underline{T}^{(m)} \right) + \Delta t \cdot \left(\underline{\underline{K}} \cdot \underline{T} \right)^{(m+\theta)} \\ - \Delta t \cdot \underline{q}^{(m+\theta)} - \Delta t \cdot \underline{f}^{(m+\theta)} = \underline{0}, \end{aligned} \tag{20}$$

where the linear operator $(\cdot)^{(m+\theta)} \equiv (1-\theta)(\cdot)^{\left(t=t^{(m)}\right)} + \theta(\cdot)^{\left(t=t^{(\ell)}\right)}$, $\ell = (m+1)$, $\underline{\underline{M}}\, \underline{\underline{K}}$ are the mass and stiffness matrix respectively. Thus the Jacobian is given by:

$$\underline{\underline{J}} = \frac{\partial \underline{R}}{\partial \underline{T}^{(\ell)}} = \underline{\underline{M}} + \frac{\partial}{\partial \underline{T}^{(\ell)}} \left(\underline{\underline{K}} \cdot \underline{T} \right)^{\left(t^{(\ell)}\right)} \tag{21}$$

this equation renders once again:

$$\underline{\underline{J}} = \underline{\underline{M}} + \Delta t \cdot \left(\underline{\underline{K}} + \delta \underline{\underline{K}} \right) \tag{22}$$

if one assumes that $\kappa(T) = (a \cdot T + b); a, b \in \mathbb{R}$, then:

$$\underline{\underline{\delta K}} = \sum_p \frac{\partial K_{ip}}{\partial T_j^{(\ell)}} \cdot T_p^{(\ell)}, \tag{23}$$

where the variation term is given by:

$$\frac{\partial K_{ip}}{\partial T_j^{(\ell)}} = \int_{\Omega^e} a\psi_j (\nabla \psi_i)^T \cdot \nabla \psi_p \cdot dx. \tag{24}$$

One often employs the Newton-Raphson algorithm to solve the linearized system of equations in every time step, namely, $\underline{\underline{J}} \cdot \underline{\Delta T^{(\ell)}} = -\underline{R}$. One can utilize the same continuous FE space that where described in Section 2. The reader may refer to [11] for a full treatment.

4. Domain decomposition methods

Domain Decomposition Methods (DDM) encompass highly efficient algorithms to obtain solutions of large-scale discrete problems on parallel super-computers. They mainly consist of partitioning the domain into various subdomains and then getting the global solution through the resolution of the subdomain problems [12, 13] often in an iterative fashion. These methods can be seen as an iterative coupling by the internal and thus unknown BCS. There is a broad literature covering these approaches, and that is why this chapter, therefore, presents a short introduction for the sake of completeness. The recommended references include Bjorstad and Widlund [14], Bramble et al. and Marini and Quarteroni [15], who considered the Dirichlet-Neumann (DN) DDM and Neumann-Neumann.

Let L be an abstract linear differential operator, such as the Laplace operator, for instance. The DN-DDM scheme implies solving a series of problems in the proper sequence that requires a coloring tool (see **Figure 1**). Let the Dirichlet subdomains be colored in white while the Neumann subdomains are in black. Notice that the interface between subdomains is denoted by Γ. After one provides the initial guess on the primary variables on Γ, i.e., γ^k must be given, then one can solve the problem on the white subdomains (Dirichlet problems), which corresponds to step 1 in Eq. (25).

$$1)\begin{cases} L{u_1}^{k+1} = f \text{ in } \Omega_1 \\ {u_1}^{k+1} = 0 \text{ on } \partial\Omega_1 \cap \partial\Omega \\ {u_1}^{k+1} = \gamma^k \text{ on } \Gamma \end{cases} \qquad 2)\begin{cases} L{u_2}^{k+1} = f \text{ in } \Omega_2 \\ {u_2}^{k+1} = 0 \text{ on } \partial\Omega_2 \cap \partial\Omega \\ \partial_n {u_2}^{k+1} = \kappa^{k+1} \text{ on } \Gamma \end{cases} \tag{25}$$

Let the primary variable be called "displacements" and their gradient "tractions," i.e., normal derivative in the boundary. Then, the tractions on the interface Γ must be computed after first solving step 1 on the white subdomains. They are then passed through communication to solve the second step on the black subdomains, i.e., Neumann subdomains. On this latter, since the tractions are known on Γ, one can solve for unknown displacements to provide feedback

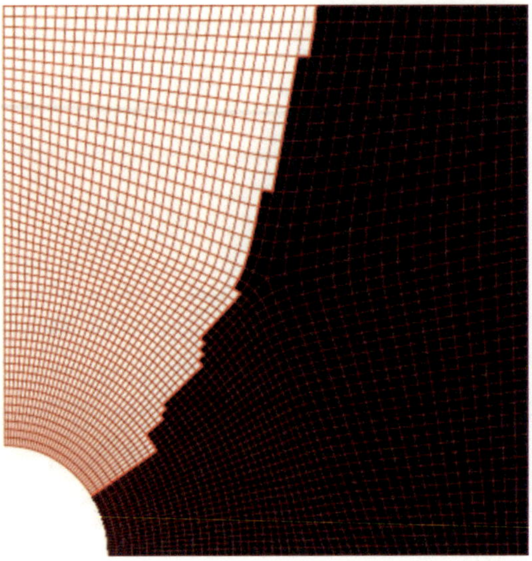

Figure 1. It depicts the DNDDM.

on the next iteration level. Both displacements and tractions are often over-relaxed to improve the convergence rate. The given relaxation parameters, referred in Eq. (26) as θ^D and θ^N, must lie between 0 and 1:

$$\begin{aligned} \kappa^{(k+1)} &= \left(-\theta^N \cdot \partial_n {u_1}^{k+1} + \left(1-\theta^N\right) \cdot \partial_n {u_2}^{k}\right) \ \text{ on } \Gamma \\ \gamma^{(k+1)} &= \left(\theta^D \cdot {u_2}^{k+1} + \left(1-\theta^D\right) \cdot {u_1}^{k}\right) \ \text{ on } \Gamma. \end{aligned} \tag{26}$$

It happens that this approach requires at least a two-entry coloring tool or even more, i.e., there may be subdomains with mixed interfaces, colored as gray [12]. There is a lack of parallelism in the sense that black subdomains must wait for the white ones to communicate their tractions. An initial guess for tractions should be prescribed to mitigate this issue, but this latter is not feasible in most cases. A straightforward way to obtain an initial estimate for the multiplier γ^k is by computing the so-called coarse-run that implies solving the same problem in a coarser mesh and interpolating over Γ by using the smaller's problem FE space. The reader may refer to the literature [16, 17] for further reading and proof of convergence and also revise [2] for a more detailed description that includes implementation details, which this chapter omits for the sake of brevity.

5. The mortar FE method (MFEM)

The primary goal here is to extend MFEM to glue curved interfaces such as the one shown in **Figure 2** where MFEM treats non-matching interfaces. The section first introduces a brief description of non-uniform rational B-Splines curves and surfaces (NURBS) in [2, 3, 18]. The reader is

Figure 2. Ω_1 is in the top, Ω_2 is in the bottom, and the interface Γ is the bold curve.

referred to those references that cover the topics of computational geometry, in particular how to build these NURBS entities. Let MFEM be described for linear isotropic elasticity regarding bilinear forms, a and Υ defined in Eq. (27) below [2, 3],

$$\begin{aligned} a\left(\underline{u},\underline{v}\right) &= \int_{\Omega} \underline{\varepsilon}(\underline{v})^T \cdot \underline{\underline{C}} \cdot \underline{\varepsilon}(\underline{u}) dx \ ; \ l(\underline{v}) = \int_{\partial\Omega^N} \underline{t}^T \cdot \underline{v} ds + \int_{\Omega} \underline{f}^T \cdot \underline{v} dx \\ \Upsilon\left(\underline{u},\underline{\Phi}\right) &= \int_{\Gamma} \lfloor \underline{u} \rfloor^T \cdot \underline{\Phi} ds \ ; \ \lfloor \underline{u} \rfloor = \left(\underline{u}^{(1)} - \underline{u}^{(2)}\right) \end{aligned} \tag{27}$$

where Υ stands for the gluing condition among subdomain interfaces and the jump $\lfloor \underline{u} \rfloor$ on the displacements is required to vanish in an integral or "weak" sense, thus:

$$\begin{cases} a\left(\underline{u}_h, \underline{v}_h\right) + \Upsilon\left(\underline{v}_h, \underline{\Lambda}_h\right) = l\left(\underline{v}_h\right) \\ \Upsilon\left(\underline{u}_h, \underline{\Phi}_h\right) = 0 \end{cases} \tag{28}$$

the parameters in Eq. (28) are as follows: $\underline{\Phi}_h$ represents the mortar space while $\underline{v}_h$ corresponds to the weighting space and $\underline{\Lambda}_h$ is the Lagrange multiplier space, i.e., the linear combination of mortar functions, often polynomial functions, and Lagrange multiplier degrees of freedom. Let $\overline{\mathcal{T}}_h^{\,M}$ be a conforming partition of the so-called parametric space, $\overline{\Omega}$, whose image serves as the mortar's geometrical entity, i.e., curve or surface, composed of line-segments ($n = 2$) or quadrilaterals ($n = 3$). One takes the mortar space as a finite-dimensional subspace of the continuous Sobolev spaces, that is:

$$\mathcal{C}_k\left(\overline{\mathcal{T}}_h^{\ M}\right) = \left\{\Phi \in L^2\left(\overline{\Omega}\right) \ : \ \forall e^M \in \overline{\mathcal{T}}_h^{\ M}, \Phi|_{e^M} \in \mathbb{P}_k\left(e^M\right)\right\} \tag{29}$$

herein $\mathbb{P}_k\left(e^M\right)$ stands for the space of polynomials of total degree less than or equal to k while $\mathcal{C}_k\left(\overline{\mathcal{T}}_h^{\ M}\right)$ represents test functions that are continuous along the edges of e^M.

One can write in a matrix or algebraic form, Eq. (28) as:

$$\begin{bmatrix} \left[k^{(1)}\right] & [0] & \left[\Upsilon^{(1)}\right]^T \\ [0] & \left[k^{(2)}\right] & -\left[\Upsilon^{(2)}\right]^T \\ \left[\Upsilon^{(1)}\right] & -\left[\Upsilon^{(2)}\right] & [0] \end{bmatrix} \cdot \begin{bmatrix} \underline{u}^{(1)} \\ \underline{u}^{(2)} \\ \underline{\Lambda} \end{bmatrix} = \begin{bmatrix} \underline{l}^{(1)} \\ \underline{l}^{(2)} \\ \underline{0} \end{bmatrix}. \tag{30}$$

The equation above corresponds to the so-called "saddle-point problem (SPP)." Notice that subdomains are only connected using the Lagrange multiplier $\underline{\Lambda}$ if they happen to be known (it is well-known that for elasticity, the multipliers are the unknown tractions on the interface), then one can decouple the system in Eq. (30) and then one just needs to perform subdomain solves. For the SPP (30), one may match displacements or tractions in the interface. The Dirichlet-Neumann scheme that the section presents is only a particular case of the most general Robin-Robin domain decomposition scheme [2, 3]. The rectangular matrices $\left[\Upsilon^{(i)}\right], i = 1\ldots2$, are denoted as projectors since they permit to map to and from the given mortar space [2, 3].

The following line integral defines the projector, for 2-D problems, as:

$$\Upsilon_{ij}^{(k)} = \int_{\overline{\Omega}} \varphi_j^{(k)}(\xi)\Phi_i(\xi) \cdot \|d_\xi \underline{\mathcal{C}}(\xi)\| \, d\xi \tag{31}$$

where $\varphi_j^{(k)}$ represents the global non-mortar side interpolation functions and Φ_i are the mortar space basis functions, while $\|d_\xi \underline{\mathcal{C}}\|$ is the length of the tangent vector associated to the B-Spline or NURBS curve. Similarly, 3-D problems imply:

$$\Upsilon_{ij}^{(k)} = \iint_{\overline{\Omega}} \varphi_j^{(k)}(\underline{\xi})\Phi_i(\underline{\xi}) \cdot \left\|\partial_\xi \underline{\mathcal{S}}(\underline{\xi}) \times \partial_\eta \underline{\mathcal{S}}(\underline{\xi})\right\| d\xi \, d\eta \tag{32}$$

where $\left\|\partial_\xi \underline{\mathcal{S}} \times \partial_\eta \underline{\mathcal{S}}\right\|$ is the norm of the surface's normal vector. Particular quadrature rules to compute these integrals must be developed. The reader should refer to [3] for a detailed explanation including the proper algorithm in pseudo-code.

6. Numerical examples

The author implemented these FE models in the Integrated Parallel Finite Element Analysis program (IPFA) that is a C++ application whose main characteristics are described in [2, 12]. IPFA employs standard continuous Lagrange polynomials as shape functions for the space discretization in each subdomain, $\mathbb{P}_k(e)$, as well as mortar space $\mathbb{P}_k(e^M)$. It also utilizes piecewise linear polynomials for the space discretizations in all examples herein that were run on a MacBook Pro laptop equipped with an Intel(R) Quad-Core(TM) i7-4870HQ CPU @ 2.5 GHz and 16 GB of RAM. The author chose this laptop for the sake of convenience, in particular, the availability of debugging tools free of charge, such as the Microsoft Visual Studio Community. Aside, one can achieve some level of parallelism due to the multi-core technology.

6.1. Example 1: Two-dimensional steady state single-phase flow

The example is a manufactured problem where the solution is a priori chosen. Then, one substitutes the given pressure field in the governing partial differential equation to obtain the source term, i.e., loading, that reproduces the input field. The problem in strong form looks like:

$$-\nabla \cdot \left(\underline{\underline{K}} \nabla p \right) = f \text{ in } \Omega \text{ ; } p = p_0 \text{ on } \Gamma_D = \Gamma, \tag{33}$$

where the domain of interest corresponds to the unitary square and Dirichlet BCS are enforced. The input pressure field is given by:

$$p(x, y) = xy \cdot (x - 1) \cdot (y - 1) \cdot \exp\left[-\left(x^2 + y^2\right)\right] \text{ ; } \underline{\underline{K}} = \underline{\underline{I}}. \tag{34}$$

Figure 3 shows the pressure field that corresponds to the problem 6.1 whose discretization encompasses three subdomains: two of them (the top and bottom ones) consist of triangular meshes while the one in the middle was discretized by a regular Cartesian quadrilateral mesh. The top-left corner of the figure shows the mesh that is employed.

The pressure field is on the right-top corner, and its horizontal derivative is in the bottom-left corner, while the discrepancy between the numerical and exact solutions, i.e., the absolute

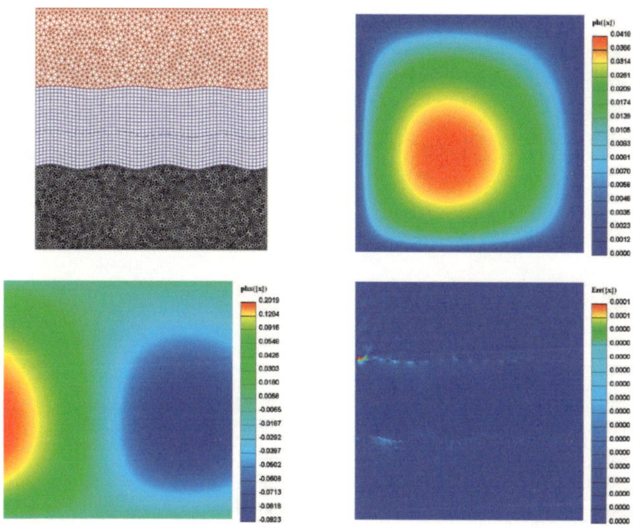

Figure 3. The MFEM solution to problem 6.1.

Points	Elements	Kind of mesh
980	1814	Triangular
1560	1472	Quadrilateral
4090	7858	Triangular

Table 1. Meshes for example 6.1.

error, was rendered in the right-bottom corner. **Table 1** represents the number of elements and points of each mesh from top to bottom. The mortars as geometrical entities correspond to two B-Splines interpolants (NURBS with all weights equal 1) that were constructed by interpolating a sinusoidal wave as the figure shows (see [3] for details). Thirty-two quadratic mortar elements per curve were utilized to glue these three subdomains. A direct frontal solver was used to solve the global SPP in Eq. (30) [3]. The results that are summarized on **Figure 3** are in good agreement with the analytical solution. The absolute error against the correct answer is also displayed. The discrepancy is of the order of 10^{-4}. Notice that besides the example only matched the displacements on the interface, a good accordance is also obtained for the horizontal derivative.

Whether or not one utilizes the SPP approach, the local problems are completely disconnected. This fact can be exploited to reduce the computational time significantly. Indeed, these sub problems can be handled in separate threads using a shared memory approach, i.e., multi-threading assembling. A convergence analysis was also performed, by successively running refined meshes [3] and by keeping a refinement ratio of 2:1 between subdomains. The exercise used a piecewise quadratic mortar space where the number of mortar elements equals the number of coarse edges in the non-mortar sides. It tackled meshes of size 8, 16, 32, 64, 128 and 256 respectively. **Figure 4** displays the resulting convergence rate in a $log - log$ plot. The slope of the least-squares straight line is 1.44143, where the coefficient of determination is $R^2 = 84\%$.

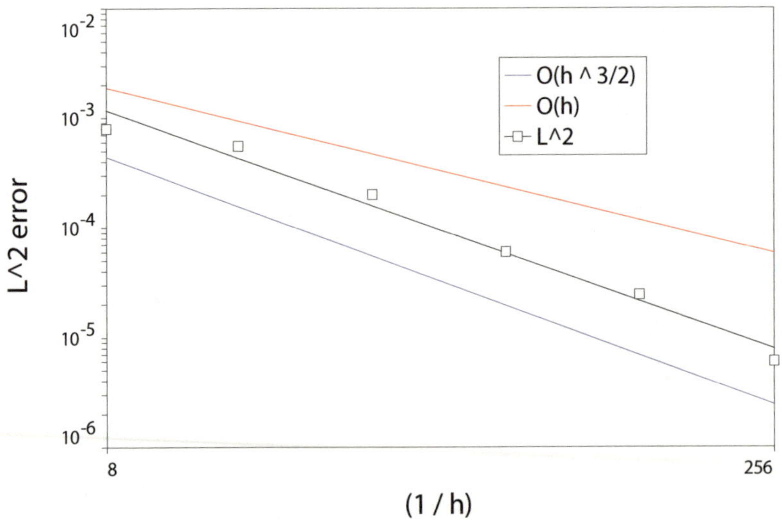

Figure 4. Snapshots showing the evolution of the DN-DDM applied to problem 6.1.

http://dx.doi.org/10.5772/intechopen.71873

This slope agrees with the theory that predicts a rate of $\mathcal{O}\left(h^{3/2}\right)$ [2, 3]. However, the resulting slope is slightly lower because of numerical errors, such as quadrature and linear system solving errors.

Finally, **Figure 5** shows pressure snapshots that represent four different Dirichlet-Neumann iteration levels evolving from left-to-right and top-to-bottom. The fact that no initial guess for pressure was provided explains the mismatch in the first snapshot. That is why one needs to eliminate discrepancies by running the process to match up those subdomains, i.e., the traction residual in the interface must vanish, which for this case occurs in just a handful of iterations. The stop criterion precisely involves the residual in the tractions in the interface that is required to fall below the given tolerance. For this particular problem, the iterative process spent six iterations to achieve a residual lower than 10^{-6} [3].

6.2. Example 2: Coupled flow and mechanics

This example analyzes a coupled flow and mechanics simulation in a reconstructed reservoir (RS) model with different meshes for the flow and mechanics physics [18]. The author proposed such a reconstruction workflow in [18] which permits this latter feature by computing a projection operator to mapping pressures from the original flow mesh into the so-called reference mechanics mesh. Toward that end, the example employs the slightly compressible flow formulation loosely combined with the mechanics model as shown in Eq. (15). The objective is to show a realistic field level RS compaction and subsidence coupled computation. The goal is thus working three different cases for the mechanics part in which one only changes the resolution of the reconstructed mechanics mesh in the pay-zone while preserving the mechanical properties constant as well as the geometry, BCS, and the depletion scenario. The exercise admits the actual static properties as being in the pay-zone such as porosity ϕ and permeability for the isotropic case $K_x = K_z = K_y$ as shown in **Figure 6**, whose depiction is three

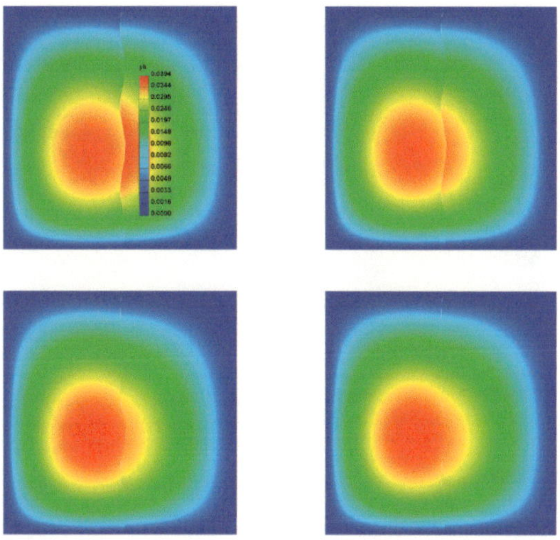

Figure 5. The numerical L^2 convergence rate for problem 6.1.

times exaggerated in the $z-$direction. The numerical values are assumed to be as follows: the fluid viscosity is 0.01325 cp and the total compressibility is $c_t = 1.4 \times 10^{-5}$ Psi^{-1} ($M^{-1} = \phi \cdot c_t$). This example does not incorporate gravity loading for both flow and mechanics.

Table 2 compiles the mesh dimensions in every direction. The example also contemplates Nz = 10, Nu = 5, No = 7, Nc = 5 (mesh patches on the corners and No and Nu stand for over- and under-burden respectively). The table also displays the number of elements, *ne*, degrees of freedom (DOF) and timing data for all three cases. The example considers 30 vertical producer wells as revealed in **Figure 6**. The initial condition encompasses a constant pressure of 10,000 Psi in the whole pay-zone while the pressure in the producer wells is set at 5000 Psi. This assumption resembles a depletion scenario. BCS correspond to no-flow on all RS faces for the pressure equation, while **Figure 7** depicts BCS for mechanics that are the typical traction free surface on the top and far-field on all remainder planes. Notice that the far-field BCS implies that the displacement in the perpendicular direction to the given plane is zero. The example also assumes a zero initial displacement field.

Figure 8 displays the mechanics mesh. The second case on **Table 2** corresponds to a layered RS with Young's modulus $E_u = 3 \times 10^4, E_p = 1 \times 10^4, E_o = 2 \times 10^4$ [Psi], while Poisson's ratio, $v = 0.25$, is constant in the whole domain. In **Figures 8** through **10** the graphs are 6 times exaggerated in the $z-$direction for better visualization. The subscript letters symbolize the

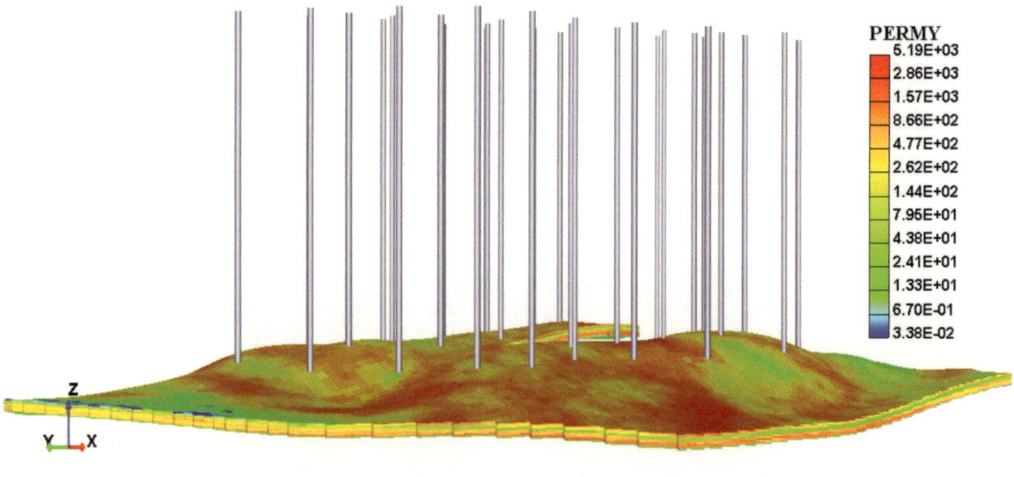

Figure 6. The reservoir's permeability K_y.

Case #	Description	Nx	Ny	*ne*	DOF	Assembling time
One	1/4 of RS	35	13	15,960	51,830	0 min, 19 s 75 ms
Two	1/2 of RS	70	26	48,279	159,120	0 min, 59 s 89 ms
Three	1/1 of RS	140	49	156,408	506,160	3 min, 14 s 89 ms

Table 2: Mesh sizes and simulations in example 6.2.

http://dx.doi.org/10.5772/intechopen.71873

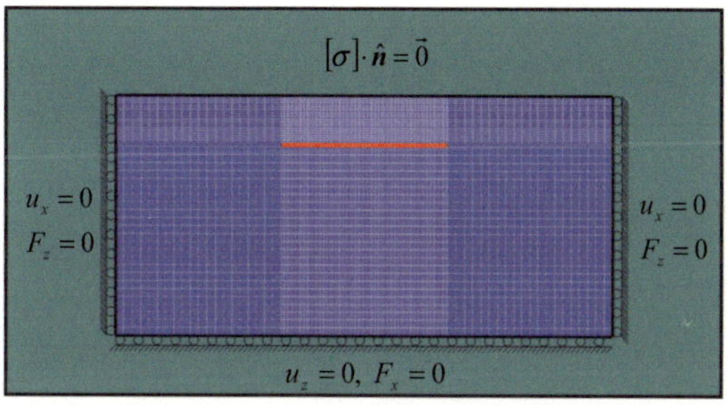

Figure 7. The BCS for the mechanics problem in the $x-z$ plane (the pay-zone is highlighted in red).

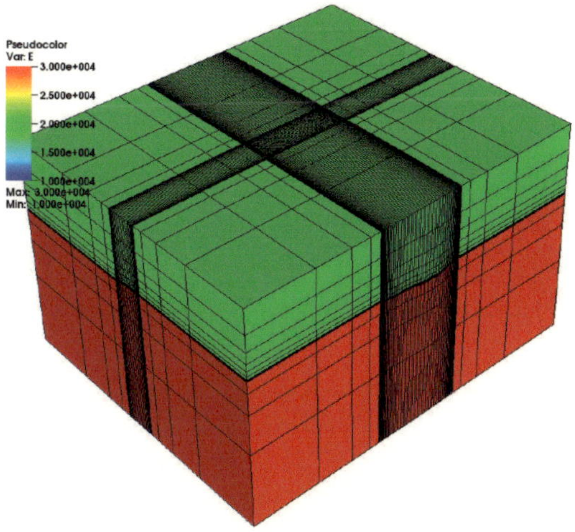

Figure 8. The hexahedral mesh generated for 2nd case in **Table 2**.

under-burden, pay-zone and over-burden levels respectively. The goal is representing a more realistic geomechanics model with stiffer surroundings around the RS.

Figure 9 pictures snapshots with the evolution of the vertical displacement u_z $[\mathrm{m}]$ and the RS pressure. A compaction dome naturally grows just above the area where the most significant pressure-drop happens. The pattern of deformation is the typical scenario where a compaction-dome rests on the top (blue color) while a build-up occurs in the bottom of the RS (rendered in red color). The deformation caused by the pressure-drop is localized because this reservoir does not entirely drain but is still a compelling case for coupled flow and mechanics.

Figure 10 renders pressure-drop snapshots at 10 years of production. Each picture draws the original RS mesh and the reference mechanic's mesh for all cases that **Table 2** covered, from top-to-bottom and left-to-right. Notice that the action of the projection operator improves with the refinement of the reference mechanics mesh as one should expect. The monotone pressure behavior, which does not drastically change across neighboring elements in the original RS mesh, may explain this improvement. Though, some items remain red-colored because they are inactive. That happens due to the interpolation error that tends to smooth out the RS topology. Perhaps it is not clear in the picture, but the reference mechanics mesh's layers (since

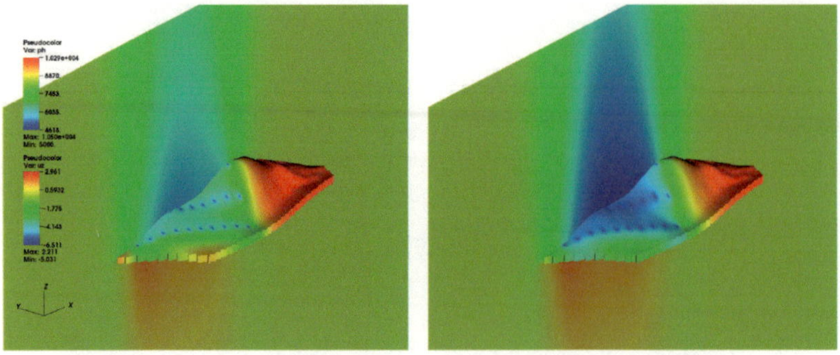

Figure 9. Snapshots at 10 and 20 years of evolution showing the vertical-displacement field u_z, the pay-zone displays pressure.

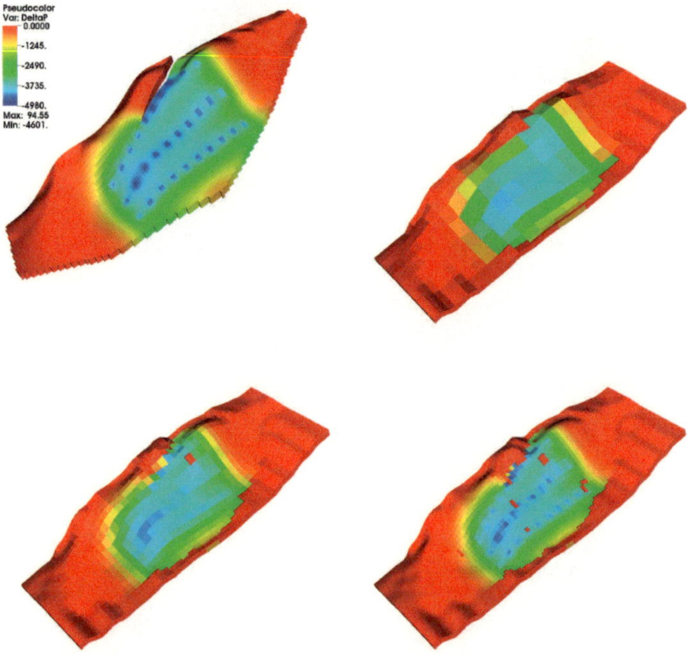

Figure 10. Snapshots showing pressure-drop [Psi] evolution at 10 years.

the thickness distribution in the $z-$direction is not uniform but instead graded toward the edge) are not evenly-spaced which tells why these inactive spots appear.

Finally, **Table 3** reviews results for the minimum and maximum vertical displacements u_z for all cases considered above. Notice that the differences between them are less than 3% for u_z min and 8% for u_z max, which proves the consistency of the projection operator. The shape of the compaction dome and the subsidence profile are alike as well. Notice that this is the case for linear isotropic elasticity. For non-linear elasticity or rate-independent plasticity probably one may expect more significant differences, though. The table also displays timing data, which reveals how the computational burden grows with the mesh refinement (see also the time spent to assemble the stiffness matrix in the last column of **Table 2**). **Figure 11** zooms out the snapshot corresponding at

Case #	u_z min	u_z max	Runtime
One	−6.652	2.693	4 min, 34 s 23 ms
Two	−6.511	2.961	7 min, 53 s 84 ms
Three	−6.469	2.752	23 min, 42 s 18 ms

Table 3. Simulations performed in example 6.2.

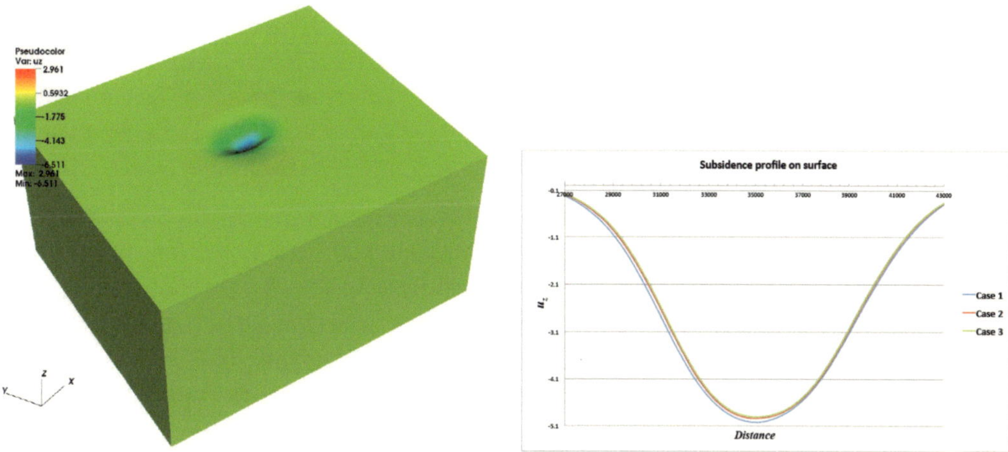

Figure 11. Subsidence profiles after 40 years of evolution.

40 years to reveal the subsidence in the surface. The plot is exaggerated several times. It also exposes the subsidence profile on the surface in the centerline of the mechanics mesh in the most extended direction. The differences between the three cases are minimal; it seems that the profile does converge toward a mesh independent solution, which is not far from the last row on the table.

The above-coupled flow and geomechanics computation, which used the reconstructed model, confirmed that the procedure is quite useful to tackle realistic reservoir compaction and subsidence simulations [18].

6.3. Example 3: Nonlinear heat transfer: arch problem

The example addresses the interesting problem that has been investigated by several researchers [9, 10]. Its distinctive features are the two re-entrant corners. Near sharp corners, there may be singularities in the solution, which cause the spatial derivatives of the solution to become unbounded. The material properties are constant density and specific heat, and a linear isotropic thermal conductivity,

$$\rho = 1.0\,\mathrm{kg/m^3};\quad C_p = 1.0\frac{\mathrm{W\cdot s}}{\mathrm{kg\cdot{}^\circ K}};\quad \kappa = \left(1 + \frac{T}{1000^\circ\mathrm{K}}\right)\frac{\mathrm{W}}{\mathrm{m\cdot{}^\circ K}}. \tag{35}$$

Figure 12 shows the domain and the mesh. The BCS are of Dirichlet type on the left- ($T = 10^3$) and right-most ($T = 0$) sides, and insulation on all other sides: $n \cdot (\kappa \nabla T) = 0$. The triangular mesh consists of 7985 points and 15,539 elements. The domain lengths are 1 m×0.5 m. The initial temperature distribution was taken to be [9]:

$$T(x, y, t^*) = 10^3 \text{erfc}\left(\frac{x}{2\sqrt{\kappa t^*}}\right)^{\circ} \text{K}, \tag{36}$$

which is the short-time linear solution at a time t^* for a plane semi-infinite medium. In the analysis, it is assumed $\kappa = 1$ and $t^* = 0.0005\,\text{s}$ in the calculation of the initial conditions.

Figure 13 shows temperature field snapshots for different times increasing from top to bottom. The example simulates 0.1 s with a fully implicit approach. It is observed that a heating front quickly travels from left to right as expected due to the temperature gradient. The temperature scale in the color maps is from 0 to 1000°K. As a qualitative benchmark, the temperature profile reported by Winget and Hughes [9] accords very well with the results herein.

The example finalizes with a simple loosely coupled thermal and mechanics computation. It takes the temperature variation that the arch problem experiences as driving force for the mechanical problem. It assumes linear isotropic elasticity with $E = 30$ Ksi and $\nu = 0.3$ and the coefficient of thermal dilatation $\beta = 1 \cdot 10^{-5} K^{-1}$ and the bulk modulus. The bottommost edges are clamped while the remainders are traction free. The right column in **Figure 13** includes three snapshots that depict the mean stress. Dilatation grows from the upper-right corner

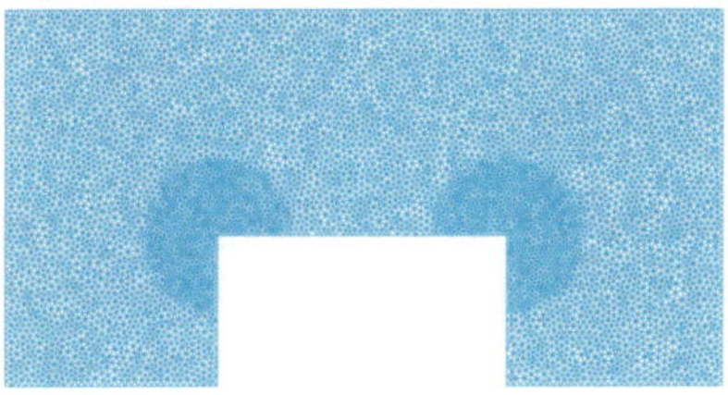

Figure 12. The mesh for the arch-problem.

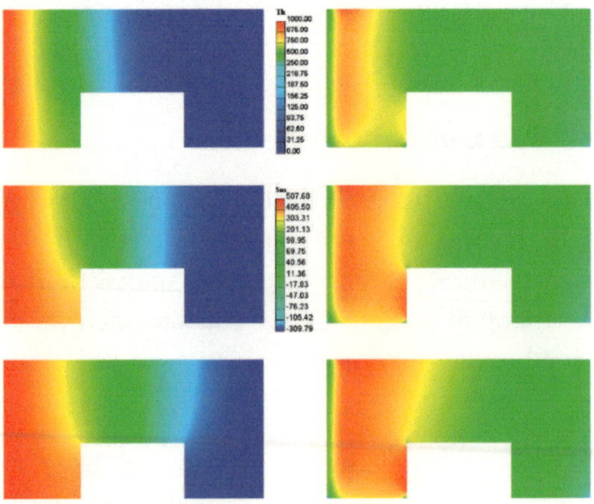

Figure 13. Temperature, T_h, (left) and mean stress, S_m, snapshots (right).

while compression appears from the upper-left corner, which are clearly observed in the results. The figure depicts the magnitude of the induced thermal stresses. The reader should refer to [10] for further details about this thermo-elasticity example.

7. Concluding remarks

This chapter introduced how to estimate stress-induced changes using elasticity simulations that are often performed through FE computations. It thus presented a formulation for linear thermo-poroelasticity. It covered the nonlinear energy equation as well. It also implemented a comprehensive MFEM on curved interfaces where the classical DN-DDM was employed to decouple the global SPP for elasticity, and steady single-phase flow. The coupled flow and geomechanics computation that utilizes the reconstructed model showed that this workflow is valuable to tackle realistic reservoir compaction and subsidence simulations. The research presented herein unfolds new prospects to further parallel codes for reservoir simulation coupled with geomechanics.

Acknowledgements

The author recognizes the financial support of the project "Reduced-Order Parameter Estimation for Underbody Blasts" financed by the Army Research Laboratory, through the Army High-Performance Computing Research Center under Cooperative Agreement W911NF-07-2-0027 and also acknowledgments Dr. Belsay Borges for proofreading the manuscript.

Author details

Horacio Florez

Address all correspondence to: florezg@gmail.com

The University of Texas at El Paso, Adelphi, Maryland, USA

References

[1] Lewis R, Schrefler B. The Finite Element Method in the Static and Dynamic Deformation and Consolidation of Porous Media. 2nd ed. New York: John Wiley and Sons; 1998

[2] Florez H. Domain decomposition methods for geomechanics [Ph.D. thesis]. The University of Texas at Austin; 2012

[3] Florez H, Wheeler M. A mortar method based on NURBS for curved interfaces. Computer Methods in Applied Mechanics and Engineering. 2016;**310**:535-566. ISSN 0045-7825. DOI: 10.1016/j.cma.2016.07.030

[4] Dean R, Gai X, Stone C, Minkoff S. A comparison of techniques for coupling porous flow and geomechanics. Paper 79709. In: SPE Reservoir Simulation Symposium; The Woodlands, Texas; 2003

[5] Gai X. A coupled geomechanics and reservoir flow model on parallel computers [Ph.D. thesis]. The University of Texas at Austin; 2004

[6] Coussy O. Poromechanics. New York: Wiley; 2004

[7] Phillips P. Finite element methods in linear poroelasticity: Theoretical and computational results [Ph.D. thesis]. The University of Texas at Austin; 2005

[8] Becker E, Carey G, Oden J. Finite Elements: An Introduction. The Texas Finite Element Series. Vol. I. Englewood Cliffs, New Jersey: Prentice-Hall Inc.; 1981

[9] Winget J, Hughes T. Solution algorithms for nonlinear transient heat conduction analysis employing element-by-element iterative strategies. Computer Methods in Applied Mechanics and Engineering. 1985;**52**:711-815

[10] Florez H. Applications of model-order reduction to thermo-poroelasticity. Paper ARMA 17-501. In: Proceedings of 51st US Rock Mechanics / Geomechanics Symposium; San Francisco, CA; 2017

[11] Florez H, Argaez M. Applications and comparison of model-order reduction methods based on wavelets and POD. Applied Mathematical Modelling. 2017;**1**:1-40

[12] Florez H, Wheeler M, Rodriguez A, Monteagudo J. Domain decomposition methods applied to coupled flow-geomechanics reservoir simulation. Paper 141596. In: SPE Reservoir Simulation Symposium; The Woodlands, Texas; 2011

[13] Maday Y, Magoules F. Absorbing interface conditions for domain decomposition methods: A general presentation. Computer Methods in Applied Mechanics and Engineering. 2006;**195**:3880-3900

[14] Bjorstad P, Widlund O. Iterative methods for the solution of elliptic problems on regions partitioned into substructures. SIAM Journal on Numerical Analysis. 1986;**23**:1093-1120

[15] Marini L, Quarteroni A. A relaxation procedure for domain decomposition methods using finite elements. Numerische Mathematik. 1989;**55**:575-598

[16] Quarteroni A, Valli A. Domain Decomposition Methods for Partial Differential Equations. Oxford: University Press; 1999

[17] Toselli A, Widlund O. Domain decomposition methods: algorithms and theory. Berlin: Springer; 2005

[18] Florez H, Manzanilla-Morillo R, Florez J, Wheeler M. Spline-based reservoir's geometry reconstruction and mesh generation for coupled flow and mechanics simulation. Computational Geosciences. 2014;**18**:949-967

Chapter 11

Numerical Analysis of the Incompressible Fluid Flow and Heat Transfer

Toshio Tagawa

Additional information is available at the end of the chapter

http://dx.doi.org/10.5772/intechopen.72263

Abstract

The present chapter introduces incompressible Newtonian fluid flow and heat transfer by using the finite difference method. Since the solution of the Navier-Stokes equation is not simple because of its unsteady and multi-dimensional characteristic, the present chapter focuses on the simplified flows owing to the similarity or periodicity. As a first section, the first Stoke problem is considered numerically by introducing the finite difference method. In the second section, natural convection heat transfer heated from a vertical plate with uniform heat flux is introduced together with the method how to obtain the system of ordinary differential equations. In the third example, linear stability analysis for the onset of secondary flow during the Taylor-Couette flow is numerically treated using the HSMAC method.

Keywords: finite difference method, similar solution, boundary layer, linear stability analysis, HSMAC method

1. Introduction

The governing equation for the fluid flow is known as Navier-Stokes equation, which is however difficult to solve analytically; and therefore, a lot of numerical techniques have been proposed and developed. Nevertheless various complex flow phenomena such as turbulent flow, multi-phase flow, compressible flow, combustion, and phase change encountered in the fields of engineering would have still difficulties to circumvent even using both present computational resources and numerical techniques. The present chapter devotes not to elucidate such complex phenomena, but to introduce rather simplified fluid flow by using the finite difference method.

One focuses on incompressible flows, in which physical properties such as the viscosity, the thermal conductivity, the specific heat are constant and even the fluid density is not a thermodynamic variable. This simplified assumption makes the fluid flow phenomena much easier to be handled and it is valid when the flow velocity is much slower than the sound velocity and/ or the temperature difference in the fluid is small enough to consider the thermal expansion coefficient is independent to the temperature. The former situation is known the *low Mach number approximation,* while the latter one the *Boussinesq approximation.*

Another simplification on the incompressible flows is the reduction of dimension due to the characteristic of similarity and periodicity. For the boundary layer flows such as the *Blasius flow,* the *stagnation-point flow,* and the *von Kármán rotating disk flow* have the similar solution where the flow transition from laminar to turbulence does not occur. In those cases, a combined dimensionless variable (similar variable) η is introduced and the velocity distribution can be only a function of η. While for the onset of instability such as the *Rayleigh-Bénard convection,* the *Bénard-Marangoni convection,* and the *Taylor-Couette flow,* the periodic characteristic of flow structure is observed. At the stage of onset of instability, the non-linear term is negligible and therefore the function of flow field is separated into the amplitude part and periodic part, respectively. This makes the effort on numerical analysis to reduce significantly and also to contribute the augmentation of accuracy of the results.

This chapter consists of three main bodies. First, a numerical technique for solving the boundary value problem called the *first Stokes problem* or the *Rayleigh problem* [1] is introduced. The differential equation is transferred into an ordinary equation and it is solved by a finite difference method using the Jacobi method. Second, similar solution of natural convection heat transfer heated from a vertical plate with uniform heat flux is introduced together with the method how to obtain the system of ordinary differential equations. The obtained Nusselt numbers are compared with some previous studies. Third, for example, of the linear stability analysis, one shows that the HSMAC method can be applied to obtain the critical values for the onset of secondary flow such as the *Taylor-Couette flow.* The Eigen functions of flow and pressure fields are visualized.

2. Unsteady flow due to sudden movement of the plate

2.1. Governing equations

An infinite length plate is set in a stationary fluid as an initial condition. Let us consider the situation that the infinite length plate suddenly moves along its parallel direction at a constant speed u_w. This problem was first solved by Stokes [2] in his famous treatment of the pendulum. Since Lord Rayleigh [3] also treated this flow, it is often called the *Rayleigh problem* in the literature. One takes that x is the plate movement direction and y is distance from the plate. Since the velocity component perpendicular to the plate v is zero, the momentum equation is simplified and is shown as a diffusion equation

$$\frac{\partial u}{\partial t} = \nu \frac{\partial^2 u}{\partial y^2} \tag{1}$$

Here, u is the velocity component parallel to the plate direction, t is the time, and ν is the kinematic viscosity. The boundary conditions for this partial differential equation are as follows:

http://dx.doi.org/10.5772/intechopen.72263

$$\begin{cases} y = 0: & u = u_w \\ y \to \infty: & u \to 0 \end{cases} \tag{2}$$

In order to reduce the partial differential equation to an ordinary equation, the following dimensionless velocity U and the similar variable η are introduced

$$u = u_w U(\eta), \quad \eta = \frac{y}{2\sqrt{\nu t}} \tag{3}$$

Then, the following ordinary differential equation can be obtained

$$\frac{d^2U}{d\eta^2} + 2\eta \frac{dU}{d\eta} = 0 \tag{4}$$

The boundary condition for the ordinary differential equation is as follows using the similar variable η instead of y:

$$\begin{cases} \eta = 0: & U = 1 \\ \eta \to \infty: & U \to 0 \end{cases} \tag{5}$$

As a consequence, one needs to solve this boundary value problem. The theoretical solution can be easily obtained and expressed using the error function

$$U = \frac{u}{u_w} = 1 - \text{erf}(\eta) = 1 - \frac{2}{\sqrt{\pi}} \int_0^{\eta} \exp\left(-\xi^2\right) d\xi \tag{6}$$

The velocity profile is shown in **Figure 1**.

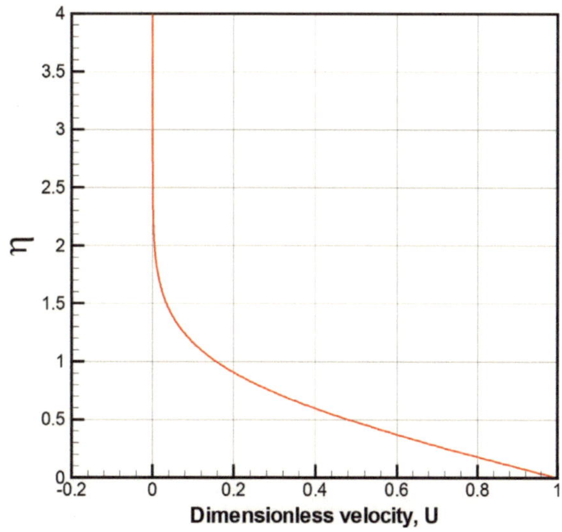

Figure 1. Velocity profile.

2.2. Numerical method for solving the ordinary differential equation using finite difference method

For numerical solution, it is necessary to define the range of η, as recognized from **Figure 1**, $\eta = 4$ is enough. Hence, the boundary condition shown below is used instead of Eq. (5)

$$\begin{cases} \eta = 0: & U = 1 \\ \eta = 4: & U = 0 \end{cases} \tag{7}$$

As illustrated in **Figure 2**, in which vertical and horizontal axes are exchanged from **Figure 1**, one needs to obtain each value of dimensionless velocity numerically. The approximated velocity profile is expressed by connecting these values smoothly. For simplicity, the intervals between neighboring two points are the same and it is noted as $\Delta\eta$. When the second-order central difference method is used, Eq. (4) is as follows:

$$\frac{U_{i+1} - 2U_i + U_{i-1}}{(\Delta\eta)^2} + 2\eta_i \frac{U_{i+1} - U_{i-1}}{2(\Delta\eta)} = 0, \quad (i = 2, 3, \cdots N - 1)$$

Here, N is total number of grids and in this chapter, the first grid point starts from 1 as its definition. The above equation becomes

$$\underbrace{\{1 - \eta_i(\Delta\eta)\}}_{\alpha_i} U_{i-1} - 2U_i + \underbrace{\{1 + \eta_i(\Delta\eta)\}}_{\beta_i} U_{i+1} = 0, \quad (i = 2, 3, \cdots N - 1). \tag{8}$$

Here, $\eta_i = (i - 1)(\Delta\eta)$ and α_i and β_i are coefficients determined by the number of grids. The boundary condition (7) is modified

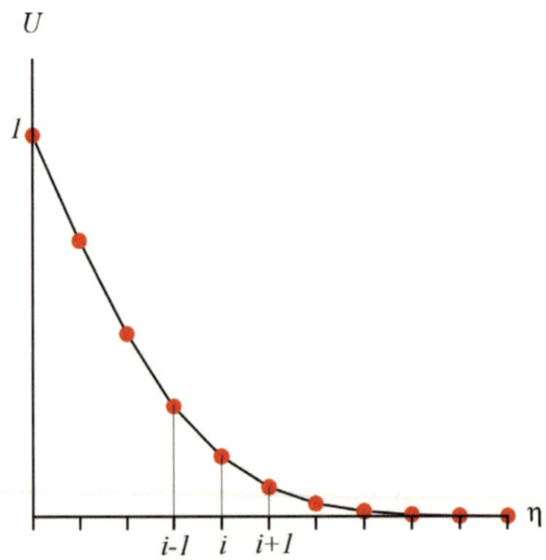

Figure 2. Equidistant grids discretized.

$$\begin{cases} \eta = 0: & U_1 = 1 \\ \eta = 4: & U_N = 0 \end{cases} \tag{9}$$

In the following, the case of $N = 7$ is considered, for example. By substituting $i = 2–6$ into Eq. (8), the following simultaneous equation is obtained:

$$\begin{pmatrix} -2 & \beta_2 & 0 & 0 & 0 \\ \alpha_3 & -2 & \beta_3 & 0 & 0 \\ 0 & \alpha_4 & -2 & \beta_4 & 0 \\ 0 & 0 & \alpha_5 & -2 & \beta_5 \\ 0 & 0 & 0 & \alpha_6 & -2 \end{pmatrix} \begin{pmatrix} U_2 \\ U_3 \\ U_4 \\ U_5 \\ U_6 \end{pmatrix} = \begin{pmatrix} -\alpha_2 U_1 \\ 0 \\ 0 \\ 0 \\ -\beta_6 U_7 \end{pmatrix} \tag{10}$$

This kind of tridiagonal matrix is often seen and can be solved by a direct numerical method, such as Tomas method. However, the rank of the matrix is usually extremely large and one introduces an iterative method for solving the king-size matrix.

2.3. Iterative method for matrix solver

In general, the rank of the matrix appearing in computational fluid dynamics (CFD) is large and iterative methods such as Jacobi, Gauss-Seidel, or successive over relaxation (SOR) methodare employed. In this subsection, the Jacobi method is explained. The matrix can be divided into three parts of lower, diagonal, and upper as follows:

$$\begin{pmatrix} 0 & 0 & 0 & 0 & 0 \\ \alpha_3 & 0 & 0 & 0 & 0 \\ 0 & \alpha_4 & 0 & 0 & 0 \\ 0 & 0 & \alpha_5 & 0 & 0 \\ 0 & 0 & 0 & \alpha_6 & 0 \end{pmatrix} \begin{pmatrix} U_2 \\ U_3 \\ U_4 \\ U_5 \\ U_6 \end{pmatrix} + \begin{pmatrix} -2 & 0 & 0 & 0 & 0 \\ 0 & -2 & 0 & 0 & 0 \\ 0 & 0 & -2 & 0 & 0 \\ 0 & 0 & 0 & -2 & 0 \\ 0 & 0 & 0 & 0 & -2 \end{pmatrix} \begin{pmatrix} U_2 \\ U_3 \\ U_4 \\ U_5 \\ U_6 \end{pmatrix}$$

$$+ \begin{pmatrix} 0 & \beta_2 & 0 & 0 & 0 \\ 0 & 0 & \beta_3 & 0 & 0 \\ 0 & 0 & 0 & \beta_4 & 0 \\ 0 & 0 & 0 & 0 & \beta_5 \\ 0 & 0 & 0 & 0 & 0 \end{pmatrix} \begin{pmatrix} U_2 \\ U_3 \\ U_4 \\ U_5 \\ U_6 \end{pmatrix} = \begin{pmatrix} -\alpha_2 U_1 \\ 0 \\ 0 \\ 0 \\ -\beta_{N-1} U_N \end{pmatrix} \tag{11}$$

In the Jacobi method, only the diagonal part is put in the left-hand side ($n + 1$ step), while the lower and upper parts are moved to the right-hand side (n step)

$$\underbrace{\begin{pmatrix} -2 & 0 & 0 & 0 & 0 \\ 0 & -2 & 0 & 0 & 0 \\ 0 & 0 & -2 & 0 & 0 \\ 0 & 0 & 0 & -2 & 0 \\ 0 & 0 & 0 & 0 & -2 \end{pmatrix}}_{D} \underbrace{\begin{pmatrix} U_2 \\ U_3 \\ U_4 \\ U_5 \\ U_6 \end{pmatrix}^{n+1}}_{\vec{U}n+1} = \underbrace{\begin{pmatrix} -\alpha_2 U_1 \\ 0 \\ 0 \\ 0 \\ -\beta_{N-1} U_N \end{pmatrix}}_{\vec{b}} - \underbrace{\begin{pmatrix} 0 & 0 & 0 & 0 & 0 \\ \alpha_3 & 0 & 0 & 0 & 0 \\ 0 & \alpha_4 & 0 & 0 & 0 \\ 0 & 0 & \alpha_5 & 0 & 0 \\ 0 & 0 & 0 & \alpha_6 & 0 \end{pmatrix}}_{L} \underbrace{\begin{pmatrix} U_2 \\ U_3 \\ U_4 \\ U_5 \\ U_6 \end{pmatrix}^{n}}_{\vec{U}n}$$

$$- \underbrace{\begin{pmatrix} 0 & \beta_2 & 0 & 0 & 0 \\ 0 & 0 & \beta_3 & 0 & 0 \\ 0 & 0 & 0 & \beta_4 & 0 \\ 0 & 0 & 0 & 0 & \beta_5 \\ 0 & 0 & 0 & 0 & 0 \end{pmatrix}}_{U} \underbrace{\begin{pmatrix} U_2 \\ U_3 \\ U_4 \\ U_5 \\ U_6 \end{pmatrix}^{n}}_{\vec{U}n} \quad (12)$$

Here, n is the old iteration step and $n + 1$ is the new iteration step. Hence, the following equation is repeatedly used:

$$\vec{U}^{n+1} = D^{-1}\left[\vec{b} - (L + U)\vec{U}^{n}\right] \quad (13)$$

This is equivalent to the following equation:

$$U_i^{n+1} = \frac{1}{2}\left(\alpha_i U_{i-1}^n + \beta_i U_{i+1}^n\right), \quad (i = 2, 3, 4, 5, 6) \quad (14)$$

By using Eq. (9), Eq. (14) is computed repeatedly and then the value of each grid gradually converges to a certain solution. The Gauss-Seidel and SOR methods are known as the faster convergence method.

3. Similarity solution for natural convection heated from a vertical plate

3.1. Introduction

In this section, let us consider the natural convection heat transfer for a vertical plate heated with uniform heat flux in the wide range of Prandtl number from zero to infinity. In order to explain the numerical method as how to solve the governing equations, one assumes that the flow and temperature fields formed in the vicinity of the heated plate have a similarity and then one introduces the finite difference method to obtain numerical results.

3.2. Governing equations

One assumes that the flow is incompressible laminar and boundary layer equations are used in this analysis. The governing equations with presuming the Boussinesq approximation are shown in Eqs. (15)–(17) together with the boundary condition (18). Here, one defines that x axis is in the vertical direction and its velocity component is u, and y axis is in the direction perpendicular to the vertical plate and its velocity component is v.

Continuity of mass

$$\frac{\partial u}{\partial x}+\frac{\partial v}{\partial y}=0 \tag{15}$$

Momentum equation

$$u\frac{\partial u}{\partial x}+v\frac{\partial u}{\partial y}=\nu\frac{\partial^2 u}{\partial y^2}+g\beta(T-T_\infty) \tag{16}$$

Energy equation

$$u\frac{\partial T}{\partial x}+v\frac{\partial T}{\partial y}=\alpha\frac{\partial^2 T}{\partial y^2} \tag{17}$$

Boundary equation

$$\begin{cases} y=0: & u=v=0, \quad q=-k(\partial T/\partial y) \\ y\to\infty: & u\to 0, \quad T\to T_\infty \end{cases} \tag{18}$$

Here, β is the thermal expansion coefficient, g is the acceleration due to gravity, α is the thermal diffusivity, k is the thermal conductivity, and T is the temperature.

3.3. Non-dimensionalization

First, dimensionless variables, such as velocity and temperature, are set as follows using the unknown reference value denoted with subscripts a and b:

$$X=\frac{x}{x_a},\quad Y=\frac{y}{y_a},\quad U=\frac{u}{u_a},\quad V=\frac{v}{v_a},\quad \theta=\frac{T-T_b}{T_a} \tag{19}$$

Equation (19) is substituted into Eqs. (15)–(18), and one gets

$$\frac{\partial U}{\partial X}+\underbrace{\frac{v_a x_a}{y_a u_a}}_{[1]}\frac{\partial V}{\partial Y}=0$$

$$U\frac{\partial U}{\partial X}+\underbrace{\frac{v_a x_a}{y_a u_a}}_{[1]}V\frac{\partial U}{\partial Y}=\underbrace{\frac{\nu x_a}{{y_a}^2 u_a}}_{[2]}\frac{\partial^2 U}{\partial Y^2}+\underbrace{\frac{g\beta(T_b-T_\infty)x_a}{{u_a}^2}}_{[3]}+\underbrace{\frac{g\beta T_a x_a}{{u_a}^2}}_{[4]}\theta$$

$$U\frac{\partial\theta}{\partial X}+\underbrace{\frac{v_a x_a}{y_a u_a}}_{[1]}V\frac{\partial\theta}{\partial Y}=\underbrace{\frac{\alpha x_a}{{y_a}^2 u_a}}_{[5]}\frac{\partial^2\theta}{\partial Y^2}$$

$$\begin{cases} Y=0: \quad U=V=0, \quad \underbrace{(qy_a)/(kT_a)}_{[6]}=-\partial\theta/\partial Y \\ Y\to\infty: \quad U=0, \quad \theta=\underbrace{(T_\infty-T_b)/T_a}_{[7]} \end{cases}$$

At the moment stage, x_a is recognized as the height of the vertical plate.

Putting [3] = 0, and one obtains $T_b=T_\infty$.Hence [7] becomes $\theta=0$.

Putting [6] = 1, and one gets $\frac{qy_a}{kT_a}=1 \quad \Rightarrow \quad T_a=\frac{qy_a}{k}$

Putting [5] = 1, and one gets $\frac{\alpha x_a}{{y_a}^2 u_a}=1 \quad \Rightarrow \quad y_a=\left(\frac{\alpha x_a}{u_a}\right)^{1/2}$

Putting [1] = 1, $\frac{v_a x_a}{y_a u_a}=1 \quad \Rightarrow \quad v_a=\frac{y_a u_a}{x_a}$

Putting [4] = 1, $\frac{g\beta T_a x_a}{{u_a}^2}=1 \quad \Rightarrow \quad u_a=(g\beta T_a x_a)^{1/2}=\left(g\beta\frac{qy_a}{k}x_a\right)^{1/2}=\left(g\beta\frac{q}{k}\left(\frac{\alpha x_a}{u_a}\right)^{1/2}x_a\right)^{1/2}$

$$\therefore \quad u_a=\left\{\left(g\beta\frac{q}{k}\right)^2\alpha {x_a}^3\right\}^{1/5}=\left(\frac{g\beta q {x_a}^4}{k\alpha^2}\right)^{2/5}\frac{\alpha}{x_a}=(Ra^*Pr)^{2/5}\frac{\alpha}{x_a}, \quad \because Ra^*=\frac{g\beta q {x_a}^4}{k\alpha\nu} \tag{20}$$

$$y_a=\left(\frac{\alpha x_a}{u_a}\right)^{1/2}=\left(\frac{\alpha x_a}{(Ra^*Pr)^{2/5}\frac{\alpha}{x_a}}\right)^{1/2}=\left(\frac{{x_a}^2}{(Ra^*Pr)^{2/5}}\right)^{1/2}=x_a(Ra^*Pr)^{-1/5} \tag{21}$$

$$T_a=\frac{qy_a}{k}=\frac{q}{k}\frac{x_a}{(Ra^*Pr)^{1/5}}=\frac{qx_a}{k}(Ra^*Pr)^{-1/5} \tag{22}$$

$$v_a=\frac{y_a u_a}{x_a}=\frac{\frac{x_a}{(Ra^*Pr)^{1/5}}(Ra^*Pr)^{2/5}\frac{\alpha}{x_a}}{x_a}=(Ra^*Pr)^{1/5}\frac{\alpha}{x_a} \tag{23}$$

In the above process, finally one obtains the dimensionless equations as follows:

$$\frac{\partial U}{\partial X}+\frac{\partial V}{\partial Y}=0 \tag{24}$$

$$U\frac{\partial U}{\partial X}+V\frac{\partial U}{\partial Y}=Pr\frac{\partial^2 U}{\partial Y^2}+\theta \tag{25}$$

$$U\frac{\partial\theta}{\partial X}+V\frac{\partial\theta}{\partial Y}=\frac{\partial^2\theta}{\partial Y^2} \tag{26}$$

$$\begin{cases} Y = 0: & U = V = 0, \quad \partial\theta/\partial Y = -1 \\ Y \to \infty: & U = 0, \quad \theta = 0 \end{cases} \tag{27}$$

The dimensionless variables are summarized as follows:

$$\begin{aligned} &X = \frac{x}{x_a}, \quad Y = \frac{y}{x_a(Ra^*Pr)^{-1/5}}, \quad U = \frac{u}{\frac{\alpha}{x_a}(Ra^*Pr)^{2/5}}, \\ &V = \frac{v}{\frac{\alpha}{x_a}(Ra^*Pr)^{1/5}}, \quad \theta = \frac{T - T_\infty}{\frac{qx_a}{k}(Ra^*Pr)^{-1/5}} \end{aligned} \tag{28}$$

Furthermore, one assumes that the velocity and temperature fields has a similarity along the direction of vertical plate, so one puts $X = 1$. These equations are useful for analyzing low Prandtl number cases and summarized as follows:

Low Prandtl number

Continuity of mass

$$\frac{dV}{d\eta} = \frac{1}{5}\left(\eta\frac{dU}{d\eta} - 3U\right) \tag{29}$$

Momentum equation

$$U\frac{dV}{d\eta} - V\frac{dU}{d\eta} + Pr\frac{d^2U}{d\eta^2} + \theta = 0 \tag{30}$$

Energy equation

$$\frac{U}{5}\left(\eta\frac{d\theta}{d\eta} - \theta\right) - V\frac{d\theta}{d\eta} + \frac{d^2\theta}{d\eta^2} = 0 \tag{31}$$

Boundary conditions

$$\begin{cases} \eta = 0: & U = V = 0, \quad d\theta/d\eta = -1 \\ \eta \to \infty: & U = \theta = 0 \end{cases} \tag{32}$$

The dimensionless variables and non-dimensional numbers are defined as follows:

$$\begin{aligned} &\eta = \frac{y}{x(Ra_x{}^*Pr)^{-\frac{1}{5}}}, \quad U = \frac{u}{\frac{\alpha}{x}(Ra_x{}^*Pr)^{\frac{2}{5}}}, \quad V = \frac{v}{\frac{\alpha}{x}(Ra_x{}^*Pr)^{\frac{1}{5}}}, \\ &\theta = \frac{T - T_\infty}{\frac{qx}{k}(Ra_x{}^*Pr)^{-\frac{1}{5}}}, \quad Ra_x{}^* = \frac{g\beta qx^4}{\alpha\nu k}, \quad Pr = \frac{\nu}{\alpha} \end{aligned} \tag{33}$$

The local Nusselt number can be obtained by the following derivation:

$$Nu_x = \frac{h_x x}{k} = \frac{qx}{(T_w - T_\infty)k} = \frac{qx}{T_a \theta_w k} = \underbrace{\frac{\left(\frac{g\beta q}{\alpha^2 k}\right)^{1/5} k}{qx^{1/5}}}_{T_a^{-1}} \frac{qx}{\theta_w k}$$
$$= \left(\frac{g\beta q}{\alpha^2 k}\right)^{1/5} \frac{x^{4/5}}{\theta_w} = \left(\frac{g\beta q x^4}{\alpha^2 k}\right)^{1/5} \frac{1}{\theta_w} = \left(Ra_x^* Pr\right)^{1/5} \frac{1}{\theta_w} \tag{34}$$

$$Nu_x = \left(Ra_x{}^* Pr\right)^{\frac{1}{5}} \left(\theta|_{\eta=0}\right)^{-1} = \left(Ra_x Nu_x Pr\right)^{\frac{1}{5}} \left(\theta|_{\eta=0}\right)^{-1} \tag{35}$$

Therefore, the local Nusselt number can be obtained just from the dimensionless temperature at the wall using Eq. (36)

$$\frac{Nu_x}{\left(Ra_x Pr\right)^{\frac{1}{4}}} = \left(\theta|_{\eta=0}\right)^{-\frac{5}{4}} \tag{36}$$

High Prandtl number

If the Prandtl number is higher than unity, the following equations are useful:

Continuity of mass

$$\frac{dV}{d\eta} = \frac{1}{5}\left(\eta \frac{dU}{d\eta} - 3U\right) \tag{37}$$

Momentum equation

$$U\frac{dV}{d\eta} - V\frac{dU}{d\eta} + Pr\frac{d^2U}{d\eta^2} + Pr\theta = 0 \tag{38}$$

Energy equation

$$\frac{U}{5}\left(\eta \frac{d\theta}{d\eta} - \theta\right) - V\frac{d\theta}{d\eta} + \frac{d^2\theta}{d\eta^2} = 0 \tag{39}$$

Boundary conditions

$$\begin{cases} \eta = 0: & U = V = 0, \quad d\theta/d\eta = -1 \\ \eta \to \infty: & U = \theta = 0 \end{cases} \tag{40}$$

The dimensionless variables and non-dimensional numbers are defined as follows:

$$\eta = \frac{y}{x\left(Ra_x{}^*\right)^{-\frac{1}{5}}}, \quad U = \frac{u}{\frac{\alpha}{x}\left(Ra_x{}^*\right)^{\frac{2}{5}}}, \quad V = \frac{v}{\frac{\alpha}{x}\left(Ra_x{}^*\right)^{\frac{1}{5}}},$$
$$\theta = \frac{T - T_\infty}{\frac{qx}{k}\left(Ra_x{}^*\right)^{-\frac{1}{5}}}, \quad Ra_x{}^* = \frac{g\beta q x^4}{\alpha \nu k}, \quad Pr = \frac{\nu}{\alpha} \tag{41}$$

http://dx.doi.org/10.5772/intechopen.72263

$$\frac{Nu_x}{(Ra_x)^{\frac{1}{4}}} = \left(\theta|_{\eta=0}\right)^{-\frac{5}{4}} \tag{42}$$

3.4. Numerical results

Figure 3 shows the numerical result for the various Prandtl number cases. The upper figures indicate the vertical velocity and lower ones the temperature. The left-hand side figures show the cases of Pr ≥ 1, while the right-hand side ones the cases of Pr ≤ 1

Table 1 shows the summary of the local Nusselt number for various Prandtl number cases together with the reference of Churchill and Ozoe for comparison [4]. The agreement is quite good except for the extreme cases such as Pr → 0 and ∞. In such extreme cases, a small amount of discrepancy exists. In this study, the boundary condition for Pr → 0

$$\begin{cases} \eta = 0: & dU/d\eta = V = 0, \quad d\theta/d\eta = -1 \\ \eta \to \infty: & U = \theta = 0 \end{cases}$$

and that for Pr → ∞

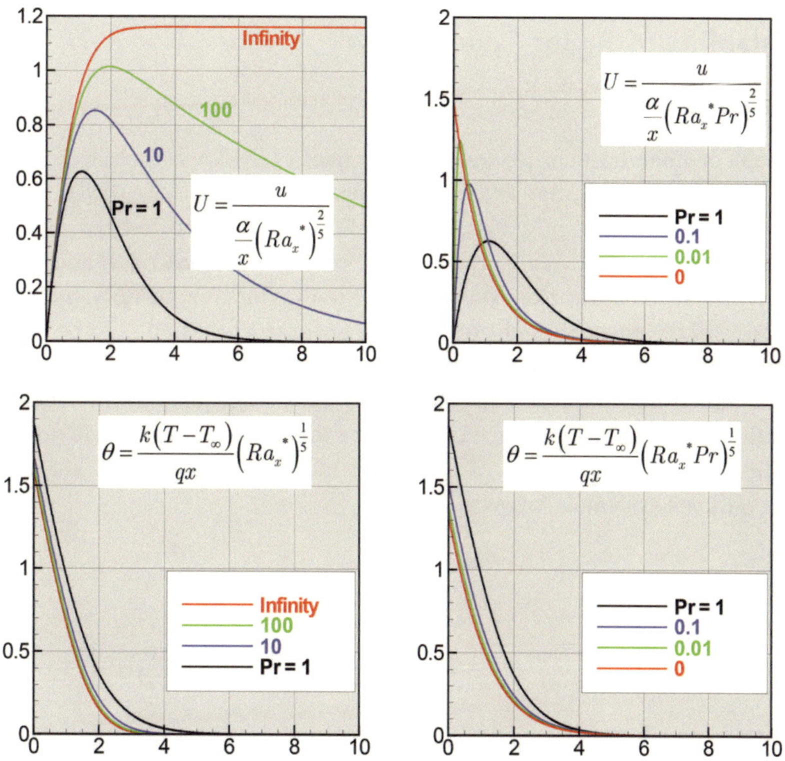

Figure 3. Vertical velocity and temperature distributions for various Prandtl numbers. The left-hand side indicates high Prandtl number cases while the right-hand side low Prandtl number cases.

Pr	0	0.01	0.1	1	10	100	∞
$\frac{Nu_x}{(Ra_x)^{1/4}}$	N/A			0.4564 0.456	0.5234 0.524	0.5495 0.550	0.5631 0.5627
$\frac{Nu_x}{(Ra_x Pr)^{1/4}}$	0.7107 0.6922	0.6694 0.670	0.5970 0.597	0.4564 0.456	N/A		

Table 1. Local Nusselt number for various values of Prandtl number (the upper: present results, the lower: Churchill and Ozoe [4]).

$$\begin{cases} \eta = 0: & U = V = 0, \quad d\theta/d\eta = -1 \\ \eta \to \infty: & dU/d\eta = \theta = 0. \end{cases}$$

are used. Owing to this kind of special treatments for the boundary condition of such extreme cases, one can obtain accurate numerical results for the system of ordinary equations. The results between the solution of the present method and that of Le Fevre [5] for the case of constant temperature of heated wall are identical to each other. The value for Pr $\to \infty$ is 0.5027 and that for Pr = 0 is 0.6004.

4. Linear stability of Taylor-Couette flow

4.1. Governing equations

In the text book of Chandrasekar [6], various examples of the linear stability analysis such as the *Rayleigh-Bénard convection*, the *Taylor-Couette flow*, and the *Rayleigh-Taylor instability* were studied extensively. More recently, Koschmieder [7] described the research focusing on the *Bénard cells* and the *Taylor vortices*. In this section, only the Taylor-Coette flow is considered. **Figure 4** shows the schematic model considered for the Taylor-Couette flow. In this section, the fluid flow inside of the co-axial double cylindrical enclosure is assumed to be incompressible Newtonian, isothermal and axisymmetric. The gray part represents the computational domain. It is known that the stationary secondary flow is generated at a certain condition under the influence of centrifugal force due to the rotation of primary basic flow which is in azimuthal direction. The continuity of mass and momentum equations are shown in the cylindrical coordinate system as follows:

$$\frac{\partial u_r}{\partial r} + \frac{u_r}{r} + \frac{\partial u_z}{\partial z} = 0 \tag{43}$$

$$\frac{\partial u_r}{\partial t} + u_r \frac{\partial u_r}{\partial r} + u_z \frac{\partial u_r}{\partial z} - \frac{u_\theta{}^2}{r} = -\frac{1}{\rho}\frac{\partial p}{\partial r} + \nu\left(\frac{\partial^2 u_r}{\partial r^2} + \frac{1}{r}\frac{\partial u_r}{\partial r} - \frac{u_r}{r^2} + \frac{\partial^2 u_r}{\partial z^2}\right) \tag{44}$$

$$\frac{\partial u_\theta}{\partial t} + u_r \frac{\partial u_\theta}{\partial r} + u_z \frac{\partial u_\theta}{\partial z} + \frac{u_r u_\theta}{r} = \nu\left(\frac{\partial^2 u_\theta}{\partial r^2} + \frac{1}{r}\frac{\partial u_\theta}{\partial r} - \frac{u_\theta}{r^2} + \frac{\partial^2 u_\theta}{\partial z^2}\right) \tag{45}$$

http://dx.doi.org/10.5772/intechopen.72263

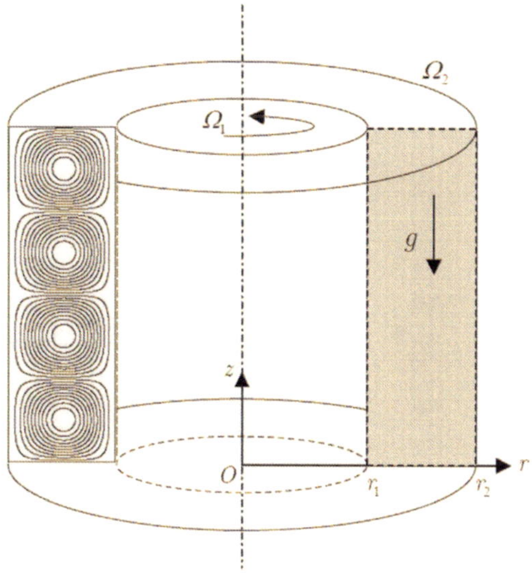

Figure 4. Schematic model for the Taylor-Couette flow.

$$\frac{\partial u_z}{\partial t} + u_r \frac{\partial u_z}{\partial r} + u_z \frac{\partial u_z}{\partial z} = -\frac{1}{\rho}\frac{\partial p}{\partial z} + \nu\left(\frac{\partial^2 u_z}{\partial r^2} + \frac{1}{r}\frac{\partial u_z}{\partial r} + \frac{\partial^2 u_z}{\partial z^2}\right) - g \tag{46}$$

Here, it is indicated that r is the radial, θ is the azimuthal, and z is the axial components.

4.2. Basic state and linearization

The cylindrical enclosure is long enough to neglect the top and bottom ends. In that situation, the basic states for the azimuthal component of velocity and pressure are as follows:

Azimuthal velocity

$$\overline{u}_\theta(r) = -\frac{r_2^2\Omega_2 - r_1^2\Omega_1}{r_1^2 - r_2^2} r + \frac{r_1^2 r_2^2(\Omega_2 - \Omega_1)}{r_1^2 - r_2^2}\frac{1}{r} \tag{47}$$

Pressure

$$\overline{p}(r, z) = \int \frac{\rho\{\overline{u}_\theta(r)\}^2}{r} dr - \rho g z + p_0 \tag{48}$$

Here, Ω_1 is the angular velocity at the inner cylinder, Ω_2 is the angular velocity at the outer cylinder, p is the pressure, ρ is the density, and g is the acceleration due to gravity. In order to derive disturbance equations for the linear stability, the three components of velocity and pressure are represented as a summation of basic state and infinitesimal disturbance as follows:

$$u_\theta(r,z,t) = \overline{u}_\theta(r) + v'(r,z,t), \quad u_r(r,z,t) = u'(r,z,t), \quad u_z(r,z,t) = w'(r,z,t),$$
$$p(r,z,t) = \overline{p}(r,z) + p'(r,z,t) \tag{49}$$

After neglecting the second-order disturbance, the following linearized equations are obtained:

$$\frac{\partial u'}{\partial r} + \frac{u'}{r} + \frac{\partial w'}{\partial z} = 0 \tag{50}$$

$$\frac{\partial u'}{\partial t} = -\frac{1}{\rho}\frac{\partial p'}{\partial r} + \nu\left(\frac{\partial^2 u'}{\partial r^2} + \frac{1}{r}\frac{\partial u'}{\partial r} - \frac{u'}{r^2} + \frac{\partial^2 u'}{\partial z^2}\right) + \frac{2\overline{u}_\theta v'}{r} \tag{51}$$

$$\frac{\partial v'}{\partial t} = \nu\left(\frac{\partial^2 v'}{\partial r^2} + \frac{1}{r}\frac{\partial v'}{\partial r} - \frac{v'}{r^2} + \frac{\partial^2 v'}{\partial z^2}\right) - \left(\frac{d\overline{u}_\theta}{dr} + \frac{\overline{u}_\theta}{r}\right)u' \tag{52}$$

$$\frac{\partial w'}{\partial t} = -\frac{1}{\rho}\frac{\partial p'}{\partial z} + \nu\left(\frac{\partial^2 w'}{\partial r^2} + \frac{1}{r}\frac{\partial w'}{\partial r} + \frac{\partial^2 w'}{\partial z^2}\right) \tag{53}$$

By considering the periodicity of the secondary flow which could be happened, each component of infinitesimal disturbance is assumed to be given in the following form. Here, a is the axial wavenumber (real number) and s is angular frequency (complex number)

$$\frac{u'}{\tilde{u}(r)} = \frac{v'}{\tilde{v}(r)} = \frac{w'}{\tilde{w}(r)} = \frac{p'}{\tilde{p}(r)} = \exp(iaz + st) \tag{54}$$

4.3. Linear stability analysis

The dimensionless simultaneous ordinary equations are summarized as follows:

Basic velocity

$$\overline{U}_\theta(R) = \frac{\mu - \eta^2}{1-\eta^2}R + \frac{\eta^2(1-\mu)}{1-\eta^2}\frac{1}{R} \tag{55}$$

Disturbance equations for amplitude functions

$$D_*\tilde{U} + ik\tilde{W} = 0 \tag{56}$$

$$S\tilde{U} = -D\tilde{P} + (DD_* - k^2)\tilde{U} + Re_\Omega\frac{2\overline{U}_\theta}{R}\tilde{V} \tag{57}$$

$$S\tilde{V} = (DD_* - k^2)\tilde{V} - Re_\Omega(D_*\overline{U}_\theta)\tilde{U} \tag{58}$$

$$S\tilde{W} = -ik\tilde{P} + (D_*D - k^2)\tilde{W} \tag{59}$$

Here, the dimensionless variables and non-dimensional numbers are as follows. The outer radius r_2 is taken as the characteristic length

$$R = \frac{r}{r_2}, \quad \overline{U}_\theta = \frac{\overline{u}_\theta}{\Omega_1 r_2}, \quad \left(\tilde{U}, \tilde{V}, \tilde{W}\right) = \frac{(\tilde{u}, \tilde{v}, \tilde{w})}{\Omega_1 r_2}, \quad \tilde{P} = \frac{\tilde{p}}{\rho \nu \Omega_1},$$
$$Re_\Omega = \frac{\Omega_1 r_2^2}{\nu}, \quad k = r_2 a, \quad \eta = \frac{r_1}{r_2}, \quad \mu = \frac{\Omega_2}{\Omega_1}, \quad S = \frac{s}{\nu / {r_2}^2}, \quad D = \frac{d}{dR}, \quad D_* = \frac{d}{dR} + \frac{1}{R} \tag{60}$$

The boundary conditions are as follows:

$$\begin{cases} R = \eta: & \tilde{U} = \tilde{V} = \tilde{W} = 0 \quad \text{(Inner wall)} \\ R = 1: & \tilde{U} = \tilde{V} = \tilde{W} = 0 \quad \text{(Outer wall)}. \end{cases} \tag{61}$$

After Chandrasekar [6], the following two non-dimensional numbers are introduced to verify the computational results:

$$Ta = \frac{4{\Omega_1}^2 r_1^4}{\nu^2} \frac{(1-\mu)(1-4\mu)}{(1-\eta^2)^2} = 4{Re_\Omega}^2 \frac{\eta^4 (1-\mu)(1-4\mu)}{(1-\eta^2)^2}, \quad \kappa = \frac{1-\mu/\eta^2}{1-\mu} \tag{62}$$

In this section, it is assumed that $S = 0$. This indicates that the secondary flow caused by the centrifugal instability is stationary and it contains toroidal vortices. To deal with the simultaneous ordinary differential equations for the boundary value problem, a one-dimensional staggered grid system is employed as shown in **Figure 5**. All the equations are discretized by the fourth order central difference method with a given wavenumber k using the HSMAC method [8] during which Re_Ω is obtained by the Newton method. The following equations are used for correction of the pressure and velocity simultaneously. Here, the subscript i indicates grid location, while the superscripts m and n indicate the iteration of the corrections for the convergence of Eq. (56) and the time step, respectively. The more detailed explanation can be found in the recent papers published by the present author [9, 10]

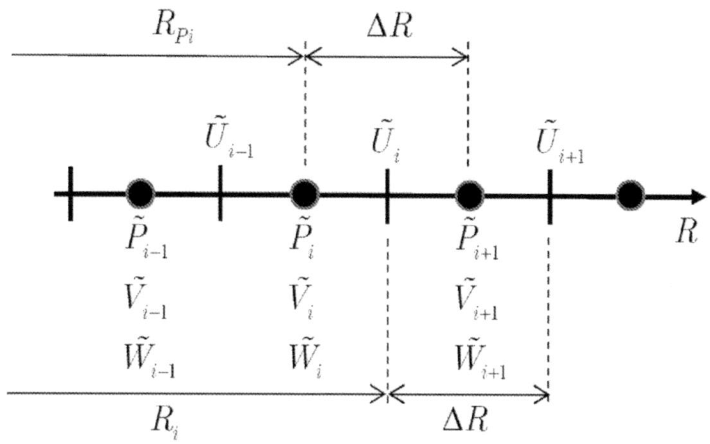

Figure 5. The staggered grids in the radius direction together with the points of each variable definition.

$$
{}^{m+1}\tilde{P}_i^{n+1} = {}^{m}\tilde{P}_i^{n+1} + {}^{m}(\delta\tilde{P})_i^{n+1}
$$

$$
= {}^{m}\tilde{P}_i^{n+1} - \frac{\dfrac{-{}^{m}\tilde{U}_{i+1}^{n+1} + 27{}^{m}\tilde{U}_i^{n+1} - 27{}^{m}\tilde{U}_{i-1}^{n+1} + {}^{m}\tilde{U}_{i-2}^{n+1}}{24(\Delta R)} + \dfrac{-{}^{m}\tilde{U}_{i+1}^{n+1} + 9{}^{m}\tilde{U}_i^{n+1} + 9{}^{m}\tilde{U}_{i-1}^{n+1} - {}^{m}\tilde{U}_{i-2}^{n+1}}{16R_{Pi}} + ik\cdot{}^{m}\tilde{W}_i^{n+1}}{\Delta\tau\{2/(\Delta R)^2 + k^2\}} \tag{63}
$$

$$
{}^{m+1}\tilde{U}_i^{n+1} = {}^{m}\tilde{U}_i^{n+1} + \frac{\Delta\tau}{\Delta R}\cdot{}^{m}(\delta\tilde{P})_i^{n+1}, \quad {}^{m+1}\tilde{U}_{i-1}^{n+1} = {}^{m}\tilde{U}_{i-1}^{n+1} - \frac{\Delta\tau}{\Delta R}\cdot{}^{m}(\delta\tilde{P})_i^{n+1} \tag{64}
$$

$$
{}^{m+1}\tilde{W}_i^{n+1} = {}^{m}\tilde{W}_i^{n+1} - ik(\Delta\tau)\cdot{}^{m}(\delta\tilde{P})_i^{n+1} \tag{65}
$$

Table 2 shows the computational results for various rotation speeds at $\eta = 0.5$. When $\mu > 0.25$, the basic flow is always stable due to the Rayleigh's criterion. The present results exhibit slightly smaller values of Taylor number than those of Chandrasekar. **Figures 6** and **7** show the amplitude functions and Eigen functions, respectively, for the case of $\mu = 0$ (the outer cylinder is stationary), and **Figures 8** and **9** show the case of $\mu = -0.5$ (the outer cylinder rotates with half angular velocity in opposite direction to the inside rotation).

The simultaneous ordinary equations from (56) to (59) were divided into the real and imaginary parts. However, only four equations among the eight equations are necessary to solve in this problem because of the symmetricity and anti-symmetricity of the complex variables. In **Figures 6** and **8**, the real part of $\tilde{U}, \tilde{V}, \tilde{P}$ and the imaginary part of $\tilde{W}$ are shown. For the visualization shown in **Figures 7** and **9**, the Stokes stream function Ψ is defined as follows:

		Present (201 grids)		Chandrasekar [6]	
κ	μ	Critical wave number	Critical *Ta* number	Wavenumber	*Ta* number
0	1/4	6.286	15316	6.4	15332
0.4	1/6	6.293	19518	6.4	19542
0.6	2/17	6.299	22617	6.4	22644
1.0	0	6.325	33062	6.4	33100
4/3	−1/8	6.403	53210	6.4	53280
1.6	−1/4	6.715	98520	6.4	99072
1.8	−4/11	7.819	197715	7.8	199540
1.9	−9/21	8.733	288761	8.6	293630
2.0	−1/2	9.602	417734	9.6	428650

Table 2. Computational results and comparison with Chandrasekar ($\eta = 0.5$).

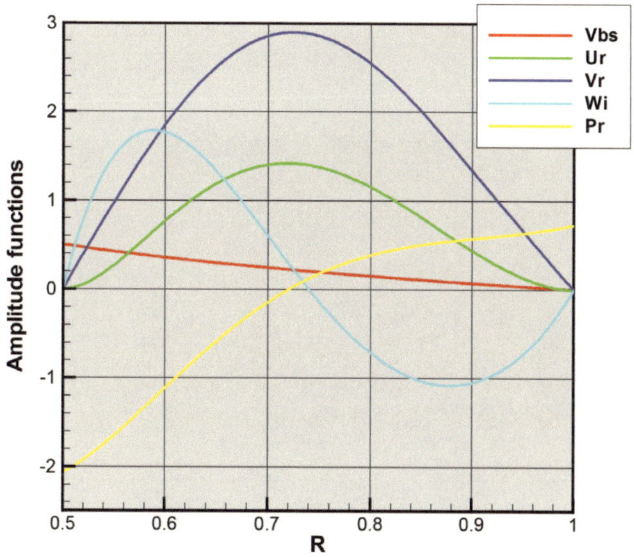

Figure 6. Amplitude functions ($\eta = 0.5$, $\mu = 0$, $k = 6.325$).

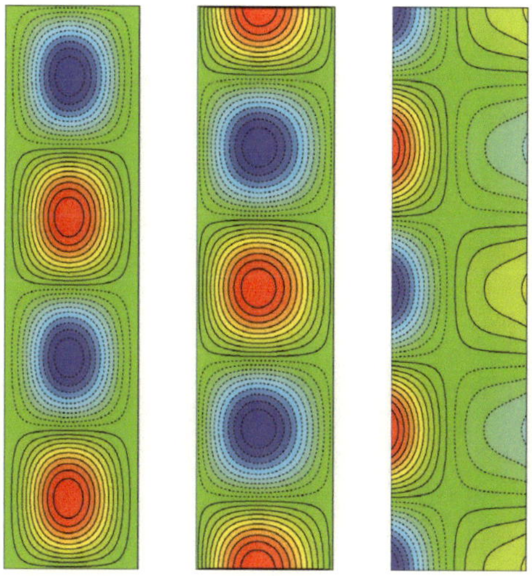

Figure 7. Visualization of Eigen functions for two wavelengths ($\eta = 0.5$, $\mu = 0$, $k = 6.325$). From left to right, Stokes stream function, azimuthal velocity, and pressure.

$$\tilde{U}_{\mathfrak{R}} \cdot \cos(kZ) = \frac{1}{R}\frac{\partial \Psi}{\partial Z}, \quad \tilde{W}_{\mathfrak{I}} \cdot \sin(kZ) = \frac{1}{R}\frac{\partial \Psi}{\partial R} \tag{66}$$

Here, the subscripts $\mathfrak{R}$ and $\mathfrak{I}$ represent the real part and the imaginary part, respectively. The visualization of other variables, such as the azimuthal velocity and the pressure, are treated in the similar manner using the trigonometric functions.

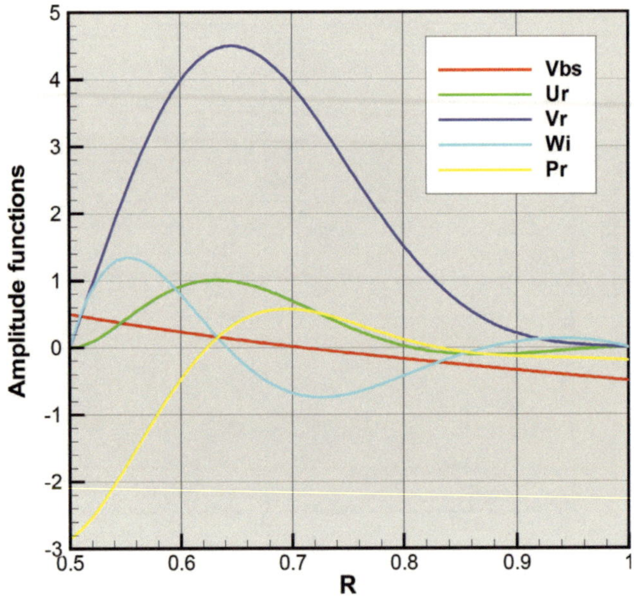

Figure 8. Amplitude functions ($\eta = 0.5$, $\mu = -0.5$, $k = 9.602$).

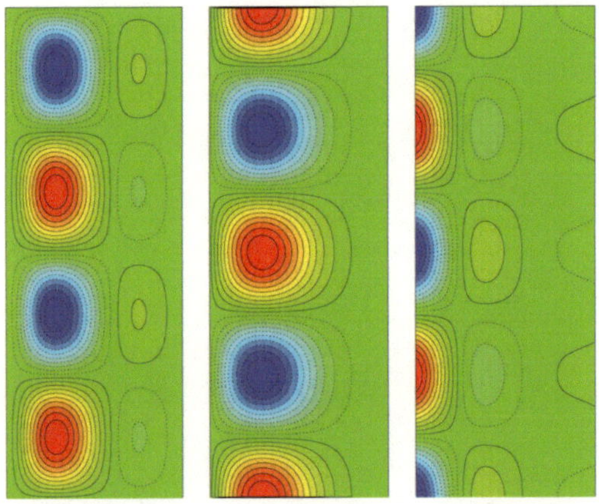

Figure 9. Visualization of Eigen functions for two wavelengths ($\eta = 0.5$, $\mu = -0.5$, $k = 9.602$). From left to right, Stokes stream function, azimuthal velocity, and pressure.

Author details

Toshio Tagawa

Address all correspondence to: tagawa-toshio@tmu.ac.jp

Department of Aerospace Engineering, Tokyo Metropolitan University, Japan

References

[1] Schlichting H, Gersten K. Boundary Layer Theory. 8th Revised and Enlarged ed. Berlin: Springer; 1999

[2] Stokes GG. On the effect of the internal friction of fluids on the motion of pendulums. Transactions of the Cambridge Philosophical Society. 1856;**9**(Part II):8-106 or Collected Papers III

[3] Rayleigh L. On the motion of solid bodies through viscous liquids. Philosophical Magazine. 1911;**21**:697-711

[4] Churchill SW, Ozoe H. A correlation for laminar free convection from a vertical plate. Journal of Heat Transfer. 1973;**95**(4):540-541

[5] Le Fevre EJ. Laminar free convection from a vertical plane surface. In: Proceedings of the 9th International Congress of Applied Mechanics; Brussels; Vol. 4; 1956. pp. 168-174

[6] Chandrasekar S. Hydrodynamic and Hydromagnetic Stability. Oxford: Clarendon Press; 1961

[7] Koschmieder EL. Bénard cells and Taylor vortices. In: Cambridge Monographs on Mechanics and Applied Mathematics. United State of America: Cambridge University Press; 1993

[8] Hirt CW, Nichols BD, Romero NC. SOLA: A Numerical Solution Algorithm for Transient Fluid Flows. Los Alamos, New Mexico, United State of America: Los Alamos Scientific Laboratory of University of California. 1975. p. LA-5852

[9] Tagawa T, Egashira R. Fluid flow of a liquid metal in a cylinder driven by a rotating magnetic field. Transactions of the Japan Society of Mechanical Engineers, Part B. 2012; **78**(794):1680-1695

[10] Tagawa T. Numerical investigation of Bénard-Marangoni convection of paramagnetic liquid in annular layers. In: The 15th International Heat Transfer Conference; Kyoto, Japan; August 2014

Chapter 12

Numerical Simulation of Wave (Shock Profile) Propagation of the Kuramoto-Sivashinsky Equation Using an Adaptive Mesh Method

Denson Muzadziwa, Stephen T. Sikwila and
Stanford Shateyi

Additional information is available at the end of the chapter

http://dx.doi.org/10.5772/intechopen.71875

Abstract

In this paper, the Kuramoto-Sivashinsky equation is solved using Hermite collocation method on an adaptive mesh. The method uses seventh order Hermite basis functions on a mesh that is adaptive in space. Numerical experiments are carried out to validate effectiveness of the method.

Keywords: adaptive mesh method, Kuramoto-Sivashinsky equation, collocation method, moving mesh partial differential equation, numerical solution

1. Introduction

The Kuramoto-Sivashinsky equation (KSe) is a non-linear fourth order partial differential equation (PDE) discovered separately by Kuramoto and Sivashinsky in the study of non-linear stability of travelling waves. Sivashinsky [1] came up with the equation while modelling small thermal diffusive instabilities in laminar flame fronts. Kuramoto [2–5] derived the equation in the study of the Belousov-Zhabotinsky reaction as a model of diffusion induced chaos. The KSe is of interest to many researchers because of its ability to describe several physical contexts such as long waves on thin films or on the interface between two viscous fluids [6] and unstable drift waves in plasmas. The equation is also used as a model to describe spatially uniform oscillating chemical reaction in a homogeneous medium and fluctuations in fluid films on inclines [7]. In one dimension, consider the KSe of the form

$$\frac{\partial u}{\partial t} + u\frac{\partial u}{\partial x} + \frac{\partial^2 u}{\partial x^2} + \frac{\partial^4 u}{\partial x^4} = 0, \qquad t > 0. \tag{1}$$

The second derivative term is an energy source and thus has a distributing effect. The non-linear term is a correction to the phase speed and responsible for transferring energy. The fourth derivative term is the dominating term and is responsible for stabilising the equation. Several methods have been used to solve the KSe numerically and these include Chebyshev spectral collocation method [8], Quintic B-spline collocation method [9], Lattice Boltzmann method [10], meshless method of lines [11], Fourier spectral method [12] and septic B-spline collocation method [13].

2. Grid generation

Generation of an adaptive mesh in the spatial domain is based on the r-refinement technique [14] which relocates a fixed number of nodal points to regions which need high spatial resolution in order to capture important characteristics in the solution. This has the benefit of improving computational effort in those regions of interest whilst using a fixed number of mesh points. The relocation of the fixed number of nodal points at any given time is achieved by solving Moving Mesh Partial Differential Equations (MMPDEs) [15, 16] derived from the Equidistribution Principle (EP). The EP [17] makes use of a measure of the solution error called a monitor function, denoted by M which is a positive definite and user defined function of the solution and/or its derivatives. Mesh points are then chosen by equally distributing the error in each subinterval. In this paper, MMPDE4 [15] is chosen to generate the adaptive mesh because of its ability to stabilise mesh trajectories and ability to give unique solutions for the mesh velocities with Dirichlet boundary conditions. MMPDE4 is given by

$$\frac{\partial}{\partial \xi}\left(M\frac{(\partial \dot{x})}{\partial \xi}\right) = -\frac{1}{\tau}\frac{\partial}{\partial \xi}\left(M\frac{\partial x}{\partial \xi}\right) \tag{2}$$

where τ is the relaxation parameter and it plays the role of driving the mesh towards equidistribution. Central finite difference approximation of MMPDE4 in space on the interval $a \le x \le b$ gives

$$\frac{M_{i+1}+M_i}{2\left(\frac{1}{N}\right)^2}(\dot{x}_{i+1}-\dot{x}_i) - \frac{M_i+M_{i-1}}{2\left(\frac{1}{N}\right)^2}(\dot{x}_i-\dot{x}_{i-1}) = -\frac{E_i}{\tau}, \tag{3}$$

where

$$E_i = \frac{M_{i+1}+M_i}{2\left(\frac{1}{N}\right)^2}(x_{i+1}-x_i) - \frac{M_i+M_{i-1}}{2\left(\frac{1}{N}\right)^2}(x_i-x_{i-1}), \qquad i = 2, \ldots, N \tag{4}$$

$$x_1 = a \qquad\qquad x_{N+1} = b. \tag{5}$$

The modified monitor function given by

$$M(x,t) = \left(1 + \alpha^2\left(\frac{\partial u}{\partial x}\right)^2 + \alpha^2\left(\frac{\partial^2 u}{\partial x^2}\right)^2\right)^{\frac{1}{2}} \tag{6}$$

is used. It is composed of the standard arc-length monitor and the curvature monitor functions. Smoothing on the monitor function is done as described in [15]. Values of the smoothed monitor function $\tilde{M}$ at the grid points are given by

$$\widetilde{M} = \sqrt{\frac{\sum_{k=i-p}^{i+p} (M_k)^2 \left(\frac{\gamma}{1+\gamma}\right)^{|k-i|}}{\sum_{k=i-p}^{i+p} \left(\frac{\gamma}{1-\gamma}\right)^{|k-i|}}} \tag{7}$$

where the parameter p is called the smoothing index which determines the extent of smoothing and is non-negative. γ is non-negative and is called the smoothing index and determines the rigidity of the grid.

3. Discretization in time

The Crank-Nicolson scheme for the KSe is

$$\left[\frac{u^{n+1} - u^n}{\delta t}\right] + \left[\frac{(uu_x)^{n+1} + (uu_x)^n}{2}\right] + \left[\frac{u_{xx}^{n+1} + u_{xx}^n}{2}\right] + \left[\frac{u_{xxxx}^{n+1} + u_{xxxx}^n}{2}\right] = 0 \tag{8}$$

where δt is the time step. Rubin and Graves [18] suggested the expression

$$uu_x^{\ n+1} = u^{n+1}u_x^n + u^n u_x^{n+1} - (uu_x)^n \tag{9}$$

for the linearization of the non-linear term $(uu_x)^{n+1}$. Expression (9) is substituted into (1) and the terms are rearranged to give

$$u^{n+1} + \frac{\delta t}{2}\left[u^{n+1}u_x^n + u^n u_x^{n+1} + u_{xx}^{n+1} + u_{xxxx}^{n+1}\right] = u^n - \frac{\delta t}{2}\left[u_{xx}^n + u_{xxxx}^n\right] \tag{10}$$

4. Septic Hermite collocation method

Consider the mesh on the domain $[a, b]$ which is a solution of MMPDE4 given by

$$a = X_1(t) < X_2(t) < \ldots < X_{N+1}(t) = b \tag{11}$$

The variable spatial length of each interval is given by H_i where $H_i = X_{i+1}(t) - X_i(t)$ for $i = 1, \ldots, N$. For some $x\epsilon[X_i(t), X_{i+1}(t)]$, define the local variable s as

$$s = \frac{x - X_i(t)}{H_i(t)} \tag{12}$$

such that $s\epsilon(0, 1)$ for every subinterval of the mesh (11). Define the septic Hermite basis functions with the local variables s as

$$
\begin{aligned}
L_{0,0} &= \left(20s^3 + 10s^2 + 4s + 1\right)(s-1)^4 \\
L_{0,1} &= s\left(10s^2 + 4s + 1\right)(s-1)^4 \\
L_{0,2} &= \frac{s^2}{2}(4s+1)(s-1)^4 \\
L_{0,3} &= \frac{s^3}{6}(s-1)^4 \\
L_{1,0} &= -\left(20s^3 - 70s^2 + 84s - 35\right)s^4 \\
L_{1,2} &= -\frac{s^4}{2}(s-1)^2(4s-5) \\
L_{1,3} &= \frac{s^4}{6}(s-1)^3
\end{aligned}
\tag{13}
$$

For $l = 0, 1, 2, 3$ the functions $L_{0,l}(s)$ and $L_{1,l}(s)$ yield the following conditions

$$
\frac{d^k}{ds^k}L_{0,l}(0) = \delta_{k,l}, \qquad \frac{d^k}{ds^k}L_{0,l}(1) = 0, \qquad k,l = 0,1,2,3
$$

$$
\frac{d^k}{ds^k}L_{0,l}(0) = 0, \qquad \frac{d^k}{ds^k}L_{1,l}(1) = \delta_{k,l}, \qquad k,l = 0,1,2,3
$$

where $\delta_{k,l}$ denotes the Kronecker delta. The physical solution $u(x,t)$ on the mesh (11) is approximated by the piecewise Hermite polynomial [19]

$$
\begin{aligned}
U(x,t) = {} & U_i(t)L_{0,0}(s) + U_{x,i}H_i(t)L_{0,1}(s) + U_{xx,i}(t)H_i^2(t)L_{0,2}(s) + U_{xxx,i}(t)H_i^3(t)L_{0,3}(s) \\
& + U_{i+1}(t)L_{1,0}(s) + U_{x,i+1}H_i(t)L_{1,1}(s) + U_{xx,i+1}(t)H_i^2(t)L_{1,2}(s) + U_{xxx,i+1}(t)H_i^3(t)L_{1,3}(s),
\end{aligned}
\tag{14}
$$

Where $U_i(t), U_{x,i}(t), U_{xx,i}(t)$ and $U_{xxx,i}(t)$ are the unknown variables. Derivatives of $U(x,t)$ with respect to the spatial variable x for $x \in [X_i(t), X_{i+1}(t)]$ are obtained by direct differentiation of (14) to give

$$
\begin{aligned}
\frac{\partial^{(l)}U(x,t)}{\partial x^{(l)}} = \frac{1}{H_i(t)^{(l)}} \Bigg[& U_i(t)\frac{d^{(l)}L_{0,0}}{ds^{(l)}} + U_{x,i}(t)H_i(t)\frac{d^{(l)}L_{0,1}}{ds^{(l)}} + U_{xx,i}(t)H_i^2(t)\frac{d^{(l)}L_{0,2}}{ds^{(l)}} \\
& + U_{xxx,i}(t)H_i^3(t)\frac{d^{(l)}L_{0,3}}{ds^{(l)}} + U_{i+1}(t)\frac{d^{(l)}L_{1,0}}{ds^{(l)}} + U_{x,i+1}(t)H_i(t)\frac{d^{(l)}L_{1,1}}{ds^{(l)}} \\
& + U_{xx,i+1}(t)H_i^2(t)\frac{d^{(l)}L_{1,2}}{ds^{(l)}} + U_{xxx,i+1}(t)H_i^3(t)\frac{d^{(l)}L_{1,3}}{ds^{(l)}} \Bigg]
\end{aligned}
\tag{15}
$$

for $l = 1, 2, 3, 4$. In each subinterval $[X_i(t), X_{i+1}(t)]$ of the mesh (11), define four Gauss-Legendre points

$$
0 < \rho_1 < \rho_2 < \rho_3 < \rho_4 < 1
$$

which are given by

$$\rho_1 = \frac{1}{2} - \frac{\sqrt{525 + 70\sqrt{30}}}{70}$$

$$\rho_2 = \frac{1}{2} - \frac{\sqrt{525 - 70\sqrt{30}}}{70}$$

$$\rho_3 = 1 - \rho_1$$

$$\rho_4 = 1 - \rho_2$$

One regards these points as the collocation points in each subinterval of the mesh (11). Scaling of the Gauss-Legendre points into subsequent intervals is done by defining the collocation points as

$$X_{ij} = X_i + H_i\rho_j, \quad i = 1, \ldots., N, \quad j = 1, 2, 3, 4. \tag{16}$$

and redefining the local variable s as

$$s_j^{(i)} = \frac{X_{ij} - X_i}{H_i} \tag{17}$$

for $i = 1, \ldots, N$ and $j = 1, 2, 3, 4$. Evaluation of the Hermite polynomial approximation (14), its first, second and fourth derivatives (15) is then done at the four internal collocation points in each subinterval $[X_i, X_{i+1}]$ and substitution of the expressions into (10) gives the difference equation

$$\beta_{j1}^{(i)}U_i^{n+1} + \beta_{j2}^{(i)}U_{x,i}^{n+1} + \beta_{j3}^{(i)}U_{xx,i}^{n+1} + \beta_{j4}^{(i)}U_{xxx,i}^{n+1} + \beta_{j5}^{(i)}U_{i+1}^{n+1} + \beta_{j6}^{(i)}U_{x,i+1}^{n+1} + \beta_{j7}^{(i)}U_{xx,i+1}^{n+1} + \beta_{j8}^{(i)}U_{xxx,i+1}^{n+1} = \psi_{ij}^n \tag{18}$$

where

$$\begin{aligned}\psi_{ij}^n = {} & U_i^n(t)L_{0,0}(s_j) + U_{x,i}^n H_i(t)L_{0,1}(s_j) + U_{xx,i}^n(t)H_i^2(t)L_{0,2}(s_j) + U_{xxx,i}^n(t)H_i^3(t)L_{0,3}(s_j)\\ & + U_{i+1}^n(t)L_{1,0}(s_j) + U_{x,i+1}^n H_i(t)L_{1,1}(s_j) + U_{xx,i+1}^n H_i(t)L_{1,1}(s_j) + U_{xxx,i+1}^n H_i(t)L_{1,1}(s_j)\\ & - \frac{\delta t}{2H_i^2}\Big[U_i^n(t)L_{0,0}''(s_j) + U_{x,i}^n H_i(t)L_{0,1}''(s_j) + U_{xx,i}^n(t)H_i^2(t)L_{0,2}''(s_j) + U_{xxx,i}^n(t)H_i^3(t)L_{0,3}''(s_j)\\ & + U_{i+1}^n(t)L_{1,0}''(s_j) + U_{x,i+1}^n H_i(t)L_{1,1}''(s_j) + U_{xx,i+1}^n H_i(t)L_{1,1}''(s_j) + U_{xxx,i+1}^n H_i(t)L_{1,1}''(s_j)\Big]\\ & - \frac{\delta t}{2H_i^4}\Big[U_i^n(t)L_{0,0}^{(iv)}(s_j) + U_{x,i}^n H_i(t)L_{0,1}^{(iv)}(s_j) + U_{xx,i}^n(t)H_i^2(t)L_{0,2}^{(iv)}(s_j) + U_{xxx,i}^n(t)H_i^3(t)L_{0,3}^{iv}(s_j)\\ & + U_{i+1}^n(t)L_{1,0}^{(iv)}(s_j) + U_{x,i+1}^n H_i(t)L_{1,1}^{(iv)}(s_j) + U_{xx,i+1}^n H_i(t)L_{1,1}^{(iv)}(s_j) + U_{xxx,i+1}^n H_i(t)L_{1,1}^{(iv)}(s_j)\Big]\end{aligned} \tag{19}$$

and

$$\begin{aligned}
\beta_{j1}^{(i)} &= L_{0,0}(s_j) + \frac{\delta t}{2}U_{x,i}^{n}L_{0,0}(s_j) + \frac{\delta t}{2H_i(t)}U_i^nL_{0,0}'(s_j) + \frac{\delta t}{2H_i^2(t)}L_{0,0}''(s_j) + \frac{\delta t}{2H_i^2(t)}L_{0,0}^{(iv)}(s_j) \\
\beta_{j2}^{(i)} &= H_i(t)L_{0,1}(s_j) + \frac{\delta t}{2}U_{x,i}^{n}H_i(t)L_{0,1}(s_j) + \frac{\delta t}{2H_i(t)}U_i^nH_i(t)L_{0,1}'(s_j) + \frac{\delta t}{2H_i^2(t)}H_i(t)L_{0,1}''(s_j) + \frac{\delta t}{2H_i^2(t)}H_i(t)L_{0,1}^{(iv)}(s_j) \\
\beta_{j3}^{(i)} &= H_i^2(t)L_{0,2}(s_j) + \frac{\delta t}{2}U_{x,i}^{n}H_i^2(t)L_{0,2}(s_j) + \frac{\delta t}{2H_i(t)}U_i^nH_i^2(t)L_{0,2}'(s_j) + \frac{\delta t}{2H_i^2(t)}H_i^2(t)L_{0,2}''(s_j) + \frac{\delta t}{2H_i^4(t)}H_i^2(t)L_{0,2}^{(iv)}(s_j) \\
\beta_{j4}^{(i)} &= H_i^3(t)L_{0,3}(s_j) + \frac{\delta t}{2}U_{x,i}^{n}H_i^3(t)L_{0,3}(s_j) + \frac{\delta t}{2H_i(t)}U_i^nH_i^3(t)L_{0,3}'(s_j) + \frac{\delta t}{2H_i^2(t)}H_i^3(t)L_{0,3}''(s_j) + \frac{\delta t}{2H_i^4(t)}H_i^3(t)L_{0,3}^{(iv)}(s_j) \\
\beta_{j5}^{(i)} &= L_{1,0}(s_j) + \frac{\delta t}{2}U_{x,i}^{n}L_{1,0}(s_j) + \frac{\delta t}{2H_i(t)}U_i^nL_{1,0}'(s_j) + \frac{\delta t}{2H_i^2(t)}L_{1,0}''(s_j) + \frac{\delta t}{2H_i^4(t)}L_{1,0}^{(iv)}(s_j) \\
\beta_{j6}^{(i)} &= H_i(t)L_{1,1}(s_j) + \frac{\delta t}{2}U_{x,i}^{n}H_i(t)L_{1,1}(s_j) + \frac{\delta t}{2H_i(t)}U_i^nH_i(t)L_{1,1}'(s_j) + \frac{\delta t}{2H_i^2(t)}H_i(t)L_{1,1}''(s_j) + \frac{\delta t}{2H_i^4(t)}H_i(t)L_{1,1}^{(iv)}(s_j) \\
\beta_{j7}^{(i)} &= H_i^2(t)L_{1,2}(s_j) + \frac{\delta t}{2}U_{x,i}^{n}H_i^2(t)L_{1,2}(s_j) + \frac{\delta t}{2H_i(t)}U_i^nH_i^2(t)L_{1,2}'(s_j) + \frac{\delta t}{2H_i^2(t)}H_i^2(t)L_{1,2}''(s_j) + \frac{\delta t}{2H_i^4(t)}H_i^2(t)L_{1,2}^{(iv)}(s_j) \\
\beta_{j8}^{(i)} &= H_i^3(t)L_{1,3}(s_j) + \frac{\delta t}{2}U_{x,i}^{n}H_i^3(t)L_{1,3}(s_j) + \frac{\delta t}{2H_i(t)}U_i^nH_i^3(t)L_{1,3}'(s_j) + \frac{\delta t}{2H_i^2(t)}H_i^3(t)L_{1,3}''(s_j) + \frac{\delta t}{2H_i^4(t)}H_i^3(t)L_{1,3}^{(iv)}(s_j)
\end{aligned} \tag{20}$$

From the boundary conditions (28) and (29), one gets

$$\begin{aligned}
U(x_1) &= \sigma \\
U_x(x_1) &= \beta \\
U(x_{N+1}) &= \omega \\
U_x(x_{N+1}) &= \zeta
\end{aligned} \tag{21}$$

which results in a consistent system of $4N + 4$ equations in $4N + 4$ unknowns.

5. Solution approach for the PDE system

The PDE system is solved using the rezoning approach which works best with the decoupled solution procedure [20]. The rezoning approach allow varying criteria of convergence for the mesh and physical equation since in practice the mesh does not require the same level of accuracy to compute as compared to the physical solution. The algorithm for the rezoning approach is as follows:

1. Solve the given physical PDE on the current mesh.
2. Use the PDE solution obtained to calculate the monitor function.
3. Find the new mesh by solving a MMPDE.
4. Adjust the current PDE solution to suite the new mesh by interpolation.
5. Solve the physical PDE on the new mesh for the solution in the next time.

6. Solution adjustment by interpolation

Discretization of the time domain $[t_a, t_b]$ is done using the following finite sequence

$$\{t_a = t_0 < \ldots < t_n < \ldots < t_k = t_b\} \tag{22}$$

At each time $t = t_n = n \times dt$, consider a non-uniform spatial mesh $\{X_i^n\}_{i=1}^{N+1}$ given by

$$a = X_1^n < \ldots < X_{N+1}^n = b \tag{23}$$

where $X_i^n = X_i(t_n)$ with $H_i^n = X_{i+1}^n - X_i^n$ being a non-uniform spatial step for $i = 1, \ldots, N$. At the same time step $t = t_n$ one also considers the approximations to the exact solution $u(x,t)$ and its derivatives given by $\{U_i^n\}_{i=1}^{N+1}$ and $\left\{\left(U_i^{(l)}\right)^n\right\}_{i=1}^{N+1}$ respectively where $\left(U_i^{(l)}\right)^n$ represents the lth derivative approximation with respect to the variable x at the time $t = t_n$ For $l = 1, 2, 3$. A new mesh $\left\{\tilde{X}_i^n\right\}_{i=1}^{N+1}$ is generated by (2) at each current time step t_n. The goal is to determine the new approximations $\left\{\tilde{U}_i^n\right\}_{i=1}^{N+1}$ and $\left\{\left(\tilde{U}_i^{(l)}\right)^n\right\}_{i=1}^{N+1}$ which are related to the new mesh $\left\{\tilde{X}_i^n\right\}_{i=1}^{N+1}$ in a similar manner the approximations $\{U_i^n\}_{i=1}^{N+1}$ and $\left\{\left(U_i^{(l)}\right)^n\right\}_{i=1}^{N+1}$ are related to the old mesh $\{X_i^n\}_{i=1}^{N+1}$ in each subinterval $[X_i, X_{i+1}]$. This process of updating the solution and its derivatives from the old mesh to the new mesh is achieved by interpolation. One considers the septic Hermite interpolating polynomial, a piecewise polynomial which allows the function values and its three consecutive derivatives to be satisfied in each subinterval $[X_i, X_{i+1}]$. The Hermite polynomial (14) is written in compact form as

$$\sum\nolimits_{l=0}^{3} (h_l)^{(l)} U_i^{(l)} L_{0,l}(s) + \sum\nolimits_{l=0}^{3} (h_l)^{(l)} U_{i+1}^{(l)} L_{1,l}(s) \tag{24}$$

where the $4(N+1)$ unknowns are given by

$$U_i^{(i)} = \frac{\partial^l u}{\partial x^l}(X_i(t), t) U_{i+1}^{(l)} \approx \frac{\partial^l u}{\partial x^l}(X_{i+1}(t), t), \qquad l = 0, 1, 2, 3.$$

Given the partition (23) and approximations $\left\{\left(U_i^{(l)}\right)^n\right\}$ for $l = 0, 1, 2, 3$, suppose interpolation of $U^{(l)}(x)$ is required at $x = \tilde{X}_i{}^n$ where $\tilde{X}_i{}^n \in [X_i^n, X_{i+1}^n]$ for $i = 1, \ldots, N$. Firstly, the local coordinate s of $\tilde{X}_i{}^n$ is defined as

$$s = \frac{\tilde{X}_i{}^n - X_i^n}{H_i^n} \tag{25}$$

$\tilde{U}^{(l)}\left(\tilde{X}_i{}^n\right)$ is then defined as

$$\tilde{U}^{(l)}\left(\tilde{X}_i^{\,n}\right) = \sum_{i=0}^{3} H_i^{l-p} U_i^{(l)} \frac{d^{(l)}L_{0,l}(s)}{ds^{(l)}} + \sum_{i=0}^{3} H_i^{l-p} U_{i+1}^{(l)} \frac{d^{(l)}L_{0,l}(s)}{ds^{(l)}} \tag{26}$$

for $l = 0, 1, 2, 3$ to give the interpolated values of $\tilde{U}$ and the first three consecutive derivatives on the new subinterval $\left[\tilde{X}_i^n, \tilde{X}_{i+1}^n\right]$. In order to compute the approximations of U at the next time step $t = t_{n+1}$ denoted by $\{U_i^n\}_{i=1}^{N+1}$, the values of the new mesh $\left\{\tilde{X}_i^n\right\}_{i=1}^{N+1}$ and the updated approximations $\left\{\tilde{U}_i^n\right\}_{i=1}^{N+1}$ are used in a septic Hermite collocation numerical scheme. The new approximations $\{U_i^{n+1}\}_{i=1}^{N+1}$ and the new mesh $\left\{\tilde{X}_i^{n+1}\right\}_{i=1}^{N+1}$ become the starting conditions for repeating the whole adaptive process.

7. Numerical results

Consider the KSe

$$\frac{\partial u}{\partial t} + u\frac{\partial u}{\partial x} + \frac{\partial^2 u}{\partial x^2} + \frac{\partial^4 u}{\partial x^4} = 0, \qquad t > 0 \tag{27}$$

in the domain $[-30, 30]$, $t > 0$ with boundary conditions

$$u(-30, t) = \sigma, \qquad u_x(-30, t) = \beta \tag{28}$$

$$u(30, t) = \omega, \qquad u_x(30, t) = \zeta \tag{29}$$

Where σ, β, ω and ζ are obtained from the exact solution

$$u(x, t) = c + \frac{15}{19}\sqrt{\frac{11}{19}}\left[-9\tanh^3(k(x - ct - x_0)) + 11\tanh(k(x - ct - x_0))\right] \tag{30}$$

With $c = 0.1, x_0 = -12$ and $k = \frac{1}{2}\sqrt{\frac{11}{19}}$.

Figures 1 and **2** show the behaviour of the numerical solution and the absolute error, respectively of the KSe equation on a stationary mesh using Hermite collocation method at $t = 4$ with $N = 100$ and $\delta t = 0.001$. In **Figure 1**, one observes that the numerical solution tracks the exact solution with the absolute error variation as shown in **Figure 2**.

Figure 3 shows the solution obtained by the collocation method on a stationary mesh for time $t = 0, 1, 2, 3, 4$. The movement of the solution is from left to right as time increases and the solution tracks the exact solution with no oscillations. One also observes that the concentration of mesh points is higher in the flatter regions of the solution profile in comparison to the concentration in the steeper region.

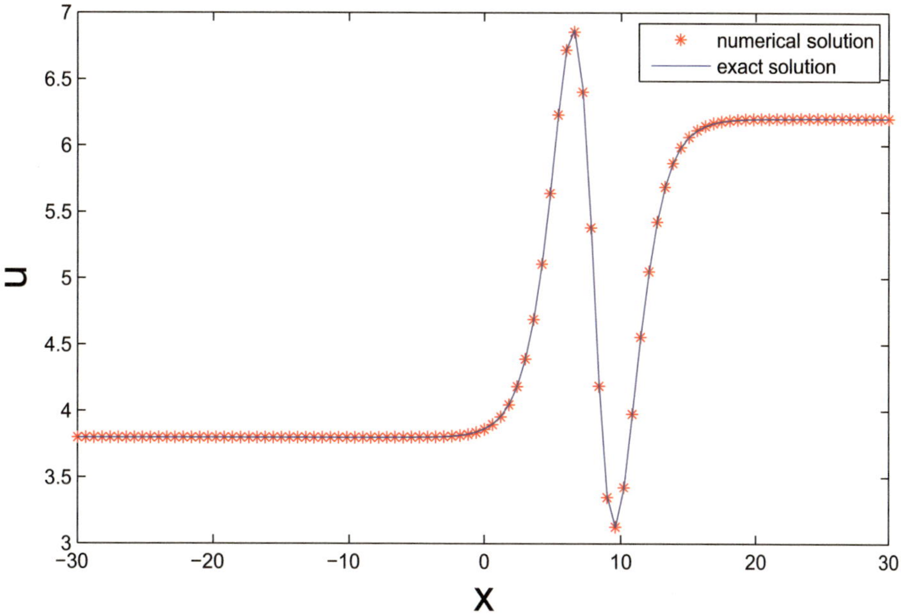

Figure 1. Hermite collocation method, uniform mesh, numerical solution behaviour of KSe at $t = 4$ with $N = 100$ and $\delta t = 0.001$.

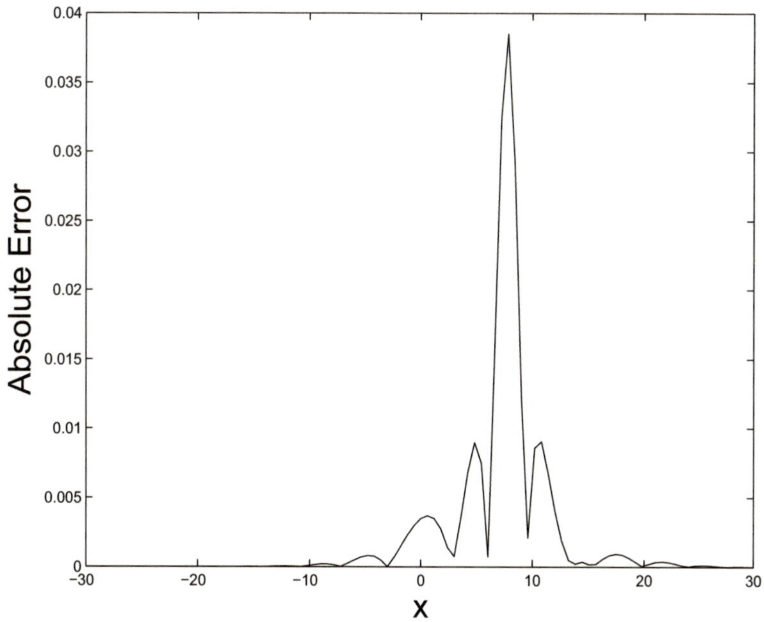

Figure 2. Hermite collocation method, uniform mesh, absolute error in numerical solution of KSe at $t = 4$, $N = 100$ and $\delta t = 0.001$.

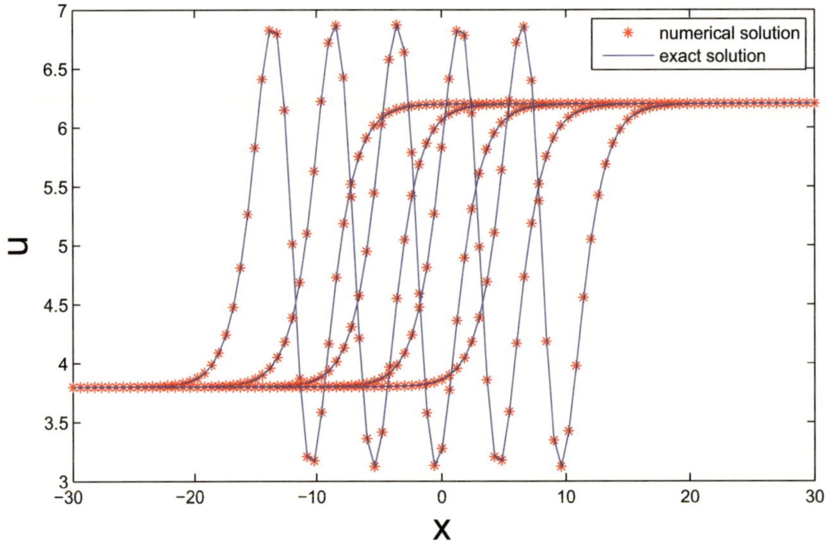

Figure 3. Hermite collocation method, stationary mesh, numerical solution behaviour of KSe problem with $N = 100$, $\delta t = 0.001$ up to final time $T = 4$.

Figures 4 and **5** show the numerical solution profile and the behaviour of the maximum absolute error, respectively at $t = 4$ with $N = 100$, $\delta t = 0.001$ and $\alpha = 8$ on an adaptive mesh. In **Figure 4**, one observes that the numerical solution is able to track the exact solution and the distribution of mesh points is almost equal along the solution profile which enables resolution of the solution with minimum errors.

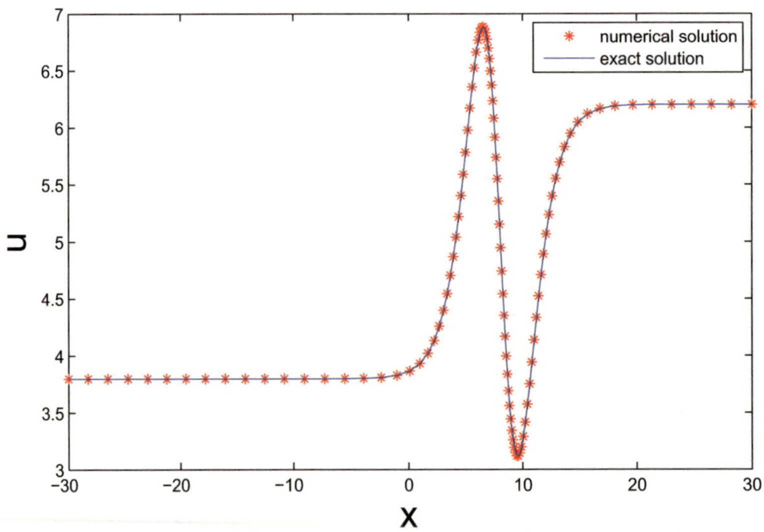

Figure 4. Hermite collocation method, non-uniform mesh, numerical solution behaviour of KSe problem at $t = 4$ with $N = 100$, $\delta t = 0.001$, $\tau = 2 \times 10^{-2}$ and $\alpha = 8$.

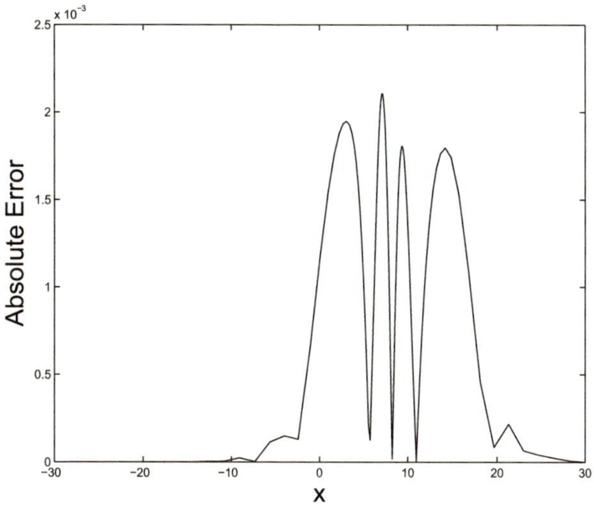

Figure 5. Hermite collocation method, non-uniform mesh, absolute error in numerical solution of KSe at $t = 100, \delta t = 0.001$, $\tau = 2 \times 10^{-2}$ and $\alpha = 8$.

Figure 6 shows the numerical solution profiles produced by the adaptive collocation method for time $t = 0, 1, 2, 3, 4$. One observes that the solution moves from left to right as time progresses. The mesh points at different times keep on tracking the solution profile and maintain an almost equal distribution along the profile up to final time $T = 4$. **Figure 7** shows the paths taken by the mesh points in tracking the solution profile. In **Table 1**, the infinity norm error for an adaptive collocation method is calculated and results are compared with the method in [13]. Results show improvements in the maximum point wise errors when an adaptive Hermite collocation method is used.

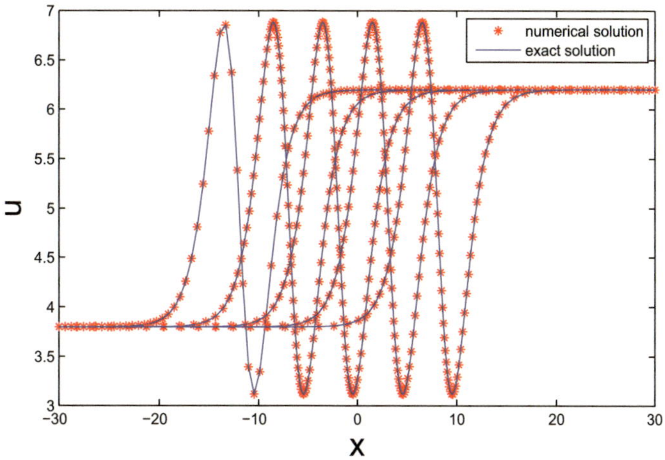

Figure 6. Hermite collocation method, adaptive mesh, numerical solution behaviour of KSe up to final time $T = 4$ for $N = 100, \delta t = 0.001, \tau = 2 \times 10^{-2}$ and $\alpha = 8$.

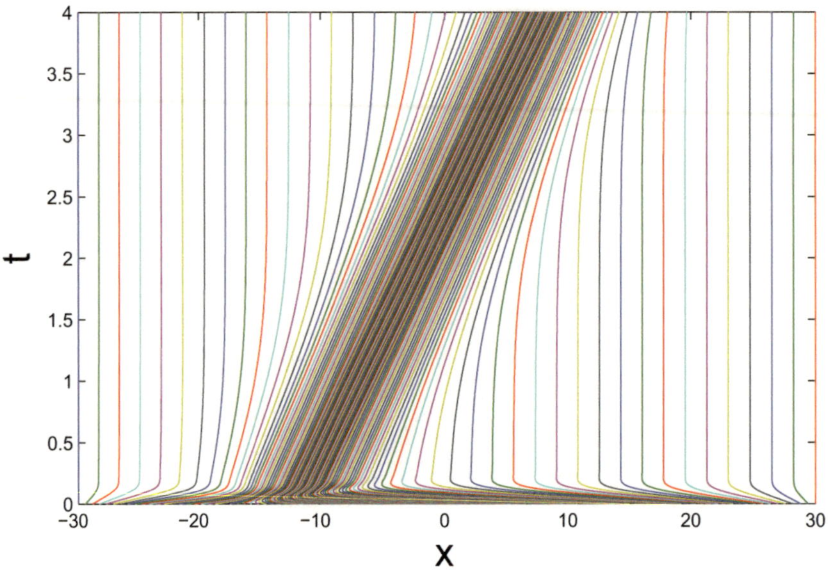

Figure 7. Hermite collocation method, mesh trajectories of KSe equation up to final time $T = 4$ with $N = 100$, $\delta t = 0.001$, $\tau = 2 \times 10^{-2}$ and $\alpha = 8$.

Time	**Hermite collocation**	**Method in [19]**
0.5	9.0×10^{-4}	1.03619×10^{-3}
1	1.4×10^{-3}	1.63762×10^{-3}
1.5	1.9×10^{-3}	2.07273×10^{-3}
2	1.7×10^{-3}	2.48375×10^{-3}
2.5	2.0×10^{-3}	2.79434×10^{-3}
3	2.1×10^{-3}	3.00439×10^{-3}
3.5	2.1×10^{-3}	3.16038×10^{-3}
4	2.1×10^{-3}	3.43704×10^{-3}

Table 1. Comparison of maximum pointwise errors in the numerical solution of the KSe on an adaptive mesh at different times with $\delta t = 0.001$ and $N = 100$.

8. Conclusions

The KSe is solved using an adaptive mesh method with discretization in the spatial domain done using seventh order Hermite basis functions. Numerical results show that Hermite collocation method on a non-uniform adaptive mesh is able to improve the accuracy of the numerical solution of the KSe. The method is able to keep track of the region of rapid solution variation in the KSe, which is one of the desired properties of an adaptive mesh method.

http://dx.doi.org/10.5772/intechopen.71875

Author details

Denson Muzadziwa[1], Stephen T. Sikwila[2] and Stanford Shateyi[3]*

*Address all correspondence to: stanford.shateyi@univen.ac.za

1 University of Zimbabwe, Harare, Zimbabwe

2 Sol Plaatje University, Kimberley, South Africa

3 University of Venda, Thohoyandou, South Africa

References

[1] Sivashinsky GI. Nonlinear analysis of hydrodynamic instability in laminar flames-I-derivation of basic equations. Acta Astronautica. 1977;**4**:1177-1206

[2] Kuramoto Y. Diffusion-induced chaos in reaction systems. Supplement of the Progress of Theoretical Physics. 1978;**64**:346-367

[3] Kuramoto Y. Instability and turbulence of wavefronts in reaction-diffusion systems. Progress of Theoretical Physics. 1980;**63**:1885-1903

[4] Kuramoto Y, Tsuzuki T. Diffusion-induced chaos in reaction systems. Progress of Theoretical Physics. 1975;**54**:689-699

[5] Kuramoto Y, Tsuzuki T. Persistent propagation of concentration waves in dissipative media far from thermal equilibrium. Progress of Theoretical Physics. 1976;**55**:356-369

[6] Hooper AP, Grimshaw C. Nonlinear instability at the interface between two viscous fluids. Physics of Fluids. 1985;**28**:37-45

[7] Sivashinsky GI, Michelson D. On irregular wavy flow of a liquid film down a vertical plane. Progress in Theoretical Physics. 1980;**63**:2112-2114

[8] Khater AH, Temsah RS. Numerical solution of the generalised Kuramoto-Sivashinsky equation by Chebyshev spectral collocation method. Computers and Mathematics Applications. 2008;**56**:1465-1472

[9] Mittal RC, Arora G. Quintic b-spline collocation method for numerical solution of the Kuramoto-Sivashinsky equation. Communications in Nonlinear Science and Numerical Simulation. 2010;**15**(10):2798-2808

[10] Huilin L, Changfeng M. Lattice Boltzmann method for the generalised Kuramoto-Sivashinsky equation. Physica A: Statistical Mechanics and its Applications. 2009;**388**(8):1405-1412

[11] Haq S, Bibi N, Tirmizi SI, Usman M. Meshless method of lines for the numerical solution of the Kuramoto-Sivashinsky equation. Applied Mathematics and Computation. 2010;**217**(6):2404-2413

[12] Zavalani G. Fourier spectral collocation method for the numerical solving of the Kuramoto-Sivashinsky equation. American Journal of Numerical Analysis. 2014;**2**(3):90-97

[13] Zarebnia M, Parvaz R. Septic b-spline collocation method for numerical solution of the Kuramoto-Sivashinsky equation. Communications in Nonlinear Science and Numerical Simulation. 2013;**7**(3):354-358

[14] Hawken DF, Gottlieb JJ, Hansen JS. Review of some adaptive node movement techniques in finite element and finite difference solutions of PDEs. Journal of Computational Physics. 1991;**95**(2):254-302

[15] Huang W, Ren Y, Russell RD. Moving mesh methods based on moving mesh partial differential equations. Journal of Computational Physics. 1994;**113**:279-290

[16] Huang W, Ren Y, Russell RD. Moving mesh partial differential equations based on equidistribution principle. SIAM Journal on Numerical Analysis. 1994;**31**(3):709-730

[17] De Boor C. Good approximation by splines with variable knots. ii. In: Conference on the Numerical Solution of Differential Equations. 1974;**363**:12-20

[18] Rubin SG, Graves RA. Cubic Spline Approximation for Problems in Fluid Mechanics. Washington DC: NASA; 1975. 93 p

[19] Russell RD, Williams JF, Xu X. MOVCOL4: A moving mesh code for fourth-order time-dependent partial differential equations. SIAM Journal on Scientific Computing. 2007;**29**(1): 197-220

[20] Weizhang H, Russell RD. Adaptive Moving Mesh Methods. New York: Springer; 2010. 432 p

Chapter 13

Numerical Analysis on the Simulated Heavy Rainfall Event of Tropical Cyclone Fung-Wong

Lei-Ming Ma and Xu-Wei Bao

Additional information is available at the end of the chapter

http://dx.doi.org/10.5772/intechopen.72264

Abstract

During landfall on the southeast coast of China, tropical cyclone (TC) Fung-Wong in the year 2008 caused torrential rainfall and flooding. In order to clarify the mechanism for the rainfall, a series of numerical simulations were conducted in this study using the National Center for Atmospheric Research (NCAR), Weather Research & Forecasting (WRF) mesoscale numerical model with three-nested domains and a highest horizontal resolution of 600 m. Numerical analysis was then performed based on the simulations. It is found that, during the evolution of heavy rainfall, quasi-frontal systems are frequently produced at the boundary of TC inflow and convective updrafts, which is more evident at the region of TC inner core and spiral rain band. The existence of energy cascading, featured by the energy transition among TC-scale inflow and convective cells, is also identified at the quasi-frontal region. These multiscale processes of Fung-Wong are further clarified by the analysis of helicity, which are believed to be responsible for the genesis and development of deep convection and rapid accumulation of rainfall. In the quasi-frontal region, numerical analysis further indicates the existence of intensive low-level wind shear as well as vertically turning of low level jet (LLJ), implying the contribution from Kelvin-Helmholtz instability (KHI).

Keywords: tropical cyclone, rainfall, landfall, helicity, CAPE

1. Introduction

Tropical cyclones (TCs) are the most devastating weather systems. Along with the direct threat from the strong winds, hazards are often brought by the torrential rainfall that causes flood and landslide. Previous studies on TC rainfall either focused on the structure and dynamics of secondary eyewalls [1] and principal rainbands [2] within the inner core or mesoscale effects such as orographically forced ascent (upslope) and coastal front in predecessor rain events

(PREs) [3]. In addition to that of TCs, suggested rainfall genesis mechanisms also include the convergence of moist outflows from previous cellular convection [4], squall line at the advance of moist cold pools [5], unorganized thermodynamic-generated tropical deep convections [6], etc. Among them, cold pools which are areas of evaporatively cooled downdraft air that spread out beneath precipitating cloud [7] have been frequently investigated because of its prominent role in growth of convection. In TCs, although cold pools are less common due to the relative lack of dry air in comparison to that in midlatitudes, they are known to be the primary mechanism for the sustenance of multicell thunderstorms and convective lines [8]. While TC outer rainband formation has been attributed to a variety of processes, including outward propagating inertia-gravity waves [9] and vortex-Rossby waves [10], it seems plausible that the cold pool played a contributory role in the intensification of TC outer rainband. Numerous TC studies [11–13] have utilized coastal buoys, instrumental towers, and aircraft data to document outer rainband and cold pool structure. When observed, cold pools are often associated with outer rainbands or bands adjacent to inward-spiraling dry air intrusions. These studies also noted decreasing storm-relative inflow, decreasing equivalent potential temperatures, and locally enhanced wind speeds in the boundary layer beneath the rainbands. Moreover, while a necessary condition for cold pool formation may be the presence of midlevel dry air, cold pool intensity appears more related to factors other than the degree of midlevel dryness. While affecting the growth of rainfall, cold pools are sometimes associated with cold fronts and cold air damming (CAD) [14]. Atallah and Bosart [15] examined aspects of the precipitation distribution of hurricane Floyd (1999) through synoptic and modeling analyses and found that precipitation ahead of Floyd's track was generally enhanced along the cold front from approximately 12 h before the time of storm passage. CAD occurs most often on the eastern side of approximately north-south-oriented mountains, as cold air moving toward the eastern slopes has insufficient kinetic energy to go over the barrier and is then forced to decelerate. The genesis of cold pool can be associated with extratropical transition (ET) [16–18], which occurs from a warm-core to cold-core cyclone and gains extratropical cyclone characteristics. Snodgrass et al. [19] found that the heaviest convective rainfall occurred in mesoscale arcs around cloud-free areas, reminiscent of outflow boundaries of cold pools created by earlier convection. However, different with the mechanism of cold pool, Tompkins [6] shows that air moistened by evaporating precipitation can be pushed outward by a drier downdraft driven by precipitation and trigger new convection when the surface air becomes sufficiently buoyant.

As the development of TC rainfall becomes quite complicated during landfall due to the interaction with midlatitude atmospheric systems and the topographical effect, these complicated processes were usually investigated with advanced atmospheric numerical models based on a series of dynamic and thermodynamic equations. TC rainfall mechanism can then be further understood with the assistance of dynamic or thermodynamic diagnosis. In this study, the mechanism of heavy rainfall associated with the frontal structure and cold pool during the landfall process of TC Fung-Wong (2008) is preliminarily examined based on the numerical simulations and numerical analysis with the special use of multiscale conception of helicity [20, 21]. The original definition of helicity [22] has been frequently employed to investigate the structure of convections and TCs [23–25]. Wu et al. [26], by investigating the relationship between helicity and nonlinear energy transition with a helicity budget of the mean and disturbance flows, indicated that the helical mean flow transfers helicity to the convective eddies and both the buoyant effect and mean-eddy exchange are important sources for disturbance. It is further indicated that the disturbances gain helicity from mean flows and the buoyancy effect amplifies it. Fei and Tan [24] reported that weak helicity is favorable for the energy cascading from large scale to convective scale at the early stage of a convective storm. Hendricks et al. [25] and Montgomery et al. [27] argued that vertical hot towers (VHTs), helical by definition because of coincident updrafts and vertical vorticity, were the preferred mode of convection in TCs. Molinari and Vollaro [28] also identified convective cells, generally favored downshear, would be stronger and longer-lived as a result of larger helicity. Although it is widely accepted that intensive helicity favors the genesis of supercell and TC intensification, it is still an open question of the connection between helicity and the evolution of TC heavy rainfall. In this regard, the mechanism for the rapid growth of TC Fung-Wong's heavy rainfall is examined based on the understanding of Fung-Wong's multiscale processes analyzed with helicity.

TC Fung-Wong, as the first strong typhoon made landfall over China mainland in 2008, was characterized by torrential rainfall, large size, and wide-range influence. It was developed at 06 UTC, 25 July 2008, over the Northwest Pacific and then intensified into a typhoon at 09 UTC, 26 July. From the morning on 27 July, it started to move northwest and approached the east coast of Taiwan Island. Fung-Wong intensified into a severe typhoon at 12 UTC, 27 July. As shown on the FY2C satellite imagery, the cloud distribution of Fung-Wong was significantly asymmetric before the occurrence of landfall. More clouds were clustered to the southwest of TC. A clear eye formed before it reached Taiwan. At 22 UTC, 27 July, Fung-Wong landed on Hualian, Taiwan, with the maximal wind speed of 45 m s^{-1} near its center. As Fung-Wong passed over Taiwan, heaviest rainfall of 818 mm was recorded near Tai-Ping Mountain. Fung-Wong landed again on Donghan, Fujian province, at 14 UTC, 28 July, with the estimated maximal wind speed of 33 m s^{-1} near its center. At that time, NASA's CloudSat satellite's Cloud Profiling Radar showed that the cloud top of Fung-Wong reached more than 15 km with estimated precipitation rate exceeding 30 mm h^{-1} on 28 Jul. After the second landfall, it was quickly reduced to a severe tropical storm, and its eyewall and spiral structure were significantly vanished. However, during its stay inland for about 52 h, it produced heavy rainfall in Zhejiang and Fujian province, leading to two rivers flooding, with an estimated total loss of CNY 3.37 billion.

To clarify the mechanism for heavy rainfall, it is helpful to carry out high-resolution simulation with mesoscale nonhydrostatic microphysical models. Recent numerical experiments using the Weather Research & Forecasting (WRF) model have shown some promise in forecasting TCs near landfall [29]. In this study, numerical experiments were designed and performed with the multiply-nested WRF model. With an inner resolution of 600 m, it provides the possibility for answering questions on the role of the energy cascading on the rainfall development of TCs.

The methods and data are described in Section 2. The numerical simulations on track, intensity, and rainfall of Fung-Wong are verified in Section 3. The numerical analysis on the multiscale mechanism of the heavy rainfall is conducted in Section 4. Section 5 is the summary.

2. Methodology

2.1. Numerical experiments

In order to clarify the multiscale mechanism for heavy rainfall, high-resolution numerical experiments were conducted with the NCAR/WRF mesoscale model [29]. The triply nested model domains (**Figure 1a**), i.e., the outermost domain (D1), the inner domain (D2), and the innermost domain (D3), are designed with horizontal spacing of 15 km, 3 km, and 600 m, respectively, with domain sizes of 281 × 281, 721 × 721, and 721 × 721 grid points, respectively. D1, which covers the northwest Pacific, eastern Tibetan plateau, Bengal Bay, and China, is employed to examine the large-scale environmental flow. D2, which covers east China, is one-way nested within D1 and is used to examine the major landfall processes. D3, which is fixed and one-way nested within D2, is used to analyze the detailed structure of rainfall system. A total of 37 vertical sigma levels are used for all the domains. The Kain-Fritsch cumulus parameterization scheme [30] with modification of convection trigger function [31] is used in D1. However, in D2 and D3, no cumulus parameterization scheme is considered to avoid its ambiguous application in high-resolution simulation. The WRF single-moment 6 (WSM6) class multiphase cloud scheme is employed in all domains to represent cloud physics. The Yonsei University (YSU) planetary boundary layer (PBL) scheme [32], using counter-gradient terms to represent nonlocal fluxes, is considered for PBL parameterization in D1 and D2. The YSU PBL scheme [33, 34] explicitly treats the entrainment layer at the PBL top with the surface buoyancy flux in line with results from large-eddy models. The PBL top is defined using a critical bulk Richardson number of zero. The turbulent kinetic energy (TKE) diffusion scheme is employed in D3 to deal with the PBL physics [35]. Furthermore, the rapid radiative transfer model (RRTM) scheme [36] and Dudhia scheme [37] are used for the parameterization of longwave and shortwave radiation, respectively.

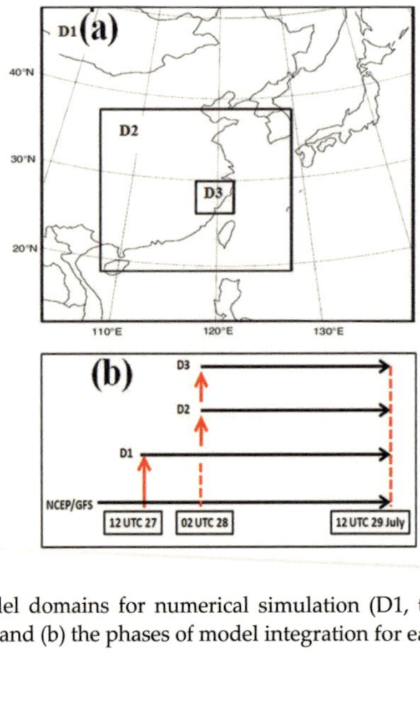

Figure 1. (a) The triply nested model domains for numerical simulation (D1, the outermost domain; D2, the inner domain; D3, the innermost domain) and (b) the phases of model integration for each model domain.

http://dx.doi.org/10.5772/intechopen.72264

Figure 1b indicates the phases for model integration in each domain. For domain D1, the time between 12UTC, 27 July, and 12UTC, 29 July, is chosen for an overall description of Fung-Wong's track and rainfall during landfall. In order to examine the detailed evolution of TC structure and rainfall, the time between 02UTC 28 and 12UTC 29 is selected for D2, and the time between 02UTC 28 and 12UTC 28 is selected for D3. The background field of D1 is interpolated from the analysis of NCEP Global Forecast System (GFS) whose horizontal resolution is 0.5°. The vortex initialization scheme developed by Ma and Tan [38] is employed to produce the initial analysis for TC simulation. In this scheme, sea level pressure (SLP) derived from satellite sea surface wind is used to generate the initial TC circulation. To ensure a reasonable simulation of Fung-Wong's track and intensity, two numerical experiments, e.g., Expt. CTRL (the one without vortex initialization) and Expt. VIRV (the one with vortex initialization), are conducted. The 3B-42 gridded rainfall datasets with the resolution of 0.25 × 0.25°, derived from the Tropical Rainfall Measuring Mission (TRMM), are employed for verification on rainfall simulation.

2.2. The multiscale conception of helicity

Helicity ($H = \vec{V} \cdot \vec{\omega}$) is originally defined as the scalar product of velocity ($\vec{V}$) and vorticity vector ($\vec{\omega} = \nabla \wedge \vec{V}$), which represents the rotational characteristics in the motion direction and the twining structure of the vortex tubes [39]. Subsequent researches [20, 21] further examined its multiscale conception.

According to Tan and Wu [20], for large-scale motion, helicity (hereafter H_1) can be approximated as

$$H_1 \approx -u\left(\frac{\partial v}{\partial z}\right) + v\left(\frac{\partial u}{\partial z}\right) \tag{1}$$

Based on the assumption of thermal wind balance, H_1 can be further expressed as

$$H_1 \approx -u\frac{\partial \theta}{\partial x} + v\frac{\partial \theta}{\partial y} = -\vec{V} \cdot \nabla\, \theta \tag{2}$$

where θ is the potential temperature.

Clearly, Eq. (2) indicates the equality between helicity and temperature advection for large-scale flow, e.g., helicity should be positive (negative) for warm (cold) air advection. Therefore, very large gradient of helicity is associated with frontogenesis.

For small-scale motion, helicity (hereafter H_2) can be rewritten as

$$H_2 \approx u\frac{\partial w}{\partial y} - v\frac{\partial w}{\partial x} + w\left(\frac{\partial v}{\partial x} - \frac{\partial u}{\partial y}\right) \tag{3}$$

Assuming $\alpha = \alpha(z)$ the angle between velocity vector $\vec{v}$ ($|\vec{v}|^2 = u^2 + v^2$) and its component u (i.e., $\tan\alpha = \frac{v}{u}$), then

$$H_1 \approx v^2\frac{\partial}{\partial z}\left(\frac{u}{v}\right) = -|\vec{v}|^2\frac{\partial \alpha}{\partial z} \tag{4}$$

The multiscale conception of helicity discussed above is fundamental for the understanding of energy cascade, which occurs either by Taylor's mechanism of stretching and spin-up of small-scale vortices due to large-scale strain or twisting of small-scale vortex filaments due to a large-scale screw.

3. Numerical experiments on TC landfall process and evolution of rainfall

The landfall process of Fung-Wong is simulated based on the experiments in Section 2. Statistical variables, including the errors of track and intensity, are calculated. The result indicates that the errors in the experiment VIRV are generally less than CTRL. For example, the errors of 24 h simulated track for the experiments CTRL and VIRV are 79 and 54 km, respectively. The improvement in TC intensity is about 27.6% in the simulation of maximum wind speed (MWS) and 16.4% in minimum sea level pressure (MSLP), respectively. Because of the "spin-up" process of numerical simulation, both the experiments exhibit smaller MWS and MSLP errors at 24 h than 12 h. However, the difference of MSLP between VIRV and CTRL increases with the model integration, indicating that the simulation of MSLP is sensitive to the initial condition. For the rainfall simulation (**Figure 2**), the rainfall pattern in VIRV agrees with the TRMM observation. In this regard, the results from VIRV simulations are used for the analysis of rainfall mechanism in the subsequent section.

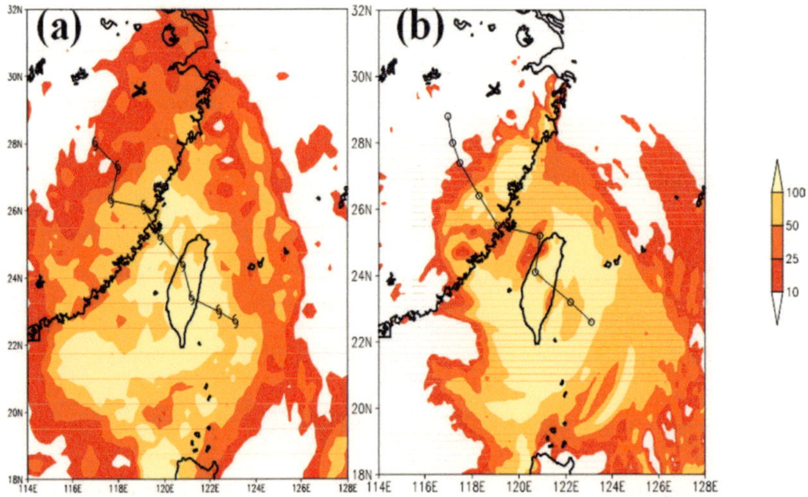

Figure 2. The accumulated rainfall (mm) during 12UTC 27–12UTC 29, Jul 2009, from TRMM 3B42 (a) and numerical simulation from D1 (b).

4. Numerical analysis on the multiscale systems associated with the torrential rainfall

4.1. Quasi-frontal structure viewed from helicity, low-level jet (LLJ), and cold pool

Numerous studies have highlighted the role of preexisting boundaries intersecting the primary convective system where cyclonic-only mesovortices were observed to form at the intersection point [40, 41]. More detailed analysis also indicated shearing instability [42] as the genesis mechanism for cyclonic-only low-level vortices formed along mesoscale boundaries such as gust fronts [43, 44]. These mesoscale boundaries are usually associated with frontal structures, which are required to be examined to clarify the mechanism of heavy rainfall. While it has long been recognized that the low-level jet (LLJ) is an efficient moisture transport mechanism [45] and a source of large-scale destabilization through warm advection [46, 47], the frontogenetical character of the boundary of LLJ can be important for the genesis of MCSs [48]. Therefore, the frontogenesis process similar to that of Augustine and Caracena [49] is investigated here to understand the characteristics of boundaries associated with MCSs. In particular, a time-averaged composite vertical cross section at 6 h preceding the mature stage shows that the LLJ in the plane of the cross section ascending the northeastward sloping frontal surface. Trier et al. [50] argued that long-lived MCSs are aided by the frontogenetical lifting of air by the LLJ, which produces a zone of elevated conditional instability favorable for rainfall genesis.

Through the analysis on the evolution of H_1 during TC landfall, this study also identifies that relative warm and moist LLJs associated with TC inflow frequently appear and move toward the TC core region and finally meet with the strong cold convective downdrafts which was induced by the convective detrainment from the middle-to-upper troposphere (PBL, **Figure 3**). As a result, quasi-frontal structure is generated at the boundary between the warm LLJ and cold downdraft. The LLJ intensifies as the front gradually sharpens. The large curvature near the quasi-front should serve to accelerate the buoyant air and the growth of convection. According to Eq. (4), the vertical shear of the angle between vector $\vec{v}$ and u component is equivalent to the ratio between helicity (H_1) and the square of total horizontal velocity. In this regard, positive helicity should be generated when the LLJ turns clockwise with height. It is interesting to find that before the occurrence of heavy rainfall, the shear vector of LLJ generally turns counterclockwise with height ($\frac{\partial \alpha}{\partial z}$ is positive). This relation indicates the existence of negative helicity and cold advection. However, as heavy rainfall occurs, the shear vector turns clockwise with height, showing a positive helicity. It is also noticed that high potential vorticity (PV, >2.5 PVU) associated with the mesoscale disturbances mainly occupies 700–950 hPa before the genesis of heavy rainfall. These PV disturbances then grow rapidly and extend to the whole troposphere, in companion with the genesis of heavy rainfall. Moreover, to evaluate the influence of the frontogenetical forcing on the growth of heavy rainfall, the Sawyer-Eliassen equation is further calculated. It is found that evident frontogenetical forcing (stream function value is −10.1 hPa m s^{-1}) is formed at the quasi-frontal area to the southeastern part of heavy rainfall. The forcing is intensified (−12.2 hPa m s^{-1}) and extended from 400 hPa to a lower level (700 hPa) at the peak time of rainfall (04UTC 28 Jul).

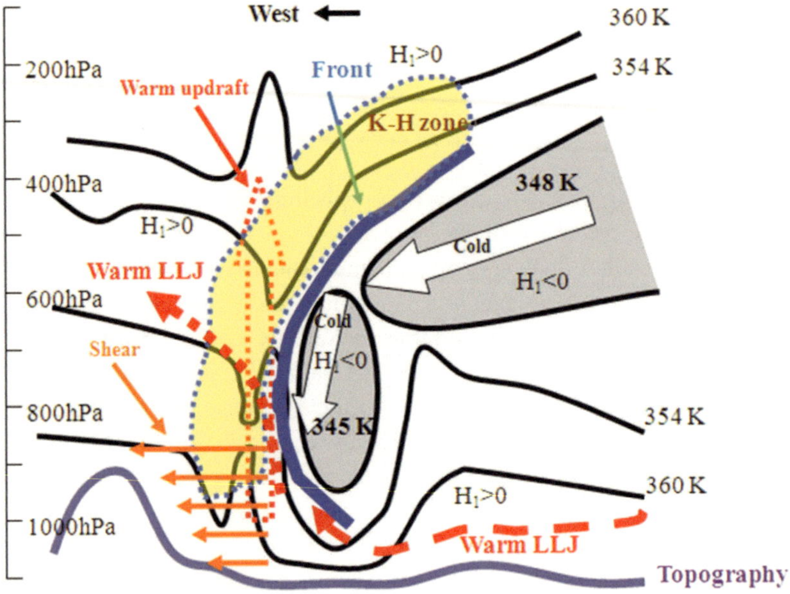

Figure 3. Schematic diagram of the multiscale quasi-frontal structure that results in the heavy rainfall.

Studies on tropical convection [51–53] suggested that convective rainfall rate is directly related to cold pool intensity. A number of idealized numerical simulations of tropical [54] and mid-latitude [55, 56] convection also have shown that cold pool may intensify when the low- to mid-level moisture is drier. Here, this study explores such relationship based on the simulation for Fung-Wong's inner rainbands where the most intensive rainfall appears. It is found that maximum $\Delta\theta$ deficits ranged from 1 to 5 K with a mean value of 2.7 K, while maximum $\Delta\theta_e$ deficits ranged from 1 to 14 K with a mean of 6.2 K. Thus, Fung-Wong's cold pools which lead to the heavy rainfall was equally intense as cold pools observed in other tropical storms. Moreover, in the cross-band direction, convergence of strong storm-relative inflow along the cold pool leading edge was coincident with a modest meso-high pressure anomaly, while inflow divergence prevailed through the collocated rainfall and cold pool maxima (figure is not given). Such structure is qualitatively consistent with many prior studies of TC outer rainbands and their associated cold pools [11, 12, 53]. In the along-band direction, several cold pools show signs of upband expansion while being advected downband by the prevailing cyclonic flow.

Meanwhile, the simulated wind profiles at the site of the most intensive cold pool exhibited easterly surface winds that veered with height, with 0–6 km shear vectors oriented toward the north at ~13 m s^{-1}. The strength and orientation (primarily crossband) of the 0–3 km shear vectors were marginally consistent with expectations for intense, long-lived rainbands [57]. Simulations further indicate a shallow moist layer near the surface (below ~1 km), drier air at mid-levels (~2–6 km), and moister air aloft. The midlevel RH minima approached 30–35% near 3–5 km AGL.

According to previous studies, the physical mechanisms for the genesis of this kind of cold pool include (1) advection of cooler and drier air from over land, (2) enhancement of rainband convection over land leading to mesoscale saturated downdrafts of cool and dry middle-level air, (3) enhanced turbulent entrainment of dry air from above the top of PBL, and (4) loss of the oceanic heat and moisture source, causing air to cool dry adiabatically while flowing toward the center. In this study, the first mechanism seems the most plausible if one examines the temperature advection disclosed by large-scale helicity. In contrast, the second mechanism seems not considerable, as the cold air is not covered by the rainband as seen from the FY2C cloud image. Based on the analysis of the simulations, the other two mechanisms should have played an additional indirect role in inducing the cold flow in the middle level.

4.2. K-H instability associated with the multiscale systems

According to Romine and Wilhelmson [58], the Kelvin-Helmholtz instability is one of the principle mechanisms that result in the genesis of spiral rain band. Based on radar data, Weckwerth and Wakimoto [59] examined a mesoscale front in association with the outflow produced by the downdraft of a supercell. They found that the K-H instability and mesoscale convective cell develop at the top of the edge of front. Detailed investigation on the important features of the quasi-frontal structure, e.g., vertical wind shear, local Richardson number (less than 1/4), and the distribution of wave structure, which is parallel to the gust-front head and perpendicular to the low-level shear vector, shows high similarity with the characteristics of K-H waves from supercells [59] and hurricanes [58]. It is also noticed that the quasi-frontal region is characterized by vertical vorticity maxima. According to Atkins and Laurent [60], as the vorticity near the front can be amplified by updraft through stretching, the vorticity maxima provides favorable locations for the growth of instability and convection. These convective cells subsequently propagated back relative to the outflow boundary while they preferentially existed along the updraft side of the K-H waves. The spacing of the cells at the leading edge of the outflow boundary, particularly along the northern part, is approximately 5 km, which compares well with the wavelength of the K-H waves. It also indicates that the static instability increases and ultimately triggered upward motion at the front. As a result, horizontal shear of vertical motion across the front develops and contributes to the growth of helicity and helical disturbance. It is also recognized that the intersections between the vortex tubes at the gust-front head are characterized by vertical vorticity maxima. In addition to the K-H instability, this study also calculated the Brunt-Vaisala frequency atop the radial inflow layer at the spiral rainband and the decrease of Scorer number [61] with height below the cold flow, which indicates the presence of gravity wave with the wave period of 220 s. It thus may mix the dynamic-unstable sheared layer and contribute to the accumulation of rainfall [58].

4.2.1. Numerical analysis on energy cascading

The vertical wind profile averaged at the quasi-frontal region is further investigated. It is found that the profile is characterized with clockwise-turning and increased curvature of hodograph through a deep layer. According to Wu et al. [26], the increased curvature of hodograph is beneficial to the development of small-scale convection due to the energy cascading from the basic flow. In this regard, the process of energy cascading is further examined based on the numerical simulation results.

Using the conception of difference in total energy (DTE), Tan et al. (hereafter T04) [62] examined the impacts of initial small-scale disturbance on a "surprise" snowstorm through the analysis of energy cascading. Similar to the definition of DTE by T04, the total energy (*TE*) is defined here by considering kinetic and internal components:

$$TE = \frac{1}{2}\left(U_{i,j,k}{}^{2} + V_{i,j,k}{}^{2} + kT_{i,j,k}{}^{2}\right) \tag{5}$$

where U, V, and T are horizontal u-wind, v-wind components, and temperature, respectively. $k = C_p/T_r$ (the reference temperature T_r=287 K). I, j, and k are the numbers of x, y, and σ grid points, respectively.

A power spectrum of *TE*, averaged in the region of heavy rainfall, is analyzed. Wavenumbers 0, 1, and 2 are the TC scales following Krishnamurti et al. [63]. Meanwhile, the scales of the individual deep convective clouds reside around the azimuthal wave numbers 20–30. According to Saltzman [64], the TC scale is about several hundreds of kilometers, whereas the scale of convection, including updrafts and adjacent downdrafts, is only a few kilometers. It shows that a sizeable portion of the variance of *TE* is contributed by the first few harmonics (0–4) in the innermost region. The contribution from wavenumbers 3 to 55 (associated with medium- to small-scale processes) accounts for less than 10% of total *TE*, which agrees with the results from quasi-geostrophic models [65].

To better understand the energy transition during rainfall, this section further examines the relation between helicity, the magnitude of which is associated with kinematic energy, and CAPE, an indicator of potential energy. Krishnamurti et al. [63], by examining the scale interaction of hurricane inferred from the decomposition of the liquid water mixing ratio fields, found that nonlinear interaction of kinetic energy and available potential energy among cloud scales and the hurricane scale provide the energy to drive the hurricane. The generation of available potential energy and its transformation to kinetic energy takes place directly on the larger scales of the hurricane. Their results among hurricane scales and smaller scales show largely a cascade of energy, that is, hurricane scales lose energy when they interact with other scales.

The evolution of CAPE and helicity of TC circulation during landfall (12UTC 27–12UTC 29 July) is investigated. It shows that an approximated negative correlation exists between H_1 and CAPE before the occurrence of rainfall, which is mainly featured by the decrease (increase) of CAPE (H_1). However after rainfall, the original negative relation is replaced by an approximate positive correlation, which decreases simultaneously. The decrease of CAPE should be associated with the significantly reduced heat flux from land surface and the large consumption of CAPE during the rainfall process. Scatter plot also shows that intensive H_1 corresponds to low CAPE (e.g., CAPE of 3500 J kg^{-1} vs. H_1 of 50–150 m^2 s^{-2}) during the growth of convection. In other words, kinematic energy increases as potential energy is consumed. However, there is no clear correlation between CAPE and H_2, indicating that the energy from CAPE might not directly fuel the growth of small-scale convection. Moreover, over the land, H_1 is positive in more than 66.6% of the rainfall region. The maximum of CAPE is 3500 J kg^{-1} with H_1 of 50–150 m^2 s^{-2}. Five percent of H_1 are greater than 400 m^2 s^{-2}, with the biggest of 800 m^2 s^{-2}. Over land, more than 95% of H_1 is positive, with H_1 decreasing with CAPE. Most of the intensive H_1 corresponds to CAPE less than 500 J kg^{-1}, while over the ocean, negative H_1 corresponds to the CAPE as low as 1000 J kg^{-1}.

The nonlinear multiscale transition of energy from basic flow to the process of disturbance (E_t) can be also represented by $E_t = -u'w'\partial\bar{u}/\partial z - v'w'\partial\bar{v}/\partial z$ (hereafter WL92) [26]. Here E_t represents the weakening phase of environmental vertical wind shear by convection, during which larger-scale instability is eliminated by the small-scale motion. Similar to WL92, this study examined the difference of E_t produced by D1 and D2. It shows that the E_t produced by D1 is generally higher than that of D2, with the difference more evident after landfall, and the E_t of D1 rapidly decreases. The amplitude of energy transition in D2 increases persistently as the typhoon makes landfall, which might relate to the development of small-scale convection. It is also noticed that the tendency of E_t evolution is nearly in positive correlation with H_2 (instead of H_1). The distribution of E_t is examined before and after the heavy rainfall, during which the maximas of E_t merged together, in concert with the rainfall intensification.

Detailed analysis also shows that the largest value of the generation of available potential energy (CAPE) and its conversion to kinetic energy occurs at the region of the heaviest rain in the simulation of TC Fung-Wong. The values decrease rapidly from TC core region to the outer radial belts. The cloud scales essentially extract energy from the TC scale (azimuthally averaged wavenumber 0) system. It implies that the TC scale is barotropically unstable to the cloud scales (wavenumbers 1 and 2). This is essentially a cascading process where energy is conveyed from the larger to the smaller scales. The generation of available potential energy and its transformation to kinetic energy takes place directly on the larger scales of TC Fung-Wong. Using a spectral closure calculation, Andre and Lesieur [66] showed that transport of energy through the inertial range is sensitive to the presence of helicity. In the calculations of this study, the time evolution of the energy spectrum toward the $k^{-5/3}$ form is slowed down when helicity is injected at small wavenumbers. It thus supports the argument by Tsinober and Levich [67] that helical structures might be an inherent part of the turbulent energy cascade and thereby suppress the nonlinear terms responsible for the cascade.

5. Summary and discussion

High-resolution simulations are performed with nonhydrostatic WRF mesoscale numerical model to clarify the multiscale mechanisms leading to the heavy rainfall of TC Fung-Wong during landfall on southwestern coast of China. Numerical analysis shows that quasi-frontal structures are frequently generated at the boundary of warm LLJs associated with TC inflow and cold convective downdrafts, which favor the genesis of intensive rainfall. Some important features of the quasi-frontal structures, e.g., intensive vertical wind shear and small local Richardson number, exhibit similarity with that of K-H waves from supercell. The hodograph of LLJ which turns clockwise with height tends to produce positive helicity and favors the genesis of convection. An evident antiphase relationship between H_1 and CAPE during heavy rainfall suggests the energy transition from CAPE to kinematic energy.

For the future study, the structure, organization, and impact of convective rainfall systems in TCs during landfall remain a fruitful area for research. Convective cells are known to be favored downshear in TCs due to the shear-induced increase in convergence and upward motion downshear [68]. The variations of helicity and CAPE described in this paper should also connect with vertical shear. As has been stated by Molinari and Vollaro [28], the helicity and CAPE in the presence of large ambient shear exceeded those in storms with small ambient shear. The reduction in stability and increase in helicity might represent the positive influence of large vertical wind shear in offsetting the greater ventilation of the storm core. Many questions about heavy rainfall in landfalling TCs remain unanswered. How about the multiscale characteristics of helicity in different situation of shear? How do the multiscale helicity affect supercells of TCs? Observation (i.e., radar) and simulations are required to confirm the processes that such cells develop in landfalling TCs. Moreover, the detailed cascading process of rainfall should be carefully examined based on energy budget. The quantitative impact of systems in various scales on rainfall deserved to be examined with sensitive numerical experiments. Additional studies should be conducted to verify and expand upon the limited observation of cold pool associated with landfalling TCs. In particular, combination of numerical simulation and datasets including both onshore and offshore observations at various intensities and evolutionary stages across a spectrum of large-scale environments would improve understanding of cold pools and their various feedbacks on convection. To enhance the simulation on cold pools, improved representation of microphysics in models would also be beneficial. Furthermore, although the orographic effect is not addressed in this study as there is no clear evident of relationship between the terrain and the amplification of rainfall, the alteration, or reorganization of the convective clouds, frontal systems associated with TC when it encounters topographic features might be possible [69], which will be examined in a next study.

Acknowledgements

This research was jointly supported by the National Science Foundation Project (no. 41475059) and China Key Research and Development Program (no. 2016YFC0201900).

Author details

Lei-Ming Ma[1,2]* and Xu-Wei Bao[3]

*Address all correspondence to: malm@mail.typhoon.gov.cn

1 Shanghai Meteorological Center, Shanghai, P. R. China

2 Shanghai Key Laboratory of Meteorology and Health, Shanghai, P. R. China

3 Shanghai Typhoon Institute, Shanghai, P. R. China

References

[1] Houze RA Jr et al. The Hurricane rainband and intensity change experiment: Observations and modeling of Hurricanes Katrina, Ophelia, and Rita. Bulletin of the American Meteorological Society. 2006;**87**:1503-1521

[2] Hence DA, Houze RA Jr. Kinematic structure of convective-scale elements in the rainbands of Hurricanes Katrina and Rita (2005). Journal of Geophysical Research. 2008;**113**: D15108

[3] Srock AF, Bosart LF. Heavy Precipitation Associated with Southern Appalachian Cold-Air Damming and Carolina Coastal Frontogenesis in Advance of Weak Landfalling Tropical Storm Marco (1990). Monthly Weather Review. 2009;**137**:2448-2470

[4] Xue H, Feingold G, Stevens B. Aerosol effects on clouds, precipitation, and the organization of shallow cumulus convection. Journal of the Atmospheric Sciences. 2008;**65**:392-406

[5] Jensen JB, Lee S, Krummel PB, Katzfey J, Gogoasa D. Precipitation in marine cumulus and stratocumulus. Part I: Thermodynamic and dynamic observations of closed cell circulations and cumulus bands. Atmospheric Research. 2000;**54**:117-155

[6] Tompkins AM. Organization of tropical convection in low vertical wind shears: The role of cold pools. Journal of the Atmospheric Sciences. 2001;**58**:1650-1672

[7] Eastin MD, Gardner TL, Link MC, Smith KC. Surface cold pools in the outer rainbands of Tropical Storm Hanna (2008) near landfall. Monthly Weather Review. 2012;**140**:471-491

[8] Markowski PM, Richardson YP. Mesoscale Meteorology in Midlatitudes. John Wiley and Sons; 2010. p. 430

[9] Willoughby HE, Marks Jr FD, Feinbergand RJ, 1984: Stationary and moving convective bands in asymmetric hurricanes. Journal of the Atmospheric Sciences, **41**: 3189-3211

[10] Montgomery MT, Kallenbach RJ. A theory for vortex Rossby-waves and its application to spiral bands and intensity changes in hurricanes. Quarterly Journal of the Royal Meteorological Society. 1997;**123**:435-465

[11] Powell MD. Boundary layer structure and dynamics in outer hurricane rainbands. Part I: Mesoscale rainfall and kinematic structure. Monthly Weather Review. 1990a;**118**:891-917

[12] Powell MD. Boundary layer structure and dynamics in outer hurricane rainbands. Part II: Downdraft modification and mixed layer recovery. Monthly Weather Review. 1990b; **118**:918-938

[13] Knupp KR, Walters J, Biggerstaff M. Doppler profiler and radar observations of boundary layer variability during the landfall of Tropical Storm Gabrielle. Journal of the Atmospheric Sciences. 2006;**63**:234-251

[14] Forbes GS, Anthes RA, Thomson DW. Synoptic and mesoscale aspects of an Appalachian ice storm associated with cold-air damming. Monthly Weather Review. 1987;**115**:564-591

[15] Atallah EH, Bosart LF. The extratropical transition and precipitation distribution of Hurricane Floyd (1999). Monthly Weather Review. 2003;**131**:1063-1081

[16] Bosart LF, Lackmann GM. Postlandfall tropical cyclone reintensification in a weakly baroclinic environment: A case study of Hurricane David (September 1979). Monthly Weather Review. 1995;**123**:3268-3291

[17] Klein PM, Harr PA, Elsberry RL. Extratropical transition of western North Pacific tropical cyclones: An overview and conceptual model of the transformation stage. Weather and Forecasting. 2000;**15**:373-395

[18] Jones SC, and Coauthors, 2003: The extratropical transition of tropical cyclones: Forecast challenges, current understanding, and future directions. Weather and Forecasting, **18**: 1052-1092

[19] Snodgrass ER, Di Girolamo L, Rauber RM. Precipitation characteristics of trade wind clouds during RICO derived from radar, satellite, and aircraft measurements. Journal of Applied Meteorology and Climatology. 2009;**48**:464-483

[20] Tan Z–M, Wu R. Helicity dynamics of atmospheric flow. Advances in Atmospheric Sciences. 1994;**11**:175-188

[21] Ma L–M, Bao X–W. Parametrization of planetary boundary-layer height with helicity and verification with tropical cyclone prediction. Boundary-Layer Meteorology. 2016;**160**: 569-593

[22] Lilly DK. The structure, energetics, and propagation of rotating convective storms. Part II: Helicity and storm stabilization. Journal of the Atmospheric Sciences. 1986;**43**:126-140

[23] Weisman ML, Rotunno R. On the use of vertical wind shear versus helicity in interpreting supercell dynamics. Journal of the Atmospheric Sciences. 2000;**57**:1452-1472

[24] Fei S, Tan Z. On the Helicity dynamics of Severe Convective Storms. Advances in Atmospheric Sciences. 2001;**18**:67-86

[25] Hendricks EA, Montgomery MT, Davis CA. The role of "vortical" hot towers in the formation of Tropical Cyclone Diana (1984). Journal of the Atmospheric Sciences. 2004;**61**: 1209-1232

[26] Wu W-S, Lilly DK, Kerr RM. Helicity and thermal convection with shear. Journal of the Atmospheric Sciences. 1992;**49**:1800-1809

[27] Montgomery MT, Bell MM, Aberson SD, et al. Hurricane Isabel (2003): new insights into the physics of intense storms. Part I. Bulletin of the American Meteorological Society. 2006; **87**:1335-1347

[28] Molinari J, Vollaro D. Distribution of Helicity, CAPE, and Shear in Tropical Cyclones. Journal of the Atmospheric Sciences. 2010;**67**:274-284

[29] Davis CA, Jones SC, Riemer M. Hurricane vortex dynamics during Atlantic extratropical transition. Journal of the Atmospheric Sciences. 2008;**65**:714-736

[30] Kain JS. The Kain–Fritsch convective parameterization: An update. Journal of Applied Meteorology. 2004;**43**:170-181

[31] Ma L-M, Tan Z-M. Improving the behavior of the cumulus parameterization for tropical cyclone prediction: Convection trigger. Atmospheric Research. 2009;**92**:190-211

[32] Hong S-Y, Noh Y, Dudhia J. A new vertical diffusion package with an explicit treatment of entrainment processes. Monthly Weather Review. 2006;**134**:2318-2341

[33] Noh Y, Cheon WG, Hong SY, et al. Improvement of the K-profile Model for the Planetary Boundary Layer based on Large Eddy Simulation Data. Boundary-Layer Meteorology. 2003;**107**:401-427

[34] Hong SY, Pan HL. Nonlocal boundary layer vertical diffusion in a medium-range forecast model. Monthly Weather Review. 1996;**124**:2322-2339

[35] Skamarock WC, Klemp JB, Dudhia J, Gill DO, Barker DM, Duda M, Huang X-Y, Wang W, Powers JG, 2008: A Description of the Advanced Research WRF Version 3. NCAR Technical Note

[36] Mlawer EJ, Taubman SJ, Brown PD, Iacono MJ, Clough SA. RRTM, a validated correlated-k model for the longwave. Journal of Geophysical Research. 1997;**102**:16 663-16 682

[37] Dudhia J. Numerical study of convection observed during the winter monsoon experiment using a mesoscale two dimensional model. Journal of the Atmospheric Sciences. 1989;**46**:3077-3107

[38] Ma L-M, Tan Z-M. Tropical cyclone initialization with dynamical retrieval from a modified UWPBL model. Journal of the Meteorological Society of Japan. 2010;**88**:827-846

[39] Moffat HK. The degree of knottedness of tangled vortex lines. Journal of Fluid Mechanics. 1969;**35**:117-129

[40] Klimowski BA, Przybylinski RW, Schmocker G, Hjelmfelt MR. Observations of the formation and early evolution of bow echoes. Preprints, 20th Conf. on Severe Local Storms, Orlando, FL, Amer. Meteor. Soc.; 2000. 44-47

[41] Schmocker GK, Przybylinski RW, Rasmussen EN. The severe bow echo event of 14 June 1998 over the mid-Mississippi Valley region: A case of vortex development near the intersection of a preexisting boundary and a convective line. Preprints, 20th Conf. on Severe Local Storms, Orlando, FL, Amer. Meteor. Soc; 2000. 169-172

[42] Miles JW, Howard LN. Note on heterogeneous shear flow. Journal of Fluid Mechanics. 1964;**20**:331-336

[43] Carbone RE. A severe frontal rainband. Part I: Stormwide hydrodynamic structure. Journal of the Atmospheric Sciences. 1982;**39**:258-279

[44] Lee BD, Wilhelmson RB. The numerical simulation of non-supercell tornadogenesis. Part I: Initiation and evolution of pretornadic misocyclone and circulations along a dry outflow boundary. Journal of the Atmospheric Sciences. 1997;**54**:32-60

[45] Means LL. A study of the mean southerly wind—Maximum in low levels associated with a period of summer precipitation in the Middle West. Bulletin of the American Meteorological Society. 1954;**35**:166-170

[46] Maddox RA. Large-scale meteorological conditions associated with midlatitude, mesoscale convective complexes. Monthly Weather Review. 1983;**11**:1475-1493

[47] Johns RH, Doswell CA III. Severe local storms forecasting. Weather and Forecasting. 1992;**7**:588-612

[48] Coniglio MC, Elmore KL, Kain JS, Weiss S, Xue M, Weisman ML. Evaluation of WRF model output for severe-weather forecasting from the 2008 NOAA Hazardous Weather Testbed Spring Experiment. Weather and Forecasting. 2010;**25**:408-427

[49] Augustine JA, Caracena F. Lower-tropospheric precursors to nocturnal MCS development over the central United States. Weather and Forecasting. 1994;**9**:115-135

[50] Trier SB, Davis CA, Ahijevych DA, et al. Mechanisms supporting long-lived episodes of propagating nocturnal convection within a 7-day WRF model simulation. Journal of the Atmospheric Sciences. 2006;**63**:2437-2461

[51] Barnes GM, Garstang M. Subcloud layer energetics of precipitating convection. Monthly Weather Review. 1982;**110**:102-117

[52] Barnes GM, Sieckman K. The environment of fast- and slow-moving tropical mesoscale convective cloud lines. Monthly Weather Review. 1984;**112**:1782-2601

[53] Skwira GD, Schroeder JL, Peterson RE. Surface observations of landfalling hurricane rainbands. Monthly Weather Review. 2005;**133**:454-465

[54] Kimball SK. A modeling study of hurricane landfall in a dry environment. Monthly Weather Review. 2006;**134**:1901-1918

[55] Gilmore MS, Wicker LJ. the influence of midtropospheric dryness on supercell morphology and evolution. Monthly Weather Review. 1998;**126**:943-958

[56] McCaul EW Jr, Cohen C. The impact on simulated storm structure and intensity of variations in the mixed layer and moist layer depths. Monthly Weather Review. 2002;**130**: 1722-1748

[57] Bryan GH, Knievel JC, Parker MD. A multimodel assessment of RKW theory's relevance to squall-line characteristics. Monthly Weather Review. 2006;**134**:2772-2792

[58] Romine GS, Wilhelmson RB. Finescale spiral band features within a numerical simulation of Hurricane Opal (1995). Monthly Weather Review. 2006;**134**:1121-1139

[59] Weckwerth TM, Wakimoto RM. The initiation and organization of convective cells atop a cold air outflow boundary. Monthly Weather Review. 1992;**120**:2169-2187

[60] Atkins NT, Laurent MS. Bow echo mesovortices, Part I: Processes that influence their damaging potential. Monthly Weather Review. 2009;**137**:1497-1513

[61] Scorer RS. Theory of airflow over mountains: II—The flow over a ridge. Quarterly Journal of the Royal Meteorological Society. 1953;**79**:70-83

[62] Tan Z–M, Zhang F, Rotunno R, Snyder C. Mesoscale Predictability of Moist Baroclinic Waves: Experiments with Parameterized Convection. Journal of the Atmospheric Sciences. 2004;**61**:1794-1804

[63] Krishnamurti TN, Pattnaik S, Stefanova L, Vijaya Kumar TSV, Mackey BP, O'Shay AJ, Pasch RJ. The hurricane intensity issue. Monthly Weather Review. 2005;**133**:1886-1912

[64] Saltzman B. Largescale atmospheric energetics in the Wave-Number Domain. Reviews of Geophysics and Space Physics. 1970;**8**:289-302

[65] Snyder C, Hamill TM, Trier S. Linear evolution of forecast error covariances in a quasi-geostrophic model. Monthly Weather Review. 2003;**131**:189-205

[66] Andre JC, Lesieur M. Influence of helicity on high Reynolds number isotropic turbulence. Journal of Fluid Mechanics. 1977;**81**:187

[67] Tsinober A, Levich E. On the helical nature of three dimensional coherent structures in turbulent flows. Physics Letters. 1983;**99A**:321

[68] Black ML, Gamache JF, Marks Jr FD, et al. Eastern Pacific Hurricanes Jimena of 1991 and Olivia of 1994: The effect of vertical shear on structure and intensity. Monthly Weather Review. 2002;**130**:2291-2312

[69] Houze RA Jr. Orographic effects on precipitating clouds. Reviews of Geophysics. 2012;**50**: RG1001. DOI: 10.1029/2011RG000365

Chapter 14

Weighted Finite-Element Method for Elasticity Problems with Singularity

Viktor Anatolievich Rukavishnikov and
Elena Ivanovna Rukavishnikova

Additional information is available at the end of the chapter

http://dx.doi.org/10.5772/intechopen.72733

Abstract

In this chapter, the two-dimensional elasticity problem with a singularity caused by the presence of a re-entrant corner on the domain boundary is considered. For this problem, the notion of the R_v-generalized solution is introduced. On the basis of the R_v-generalized solution, a scheme of the weighted finite-element method (FEM) is constructed. The proposed method provides a first-order convergence of the approximate solution to the exact one with respect to the mesh step in the $\mathbf{W}^1_{2,\nu}(\Omega)$-norm. The convergence rate does not depend on the size of the angle and kind of the boundary conditions imposed on its sides. Comparative analysis of the proposed method with a classical finite-element method and with an FEM with geometric mesh refinement to the singular point is carried out.

Keywords: elasticity problem with singularity, corner singularity, R_v-generalized solution, weighted finite-element method, numerical experiments

1. Introduction

The singularity of the solution to a boundary value problem can be caused by the degeneration of the input data (of the coefficients and right-hand sides of the equation and the boundary conditions), by the geometry of the boundary, or by the internal properties of the solution. The classic numerical methods, such as finite-difference method, finite- and boundary-element methods, have insufficient convergence rate due to singularity which has an influence on the regularity of the solution. It results in significant increase of the computational power and time required for calculation of the solution with the given accuracy. For example, the classic finite-element method allows the finding of the solution for the elasticity problem posed in a two-dimensional domain containing a re-entrant corner of on the boundary with convergence rate $O(h^{1/2})$. In this case to compute the solution with the accuracy of 10^{-3} requires a computational power that is one million times greater than in the case of the weighted finite-element method used for the solution of the same problem.

By using meshes refined toward the singularity point, it is possible to construct schemes of the finite-element method with the first order of the rate of convergence of the approximate solution to the exact one [1–3].

In [4, 5], for boundary value problems with strongly singular solutions for which a generalized solution could not be defined and it does not belong to the Sobolev space H^1, it was proposed to define the solution as a R_v-generalized one. The existence and uniqueness of solutions as well as its coercivity and differential properties in the weighted Sobolev spaces and sets were proved [5–10], the weighted finite-element method was built, and its convergence rate was investigated [11–15].

In this chapter, for the Lamé system in domains containing re-entrant corners we will state construction and investigation of the weighted FEM for determination of the R_v-generalized solution [16, 17]. Convergence rate of this method did not depend on the corner size and was equal $O(h)$ (see [18], Theorem 2.1). For the elasticity problems with solutions of two types—with both singular and regular components and with singular component only—a comparative numerical analysis of the weighted finite-element method, the classic FEM, and the FEM with meshes geometrically refined toward the singularity point is performed. For the first two methods, the theoretical convergence rate estimations were confirmed. In addition, it was established that FEM with graded meshes failed on high dimensional meshes but weighted FEM stably found approximate solution with theoretical accuracy under the same computational conditions. The mentioned failure can be explained by a small size of steps of the graded mesh in a neighbourhood of the singular point. As a result, for the majority of nodes, the weighted finite-element method allows to find solution with absolute error which is by one or two orders of magnitude less than that for the FEM with graded meshes.

2. R_v-generalized solution

Let $\Omega = (-1,1)\times(-1,1)\backslash[0,1]\times[-1,0]\subset R^2$ be an L-shaped domain with boundary $\partial\Omega$ containing re-entrant corner of $3\pi/2$ with the vertex located in the point $O(0,0)$, $\overline{\Omega} = \Omega\cup\partial\Omega$.

Denote by $\Omega' = \left\{x\in\Omega : \left(x_1^2 + x_2^2\right)^{1/2} \leq \delta < 1\right\}$ a part of δ-neighbourhood of the point (0,0) laying in the $\overline{\Omega}$. A weight function $\rho(x)$ can be introduced that coincides with the distance to the origin in $\overline{\Omega}'$, and equals δ for $x\in\overline{\Omega}\,\overline{\Omega}'$.

Let $W^1_{2,\alpha}(\Omega,\delta)$be the set of functions satisfying the following conditions:

a. $\left|D^k u(x)\right| \leq c_1(\delta/\rho(x))^{\alpha+k}$ for $x\in\overline{\Omega}'$, where $k = 0,1$ and c_1 is a positive constant independent on k,

b. $\|u\|_{L_{2,\alpha}(\Omega-\Omega')} \geq c_2 > 0,$

with the norm

$$\|u\|_{W^1_{2,\alpha}(\Omega)} = \left(\sum_{|\lambda|\leq 1}\int_\Omega \rho^{2\alpha}\left|D^\lambda u\right|^2 dx\right)^{1/2}, \tag{1}$$

where $D^{\lambda} = \partial^{|\lambda|}/\partial x_1^{\lambda_1}\partial x_2^{\lambda_2}$, $\lambda = (\lambda_1, \lambda_2)$, and $|\lambda| = \lambda_1 + \lambda_2$; λ_1, λ_2 are nonnegative integers, and α is a nonnegative real number.

Let $L_{2,\alpha}(\Omega, \delta)$ be the set of functions satisfying conditions (a) and (b) with the norm

$$\|u\|_{L_{2,\alpha}(\Omega)} = \left(\int_{\Omega} \rho^{2\alpha} u^2 \, dx \right)^{1/2}.$$

The set $\overset{\circ}{W}{}^1_{2,\alpha}(\Omega, \delta) \subset W^1_{2,\alpha}(\Omega, \delta)$ is defined as the closure in norm (1) of the set $C_0(\Omega, \delta)$ of infinitely differentiable and finite in Ω functions satisfying conditions (a) and (b).

One can say that $\varphi \in W^{1/2}_{2,\alpha}(\partial\Omega, \delta)$ if there exists a function Φ from $W^1_{2,\alpha}(\Omega, \delta)$ such that $\Phi(x)|_{\partial\Omega} = \varphi(x)$ and

$$\|\varphi\|_{W^{1/2}_{2,\alpha}(\partial\Omega,\delta)} = \inf_{\Phi|_{\partial\Omega} = \phi} \|\Phi\|_{W^1_{2,\alpha}(\Omega,\delta)}.$$

For the corresponding spaces and sets of vector-functions are used notations$\mathbf{W}^1_{2,\alpha}(\Omega, \delta)$, $\mathbf{L}_{2,\alpha}(\Omega, \delta)$, $\overset{\circ}{\mathbf{W}}{}^1_{2,\alpha}(\Omega, \delta)$.

Let $\mathbf{u} = (u_1, u_2)$ be a vector-function of displacements. Assume that $\overline{\Omega}$ is a homogeneous isotropic body and the strains are small. Consider a boundary value problem for the displacement field $\mathbf{u}$ for the Lamé system with constant coefficients λ and μ:

$$-(2\mathbf{div}(\mu\varepsilon(\mathbf{u})) + \nabla(\lambda \mathrm{div}\mathbf{u})) = \mathbf{f}, \quad x \in \Omega, \tag{2}$$

$$u_i = q_i, \quad x \in \partial\Omega, \tag{3}$$

Here, $\varepsilon(\mathbf{u})$ is a strain tensor with components $\varepsilon_{ij}(\mathbf{u}) = \frac{1}{2}\left(\frac{\partial u_i}{\partial x_j} + \frac{\partial u_j}{\partial x_i}\right)$.

Assume that the right-hand sides of (2), (3) satisfy the conditions

$$\mathbf{f} \in \mathbf{L}_{2,\beta}(\Omega, \delta), \quad q_i \in W^{1/2}_{2,\beta}(\partial\Omega, \delta), \quad i = 1, 2, \quad \beta > 0. \tag{4}$$

Denoted by

$$a_1(\mathbf{u}, \mathbf{v}) = \int_{\Omega} \left[(\lambda + 2\mu) \frac{\partial u_1}{\partial x_1} \frac{\partial(\rho^{2\nu} v_1)}{\partial x_1} + \mu \frac{\partial u_1}{\partial x_2} \frac{\partial(\rho^{2\nu} v_1)}{\partial x_2} + \lambda \frac{\partial u_2}{\partial x_2} \frac{\partial(\rho^{2\nu} v_1)}{\partial x_1} + \mu \frac{\partial u_2}{\partial x_1} \frac{\partial(\rho^{2\nu} v_1)}{\partial x_2} \right] dx,$$

$$a_2(\mathbf{u}, \mathbf{v}) = \int_{\Omega} \left[\lambda \frac{\partial u_1}{\partial x_1} \frac{\partial(\rho^{2\nu} v_2)}{\partial x_2} + \mu \frac{\partial u_1}{\partial x_2} \frac{\partial(\rho^{2\nu} v_2)}{\partial x_1} + (\lambda + 2\mu) \frac{\partial u_2}{\partial x_2} \frac{\partial(\rho^{2\nu} v_2)}{\partial x_2} + \mu \frac{\partial u_2}{\partial x_1} \frac{\partial(\rho^{2\nu} v_2)}{\partial x_1} \right] dx,$$

$$l_1(\mathbf{v}) = \int_{\Omega} \rho^{2\nu} f_1 v_1 dx, \quad l_2(\mathbf{v}) = \int_{\Omega} \rho^{2\nu} f_2 v_2 dx$$

the bilinear and linear forms and $a(\mathbf{u}, \mathbf{v}) = (a_1(\mathbf{u}, \mathbf{v}), a_2(\mathbf{u}, \mathbf{v}))$, $l(\mathbf{v}) = (l_1(\mathbf{v}), l_2(\mathbf{v}))$.

Definition 1

A function $\mathbf{u}_v$ *from the set* $\mathbf{W}^1_{2,\nu}(\Omega,\delta)$ *is called an* R_v*-generalized solution to the problem (2), (3) if it satisfies boundary condition (3) almost everywhere on* $\partial\Omega$ *and for every* $\mathbf{v}$ *from* $\mathbf{W}^1_{2,\nu}(\Omega,\delta)$ *the integral identity*

$$a(\mathbf{u}_\nu, \mathbf{v}) = l(\mathbf{v}) \tag{5}$$

holds for any fixed value of ν *satisfying the inequality*

$$\nu \geq \beta. \tag{6}$$

In [17], for the boundary value problem (2)–(3) with homogeneous boundary conditions, existence and uniqueness of its R_v-generalized solution were established.

Theorem 1

Let condition (4) be satisfied. Then for any $\nu > \beta$ *there always exists parameter* δ *such that the problem (2)–(3) with homogeneous boundary conditions has a unique* R_v*-generalized solution* $\mathbf{u}_v$ *in the set* $\mathbf{W}^{\circ 1}_{2,\alpha}(\Omega,\delta)$. *In this case*

$$\|\mathbf{u}_\nu\|_{\mathbf{W}^1_{2,\nu}(\Omega)} \leq c_3 \|\mathbf{f}\|_{\mathbf{L}_{2,\beta}(\Omega)}, \tag{7}$$

where c_3 *is a positive constant independent of* $\mathbf{f}$.

Then for any $\nu > \beta$*, there always exists parameter* δ *such that the problem (2)–(3) with homogeneous boundary conditions has a unique* R_v*-generalized solution* $\mathbf{u}_v$ *in the set* $\mathbf{W}^{\circ 1}_{2,\alpha}(\Omega,\delta)$.

Comment 1

At present, there exists a complete theory of classical solutions to boundary value problems with smooth initial data (equation coefficients, right hands of solution and boundary conditions) and with smooth enough domain boundary [19–22].

On the basis of the generalized solution-wide investigations of boundary value problems with discontinuous initial data and not smooth domain boundary were performed in Sobolev and different weighted spaces [23–26]. On the basis of the Galerkin method, theories of difference schemes, finite volumes, and finite-element method were developed to find approximate generalized solution [27].

Let us call boundary value problem a problem with strong singularity if its generalized solution could not be defined. This solution does not belong to the Sobolev space W^1_2 (H^1), or, in other words, the Dirichlet integral of the solution diverges. In [4, 5], we suggested to define a solution to the boundary value problems with strong singularity as an R_v-generalized one in the weighted Sobolev space. The essence of this approach is in introducing weight function into the integral equality. The weight function coincides with the distance to the singular points in their neighbourhoods. The role (sense, mission) of this function is in suppressing of the solution singularity caused by the problem features and is in assuring convergence of integrals in both parts of the integral equality. Taking into account the local character of the singularity, we define weight function as the distance to each singularity point inside the disk of radius δ centered in that points, and outside these disks the weight function equals δ. An exponent of the weight function in the definition of the R_ν-generalized solution as well as weighted space containing this solution depend on the spaces to which problem initial data belongs, on geometrical features of the boundary (re-entrant corners), and on changing of the boundary condition type.

In [13, 14], for the transformed system of Maxwell equations in the domain with re-entrant corner in which the solution does not depend on the space W_2^1, the weighted edge-based finite-element method was developed on the basis of introducing the R_ν-generalized solution. Convergence rate of this method is $O(h)$, and it does not depend on the size of singularity as opposed to other methods [28, 29].

The proposed approach of introducing R_ν-generalized solution allows to effectively find solutions not only to the boundary value problems with divergent Dirichlet integral but also to problems with weak singularity when the solution belongs to the W_2^1 and does not belong to the space W_2^2.

3. The weighted finite-element method

A finite-element scheme for problems (2)–(3) is constructed relying on the definition of an R_ν-generalized solution. For this purpose, a quasi-uniform triangulation T^h of $\overline{\Omega}$ and introduction of special basis functions are constructed.

The domain $\overline{\Omega}$ is divided into a finite number of triangles K (called finite elements) with vertices P_k ($k = 1,\dots,N$), which are triangulation nodes. Denoted by $\Omega^h = \cup_{K\in T^h} K$—the union of all elements; here, h is the longest of their side lengths. It is required that the partition satisfies the conventional constraints imposed on triangulations [10]. Denote by $P = \{P_k\}_{k=1}^{k=n}$, the set of triangulation internal nodes; by $P = \{P_k\}_{k=n+1}^{k=N}$, the set of nodes belonging to the $\partial\Omega$.

Each node $P_k \in P$ is associated with a function Ψ_k of the form

$$\Psi_k(x) = \rho^{\nu^*}(x)\phi_k(x), \quad k = 1, \dots, n,$$

where $\phi_k(x)$ is linear on each finite element, $\phi_k(P_j) = \delta_{kj}$, $k, j = 1, \dots, n$ δ_{kj} is the Kronecker delta, and ν^* is a real number.

The set V^h is defined as the linear span of the system of basis functions $\{\Psi_k\}_{k=1}^{k=n}$. Denote the corresponding vector set by $\mathbf{V}^h = \left[V^h\right]^2$. In set $\mathbf{V}^h$, one singled out the subset $\mathbf{V}^{\circ h} = \{\mathbf{v}\in\mathbf{V}^h, v_i (P_k)|_{P_k\in\partial\Omega} = 0, i = 1, 2\}$.

Associated with the constructed triangulation, the finite-element approximation of the displacement vector components has the form

$$u_{\nu,1}^{h}=\sum_{k=1}^{n}d_{2k-1}\Psi_{k},\quad u_{\nu,2}^{h}=\sum_{k=1}^{n}d_{2k}\Psi_{k},\quad d_{j}=\rho^{-\nu^{*}}\left(P_{\left[\frac{j+1}{2}\right]}\right)c_{j},\quad j=1,\dots,2n.$$

Definition 2

An approximate R_ν-generalized solution to the problems (2)–(3) by the weighted finite-element method is a function $\mathbf{u}_\nu^h \in \mathbf{V}^h$ such that it satisfies the boundary condition (3) in the nodes of the boundary $\partial\Omega$ and for arbitrary $\mathbf{v}^h(x) \in \mathbf{V}^h$ and $\nu > \beta$ the integral identity

$$a\left(\mathbf{u}_\nu^h, \mathbf{v}^h\right) = l\left(\mathbf{v}^h\right),$$

holds, where $\mathbf{u}_\nu^h = \left(u_{\nu,1}^h, u_{\nu,2}^h\right)$.

In [18], it was shown that convergence rate of the approximate solution to the exact one does not depend on size of the re-entrant corner and is always equal to $O(h)$ when weighted finite-element method is used for finding an R_ν-generalized solution to elasticity problem. The next section explains results of comparative numerical analysis for the model problems (2)–(3) of the weighted FEM using the classical finite-element method and the FEM with geometrically graded meshes of two kinds.

4. Results of numerical experiments

In the domain, Ω is considered a Dirichlet problem for the Lamé system (2), (3) with constant coefficients $\lambda = 3$ and $\mu = 5$. Two kinds of vector-function $\mathbf{u} = (u_1, u_2)$ were used as a solution to the problem.

Problem A

Components of the solution $\mathbf{u}$ of the model problem (2), (3) contain only a singular component

$$u_1 = \cos(x_1)\cos^2(x_2)\left(x_1^2 + x_2^2\right)^{0.3051},$$

$$u_2 = \cos^2(x_1)\cos(x_2)\left(x_1^2 + x_2^2\right)^{0.3051}.$$

Singularity order of u_1, u_2 corresponds to the size of the re-entrant corner $\gamma = 3\pi/2$ on the domain boundary [30].

Problem B

Solution $\mathbf{u}$ of the model problems (2, 3) contains both singular and regular components—regular part belongs to the $\mathbf{W}_2^2(\Omega)$

$$u_1 = \cos(x_1)\cos^2(x_2)\left(x_1^2 + x_2^2\right)^{0.3051} + \left(x_1^2 + x_2^2\right),$$

$$u_2 = \cos^2(x_1)\cos(x_2)\left(x_1^2 + x_2^2\right)^{0.3051} + \left(x_1^2 + x_2^2\right).$$

4.1. Comparative analysis of the generalized and R_ν-generalized solutions

Results of numerical experiments presented in this subsection were obtained using the code "Proba-IV" [31] with regular meshes which were built by the following scheme:

Domain Ω was divided into squares by lines parallel to coordinate axis, with distance equal to $1/N$ between them, where N is a half of number of partitioning segments along the greater side;

Each square was subdivided into two triangles by the diagonal.

In this case, size of the mesh-step h could be computed by $h = \sqrt{2}/N$. Example of the regular mesh for $N = 4$ is presented in **Figure 1**.

Calculations were performed for different values of N. Optimal parameters δ, ν, and ν^* were obtained by the program complex [32]. Generalized solution was determined by the integral equality (5) for $\nu = 0$.

One calculated the errors $\mathbf{e} = (e_1, e_2) = \left(u_1 - u_1^h, u_2 - u_2^h\right)$ and $\mathbf{e}_\nu = (e_{\nu,1}, e_{\nu,2}) = \left(u_1 - u_{\nu,1}^h, u_2 - u_{\nu,2}^h\right)$ of numerical approximation to the generalized $\mathbf{u}^h = \left(u_1^h, u_2^h\right)$ and R_ν-generalized $\mathbf{u}_\nu^h = \left(u_{1,\nu}^h, u_{2,\nu}^h\right)$ solutions, respectively. Problems A and B in **Tables 1** and **4**, respectively, present values of relative errors of the generalized solution in the norm of the Sobolev space $\mathbf{W}_2^1\left(\eta = \frac{\|\mathbf{e}\|_{W_2^1}}{\|\mathbf{u}\|_{W_2^1}}\right)$ and the R_ν-generalized one in the norm of the weighted Sobolev space $\mathbf{W}_{2,\nu}^1$ $\left(\eta_\nu = \frac{\|\mathbf{e}_\nu\|_{W_{2,\nu}^1}}{\|\mathbf{u}\|_{W_{2,\nu}^1}}\right)$ with different values of h. In addition, these tables contain ratios between error norms, obtained on meshes with step reducing twice. **Figures 2** and **3** show the convergence rates of the generalized and R_ν-generalized solutions to the corresponding problems with the logarithmic scale. The dashed line in the figures corresponds to convergence with the rate $O(h)$. **Tables 2** and **3** (Problem A) and **Tables 5** and **6** (Problem B) give limit values: number of nodes where $|e_1|$, $|e_2|$, $|e_{v,1}|$, and $|e_{v,2}|$ belong to the giving range, this number in percentage to the total number of nodes, and pictures of the absolute error distribution in the domain Ω.

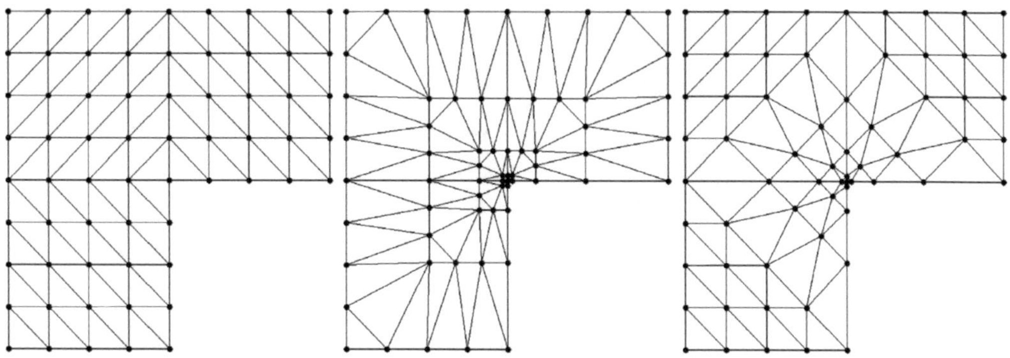

Figure 1. Example of regular mesh (**a**), and graded meshes I (**b**) and II (**c**) ($N = 4$, $\kappa = 0.4$).

4.1.1. Problem A

$2N$	128		256		512		1024		2048		4096
h	1.105e-2		5.524e-3		2.762e-3		1.381e-3		6.905e-4		3.453e-4
η	6.963e-2	1.52	4.579e-2	1.52	3.007e-2	1.52	1.972e-2	1.53	1.293e-2	1.53	8.476e-3
η_ν	7.011e-2	1.55	4.522e-2	1.64	2.756e-2	2.17	1.272e-2	2.21	5.745e-3	1.98	2.902e-3

Table 1. Dependence of relative errors of the generalized (η) and R_ν-generalized (η_ν) ($\delta = 0.0029$, $\nu = 1.2$, $\nu^* = 0.16$) solution to problem A on mesh step.

$\lvert e_1 \rvert$	$\lvert e_2 \rvert$	**Limit values**	$\lvert e_1 \rvert$		$\lvert e_2 \rvert$	
Distribution				**Number**	**%**	**Number**
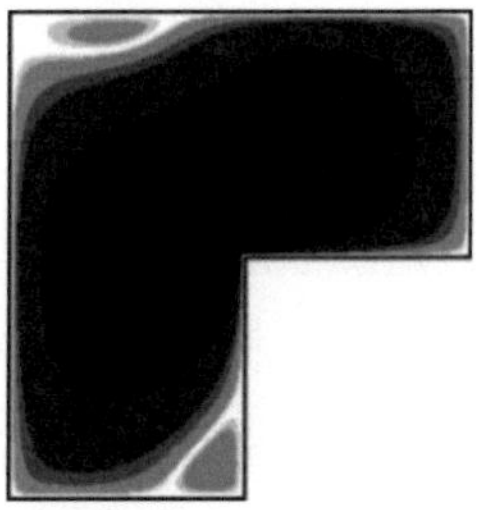	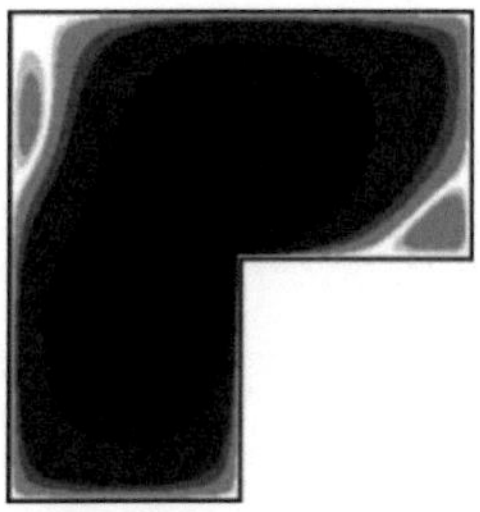	● $\geq 5e-6$	48.077	6045579	48.077	6045579
		● $\geq 1e-6$	29.387	3695290	29.387	3695290
		● $\geq 5e-7$	6.724	845468	6.724	845468
		● $\geq 1e-7$	9.624	1210192	9.624	1210192
		● $\geq 5e-8$	2.564	322449	2.564	322449
		○ ≥ 0	3.624	455743	3.624	455743

Table 2. Number, percentage equivalence, and distribution of nodes where absolute errors $|e_i|$ ($i = 1,2$) of finding components of the approximate generalized solution to problem A are not less than given limit values, $2N = 4096$.

$\lvert e_1 \rvert$	$\lvert e_2 \rvert$	**Limit values**	$\lvert e_1 \rvert$		$\lvert e_2 \rvert$	
Distribution			**%**	**Number**	**%**	**Number**
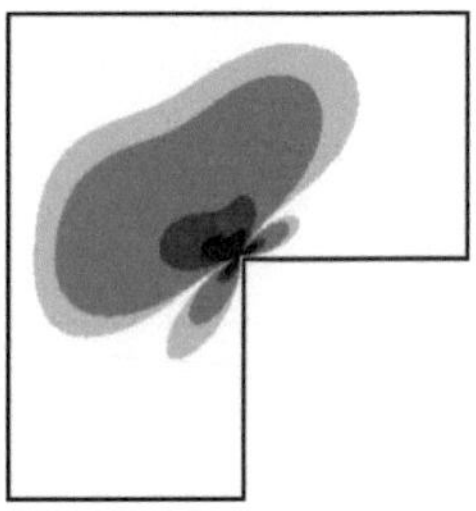	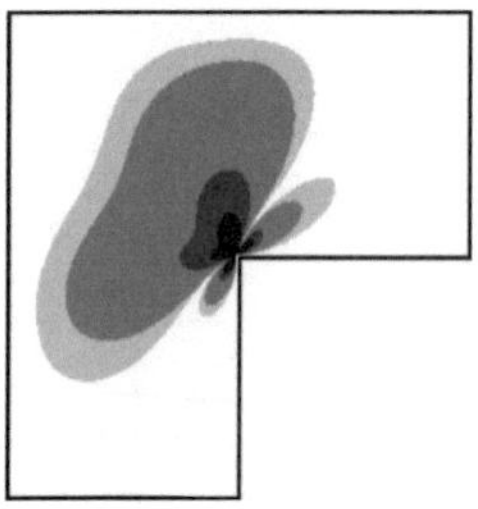	● $\geq 5e-6$	0.033	4102	0.033	4102
		● $\geq 1e-6$	0.764	96075	0.764	96075
		● $\geq 5e-7$	2.457	308985	2.457	308985
		● $\geq 1e-7$	21.704	2729186	21.704	2729186
		● $\geq 5e-8$	12.589	1582976	12.589	1582974
		○ ≥ 0	62.454	7853397	62.454	7853399

Table 3. Number, percentage equivalence, and distribution of nodes where absolute errors $|e_{\nu,i}|$ ($i = 1,2$) of finding components of the approximate R_ν-generalized solution to problem A ($\delta = 0.0029$, $\nu = 1.2$, $\nu^* = 0.16$) are not less than given limit values, $2N = 4096$.

4.1.2. Problem B

2N	128		256		512		1024		2048		4096
h	1.105e-2		5.524e-3		2.762e-3		1.381e-3		6.905e-4		3.453e-4
η	2.849e-2	1.54	1.850e-2	1.53	1.205e-2	1.53	7.870e-3	1.53	5.146e-3	1.53	3.367e-3
η_ν	2.868e-2	1.57	1.827e-2	1.65	1.107e-2	2.16	5.117e-3	2.21	2.319e-3	1.98	1.171e-3

Table 4. Dependence of relative errors of the generalized (η) and R_ν-generalized (η_ν) ($\delta = 0.0029$, $\nu = 1.2$, $\nu^* = 0.16$ solution of the problem B on the mesh step.

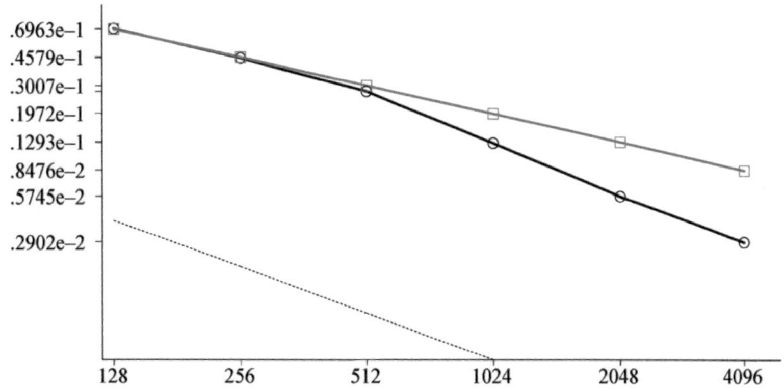

Figure 2. Chart of η for the generalized (squared line) and of η_ν for R_ν-generalized (circled line) (δ=0.0029, ν=1.2, ν^*=0.16) solutions to the problem A in dependence on the number of subdivisions 2N.

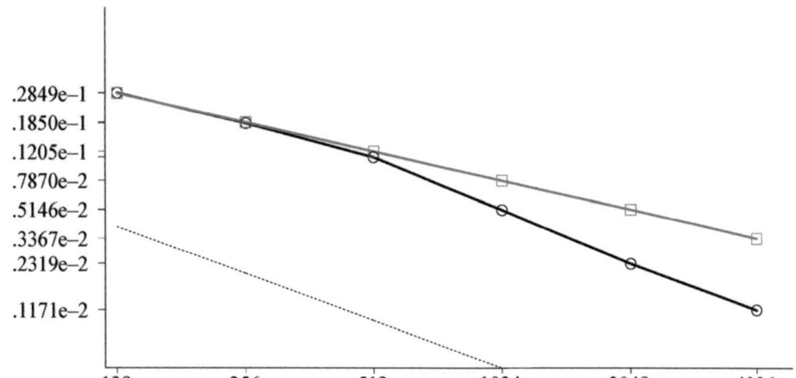

Figure 3. Chart of η for the generalized (squared line) and of η_ν for R_ν-generalized (circled line) ($\delta = 0.0029$, $\nu = 1.2$, $\nu^* = 0.16$) solutions to the problem B in dependence on the number of subdivisions 2N.

$\|e_1\|$	$\|e_2\|$	Limit values	$\|e_1\|$		$\|e_2\|$	
Distribution				**Number**	%	**Number**
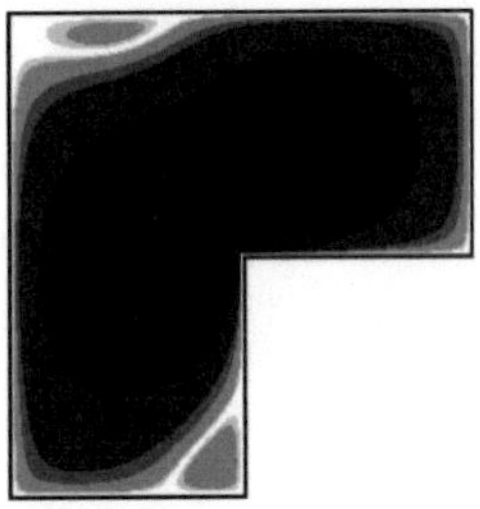	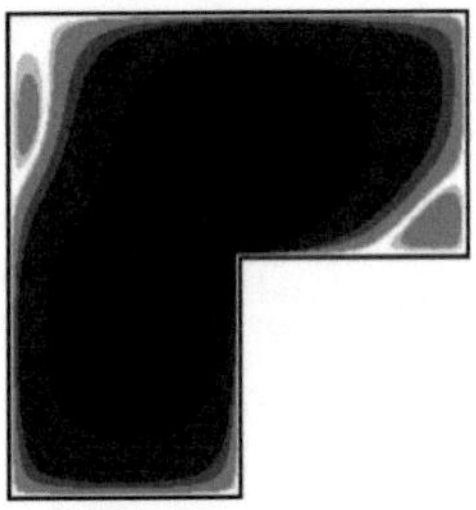	● $\geq 5e-6$	48.078	6045622	48.078	6045622
		● $\geq 1e-6$	29.387	3695278	29.387	3695278
		● $\geq 5e-7$	6.724	845466	6.724	845466
		● $\geq 1e-7$	9.624	1210158	9.624	1210159
		● $\geq 5e-8$	2.564	322439	2.564	322438
		○ ≥ 0	3.624	455758	3.624	455758

Table 5. Number, percentage equivalence, and distribution of nodes where absolute errors $|e_i|$ $(i = 1, 2)$ of finding components of the approximate generalized solution to problem B are not less than given limit values, $2N = 4096$.

$\|e_1\|$	$\|e_2\|$	Limit values	$\|e_1\|$		$\|e_2\|$	
Distribution			%	**Number**	%	**Number**
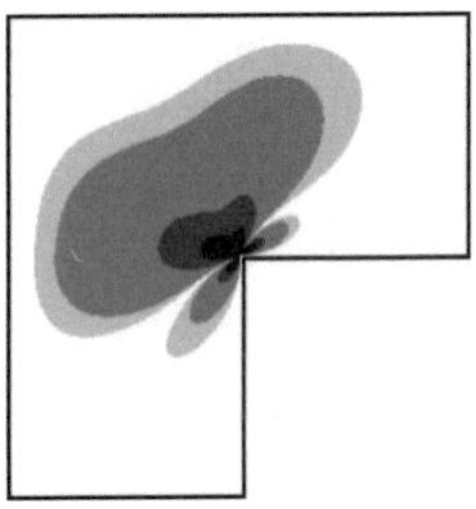	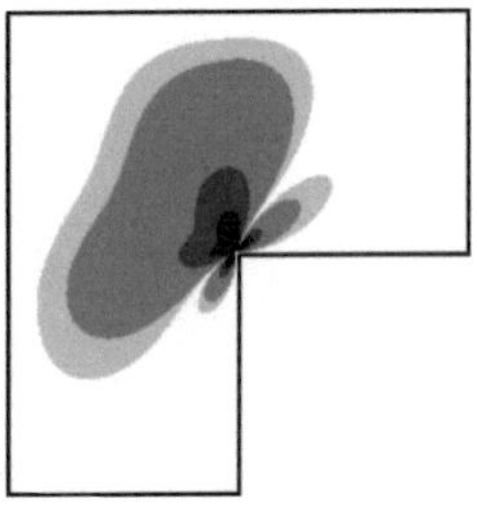	● $\geq 5e-6$	0.033	4108	0.033	4108
		● $\geq 1e-6$	0.771	96899	0.771	96899
		● $\geq 5e-7$	2.481	311996	2.481	311996
		● $\geq 1e-7$	21.789	2739862	21.789	2739863
		● $\geq 5e-8$	12.588	1582876	12.588	1582876
		○ ≥ 0	62.339	7838980	62.339	7838979

Table 6. Number, percentage equivalence, and distribution of nodes where absolute errors $|e_{\nu,i}|$ $(i = 1, 2))$ of finding components of the approximate R_ν-generalized solution to problem B $((\delta = 0.0029,\ \nu = 1.2,\ \nu^* = 0.16)$ are not less than given limit values, $2N = 4096$.

4.2. FEM with graded mesh: comparative analysis

This subsection presents results of error analysis for finding generalized solution to the problems A and B by the FEM with graded meshes of two kinds (for detailed information about graded meshes, see [2, 33, 34]).

Mesh I. This partitioning was built by the following scheme

1. In the domain Ω, for a given N, regular mesh was constructed as described in section 4.1.
2. Level $l = \max_{i=1,2}(|N - [(x_i + 1)N]|)$ was determined for each node. Here, x_i $(i = 1, 2)$ are initial node coordinates on the regular mesh, $[\cdot]$ means integer part.
3. New coordinates of nodes of the graded mesh are calculated by the formula $([(x_i + 1)N] - N)l^{-1}(l/N)^{1/\kappa}$ $(i = 1, 2)$.

Mesh II. Constructing process for this mesh differs from the one described earlier in the level-calculating mode. Here, $l = \sum_{i=1}^{2} |N - [(x_i + 1)N]|$. In this case, new coordinates are determined only for nodes with $l \leq N$.

Examples of meshes I and II are shown in **Figure 1(b)** and **(c)**, respectively.

The FEM solution obtained on described graded meshes converges with the first rate on the mesh step when the value of the parameter κ is less than the order of singularity [2, 33].

Calculations were performed for different values of N and κ. For each node, one calculated the errors $\mathbf{e}_I = \mathbf{u} - \mathbf{u}_I^h$ and $\mathbf{e}_{II} = \mathbf{u} - \mathbf{u}_{II}^h$ of the approximate generalized solutions $\mathbf{u}_I^h$, $\mathbf{u}_{II}^h$ obtained on meshes I and II, respectively. The values of relative errors of the generalized solution to the problems A and B in the norm of the Sobolev space $\mathbf{W}_2^1$ for different values of h and κ for mesh I $\left(\eta_I = \frac{\|\mathbf{e}_I\|_{W_2^1}}{\|\mathbf{u}\|_{W_2^1}}\right)$ are presented in **Tables 7** and **10**, respectively, and for mesh II $\left(\eta_{II} = \frac{\|\mathbf{e}_{II}\|_{W_2^1}}{\|\mathbf{u}\|_{W_2^1}}\right)$ are presented in **Tables 8** and **11**, respectively. In addition, these tables contain ratios between error norms and between mesh steps obtained with nodes number increasing four times. **Figures 4** and **5** show the convergence rates of the generalized solutions to the corresponding problems for meshes I and II with the logarithmic scale. Dashed line in the figures corresponds to convergence with the rate $O(h)$ as in paragraph 1. Besides, for the problems A and B, **Tables 9** and **12**, respectively, contain limit values for the following data: number of nodes where $|e_{1,II}|$, $|e_{2,II}|$ belong to the giving range, this number in percentage to the total number of nodes, and pictures of the absolute error distribution in the domain Ω.

4.2.1. *Problem A*

$2N$	128		256		512		1024		2048		4096
$\kappa = 0.3$											
η_I	2.659e-2	2.00	1.332e-2	2.00	6.675e-3	1.91	3.501e-3	0.75	4.650e-3	0.27	1.741e-2
h	0.062263	1.979	0.031459	1.99	0.015812	1.995	0.007926	1.997	0.003968	1.999	0.001985
$\kappa = 0.4$											
η_I	2.111e-2	2.00	1.057e-2	1.99	5.302e-3	1.78	2.971e-3	0.53	5.559e-3	0.26	2.154e-2
h	0.044928	1.986	0.02262	1.993	0.011349	1.997	0.005684	1.998	0.002845	1.999	0.001423
$\kappa = 0.5$											
η_I	1.990e-2	1.99	1.001e-2	1.99	5.038e-3	1.71	2.940e-3	0.46	6.401e-3	0.25	2.513e-2
h	0.034611	1.99	0.017387	1.995	0.008714	1.998	0.004362	1.999	0.0021823	1.999	0.001092
$\kappa = 0.6$											
η_I	2.315e-2	1.92	1.204e-2	1.93	6.254e-3	1.70	3.678e-3	0.50	7.292e-3	0.26	2.818e-2
h	0.030169	1.993	0.015135	1.997	0.007580	1.998	0.003793	1.999	0.0018973	1.9996	0.0009489

Table 7. Dependence of relative errors of the generalized solution to problem A with mesh I on the mesh step for different κ.

$2N$	128		256		512		1024		2048		4096
$\kappa = 0.3$											
η_{II}	2.392e-2	2.00	1.196e-2	2.00	5.982e-3	1.99	3.012e-3	1.46	2.059e-3	0.36	5.687e-3
h	0.05114	1.982	0.025805	1.99	0.012962	1.995	0.006496	1.998	0.003252	1.999	0.001627
$\kappa = 0.4$											
η_{II}	1.974e-2	2.00	9.879e-3	2.00	4.942e-3	1.97	2.511e-3	1.16	2.167e-3	0.30	7.154e-3
h	0.038606	1.988	0.019417	1.994	0.009737	1.997	0.004876	1.999	0.00244	1.999	0.001220
$\kappa = 0.5$											
η_{II}	1.954e-2	1.98	9.857e-3	1.99	4.963e-3	1.93	2.565e-3	0.94	2.726e-3	0.28	9.725e-3
h	0.031006	1.99	0.015564	1.996	0.007797	1.998	0.003902	1.999	0.001952	1.9995	0.000976
$\kappa = 0.6$											
η_{II}	2.339e-2	1.91	1.225e-2	1.92	6.386e-3	1.90	3.368e-3	1.14	2.966e-3	0.31	9.712e-3
h	0.025906	1.995	0.012987	1.997	0.006502	1.999	0.003253	1.999	0.001627	1.9997	0.000814

Table 8. Dependence of relative errors of the generalized solution to problem A with mesh II on the mesh step for different κ.

$\|e_1\|$	$\|e_2\|$	Limit values	$\|e_1\|$		$\|e_2\|$	
Distribution			%	**Number**	%	**Number**
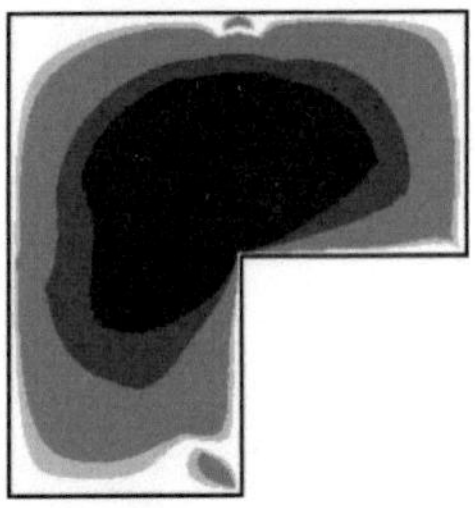	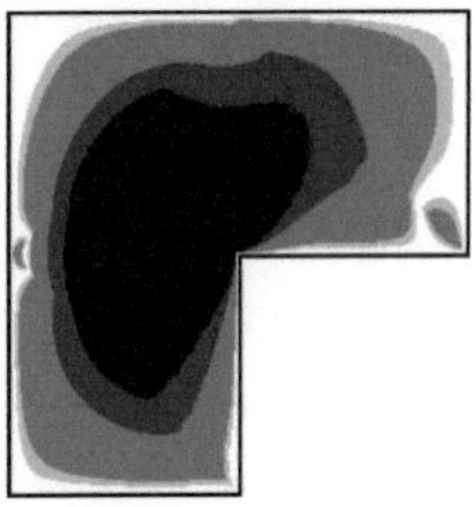	$\geq 5e-6$	0.001	6	0.001	6
		$\geq 1e-6$	35.524	278645	35.479	278292
		$\geq 5e-7$	13.631	106920	13.770	108011
		$\geq 1e-7$	33.363	261697	33.377	261808
		$\geq 5e-8$	7.020	55066	6.984	54782
		≥ 0	10.461	82051	10.389	81486

Table 9. Number, percentage equivalence, and distribution of nodes where absolute errors $|e_{i,II}|$ $(i = 1, 2)$ of finding components of the approximate generalized solution to problem A obtained with mesh II ($\kappa = 0.5$) are not less than given limit values, $2N = 1024$.

4.2.2. *Problem B*

$2N$	128		256		512		1024		2048		4096
$\kappa = 0.3$											
η_I	9.851e-3	1.99	4.955e-3	1.97	2.510e-3	1.36	1.845e-3	0.33	5.639e-3	0.25	2.247e-2
h	0.062263	1.979	0.031459	1.99	0.015812	1.995	0.007926	1.997	0.003968	1.999	0.001985
$\kappa = 0.4$											
η_I	7.712e-3	1.99	3.870e-3	1.95	1.988e-3	0.98	2.034e-3	0.28	7.218e-3	0.25	2.866e-2
h	0.044928	1.986	0.02262	1.993	0.011349	1.997	0.005684	1.998	0.002845	1.999	0.001423

$\kappa = 0.5$											
η_I	7.625e-3	1.99	3.839e-3	1.92	1.995e-3	0.87	2.301e-3	0.27	8.676e-3	0.25	3.454e-2
h	0.034611	1.99	0.017387	1.995	0.008714	1.998	0.004362	1.999	0.002182	1.999	0.001091
$\kappa = 0.6$											
η_I	9.330e-3	1.92	4.849e-3	1.88	2.584e-3	0.91	2.847e-3	0.28	1.016e-2	0.25	4.001e-2
h	0.034611	1.99	0.017387	1.995	0.008714	1.998	0.004362	1.999	0.002182	1.999	0.001091

Table 10. Dependence of relative errors of the generalized solution to problem B with mesh I on the mesh step for different κ.

$2N$	128		256		512		1024		2048		4096
$\kappa = 0.3$											
η_{II}	5.963e-3	2.00	2.982e-3	2.00	1.492e-3	1.91	7.819e-4	0.77	1.013e-3	0.27	3.757e-3
h	0.05114	1.982	0.025805	1.99	0.012962	1.995	0.006496	1.998	0.003252	1.999	0.0016267
$\kappa = 0.4$											
η_{II}	6.349e-3	2.00	3.178e-3	2.00	1.591e-3	1.87	8.490e-4	0.67	1.263e-3	0.26	4.805e-3
h	0.038606	1.988	0.019417	1.994	0.009737	1.997	0.004876	1.999	0.00244	1.999	0.0012203
$\kappa = 0.5$											
η_{II}	7.441e-3	1.98	3.756e-3	1.98	1.894e-3	1.83	1.037e-3	0.60	1.717e-3	0.26	6.606e-3
h	0.031006	1.99	0.015564	1.996	0.007797	1.998	0.003902	1.999	0.001952	1.9995	0.0009763
$\kappa = 0.6$											
η_{II}	9.574e-3	1.91	5.000e-3	1.92	2.602e-3	1.85	1.409e-3	0.78	1.804e-3	0.27	6.660e-3
h	0.025906	1.995	0.012987	1.997	0.006502	1.999	0.003253	1.999	0.001627	1.9997	0.00081366

Table 11. Dependence of relative errors of the generalized solution to problem B with mesh II on the mesh step for different κ.

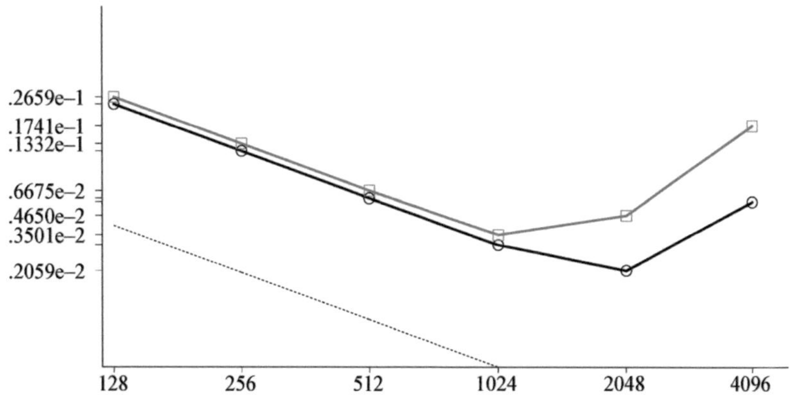

Figure 4. Chart of η_I for mesh I (squared line) and of η_{II} for mesh II (circled line) for problem A depending on the number of subdivisions $2N$; $\kappa = 0.3$.

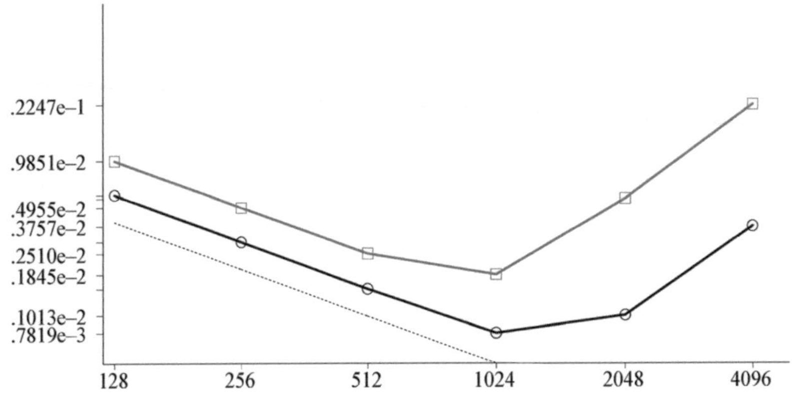

Figure 5. Chart of η_I for mesh I (squared line) and of η_{II} for mesh II (circled line) for problem B depending on the number of subdivisions $2N$; $\kappa = 0.3$.

$\lvert e_1\rvert$	$\lvert e_2\rvert$	Limit values	$\lvert e_1\rvert$		$\lvert e_2\rvert$	
Distribution			%	Number	%	Number
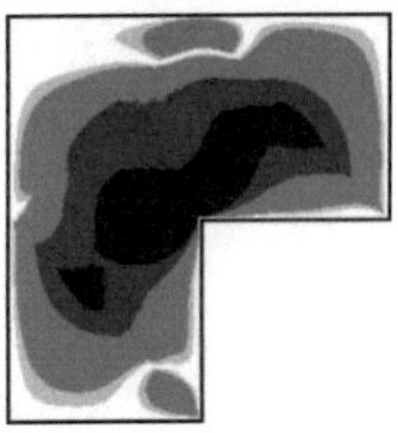	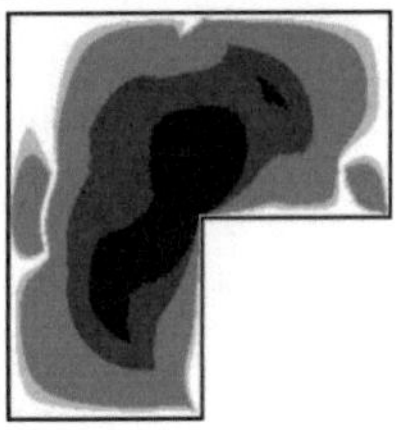	● $\geq 5e-6$	0.001	6	0.001	6
		● $\geq 1e-6$	23.718	186038	23.282	182623
		● $\geq 5e-7$	18.518	145255	19.047	149398
		● $\geq 1e-7$	34.864	273467	35.327	277097
		● $\geq 5e-8$	8.084	63407	7.899	61956
		○ ≥ 0	14.816	116212	14.445	113305

Table 12. Number, percentage equivalence, and distribution of nodes where absolute errors $|e_{i,II}|$ $(i = 1, 2)$ of finding components of the approximate generalized solution to problem B obtained with mesh II ($\kappa = 0.5$) are not less than given limit values, $2N = 1024$.

5. Conclusions

Presented numerical results have demonstrated that:

1. An approximate R_ν-generalized solution to the problem (2)–(4) converges to the exact one with the rate $O(h)$ in the norm of the set $\mathbf{W}^1_{2,\nu}(\Omega, \delta)$ in contrast with the generalized solution, which converges with the rate $O(h^{0.61})$ for the classical FEM;
2. FEM with graded meshes fails on high-dimensional grids because of the small mesh size near the singular point, but the weighted FEM stably allows to find approximate solution with the accuracy $O(h)$ under the same computational conditions;

For the approximate R_ν-generalized solution obtained by the weighted finite-element method, an absolute error value is by one or two orders of magnitude less than the approximate generalized one obtained by the FEM or by the FEM with graded meshes; this holds for the overwhelming majority of nodes.

Author details

Viktor Anatolievich Rukavishnikov[1,2]* and Elena Ivanovna Rukavishnikova[1,2]

*Address all correspondence to: vark0102@mail.ru

1 Far Eastern Branch, Russian Academy of Science, Khabarovsk, Russian Federation

2 Far Eastern State Transport University, Khabarovsk, Russian Federation

References

[1] Szabó B, Babuška I. Finite Element Analysis. New York: Wiley; 1991. 368 p

[2] Apel T, Sändig A-M, Whiteman JR. Graded mesh refinement and error estimates for finite element solutions of elliptic boundary value problems in non-smooth domains. Mathematical Methods in the Applied Sciences. 1996;**19**(1):63-85

[3] Nguyen-Xuan H, Liu GR, Bordas S, Natarajan S, Rabczuk T. An adaptive singular ES-FEM for mechanics problems with singular field of arbitrary order. Computer Methods in Applied Mechanics and Engineering. 2013;**253**:252-273

[4] Rukavishnikov VA. The weight estimation of the speed of difference scheme convergence. Doklady Akademii Nauk SSSR. 1986;**288**(5):1058-1062

[5] Rukavishnikov VA. On the differential properties of R_ν-generalized solution of Dirichlet problem. Doklady Akademii Nauk SSSR. 1989;**309**(6):1318-1320

[6] Rukavishnikov VA. On the uniqueness of the R_ν-generalized solution of boundary value problems with noncoordinated degeneration of the initial data. Doklady Mathematics. 2001;**63**(1):68-70

[7] Rukavishnikov VA, Ereklintsev AG. On the coercivity of the R_ν-generalized solution of the first boundary value problem with coordinated degeneration of the input data. Differential Equations. 2005;**41**(12):1757-1767. DOI: 10.1007/s10625-006-0012-5

[8] Rukavishnikov VA, Kuznetsova EV. A coercive estimate for a boundary value problem with noncoordinated degeneration of the input data. Differential Equations. 2007;**43**(4): 550-560. DOI: 10.1134/S0012266107040131

[9] Rukavishnikov VA, Kuznetsova EV. The R_ν-generalized solution with a singularity of a boundary value problem belongs to the space $W^{k+2}_{2,\nu+\beta/2+k+1}(\Omega,\delta)$. Differential Equations. 2009;**45**(6):913-917. DOI: 10.1134/S0012266109060147

[10] Rukavishnikov VA. On the existence and uniqueness of an R_{ν}-generalized solution of a boundary value problem with uncoordinated degeneration of the input data. Doklady Mathematics. 2014;**90**(2):562-564. DOI: 10.1134/S1064562414060155

[11] Rukavishnikov VA. The Dirichlet problem with the noncoordinated degeneration of the initial data. Doklady Akademii Nauk. 1994;**337**(4):447-449

[12] Rukavishnikov VA, Rukavishnikova HI. The finite element method for a boundary value problem with strong singularity. Journal of Computational and Applied Mathematics. 2010;**234**(9):2870-2882. DOI: 10.1016/j.cam.2010.01.020

[13] Rukavishnikov VA, Mosolapov AO. New numerical method for solving time-harmonic Maxwell equations with strong singularity. Journal of Computational Physics. 2012;**231**(6): 2438-2448. DOI: 10.1016/j.jcp.2011.11.031

[14] Rukavishnikov VA, Mosolapov AO. Weighted edge finite element method for Maxwell's equations with strong singularity. Doklady Mathematics. 2013;**87**(2):156-159. DOI: 10.1134/S1064562413020105

[15] Rukavishnikov VA, Rukavishnikova HI. On the error estimation of the finite element method for the boundary value problems with singularity in the Lebesgue weighted space. Numerical Functional Analysis and Optimization. 2013;**34**(12):1328-1347. DOI: 10.1080/01630563.2013.809582

[16] Rukavishnikov VA, Nikolaev SG. Weighted finite element method for an elasticity problem with singularity. Doklady Mathematics. 2013;**88**(3):705-709. DOI: 10.1134/S1064562413060215

[17] Rukavishnikov VA, Nikolaev SG. On the R_{ν}-generalized solution of the Lame system with corner singularity. Doklady Mathematics. 2015;**92**(1):421-423. DOI: 10.1134/S1064562415040080

[18] Rukavishnikov VA. Weighted FEM for two-dimensional easticity problem with corner singularity. Lecture Notes in Computational Science and Engineering. 2016;**112**:411-419. DOI: 10.1007/978-3-319-39929-4_39

[19] Douglis A, Nirenberg L. Interior estimates for elliptic systems of partial differential equations. Communications on Pure and Applied Mathematics. 1955;**8**:503-538

[20] Agmon S, Douglis A, Nirenberg L. Estimates near the boundary for solutions of elliptic partial differential equations satisfying general boundary conditions, I, II. Communications on Pure and Applied Mathematics. 1959/1964;**12/17**:623-727, 35-92

[21] Hörmander L. Linear Partial Differential Operators. Berlin: Springer; 1963

[22] Lopatinsky YB. On a method of reducing boundary problems for a system of differential equations of elliptic type to regular integral equations. Ukrains'kyi Matematychnyi Zhurnal. 1953;**5**:123-151

[23] Ladyzhenskaya OA. The Boundary Value Problems of Mathematical Physics. Moscow: Nauka; 1973. 408 p

[24] Maz'ya VG, Plamenevskii BA. L_p-estimates of solutions of elliptic boundary value problems in domains with ribs. Trudy Moskovskogo Matematicheskogo Obshchestva. 1978;**37**:49-93

[25] Grisvard P. Elliptic Problems in Nonsmooth Domains. London: Pitman; 1985. 410 p

[26] Dauge M. Elliptic Boundary Value Problems on Corner Domains. Berlin: Springer; 1988. 264 p

[27] Samarski AA, Andreev VB. Finite Difference Methods for Elliptic Equations. Moscow: Nauka; 1976. 352 p

[28] Assous A, Ciarlet P Jr, Segré J. Numerical solution to the time-dependent Maxwell equations in two-dimensional singular domains: The singular complement method. Journal of Computational Physics. 2000;**161**:218-249

[29] Costabel M, Dauge M. Weighted regularization of Maxwell equations in polyhedral domains. Numerische Mathematik. 2002;**93**:239-277

[30] Rössle A. Corner singularities and regulatiy of weak solutions for the two-dimensional Lamé equations on domains with angular corners. Journal of Elasticity. 2000;**60**(1):57-75

[31] Nikolaev SG, Rukavishnikov VA. Proba IV, programm for the numerical solution of the two-dimensional elasticity problems with singularity: 2013616248 Russian Federation. Computer programms. Data bases. IC Chips Topology. 2013;**3**(84)

[32] Rukavishnikov VA, Maslov OV, Mosolapov AO, Nikolaev SG. Automated software complex for determination of the optimal parameters set for the weighted finite element method on computer clusters. Computational Nanotechnology. 2015;**1**:9-19

[33] Oganesyan LA, Rukhovets LA. Variational-difference methods for solving elliptic equations. Yerevan: Izdatel'stvo Akad. Nauk. Arm. SSR; 1979. 235 p

[34] Raugel G. Résolution numérique par une méthode d'éléments finis du probléme Dirichlet pour le Laplacien dans un polygone. Comptes Rendus de l'Académie des Sciences. 1978;**286**: A791-A794